Marketing strategy and competitive positioning

— MARKETING MODELS
— STRATEGIC PLANNING TOOL

Graham

To Jackie, Tom and Katy

John

To Veronica, Carolyne and Paul

Nigel

To Nikala

Marketing strategy and competitive positioning

second edition

Graham J. Hooley
Aston Business School
Aston University

John A. Saunders
Aston Business School
Aston University

Nigel F. Piercy
Cardiff Business School
University of Wales

PRENTICE HALL
LONDON · NEW YORK · TORONTO · SYDNEY · TOKYO
SINGAPORE · MADRID · MEXICO CITY · MUNICH · PARIS

Pearson Education Limited
Edinburgh Gate
Harlow
Essex CM20 2JE
England

and Associated Companies throughout the world

Visit us on the World Wide Web at: http://www.pearsoneduc.com

First published 1993
as *Competitive Positioning: The key to market success*
This second edition published 1998 by
Prentice Hall Europe

Typeset in 10/12 Plantin Light
by Mathematical Composition Setters Ltd, Salisbury, Wiltshire

Printed and bound in Great Britain by
Redwood Books, Trowbridge, Wiltshire

Library of Congress Cataloging-in-Publication Data

Hooley, Graham J.
   Marketing strategy and competitive positioning / Graham J. Hooley,
John A. Saunders, Nigel F. Piercy. — 2nd ed.
      p.   cm.
   Includes bibliographical references and index.
   ISBN 0-13-371253-2 (alk. paper)
   1. Target marketing. 2. Marketing—Management. I. Saunders,
John A., 1946– . II. Piercy, Nigel. III. Title.
HF5415. 127.H66 1998
658.8'02 — DC21   97-45173
                                                             CIP

British Library Cataloguing in Publication Data

A catalogue record for this book is available from
the British Library

ISBN 0-13-371253-2

4 5   02 01 00

Contents

Part II Competitive market analysis

Part V Conclusions

Preface to the second edition

Like its predecessor, the second edition of this book is about creating and sustaining superior performance in the marketplace. While its focus remains the two central issues in marketing strategy formulation – the identification of target markets and the creation of a differential advantage – the treatment has been substantially expanded to cover new developments in strategic thinking that have emerged in recent years. In particular, our approach emphasizes the very different role that organizations are defining for marketing as a strategic force rather than just as an operational department. The change in the title reflects this breadth and changing perspective. It also represents our goal of reaching a broader audience to include strategic decision-makers as well as marketing specialists.

New topics include service quality and relationship marketing, networks and alliances, innovation, internal marketing and market forecasting. Greater emphasis is given to the development of marketing resources and capabilities, together with the need to reassess the role of marketing in the organization as a critical process and not simply as a conventional functional specialization. In addition to the new chapters, all original chapters have been extensively updated to take into account new theoretical perspectives, and many new examples have been included.

The structure of the first edition has been retained:

Part I is concerned with the fundamental changes that are taking place in how marketing operates in organizations and the increasing focus on marketing as a process rather than as a functional specialization. The central questions of the market orientation of organizations and the need to find better ways of responding to turbulent and ambiguous environments lead us to the proposal for market-led strategic management and the framework for developing marketing strategy which provides the structure for the rest of the book. Discussion of strategic marketing planning and portfolio analysis provides the groundwork for two critical issues on which we focus throughout this volume: the choice of market targets and the building of strong competitive positions.

Part II deals with the competitive environment in which the company operates. Different types of strategic environment are first considered, together with the critical success factors for dealing with each type. Discussion then focuses on the 'strategic triangle' comprised of customers, competitors and company. To this triangle is now added the 'virtual' organization created through strategic alliances and networks that is the hallmark of many industries today as the basis for new types of competition. Ways of analyzing each in turn are explored to help identify the options open to the company. The emphasis is on matching corporate resources, assets and capabilities to market opportunities.

Part III examines in more detail the techniques available for identifying market segments (or potential targets) and current (and potential) positions. Alternative bases for segmenting consumer and industrial markets are explored, as are the data collection and analysis techniques currently available. A new chapter focuses specifically on forecasting approaches and methods that can help identify changes in markets and customer requirements.

Part IV returns to strategy formulation. Selection of market targets through consideration of market attractiveness and business strength is followed by a discussion of how to create a defensible position in the marketplace. Strategies for attacking competitor positions and effectively defending current positions in the market are explored in detail. Three new chapters concerned with specific aspects of strategy formulation and execution are added to this part. The roles of customer service in relationship-building, innovation to create competitive advantage and internal marketing to gain the implementation of marketing strategies throughout the company and its sales organization are all discussed in depth.

Part V provides a new perspective on competition for the twenty-first century. The various themes from the earlier parts of the book are drawn together in order to identify the major changes taking place in markets, the necessary organizational responses to those changes and the competitive positioning strategies that could form the cornerstones of effective future marketing.

This book is intended for readers in the academic, professional and practitioner markets, who are linked by the need for an up-to-date understanding of the meaning and scope of marketing strategy and a framework to manage the critical issues of market choice and competitive positioning. The material covered will be of direct importance to students of marketing strategy on both postgraduate (MBA, MA and MSc) and undergraduate programmes as a marketing strategy textbook. It will also be useful for those undertaking professional qualifications in marketing and business who need to build their understanding of marketing as a strategic issue. We believe that the book will also be of value to marketing practitioners who wish to explore new ways of looking at the marketing process and their target markets, with a view to managing marketing better as a route to gaining an edge over their competitors.

Graham Hooley
John Saunders
Nigel Piercy

Acknowledgements

This second edition gives us the opportunity to make fuller acknowledgement to the many friends, colleagues, students and managers who have helped shape our ideas over the years. In particular, we would like to acknowledge a number of outstanding management and marketing scholars that we have been fortunate to work with over recent years: Professors Gary Armstrong, George Avlonitis, Jozsef Beracs, Pierre Berthon, Günther Botschen, Martina Botschen, Amanda Broderick, Peter Buckley, Frank Cespedes, David Cook, Tony Cox, David Cravens, Ted Davis, Adamantios Diamantopoulos, Susan Douglas, Peter Doyle, Colin Egan, John Fahy, Krzysztof Fonfara, Gordon Foxall, Fu Gouqun, Gordon Greenley, Salah Hassan, J. Mac Hulbert, David Jobber, Costas Katsikeas, Philip Kotler, Giles Laurent, Gary Lilien, Ray Loveridge, Jim Lynch, Malcolm MacDonald, Hafiz Mizra, Kristian Möller, Neil Morgan, Hans Mühlbacher, Leyland Pitt, Bodo Schlegelmilch, David Shipley, Stan Slater, Jan-Benedict Steenkamp, Rajan Varadarajan, Michel Wedel, David Wilson, Berend Wirenga, Veronica Wong, Oliver Yau.

In addition, the help of Chris Stagg in preparing the manuscript is gratefully acknowleged.

PART I

Marketing strategy

The first part of the book is concerned with the role of marketing in strategy development and lays the groundwork for analyzing the two critical issues of competitive positioning and market choices.

Chapter 1 discusses the modern challenges to the conventional view of marketing as simply a specialized function in an organization, and the move towards examining marketing as a process of value-creation and delivery to customers, which transcends traditional departmental boundaries. We examine the issue of our growing understanding of market orientation as a way of doing business which places the customer at the centre of operations, and aligns people, information and structures around the value creation process. The context is seen to be the dynamic and turbulent market environment, which can be assessed in terms of political, economic, social, cultural and technological change, with many implications for marketing management. The chapter concludes with a set of fundamental marketing principles to guide the actions of organizations operating in competitive markets, and by identifying the role of marketing in leading and shaping strategic management.

Chapter 2 presents a framework for developing a marketing strategy which is then adopted throughout the rest of the book. A three-stage process is proposed. First, the establishment of the core strategy. This involves defining the business purpose, assessing the alternatives open to the organization through an analysis of customers, competition and the competencies of the organization, and deciding on the strategic focus that will be adopted. Second is the creation of the competitive positioning for the company. This boils down to the selection of the target market(s) (which dictates where the organization will compete) and the establishment of a differential advantage (which spells out how it will compete). Third, implementation issues are discussed, such as the achievement of positioning through the use of the marketing mix, organization and control of the marketing effort.

Chapter 3 examines portfolio planning in a multi-business organization. Different product types are considered, together with various techniques for modelling portfolio balance (in terms of today and tomorrow, cash use and generation, and risk and return). The concept of a competence portfolio is introduced.

The ideas and frameworks presented in Part I are used to structure the remainder of the book, leading into a more detailed discussion of market analysis in Part II, segmentation and positioning analysis in Part III, and implementation of positioning strategies in Part IV.

CHAPTER 1

Market-led strategic management

The successful organization of the future will be customer-focused, not product or technology focused, supported by a market-information competence that links the voice of the customer to all the firm's value-delivery processes .... Successful marketing organizations will have the skills necessary to manage multiple strategic marketing processes, many of which have not, until recently, been regarded as within the domain of marketing.
Frederick E. Webster (1997)

Introduction

In looking at how we will be doing business in the new millennium, there is some debate about whether marketing, as an approach to business and as a business function, has come of age, has reached maturity or is in decline. While a decade ago marketing was misunderstood by many senior managers and typically thought to be just a new name for selling and advertising, today most senior managers could offer passably accurate textbook definitions of marketing, centring on identifying and satisfying customer requirements at a profit, and most would probably also claim that their businesses were 'market-oriented'. In Stephen Greyser's terms, marketing has successfully 'migrated' from being a functional discipline to being a concept of how businesses should be run (Greyser, 1997). Similarly, marketing is talked of as a key function in organizations other than the conventional commercial company – in not-for-profit enterprises like charities and the arts; in political parties; and even in public sector organizations like the police service.

However, the paradox is that this is also a time when many companies are abandoning marketing departments as they prepare to cope with new types of market and increasingly sophisticated customers, through new types of organizations and collaborations between organizations.

In fact, as we shall see in chapter 18, there have been recent challenges to the function of marketing from sources as diverse as McKinsey consultants (e.g. Brady and Davis, 1993) and by theoreticians of a purportedly 'postmodern' persuasion (e.g. Brown, 1995). We shall evaluate the credibility of these challenges in chapter 18, although broadly they appear more concerned with the operational aspects of marketing than the strategic. We shall argue throughout that while the organization structures, operational methods and formal 'trappings' of marketing can and should change to reflect new developments and market opportunities, the philosophy and concept of marketing, as described in this chapter, are even more relevant in the marketing environment faced now than ever before.

Indeed, some suggest that many companies have anyway done little more than pay lip-service to marketing and to the fundamental marketing principle of making focus on the customer a strategic priority. For example, a recent survey of major British companies found the following evidence suggesting lip-service rather than a real commitment to customers:

➤ One hundred per cent of a sample of senior management from *Times 1000* companies said that customer satisfaction was their real measure of success – in fact, most measure successful performance by short-term financials like pre-tax profit, and only 60 per cent use *any* form of customer-based criteria to evaluate staff performance.
➤ Seventy per cent of executives said the customer was their first or second priority; at the same time less than 24 per cent believed management time spent with customers was important, and only 34 per cent saw it as important to train staff in customer service skills.
➤ Seventy-six per cent said they had a database for target marketing – however, almost none placed any value at all on developing relationships with those same customers.
(*Marketing Business*, 1997)

It may be less a case of marketing 'failing' or being in decline, than not been properly understood or effectively implemented in the first place.

Indeed, Doyle (1997) has claimed that relatively few companies have succeeded in moving beyond the 'marketing' trappings of advertising, short-term sales growth and flamboyant innovation to achieve the substance of a robust marketing strategy that produces long-term performance and strong shareholder value. Doyle distinguishes between:

➤ **Radical strategies**: Companies may achieve spectacular growth in sales and profits, but because they do not build customer value through superior products and services, they do not create long-term shareholder value. Characteristics of such strategies are that they are acquisition-based (e.g. Ratners, WPP), or they are marketing department-based (e.g. high levels of advertising and proliferating product-lines), or they are public relations-based (media hype to attract customers).
➤ **Rational strategies**: Some achieve high short-term performance by creating new products which are significantly superior or cheaper than traditional competitors. Examples of such strategies are major innovations in technology, marketing methods or distribution channels (e.g. Amstrad in electronics and personal computers (PCs), Direct Line in the telemarketing of financial services, Sock Shop in speciality retailing). Their weakness is these strategies offer no defensible, sustainable competitive advantage (e.g. Direct Line's

innovatory telephone marketing for financial services gained spectacular short-term competitive advantage but was easily imitated by competitors). They do not build long-term customer relationships, and ultimately fail to produce long-term shareholder value.

➤ **Robust strategies**: These companies achieve steady performance over the long term by creating superior customer value and building long-term customer relationships. Characteristics of these strategies are: focus on superior customer value but recognizing that no innovation on its own can offer long-term advantage; making long-term investments in relationships with suppliers, distributors, employees and customers; processes of continuous learning, innovation and improvement; and developing effective supply-chains and information technology to deliver superior operating performance. Examples include Marks & Spencer, Johnson & Johnson and Toyota.

The implication is that the real challenge facing companies as they move into the twenty-first century is to move past mere lip-service to 'marketing', and to get to grips with what is required to achieve a sustainable, long-term competitive position in the marketplace, which will yield profit and shareholder value. Meeting this challenge may or may not involve a marketing department. It will certainly involve developing a marketing strategy that is based on a profound understanding of the marketplace to define a competitive position that is defensible, and that is supported by a continuous process of learning and improvement in customer value. It will certainly involve competing against new benchmarks of superior service and relationship-building. It will certainly involve the successful management of implementation of marketing strategy, and all that this implies for organizational change.

Indeed, our understanding of the fundamentals of marketing in increasingly enhanced by looking at marketing as 'the process of going to market' (Piercy, 1997), rather than a functional or departmental activity in companies, and as a process which is driven by value-creation for customers. Webster (1997), for example, proposes that marketing should be thought of as the design and management of all the business processes necessary to define, develop and deliver value to customers. He suggests that a list of marketing processes would include the following:

➤ **Value-defining processes**: processes that enable the organization to understand the environment in which it operates better (such as market research, studies of customer needs and preferences, buying behaviour, product use, and so on), to understand its own resources and capabilities more clearly, to determine its own position in the overall value-chain, and to assess the value it creates through economic analysis of customer use systems.

➤ **Value-developing processes**: processes that create value throughout the value chain, such as procurement strategy, new product and service development, design of distribution channels, vendor selection, strategic partnership with service providers (e.g. credit, database management, product service and disposal), pricing strategy development and, ultimately, the development of the value proposition for customers.

➤ **Value-delivering processes**: processes that enable the delivery of value to customers including service delivery, customer relationship management, management of distribution and logistics, communications processes (such as advertising and sales promotion), product and service enhancement, customer support services, and the deployment of the field salesforce.

In the context of managing the process of going to market – value definition, value development and value delivery – we see that the goal of this book is to provide a rigorous analytical framework for developing effective and robust marketing strategies applicable both today and, critically, in the future. A process perspective implies constant effort to increase value. We are interested not only in finding solutions to today's problems, but also in building approaches that will enable organizations to change and adapt as new opportunities and threats arise.

This first chapter sets the scene by examining the marketing concept and market orientation as the foundations of strategic marketing, the impact of a dynamic and changing marketing environment, and the emerging era of market-based strategic management.

1.1 *The marketing concept and market orientation*

1.1.1 Evolving definitions of marketing

One of the earliest pieces of codification and definition in the development of the marketing discipline was concerned with the marketing concept. Nearly forty years ago, Felton (1959) proposed that the marketing concept is:

> A corporate state of mind that exists on the integration and co-ordination of all the marketing functions which, in turn, are melded with all other corporate functions, for the basic objective of producing long-range profits.

More recently, Kotler *et al.* (1996) have suggested that the defining characteristic is that:

> The marketing concept holds that achieving organizational goals depends on determining the needs and wants of target markets and delivering the desired satisfactions more effectively and efficiently than competitors do.

At its simplest, it is generally understood that the marketing concept holds that, in increasingly dynamic and competitive markets, the companies or organizations that are most likely to succeed are those that take notice of customer expectations, wants and needs and gear themselves to satisfying them better than their competitors. It recognizes that there is no reason why customers should buy one organization's offerings unless they are in some way better at serving their wants and needs than those offered by competing organizations.

In fact, the meaning and domain of marketing remains controversial. In 1985 the American Marketing Association reviewed more than twenty-five marketing definitions before arriving at their own, now more or less universally accepted definition (see Ferrell and Lucas, 1987):

> Marketing is the process of planning and executing the conception, pricing, planning and distribution of ideas, goods and services to create exchanges that satisfy individual and organizational objectives.

This definition places marketing as a process that is performed within an organization. This process may or may not be managed by a marketing department or function. It leads to a model of 'mutually beneficial exchanges' as an overview of the role of marketing, as shown in Figure 1.1.

However, moving from textbook definitions of marketing to the realities of what marketing means operationally is more difficult. Webster (1997) points out that of all the management functions, marketing has the most difficulty in defining its position in the organization, because it is simultaneously culture, strategy and tactics. Webster's argument is that marketing involves:

➤ **Organizational culture**: Marketing may be expressed as the 'marketing concept' (Drucker, 1954; McKitterick, 1957; Keith, 1960), i.e. a set of values and beliefs that drives the organization through a fundamental commitment to serving customers' needs as the path to sustained profitability.
➤ **Strategy**: As strategy marketing seeks to develop effective responses to changing market environments by defining market segments, and developing and positioning product offerings for those target markets.
➤ **Tactics**: Marketing as tactics is concerned with the day-to-day activities of product management, pricing, distribution and marketing communications, such as advertising, personal selling, publicity and sales promotion.

The challenge of simultaneously building a customer orientation in an organization (culture), developing value propositions and competitive positioning (strategy) and developing detailed marketing action plans (tactics) is massive and complex. It

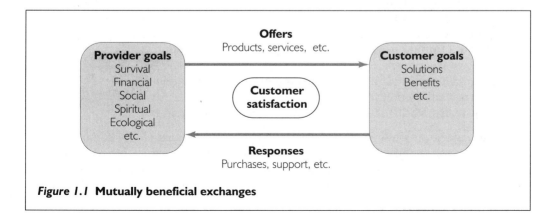

Figure 1.1 **Mutually beneficial exchanges**

is perhaps unsurprising that the organizational reality of marketing often falls short of these demands.

1.1.2 Market orientation

Marketing Science Institute (MSI) studies during the 1990s have attempted to identify the specific activities which translate the philosophy of marketing into reality, i.e. to achieve market orientation. In one of the most widely quoted research streams in modern marketing, Kohli and Jaworski (1990) define market orientation in the following terms:

> a market orientation entails (1) one or more departments engaging in activities geared toward developing an understanding of customers' current and future needs and the factors affecting them, (2) sharing of this understanding across departments, and (3) the various departments engaging in activities designed to meet select customer needs. In other words, a market orientation refers to the organization-wide generation, dissemination, and responsiveness to market intelligence.

This view of market orientation is concerned primarily with the development of what may be called market understanding throughout an organization, and poses a substantial challenge to the executive to develop ways to build this market understanding (see e.g. Piercy and Lane, 1996).

In parallel studies, Narver and Slater (1990) defined market orientation as:

> The organizational culture ... that most effectively and efficiently creates the necessary behaviors for the creation of superior value for buyers and, thus, continuous superior performance for the business.

This work proposes the model shown in Figure 1.2, identifying the components of market orientation as:

➤ **Customer orientation** – understanding customers well enough continuously to create superior value for them.
➤ **Competitor orientation** – awareness of the short- and long-term capabilities of competitors.
➤ **Interfunctional co-ordination** – using all company resources to create value for target customers.
➤ **Organizational culture** – linking employee and managerial behaviour to customer satisfaction.
➤ **Long-term profit focus** – as the overriding business objective.

Although the study findings are somewhat mixed, there appears to be some empirical support for the belief that achieving market orientation is associated with superior performance on the one hand, and internal company benefits like employee commitment and *esprit de corps* on the other (Jaworski and Kohli, 1993; Slater and Narver, 1994).

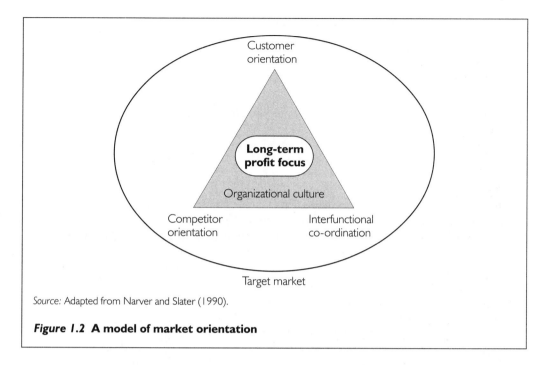

Source: Adapted from Narver and Slater (1990).

Figure 1.2 A model of market orientation

However, what has also been suggested is that there may be substantial barriers to achieving market orientation (Harris, 1996, 1998), and the reality may be that executives face the problem of creating and driving marketing strategy in situations where the company is simply not market-oriented in any real way. This is probably the heart of the implementation problem in marketing (see pp. 389–91 below).

An interesting attempt to 'reinvent' the marketing concept for a new era of different organizational structures, complex relationships and globalization, which may be relevant to overcoming the barriers to market orientation, is made by Frederick Webster (1994). Webster presents 'the new marketing concept as a set of guidelines for creating a customer-focused, market-driven organization', and develops fifteen ideas which weave the 'fabric of the new marketing concept':

1. Create customer focus throughout the business.
2. Listen to the customer.
3. Define and nurture the organization's distinct competencies.
4. Define marketing as market intelligence.
5. Target customers precisely.
6. Manage for profitability, not sales volume.
7. Make customer value the guiding star.
8. Let the customer define loyalty.
9. Measure and manage customer expectations.
10. Build customer relationships and loyalty.

11. Define the business as a service business.
12. Commit to continuous improvement and innovation.
13. Manage culture along with strategy and structure.
14. Grow with partners and alliances.
15. Destroy marketing bureaucracy.

Webster's conceptualization represents a useful attempt to develop a pragmatic operationalization of the marketing concept.

We can summarize the signs of market orientation in the following terms, and underline the links between them and our approach here to marketing strategy and competitive positioning:

➤ Reaching marketing's true potential may rely mostly on success in moving past marketing activities (tactics), to marketing as a company-wide issue of real customer focus (culture) and competitive positioning (strategy). The evidence supports suggestions that marketing has generally been highly effective in tactics, but only marginally effective in changing culture, and largely ineffective in the area of strategy (Day, 1992; Varadarajan, 1992; Webster, 1997).

➤ One key is achieving understanding of the market and the customer throughout the company and building the capability for responsiveness to market changes. The real customer focus and responsiveness of company is the context in which marketing strategy is built and implemented. Our approach to competitive market analysis in Part II provides many of the tools that can be used to enhance and share an understanding of the customer marketplace throughout the company.

➤ Another issue is that the marketing process should be seen as interfunctional and cross-disciplinary, and not simply the responsibility of the marketing department. We shall see in Part IV on competitive positioning strategies that superior service and value, and innovation to build defensible competitive positions, rely on the co-ordinated efforts of many functions and people within the organization.

➤ It is also clear that a deep understanding of the competition in the market from the customer's perspective is critical. Viewing the product or service from the customer's viewpoint is often difficult, but without that perspective a marketing strategy is highly vulnerable to attack from unsuspected sources of competition. We shall confront this issue in Part III, where we are concerned with competitive positioning.

➤ Finally, it follows that the issue is long-term performance, not simply short-term results, and this perspective is implicit in all that we consider in building and implementing marketing strategy.

A framework for executives to evaluate market orientation in their own organizations is shown in Exhibit 1.1. However, it is also important to make the point at this early stage that marketing as organizational culture (the marketing concept and market orientation), must also be placed in the context of change in the external environment.

Exhibit 1.1 **Market orientation assessment**

1 CUSTOMER ORIENTATION

	Strongly agree	Agree	Neither	Disagree	Strongly disagree	Don't know
Information about customer needs and requirements is collected regularly	5	4	3	2	1	0
Our corporate objective and policies are aimed directly at creating satisfied customers	5	4	3	2	1	0
Levels of customer satisfaction are regularly assessed and action taken to improve matters where necessary	5	4	3	2	1	0
We put major effort into building stronger relationships with key customers and customer groups	5	4	3	2	1	0
We recognize the existence of distinct groups or segments in our markets with different needs and we adapt our offerings accordingly	5	4	3	2	1	0

Total score for customer orientation (*out of 25*)

2 COMPETITOR ORIENTATION

	Strongly agree	Agree	Neither	Disagree	Strongly disagree	Don't know
Information about competitor activities is collected regularly	5	4	3	2	1	0
We conduct regular benchmarking against major competitor offerings	5	4	3	2	1	0
There is rapid response to major competitor actions	5	4	3	2	1	0
We put major emphasis on differentiating ourselves from the competition on factors important to customers	5	4	3	2	1	0

Total score for competitor orientation (*out of 20*)

(continued)

Exhibit 1.1 **Continued**

3 LONG-TERM PERSPECTIVES

	Strongly agree	Agree	Neither	Disagree	Strongly disagree	Don't know
We place greater priority on long-term market share gain than short-run profits	5	4	3	2	1	0
We put greater emphasis on improving our market performance than on improving internal efficiencies	5	4	3	2	1	0
Decisions are guided by long-term considerations rather than short-run expediency	5	4	3	2	1	0

Total score for long-term perspectives (*out of 15*)

4 INTERFUNCTIONAL CO-ORDINATION

	Strongly agree	Agree	Neither	Disagree	Strongly disagree	Don't know
Information about customers is widely circulated and communicated throughout the organization	5	4	3	2	1	0
The different departments in the organization work effectively together to serve customer needs	5	4	3	2	1	0
Tensions and rivalries between departments are not allowed to get in the way of serving customers effectively	5	4	3	2	1	0
Our organization is flexible to enable opportunities to be seized effectively rather than hierarchically constrained	5	4	3	2	1	0

Total score for interfunctional co-ordination (*out of 20*)

(continued)

Exhibit 1.1 **Continued**

5 ORGANIZATIONAL CULTURE

	Strongly agree	Agree	Neither	Disagree	Strongly disagree	Don't know
All employees recognize their role in helping to help create satisfied end-customers	5	4	3	2	1	0
Reward structures are closely related to external market performance and customer satisfaction	5	4	3	2	1	0
Senior management in all functional areas give top importance to creating satisfied customers	5	4	3	2	1	0
Senior management meetings give high priority to discussing issues which affect customer satisfaction	5	4	3	2	1	0

Total score for organizational culture (out of 20)

Summary

Customer orientation (*out of 25*)

Competitor orientation (*out of 20*)

Long-term perspectives (*out of 15*)

Interfunctional co-ordination (*out of 20*)

Organizational culture (*out of 20*)

Total score (*out of 100*)

Interpretation

80–100 indicates a high level of market orientation. Scores below 100 can still, however, be improved!

60–80 indicates moderate market orientation – identify the areas where most improvement is needed.

40–60 shows a long way to go in developing a market orientation. Identify the main gaps and set priorities for action to close them.

20–40 indicates a mountain ahead of you! Start at the top and work your way through. Some factors will be more within your control than others. Tackle those first.

Note: If you scored '0' on many of the scales you need to find out more about your own company!

1.2 *The changing marketing environment*

Of critical importance in developing and implementing a market orientation, and in developing robust marketing strategies, is awareness of how the environment in which marketing takes place is changing. At its simplest, the marketing environment can be divided into the *competitive environment* (including the company, its immediate competitors and customers) and the *macroenvironment* (the wider social, political and economic setting). Understanding and analyzing the competitive environment is dealt with in detail in Part II of this book as a foundation for developing marketing strategy. Here we deal briefly with the nature of the changes in the macroenvironment that affect all marketers.

The importance of understanding the macroenvironment is two-fold: we should recognize the marketing impact of fundamental environmental change, but we should also be alert to the fact that the nature of the change facing companies is itself changing. For example, Stephen Haeckel (1997) writes that of all the pressures driving companies to revitalize their marketing processes 'the leading candidate is a change in the nature of change: from continuous (but incremental) to discontinuous [because] when discontinuous change makes customer requests unpredictable, strategic leverage shifts from efficiency to flexibility and responsiveness – and to investments that enable a firm to sense unanticipated change earlier and co-ordinate an unprecedented response to it faster.'

Many important changes are taking place in the environment in which marketing operates and some important examples are summarized briefly below; however, this cannot be a comprehensive list for the reason discussed above. For these purposes change is discussed under four main headings: economic and political change, social/cultural change, technological change, and the resulting marketing change, as shown in Figure 1.3.

1.2.1 Economic and political change

In the last decade major changes have revolved around questions like the following.

The slowing of economic growth experienced in most of the developed economies has brought many consequences. It is still not clear whether this slowdown is temporary or structural. While growth is undoubtedly cyclical, the indications are that the developed economies are unlikely to see again the rates of growth experienced in the years after the Second World War. Many organizations will have to learn to live with low growth in their once buoyant markets. Where growth objectives once dominated management thinking, other criteria are now becoming more important. Market choices may be affected radically: John Farley (1997) ranks the most attractive international markets for the year 2003 not as the United States (US) or the European marketplace, but as India, China, Brazil, Indonesia and Nigeria.

The continuing North–South divide between the rich and poor nations, the developed and the underdeveloped, is accompanied by a growing recognition by

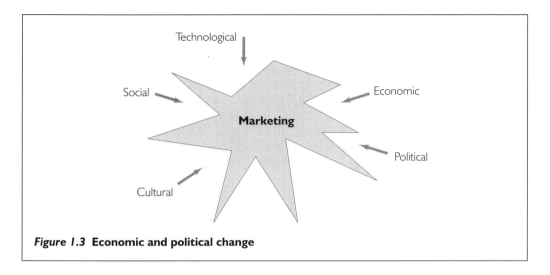

Figure 1.3 Economic and political change

Third World raw materials producers of the power they hold over the Western, developed economies. This was sharply demonstrated by the formation of OPEC in the early 1970s and the immediate effect on world energy prices. At that time energy costs soared and other Third World countries with valuable raw materials realized the power their resources gave them.

More recently the late 1980s/early 1990s saw dramatic changes in East/West relationships. The dismantling of the Berlin Wall, the liberalization of the economies of Central Europe (Poland, Hungary, Czechoslovakia, Bulgaria) and the break-up of the Soviet Union into the new Commonwealth of Independent States, signalled many potential changes in trading patterns.

While the political barriers have been coming down in Europe, there is some concern that the emergence of regional trading blocs ('free trade areas') will have a dramatic impact on the future of free world trade. The Single European Market post-1993, closer economic relations in the Asia Pacific region (Australia, Singapore, Thailand, South Korea, etc.) and the North American Free Trade Alliance zone (US, Canada and Mexico) are emerging as massive internal markets where domestic-based, 'international' trade will become freer, to the disadvantage of those outside.

At the same time, trade between trading blocs or nations outside them may become more restricted. Major trading partners such as the US and Japan are increasingly entering into bilateral trade deals (e.g. the US–Japan deal on semiconductors). While most politicians espouse the goals of free international trade (see, for example, Sir Leon Brittan (1990), EC Competition Commissioner, speaking at the EC/Japan Journalists' Conference), the realities of the 1990s are a concentration of trade within blocs and reduced trade between them.

The United Kingdom (UK) approaches the new century with a 'New Labour' government with many policies directly affecting business: high-profile ministerial support for retailers breaking price-fixing deals espoused by branded goods manufacturers like Adidas and Levi-Strauss; a new and potentially restrictive morality relating to international arms and munitions sales; banning tobacco companies from sponsoring sports; governmental attacks on breweries for attracting under-age drinkers to 'alco-pops' leading to major changes in product names and distribution; the banning of handguns for the whole population in response to pressure from a handful of 'politically correct' lobbyists; and so on. In fact, these changes are modest compared to those faced, for example, by companies operating in Hong Kong after its return to Chinese sovereignty in 1997. Companies have to learn to adjust quickly to a new political will in a country.

1.2.2 Social and cultural change

Coupled with the changing economic environment has been a continuous change in social attitudes and values (at least in the developed West) that are likely to have important implications for marketing management. Examples include the following.

Increased questioning of the industrial profit motive as the main objective for commercial enterprises has grown. More stakeholders are being recognized as having a legitimate input into the setting of organizational objectives. Stakeholders include the owners of the organization (usually shareholders), the managers who run the business (increasingly management and ownership is being divorced as more professional managers move from one company to another during their careers), the people who work for the organization, the customers of the organization, the suppliers who depend on the organization for their livelihoods, and the wider society on which the organization has an impact. Managers and workers have changing expectations from work as standards of living increase.

A further social/cultural change has been in attitudes to, and concern for, the physical environment. Environmental pressure groups impact on businesses, so much so that major oil multinationals and others spend large amounts on corporate advertising each year to demonstrate their concern and care for the environment. The activities of Greenpeace have begun to have a major impact on public opinion and now affect policy-making at the national and international levels. It is to be expected that concern for the environment will increase and hence will be a major factor in managing that prime marketing asset – company reputation. The significance of the impact on business is underlined by BP's recent court action against Greenpeace to constrain their actions.

None the less, the 'green' movement has seen the emergence of new consumer market segments based on attitudes towards green issues:

➤ **Affluent greens and young greens** – some 36 per cent of the population, who are committed to green consumerism.
➤ **Recyclers and careful spenders** – around 38 per cent of the population, who act in an environmentally friendly way, but do not usually 'buy green'.

➤ **Sceptics** – about 26 per cent of the population, who are determined not to buy green under any circumstances (Clover, 1996).

New cars like the Ford Ka, the Renault Twingo and the Mercedes Smart car are examples of compact, fuel-economical, low-emission vehicles, designed and produced for city use, in anticipation of environmental pressure and stricter legislation on pollution levels in cities.

Even more surprising, the much vilified Reliant Robin (a three-wheel car with a fibreglass body originally positioned as the cheapest motoring for low-income consumers) has been saved from bankruptcy by the Green movement. In 1997 the Reliant Robin was selling as a status symbol for young professionals in Austria, Monaco and California, because it uses very little petrol, does not rust and causes little pollution (and is fun) (Self, 1997).

Coupled with greater concern for the environment is greater concern for personal health. There has been a dramatic movement in the grocery industry, for example, towards healthier food products, such as wholemeal bread and bran-based cereals. This movement, originally dismissed by many food manufacturers as a passing fad amongst a minority of the population, has accelerated with the marketing of low-sugar, salt-free products, free from additives, colourings and preservatives. Fitness products in general, such as jogging suits and exercise machines, have enjoyed very buoyant markets.

The 'demographic timebomb' has started to have an impact on diverse businesses. With generally better standards of living, life expectancy has increased. Death rates have declined in all age groups but most significantly in the older age categories. For males in Britain life expectation has risen from 48 years in 1901, to 68 years in 1961 and 73 years in 1991. For females it has risen from 52 years in 1901, to 74 years in 1961 and 78 years in 1991. By 1985 15 per cent of the population were over the age of 65. Barratt Developments in Britain, for example, have particularly quick to capitalize on this change in the demographic profile and have specialized in providing retirement homes for the elderly. Demographic changes of this type vary significantly between countries and regions throughout the world, and warrant serious study as a fundamental influence on demand for different products and services.

At the other end of the spectrum the youth market has recently become more affluent and poses new opportunities for marketers. Fashion and music industries have been quick to recognize this newfound affluence. Much of the success of Virgin Records (sold to Thorn EMI for over £500 million in early 1992) was based on understanding and catering for this market. Clothes stores too such as Now and Next built their early successes on catering to the teenager market.

Related to this youth market has been the emergence of the enigmatic 'Generation X' consumer – the cynical, world-weary 'twenty-somethings', who are hostile to business values and traditional advertising and branding, and reject many conventional product offers. The payoff in understanding the values and preferences of this type of consumer has been substantial for companies like Nike in clothing and footwear and Boss in fragrances and clothing – these consumers react positively to pictures of athletes vomiting on their sport shoes at the end of the race, and Nike's advertising copy: 'We don't sell dreams. We sell shoes … Don't insult our intelligence. Tell us what it is. Tell us what it does. And don't play the national anthem while you do it.'

The UK has become an increasingly multi-ethnic society – by the late 1990s ethnic minorities comprised 5.5 per cent of the population and forecasts predicted the number would double in the next 50 years. This group currently spends some £10 billion a year, and includes many socially mobile and affluent groups. As well as a target for specialized products and services, ethnic minorities are increasingly vocal about what they object to in conventional marketing and advertising. For example, some brands have been labelled as 'ethnically insensitive', such as Persil's TV advertisement showing a Dalmation dog shaking off its black spots, or McDonald's TV advertisement showing a stereotypical young black man listening to very loud music while driving. On the other hand, some marketers have earned praise for being 'ethnically sensitive': for example, BT's radio advertisements in Hindi to promote long-distance phone calls, and W.H. Smith for stocking ethnic greetings cards (Dwek, 1997).

There has also been an increase in single-person households, so much so that the BBC launched a television series on cooking for one. Barratt Developments have complemented their success in the retirement homes market by successfully developing 'Studio Solos', housing accommodation for the young, single but more affluent individual.

Even during the period of increasing unemployment there was a significant growth in the numbers of women in employment, be it full- or part-time. This led to changes in household eating patterns, with an emphasis on convenience foods and cooking. It has, in turn, led to increased markets for products to make cooking and meal preparation easier and quicker, such as the deep freeze, the food processor and the microwave oven.

1.2.3 Technological change

The latter part of the twentieth century has seen technological change and development impact on virtually every industry. Key points include the following.

The microprocessor has been attributed with heralding the post-industrial age and it is probably this invention above all others that has had the most profound effect on our lives today. Microprocessors have revolutionized data collection, processing and dissemination. They have caused major changes in production technology and have served to increase the rate of technological change. As Kotler (1997) points out, around 90 per cent of all scientists who ever lived are alive and working today contributing to this increased rate of change in the technologies and processes available to us.

This has been associated with a shortening of commercialization times of new inventions. Photography, for example, took over 100 years from initial invention to commercial viability. The telephone took 56 years, radio 35 years, TV 12 years and the transistor only 3 years.

This shortening of commercialization times has, in turn, led to a shortening of product life cycles with products becoming obsolete much more quickly than previously. In the Japanese electronics industry, for example, the time between perception of a need or demand for a new product and shipment of large quantities of that product can be under five months (e.g. Matsushita colour TVs). Computer integration of manufacturing and design is helping to shorten product development times. It has been estimated that in automobiles this has been in the order of 25 per cent.

Through technological changes whole industries or applications have been wiped out almost overnight. In 1977/8 cross-ply tyre manufacturers in the US lost 50 per cent of the tyre market to radials in just 18 months (Foster, 1986).

Newer technology has a major impact on particular aspects of marketing. The advent of the microcomputer and its wide availability to management has led to increased interest in sophisticated market modelling and decision support systems. Increased amounts of information can now be stored, analyzed and retrieved very much more quickly than in the past. Innovative marketing research companies have been quick to seize on the possibilities afforded by the new technology for getting information to their clients more quickly than competitors. Suppliers of retail audits (see chapter 6) can now present their clients with on-line results of the audits completed only 24 hours previously. In a rapidly changing marketplace the ability to respond quickly afforded by almost instantaneous information can mean the difference between success and failure.

The 'data warehouses' created by the capture of customer data are increasingly a major marketing resource for companies, which has the potential for achieving stronger and more enduring relationships than competitors – examples include the data collected by retailers like Tesco and Sainsbury through their loyalty card schemes; the customer information held by airlines to monitor the purchase behaviour of their frequent flyer customers; and the customer data gained through the direct marketing of products like financial services.

The Internet – the global electronic communications network – is fast emerging as not simply a new marketing communications vehicle, but potentially a whole new way of going to market, which may change the competitive structures of industries irrevocably. Already the consumer can browse through the 'virtual shopping mall' and make direct purchases of products varying from groceries to car insurance to travel tickets. Even the small business (if it invests in the modest costs of establishing a web site) can access markets throughout the world at almost no cost. This changes fundamentally the costs of market entry and the competitive structures of the markets affected.

1.2.4 Marketing changes

In addition to the changes noted above there are several important changes taking place in the general marketing environment and in marketing practices.

In many markets, increased levels of competition, both domestic and international, are reaching unprecedented levels. In the period 1983–84 for example, UK trade with the rest of the world expanded dramatically. In 1983 exports from the UK were £61 billion. By 1993, they had almost doubled to £121 billion (*Annual Abstract of Statistics*, 1995). Yet, by the late 1990s, exports in many sectors were under threat as the strength of sterling forced up the UK's export prices.

Some writers (e.g. Farley, 1997) have argued that many markets are becoming increasingly global in nature and no business, however big or small, is exempt from global competition. The reasoning centres on the impact of technology on people throughout the world. Technology has made products more available and potential consumers more aware of them. Farley believes we are currently experiencing a move towards gigantic, world-scale markets where economies of scale in production, marketing and distribution can be vigorously pursued. The result will be significantly lower costs creating major problems for competitors that do not operate on a global scale. Many of these cost advantages are being realized as companies operating within the EU's Single Market rationalize their production and distribution facilities.

The counter-argument to the globalization thesis is that markets are becoming more fragmented, with consumers more concerned to express their individuality (King, 1985) than to buy mass-produced, mass-marketed products. In addition, there is little evidence of the existence of widespread preference for the cheapest products available. The demand for low prices, relative to other product benefits and extras, is not proven in many markets. Each market should be examined individually and the factors likely to affect it explored.

Whether one subscribes to the globalization argument or not, one factor is clear – that organizations ignore international competition at their peril. The British motor-cycle industry is a textbook example of a once supreme industry now virtually non-existent because of its failure to recognize and respond to the threat posed by cheap, good quality, Japanese motor-bikes.

At the same time as markets are becoming more global so the existence of distinct market segments is becoming clearer. The most successful firms are those that have recognized this increasing importance of segmentation and positioned their companies so as to take best advantage of it. Van den Berghs is a prime example in the UK 'yellow fats' (butter and margarine) market. They have clearly identified several main segments of the market and positioned individual brands to meet the needs of those segments (see chapter 9). The company now commands in excess of 60 per cent of the margarine market through a policy of domination of each distinct market segment.

The role of marketing in the modern corporation has been subject to far-reaching reappraisal in many cases (e.g. Webster, 1992). It is possible to argue that the marketing function has a major role to play in keeping the company up-to-date with changes in its broader environment and the competitive environment. However, the way that role is fulfilled is likely to reflect major forces of change, such as: increasingly sophisticated customers; the move from an emphasis on single sales transactions to long-term customer relationships; the role of information technology

(IT) in changing how markets and organizations work; and the development of the network organization consisting of a group of companies collaborating to exploit their core competencies linked together by a mix of strategic alliances, vertical integration and looser partnerships (Webster, 1994). The implications for how marketing will operate are profound (see chapters 8 and 19).

1.2.5 The impact of change

Several broad conclusions can now be drawn and their implications for marketing management identified.

First, in many industries the days of fast growth are gone forever. In those where high rates of growth are still possible competition is likely to be increasingly fierce and of an international nature. It is no longer sufficient for companies to become marketing oriented. That is taken for granted. The keys to success will be the effective implementation of the marketing concept through clearly defined positioning strategies.

Second, change creates opportunities for innovative organizations and threats for those who, Canute-like, attempt to hold them back. It is probable that there will be a redefinition of 'work' and 'leisure' which will provide significant new opportunities to those companies ready and able to seize them. The changing demographic profile, particularly in terms of age, marital status and income distribution, also poses many opportunities for marketing management.

Third, the speed of change in the environment is accelerating, leading to greater complexity and added 'turbulence', or discontinuity. Technological developments are combining to shorten product life cycles and speed up commercialization times. The increasing turbulence in the market makes it particularly difficult to predict. As a result planning horizons have been shortened. Where long-range plans in relatively predictable markets could span 10–15 years, very few companies today are able to plan beyond the next few years in any but the most general terms.

Fourth, successful strategies erode over time. What has been successful at one point in time, in one market, cannot guarantee success in the future in the same or other markets. The following examples underline that fact, and should discourage complacency that any company need not continually evaluate its marketing strategy.

J. Sainsbury plc is a family-dominated business which operates the supermarket chain that has changed the food and wine that British consumers buy in fundamental ways. For a generation, Sainsbury was the market leader in the grocery business and was the watchword for quality, choice and innovation in food and wine – by the 1990s the company had become a British 'institution'. Tesco Stores, by contrast, was the second player, which had grown from a downmarket discount retailer into a supermarket operator, forever associated with its founder's slogan of 'pile it high, sell it cheap'. In 1995, Sainsbury lost market leadership to Tesco. This trauma was accompanied by a massive slump in Sainsbury's share value, and continued losses of market share to Tesco. Sainsbury had continued its strategy of the 1980s into the 1990s. Tesco had developed a repositioning strategy based on product and store quality (and persevered with this strategy through the recession, when many commentators said they had got it wrong), backed by a massive investment in information technology to dramatically improve operational efficiency and value to customers. Sainsbury's strategy became outdated, but worse the company shows no sign of being able to develop a coherent response to the new situation (Piercy, 1997).

Founded in 1953 by Bernard and Laura Ashley, the Laura Ashley company was based on a quintessentially British design concept, characterized by the long flowing skirts and romantic floral designs which were the foundation of the company's success in the 1960s and 1970s. With its Victorian and Edwardian-style designs, Laura Ashley wallcoverings were favoured in locations like the British embassy in Washington and Highgrove, home of the Prince of Wales, and its floral smocks and chintzes were favoured by a young Princess Diana. From its early designs for women's clothes, the company had expanded rapidly into fabrics, wallcoverings and paints, linked by the central design concept. Manufacturing plants were established in Wales, and by 1997 the company operated more than 400 retail stores worldwide covering dozens of countries, including more than 150 in the USA. By 1997 the company had sales of £320 million, but was issuing repeated profit warnings, and its shares had lost three-quarters of their value in 12 months. The loss-making manufacturing units started to declare redundancies. The death of the founder in 1985 had marked a turning point. The loss of vision for the company at that point was accompanied by losses in most of the following 12 years. Ann Iverson (then Chief Executive) faced the problem of turning the company around and reclaiming its position with the affluent 35–50-year-old female fashion buyer. City commentators point to the strength of new competitors like Ralph Lauren in this core market, and conclude that 'Its management must decide what to be, preferably before the money runs out' (*Daily Telegraph*, 1997; Olins, 1997a).

Almost every British high street and rail station has a W.H. Smith retail outlet, selling magazines and newspapers, books, stationery, cassettes/compact discs and videos. Its bookstalls first appeared in 1792, and W.H. Smith had a market value of £1.1 billion in 1997 with 10 million customers a week buying in its stores. However, during the 1980s and 1990s, W.H. Smith's traditional core market has been attacked by strong competitors. On the one side, there has been a growth in specialist retailers like Dillons, and the other side there has been a dramatic expansion by the main supermarket groups in selling books, newspapers and music/videos. Smiths has bought its own specialists, like Dillons and Our Price, but the commercial position of the core retail chain has continued to decline. Many of the peripheral businesses were sold by Bill Cockburn, the chief executive who spent the mid-1990s trying to position the company as a 'world-class retailer', before resigning in 1996. Management at the problematic retail chain claim that W.H. Smith is a middle-of-the-market variety chain, serving consumers who are not Dillons customers or Tesco customers. The retail business is struggling to find a role and has been left behind by market change. Some commentators in the city accuse W.H. Smith of smugness. Analysts suggest that the underlying retail concept and trading format has had its day, leaving the business with no credible growth strategy in its core business (Olins, 1997b; Weyer, 1997).

1.2.6 New strategies for changing environments

However, to suggest that firms need to develop new strategies as times change may not go far enough. The problem may not just be that we need to develop new strategies, but that we have to develop wholly new approaches to strategy. For example, at the 1997 Academy of Marketing Science conference, two leading marketing thinkers spoke of the trends in strategic development which they believe have to be confronted.

Jagdish Sheth challenged conventional marketing thinking along the following lines:

➤ **Global positioning**: Sheth urges strategists to think about globalization and a focus on core competencies, instead of thinking about the domestic market and a portfolio of business and brands. He suggests the need for a different approach to delivering shareholder value (see Figure 1.4).

➤ **The master brand**: Sheth argues that strength comes from a brand identity that links all parts of the business – this is the fundamental strength of Toyota and Honda compared to the dozens of brands operated by General Motors.

➤ **The integrated enterprise and end-user focus**: the challenge of managing people, processes and infrastructure to deliver value to an end-user.

➤ **Best-in-class processes**: customers do not, for example, compare an airline's service just to that of other airlines; the new standards for the airline to meet come from service excellence at companies like Federal Express and Marriott hotels – the challenge is to meet world-class standards from wherever they come.

➤ **Mass customization**: the imperative is to achieve scale economies, but at the

Source: Adapted from Sheth (1994).

Figure 1.4 The shift in strategy for delivering shareholder value

same time to produce a product or service tailored to the individual customer's requirements.

➤ **Breakthrough technology**: new technology will underpin every aspect of the marketing process, even the product itself, in ways which may seem outlandish. For example, a new product in Japan is the 'smart toilet'. Avoiding technical details, basically the person just sits there and the machine does the rest. However, the machine also produces a diagnosis of waste output, as well as measuring the user's temperature and blood pressure. Useless technology? Not in situations where there is an ageing population with potential medical problems and insufficient hospital places. For around $600 the home has a first line of medical diagnosis, which may save many lives.

David Cravens underlined the message that traditional views of strategy may quickly become obsolete. He argued that the strategy paradigms of the last twenty years are increasingly inadequate as we enter a new era of 'market-based strategy'. His predictions took the following forms:

➤ **Markets shape business strategy**: Cravens suggests that the market will be seen as the dominant force shaping how business operates – this is the factor that links industrial economics, total quality management (TQM), financial investment appraisal and business process re-engineering.

➤ **Networks of interlinked product markets**: he notes that traditional boundaries based on conventional product markets will blur and become irrelevant, and this blurring will become the norm. Look, for example, at the move of grocery supermarkets like Sainsbury and Tesco into banking and financial services. How else do we make sense of Virgin moving from music to retailing to airlines to rail transport to financial services to cosmetics to drinks to clothes, all under the single Virgin brand?

➤ **The move from functions to processes**: he also suggests that the new era of market-based strategy is one where we will increasingly focus on the process of going to market not the interests of traditional departments and specialists.

➤ **Strategic alliances**: for many companies the future will be one of collaboration and partnership to allow them to focus on core competencies, not one of traditional competition.

➤ **The balanced scorecard**: keeping score involves evaluating the benefits we deliver to all the stakeholders in the organization.

These predictions imply the need to create new types of strategies, not just more of the same. They also underline the critical importance of building market sensing and organizational learning capabilities, to allow organizations to understand what is happening and to act accordingly.

The above factors all combine to make strategic planning in general, and marketing planning in particular, more difficult now than they have ever been before. They also make them more vital activities than they have ever been before. Strategic marketing planning today attempts to build flexibility into the organization to enable it to cope with this increased level of complexity and uncertainty and to take full advantage of the changing environment. At the heart of that planning process is the creation of a strong competitive position and a robust marketing strategy, the subject of the remainder of this book.

1.3 *Marketing fundamentals*

Following from the underlying marketing concept outlined above and the changes identified in the context in which marketing takes place we can distil a set of basic and very pragmatic marketing principles which serve to guide marketing thought and action. The principles follow the logic of value-based processes described by Webster (1997) (see pp. 5–6 above). Each of these principles seems so obvious as not to require stating. However, recognition of these principles and their application can revolutionize how organizations respond to, and interact with, their customers.

Principle 1: The customer is the centre of everything

A first principle of marketing which emerges from our comments throughout goes back to the marketing concept itself. This recognizes that the long-run objectives of the organization, be they financial or social, are best served by achieving a high degree of customer focus. From that recognition flows the need for a close investigation of customer wants and needs, followed by a clear definition of how the company can best serve them.

It also follows that the only arbiters of how well the organization satisfies its customers are the customers themselves. The quality of the goods or services offered to the market will be judged by the customers on the basis of how well their requirements are satisfied. A quality product or service, from the customers' perspective, is one that satisfies or is 'fit for purpose' rather than one that provides unrequired luxury.

As Levitt (1986) demonstrates, adopting a market-led approach poses some very basic questions. The most important include:

What business are we in?
What business could we be in?
What business do we want to be in?
What must we do to get into or consolidate in that business?

The answers to these fundamental questions can often change a company's whole outlook and perspective. In chapter 2 we discuss more fully business definition and show how it is fundamental to setting strategic direction for the organization.

Principle 2: Customers do not buy products

The second basic marketing principle is that customers do not buy products, they buy what the product can do for them – the problem it solves. In other words, customers are less interested in the technical features of a product or service than in what benefits they get from buying, using or consuming the product or service. For example, a classic example is that the DIYer does not want a quarter-inch drill bit, but a quarter-inch hole. The drill bit is merely a way of delivering that benefit (the hole) and will only be the solution to the basic need until a better method or solution is invented (Kotler, 1997). We can go further – what s/he probably wants is storage for books. Competition will not come just from other manufacturers of drill bits, but from laser techniques for making holes in the wall; wall designs that incorporate shelving studs in their design; adhesives that will support shelves; or alternative ways of storing books. This is the difference between an industry – firms with similar technology and products – and a market – customers with a problem to solve or a need to meet. In this sense, white goods manufacturers may see themselves as an industry – they all produce white boxes with electric motors – but the markets they serve are the laundry market, the food storage market, and so on. Similarly the gardener does not really want a lawnmower. What s/he wants is grass that is 1 inch high. Hence a new strain of grass seed, which is hardwearing and only grows to 1 inch in height, could provide very substantial competition to lawnmower manufacturers, as could artificial grass substitutes or fashions for grass-free garden designs.

This is far from mere academic theorizing. One trend in retail marketing in the grocery business is category management. Retailers are attempting to define categories around customer needs, not manufacturers' brands. For example, one common category is 'meal replacement' – the challenge to manufacturers is to prove the retailer with what their products and brands add to the value of the category. Putting category definition at its simplest:

The manufacturer makes	potato crisps
The retailer merchandizes	salty snacks
The customer buys	lunch!

Looking at a market from the customer's perspective may suggest a very different view of market opportunities and the threats to our competitive position.

Some effects are surprising: Wal-Mart, the US discount retailer, merchandizes disposable nappies and packs of beer together on Fridays. The reason? Their point-of-sale data analysis shows that these products are bought together. Young parents are asked to pick-up a pack of disposable nappies on the way home from work by their partners, and use the opportunity to buy beer as well (these purchase needs may be causally linked!) – and this starts to identify a category for the retailer.

It is critical that marketers view products and services as 'bundles of benefits', or a combination of attractions that all give something of value to the customer.

One mission for the marketing executive is to ensure that the organization should gear itself to solving customers' problems, rather than exclusively promote its own current (and often transitory) solutions.

Principle 3: Marketing is too important to leave to the marketing department (even if there still is one)

It is increasingly the case that marketing is everyone's job in the organization. The actions of all can have an impact on the final customers and the satisfaction the customer derives.

King (1985) has pointed to a number of misconceptions as to what marketing is. One of the most insidious misconceptions he terms 'marketing department marketing' where an organization employs marketing professionals who may be very good at analyzing marketing data and calculating market shares to three decimal points, but who have very little real impact on the products and services the organization offers to its customers. The marketing department is seen as the only department where 'marketing is done' so that the other departments can get on with their own agenda and pursue their own goals.

As organizations become flatter, reducing layers of bureaucracy, and continue to break down the spurious functional barriers between departments, so it becomes increasingly obvious that marketing is the job of everyone. It is equally obvious that marketing is so central to both survival and prosperity that it is far too important to leave only to the marketing department.

However, it is clear that we must avoid simply stating that marketing is 'everyone's job' and leaving it at that. If marketing is 'everyone's job', it may become 'no one's job'. Stephen Greyser (1997) points to the need for simultaneous upgrading of market orientation and downsizing of the formal marketing function, as two sides of the same issue:

> While the marketing function ('doing marketing') belongs to the marketing department, becoming and being marketing-minded is *everybody's* job. What happens when (almost) everybody is doing that job? As companies have become more marketing-minded, there have been substantial reductions in the formal 'marketing departments' which *do* marketing. In short, a corollary of the trend to better organizational *thinking* about marketing is the dispersion of the *activity* of marketing, e.g. via task forces.

Principle 4: Markets are heterogeneous

It is becoming increasingly evident that most markets are not homogeneous, but are made up of different individual customers, sub-markets or segments. While some customers, for example, may buy a car for cheap transport from A to B, others may buy for comfortable travel, or safe travel, and still others may buy for status reasons or to satisfy and project their self-image. Products and services that attempt to satisfy a segmented market through a standardized product almost invariably fall between two or more stools and become vulnerable to more clearly targeted competitors.

Picking up on Principle 2, it is evident that a basic way of segmenting markets is on the basis of the benefits customers get in buying or consuming the product or service. Benefit segmentation (see chapter 10) has proved to be one of the most useful ways of segmenting markets for the simple reason that it relates the segmentation back to the real reasons for the existence of the segments in the first place – different benefit requirements.

Principle 5: Markets and customers are constantly changing

It is a truism to say that the only constant is change. Markets are dynamic and virtually all products have a limited life which expires when a new or better way of satisfying the underlying want or need is found; in other words, until another solution or benefit provider comes along.

The fate of the slide rule, and before that logarithmic tables, at the hands of the pocket calculator is a classic example where the problem (the need for rapid and easy calculation) was better solved through a newer technology. The benefits offered by calculators far outstripped the slide rule in speed and ease of use.

This recognition that products are not omnipotent, that they follow a product life cycle (PLC) pattern of introduction, growth, maturity and decline, has led companies to look and plan more long term; to ensure that when the current breadwinners die there are new products in the company's portfolio to take their place. The development of product portfolio planning has been one of the most far-reaching contributions of marketing to strategic management in recent years. These developments are discussed in chapter 3.

Also evident is the need for constant product and service improvement. As customer expectations change, usually becoming more demanding in the benefits they expect from a given product or service, so organizations need continuously to upgrade their offerings to retain, let alone improve, position.

There are two main processes of improvement. The first is through innovation where a relatively large step is taken at one point in time. The advent of the pocket calculator was a significant innovation which virtually wiped out the slide rule industry overnight. Other step changes in technology such as the advent of colour television and the compact disc have served to change whole industries in a similarly short period of time.

The second approach to improvement is a more continuous process whereby smaller changes are made but on an insistent basis. This approach has been identified by a number of writers (e.g. Imai, 1986) as a major contributor to the success of Japanese businesses in world markets since the early 1950s. The Japanese call continuous improvement *Kaizen* and see it as an integral part of business life. Increasingly, organizations are attempting to marry the benefits of step change innovation with continuous (*Kaizen*) improvement. Figure 1.5 illustrates this process diagramatically.

The impact of technological change has been felt most, perhaps, in the computer industry. It is sometimes hard to remember that computers were invented *after* the Second World War because they are now such a pervasive part of both business and

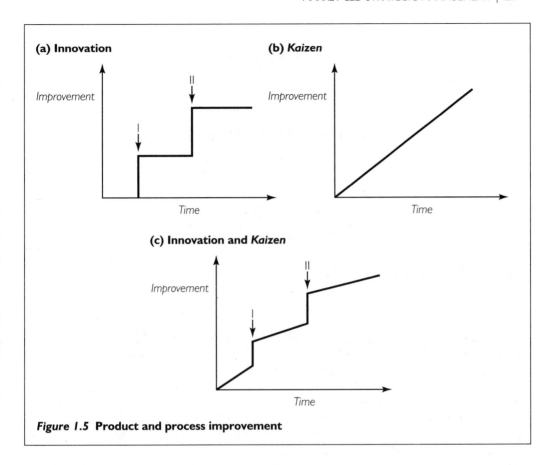

***Figure 1.5* Product and process improvement**

home life. Toffler (1981) noted in *Computer World* magazine:

> If the auto industry had done what the computer industry has done over the last thirty years, a Rolls Royce would cost $2:50, get around 2,000,000 miles to the gallon and six of them would fit on the head of a pin!

1.4 *The role of marketing in leading strategic management*

In order for strategic management to cope with the changing marketing environment there is a need for it to become increasingly market-led. In taking a leading role in the development and the implementation of strategy the role of marketing can be defined in the way shown in Figure 1.6. That role is threefold:

1.4.1 Identification of customer requirements

The first critical task of marketing is to identify the requirements of customers and

Figure 1.6 **The role of marketing in leading strategic management**

to communicate them effectively throughout the organization. This involves conducting or commissioning relevant customer research to uncover first, who the customers are, and second, what will give them satisfaction.

Who the customers are is not always obvious. In some circumstances buyers may be different from users or consumers; specifiers and influencers may also be different. Where services are funded, for example, by central government the suppliers may be forgiven for the (mistaken) view that government is their customer.

Customers may expect a degree of benefit from purchasing or using a product or service. They may actually want something more, but believe they have to settle for second best because of budget or other constraints. The organization that can give customers something closer to what they want than what they expect has an opportunity to go beyond customer satisfaction and create 'customer delight'.

Customer expectations, wants and needs must all be understood and clearly communicated to those responsible for designing the product or service, those responsible for creating or producing it, and those responsible for delivering it.

Identifying what customers require is discussed in chapter 6.

1.4.2 Deciding on the competitive positioning to be adopted

Recognizing that markets are heterogeneous and typically made up of various market segments each having different requirements from essentially similar offerings leads to the need to decide clearly which target market or markets the organization will seek to serve.

That decision is made on the basis of two main sets of factors. First, how attractive the alternative potential targets are. And second, how well the company can hope to serve each potential target relative to the competition. In other words, the relative strengths or competencies it can bring into play in serving the market. These two related issues are discussed at length in Part IV.

1.4.3 Implementing the marketing strategy

The third key task of marketing is to marshal all the relevant organizational resources to plan and execute the delivery of customer satisfaction. This involves ensuring that all members of the organization are co-ordinated in their efforts to satisfy customers, and that no actual or potential gaps exist between offer design, production and delivery.

In the field of services marketing there has been a great deal of work aimed at identifying the factors that can create gaps in the process from design through to delivery of offer to customers. Parasuraman, Zeithaml and Berry (1985), for example, have studied each of the potential gaps and concluded that a central role of marketing is to guide design so as to minimize the gaps and hence help to ensure customer satisfaction through the delivery of high quality (fit for the purpose) services (see chapter 15).

Chapters 17 and 18 address implementation and co-ordination issues more fully.

1.5 Conclusions

This chapter has sought to review the marketing concept and demonstrate its importance in providing a guiding approach to doing business in the face of increasingly competitive and less predictable marketing environments. This approach we term market-led strategic management. A number of marketing principles were discussed, together with the role of marketing in strategic management. The remainder of Part I presents a framework for developing a market-led approach.

CHAPTER 2

Strategic marketing planning

Strategy is the matching of the activities of an organisation to the environment in which it operates and to its own resource capabilities.

Johnson and Scholes (1988)

Introduction

The essence of developing a marketing strategy for a company is to ensure that the company's capabilities are matched to the competitive market environment in which it operates not just for today, but into the foreseeable future. This involves assessing the company's strengths and weaknesses, and the opportunities and threats facing it.

Strategic planning attempts to answer three basic questions:

1. What is the business doing now?
2. What is happening in the environment?
3. What should the business be doing?

Strategy is concerned primarily with effectiveness (doing the right things) rather than efficiency (doing what you do well). The vast bulk of management time is, of necessity, concerned with day-to-day operations management. A time audit for even senior management will often reveal a disproportionate amount of time spent on routine daily tasks, with the more difficult and demanding task of planning further into the future relegated to a weekend or one-week conference once a year. In the most successful companies, however, thinking strategically, sitting back from the present concerns of improving what you do now and questioning what it is you are doing, is a constant process.

As with the adoption of a marketing philosophy throughout the organization the adoption of strategic thinking goes beyond the brief of marketing management alone. All senior executives in the company or organization have a responsibility for developing the strategic profile of the company and giving it a strategic focus. Strategic planning and strategic marketing planning share many activities, although strategic planning has more breadth and covers all business activities. A marketing orientation must permeate the whole of an organization, but the strategic marketing plan is just one of several functional plans that feed into the overall strategic plan of a company. Marketing management, however, with its specific responsibility for managing the interface between the organization and its environment (both customers and competitors), has an increasingly important role to play in overall strategy development.

2.1 *The marketing strategy process*

The development of a marketing strategy can be viewed at three main levels: the establishment of a core strategy, the creation of the company's competitive positioning and the implementation of the strategy (see Figure 2.1).

The establishment of an effective marketing strategy starts with a detailed, and creative, assessment both of the company's capabilities – its strengths and weaknesses relative to the competition – and the opportunities and threats posed by the environment. On the basis of this analysis the core strategy of the company will be selected, identifying marketing objectives and the broad focus for achieving them.

At the next level market targets (both customers and competitors) are selected and/or identified. At the same time the company's differential advantage, or competitive edge, in serving the customer targets better than the competition is defined. Taken together the identification of targets and the definition of differential advantage constitute the creation of the competitive positioning of the organization and its offerings.

At the implementation level a marketing organization capable of putting the strategy into practice must be created. The design of the marketing organization can be crucial to the success of the strategy. Implementation is also concerned with

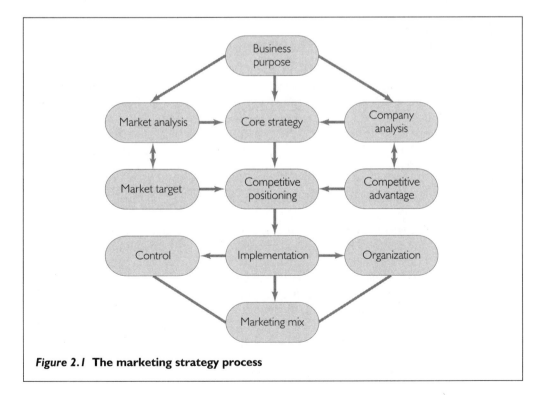

Figure 2.1 **The marketing strategy process**

establishing a mix of products, price, promotion and distribution that can both convey the positioning and the products and services themselves to the target market. Finally, methods of control must be designed to ensure that the strategy implementation is successful. Control concerns both the efficiency with which the strategy is put into operation and the ultimate effectiveness of that strategy. Each of the three main levels of strategy is now considered in more detail.

2.2 *Establishing the core strategy*

The core strategy is both a statement of the company's objectives and the broad strategies it will use to achieve them. The three main ingredients for establishing the core strategy are: (1) defining the business purpose or mission; (2) analyzing the company's capability profile or strengths and weaknesses; and (3) examining the industry (customers and competitors) in which the company operates or wishes to operate.

2.2.1 **Defining the business purpose**

Defining the business purpose or mission requires the company to ask the fundamental questions first posed by Levitt more than a quarter of a century ago (see Levitt, 1960):

> **What business are we in?**
> **What business do we want to be in?**

Several years ago, so marketing folklore has it, a new managing director took over at Parker Pens. One of his first actions was to assemble the board of directors, stand before them holding the top of the range Parker of the day and ask, 'Who is our greatest competitor?'

The first answer to emerge from the board was Shaeffer. Shaeffer produced a pen very similar to the Parker. It had a good reputation for quality, had a similar stylish finish and was similarly priced at the top end of the market. The new managing director was not, however, impressed with this answer. 'We certainly compete to some extent with Shaeffer, but they are by no means our major competitor.'

A newer member of the board then suggested that the major competitor might be Biro-Swan, the manufacturers and marketers of a range of ballpoint pens. While these retailed considerably cheaper than the Parker he reasoned that they were used for the same purpose (writing) and hence competed directly with Parker. The business definition was now changing from 'quality fountain pens' to 'writing implements' and under this definition pencils could also be considered as competitors, as could the more recent developments in the market of fibre tip pens and roller ball pens. 'Your thinking is getting better', said the MD, 'but you're still not there.'

Another board member then suggested that perhaps the major competitor was the telephone which had been gaining more widespread use in recent years. Under this view of the market they were in 'communications' and competing with other forms of communication including the written word (perhaps competing here with typewriters and more recently word processors) and other (verbal) means of communication. 'More creative thinking', said the MD, 'but you still haven't identified the main competitor.'

Eventually the MD gave his view of the major competitor. To an astonished board he announced 'Our major competitor is the Ronson cigarette lighter!' When asked to explain his reasoning he defined the market that the company was in as the 'quality gift market'. Analysis of sales of Parker Pens showed that the majority of purchases were made by individuals buying them as gifts for other people. When they considered what to buy often a major alternative was a quality cigarette lighter and hence the definition of the market (example courtesy of Graham Kenwright, Birmingham Chamber of Commerce).

This definition has widespread implications for the marketing of the product. Packaging assumes a more important role, as does the development and maintenance of a superior quality image. Price is perhaps less important than might have been thought under alternative market definitions. Distribution (through the outlets where potential customers buy gifts) also becomes more important.

This example serves to illustrate how asking a basic question such as 'who is our major competitor?' or 'what market are we in?' can affect the whole of the strategic direction of the company.

Mission formulation and statement
Hooley, Cox and Adams (1992) discuss the elements that go to make up an effective statement of mission. These are shown in Figure 2.2. The mission statement

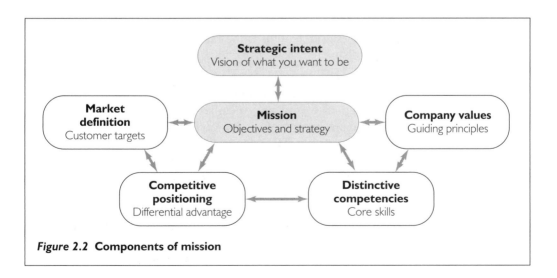

Figure 2.2 **Components of mission**

needs to spell out:

(i)   The Strategic Intent (see Hamel and Prahalad, 1989), or Vision of where the organization wants to be in the foreseeable future. Hamel and Prahalad cite examples of strategic intent for Komatsu (earthmoving equipment manufacturers) as to 'encircle Caterpillar' and for the American Apollo space programme as 'landing a man on the moon ahead of the Soviets'. Vision need not be as competitive as these examples. The vision of an organization such as a university might be set in the achievement of a set of worthy social goals.

(ii)   The value to the organization should be spelled out to set the ethical and moral tone to guide operations. Fletcher Challenge, the New Zealand-based multinational, sets down its values in its Statement of Purpose (Company Report, 1991) as follows:

> Fletcher Challenge will operate with integrity and a people oriented management style which stresses openness, communication, commitment, innovation and decentralisation of authority, responsibility and accountability.

(iii) The distinctive competencies of the organization should be articulated, clearly stating what differentiates the organization from others of its kind, what is the distinctive essence of the organization.

(iv)   Market definition, in terms of major customer targets that the organization seeks to serve and the functions, or needs of those customers that will be served. The retail store Mothercare has clearly focused on the needs of a well-defined market target as exemplified by its slogan 'everything for the mother-to-be and baby'. Many successful entrepreneurs such as Richard Branson of Virgin have built their businesses around a clear definition of customer targets and their needs.

(v)   Finally, the mission should spell out where the organization is, or intends to be, positioned in the marketplace. This is the result of bringing together market definition and distinctive skills and competencies.

Business definitions that are too narrow in scope are dangerous. They should include definition of both target market and function served. A camera manufacturer that defines its function in a way that includes only photochemical image storage ignores at its peril digital means of storing and manipulating images. The key to definition by function is not to be blinded by the company's perception of the function but to allow the customer view to come through.

Levitt (1960) provided many examples of companies adopting a myopic view in defining their businesses. The railroads believed they were in the railroad business, not transportation, and failed to take note of alternative means of transport. The oil industry believed they were in the business of producing oil, not in the business of producing and marketing energy.

In defining the business it is necessary to understand the total product or service the customer is buying, and avoid the trap of concentrating too much on the physical product on offer. In many markets the augmented or extended product (see chapter 13) can be as important, or more important, than the core product.

There are several techniques that can be used to help define the current business that the company is in. Perhaps one of the simplest to use is Item by Use analysis. Under this marketing research technique consumers are shown a product (e.g. a packet of potato crisps, see Figure 2.3) and asked on what occasions they have used that product. The various responses are recorded (e.g. for elevenses. when friends drop round for a drink, to keep the kids quiet, in a pub, etc.). For each of the uses given the respondent is then asked what other products would be considered as alternatives if the original product were not available.

These alternatives may be general alternatives that could be used on all the occasions listed (e.g. peanuts) or specific to a particular occasion (e.g. biscuits with elevenses but not when in a pub). Respondents can also be asked to gauge the proportion of uses associated with each occasion and, using a large enough sample, a clear picture can be built up of the current market and competition. This approach combines both business definition by market (identifying who existing and potential customers are) and by function (the use or uses to which the product is put).

The second question posed at the start of this section – what business do we want to be in? – is often more difficult to answer. It requires a thorough analysis of the options open to the company and an understanding of how the world in general, and the company's markets in particular, is changing.

Item	Use	Item
Potato crisps	'Elevenses'	Biscuits Piece of cake Bar of chocolate Toast and jam
	When friends drop in for a drink	Peanuts Olives Cocktail biscuits Cheese and biscuits
	In a pub	Sandwich Peanuts Cocktail biscuits Pork scratchings
	When watching TV	Sweets/chocolates Cup of soup Peanuts

Figure 2.3 **Item-by-use analysis**

2.2.2 Company analysis

In deciding on core strategy full regard must be taken of the skills and distinctive competencies of the company, defining what the company is good at, be that a technologically based definition or a market-based definition. This can help to set the bounds on what options are open to the organization and to identify where its strengths can be utilized to the full. Core competencies or core skills may result from any aspect of the operation. They may stem from the skills of the workforce in assembling the product effectively or efficiently, from the skills of management in marketing or financial planning, or from the skills of the R&D department in initiating new product ideas or creating new products on the basis of customer research.

One of the core skills of Royal Doulton was identified in their thorough understanding of porcelain technology. Traditionally this skill has been put to use in producing tableware and ornamental porcelain but more recently the skills have also been exploited in a totally new area, in dealing with rising damp! The Doulton Wallguard system offered a relatively cheap and, importantly, less disruptive, solution to the problems of rising damp through exploiting the properties of porcelain in attracting and expelling moisture.

The distinctive competencies of the company may be its marketing assets of image and market presence or its distribution network or after-sales service. The crucial issue in identifying distinctive competence is that it be something exploitable in the marketplace. Having distinctive technological skills in producing a product are of little value if there is no demand for that product. Hence an important role of marketing management is to assess the potential distinctive competencies of the organization in the light of exploitability in the market.

The counterbalance to distinctive competencies, or exploitable strengths, are weaknesses relative to the competition. Where, for example, competitors have a more favourable or protected supply of raw materials, or a stronger customer loyalty, the company must be fully aware of its limitations and generate strategies to overcome, or circumvent, them. Structural weaknesses, those inherent in the firm's operations, brought about by its very mode of doing business, may be difficult or even impossible to eliminate. Strategies should be developed to shift competition away from these factors, to make them less important to competitive success. Other weaknesses may be more easily avoided once they have been identified, or even changed to strengths by exploiting them in a different way.

Strengths and weaknesses can only be effectively determined through a systematic and comprehensive audit of the firm's resources and their utilization relative to the competition. Chapter 5 describes in more detail how this can be accomplished.

2.2.3 Industry analysis

An analysis of the industry or industries in which the company operates can serve to throw into focus the opportunities and threats facing the company. Those opportunities and threats stem from two main areas: the customers (both current and potential) of the company, and its competitors (again both current and potential).

Most markets are segmented in one way or another. They consist of heterogeneous customers, or customers with varying needs and wants. Asking 'how is the market segmented?' can provide valuable insights into customer requirements and help in focusing on specific market targets.

In computers, for example, there are several ways in which the total market could be segmented. A simple, product-based segmentation is between mainframe, minicomputers and micros. IBM has long dominated the mainframe market. Recognizing the difficulties in tackling such a giant head on Hewlett Packard sensibly focused their efforts on the minicomputer market, for smaller users with different requirements, and established dominance of that market. Similarly in the microcomputer market Apple were very successful in leading the market prior to the dominance of 'IBM-compatible' machines using successive generations of Intel microprocessors and Microsoft operating systems.

Canon is also in the computer market but have taken a different tack. They recognized that computer users do not just need computers. They also need peripheral devices to enable them to use the computer to the best advantage. Canon carved a strong niche in the market as suppliers of laser printers while Hewlett Packard focus on inkjet colour printers.

Even within these broad product-based definitions of the market, however, further segmentation exists. Apple still holds their niche for desktop publishing while Psion's palm top machines are world leaders in that segment.

In the 1990s Sega, Nintendo and Sony were hugely successful in developing the computer games market with cheap machines and addictive software. Late entrants Sony are now leaders with their Playstations but the market is forecast to decline as the games and PC markets converge because of the increased power, availability and lower cost of Pentium-powered PCs.

Having examined the current and potential segmentation of the market, the next step in assessing alternatives is to search for untapped, or under-tapped, opportunities in the market. In the food market, for example, fundamental changes in eating habits are currently taking place. Two of the most important are the increased emphasis on convenience foods and the trend towards healthier eating. Both changes have opened up new opportunities to those companies willing and able to take advantage of them.

Yeoman instant mashed potato has, for example, been promoted with added emphasis on fibre content and vitamin C. Interestingly the claim that the instant product contains more fibre and vitamin C than 'real' potatoes is based on the normal method of preparation of real potatoes. The peeling of the outer skin prior to cooking takes with it much of the fibre and vitamin C (which is located just below the surface of the skin). The instant product, however, utilizes the entire original product in its manufacture. The marketers of Marvel, dried milk, have similarly attempted to take advantage of increasing health awareness by adding extra vitamins to their product.

Opportunities are created through fundamental changes taking place (as with increased health awareness and its impact on eating habits) in the market or through competitor inability to serve existing needs. Apple's initial success in the micro-computer market was in part due to the fact that IBM originally chose not to enter the market, while Compaq and Dell's success rested upon IBM's neglect of changing distribution channels. Market gaps can exist because existing companies cannot fill them (they do not have the skills and competencies to do so) or they choose not to fill them for one reason or another.

Abell (1978) has discussed the importance of timing in recognizing and capitalizing on opportunities. His concept of strategic windows focuses attention on the fact that there are only limited periods during which the fit between the requirements of the market and the capabilities of the firm is at an optimum. Investment should be timed to coincide with periods when such strategic windows are open, and conversely disinvestment should be considered once a good fit has been eroded. A good deal of the success of Japanese companies in world markets has been attributed to an ability to time their entry such that their competencies and the market requirements are closely in tune.

An example of the concept of strategic windows at work in the UK was the spotting of an opportunity to break into the educational computing market by the microcomputer manufacturer Acorn. This Acorn did by securing a contract with the British Broadcasting Corporation (BBC) to produce what became known as the BBC microcomputer in the early 1980s. In the longer term, however, Acorn suffered from not having the 'Acorn' name on the product and their subsequent attempts to launch their own brands into the home computer market (the Acorn Electron) were less successful.

In addition to considering the opportunities open to the organization it is important to examine the threats facing it. These threats stem from two main sources – a changing marketplace that the firm is not aware of or capable of keeping up with, or competitive activity designed to change the balance of power within the market.

A changing world requires constant intelligence-gathering on the part of the organization to ensure that it can keep abreast of customer requirements. Keeping up with technological developments can be particularly important in many markets. The pocket calculator destroyed the slide rule market in the early 1970s and the digital watch caused severe problems for Swiss watch manufacturers in the mid-1970s. Changes also occur in customer tastes. Fashions come and go (many of them encouraged by marketers), but in markets where fashion is important keeping up is crucial. Chapter 6 deals in more detail with customer analysis.

The second major type of threat an organization may face is from its competition. Increasing competition, both from domestic and international sources, is the name of the game in most markets. As competitors become more sophisticated in seeking out market opportunities and designing marketing programmes to exploit them, so the company itself needs to improve its marketing activities. In the UK many industries have failed or have been unable to respond adequately to increased international competition and have suffered the consequences. In the more sophisticated marketing companies competitor analysis commands almost as much time as customer and self-evaluation. Effort is geared to identifying competitors' strengths and weaknesses and their likely strategies (see chapter 7).

2.2.4 Core strategy

On the basis of the above analysis the company seeks to define the key factors for success (KFS, sometime termed critical success factors – CSF) in its particular markets. Key factors for success in the industry are those factors that are crucial to doing business (see Ohmae, 1982). The KFS are identified through examining the differences between winners and losers, or leaders and also-rans in the industry. They often represent the factors where the greatest leverage can be exerted, i.e. where the most effect can be obtained for a give amount of effort.

In the grocery industry. for example, the KFS can centre on the relationships built up between the manufacturer and the retailer. The power of the major multiples (less than a dozen major food retail chains now account for around 80 per cent of food sales in the UK) is such that if a new food product does not obtain distribution through the major outlets a substantial sector of the potential market is denied. In commodity markets the KFS often lie in production process efficiency, enabling costs to be kept down, where pricing is considered the only real means of product differentiation. As Ohmae (1982) points out, for the Japanese elevator business the KFS centre on service – it is essential that breakdown is rectified immediately as the Japanese hate to be stuck in lifts!

A further consideration when setting the core strategy for a multi-product or multi-divisional company is how the various corporate activities add up, i.e. the role in the company's overall business portfolio (see chapter 3) of each activity.

Having identified corporate capabilities, market opportunities and threats, the key factors for success in the industry in which the firm operates and the role of the particular product or business in the company's overall portfolio the company sets its marketing objectives. The objectives should be both long- and short-term. Long-term objectives indicated the future overall destination of the company: its long-term goals. To achieve those long-term goals, however, it is usually necessary to translate them into shorter-term objectives, a series of which will add up to the longer-term goals. Long-term objectives are often set in terms of profit or market domination for a firm operating in the commercial sector. Non-profit-making organizations, too, set long- and short-term goals. The long-term goal of Greenpeace, for example, is to save the world's environment. Shorter-term goals in the 1990s centred on single, high-profile events, such as Shell's disposal of oil platforms in the North Atlantic, to global issues, such as the destruction of the environment by hydroelectric schemes in developing countries.

Often short-term and long-term goals can become confused, and there is always the danger that setting them in isolation can result in a situation where the attainment of the short-term goals does nothing to further the long-term objectives and may, in some instances, hinder them. For example, a commercial company setting long-term market domination goals will often find short-term profit-maximization at odds with this. Many of the managers, however, will be judged on yearly, not long-term performance, and hence will be more likely to follow short-term profit objectives at the expense of building a stronger market position.

The core strategy of the organization is a statement of how the organization intends to achieve its objectives. If, for example, the long-term objective is to be market leader in market X with a share of market at least twice that of the nearest competitors, the core strategy may centre on using superior technology to achieve this, or it may centre on lower prices, or better service or quality. The core strategy will take advantage of the firm's core competencies and bring them to bear wherever possible on the KFS to achieve the corporate objectives of the company.

The core strategy to be pursued may vary at different stages of the product or service's life cycle. Figure 2.4 shows alternative ways in which a company may go about improving the performance of its products or services.

A basic choice is made between attempting to increase sales or improve the level of profitability achieved from existing sales (or even reduced sales in a declining market). When the objectives are to increase sales again two fundamental approaches may be taken: to expand the total market (most easily, though not exclusively, achieved during the early, growth stages of the life cycle) or to increase share of the existing market (most often pursued during the late growth/maturity phases).

2.2.5 Expand market

Market expansion can be achieved through attraction of new users to the product or service, identifying new uses for the product or developing new products and

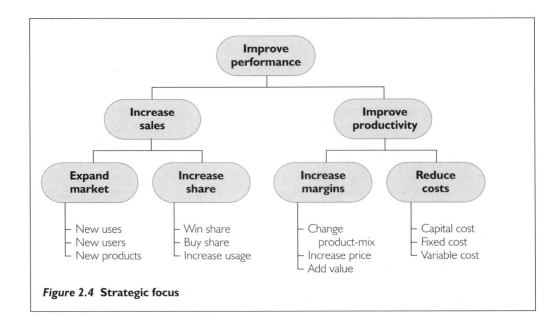

Figure 2.4 **Strategic focus**

services to stimulate the market. New users can be found through geographical expansion of the company's operations (both domestically and internationally). Asda, for example, pursued new customers for their grocery products in their move south from the Yorkshire home base while Sainsbury attacked new markets in its march north from the southeast. Alternatively, new segments with an existing or latent need for the product may be identifiable. Repositioning Lucozade as a high-energy drink found a new segment for a product once sold exclusively to parents of sick children.

For some products it may be possible to identify new uses. An example is the use of the condom (largely abandoned as a means of contraceptive to the more popular pill and IUD in the 1960s and 1970s) as a defence against contracting HIV. In household cleaners Flash was originally marketed as a product for cleaning floors, but now is also promoted as an all-purpose product for cleaning baths and wash basins.

Increase share

Increasing market share, especially in mature markets, usually comes at the expense of existing competition. The main routes to increasing share include: winning competitors' customers, merging with (or acquiring) the competitors or entering into strategic alliances with competitors, suppliers and/or distributors. Winning competitors' customers requires that the company serve them better than the competition. This may come about through identification of competitor weaknesses, or through better exploitation of the company's own strengths and competencies. Each of the elements of the marketing mix, products, price, promotion and distribution, could be used to offer the customer added value, or something extra, to induce switching.

Increasing usage rate may be a viable approach to expanding the market for some products. An advertising campaign for Guinness (the 'Guinnless' campaign devised by the ad agency Ogilvy and Mather) sought to convert irregular users (around one bottle per month) to regular use (at least one bottle per week). Similarly Coleman have attempted to encourage more frequent use of mustard, and Hellman more varied use of mayonnaise.

Improving profitability

With existing levels, or even reduced levels, of sales, profitability can be improved through improving margins. This is usually achieved through increasing price, reducing costs, or both. In the multi-product firm it may also be possible through weeding of the product line, removing poorly performing products and concentrating effort on the more financially viable. The longer-term positioning implications of this weeding should, however, be carefully considered prior to wielding the axe. It may be, for example, that maintenance of seemingly unprofitable lines is essential to allow the company to continue to operate in the market as a whole or its own specifically chosen niches of that market. They may be viewed as the groundstakes in the strategic game essential to reserve a seat at the competitive table.

2.3 *Creation of the competitive positioning*

The competitive positioning of the company is a statement of market targets, i.e. where the company will compete, and differential advantage, or how the company will compete. The positioning is developed to achieve the objectives laid down under the core strategy. For a company whose objective is to gain market share and the broad approach to that is to win competitors' customers, for example, the competitive positioning will be a statement of exactly how and where in the market that will be achieved.

2.3.1 Market targets

While the discussion of core strategy required an analysis of customers and competitors to identify potential opportunities and threats, competitive positioning selects those targets most suited to utilizing the company's strengths and minimizing vulnerability due to weaknesses.

A number of factors should be considered in choosing a market target. Broadly they fall into two categories: assessing market attractiveness, and evaluating the company's current or potential strengths in serving that market (see Robinson, Hichens and Wade, 1978; Porter, 1987).

Market attractiveness is made up of many, often conflicting, factors. Other things being equal, however, a market will generally be more attractive if:

it is large;
it is growing;
contribution margins are high;
competitive intensity and rivalry are low;
there are high entry and low exit barriers;
the market is not vulnerable to uncontrollable events.

Markets which possess all these features do not exist for long, if at all. They are, almost by definition, bound to attract high levels of competition and hence become less attractive to other entrants over time. For small or medium-sized companies small and/or static markets, which do not attract more powerful competitors, may be more attractive. In a market where high entry barriers (such as proprietary technology, high switching costs, etc.) can be erected, the company will be better able to defend its position against competitive attack (see chapter 14).

All markets are vulnerable to some extent to external, uncontrollable factors such as general economic conditions, government legislation or political change. Some markets, however, are more vulnerable than others. This is especially true when selecting amongst international market alternatives. In the international context one way companies assess vulnerability to external political events is through the British Overseas Trade Board (BOTB) and its Export Credit Guarantee Scheme (ECGS). Under the scheme advice about the risks involved in entering a particular market is freely available and insurance against default in payments made available.

Domestically, the company must weigh the power of various pressure groups in determining market vulnerability.

The company's strengths and potential strengths in serving a particular market must be considered relative to customer requirements and to competitor strengths in serving the market. Other things being equal, the company's existing strength in a market will be greater where (relative to the competition):

it commands a high market share;
it is growing faster than the market;
it has unique and valued products or services;
it has superior quality products;
it has better margins;
it has exploitable marketing assets;
it can achieve production and marketing efficiencies;
it has protected technological leadership.

As with assessing market attractiveness it is unlikely that in any market a particular company will enjoy all the above favourable characteristics. In any situation the management will have to assess the relative importance of each aspect of strength in evaluating overall strength in serving that market (target market selection is covered in more detail in chapter 12).

Having selected the market target or targets on the basis of market attractiveness and current, or potential, business strength in serving the market, the company creates its differential advantage, or competitive edge in serving the market.

2.3.2 Differential advantage

A differential advantage can be created out of any of the company's strengths, or distinctive competencies relative to the competition. The essential factors in choosing how to create the advantage are that it must be on a basis of value to the customer (e.g. lower prices, superior quality and better service) and should be using a skill of the company that competitors will find hard to copy.

Porter (1980) has argued that a competitive advantage can be created in two main (though not exclusive) ways: through cost leadership or differentiation (see Figure 2.5).

Cost leadership
The first type of advantage involves pursuing a cost leadership position in the industry. Under this strategy the company seeks to obtain a cost structure significantly below that of competitors while retaining products on the market that are in close proximity to competitors' offerings. With a low cost structure above-average returns are possible despite heavy competition.

Cost leadership is attained through aggressive construction of efficient scale economies, the pursuit of cost reductions through experience effects, tight cost and overhead control, and cost minimization in R&D, services, sales force, advertising,

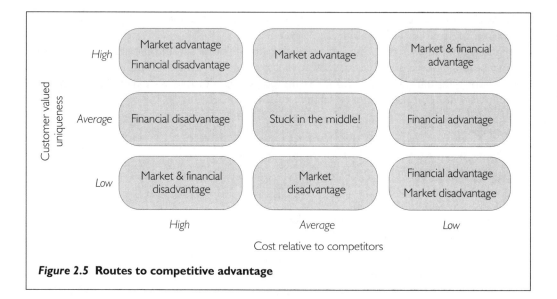

Figure 2.5 **Routes to competitive advantage**

etc. The cost leadership route is that followed aggressively by Casio in the calculator market and Seiko in watches.

Cost leaders typically need high market shares to achieve the above economies and favourable access to raw materials. If, for example, efficient production processes, or superior production technology enabling cheaper production, were identified as company strengths or distinctive competencies, they could be effectively translated into a competitive advantage through cost leadership. Similarly, if backward integration (merger with, or acquisition of, suppliers) has secured relatively cheaper supply of raw materials, that asset could also be converted into a competitive advantage.

This strategy is particularly suitable in commodity markets where there is little or no differentiation between the physical products offered. Where products are highly differentiated, however, the strategy has the major disadvantage that it does not create a reason why the customer should buy the company's offering. Low costs could be translated into lower price, but this would effectively be a differentiation strategy (using price as the basis on which to differentiate).

Differentiation
The second approach to creating a differential advantage is differentiation; i.e. creating something that is seen as unique in the market. Under this strategy company strengths and skills are used to differentiate the company's offerings from those of its competitors along some criteria that are valued by consumers.

Differentiation can be achieved on a variety of bases, for example by design, style, product or service features, price, image, etc. The major advantage of a differentiation strategy, as opposed to a cost leadership strategy, is that it creates, or emphasizes, a reason why the customer should buy from the company rather than from its competitors. While cost leadership creates an essentially financially based advantage for the company, differentiation creates a market-based advantage (see Hall, 1980; and Figure 2.4). Products or services that are differentiated in a valued way can command higher prices and margins and thus avoid competing on price alone. An example of this in the market for blue jeans would be designer jeans. In the same market Levi-Strauss and Co.'s offerings are differentiated by the 'Levi' name from the competition.

Fulmer and Goodwin (1988) point out that the two strategies are not mutually exclusive, but could both be pursued simultaneously. Buzzell and Gale (1987) demonstrate that differentiation, especially through superior quality, can often result in lower units costs through achieved gains in market share and attendant economies of scale and/or experience effects.

Each of the two basic approaches to creating a differential advantage has its attendant risks. Cost leadership may be impossible to sustain due to competitor imitation (using, for example, similar technology and processes), technological change occurring that may make it cheaper for newer entrants to produce the products or services, or alternatively competitors find and exploit alternative bases for cost leadership (see the discussion of cost drivers in chapter 13). Cost leadership is also a risky strategy where there is a high degree of differentiation between competitive offerings. Differentiation creates reasons for purchase, which cost leadership does not. In addition, cost leadership typically requires minimal spending on R&D, product improvements and image creation, all of which can leave the product vulnerable to competitively superior products.

Differentiation as a strategy is also open to a variety of risks. If differentiation is not based on distinctive marketing assets, it is possible that it will be imitated by competitors. This risk can be minimized by building the differentiation on the basis of skills or marketing assets that the company alone possesses and cannot be copied by competitors. In addition the basis for differentiation may become less important to customers or new bases become more important. These latter points should be guarded against by constant customer and competitor monitoring. A further danger of the differentiation strategy is that the costs of differentiating may outweigh the value placed on it by customers.

For both the cost leadership and differentiation approaches which seek to appeal industry-wide there is the added risk that focusers or nichers in the market (those competitors that focus their activities on a selected segment) may achieve lower costs or more valued differentiation in specific segments. Thus in markets where segmentation is pronounced both the basic approaches carry high risks. Chapter 13 explores further these approaches to creating a defensible position in the marketplace.

2.4 *Implementation*

Once the core strategy and the competitive positioning have been selected the task of marketing management is to implement those decisions through marketing effort.

The three basic elements of implementation – marketing mix, organization and control – are discussed next.

2.4.1 Marketing mix

The marketing mix of products, price, promotion and distribution are the means by which the company translates its strategy from a statement of intent to effort in the marketplace. Each of the elements of the mix should be designed to add up to the positioning required.

Viewed in this light it is evident that decisions on elements of the mix, such as pricing or advertising campaigns, cannot be considered in isolation from the strategy being pursued. A premium positioning, for example, differentiating the company's offerings from the competition in terms of high product quality could be destroyed through charging too low a price. Similarly, for such a positioning to be achieved the product itself will have to deliver the quality claimed and the promotions used communicate its quality. The distribution channels selected, and the physical distribution systems used or created, must ensure that the products or services get to the target customers.

Where elements of the mix do not pull in the same direction but contradict each other, the positioning achieved will be confused and confusing to customers.

2.4.2 Organization

How the marketing effort and the marketing department are organized will have an effect on how well the strategy can be carried through.

At a very basic level it is essential for the required manpower, as well as financial resources, to be made available. Given the resources, however, their organization can also affect their ability to implement the strategy effectively. The traditional organizational forms found in marketing are functional and product (brand) management.

Under a *functional organization* the marketing department consists of specialists in the various marketing activities reporting to a marketing co-ordinator (manager or director). Typical functions include sales management, advertising and promotions management, market research and new product development. An extension of the functional design is geographic organization where, within the functions (such as sales management), managers have a responsibility for specific geographic markets. Functional designs offer simplicity of structure and foster a high level of expertise in each function. They are often the first step in a company adopting a higher profile for the marketing function as a whole. They are most applicable where the number and complexity of products or services the company has on the market are limited.

Product (or brand) management, pioneered in 1927 by the American multinational Procter & Gamble for its ailing Camay soap brand, vests responsibility for all the marketing activities of a particular product in one product manager. In diversified companies with many different products the system has the major advantage in co-ordinating under one individual the entire mix of marketing activities, and hence making it more likely that they will all pull in the same direction. In the larger companies product managers are able to call on the talents of functional specialists as and when necessary.

Recent dramatic changes in the marketing environment have caused many companies to rethink the role of the product manager. Today's consumers face an ever-growing set of brands and are now more deal-prone than brand-prone. As a result, companies are shifting away from national advertising in favour of pricing and other point-of-sale promotions. Brand managers have traditionally focused on long-term, brand-building strategies targeting a mass audience, but today's marketplace realities demand shorter-term, sales-building strategies designed for local markets.

A second significant force affecting brand management is the growing power of retailers. Larger, more powerful, and better informed retailers are now demanding and getting more trade promotions in exchange for their scarce shelf space. The increase in trade promotion spending leaves fewer dollars for national advertising, the brand manager's primary marketing tool (Teinowitz, 1988; Dewar and Schultz, 1989).

To cope with this change Campbell Soups created *brand sales managers*. These combine product manager and sales roles charged with handling brands in the field, working with the trade, and designing more localized brand strategies. The managers spend more time in the field working with salespeople, learning what is happening in stores and getting closer to the customer.

Other companies, including Colgate-Palmolive, Procter & Gamble, Kraft and Lever Bros., have adopted *category management* (Spethman, 1992). Under this system, brand managers report to a category manager, who has total responsibility for an entire product line. For example, at Procter & Gamble, the brand manager for Dawn liquid dishwashings detergent reports to a manager who is responsible for Dawn, Ivory, Joy and all other light-duty liquid detergents. The light-duty liquids manager, in turn, reports to a manager who is responsible for all of P&G's packaged soaps and detergents, including dishwashing detergents, and liquid and dry laundry detergents. This offers many advantages. First, the category managers have broader planning perspectives than brands managers do. Rather than focusing on specific brands, they shape the company's entire category offering. Second, it better matches the buying processes of retailers. Recently, retailers have begun making their individual buyers responsible for working with all suppliers of a specific product category. A category management system links up better with this new retailer 'category buying' system.

Some companies, including Nabisco, have started combining category management with another idea: *brand teams* or *category teams*. Instead of having several brand managers, Nabisco has three teams covering biscuits: one each for adult rich, nutritional and children's biscuits. Headed by a category manager, each category team includes several marketing people/brand managers, a sales planning manager and a marketing information specialist handling brand strategy, advertising and sales promotion. Each team also includes specialists from other company departments: a finance manager, an R&D specialist, and representatives from manufacturing, engineering and distribution. Thus category managers act as a small business, with complete responsibility for the performance of the category and with a full complement of people to help them plan and implement category-marketing strategies.

For companies that sell one product line to many different types of market that have different needs and preferences, a *market management organization* might be best. Many companies are organized along market lines. A market management organization is similar to the product management organization. Market managers are responsible for developing long-range and annual plans for the sales and profits in their markets. This system's main advantage is that the company is organized around the needs of specific customer segments.

In 1992 Elida-Gibbs, Unilever's personal care products division, scrapped both brand manager and sales development roles. They had many strong brands, including Pears, Fabergé Brut, Signal and Timotei, but sought to improve their service to retailers and pay more attention to developing the brands. To do this they created two new roles: brand development managers and customer development managers. *Customer development managers* work closely with customers and have also taken over many of the old responsibilities of brand management. This provides an opportunity for better co-ordination of sales, operations and marketing campaigns. The change leaves *brand development managers* with more time to spend on the strategic development of brands and innovation. They have the authority to pull together technical and managerial resources to see projects through to their completion.

Elida-Gibbs' reorganization goes beyond sales and marketing. Cross-functional teamwork is central to the approach and this extends to the shop floor. The company is already benefiting from the change. Customer development managers have increased the number of correctly completed orders from 72 per cent to 90 per cent. In addition, brand development managers developed Aquatonic (an aerosol deodorant) in six months – less than half the usual time.

Whichever structure or organization is adopted by the company individuals with the skills necessary to carry out the various marketing tasks is needed. Two sources of personnel emerge: internal to the company or brought in from outside. When entering new markets bringing in external expertise can be a shortcut to creating in-house the knowledge needed. Skills can be improved and extended through training programmes held within the company or through outside training agencies.

2.4.3 Control

As the marketing strategy is being executed an important role of the marketing department is to monitor and control the effort.

Performance can be monitored in two main ways: on the basis of market performance and on financial performance. Market performance measures such as sales, market share, customer attitudes and loyalty and the changes in them over time can be related back to the original objectives of the strategy being pursued. Performance measures should, however, include factors other than those used to set objectives to ensure that pursuit of those objectives has not lost sight of the wider implications.

Financial performance is measured through a monitoring of product contribution relative to the resources employed to achieve it. Often a basic conflict between marketing and financial performance may arise. Where the marketing objectives are long-term market domination, short-term financial performance may suffer. Where managers are rewarded (i.e. promoted or paid more) on the basis of short-term financial performance it is likely that long-term marketing objectives may be sacrificed to short-term profit. In comparing the strategies pursued in number of UK markets by Japanese firms and their UK competitors, Doyle, Saunders and Wong (1986) found that the Japanese were more prepared to take a longer view of market performance, compared to the short-term profit orientation pursued by many of the British firms.

The efficiency with which the strategy is being executed can be monitored through a detailed evaluation of each of the elements of the marketing mix. Many companies benefit from regular, independent marketing audits (McDonald, 1984; Brownlie, 1996). These are designed to offer an objective, external evaluation of both the effectiveness and the efficiency of marketing operations.

A final important element in implementation is contingency planning, i.e. answering the question: 'What will we do if?' Contingency planning requires a degree of forecasting competitive reaction to the plans developed should they be implemented and then estimation of the likely competitive moves. Forecasting a range of likely futures and making plans to deal with whichever occur is termed scenario planning.

2.5 Conclusions

Strategic marketing planning involves deciding on the core strategy, creating the competitive positioning of both the company and its offerings, and implementing that strategy.

The above is equally true of the one product firm as it is of the large conglomerate containing many different businesses. For the conglomerate, however, there is an added dimension to planning. That extra dimension consists of portfolio planning, ensuring that the mix of businesses within the total corporation is suitable for achieving overall corporate objectives. Portfolio planning is discussed in chapter 3.

CHAPTER 3

Portfolio analysis

*Each man plays his own important part, whether he is in the
lead, finding and preparing a passage, or acting as a second man
on the rope, carrying the gear, perhaps improving the track,
safeguarding and advising his leader. The bigger the scale or
technical difficulty the more vital this teamwork and, probably,
the larger the team required to accomplish the task. To achieve
a potential of three assaults a total of ten climbers has been
decided in the ratio of 6 (assault) to 4 (support). To the latter
should be added the physiologist and the photographer who may
be expected to take their share in the build-up. We also
recruited 36 Sherpas in addition to two cooks, not counting
Tenzing himself.*

John Hunt, The Ascent of Everest (1953)
*on the portfolio of skills and competencies necessary to put two people,
Edmund Hillary and Sherpa Tenzing, on the summit of Everest*

Introduction

Being 'one or two in all we do' is the driving philosophy of General Electric (GE),
the American power station to electric light bulb conglomerate. The businesses of
GE are amazingly diverse. One of its most successful subsidiaries is market leader
in America for electric light bulbs, a mature, high-volume, low-priced commodity.
Other divisions make domestic electrical appliances of all types, another makes
medical equipment including body scanners, and one of the most successful parts
of the company is market leader in the military and commercial aeroengine markets.
It is clear that the different businesses within the company are operating in different markets, with different opportunities and threats, and utilizing different corporate skills and resources. It is therefore important to ensure that appropriate
objectives and strategies are formulated for each business unit and that these objectives and strategies support each other. The process of balancing the activities
across this variety of business units involves portfolio planning which is the subject
of this chapter.

Consider, for example, the challenge for Virgin of managing a group of businesses spanning airlines and rail travel, music and cinemas, financial services,
drinks, clothing and cosmetics, and a variety of smaller enterprises. We shall see that
this is an excellent example of growth by collaboration (chapter 8) and of portfolio
management. The sale, for example, of Virgin Megastores has provided the capital

for most of the subsequent investments in new areas to exploit the Virgin brand. Notwithstanding the Virgin example, the 1990s have seen renewed emphasis by organizations on focus and concentration of resources on core businesses and brands by major corporations. Portfolio decisions by Niall FitzGerald at Unilever are based on his strategy: 'we will focus on branded consumer goods – ice cream, spreads, tea, beverages, personal products'. This has led to the disposal of 'non-core' business from the portfolio, such as speciality chemicals.

These examples underline the importance of portfolio issues and the central role of marketing variables, as opposed to purely financial criteria, in making portfolio choices.

More than two decades ago Drucker (1973) identified seven types of businesses which still find resonance today:

1. **Today's breadwinners** – the products and services that are earning healthy profits and contributing positively to both cash flow and profits.
2. **Tomorrow's breadwinners** – investments in the company's future. Products and services that may not yet be making a strong financial contribution to the company, but that are in growth or otherwise attractive markets and are expected to take over the breadwinning role in the future, when today's breadwinners eventually fade.
3. **Yesterday's breadwinners** – the products and services that have supported the company in the past, but are not now contributing significantly to cash flow or to profits. Many companies have a predominance of businesses of this type, indicating that they have been slow to invest in future developments.
4. **Developments** – the products and services recently developed that may have some future, but where greater investment is needed to achieve that future.
5. **Sleepers** – the products and services that have been around for some time, but have so far failed to establish themselves in their markets or, indeed, their expected markets have failed to materialize. These are allowed to remain in the portfolio in the hope that one day they will take off.
6. **Investments in managerial ego** – the products and service that have strong product champions amongst influential managers, but for which there is little proven demand in the marketplace. The company, because of the involvement of powerful managers, continues to put resources into these products in the hope of their eventually coming good.
7. **Failures** – the products and services that have failed to play a significant role in the company's portfolio and have no realistic chance of doing so. These are kept on the company's books largely through inertia. It is easier to do so than admit defeat and withdraw or divest them.

The product life cycle (or death cycle) provides a link between the businesses identified by Drucker (see Figure 3.1). As they stand, developments, sleepers or ego trips contribute little to the company, but it is hoped that they may one day do so. The markets they are in may be highly attractive but, because of under-investment, the company has little ability to serve them. If left alone as they are, with no extra

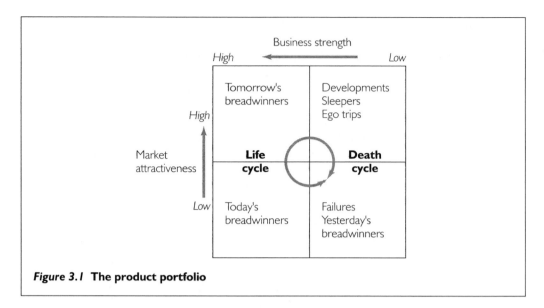

***Figure 3.1* The product portfolio**

investment being made in them, the businesses will follow the death cycle and become failures.

Strategically a company is facing a dilemma with these businesses. If left alone they are unlikely to succeed, so a choice has to be made between investing in them or getting out. In even the largest companies it is impossible to pursue all attractive markets, so the first portfolio decision is one of double or quits. If the choice is to invest, then the aim is to build the business until it is strong enough to become one of tomorrow's breadwinners. This usually means achieving some degree of market dominance in a growth sector. If successfully managed, the product will mature to become one of today's breadwinners and, as it ages, one of yesterday's. As with all things, the difficulty in the portfolio is not starting ventures, but knowing when to kill them and when to concentrate resources where success can be achieved.

3.1 *Portfolio planning*

Any diversified organization needs to find methods for assessing the balance of businesses in its portfolio and to help guide resource allocation between them. A number of portfolio planning models have been developed over the past thirty years to facilitate this process. The earliest and most basic model was the Growth-Share Matrix, developed by the Boston Consulting Group. More sophisticated models have been developed by consultants Arthur D. Little and McKinsey, as well as by commercial companies such as Shell and General Electric. All, however, share a number of key objectives (Grant, 1995):

1. Development of business strategies and allocation of resources (both financial and managerial). By assessing the position of a business in its industry,

together with the prospects for that industry over the medium to long term, investment priorities can be set for individual businesses. Those businesses that are strong in attractive markets are likely to be self-sustaining financially. They will require, however, attentive management to ensure they continue to achieve their potential. Hold or build strategies will typically be indicated. Weak businesses in attractive markets may require further investment to build position for the future. Products in declining sectors may be less deserving of resource allocation unless turnaround strategies are likely to reverse market trends. In declining markets, products are often managed for cash flow to enable resources to be reallocated to areas of the portfolio with more potential.

2. Analyzing portfolio balance. In addition to suggesting strategies for individual businesses, portfolio analysis assists assessment of the overall portfolio balance in terms of cash flow, future prospects and risk. Cash flow balance is achieved where investments in businesses with potential are met through surpluses from current or past breadwinners. The extent to which the cash flow is out of balance suggests opportunities for expansion or acquisition (in the mid-1990s Microsoft was said to be sitting on a cash mountain of around $7 billion and looking for profitable new, synergistic businesses in which to invest) or the need to raise capital from external investors. A crucial element of portfolio planning is to help assess the future prospects of the organization as a whole. Too heavy a dependence in the portfolio on yesterday's products may indicate a healthy current cash flow, but unless that is invested in tomorrow's products the longer-term future may be in doubt. Too many future investments without a solid enough current cash generation may suggest an overstretched portfolio. Finally, assessing the risks associated with individual businesses enables a firm to spread its overall risk, ensuring not all its ventures are high risk but allowing some more risky ventures to be balanced by perhaps less rewarding but more predictable activities.

The success of any portfolio planning technique – and there are many competing approaches on the market – depends ultimately on its ability to help managers make the above types of decisions. Some have been criticized for being too simplistic, while others have been criticized for being too subjective (Haspeslagh, 1982; Doyle, 1994). Below, we examine the main approaches in use today.

3.2 The Boston Consulting Group Growth-Share Matrix

In the mid-1960s many companies were looking for ways of assessing the balance of their portfolio of activities. Some companies called in the newly formed Boston Consulting Group who, through their work with the Mead Paper Corporation, developed a way of classifying their acquisitions into four categories. By 1970 this had developed into what was then called their Growth-Share Matrix or the 'Boston Box' (Henderson, 1970). Figure 3.2 shows the two dimensions which underlie the Boston Consulting Group's approach.

3.2.1 **Market growth rate**

The first dimension, along the vertical axis, recognizes the impact of market growth rate on cash flow. This dimension acts as a proxy, or more easily measured substitute, for the more difficult to assess product life cycle (see Hooley, 1994) and reflects the strategies and associated costs typical over the cycle. At product launch costs are likely to far outstrip revenues. Research and development (R&D) costs will need to be recouped, production capacity created and marketing bridgeheads established. Typically during the launch and introductory phases of the life cycle cash flow will be negative and hence there will be a need to invest cash generated elsewhere (or borrowed from external sources) in the venture.

As the product becomes established in the market, revenues will pick up, but the venture is likely to remain cash-hungry because of the need to make further capital investments. This problem is increased by the disequilibrium which occurs in growth markets where sales are at a lower level than production, and production is at a lower level than raw material purchases. During rapid growth profits may peak, but the need for reinvestment (second- and third-generation products, expansion of product range to meet emerging segment requirements, etc.) is high. During this phase cash flow may be in balance or show a small surplus overall.

As the life cycle is followed from growth to maturity, profits decline as know-how becomes more available and differentiation diminishes. Increased competition through new entrants can cause a downward pressure on margins achieved but, at the same time, capital investments are lower and the potential to generate excess

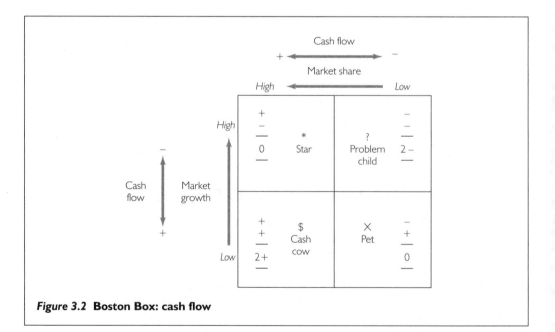

Figure 3.2 Boston Box: cash flow

cash is greatest. This cash-generation potential in companies in mature markets provides the strength of many blue chip companies such as Unilever, Marks & Spencer, Sainsbury, etc. In Figure 3.2 the change is shown as a negative cash flow when the growth rate is high and a positive cash flow when the growth rate is low (mature markets). During the decline phase of the life cycle margins are likely to come under increasing pressure, but investments can be kept to a minimum. Products at this phase of the cycle are typically managed for cash, which is then invested in the next generation of products to ensure life (from new products) after death (of the old ones).

3.2.2 Relative market share

The horizontal axis of the Boston Box depicts relative market share. While market growth rate has been found to be a useful indicator of cash use (or the need for investment), market share has been found to be related to cash generation. Higher market shares, relative to competitors, are associated with better cash generation because of economies of scale and experience curve effects. The experience curve concept, also developed by the Boston Consulting Group in the 1960s, forms the foundation for this relationship, but further supporting evidence comes from the influential Profit Impact of Marketing Strategy (PIMS) study of the 1970s and 1980s. Relative market share is in effect used as a proxy for profitability, the underlying premise being that dominant share leads to superior profitability. Further support for this has come more recently from Doyle (1994: 171) who reports that return on sales in fast-moving consumer goods averages around 18 per cent for market leaders, 3 per cent for number 2 brands, and the rest are unprofitable.

Negative cash generation is, therefore, associated with low market share and positive cash generation flows where market share is higher. The Boston Consulting Group poses this relationship on the basis of experience effects. These show a company's operating costs decreasing as it gains experience in the market. Some of this is due to the learning curve as a company finds a task easier to do. But there are also other returns from scale economies and capital investment.

Experience curves are linked to market share through a cycle of virtue where a company with high market share gains more experience than its competitors. This experience results in lower costs; the lower costs mean that, at a given market price, the company with the highest market share has the highest profits and the company with the highest profits or contributions from sales has more to spend on research and development or marketing, which allows it to maintain its high market share.

The Boston Box received fresh impetus from the PIMS study (Buzzell and Gale, 1987) which showed a very strong relationship between market share and return on investment. Figure 3.3 shows a variation on these results, where the variation in the return on investment doubles for manufacturing-intensive companies as their market share rank increases from 5th to 1st, and more than trebles for R&D and marketing-intensive companies as they improve. These very powerful empirical results lend credibility to GE's strategy of being number 1 or 2 in everything they do.

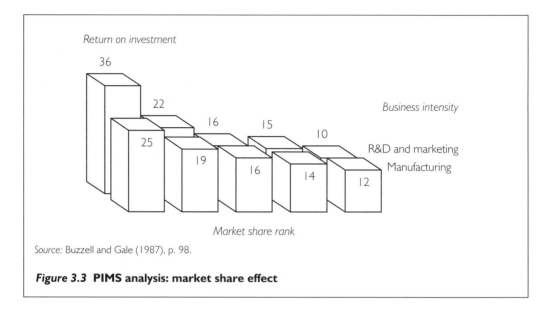

Source: Buzzell and Gale (1987), p. 98.

***Figure 3.3* PIMS analysis: market share effect**

3.2.3 Putting the dimensions together

The portfolio implications of combining the cash requirements of market growth and the cash-generation potential of market share achieved are shown graphically in the two dimensional Growth-Share Matrix. The lower left-hand quadrant of Figure 3.2 looks particularly attractive where the low cash requirements of a low-growth market and the high cash generation of high market share are brought together. These businesses have the benefit of experience effects from high market share and, because they are in mature markets, have a limited need for investment. They have become cash generators and potentially a source of funds to be invested elsewhere in a business's portfolio. The Boston Consulting Group termed these businesses 'cash cows' as they can be milked to produce excess cash which can be used elsewhere in the portfolio.

Several companies can be identified which have many of their activities in this sector. In the UK, GEC is renowned for its cash mountain which it has generated from its mature businesses. RTZ is another British company which has used the funds generated from its mineral extraction to good effect in diversifying into other sectors where it is a market leader. These cash cows are clearly today's breadwinners, but the danger is they are milked to excess and therefore lose their competitiveness or become indulgent consumers of their own surpluses. At a corporate level there is a danger of complacency, since companies which have a preponderance of cash cows may fail to develop tomorrow's breadwinners.

The beneficial qualities of the cash cows can be contrasted with the 'pets' which have low market share in low growth markets (bottom right-hand corner of the matrix). Maturity of the market means little investment needs to be made, but the low market share means that their profit margins and cash flows are well below those of the market leaders. The simple summation shown in Figure 3.2 indicates a cash flow of zero. More realistically, there may be a modest cash flow, which can be either positive or negative. Businesses in this quadrant are called pets because they do not cost much to keep and give a little pleasure. They are, however, of little financial significance to the company. The danger is the distraction of managerial time and resources which are out of proportion to their worth. Here may lie once profitable businesses which, because of competition from new technologies or global competitors, are no longer what they used to be; one-time breadwinners, which have fallen on bad times – or yesterday's breadwinners in Drucker's terminology. As yesterday's breadwinners in mature markets with low market share, the pets (or 'dogs' as they are often called in connection with the Boston Box) tend to make little money now and have little prospect of making money in the future.

Many companies have a predominance of dogs in their portfolio. This is almost tautological. Given that many markets (in developed economies at least) are mature, and that only one product, by definition, can be market leader, a significant proportion of all products will be classed as dogs. For firms with significant proportions of dogs it is clearly impossible to follow GE's strategy of being 1st or 2nd in the markets in which they compete. There are also many examples of relatively low market share companies in mature markets which are making good returns. To reflect the value in these companies, the term 'cash dog' is used to refer to businesses which are close to the border between the cash cows and pets. Strategies for these will be discussed later.

Business units with a high market share and high market growth tend to have a cash flow which is similar to that of pets, but their prospects are very different. This is a case where static analysis of the company's accounts could be very dangerous in categorizing these businesses and the pets together. Companies in this quadrant have a business strength because of their market share, but are not generators of large volumes of cash surplus because of the need to invest in their growth. They may not be making money now, but if properly nurtured and supported they can become tomorrow's breadwinners. Failure to distinguish between the pets and the stars is one of the most important lessons of portfolio analysis. Whereas the poor cash flow of the pets suggests they should be divested or milked and that a company should be wary of investing in them, a similar result for high market share businesses in growth markets suggests there could be good reasons for investing in them in order to gain or hold share. Not surprisingly, these businesses are called the 'stars'.

The last quadrant suggests that businesses with low market share in high growth markets could show a negative cash flow. They lack the experience or scale economics to have a high margin and yet their presence in a growth market demands investment. The label 'problem children' or 'dilemma' reflects the position which companies face with these business units. If they fail to invest in them, they are likely to follow a death cycle and proceed from being a development that is losing money at present, to a failure that will not make any money in the future. The alternatives to this are double or quits: invest heavily to gain market share in order to achieve star status; or get out of the market altogether. Since the market is growing there are clear opportunities to build as technologies shift, dominant designs emerge and new segments appear. Competitors' 'stars' will dominate mainstream markets, but opportunities may be exploited through innovative positioning and targeting.

In the UK Amstrad did this in the personal computer (PC) market during the 1980s, when they launched late against established competition and succeeded by offering a cheap and simple word processor sold through electrical retailers. This initial success was followed by the launch of an inexpensive PC compatible with high service back-up, once again sold through low-cost retailers rather than more expensive computer retailers to enable a different target market (home and home professionals) to be reached while competitors were concentrating on the business sector. In America Compaq achieved similar success against IBM for several years until the maturity of the mainframe market forced IBM to take the PC market more seriously. Indeed, some say that the pioneering IBM never recovered from the impact of later entrants to the PC market.

3.2.4 Virtuous circles

As an alternative to the death cycle, the Growth-Share Matrix proposes a life cycle where funds are invested in the problem children in order to make them stars (tomorrow's breadwinners) which will, one day, become cash cows (today's breadwinners). In the end these cash cows may decay to become pets. Figure 3.4 illustrates this sequence, cash being taken from the cash cows and invested in the problem children in order to make them stars. The success sequence is closed by the stars one day themselves becoming cash cows.

The alternative disaster sequence shows the danger that can occur if companies enter a market early and gain high market share which they fail to support. The star may then degenerate from being a reasonably profitable star into a loss-making cash cow and from there into a pet or dog. Ironically this progression covers the results of short-termism where a company fails to see the value of investing in a market and tries to take money out of it quickly. This partly explains the failure of EMI with their world-beating body scanner, which then failed to invest in product quality and technological development, and so lost their early lead to the large competitors attracted to the market. Ironically, one of their early competitors, GE, eventually acquired EMI's ailing subsidiary.

Another disaster sequence could occur if, in a desire to take profits, a cash cow is over-milked and therefore becomes vulnerable to competition. The British motorcycle manufacturers fell foul of this when they became complacent in the world market, which they dominated. They paid for their lack of investment in current development and production technology when Honda, Yamaha and Suzuki decimated such firms as BSA, Norton, Triumph and Royal Enfield.

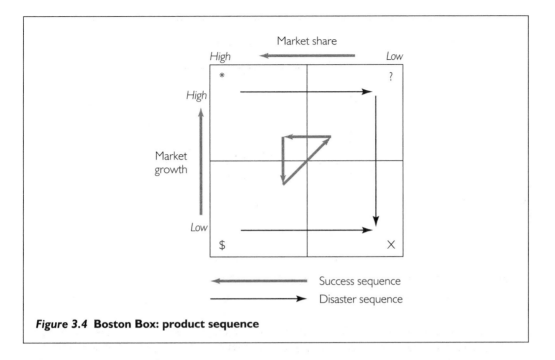

Figure 3.4 Boston Box: product sequence

3.2.5 The pros and cons of the Growth-Share Matrix

The Boston Box, along with Peters and Waterman's view of excellence and Porter's more recent views on competitive strategy, is one of the few business ideas with the subtlety and attractiveness to become well known within business circles. The very success of these ideas means that they become controversial and their simplicity, which is such an important factor in their diffusion, makes them vulnerable to accusations of lack of sophistication. In using any tool, however, it is essential that users are aware of its limitations, its strengths and its weaknesses.

The success of the Growth-Share Matrix has been lucidly explained by Morrison and Wensley (1991). On psychological grounds it fulfils a human desire for taxonomy, classifying a complex mix of different businesses. It is easy to grasp, has an attractive presentation and uses catch-phrases and terms which are easy to memorize and have a clear link to strategy. These may be poor reasons for using a strategic tool, but they make it an effective means of communication in an area where little else is clear.

Research has provided some evidence to support the Boston Box. It embodies simple ideas with the cash flow implications which are intuitively appealing to managers. The PIMS study has been a particularly fruitful source of support for the Boston Box. Figure 3.5 provides some evidence and shows the percentage of businesses with positive cash flows in each of the four categories. The difference is strong along the market share axis, but less strong along that for market growth. It is also

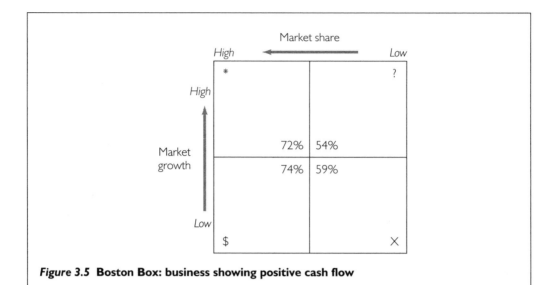

Figure 3.5 **Boston Box: business showing positive cash flow**

noticeable that the much maligned dogs do provide a positive cash flow in many cases. These reflect a strategy which does not come within the remit of the Boston Box where business units with low market share can find niche opportunities. For example, in the car market the BMW was a relatively small player but is often regarded as the most successful competitor. Its quality and sporting image allow the company to charge more than competitors with a similar car of a similar size.

Fashion has led to the Boston Box being popular. This means it is an idea that is well understood and liked by many managers and therefore one which allows communication between headquarters and SBUs. It has become part of the common business vocabulary; its use and terminology have become symbols of membership of the informal executive club. Strategically, it allows companies to pursue a purposive strategy rather than to follow the vagaries of the marketplace. It gives the illusion of control to managers by suggesting they could move SBUs around the chart like pieces around a chessboard. But of course, it is not possible for a single player to decide where each SBU should be moved to, no more than it is possible for a single player to decide where all the pieces in a chessboard should be positioned.

Simplicity is probably the Boston Box's greatest virtue. It brings together a number of very important strategic issues and allows them to be presented and understood quickly. Perhaps this is also the greatest danger of the Boston Box. It would be ridiculous for an organization to follow it blindly as the only guide to strategy.

It is as easy to enunciate the limitations of the Boston Box as it is to praise its elegance. There is no rigid definition of what an SBU is or how a market may be defined. For example, British Aerospace with their Harrier Jump Jet could easily define themselves as being totally dominant in the market since there is no other vertical take-off fighter. Alternatively, it could be seen as a very small producer of tactical support aircraft, since the Harrier is one of many answers to general defence problems. This problem of definition of the product market leads to the difficulty of measurement of market growth and market share. These can be difficult to obtain, but even if a company is not using the Boston Box, it is hard to defend failure to gather information so vital to their operations. Moreover the tool is not so much concerned with odd percentage points as it is with broad classifications and shifts.

The tool is certainly prone to over-use because of its very simplicity. But perhaps there is even more danger of misuse of more complex tools when even the under-lying assumptions are difficult to grasp. Take, for example, regression analysis which is often used to analyze markets, but is understood by few marketers.

Perhaps the major problem with the Boston Box is the euphoria with which it was first received and the exaggerated claims which were made for it. The developers claimed in 1972 that 'Such a simple chart with a projected position for five years out, is sufficient alone to tell a company's profits ability, debt capacity, growth potential and competitive strength.' Would it were true. The Boston Box certainly has its deficiencies, but it also has great advantages. It is clearly inadequate as a complete solution, but is of undisputed value as a starting point in many analyses.

If it is to be used, it should be audited carefully to ensure its validity rather than followed blindly. A number of basic questions should be asked:

➤ How has the market or industry been defined, and is this the most useful way to define it? The results and conclusions from the model can alter radically if market definitions are changed.

➤ Does the product life cycle concept (as measured by market growth rate) make sense in this market? If there is no relationship between market growth rate and both cash use and cash generation the model has little meaning.

➤ Does the link between profitability and market share (as measured by relative market share) hold true in this business? If experience effects are small, or alternative technologies negate volume economies, the profit potential of high market share businesses may be overestimated.

➤ Are we confident that the model is not leading us to ignore major changes in technology, competition or other fundamentals that invalidate the approach? New market entrants, doing business in new ways or employing fresh competitive advantages can invalidate the conclusions.

➤ Are there any interdependencies between businesses that mean actions taken on one will affect others? Where a 'dog' has a role in supporting a 'star' or 'cash cow' (maybe as a 'loss leader') the knock-on effects of its deletion should be fully considered before action is taken.

3.3 *Multi-factor approaches to portfolio modelling*

Relative market share is just one business strength of a company. There are other strengths that a company could have, such as an exploitable brand name, exclusive access to distribution channels, unique product features or particular financial strengths. It is also quite possible that a company willing to commit vast resources to new technology could achieve lower costs than the market leader, thereby rendering the higher market share generated through experience of little advantage. Toyota's success relative to the market leading General Motors is a case in point. It is also clear that the British motor-cycle industry's dominance of the market did not help defend against the Japanese onslaught.

Just as market share is only one business strength, market growth is only one dimension of market attractiveness. The low market growth rate of the UK grocery trade may not make it attractive in itself, but when its margins are compared across Europe it seems a very good one to exploit – hence the movement of the German grocery retailer Aldi against the long-established and strong competitors, such as Sainsbury and Tesco. Stability in a market may be another attractive feature. Although small, the market for academic journals is very attractive and has been exploited very successfully by MCB. Its two attractive features, beside the low fluctuation in demand, are the relatively low price sensitivity of subscribers, particularly in the supposedly hard-pressed libraries, and the mailing list associated with the publications. Certainly, if the desire is to generate a regular income, it is probably a better idea to invest in a company that occupies a dominant position in a mature market than one in a growth market of uncertain future. Note how long the leading brands in mature markets have survived and how short has been the life of companies in the electronics industry.

In order to understand their own portfolio more fully, General Electric (GE) devised a matrix which was able to show business strength and market attractiveness across a multitude of dimensions. Figure 3.6 shows a typical example. The GE Market Attractiveness-Business Position Matrix considers two sets of factors which appear to influence the relative attractiveness of investing in a business. Business in this context could conceivably be defined as an individual product, a product line, a market segment, a business unit or even a division.

The first set of factors addresses the favourability of the market in which the business is located. The second refers to criteria by which the business or company's position in a market is judged to be weak or strong. All these criteria are then employed to construct scores of market attractiveness and of business position. These are plotted usually on a 3 × 3 matrix depicting the relative investment opportunity for a business. Normally, as in the Boston Box, the business unit is represented on the chart by a circle, the diameter or area of which corresponds to the sales volumes of the business. Sometimes, the size of the circle represents the market size rather than the size of the company's business, and parts of the circle are shaded to represent the business's absolute market share.

3.3.1 By any other name

The GE matrix is often known by other names, such as the Multi-factor Portfolio Matrix or the Stoplight Matrix. Another similar model, and a refinement on the GE

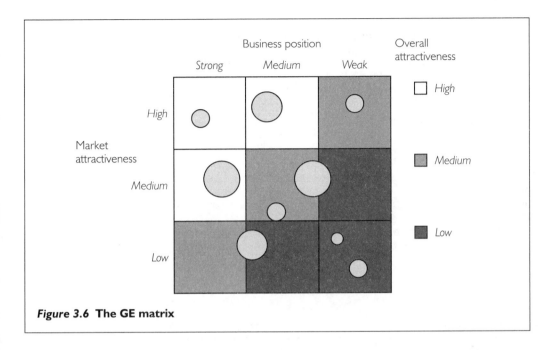

***Figure 3.6* The GE matrix**

matrix, which evaluates business sector prospects together with the company's competitive position, is the Directional Policy Matrix, developed by Shell. Either technique is applicable to almost any diversified business with separately identifiable sectors: for example, an engineering company offering a range of products and services, or an electrical company where the separate business sectors might be different types of electrical appliances. The main issue is to measure the two dimensions forming the axes of the matrix. To do this, the factors underlying each dimension must be identified, measured and brought together to provide an index or value.

3.3.2 Identifying the factors

Each company has to decide on its list of factors which make a market 'attractive' or a business position in a market 'strong'. Experience suggests the factors listed in Table 3.1 to be among the most important.

The importance of each factor depends primarily on the nature of the product, customer behaviour, the company itself and the industry in which it operates. For example, for commodity products, low production costs and high entry barriers may be important contributors to business position and industry attractiveness respectively. With more highly differentiated products (for example, precision measurement instruments, specialized machine tools, and so forth) the customer seeks technical innovation, accuracy or other benefits. Relative technological status may be a prime contributor to business position and being 'first in' with new processes

Table 3.1 **Factors contributing to market attractiveness and business position**

Attractiveness of your market	Status/position of your business
Market factors	
Size (value, units or both)	Your share (in equivalent terms)
Size of key segments	Your share of key segments
Growth rate per year:	Your annual growth rate:
Total	Total
Segments	Segments
Diversity of market	Diversity of your participation
Sensitivity to price, service features and external factors	Your influence on the market
Cyclicality	Lags or leads in your sales
Seasonality	
Bargaining power of upstream suppliers	Bargaining power of your suppliers
Bargaining power of downstream suppliers	Bargaining power of your customers
Competition	
Types of competitor	Where you fit, how you compare in terms of products, marketing capability
Degree of concentration	
Changes in type and mix	Service, production strength, financial strength, management
Entries and exits	Segments you have entered or left
Changes in share	Your relative share change
Substitution by new technology	Your vulnerability to new technology
Degrees and types of integration	Your own level of integration
Financial and economic factors	
Contribution margins	Your margins
Leveraging factors, such as economies of scale and experience	Your scale and experience
Barriers to entry or exit (both financial and non-financial)	Barriers to your entry or exit (both financial and and non-financial)
Capacity utilization	Your capacity utilization
Technological factors	
Maturity and volatility	Your ability to cope with change
Complexity	Depths of your skills
Differentiation	Types of your technological skills
Patents and copyrights	Your patent protection
Manufacturing process technology required	Your manufacturing technology
Sociopolitical factors in your environment	
Social attitudes and trends	Your company's responsiveness and flexibility
Law and government agency regulations	Your company's ability to cope
Influence with pressure groups and government representatives	Your company's aggressiveness
Human factors, such as unionization and community acceptance	Your company's relationships

or technology having patent protection may be a major factor determining market attractiveness.

Identification of the relevant factors requires detailed examination of customers, competitors, market characteristics, the external environment and the organization itself. It also relies on management judgement, experience and an appreciation of the technique's limitations. The latter, hopefully, avoids easy generalizations made by management.

3.3.3 Scoring the factors

Having identified the relevant factors, the analyst has to summarize them into measures of market attractiveness and business position. This can usually be done by assigning scores to each factor (0.0 = low; 0.5 = medium; 1.0 = high), then weighting each factor depending on its relative importance. Finally, the score and weighting for each factor are multiplied together to obtain the factor's rating or value in respect of the two variables – market attractiveness and business position.

Tables 3.2 and 3.3 provide hypothetical examples of the scheme. The sum of the values under each variable would then be used to plot the location of the business analyzed in the matrix. Scores and weighting are a matter of managerial judgement and experience, but in practice the weightings have much less impact on the final outcome than one might expect.

3.3.4 Implications for marketing strategy

The GE model uses return on investment (ROI) as the criterion for assessing an investment opportunity in contrast to the cash flow criterion used in the BCG Growth-Share Matrix. A business located in the upper left part in the matrix, that is one showing high overall attractiveness, would be indicative of one showing good investment opportunity: the business shows a high ROI.

The GE model has useful implications for marketing strategy. The analyst or planner can use it to plan in three stages. First, the model could be used to classify

Table 3.2 **Market attractiveness**

Factor	Score	Weighting	Rating
1 Market size	0.5	15	7.5
2 Volume growth (units)	0.0	15	0.0
3 Concentration	1.0	30	30.0
4 Financial	0.5	25	12.5
5 Technology	0.5	15	7.5
		100	**57.5**

Table 3.3 **Business position**

Factor	Score	Weighting	Rating
1 Product technology			
Current quality	0	20	0
New technology	0.5	20	10
2 Manufacturing			
Scale	0.5	10	5
Efficiency	0.5	10	5
Physical distribution	0.5	10	5
3 Marketing			
Expertise	0	10	0
Sales	0.5	10	5
Service	0.5	10	5
		100	**35**

the present opportunity facing the business given the present business strategy, industry character and competitive structure. Second, an analysis of future market environment and position could be conducted assuming no major changes in strategy are made. Third, the latter process could be repeated several times but with new and alternative strategic options explored. Different assumptions can be made about objectives and investments to be put into the business each time the process is repeated.

The final choice of strategy requires estimation of long-term costs and benefits of contemplated changes, as well as consideration of competitors' reaction to any strategic change. Several major strategic options are usually available in terms of changes in business position. These are:

1. **Invest to hold or maintain current business position**. The investment has to be sufficient to keep up with market changes. This option is likely to make sense in a market of declining attractiveness.
2. **Invest to improve market position of the business**. Such a strategy requires sufficient investment to penetrate the market, thereby strengthening the business. It is usually undertaken in the early development or growth phase of the market.
3. **Invest to rebuild**. This is a high investment strategy aimed at restoring or revitalizing business position in a maturing or declining market.
4. **Selectivity**. This strategy aims at strengthening position in segments where benefits of penetration or rebuilding exceed the costs, for example building 'problem children' up to 'stars' or letting them turn into 'pets'.
5. **Low investment or harvest the business**. This option is usually effected

over a period of time. The business tends to be subject to selective investment over the short term and eventually 'cashed in' when the price is right. The strategy may be appropriate for businesses holding strong positions in declining markets, 'cash cows', for example.

Other strategic options are also available, such as investing heavily to enter new markets, or to withdraw or divert from the market because the business is not viable at all.

3.3.5 Limitations of multi-factor approaches

Market attractiveness–business position analysis focuses on the ROI potential of alternative business strategies. In a way it can be used to complement traditional portfolio analysis which looks at the cash flow implications of strategy. The technique does, however, contain practical limitations.

Many factors influencing the two major variables might have been considered. These are not specified but are based on managers' subjective judgement. The problem is whether all relevant contributory factors are identified by planners. Weightings of relative importance of factors are also decided subjectively, not specified by any objective procedure. Subjectivity can be a problem, especially if planners are inexperienced or incapable of exercising the judgement required. The other side of this coin, however, is that its very subjectivity makes it easier to tailor to the specific conditions facing an individual firm. Indeed, much of the value of such as tool lies in the discussions and debates necessary to identify and weight relevant factors.

Another limitation is the unproven relationship between influencing factors and the overall dimensions (market attractiveness and business position) themselves. For instance, management recognizes that their company's technological innovativeness gives them a strong status in the market, but the form and direction of that relationship is not specified or easily quantifiable. Again, informed debate about the nature and form of such relationships can be highly beneficial.

Despite the limitations and practical difficulties in assessing future changes and strategic choices to deal with them, the technique has useful implications for marketing strategy. The limitations may be somewhat minimized if management uses informed judgement throughout the assessment (that is judgement based on detailed examination of information about customers, markets, competitors, and so on). The model can be used to build up a qualitative picture of the product portfolios of other companies hence providing useful insight into competitors' market positions and business strength.

3.4 *The process of portfolio planning*

Whichever portfolio model is used the portfolio planning process has four stages: defining the unit of analysis, analyzing the current position of each business unit, examining the interrelationships between the business units and, finally, projecting the future portfolio. The Growth-Share Matrix will be used to illustrate the portfolio planning process.

3.4.1 Define the unit of analysis

The definition of the unit of analysis for portfolio planning is a critical stage and one that is often poorly done in practice. The Boston Box was originally intended for use at the strategic business unit (SBU) level, where these are generally defined as subsidiaries who can operate independently as businesses in their own right. In reality, however, boundaries are seldom clear-cut and the problems of definition can be substantial (see Haspeslagh, 1982; Gluck, 1986).

Practitioners have often used the Boston Box to look at products rather than business units or to provide a pictorial presentation of international markets. These applications do not conform strictly to those for which it was originally intended, but its value as a means of presenting much information still remains and there is no danger, providing the limitations of the matrix are kept in mind.

Where products are selected as the unit of analysis it is important that market shares and growth rates reflect the more specific market sectors in which they are operating. In the yellow fats market, for example, Van den Bergh has an extensive portfolio of products in the various segments of the market. For the portfolio planning model to be of value at the product level each would need to be assessed in the light of its share of its chosen segment and the dynamics of that segment, rather than assessed in relation to the market overall. Similarly computer manufacturers will need to assess market shares and growth rates of specific sectors of the market (desk top, notebook, etc.) to enable useful conclusions to be drawn.

3.4.2 Analyze the current position of each SBU

For illustrative purposes the Boston Box has been drawn to show the position of individual SBUs for a fictitious company in Figure 3.7. The calibration of the vertical axis is somewhat arbitrary but the central point (which in this case is set at a 10 per cent market growth rate) would logically refer to the rate of growth which reflects a switchover from the growth phase of the product life cycle to early maturity. In other words, the point at which investment in growth (capacity, R&D, marketing expenditure) becomes less necessary and cash surplus can begin to be diverted to other activities rather than ploughed back in.

The upper and lower limits of the axis should be set to ranges which are typical of the industry concerned. In the example these are set at between 25 per cent growth and a 5 per cent decline. Whereas the scale suggested may be quite adequate for an evolving industry, in some markets a 25 per cent rate of growth would be way below what was expected. Whatever scales are chosen, users should expect that sometimes business units will fly off the scale or be congregated in markets with similar growth rates.

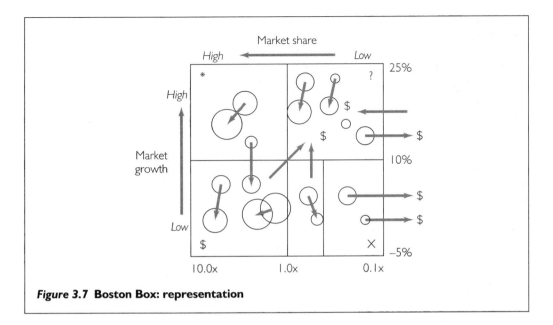

***Figure 3.7* Boston Box: representation**

It is most important to note that the vertical axis refers to the market growth rate and not the growth rate achieved by business units. All competitors within a market should be in a horizontal line across the plot. This means that a company which gains market share and sales would be shown as moving across the Boston Box from right to left rather than up it. Conversely, a fall in market share will result in movement to the right rather than down.

The horizontal axis, market share, is much more rigidly defined by the originators of the model. It is a logarithmic scale with the centre being at 1.0, the left-hand limit being at 10 and the right-hand limit being at 0.1. Here it must be remembered that the appropriate measure is not market share but relative market share. In the original model the Boston Consulting Group advocated measuring market share relative to the largest competitor. Hence a score of '1' indicates a share equal to the biggest competitor (the sort of head-to-head battle experienced between equally placed rivals such as Cadbury and Nestlé in the UK confectionery market), '10' indicates a massive market dominance where the focal business is ten times larger than its nearest rival (this indicates essentially a monopoly position), and '0.1' indicates a weak follower with one tenth the share of the market leader.

An alternative measure of relative share is to compare own share with the average size of the top three players in the market. Both measures of relative market share tend to be rather brutal since they mean it is impossible for anyone other than the market leader to be shown on the left-hand, high-rated market share side of the box.

As a final pictorial aid to representation each SBU is represented as a circle with its centre corresponding to its market share and growth rates, and an area proportional to its sales. In Figure 3.7 the current position of SBUs are represented by circles. The arrows emanate from the current position of the SBUs and point to their projected positions in the next planning period.

The impact of this summary presentation is a reason for the popularity of the Boston Box. It provides an easy to understand portrayal of the business units of a company where their size and position have clear managerial implications.

3.4.3 Examine interrelationships

The proposed interrelationships between the SBUs has been suggested in the success sequence in Figure 3.4 and the life cycle and death cycle in Figure 3.1. These ideas are projected onto Figure 3.7 to show the sources and applications of funds. Two pets and a problem child are shown as being divested and therefore generating funds. Potential fund flows are also indicated from the cash dog which is being harvested, and from the cash cows. It is likely that most of the cash generated by the stars and the cash cows remains within their business units, but some of the cash taken from them and that from the divestments is shown as invested in the problem children, where it could be used in an attempt to shift them close to being stars or to start new ventures.

This rationale for the sources and allocation of funds has been described by practitioners as one of the major values of the box. It is on call for headquarters to explain how the SBUs need to be managed and it can help SBU managers argue for the cash they need.

3.4.4 Project the future for each SBU

The model can be used to represent the likely future of each SBU and to help choose strategies appropriate for them. Problem children which are to be retained must break even so as not to be a drain on cash, or be grown aggressively before a slowdown in their markets, and dominance by competitors, make this too difficult or costly to achieve. Since the problem children are in growth markets, it is particularly important to see market share gain rather than merely sales improvement. If the assumptions of the Boston Consulting Group are correct, it would be wrong to anticipate that these problem children, who are set to grow, would be able to do so on the basis of internally generated funds alone.

Stars may be given growth objectives which are difficult to achieve for political or competitive reasons. It is not uncommon to see an early market leader slowly lose share as more companies enter the market. What is important is to retain market share and grow with the market, maybe taking market share gains as a shake-out occurs. This may appear to be a smooth process but the shifts which do occur are often the result of discontinuity in product, technology or market development, discontinuities which can be to the advantage of aggressive entrants.

Two main dangers for a star business are excessive milking and satisfaction with sales growth levels which leave market share eroded. A company that is over-stretched by trying to cultivate too many problem children or maintaining too many pets may find the milking of its stars to support them an irresistible temptation.

The main concern for cash cows is the generation of cash now. There may occasionally be opportunities for further market share gain, but experience shows that once markets are mature companies and brand shares remain stable for a long time. Attempts to build share further, especially through price wars during maturity, can be costly and may reduce cash flow significantly. For these business units appropriate strategies will focus on the maintenance of market share and the generation of adequate profit levels. Future funds for the company's development may depend on the continued success of the cash cows but growth is likely to come from the growth markets occupied by the problem children or the stars.

The future for each SBU is represented by an arrow connecting its present and projected position. This direction is a function of the uncontrolled change in market growth and the market share strategy being pursued by the SBU. For a successful company many of these improvements will show market share gain but it may also be appropriate to show a decline in market share where competition is intensifying and an early lead is being lost or, as is the case in Figure 3.7, a cash dog is being milked to provide funds for SBUs with greater promise.

3.4.5 Project the future portfolio

If left to their own devices SBUs will tend to drift down the Boston Box as markets mature and from left to right as competitors win share. This drift to bottom right suggests the need for a company to view its future portfolio and seek out opportunities and markets which may create tomorrow's breadwinners. This has proved one of the most difficult tasks of large mature companies, which inevitably find it hard to find new growth industries to replace those on which they have depended for so long. Many of the blue chip companies in retailing, groceries and the oil industry fall into this category. Global expansion provides some opportunities for growth but when that has been achieved it is maybe time to give the profits back to the shareholders. In addition to product portfolio planning models described above, other researchers have suggested the value of financial portfolio planning techniques. These and newer approaches to planning the competence portfolio are discussed below.

3.5 *Financial portfolio theory*

The mean variant rule suggested by Markowitz (1952) has led financiers into developing an approach which is quite different from those already discussed. This is most frequently thought of in the context of a way of examining a portfolio of investments in the Stock Exchange but it has also been found to be fairly robust at the firm level.

The *capital asset pricing model* (CAPM) applies Markowitz's portfolio theory to the resource allocation decision. It focuses on the rate of return that should be obtained from an investment with a certain risk level. The underlying principle is portrayed diagrammatically in Figure 3.8 where the line is used to portray the relationship between the risk of the investment and its appropriate rate of return. At zero risk, the rate of return expected is the lowest and is called the risk free rate of return. This is akin to the safe but low rates of return that an individual can obtain by investing cash in a building society or a bank deposit account. A more risky investment would be to put some money into a wide spread of shares on the Stock Market. In this case, the investor suffers the uncertainty of dividends going up and down with economic cycles and potential capital loss if share prices as a whole go down. To compensate the investor for this new level of risk (rm) the investor would expect a higher rate of return (Rm). Riskier still would be investing in a single firm where it is to be expected the share price will oscillate more than the market itself and there is much greater likelihood of fluctuation in dividends. Counted against this could be expectation of high capital gains if the investment performs well. There is clearly much higher risk in this investment (rc) so for this the investor would demand a much higher rate of return (Rc). In a sense the line in Figure 3.8 relating the risk levels to the rates of return is an indifference curve where all investments with their appropriate levels of risk and return are of equal utility to an investor.

The level of risk of a particular investment can be represented using the CAPM formula:

$$b = (Rc - R0)/(rc - r0)$$

which gives the b coefficient for stock C. This is known as the *systematic risk* to the investor.

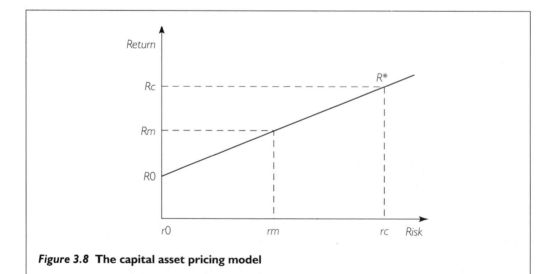

Figure 3.8 **The capital asset pricing model**

This has interesting implications for the portfolio manager. Clearly everyone is looking for an investment which is likely to perform above the line R^* which has a higher rate of return than the level of risk implies; of course these are very easy to identify after the event. A number of financial analysts have argued that there is a general relationship between increased market uncertainties and systematic risk (b). This could imply, for instance, that an investment in a new venture may involve higher systematic risk than an investment associated with a mature product. On this basis, Franks and Broyles (1979) suggest that products should be grouped into Class A projects which are lower-risk, cost-reducing products, Class B projects with average risks which are skill expansion projects, and Class C, new projects which are high-risk. Using the Boston Box terminology this has interesting implications for it suggests that the question marks and stars are likely to be in high-growth and uncertain markets where new projects Class C and skill expansions Class B are likely. This then overlays the cycle of cash investment from marketing portfolio theory with the expectation that this higher-risk investment in the question marks and stars should be expected to gain a higher return than the investments in cash cows. This requirement is realistic since there is a hope that increased market share in the early days of the product life cycle will be an investment which will allow the company to grow with the market and reap long-term cash benefits in the future.

At first sight it is easy to draw the conclusion from the CAPM model that it is the corporate manager's task to invest in a diversified portfolio of product markets and so reduce the risk of the overall investment. In particular, it looks like a good idea to invest in a number of investments with high specific risk (b) where the risks will tend to cancel out and the average returns will be high. In reality analysis of the CAPM model suggests that stockholder wealth is maximized if the investor is allowed to diversify his portfolio rather than the firm making its own series of relatively restricted investments. The conclusion is, therefore, that the management should concentrate on achieving a return appropriate to the risk level involved, rather than diversifying in a portfolio. Other evidence suggests this is clearly the case, for to develop the portfolio product market investments which are sufficiently diverse to move independently means a firm has to become a conglomerate of unrelated businesses. Although conglomerates of such businesses tend to form very quickly in periods of growth when firms are cash-rich and share prices are high, evidence suggests that these firms rarely survive cyclical downturns in the economy and often end up performing poorly or being broken up by a more conservative and thoughtful predator.

Kellogg's is a very good example of a company which avoided the temptation of diversifying out of trouble. In the late 1970s, 75 per cent of Kellogg's revenue and 80 per cent of its profits came from the cereal market, an environment which was becoming increasingly risky and hostile. The company's pre-sweetened cereals were being denounced by consumer groups, anti-trust legislation was being mounted against its dominant position in the market, and the proportion of children in the population (high consumers of cereals) was declining. Faced with this uncertainty, the competitors of Kellogg's, General Mills and General Foods, diversified into other food and non-food products. In contrast, Kellogg's stuck to the business they knew and have since outperformed the firms that tried to escape the rigours of the cereal market. In fact, Kellogg's learned from their experiences when they failed to become the 'king of breakfast' by putting their brand on juices and other breakfast products, and have settled for being 'king of breakfast cereals'.

Being based on financial theory the CAPM approach to portfolio analysis is far better founded than the Boston Box or the Multi-factor Matrix approach of portfolio analysis. Empirical evidence supports the descriptive validity of the CAPM but in practice there is great difficulty in the prior determination of the b coefficient. Finally, as Wensley (1981) suggests, the actual investment decision goes beyond the estimation of the positive net value of an investment. The basic application of CAPM must be compared with the strategic analysis of competitive advantage in any resource allocation decision.

3.6 Competence portfolio

In addition to consideration of portfolios of SBUs, divisions or products many organizations are now concentrating on planning their portfolios of competencies. The resource-based view (RBV) of the firm (see chapter 5), which became a highly influential theme in strategic thinking during the 1990s (see Grant, 1995, for an excellent summary of the approach) stressed the central importance of managing and developing the firm's competencies as well as its existing products.

The resource-based view holds that, particularly during periods of market turbulence, firms need to ensure that strategies are based on the resource endowments of the firm that differentiate it from its competitors. Resources take the form of assets and capabilities. Assets may include physical assets such as plant and machinery, and intangible assets, such as brand names and goodwill (see section on marketing assets in chapter 5). Capabilities are skills and competencies that are brought to bear in utilizing those assets in the marketplace. They can include marketing capability, operations capability, financial capability, and so on. Day (1994) classifies competencies as outward-in (the ability to identify customer needs and build relationships with key customers), inward-out (technical and process capabilities such as financial control which can provide advantages such as lower costs) and spanning capabilities (those that require both an external and an internal focus).

Any analysis of a company's current strengths and weaknesses will include an assessment of assets and capabilities. These can then be viewed as a portfolio that are available for deployment (Hamel and Prahalad, 1994). When developing strategy the key questions are: How can we exploit our capabilities more fully? What new capabilities will we need to build to enable us to compete in the future?

Unlike the traditional portfolio planning techniques discussed above, the interdependence of capabilities and their potential for combination can be the essence of their value. Yamaha, for example, developed the DC11 Digital Piano by combining their craft competencies in quality acoustic piano manufacture with their digital technology skills developed from successes in electronic keyboards (see chapter 19).

Hamel and Prahalad (1994) suggest that in future firms will define themselves more as portfolios of competencies than as portfolios of products or SBUs. That, indeed, the roots of successful products essentially lie in created and acquired competencies and that the key to future strategy is to further develop, extend and deepen them so that they are available for configuration and deployment in new and innovative ways.

3.7 Conclusions

Portfolio theories provide a link between the wide activities of a company and appropriate strategies for individual product markets. They provide ways of viewing the pattern of all of a company's product market activities, drawing conclusions about their interactions and considering appropriate strategies for them.

Portfolio theories have certainly not provided the answers hoped for by the early pioneers, but they remain valuable tools which need to be used with some concern for their limitations. Table 3.4 provides an overview of them.

The Growth-Share Matrix or Boston Box is the most seductive of the approaches. It is simple, intuitively appealing and there is some moderate evidence in support of the underlying ideas. It is easy to use, although there can be some difficulty in determining the business units involved. The strategic implications of the Box can be important, even though the tool is very simple. It is clearly important that the company develops tomorrow's breadwinners while benefiting from today's. The simplicity of the Box makes it operationally useful and its ease of understanding makes it a useful operational tool provided its limitations are kept clearly in mind.

Multi-factor matrices, such as the GE matrix, recognize the need to take a broad view of business strengths and market attractiveness. The danger in their application is the tendency of the weightings and scorings used to push all the business units investigated towards the central, medium or overall attractiveness area. Theoretical and empirical support for the multi-factor matrices is low but the message is simple and companies should certainly consider very carefully investments in markets with low or medium overall attractiveness or where they are competitively weak. The matrix is certainly more cumbersome to use than the Boston Box and depends upon far more subjective decisions, but it is easy to understand and operate. As a way of analyzing the overall portfolio of a company's activities, the Boston Box and the GE matrix complement each other very well.

The CAPM approach has the elegance and simplicity of a great scientific discovery. It contains very important truths about portfolio investments and provides counter-intuitive implications about how firms should manage themselves. The strategic importance of the theory is very high and this is backed by theoretical underpinning and empirical support of the descriptive ability of the model. Unfortunately, at a practical level, it is not easy to use and, in a marketing sense, it is of little operational value. Maybe one danger of the CAPM is its application without strategic vision. It is easy to see the risk of new ventures but much more

Table 3.4 Portfolio models

Model	Focus	Measure	Completeness	Theoretical support	Empirical support	Ease of use	Strategic value	Operational value
Boston Box	Cash flow	Market share vs market growth	Low	Moderate	Moderate	Good	Moderate	Good
GE Matrix	ROI	Business strength vs market attract.	High	Low	Low	Moderate	Moderate	Good
CAPM	Beta ratio	Risk vs return	Very low	High	High	Low	High	Low

difficult to calculate the high, long-term return that could exist. It may lead companies to veer towards supporting today's breadwinners and the cost-cutting support of these, rather than investing in the more risky ventures. These models do not provide a complete answer to analyzing a company's portfolio, but they do provide a very useful starting point.

Finally, recent thinking on portfolio management has highlighted the underlying reasons for business strength – the assets and capabilities a firm has at its disposal. Increasingly, firms are being managed as portfolios of competencies and managers are seeking to build, extend and reconfigure those competencies in ways that enable existing offerings to reach their potential and new opportunities to be created and exploited.

Competitive market analysis

Part II examines the analysis of competitive markets in finer detail. This is pursued through the five chapters described below.

Chapter 4 examines industry analysis. The discussion commences with a review of strategic groups, followed by analysis of industry evolution. Environmental stability is assessed, together with SPACE analysis. Finally, the Advantage Matrix is reviewed as a means of assessing the key characteristics of an industry when forming strategy.

Chapter 5 is concerned with the internal analysis of a company's competitive capabilities in its target markets. Starting from a broad, resource-based view of the firm and the identification of its core competencies, the chapter moves to the more detailed issues of auditing resources and itemizing specific marketing assets, such as brands, reputation, supply chain strengths and partnerships. The chapter concludes with a framework to build a profile of a company's marketing capabilities.

Chapter 6 considers customer analysis. Information requirements are first discussed followed by sources of customer information. The variety of marketing research techniques available to aid customer analysis is examined. The discussion then turns to the processes by which customer data are collected and how those data can be turned into information to aid marketing decision-making.

Chapter 7 addresses competitor analysis. Following a discussion of competitive benchmarking, the dimensions of competitor analysis are discussed, together with techniques for identifying competitor response profiles. The chapter concludes with a review of sources of competitor information.

Chapter 8 examines recent developments in strategic alliances and the development of networks of collaborating firms, as a major influence on the competitive structure of markets. The chapter considers the forces driving firms towards partnerships with others in a new era of collaboration replacing some aspects of conventional competition, forming different types of network organizations. A cautionary note is sounded regarding the potential risks in strategic alliance, and a management agenda proposed to evaluate the real attractiveness of these approaches.

CHAPTER 4

Industry analysis

Success breeds failure ... the historical success model becomes the major obstacle to the firm's adaptation to the new reality.
H. Igor Ansoff (1984)

Introduction

Competition between firms to serve customers is the very essence of modern, market-led economies. During the 1990s competition has intensified as firms have sought to create competitive advantage in ever-more crowded markets and with increasingly demanding customers. This chapter provides a number of tools for understanding the competitive environments in which firms operate and recognizing the opportunities and threats that they present. It can provide no simple rules for achieving competitive success, but can explain the forms of industry environment that exist, the competition within them, and when and why certain strategies succeed.

It should be borne in mind, however, that *industries* and *markets* are not the same thing – industries are collections of organizations with technologies and products in common, whereas markets are customers linked by similar needs. For example, white goods firms comprise an industry – companies that make refrigerators, washing machines, and so on. On the other hand, laundry products constitute a market – the products and services customers use to clean their clothes. This distinction is important for two reasons. First, if we only think about the conventionl industry we may ignore the potential for competition for our customers from companies with different products and technologies that meet the same need. For example, conventional financial services companies were wrong-footed by Virgin's entry into the market with simplified products and direct marketing techniques, and seem unable to respond to the entry of diverse firms like supermarkets and airlines into financial services.

Second, there are some signs that many companies are having to abandon traditional industry definitions under pressure from distributors and retailers. For example, *category management* in grocery retailing is fundamental, the retailers concerned with managing a category of products that meet a particular need such as laundry, meal replacement or lunch, not with individual products or brands. The effects of category management can be bizarre – WalMart discovered, for example, a relationship between the purchase of disposable nappies and beer on Friday evenings. The explanation was that young fathers were being told by their partners to stock up on nappies on the way home from work. They reasoned this was a good opportunity (or reason?) to stock up on beer as well. These products are now merchandized together on Fridays. The point is that we should temper any conclusions we draw about the industry by recognizing that markets may change in ways that invalidate conventional industry definitions.

Systematic analysis of the business environment typically commences at the macro level, highlighting aspects of the broader environment that may impinge on the specific markets the firm operates in. These can be summarized as *PEST* analysis – analysis of the *P*olitical, *E*conomic, *S*ocial/Legal and *T*echnological background in which all firms operate. At a more specific, industry level, however, the identification of strategic groups within industries can provide the most fruitful basis for understanding opportunities and threats facing individual firms. It is within those strategic groups that firms compete to grow, survive or decline.

4.1 *Strategic groups*

A strategic group is composed of firms within an industry following similar strategies aimed at similar customers or customer groups. Coca-Cola and Pepsi, for example, form a strategic group in the soft drinks market (Kay, 1993). The identification of strategic groups is fundamental to industry analysis since, just as industries can rise or fall despite the state of the overall business environment, so strategic groups with the distinctive competencies of their members can defy the general fluctuations within an industry.

Indeed, understanding the dynamics of existing strategic groups can be productive to understanding their vulnerability to competitive attack. For example, pursuing the Coca-Cola and Pepsi example, these firms compete on the basis of massive advertising spend on image and packaging to position against each other. They will respond to each other's advertising and promotion with anything except one thing – price. Coca-Cola and Pepsi have experienced price wars and they do not like them. This made the big brands highly vulnerable to attack by cheaper substitutes – Sainsbury own label and Virgin Cola have taken significant market share in the UK market driven mainly by lower prices.

The separation of strategic groups within a market depends on the barriers to mobility within the industry. For instance, all the companies within the British shipbuilding industry tend to compete with each other for high value added defence contracts, but their lack of cheap labour and resources mean that they are not in the same strategic group as the Korean or Japanese suppliers or bulk carriers. Other barriers may be the degree of vertical integration of companies, as in the case of British Gypsum and their source of raw materials for making plasterboard within the UK, or Boots Pharmaceuticals with their access to the market via Boots retailing chain. At a global level, geopolitical boundaries can also cause differences. For instance, the fragmented buying of the European military and the small production runs which result tend to position European defence contractors in a different strategic group from their American counterparts. Similarly, the differences in technology, reliability and safety standards form barriers between Russian and Western aerospace manufacturers.

As well as the barriers surrounding them, strategic groups also share competitive pressures. Within the American defence industry firms share similar bargaining power with the Pentagon and influence through the political lobbying system. This can help protect them from non-American suppliers but does not give them an advantage within their home market. The threat from substitutes or new entrants may also provide a unifying theme for strategic groups. Within the computer industry suppliers of low-cost products such as Compaq are facing intense competition from inexpensively manufactured alternatives including desktop, laptop and even palmtop machines. Companies within the higher value added mainframe businesses are under less threat from low-cost mainframe manufacturers, but are being squeezed by increasingly sophisticated and networked PCs. Finally, strategic groups often share common competitors because they are often competing to fulfil similar market needs using similar technologies.

The map of strategic groups within the US automobile market shows their dynamics (Figure 4.1). The presentation is simplified into two dimensions for ease of discussion but in reality a full analysis may use more. In this case the strategic groups show their clear geographical and historic origins. The Big Three – GM, Ford and Chrysler – remain dominant in supplying a broad range of cars with high local content. In this they retain some technological and styling expertise in the supply of regular and luxury sedans but until recently had the common basic defence of promoting import restrictions.

Another group is the Faded Champions who were once the major importers into the American market. Both are European companies whose American ventures have either seen better days, in the case of Volkswagen/Audi, or much better days, in the case of the Rover Group. Once suppliers of a relatively broad range of vehicles, both these companies retreated towards the luxury car sector where they appeared to have little competitive edge. More recently Rover has been acquired by the German luxury car manufacturer BMW and has reconfirmed its positioning at the cheaper end of the market, complementary to, rather than in direct competition with, the BMW range. The demise of the Faded Champions in the US is not due to the Big Three, but to the entry of the Samurai into the American market. Initially, the quality and low cost of the Japanese strategic group gave them an advantage over the European broad-range suppliers. But now the Japanese are gaining even more power by becoming local manufacturers and therefore overcoming the local content barriers.

High European labour costs have meant that they operate in strategic groups selling high added value luxury cars or specialist cars: the luxury cars being supplied by relatively large-scale manufacturers with moderately wide product ranges (e.g. the German firm Mercedes-Benz), or the specialist manufacturers producing the very expensive, small volume products (e.g. the British Morgan cars).

The strength of the barriers surrounding the industries is reflected by recent shifts that have taken place. Although the Samurai have never attacked the hard core of the Big Three, they have continued to nibble away at the weaker imports. First the Faded Champions with cheap, reliable family cars and now the luxury car

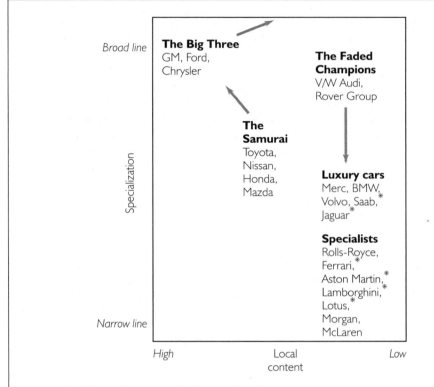

NB: This map is not comprehensive, but illustrative.
*Brands now owned by large-scale American or European automobile manufacturers.

Figure 4.1 **Map of strategic groups in the US automobile market (brands now owned by large-scale American or European automobile manufacturers)**

makers with the advent of the Lexus and other luxury offerings. Even though they are very large, the Big Three have found it difficult to defend their position by developing their own luxury cars and so have been seeking to defend their flanks against the Samurai by purchasing European manufacturers such as Jaguar, Saab, Lamborghini, Aston Martin and Lotus. After years of the Big Three and the Samurai avoiding direct competition, the luxury car market has become the point where the two meet. Although the Samurai have not found it appropriate to purchase European companies in order to overcome entry barriers to those sectors (with the exception of Toyota which has bought, and sold, Lotus), so distinct are the luxury car markets that both Toyota and Honda launched totally new ranges with new brand names and distribution systems to attack the market (the Acura and the Lexus).

With the luxury car market already being fought over, the next stand-up battle between the Big Three and the Samurai is in the specialist market where the Americans have again been purchasing European brands and the Japanese have been aggressively developing 'Ferrari bashers'. Although the one-time distinct strategic groups are becoming blurred as the main protagonists enter new markets, it is to be noted that in all cases the strategy involves establishing distinct business units with the skills appropriate for the strategic groups being fought over. Examination of the US automobile market shows that even when markets are mature there can be areas of rapid growth and competition, such as the luxury car and specialist markets. And the different expertise and situation of the strategic groups means that the protagonists from the different groups may well compete in different ways.

The inability of companies to understand the differences in strategic groups is one that causes the frequent failures of companies entering new markets by acquisition. Although the broad business definition, products being sold and customers may be similar within the acquired and the acquiring company, where the two are in different strategic groups there can be major misunderstandings. Although having great expertise in the British market, many British retailers have found international expansion very difficult because of the competition they face in the new markets and failure to understand the strategic groups they are entering. Examples include Boots' acquisition in Canada and Dixons' in the United States where, although their international diversification was into the same industries as those with which they were familiar in the UK, those skills which allowed them to beat competition within their strategic groups at home did not transfer easily internationally. Were the companies facing the same competition within the European markets it is likely that their ventures would have been more successful. In a sense that is what the Japanese have been doing, as their industries have rolled from country to country across the world, where their major competitors are their own compatriots who they have faced in many markets in the past.

4.2 *Industry evolution*

The critical issues to be addressed within an industry depend on its evolutionary stage. Porter (1980) discusses the evolution of industries through three main stages: emergence; transformation to maturity; and decline (see Figure 4.2). These stages follow in much the same way as products are represented as following more or less identifiable life cycle stages (see O'Shaughnessy, 1995, for a comparison of the product life cycle and Porter's Industry Evolution model). However, industry evolution is to the product what the product life cycle is to the brand. For example, whereas in the music industry the product life cycle may relate to vinyl records, industry evolution embraces the transition from cylinders to 78s, 45s, vinyl albums, 8-track cartridges, cassettes, compact discs, DAT and subsequent technologies.

Uncertainty is the salient feature within emerging industries. Recent developments in broadcasting show this most clearly. There is no technological uncertainty about the basic technologies involved in achieving the direct broadcasting of

Stage	Issues	Strategies
Emergence	Technological uncertainty Commercial uncertainty Customer uncertainty Channel uncertainty	Establish standard Reduce switching cost/risk Cost leadership Finding customers Locating early adopters Encourage trials
Transition to maturity	Slow growth Falling profits Excessive capacity Intense competition Extended product Customer power	4P marketing Efficiency Better co-ordination Retaining customers Segmentation
Decline	Substitution Demographic shift	Divest Focus

Source: Based on O'Shaughnessy (1988), Table 8.1, p. 183. Reproduced by kind permission of Unwin Hyman Ltd.

Figure 4.2 Industry evolution

television programmes by cable or satellite, but there are vast uncertainties about the combination of technologies to be used and how they should be paid for. In the early 1980s the discussion was about cable and the terrific opportunities offered for industrial redevelopment by cabling declining British cities such as Liverpool. In America, many cable channels emerged, but with no particular standard and with numerous channels that had a short life. In only a few years the vast infrastructure requirements of cable have been replaced by the equally capital intensive but more elegant solution of satellite television. Even there, however, there is uncertainty about whether to use high-, low- or medium-powered satellites and the means of getting revenue from the customers. In the UK, to that brawl has been added uncertainty concerning British regulations, those of the EU and the activities of the broadcasting channels, which were once the oligopolistic supplier. It is not surprising that with this uncertainty consumers have shown reluctance in adopting the new viewing opportunities open to them.

The high losses that can be associated with the emergent stage of an industry are shown by the losses incurred by the pioneers of the competing technologies in the video industry. Out of three competing video disc and video cassette recording technologies in the mid-1980s only one, VHS, has survived. Two of the losers in that round (Philips with the laser disc and V2000 VCRs, and Sony with the BetaMax format) managed the emergence of laser-based reproduction in the late 1980s and 1990s more carefully. The two industry leaders collaborated in the development of a compact disc (CD) standard and licensed the technology widely in order to accelerate its diffusion and reduce customer uncertainty. With the establishment of a single technology, the compact disc was less prone to the software shortages that made video discs so unattractive to customers. Customers still faced potentially high switching costs if they traded in their existing album collection for CDs, but the impact of this was reduced by focusing on segments which were very conscious of hi-fi quality and heavy users. The CD was also capable of being integrated into existing hi-fi systems and quickly became an established part of budget rack systems.

In the transition to maturity, uncertainty declines but competition intensifies. Typically, the rapid growth, high margins, little competition and apparent size of industries within the late stage of emergence attracts many competitors. Those who sought to avoid the uncertainty in the early stages now feel the time is right for them to enter the market. This decision usually coincides with a transition to maturity within a marketplace where competition increases, profits fall, growth slows and capacity is excessive as more producers come on stream. Also by now a dominant design has typically emerged, and hence competitors are forced to compete on a basis of price or the extended/augmented product. In technological terms, there is a switch to process technology; in marketing terms, a switch from entrepreneurship to the management of the marketing mix. That is, towards efficiency, coupled with the careful identification of market segments with a marketing mix to address them.

Not unexpectedly, companies that fail to notice this transition from entrepreneurial to more bureaucratic management find things difficult. Take, for instance, Sinclair, which were still seeking to differentiate the market in the mid-1980s with the QL microcomputer after the emergence of the IBM PC had established industry standards. Equally, examine the increasing difficulties which Amstrad faced once their entrepreneurial, cost-cutting and channel strategies had been followed by industry leaders such as IBM and Olivetti.

An industry's decline is usually caused by the emergence of a substitute or a demographic shift. Two main strategies are usually appropriate: either divest or focus upon the efficient supply of a robust segment. Although the basic options are few, industries often find this decision a difficult one because of the vested interests within the sector declining. It is extraordinary that at this last stage there seem to be more organizational choices about how to implement the basic strategies than at any other stage in an industry's evolution. At a clinical level there can be the decision to divest or milk a company within a declining sector. There is the option of carefully nurturing a long-lasting, lingering target market; or for the entrepreneurial zest of an opportunist who can take advantage of the shifting needs. There is certainly much money to be made in the remnants of industries as AEM, a subsidiary of RTZ, have found. They specialize in aviation engineering and maintenance of products which are no longer the main focus of the leading airframe and aeroengine manufacturers.

Industry evolution shows the violent shifts that occur within an industry as it progresses from stage to stage. Not only do the major issues change, but the management tasks and styles appropriate are equally shifting. Industry evolution also shows that their very success can lead to failure for some firms which do not adapt their approaches and styles to changing conditions. Firms that have been highly successful in entrepreneurial mode during emergence may find it difficult to make the transition to a more bureaucratic way of operating. Similarly, those that have learned to live with stability and maturity may find difficulty managing the business during industry decline where a highly focused, cost-restrained way of operating is appropriate. Understanding the stage of industry evolution is essential if a company is to avoid managing in an environment with which it is unfamiliar, with an inappropriate management style.

4.3 *Environmental stability*

A limitation of Porter's industry evolution model is the rigid association of techno-logical and marketing uncertainty with only the emerging stage of an industry. This may not be so. For instance, the UK grocery trade has certainly been mature for generations, but the growth of supermarkets and hypermarkets, the removal of retail price maintenance and the move towards out-of-town shopping have meant the market has faced great turbulence, despite its maturity. Ansoff's (1984) theory is that environmental turbulence is fundamental to understanding industries, but it should not be seen as relating only to the early stages of industry life cycle.

A distinction is drawn between marketing and innovation turbulence (Table 4.1). The reason for this is apparent when one considers many industries, such as the automobile industry, where competition has been rapidly changing but for which the competing technologies have changed little. The determinants of envir-onmental turbulence parallel industry evolution in relating uncertainty to the stage

---

Table 4.1 **Determinants of environmental turbulence**

Association of high marketing turbulence	Association of high innovative turbulence
High % of sales spent on marketing	High % of sales spent on R&D
Novel market entrant	Frequent new products in the industry
Very aggressive leading competitor	Short PLCs
Threatening pressure by customers	Novel technologies emerging
Demand outstripping industry capacity	Many competing technologies
Emergence, decline or shifting stage of PLC	Emergence, decline or shifting stage of PLC
Low profitability	Low profitability
High product differentiation	Creativity is a critical success factor
Identification of latent needs a critical success factor	

of the product life cycle for both marketing and innovation turbulence. However, along with the emerging stage, decline and the transition from stage to stage can spell danger for the unwary company. And in some markets the antecedents of marketing and innovation turbulence are quite different.

Figure 4.3 provides a mechanism for combining two dimensions of turbulence and shows how two strategic groups in the same industry can be facing different

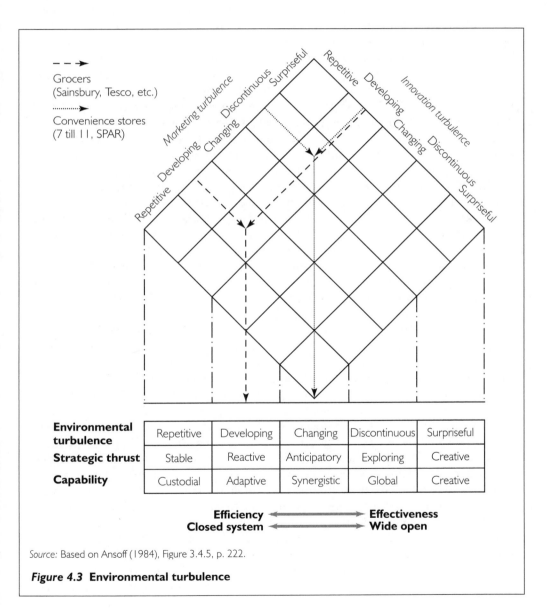

Environmental turbulence	Repetitive	Developing	Changing	Discontinuous	Surpriseful
Strategic thrust	Stable	Reactive	Anticipatory	Exploring	Creative
Capability	Custodial	Adaptive	Synergistic	Global	Creative

Efficiency ⟷ Effectiveness
Closed system ⟷ Wide open

Source: Based on Ansoff (1984), Figure 3.4.5, p. 222.

Figure 4.3 Environmental turbulence

environments. Within the UK food retailing trade, the environment for the leading grocers, such as Sainsbury and Tesco, is *developing* in terms of both marketing and innovation. The shift out of town is continuing (though there are signs that concerns for the environmental impact of out-of-town shopping may lead to a slowdown of this trend) as is the move towards larger establishments, but the pattern is well understood, as is the position of the main protagonists within the industry. Similarly major changes with electronic point of sale (EPOS) and stock control technologies have been absorbed by this sector and are now a well-established part of their activities. The intersection of the developing market turbulence and developing innovation turbulence not surprisingly indicates that the overall environmental turbulence is appropriately classified as *developing*.

The situation of the leading grocers contrasts with the convenience stores, which form another strategic group within the same industry. Although their innovation turbulence is similar to leading grocers, they face *discontinuous marketing* turbulence. This is due to their not yet having faced the shift from in-town to out-of-town shopping and their existence within the emergent phase of an industry in which many new entrants are appearing. Although in the same industry as the leading grocers, the convenience stores, therefore, face *changing environmental* turbulence.

Ansoff draws broad strategic and managerial conclusions from the differences in environmental turbulences that companies face. Whereas, he suggests, the leading retailers see the need to be *reactive* in terms of their strategic thrust and have the ability to adapt, he would suggest that the convenience stores need a more dynamic management style where they *anticipate* shifts in the environment and look for synergistic opportunities. Within that context the convenience stores have concentrated upon a series of goods for which their position is critical, such as alcoholic beverages, milk and soft drinks, which constitutes a very large proportion of their sales. Many have also opened video libraries.

From a marketing point of view, there is great importance in correctly assessing environmental turbulence. A firm must try to match its capability to appropriate environments or develop capabilities which fit new ones. The Trustee Savings Bank (TSB) and many other retailing banks in the UK have shown the dangers of believing their resources can enable them to operate in unfamiliar style. TSB in particular almost epitomized custodial management where it provided an efficient service in a standard way to a very stable market, for a long time. Even more than other banks it meant the company was built around closed systems and operations where there was little need for entrepreneurship. The privatization of TSB gave it a dangerous combination of a large amount of money and wider opportunities, together with a massively changed banking environment. Two almost inevitable developments have occurred: (a) the bank has shown its inability to manage businesses with a more dynamic environment; and (b) it has found itself unable to work out what to do with its cash mountain. A solution was eventually found in the merger with Lloyds Bank, which could provide the necessary capabilities. Similar examples within the British financial market are legion where the very mentality paramount in providing security and correct balances at the end of each trading day left management with completely inappropriate skills to manage modern, fast-moving trading houses. The conversion into banks of some of the leading building societies such as Alliance & Leicester and the Halifax will be watched with interest as they begin to come to terms with very different operating environments.

4.4 SPACE analysis

SPACE (Strategic Position and ACtion Evaluation) (Rowe *et al.*, 1989) analysis extends environmental analysis beyond the consideration of turbulence to look at industry strength and relates this to the competitive advantage and financial strength of a company. Like Shell's Directional Policy Matrix and other multidimensional portfolio planning devices, it is a method of summarizing a large number of strategic issues on a few dimensions. One of the dimensions is of environmental stability (Table 4.2), which includes many of the facets of environmental turbulence. But with SPACE analysis environmental instability is seen as being counterbalanced by financial strength, a company with high liquidity or access to other reserves being able to withstand environmental volatility.

Industry strength is the second environmental dimension considered. This focuses upon attractiveness of the industry in terms of growth potential, profitability

---

Table 4.2 SPACE analysis: components

Company dimensions	Industry dimensions
Financial strengths	*Environmental stability*
Return on investment	Technological changes
Leverage	Rate of inflation
Liquidity	Demand variability
Capital required/available	Price range of competing products
Cash flow	Entry barriers
Exit barriers	Competitive pressures
Risk	Price elasticity of demand
Competitive advantage	*Industry strength*
Market share	Growth potential
Product quality	Profit potential
Product life cycle	Financial stability
Product replacement cycle	Technological know-how
Customer loyalty	Resource utilization
Competition's capacity utilization	Capital intensity
Technological know-how	Market entry ability
Vertical integration	Productivity

and the ability to use its resources efficiently. For a company within the industry, these strengths are no virtue unless a company has a competitive advantage. SPACE analysis, therefore, opposes industry strength by competitive advantage (Figure 4.4) to provide a gauge of a company's position relative to the industry.

Rating a company and the industry on each of the four dimensions gives the competitive profile abAB in Figure 4.4. The example clearly shows a company in a weak position: moderately high environmental instability is not balanced by financial strength, and the competitive advantage of the company is not great compared with the overall industry strength.

The relative size of the opposing dimension gives the guide to the appropriate strategic posture of a firm. For example, from Figure 4.4, A + a and B + b show the overall weight of the SPACE analysis to be towards the bottom right-hand quadrant. This indicates a *competitive posture*, which is typical of a company with a competitive advantage in an attractive industry. However, the company's financial strength is insufficient to balance the environmental instability it faces. Such firms clearly need more financial resources to maintain their competitive position. In the long term this may be achieved by greater efficiency and productivity, but likely is the need to raise capital or merge with a cash-rich company.

Firms that find their strategic posture within the *aggressive quadrant* are enjoying

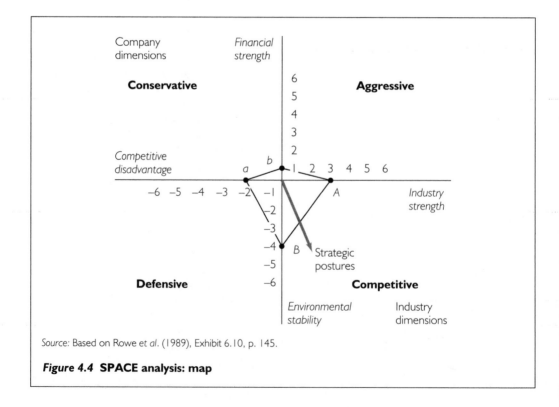

Source: Based on Rowe *et al.* (1989), Exhibit 6.10, p. 145.

***Figure 4.4* SPACE analysis: map**

significant advantages yet are likely to face threats from new competition. The chief danger is complacency, which prevents them gaining further market dominance by developing products with a definite competitive edge. The excessive financial strength of these companies may also make it attractive for them to seek acquisition candidates in their own or related industries.

A *conservative posture* is typical of companies in mature markets where the lack of need for investment has generated financial surpluses. The lack of investment can mean that these companies compete at a disadvantage and lack of opportunities within their existing markets makes them vulnerable in the long term. They must, therefore, defend their existing products to ensure a continued cash flow while they seek new market opportunities.

Companies with a *defensive posture* are clearly vulnerable. Having little residual strength to combat competition, they need to foster resources by operating efficiently and be prepared to retreat from competitive markets in order to concentrate on ones they have a chance of defending. For these it just appears to be a matter of time before either competition or the environment gets the better of them.

4.5 *The Competitive Advantage Matrix*

Once strategic groups within a market have been identified, it becomes apparent that the groups have differing levels of profitability. For instance, in the machine tool industry conventional lathes are almost a commodity and frequently produced at low cost in the Third World. But, in another part of the industry, say flexible manufacturing systems, profits can be quite high for those companies with special skills. Recognition of this pattern in the 1970s led the Boston Consulting Group (1979) to develop the Advantage Matrix, which helps to classify the competitive environments that can coexist within an industry. The framework identifies two dimensions: the number of approaches to achieving advantage within a market and the potential size advantage. In Figure 4.5 the quadrants of the Advantage Matrix show how relationships between relative size and return on assets for companies can differ.

The *stalemate* quadrant represents markets with few ways of achieving advantage and where the potential size advantage is small. Companies in such a strategic group would therefore find trading akin to a commodity market. These can be relatively complex products, as in the case of desktop computers, where the technologies are well known, product designs are convergent despite constant technological improvement, and similar sources of supply used by everyone. Both large and small manufacturers are using overseas suppliers, and consumers are well able to compare product with product. Attempts to differentiate the market, as tried by IBM with their PS$_2$, have failed. Therefore competitors are forced to compete mainly on the basis of efficient manufacturing and distribution.

The *volume* quadrant represents markets where the opportunities for differentiation remain few yet where potential size advantages remain great. This has occurred within some of the peripheral markets which support desktop computers.

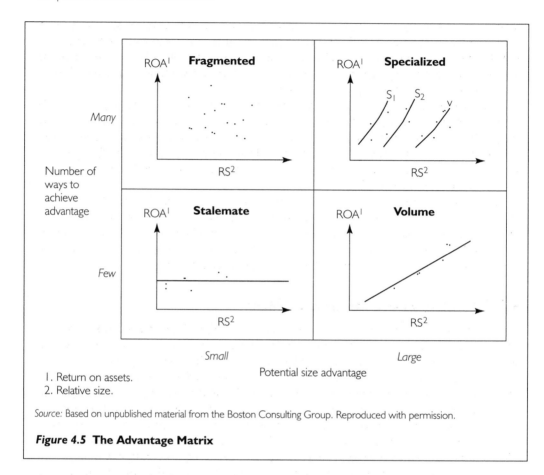

Source: Based on unpublished material from the Boston Consulting Group. Reproduced with permission.

Figure 4.5 The Advantage Matrix

In particular, the printer industry has come to be dominated by Canon, Hewlett Packard (HP) and IBM. The reason for this is the convergence in needs of users of printers and the mass production of the intrinsically mechanical printer units. Unlike microcomputers where the manufacturing process is one of assembly of basically standard components in a very fixed fashion, as any user of printers will know, there are numerous ways of solving the printing and paper-feed problems. This results in an industry where large economies of scale can be achieved by a few dominant suppliers. Where there are markets of this form, battles to achieve volume and economies of scale are paramount. Dominant companies are likely to remain dominant for some time once their cost advantage is achieved, although there is always a threat from a new technology emerging which will destroy the cost advantage they have fought to obtain. In this way, HP joined the band of leaders within the printer market by becoming the industry standard in the newly emerged market for laser printers.

Specialized markets occur when companies within the same market have differing returns on scale. This occurs most conspicuously among suppliers of software for microcomputers. Within the overall market for software there are clear subsectors with dominant leaders. It is also apparent that the market leaders, because of their familiarity and proven reliability, are able to charge a price premium. Microsoft Office, for example, is fast establishing leadership of the integrated office software sector at prices ahead of its major competitors. Within the games sector Atari are less able to command premium prices, although their dominance does mean they are reaping size advantages within their own segments. The result in these specialized markets is therefore a series of experience curves being followed by different companies. Within these specialized markets the most successful companies will be those that dominate one or two segments. Within the market for microcomputer software this has often meant that they will be the companies creating new generic class of product as Microsoft achieved with its Windows products making the IBM PC as user-friendly as its Apple Mac rival.

Fragmented markets occur when the market's requirements are less well defined than the stalemate, volume or specialized cases. Several parts of the computer peripheral market conform to this pattern. In contrast to the demand for printers, the specialized users of plotters have a wide variety of requirements and the opportunity for colour and high resolution mean there is an unlimited variety of differentiated products that can be made. Similarly in the provision of accounting software, alternative specifications are numerous and therefore many different prices and products coexist in the same market. Where this fragmentation has occurred success depends on finding niches where particular product specifications are needed. Each niche provides little opportunity for growth, therefore a company hoping to expand depends on finding a multiplicity of niches where, hopefully, some degree of commonality will allow economies to be achieved.

4.6 Conclusions

Industry analysis has three main components: (1) the recognition of the strategic groups within a market which can allow a company to address its efforts towards specific rather than general competitors; (2) the recognition of the different competitive environments and scale economies that can exist within the sub-markets in which the strategic clusters operate; and (3) the degree of turbulence within markets. Through understanding these, a company can identify the sort of competition that is likely to exist within chosen segments and the types of strategy that are likely to lead to success. From the study of turbulence they can also find a guide to necessary orientation of the company and the blend of custodial management and entrepreneurial flair which will be needed to manage the venture. Just as segmentation allows a company to direct its resources towards fulfilling a particular set of customer needs, the industry analysis helps a company to build its defences towards a specific group of competitors, and build its strengths in accordance with the type of market it faces.

At the outset we noted, however, that studying the industry alone is not enough – it may blind us to changes in the sources and type of competition we will face in the future and fundamental changes in the structure of markets. To our analysis of industry we must add our understanding of customers and competitors, as well as our real capabilities as an organization. These are the topics of the chapters that follow.

CHAPTER 5

Assessment of corporate capabilities

The most important assets a company has are its brand names. They should appear at the head of the assets list on the balance sheet.

Marketing Director, International Food Marketing Company

Introduction

The realistic identification of a company's marketing strategy options can only be undertaken in the context of that company's capabilities, competencies, resources and assets, although we should recognize both existing and potential capabilities. This is the base from which we have to build a competitive position, and any marketing strategy which is not grounded in these realities faces two major risks: it may ignore those capabilities that could provide us with a unique differentiation in the customer's eyes; or it may rely for success on resources and abilities we simply do not have at our disposal and cannot acquire – these strategies will inevitably fail at the implementation stage.

This chapter is structured around the following issues which provide a framework for assessing corporate capabilities:

➤ insights from the emerging resource-based theory of the firm;
➤ the issue of the identification of the corporate competencies of the firm and the link between competencies and competitive differentiation;
➤ auditing a company's resource and competence base, leading to an evaluation of the particular issue of marketing assets – those intangibles like reputation, brands, distribution strength, and the like, which are sources of competitive strength;
➤ integrating these perspectives into a framework of marketing capabilities as the basis for marketing strategy development.

This is shown schematically in Figure 5.1, starting from the most general issues and moving progressively to the more specific.

5.1 Understanding corporate capabilities

Before moving to a more detailed consideration of corporate resources, competencies and strengths and weaknesses, it is worth underlining the importance of gaining a profound understanding of our company's capabilities, as well as some of

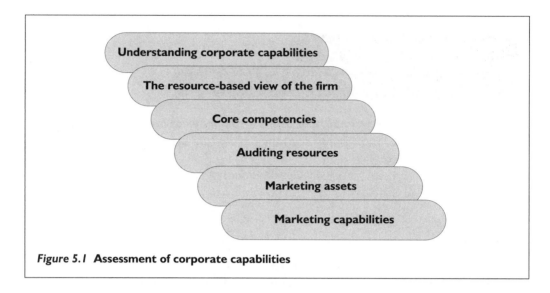

Figure 5.1 **Assessment of corporate capabilities**

the difficulties which may be faced in achieving that understanding in reality. What we are discussing should be seen, not as a routine appraisal of resources, but as a process of 'looking inside for competitive advantage', i.e. identifying those resources and capabilities which are value-creating, rare in the marketplace, and hard for competitors to imitate (Barney, 1997).

5.1.1 Interpreting corporate characteristics

First, we should note that interpreting a corporate characteristic as a competence or as a strength or weakness, or as an asset or liability, risks presuming that we know already what our marketing strategy will be. George Day (1997) points out that 'every business acquires many capabilities that enable it to move its products through the value chain. Only a few of these need to be superior to competition. These are the distinctive capabilities that support a value proposition that is valuable to customers and hard for competitors to match'. In fact, it is clear that different ways of delivering superior customer value require quite different capabilities. For example, Treacy and Wiersema (1995) point to three different 'value disciplines', each of which excels at meeting the distinctive needs of one customer type, and each of which requires different capabilities:

1. **Operational excellence** – providing middle-of-market products at the best price with the least inconvenience, examples are no-frills mass-market retailers, or McDonald's in fast food. This strategy requires an organization achieving excellence in the core processes of order fulfilment, supply-chain management, logistics, service delivery and transaction processing.
2. **Product leadership** – offering products that push the boundaries of product

and service performance: Intel is a product leader in computer chips, as is Nike in athletic footwear. A prime example is Hewlett Packard's computer printer business, which has achieved market dominance through major technology advances, rapid product variations, price-cuts and a willingness to attack competitors. The core processes that underpin this strategy include market sensing (of latent customer needs), openness to new ideas, fast product development and launch, technology integration and flexible manufacturing. Management and structure will probably be decentralized, team-oriented and loose-knit.

3. **Customer intimacy** – deliver what specific customers want in cultivated relationships. The core requirements are flexibility, a 'have it your way' mindset, mastery of 'mass customization' to meet the distinct needs of micro-segments of the market, and the ability to sustain long-term customer relationships.

Gary Hamel (1996) points out cogently that in an effective strategy-making process, 'you can't see the end from the beginning'. We need to be flexible enough to change our ideas about corporate capabilities as marketing strategy options emerge from our analysis (and vice versa), and if necessary rethink the attractiveness of strategy options as a result.

5.1.2 The search for differentiation

Second, we should be wary of the trap of 'competitive convergence' (Porter, 1996). Porter argues that the danger inherent in the pressure on companies to improve operational efficiency is not simply that we substitute operational efficiency for strategy, but that competing companies become more and more similar: 'The more benchmarking companies do, the more they look alike.... Continuous improvement has been etched on managers' brains. But its tools unwittingly draw companies toward imitation and homogeneity.' When we attempt to assess corporate capabilities, our search should be for sources of competitive differentiation and advantage in activities and areas that matter to customers, not simply sources of operational efficiency.

5.1.3 Grouping competencies

Third, we should be aware that how we group or categorize or label what we see as our company's competencies is also critical. Michael Porter's powerful argument is that while strategy does not consist of mere operational improvement, neither does it consist of focusing on a few core competencies (especially if they are the same things our competitors would claim as their own competencies). He argues that real sustainable advantage comes from the way the activities of a company fit together (Porter, quoted in Jackson, 1997).

Porter illustrates this with the example of the car hire business. Companies like

Hertz, Avis and National are the brand leaders, but profitability is generally low – these firms are locked into an operational effectiveness competition, offering the same kind of cars at the same kind of airports with the same kind of technology. Enterprise, on the other hand, achieves superior performance in this same industry with smaller outlets which are not at airports, little advertising, and older cars. Enterprise does everything differently. Enterprise employs more experienced staff and operates a business-to-business sales force – it specializes in a temporary car replacement for those whose own vehicle is off the road, and has turned its back on the business travel market at major airports. The point is that on its own each of the Enterprise capabilities is unremarkable: together they comprise a powerful route to a differentiated competitive position and superior performance.

In reviewing our own companies, we have to search for advantage from the way we fit things together, not just the individual resources or abilities we may have. Indeed, the critical question may be whether capabilities can be managed success-fully across alliances of companies (see chapter 8).

5.1.4 The pressure of the status quo

Fourth, we have to give thought to whose view of competencies and capabilities we should follow – much in this is subjective and judgemental. Indeed, Hamel (1996) suggests that 'the bottleneck is at the top of the bottle'. A crueller statement of the problem is that 'the fish rots from the head'! Senior managers may tend to defend orthodoxy because it is what they know, and what they have built their careers on: 'Where are you likely to find people with the least diversity of experience, the largest investment in the past, and the greatest reverence for strategic dogma? At the top' (Hamel, 1996).

New perspectives on our company may come from surprising places. Hamel describes how in one company the idea for a multi-million dollar opportunity came from a twenty-something secretary, and in another some the best ideas about an organization's core competencies came from a forklift operator, while in an account-ing company the partners learned about virtual reality from a junior employee aged 25.

At the very least, when we try to assess corporate capabilities we should include the views of those who run the business, and outsiders who may have insights that are valuable. For example, the world-famous Avis campaign 'We Try Harder' came from the advertising agency hired by Robert Townsend to search for a competitive advantage that would enable him to turn around the then ailing Avis company. The agency view was that there was no competitive advantage other than the fact that Avis employees seemed to 'try harder', probably because they had to. This was the core of the highly successful turnaround strategy at Avis – and, it should be noted, it was resisted from the outset by executives who had a more conventional view of the car rental business.

With these issues in mind, we can turn to consider the resource-based view of the firm and the issue of corporate capabilities.

5.2 *The resource-based view of the firm*

There is a growing literature propounding a resource-based view of the firm. Indeed, it has been argued (Hooley *et al.*, 1997) that two main themes have come to dominate thinking about marketing strategy during the 1990s: market orientation and the resource-based view (RBV) of the firm. They argue that while the market orientation literature (see chapter 1) emphasizes the superior performance of companies with high quality, organization-wide generation and sharing of market intelligence leading to responsiveness to market needs, the RBV suggests that high performance strategy is dependent primarily on historically developed resource endowments (e.g. Grant, 1995; Wernerfelt, 1995).

There is, however, a potential conflict between these two literatures in the sense that one advocates the advantages of outward-looking responsiveness in adapting to market conditions, while the other is inward-looking and emphasizes the rent-earning characteristics of corporate resources (Amit and Shoemaker, 1993) and the development of corporate resources and capabilities (Mahoney, 1995). Quite simply, from a marketing viewpoint, if strategy becomes too deeply embedded in corporate capabilities, it runs the risk of ignoring the demands of changing, turbulent marketing environments. Yet from a resource-based perspective, marketing strategies that do not exploit a company's distinctive competencies are likely to be ineffective and unprofitable.

However, we argue that competitive positioning provides a way of reconciling this potential conflict. We argue that competitive positioning provides a definition of how the firm will compete by identifying target markets (see chapter 13) and the competitive advantage that will be pursued in serving these target markets. The attractiveness of markets will depend, in part, on the resources available to the firm to build a strong competitive position. Similarly, the positioning perspective recognizes that for corporate resources to be leveraged for economic benefit requires their application in the marketplace. However, it also recognizes that if that application is to be sustainable in the face of competition from rivals, the competitive advantage must be built on the firm's distinctive resources and capabilities (Hamel and Prahalad, 1994; Webster, 1994). Indeed, market orientation itself may be enumerated as a key corporate resource, accumulated and learned over a substantial time period.

This iterative relationship between the pressures of market orientation and the RBV, and the linkage in competitive positioning is shown in Figure 5.2. In this simplified view, the issue becomes one of responding to markets in applying corporate resources to the opportunities and customer needs identified. The outcome is competitive positioning. However, the theories of the RBV of the firm are worth consideration as a further source of insight into assessing corporate capabilities as a basis for competitive positioning.

5.2.1 Sources of the resource-based view of the firm

The RBV is current in much of the modern literature of strategy (e.g. see Grant,

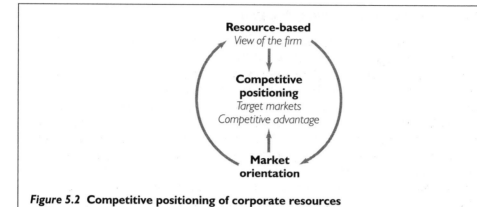

Figure 5.2 **Competitive positioning of corporate resources**

1995; Mahoney, 1995; and Wernerfelt, 1995, for extensive summaries of the theory). The central tenet of the RBV is that for strategy to be sustainable, it must be embedded in the firm's resources and capabilities. Indeed, the potential incompatibility with the principles of market orientation is illustrated by Grant's (1995) view that:

> In general, the greater the rate of change in a company's external environment, the more it must seek to base long term strategy upon its internal resources and capabilities, rather than upon an external market focus.

Grant uses the example of typewriter manufacturers faced with the PC revolution of the 1980s. He suggests there were only two available strategies: pursue the traditional market and attempt to acquire the technology for word processing; or seek other markets where existing competencies and capabilities could be exploited. The move of Olivetti from typewriter to PC is an example of the first strategy. The move of other companies into the printer market to exploit existing resources is an example of the second strategy. However, to assume that these are the only strategies or that they are mutually exclusive is somewhat myopic.

Notwithstanding this limitation in perspective, the RBV offers a number of useful insights into the nature of corporate resources. There are a number of different views of how to define and classify resources:

➤ anything that can be thought of as a strength or weakness of a firm (Wernerfelt, 1984);
➤ stocks of available factors that are owned or controlled by the firm (Amit and Shoemaker, 1993);
➤ a bundle of assets, capabilities, organizational processes, firm attributes, information and knowledge (Barney, 1991).

However, one particularly useful framework is proposed by Day (1994) in distinguishing between a company's *assets* and its *capabilities*. In Day's terms, organizational assets are the endowments a business has accumulated, such as those resulting from investments in scale, plant, location and brand equity, while capabilities reflect the synergy between these assets and enable them to be deployed to the company's advantage. In these terms capabilities are complex bundles of skills and collective learning, which ensure the superior co-ordination of functional activities through organizational processes.

For present purposes, we take resources to contain both assets and capabilities, and use the terms capabilities and competencies interchangeably. The structure for the discussion below is shown schematically in Figure 5.3.

5.2.2 Organizational assets

As resource endowments, organizational assets may generally be tangible or intangible, and include the following:

> **Physical assets** – such as land and facilities, etc. owned or controlled.
> **Financial assets** – in the tangible form of cash in hand, and intangibles like credit-worthiness or credit rating.
> **Operations assets** – the tangible plant and machinery to produce products and services, and the intangibles of systems and processes.
> **Human assets** – the people employed by the firm (tangible) and their qualities, traits and abilities (intangible).
> **Marketing assets** – primarily intangibles, such as relationships built with customers and distribution intermediaries, brand name and reputation, customer loyalty and current positioning in the market (see customer-based assets, pp. 115–23 below).
> **Legal assets** – such as patents and copyrights, or the litigiousness of the firm (companies like McDonald's and Virgin have a reputation of willingness to go to court to protect their rights which may deter competitors).
> **Systems** – the tangibles of databases and management information systems, and the intangibles of decision support.

Our approach to evaluating these types of resource is detailed below, pp. 111–14.

5.2.3 Company capabilities

While assets are one type of resource in the RBV of the firm, capabilities or competencies are the other. This refers to the abilities of an enterprise to organize, manage, co-ordinate or undertake specific sets of activities (Teece *et al.*, 1992). This is closely related to the consideration of core competencies below (see pp. 107–11). In essence, capabilities refer to a firm's ability to deploy assets through organizational processes to achieve a desired result. Hooley *et al.* (1997) propose a typology along two main dimensions, as shown in Figure 5.3, depending on whether they are strategic or operational, and whether they are based in individuals or at some corporate level.

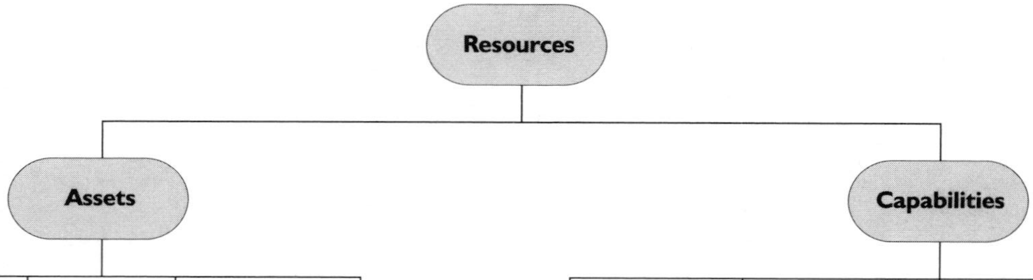

	Tangible	Intangible
Physical	Land	—
Financial	Cash in hand	Creditworthiness
Operations	Plant & machines	Procedures & systems
Human	The people	Their abilities
Marketing	Customer database	Brands & reputation
Legal	Copyrights & patents	Reputation in litigation
Systems	Databases & MIS	Knowledge & DSS
Other	?	?

	Individual	*Group*	*Corporate*
Orientation, Dominant logic	Customer care	Customer orientation	Market orientation
Learning	Individual learning	Group learning	Organizational learning
Organizing/ Managing	Self-management	Interpersonal skills	Portfolio management
Outside-in	External focus	Marketing	Market sensing
Inside-out	Internal focus	Operations	Resource utilization
Spanning	Co-ordinating skills	New product development	Innovation
Task skills	Individual tasks	Group tasks	Planning processes
Other	?	?	?

Strategic — *Functional* — *Operational* (row groupings on Capabilities table)

Note: Items not in italic are examples only, and are not intended to be exhaustive.

Source: Hooley *et al.* (1997).

Figure 5.3 A framework for analyzing corporate resources

First, capabilities can be seen as strategic, functional or operational:

➤ **Strategic capabilities** underpin the definition of direction for the firm. They include issues such as the dominant logic or orientation guiding management (which will strongly influence strategic direction), the ability of the organization to learn (to acquire, assimilate and act on information), and the ability of senior managers to manage the implementation of strategy.

➤ **Functional capabilities** lie in the execution of functional tasks. These include marketing capabilities (see below), financial management capabilities and operations management capabilities. These have been usefully categorized by Day (1994) as inside-out, outside-in and spanning capabilities (see below).

➤ **Operational capabilities** are concerned with undertaking individual line tasks, such as operating machinery, the application of information systems and completion of order processing.

Second, capabilities may lie with individuals, with groups, or at the corporate level:

➤ **Individual competencies** are the skills and abilities of individuals within the organization. They include the ability of the individual to analyze critically and assess a given situation (whether this is a CEO assessing a strategic problem, or the shop-floor worker assessing the impact of a machine failure – or vice versa).

➤ **Group competencies** are where individual abilities come together in teams or *ad hoc*, informal, task-related teams. While the abilities of individuals are important, so too is their ability to work constructively together.

➤ **Corporate-level competencies** relate to the abilities of the firm as a whole to undertake strategic, functional or operational tasks. For example, this could include the ability of the firm to internalize learning, so that critical information is not held just by individuals, but is shared throughout the firm.

There is always a risk that such lists are arbitrary and simplistic when we come to study a real organization, but perhaps the most fundamental importance of the RBV of the firm is that it underlines the fact that many important resources and capabilities are created through company history; they are the results of enduring accumulation and learning processes. Often, they cannot be changed easily or rapidly. This approach should enrich our understanding of a company's potential in the marketplace, and we saw that it can be linked to the issue of market orientation through the competitive positioning of the firm (i.e. choice of market targets and pursuit of competitive advantage).

The RBV can be linked also to the core competencies issue considered below. They are attacks on a similar issue – understanding what a company is capable of achieving by exploiting its capabilities in the marketplace.

5.3 *Identifying the core competencies of the organization*

In recent years, much attention has been devoted to identifying and understanding the 'core competencies' of organizations. For example, Rentokil is a diversified services group, which has defined its core competence as:

> the ability to carry out high-quality services (from pest control through healthcare to manned guarding) on other people's premises through well-recruited, well-trained and well-motivated people. (Simms, 1996)

The need to identify the 'distinctive competence' of a company is underlined by a very influential analysis of successful international businesses by Prahalad and Hamel (1990), who argued that the most fundamental source of competitiveness lies in the core competencies of the organization. We saw in chapter 1 that it is being argued that one of the challenges we face in developing new strategies is to focus on core competencies as the basis for strategy – the 'master brand' – instead of thinking of managing a portfolio of brands and businesses. At its simplest the argument is that a company is likely to be genuinely world class at perhaps five or six activities, and superior performance will come from focusing on those to the exclusion of others. The late 1990s have seen much effort to refocus major organization onto their core activities. For example:

> ➤ In 1996, Grand Metropolitan announced plans to sell £150 million-worth of brands and business units. The company is in the process of shedding two-thirds of its European food businesses, to concentrate on four key global brands: Pillsbury, the chilled dough maker; Green Giant, the canned sweetcorn brand; Häagen-Dazs ice-cream; and Old El-Paso Mexican foods.
> ➤ At Unilever, Niall Fitzgerald is committed to a strategy of narrowing the company's focus around the core food and detergent brands and divesting operations like the European fishery businesses and brands like John West (Wheatcroft, 1997).
> ➤ Meanwhile at Procter & Gamble, the company is removing numerous soap powder sub-brands and pack variations, in a campaign called the 'Great Soap Simplification' (Mazur, 1996).
> ➤ At ICI, the company continues a programme of divesting non-core activities, with the pigments business being demerged following the earlier split from Zeneca. In 1997 most of its industrial chemicals operations were sold to DuPont in the US. Together with the purchase of Unilever's speciality chemicals businesses, this marks a shift in ICI's core business away from commodity bulk chemicals towards the higher margin speciality chemicals business, such as those making coatings for the Pentium computer chip, and the glue for disposable nappies (Blackwell, 1997).

Prahalad and Hamel (1990) define core competencies as the underlying skills, technologies and competencies that can be combined in different ways to create the next generation of products and services:

> ➤ For Canon the core competencies are their skills and technologies in optics, imaging and microprocessor controls that have enabled it to survive and thrive in markets as diverse as copiers, laser printers, cameras and image scanners.

➤ At 3M a core competence in sticky tape has led the company into markets as diverse as 'Post-It' notes, magnetic tape, photographic film, pressure sensitive tapes and coated abrasives.
➤ Black and Decker's competence is in small electrical motors, which can be used to power many tools and appliances.

Three tests are suggested by Prahalad and Hamel for identifying core competencies:

1. A core competence provides potential access to a wide variety of markets. Competencies in display systems are needed, for example, to enable a company to compete in a number of different markets including miniature TV sets, calculators, laptop or notebook computers.
2. A core competence should make a significant contribution to the benefits the customer derives from using the ultimate product or service. In other words, the competence is important where it is a significant determinant of customer satisfaction and benefit.
3. A core competence should be difficult for competitors to copy. Clearly, a competence that can be defended against competitors has greater value than one which other companies can share.

To these three characteristics identified by Prahalad and Hamel, a further useful test is whether the competence can be combined with other skills and capabilities to create unique value for customers – the grouping of competencies we discussed earlier (see pp. 101–2). It could be, for example, that a competence on its own does not fulfil the above criteria, but when combined with other competencies is an essential ingredient in defining the firm's uniqueness. Put another way: what would happen if we did not have that competence?

Prahalad and Hamel argue that the critical management ability for the future will be to identify, cultivate and exploit the core competencies that make growth possible. The argument about core competencies is compelling, and it is certainly driving major corporate changes, such as:

➤ the demerger and sale of non-core activities and brands, for example;
➤ the emergence of network of strategic alliances, where each partner brings its core competence into play to build a market offering (see p. 180);
➤ organizational changes away from SBUs to a new 'strategic architecture' (Prahalad and Hamel, 1990).

However, we should bear in mind the admonition by Michael Porter that strategy is about more than simply choosing to focus on a few core competencies. To be world-class in an activity that does not create superior value for a customer is expensive and dangerous.

For example, in the 1960s and 1970s, IBM built an awesome degree of dominance in the world computer market. By the mid-1980s, IBM had 40 per cent of the computer industry's entire worldwide sales, and 70 per cent of all the profits made in the industry. The core competence at IBM was 'big iron' – dealing with large customers and large mainframe computer systems. In the 1980s the market changed fundamentally with the rapid diffusion of the inexpensive personal computer throughout business and consumer markets. IBM was poorly positioned to compete in this new market, which was dominated by small suppliers dealing with large numbers of small customers. IBM's traditional core competence gave little competitive advantage in this new market reality. John Akers' strategy of attacking Intel and Microsoft was a failure. In fact, in the 1990s Lou Gerstner brought IBM his vision for an IBM Global Network as a turnaround strategy – global networking exploits IBM's core competence in 'big iron' (Lattice, 1996).

It is very easy to be impressed with excellence in the way a company performs an activity or produces a product or service, and to believe this to be a core competence. This must be tested against the market before we accept it as a foundation for our competitive positioning. It may be helpful to identify core competencies, but then to see which are 'differentiating capabilities' (Piercy, 1997), i.e. which produce competitive advantage of the type described by Porter (1996).

Snyder and Ebeling (1997) suggest that while identifying and exploiting core competencies lie at the heart of competitive advantage and superior performance, there are a number of important imperatives to bear in mind in assessing core competencies, or the analysis will be unhelpful and possibly even counter-productive:

➤ **Activities are not the same as competencies** – 'quality products' and 'marketing strength' are not competencies, they are attributes emerging from core competencies. In the 1980s, General Electric focused on marketing to build a strong brand image, but lost to Panasonic (Matsushita) which understood that excellence in components and assembly had a greater impact on value-added for the customer. Honda's core competency is in small engine manufacture. Honda has moved from an initial position in motor-cycles, and transferred its small engine expertise into small cars, pumps, lawnmowers and other products where engines were the significant value-added element. Snyder and Ebeling (1997) note: 'Had Honda determined that its core competence was in supplying motorcycles and related products, lawn mower manufacturers around the globe might be a lot better off today.'

➤ **Avoid laundry lists** – by definition, core competencies should be no more than a handful of activities. Most successful companies have targeted one or two key activities – their identification is a major management issue.

➤ **Achieve management consensus** – if competencies are to be nurtured and shared widely in the organization as the basis for strategy, then management must agree what they are, and act accordingly. We noted earlier, this may not be straightforward (see p. 102).

➤ **Leverage core competencies** – it is not enough to identify core competencies and agree what they are. This is pointless unless they underpin all strategic decision-making.

➤ **Share core competencies outside the organization** – focusing on core competencies may well favour the use of collaboration to link to the value-adding competencies of other companies. Indeed, the logic of the 'lean enterprise' spanning the firms in the value chain explicitly requires companies to share their specialist expertise with others, the exemplar being the automotive sector (Womack and Jones, 1996). A similar approach is seen in the Intra-Firm Transfer of Best Practices Project (Szulanski, 1997). Further comments on the move from competition to collaboration between firms is made in chapter 8.

However, the practicalities of addressing these fundamental issues operationally may be facilitated by the framework below for assessing corporate resources in terms of strengths and weaknesses.

5.4 Auditing resources

In the context of understanding corporate competencies and the resource-based view of the firm, we can move to a more specific framework for assessing corporate strengths and weaknesses. The goal is to progress from the theory to an operational approach.

Assessing an organization's capabilities in terms of its specific strengths and weaknesses commences with a thorough audit of the resources of the organization that can be brought to bear in the marketplace. The assessment needs to go beyond a mere listing of resources to identify those resources which make the organization strategically distinct from its competitors.

For these purposes the marketing audit (see Kotler et al., 1989 for a classic description) has been suggested as a systematic approach to assessing marketing resources and their utilization within the organization. Strengths and weaknesses exist, however, only in relation to the tasks the organization is seeking to achieve, the priorities of customers and the capabilities of competitors (see Piercy, 1997). These analyses should help to identify the distinctive competencies of the organization in a practical way and the core weaknesses inherent in its current operations and activities (see Prahalad and Hamel, 1990).

The RBV of the firm discussed above implies that the first stage in assessing strengths and weaknesses should be to conduct an audit of the resources available to the company including both the tangible and intangible. The types of resource and capabilities listed earlier can be simplified into:

Technical resources: A key resource in many organizations, and one becoming increasingly important in a world of rapidly changing technology, is technical skill. This involves the ability of the organization to develop new processes and products through research and development (R&D), which can be utilized in the marketplace.

Financial standing: A second important resource is the organization's financial standing. This will dictate, to a large extent, its scope for action and ability to put its strategies into operation. For example, in 1997 Microsoft was reported as holding $7 billion in cash reserves available for investment in new projects such as developing Internet-based products and services, and partnership with Comcast to develop interactive and video services (*Economist*, 14 June 1997). Indeed, an organization of sound financial standing can raise capital from outside to finance ventures. In deciding marketing strategy a major consideration is often what financial resources can or cannot be put into the programme.

Managerial skills: Managerial skills in the widest possible sense are a further resource of the organization. The experience of managers and the way in which they discharge their duties and motivate their staff, have a major impact on corporate performance.

Organization: The very structure of the organization can be a valuable asset or resource. Some structures, such as the matrix organization, are designed to facilitate wide use of skills throughout the organization. For organizing the marketing effort product management, as pioneered by Procter & Gamble in the early years of this century, has proved particularly successful in developing brand champions. The system has proved useful in focusing control at the brand level, encouraging a co-ordinated marketing mix and facilitating a flexible, rapid response to changing circumstances. It is not without its drawbacks, however. The product management system can lead to responsibility without authority, conflicts between product managers within the same organization and the 'galloping midget' syndrome (managers moving on to the next product management job having maximized short-term returns at the expense of longer-term market position).

Information systems: The information and planning systems in operation also provide a valuable resource. For example, those organizations such as banks dealing in foreign currency speculation rely heavily on up-to-the-minute and accurate information systems. New technological developments, such as electronic point of sale scanning (EPOS) allow data to be collected and processed in a much shorter time than a few years ago. The companies with the systems to cope with the massive increases in data that such newer collection procedures are creating will be in a stronger position to take advantage of the opportunities afforded.

5.4.1 The marketing audit

More specifically in the marketing activities of the firm the marketing audit has been developed as a systematic approach to identifying and evaluating marketing practices, resources and their utilisation (see Kotler *et al.*, 1989). Often, especially in the major marketing textbooks (see, for example, Kotler, 1997), the marketing audit is presented as a means of controlling the marketing effort. While in its fullest and most comprehensive sense it is often used this way, it also has great value in helping to define marketing capabilities.

A full marketing audit consists of an examination of the marketing environment, the marketing strategy currently being pursued, the organization of the marketing function, an analysis of the marketing systems in use (e.g. decision support systems and new product development systems), an assessment of marketing productivity and a marketing functions audit covering the marketing mix:

➤ The marketing environment audit examines changes both in the broader economic, technical social and cultural environment and in the more immediate task environment of markets, customers, competitors, suppliers and distributors. These are discussed more fully in chapters 6 and 7.

➤ A strategy audit examines the appropriateness and clarity of corporate and marketing objectives. In addition, it ensures that the resources needed to carry out the strategy are available and optimally allocated.

➤ The formal structure of the marketing department, its functional efficiency and its interface efficiency (with other departments such as finance, production and R&D) is examined in an organization audit.

➤ A marketing systems audit examines the information systems, planning systems, control systems and new product development systems of the company.

➤ Productivity auditing involves profitability and contribution analysis of the organizations various offerings together with a cost-effectiveness analysis to identify areas where costs may be excessive in relation to returns.

➤ Finally, a marketing functions audit examines in more detail the elements of the marketing mix. The products and services on offer, the prices charged, the distribution system employed, the sales force effort, advertising, promotion and publicity.

5.4.2 Balance and flexibility

A company with many strengths over its competitors may not, necessarily, be in a healthy position. Crucial to diagnosing overall strength is assessing the balance of activities within the organization. Product portfolio analysis techniques (see chapter 3) can be useful here for assessing the balance of cash use and generation, today's and tomorrow's breadwinners and vulnerability to major changes in competitive action or the broader marketing environment.

A truly balanced organization has a built-in flexibility to allow it to respond to uncertain events. In an effort to increase flexibility of response, some companies are buying in services that once were done in-house. An example is the use of contractors to handle distribution for companies that no longer wish to tie up resources with large scale distribution fleets. Contracting offers the flexibility to expand or contract distribution capability without incurring substantial fixed costs or penalties. Outsourcing and partnership strategies are examined in detail in chapter 8.

There is evidence too that in other aspects of marketing there is greater use of specialized services rather than developing skills as fixed resources in-house. There have been a plethora of specialist marketing services agencies launched in recent years covering aspects such as design, branding and public relations. The modern marketing organization stays lean in its internal staff structures and buys in specialist expertise as and when needed.

A helpful technique – flexibility analysis – is explained by Johnson and Scholes (1993). Under this approach a company's flexibility to respond to uncertain events is assessed and action to increase flexibility suggested where necessary. For example, an area of uncertainty may be an expectation that a competitor could launch a new brand. The flexibility required to respond to this event, should it occur, may be the requirement of a 'better' brand than the company's present offering (in terms, say, of quality or design features).

The actual flexibility in the company may not be adequate should the competitor go the anticipated route (i.e. there is currently no suitable brand available for launch by the company). It is clear that the action required is to do further R&D to improve on current brands offered or to develop new ones that will become available should the need arise. Thus an R&D programme would be set in train to increase flexibility of response of the organization to the identified uncertain event.

This is an important corporate capability in its own right. Indeed, major organizations show many examples of significant realignments to enhance their flexibility and speed of response to market change:

➤ **Breaking hierarchies** – speed and flexibility come from reducing organizational levels, creating smaller business units and empowering line management to manage key business processes.
➤ **Self-managing teams** – critical change managed by high-performance multi-functional teams to achieve fast, precise and flexible execution of plans, possibly organized around market segments and possibly temporary in duration.
➤ **Re-engineering** – critical organizational processes are radically restructured to reduce cost, and increase speed, flexibility and responsiveness to customers.
➤ **Learning organizations** – organizations require the continual upgrading of skills and the corporate knowledge base, leading to adding value for customers through knowledge feedback to create competitive advantage (Piercy and Cravens, 1996).

5.4.3 Evaluating resources

Resources and their utilization do not constitute the strengths and weaknesses of an organization. Potentially useful resources may be under-utilized and present scope for further development. Other resources may be stretched to breaking-point and need additional support. To assess whether the organization has a strength or weakness requires comparisons to be made between the organization's resource utilization and that of its competitors. There are two main ways in which the organizations can assess their relative strengths and weaknesses:

➤ **Historical comparison** – shows corporate capabilities now relative to capabilities in the past. An improvement in productivity from one time period to another may be seen as a corporate strength.
➤ **Competitor comparison** – The second approach to assessing strengths and weaknesses – compares the resources and their utilization with major

competitors. These may be direct competitors (those that produce the same goods and services for the same target markets) or indirect competitors (those that offer similar products and services to different target markets or other satisfactions to the same target market).

5.5 *Itemizing marketing assets*

Of particular note in developing effective marketing strategies is the issue of marketing assets. The term 'marketing assets' was first used in a series of articles in *Marketing* magazine by Hugh Davidson in 1983. Marketing assets are essentially properties – normally intangible – that can be used to advantage in the marketplace. Davidson (1983) gave a good example of this:

> In the early 80's the brand share of Kellogg's Corn Flakes, while still in the low 20's, was in long term decline. The company had spare capacity, but did not produce corn flakes for private label store brands. Kellogg solved this problem by launching Crunchy Nut Corn Flakes which used the Kellogg name and the corn flakes plant. It was priced at a heavy premium, but it gained 2–3% market share, mainly incremental to the share of other Kellogg's brands, at very attractive margins. The new product exploited the existing brand name, flake technology and plant, but did so in a way that attracted new customers at high margins.

Essentially, an asset-based approach to marketing attempts to match the assets of the organization to the needs and wants of its chosen customers. In that sense it is different from a product orientation (which starts from what the company is – or believes it is – good at producing, irrespective of market requirements) and from a pure marketing orientation (where markets are chased because they are attractive, possibly irrespective of the company's long-term ability to serve the market more effectively than its competitors).

The distinction is shown in Figure 5.4. The asset-based approach is similar in concept to the core competencies argument – and some of the same limitations apply (see pp. 110–11 above).

In fact, a wide variety of company properties can be converted into marketing assets. As shown in Figure 5.5, they can be usefully grouped into:

➤ customer-based marketing assets;
➤ distribution-based marketing assets;
➤ internal marketing assets;
➤ alliance-based marketing assets.

5.5.1 Customer-based marketing assets

Customer-based marketing assets are those assets of the company, either tangible or intangible, valued by the customer or potential customer. Often they exist in the

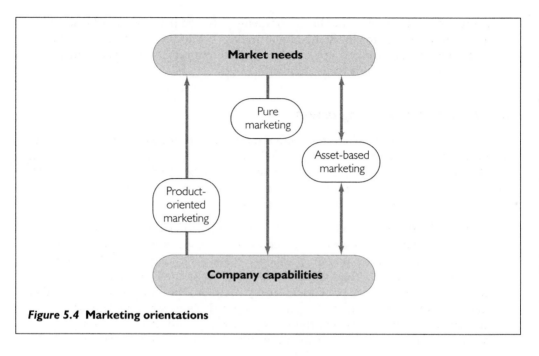

Figure 5.4 **Marketing orientations**

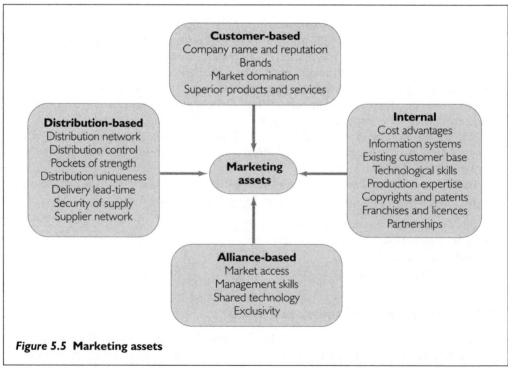

Figure 5.5 **Marketing assets**

mind of the customer and they are essentially intangible in nature. They may, however, be one of the most critical issues in building a defensible competitive position in the marketplace.

Company name and reputation
One of the most important customer-based assets a company can possess is its reputation or image. Companies such as Marks & Spencer and Rolls-Royce have a clear image of supplying a particular set of customer benefits (reliability, durability, prestige, overall quality) in the markets in which they operate.

Company name confers an asset on all products of the company where it is clearly identified. Indeed in many cases where the company identity is a strong asset it has been converted into a brand name for use on a wide variety of products (e.g. Virgin, Kodak and Sainsbury are not only company names but also brands with strong customer franchises).

Image and reputation can also, however, be a negative asset or a liability. This may go far beyond what customers think about product quality. An Ogilvy & Mather study in 1996 contrasted the views of consumers of some companies as 'efficient bastards' compared to the 'Mr Cleans' at the other end of the scale. The top end of the ethical scale was occupied by companies like Marks & Spencer, Boots, Virgin Atlantic, Cadbury and The Body Shop. The other end of the scale was occupied by Camelot, *The Sun*, Yorkshire Water, William Hill, Ladbrokes and Sky TV (Bell, 1996). The seriousness of this issue is underlined by evidence that consumers are increasingly reluctant to deal with companies they regard as unethical (Bernoth, 1996).

Indeed, company reputation may be a 'marketing liability' in some cases. Skoda cars are best known in Britain as the butt of bad jokes, reflecting a widespread but erroneous belief that the cars are very low quality. In 1995, Skoda was preparing to launch a new model in the UK, and did 'blind and seen' tests of the consumers' judgement of the vehicle. The vehicle was rated as better designed and worth more by those who did not know the make. With the Skoda name revealed, perceptions of the design were less favourable and estimated value was substantially lower. This leads us from company name and reputation to branding.

Branding
The identity and exploitation of brands remain central to many views of marketing. For example, the Interbrand agency reports the ten most valuable brand names in the world. The results are presented in Table 5.1.

This listing attracted much comment because Coca-Cola overtook McDonald's for the first time. The highest placed British brands on the Interbrand listing were: The Body Shop (36th), Harrods (41st), the BBC (50th) and Virgin (91st). Such lists are, of course, limited, in that the 'winners' are selected by the nature of the criteria chosen more than the real value of the brand in question.

More importantly, for companies where corporate identity is a liability or a non-existent asset, more emphasis is placed on building or acquiring individual brand

Table 5.1 The top ten brand names

Rank*	1990	1996
1	Coca-Cola	McDonald's
2	Kellogg	Coca-Cola
3	McDonald's	Disney
4	Kodak	Kodak
5	Marlboro	Sony
6	IBM	Gillette
7	American Express	Mercedes Benz
8	Sony	Levis
9	Mercedes Benz	Microsoft
10	Nescafé	Marlboro

* Ranking based on: (1) Weight – dominance of the market, (2) Length – extension into other markets, (3) Breadth – approval across age, religion or other divides, and (4) Depth – customer commitment.
Source: Interbrand (1996).

names as assets. Beechams, for example, deliberately set out to acquire brands with a marketable reputation. The Bovril brand was purchased to ease the company's launch into the stock cubes market (Bovril being an established brand property in the similar meat extracts market).

Companies with little customer-based corporate identity, such as Rank Hovis MacDougal (RHM), have developed their various brands into major assets: the Bisto brand, famous as the UK market leader in gravy making, for example, has been used to good effect by RHM in their move into the soups and sauces market.

As with company reputation the value of brands has long been recognized as 'goodwill' in valuing companies. When the Rowntree confectionery company was purchased by Nestlé in 1988, the buyer paid six times the book value of the company's assets to acquire brands such as Kit-Kat, Quality Street, Smarties, Rolo and Yorkie.

The British car industry is perhaps one of the best examples of assets based in brand names or marques. Over the years Rover Group and its predecessors have had valuable assets in marques such as Rover, Wolsey, MG, Austin Healey and Jaguar. Since BMW purchased the ailing Rover Group in 1994, part of the BMW approach has been to embed the vision of the brand as the unifying focus throughout the company and its supply chain.

In another part of the car market, Rolls-Royce cars, now part of Vickers (and completely independent of the Rolls-Royce Aero Engine company), rejuvenated the Bentley name. Bentley became part of Rolls-Royce in the 1930s as a successful, 'sporty' car, but was never developed to its full potential – it was used essentially as a different badge on the front of the same car. Market research showed, however, that 'Bentley' and 'Rolls-Royce' meant very different things to customers and potential customers. While the Rolls was seen as the car in which those who have 'arrived' are driven, the Bentley was 'the sporty car you drive yourself'. Bentley stands for understated wealth rather than the blatant wealth of the Rolls owner. The Bentley has now been relaunched to take advantage of this with a sportier, turbo engine appealing directly to the younger, sportier, but still wealthy driver. In this market it is doing well in competition with Porsche and Mercedes.

Branding can operate at the individual level too. For example, recently sportsmen and sportswomen have begun taking out patents on their names and nicknames, as these are used in merchandising and advertising. Footballers such as Alan Shearer, Paul Gascoigne and Ryan Giggs have registered their surnames and the nicknames 'Gazza', 'Giggsy' and 'Giggs 11'. Eric Cantona, the former Manchester United player, has patented his name and the slogan 'Ooh Aah Cantona', which fans chanted. Damon Hill, the racing driver, has registered the image of his eyes looking out of his driving helmet (subsequently used in advertisements like those by Anderson Consulting), and Dickie Bird, the former international cricket umpire, has launched his own personality Toby jug. Each of these could get about 10 per cent royalties on product sales, when their names, slogans and nicknames are used. The football kit business in the UK alone was worth £100 million in 1996, and football boots a further £110 million. Many of these products are now marketed with players' names on them (*The Guardian*, 30 August 1997). Similar developments can be seen with major basketball and football stars in the US.

In fact, branding remains a highly topical marketing issue for a number of reasons:

> **Brands are difficult to build** – for example, in the top fifty grocery brands in the UK, very few are new: four were launched in the 1800s; sixteen were launched between 1900 and 1950; twenty-one were launched between 1950 and 1975; and nine have been launched since 1975. Once established, simple economics suggests brands must be fully exploited.

> **Brands add value for customers** – the classic example is that in blind tests 51 per cent of consumers prefer Pepsi to Coca-Cola, but in open tests 65 per cent prefer Coca-Cola to Pepsi: soft drink preferences are based on brand image not taste (de Chernatony and MacDonald, 1992).

> **Brands create defensible competitive positions** – Heinz baked beans is a cliché and an old brand. In 1996, some supermarket own-label baked beans were priced as low as 3p a can. The power of this brand is such that not only did Heinz customers stay loyal while paying fully nine times as much, Heinz was actually able to increase its prices at this time. In the whole war, Heinz saw only a 4 per cent dip in revenue.

> **Brands build customer retention** – research sponsored by the US Coalition for Brand Equity shows that brand loyalty makes customers less sensitive to competitors' promotions and more likely to try new products and services from

that brand. A study of 400 brands over eight years by Information Resources found that with successful brands 30 per cent of the sales increase attributable to new advertising came from new customers, but 70 per cent came from the increased loyalty of existing customers (Kanner, 1996).

➤ **Brands can transform markets** – the British financial services sector has long been associated with weak branding and low brand awareness: names like Provident, Perpetual and Scottish imply thriftiness, but little else. Virgin Direct and the Sainsbury Bank have taken market share in financial services quickly and cheaply by extending their strong brands into this sector.

➤ **Brands perform financially** – a study by Citibank and Interbrand in 1997 found that companies basing their business on brands had outperformed the stock market for fifteen years. The same study does, however, note the risky tendency of some brand owners to have reduced investment in brands in the mid-1990s with negative impacts on their performance (Smith, 1997).

Putting a value on brand names

For some time, accountants have grappled with the problem of attempting to put a value on a company's brand names, and then to enter them on the balance sheet as assets distinguished from goodwill. This is technically complex. While Saunders (1990) has questioned the case for valuing brands, it is clear that many companies are now adopting this policy. Recent years have seen growing emphasis on the sale of brands as assets: in 1996 Grand Metropolitan raised some £300 million by the sale of brands like Shippams Paste, Memory Lane Cakes and Peters Savoury Products. Highland Distilleries valued the Macallan brand of whisky at £60 million in its 1997 accounts and in the same year, Manchester United football club raised £2.2 million by a trademark licensing deal for the 'Man U' brand.

Brand valuation remains highly controversial. However, a number of factors are taken into account when valuing brands for accounting purposes (see Murphy, 1991). They are all, however, related to the ability of the brand to produce a better return than competitors now or in the future:

➤ **Current market position**: Brands that are market leaders are typically valued more highly than brands that may have good market shares, but operate in markets where another brand is dominant. This is because, particularly in consumer markets, buyers often have a strong tendency to purchase leading brands and this is not easily overcome by competitors or newcomers. Market leadership can, therefore, create a barrier to competitor entry or development.

➤ **Market type**: Brands are more valuable in established, high-volume markets with further potential for growth. They are more valuable in markets where margins are high, rather than markets which are highly price-competitive (indeed, valuable brands are those which enable the company to compete on grounds other than price), and in markets which are less prone to technological or fashion change (e.g. confectionery or beer).

➤ **Durability**: Brand names which have lasted for many years are likely to have developed stronger customer loyalty and become part of the 'fabric' of the market. IBM is a prime example in the computer hardware market. Brands which have become generically associated with the product, e.g. Formica in kitchen work surfaces and Hoover in carpet vacuum cleaners, also have higher value. While specific products may have increasingly short life cycles due to rapid technological or market change durable brands can survive through product change and improvement. Persil has remained market leader (or thereabouts) in washing powders for nearly fifty years through continuous product improvement and adaptation to changing washing habits and conditions. Blackett (in Murphy, 1991) notes that Stork (margarine), Kellogg (cornflakes), Cadbury (chocolate), Gillette (razors), Schweppes (mixers), Brooke Bond (tea), Colgate (toothpaste), Kodak (film) and Hoover (vacuum cleaners) were all brands that led their product categories in 1931 and continued to do so in 1991, though few have survived in their original form. Brands that can remain contemporary and relevant to customers over an extended period constitute greater assets.

➤ **Global presence**: Those brands that are, or can be, exploited internationally are generally more valuable than those restricted to domestic markets. Recent developments in global media and global advertising have enhanced the value of international or global brands. We discussed earlier the power of the 'master brand' in global positioning (see pp. 23–4).

➤ **Extendibility**: Brands that can be extended and exploited in the same or new markets have greater value than brands that are more limited in their scope. The Gillette brand, for example, has been successfully extended across a number of 'disposable' markets; the Guinness name has been used to sell books; and the Levi name has been extended to other garments and accessories over and above five pocket blue jeans. Fashion house names such as Dunhill, Gucci and Yves Saint Laurent have proved to be particularly successful at extension beyond their original product fields.

➤ **Protection**: Brands that can be protected through registered trademarks, patents and/or registered designs can potentially offer greater value than those that can be easily copied. Brand value is vulnerable to attack by retailer own-brands (e.g. Virgin Cola and Sainsbury's Classic Cola knocked Coca-Cola's share of the British market to less than 50 per cent for the first time in 1995); brand copying (the retailer Asda has been defending a series of actions by brand owners following the remarkable similarity between some of their own-labels and the brand leaders); brand counterfeiting (the illegal falsifying of brand identities has plagued firms like Nike, Reebok, Levi Strauss, BP motor oils and many computer software producers); and retailer strategies (Tesco is selling branded products like Levi Strauss blue jeans, Chanel fragrances and Clarins cosmetics at cut-prices against the will of the brand owners, who see their brand equity diminishing as their brands are sold in 'unsuitable' places).

It should be noted that to date much of the interest in brand valuation has come from accountants and valuers attempting to get a truer picture of the value of companies for the purposes of takeovers and defences against takeovers. Hence much of the debate on valuation has centred on methods for putting a current value on the brand. Marketers are more concerned with the potential value of a brand and how it can be extended or better exploited in the marketplace.

Country of origin

For companies operating in international markets, the identity of the home country can contribute either an asset or a liability. Japanese firms, for example, collectively enjoy a good reputation for quality and value for money. Similarly 'made in Hong Kong' or 'Taiwan' still gives the impression, rightly or wrongly, of poor workmanship and cheap materials. British-made goods, such as Barbour, The Body Shop and Church's shoes, are enjoying a revival in the US due to the favourable image of Britain in this market.

The value of image of home country, company or brand should not be underestimated. Image often takes a long time to build up, but can be destroyed very quickly by mistakes. Conversely, it is often more difficult, though not impossible, for competitors to destroy a company's image-based assets, than, say, copy its technology or imitate its products.

Market domination

In addition to image, the domination or apparent domination of the market can constitute an asset. As discussed above, market presence or domination has been used as a criterion for valuing brands. Market leaders typically enjoy good coverage of the market, wide distribution and good shelf positions. In addition, market leaders are often believed by consumers to be better in some way than the rest of the market. Simply being there and highly visible may confer an asset on the product. There is, however, a counter-argument emerging. There is some evidence of an increasing desire amongst more affluent consumers to demonstrate their independence and sophistication by not buying the same goods and services that others buy. In some product areas this could lead to the situation where being popular and widely used actively discourages some customers who wish to feel they are different from the mass.

For example, in Japan there has been a surge in the sales of unbranded goods in an attempt by conspicuous consumers to stand out from the mass in their Jean Paul Gaultier dresses, Hermes scarves, Cartier gold watches and Chanel handbags. *The Economist* (14 March 1992) reported the success of the clothes retail store Seibu in Tokyo, which sells only *Mujirushi ryohin* ('no brand/good quality') products. Their labels say only what materials are used and the country of manufacture. The clothes have simple designs, plain colours, high quality and reasonable pricing. Seibu's parent group have also developed the no-brand idea for tinned food and household items in its Seiyu supermarkets.

Superior products and services

It is still worth saying that having superior products and services on the market – products that are, or are believed to be, better in some way (e.g. cheaper, better quality, more stylish and up-to-date) than the competitors' – can be a marketing asset for the company. Unique products or services, until they are imitated, can provide marketing assets, so long as customers want them and are prepared to pay for them.

5.5.2 Distribution-based marketing assets

Distribution-based assets are concerned with the manner in which the product or service is conveyed to the customer. They include the distribution network, its control and its uniqueness and pockets of strength.

Distribution network

The physical distribution network itself can be a major asset. Hertz, for example, in the car hire business owe much of their success to a very wide network of pick-up and drop-off centres, especially in the US. This wide network ensures availability of the required services in the right place increasing convenience of use for the customers. Similarly, in the UK, the Post Office found their distribution system a major asset in offering new postal services to potential customers when deregulation permitted increased competition from other parcel carriers. The supply-chain partnerships created by Federal Express are what enables the company to guarantee overnight delivery.

Distribution control

Investments in dominating some or all of the channels for a product can be a powerful asset. Mars launched the Mars Ice-Cream Bar as a child's treat transformed into an adult indulgence – a strategy since imitated by countless competitors. The product has yet to show a profit (Mitchell, 1995). The Unilever-owned competitor Walls 'owns' the distribution channel that matters: small convenience stores. Indeed, Walls quite literally does own the freezers and display cabinets in many of these outlets, and does not share them with competitors. The critical marketing asset is distribution channel control.

Pockets of strength

Selective but close relationships between a company and its distribution outlets can lead to pockets of strength. Where a company is unable, through size or resource constraints, to serve a wide market concentrating effort, either geographically on specific regions of the market (Wm Morrisons supermarkets are particularly strong in Yorkshire), or through specific outlets, can enable a pocket of strength to be developed.

Companies adopting the latter approach of building up a strong presence with selective distributors, or even end-users in many industrial markets, often achieve that pocket of strength through key account marketing, i.e. giving full responsibility for each key account development to a specific, normally quite senior, executive. Pockets of strength are typically built up on the basis of strong relationships with those selected distributors and hence require a pro-active relationship marketing strategy to ensure their development (see chapter 16).

Distribution uniqueness

Further distribution-based assets can be built through uniqueness, reaching the target market in a novel, or innovative way. For instance, Ringtons sell tea and coffee door to door in the North of England and the Avon Cosmetics company have built a strong door-to-door business in cosmetics sales through the 'Avon Calling' campaign.

Similarly, Dell computers has achieved a uniquely strong position in the personal computer market by using a direct distribution approach, which enables almost all the computers sold to be built to the specifications of the customer, while at the same time giving Dell a much faster stockturn than its competitors. Dell has been growing at 50 per cent a year in a market growing at 20 per cent a year, and is now the fifth largest computer manufacturer in the world (*Economist*, 5 October 1996).

Delivery lead-time and security of supply

Delivery lead-time is a function of at least three main factors – physical location, order through production systems and company delivery policy. In an increasing number of situations the ability to respond quickly, at no compromise to quality, is becoming more important. Deliberately creating a rapid response capability can constitute a significant marketing asset (see Stalk, 1988).

Similarly, particularly in volatile markets, where the supplier's offering is on the critical path of the customer company, the ability to guarantee supply can be a major asset. As with lead-time that ability will be a function of several factors, but perhaps central is the desire on the part of the supplier to meet agreed targets.

Supplier network

At the other end of the supply chain, well-developed or unique links with key suppliers can be important marketing assets. These can help to secure continuity of supply of raw or semi-finished materials at required standards for negotiated prices. The suppliers to Marks & Spencer, for example, are seen by that retailer as essential assets in their total value chain (see chapter 8).

Nissan, the Japanese car producer, operates a computerized supply-chain linking itself to its suppliers and distributors. The company claims it has increased by 80 per cent the number of customers who get exactly the car specifications they want from the dealer within 48 hours of deciding what they want. This precision in meeting exact customer needs is a potential competitive advantage that results in no increase in stock in the supply chain (Tighe, 1997).

5.5.3 **Internal marketing assets**

Many of the factors discussed above under resource auditing can be converted into marketing assets. A resource becomes an asset when it is actively used to improve the organization's performance in the marketplace. Consider the following examples.

Cost advantages
A cost advantage brought about by employing up-to-date technology, achieving better capacity utilization than competitors, economies of scale or experience curve effects, can be translated into lower prices for products and services in the marketplace. Where the market is price-sensitive, for example, with commodity items, lower price can be a major asset. In other markets where price is less important, cost advantages may not be translated into marketing assets; rather they are used to provide better margins.

Information systems and market intelligence
Information systems and systematic marketing research can be valuable assets in that they keep the company informed about its customers and its competitors. Information is a major asset which many firms guard jealously but until it is utilized to make better decisions it does not convert to a marketing asset.

Of particular note is the use of 'data warehouses' of customer information – collected in loyalty schemes or as part of the purchase process, to develop very specific offerings to customers based on their interests and key characteristics. This is why Virgin Atlantic knows which newspapers and seats its frequent fliers prefer.

As well as understanding customers better than competitors do, the owners of data warehouses can create marketing strategies that exploit this resource as a differentiating capability. For example, Nestlé's attack on the pasta market in the UK involved major brand-building activities around the Buitoni subsidiary, entailing the creation of a large database of consumers attracted to traditional Italian cuisine, and the launch of the *Casa Buitoni Club*. To overcome the problems of a market where consumers were not well educated about pasta products and were confused by the variety on offer, as well as the problem of being cut off from the consumer by retailers, Nestlé used direct response advertising to establish the customer database, and the *Casa Buitoni Club* as a communications channel with its chosen market segment, allowing one-to-one marketing.

Existing customer base
A major asset for many companies is their existing customer base. Particularly where a company is dealing with repeat business, both consumer and industrial, the existence of a core of satisfied customers can offer significant opportunities for further development.

For example, Boots, the high street chemist and health products manufacturer, is planning to sell private medical insurance and may provide medical practitioner services at big stores to exploit its national distribution network of more than 1,200 shops, and its brand identity as a health care company (Wall, 1997).

This has been especially noted in the recent development of the direct marketing industry (accounting for around half of all marketing expenditure in the US), where it is recognized that the best customer prospects for a business are often its existing customers. Where customers have been satisfied with previous company offerings they are more likely to react positively to new offers. Where a relationship has been built with the customer this can be capitalized on both for market development and employed as a barrier to competitive entry.

The converse is, of course, also true. Where a customer has been dissatisfied with a product or service offering they may not only be negative towards new offers, but also may act as 'well poisoners' in relating their experiences to other potential customers. There is an old marketing adage: 'Each satisfied customer will tell three others, each dissatisfied customer will tell 33!'

The issue of customer retention and customer loyalty has become extremely important, and we will consider this in more detail in chapter 16.

Technological skills
The type and level of technology employed by the organization can be a further asset. Technological superiority can aid in cost reduction or in improving product quality. For example, the high rate of growth of a company like Amersham International (specializing in high technology medical products for diagnosis of cancers) is largely based on its ability to stay ahead of its competitors in terms of new product development, but also the capability for distributing highly toxic substances safely throughout the world – many of the products are radioactive and extremely dangerous. In the automotive industry, German manufacturers of BMW, Audi and Mercedes Benz are successfully positioned at the high-quality end of the spectrum on the basis of their superior design, technical engineering excellence and quality controls. The strategy is encapsulated in the Audi slogan 'Vorsprung durch Technik' (leading through technology).

Production expertise
Production know-how can be used to good effect as a marketing asset. Mars, for example, are particularly good at producing high quality nougat (a great deal of effort has been put into quality control at Mars developing their production processes as a core competence). This asset has been turned into a marketing asset in a number of leading products such as Mars Bar, Milky Way, Topic and Snickers, all of which are nougat-based.

Copyrights and patents
Copyright is a legal protection for musical, literary or other artistic property, which prevents others using the work without payment of an agreed royalty. Patents grant persons the exclusive right to make, use and sell their inventions for a limited period. Copyright is particularly important in the film industry to protect films from

illegal copy ('pirating') and patents are important for exploiting new product inventions. The protection of copyrights and patents, in addition to offering the holder the opportunity to make and market the items protected, allows the holder to license or sell those rights to others. They therefore constitute potential marketing assets of the company.

Franchises and licences
The negotiation of franchises or licences to produce and/or market the inventions or protected properties of others can also be valuable assets. Retailers franchised to use the 'Mitre 10' name in hardware retailing in New Zealand, for example, benefit from the strong national image of the licenser and extensive national advertising campaigns.

Similarly, in many countries American Express cards and products are marketed under licence to the American Express Company of the US. The licence agreement is a significant asset for the licensee.

Partnerships
As we shall see in more detail in chapter 8, increasingly companies are going to market in collaborative or alliance-based strategies. We should not neglect the importance of existing partnerships as marketing assets, and also the management capability to manage marketing strategy in alliance-based networked organizations.

Corporate culture
One of the resources that is least easy for competitors to imitate and particularly distinctive of a company is its culture. The formation of culture and the capacity to learn are complex issues. None the less, for many successful companies culture represents one of the most unique resources. For example, Hewlett Packard (HP) has a culture which encourages teamwork and cross-functional and cross-divisional working. This has allowed HP to use its core technologies in many diverse products – printers, plotters, computers, electronic instruments – and to make these products compatible. Competitors can imitate HP's technology relatively easily, but it is far less straightforward to imitate the culture and organization that underpins HP's marketing effectiveness (Barney, 1997).

5.5.4 Alliance-based marketing assets

All the assets discussed above can be held internally in the firm itself or gained through strategic alliances and partnerships. Although there are strategic risks involved, strategic alliances can be seen as one way of increasing a company's pool of assets and capabilities without incurring the expense and loss of time in developing them in-house. The importance of strategic alliances and different forms of partnership is discussed in detail in chapter 8, but for present purposes we should note the significance of such alliance-based marketing assets as:

➤ **Market access** – for example, alliances with local distributors are frequently the only way open to the exporter to enter protected overseas markets.

➤ **Management skills** – partnerships may bring access to abilities not held in-house, both in technology management and marketing management.
➤ **Shared technology** – alliances are often the basis for sharing and combining technologies to create market offerings with higher customer value, which neither partner could achieve alone.
➤ **Exclusivity** – partnerships may create monopolistic conditions: for example, the close relationship between McDonald's and Coca-Cola denies access to these outlets for other cola producers.

5.6 *Assessing marketing capabilities*

The discussion above provides the foundations for understanding and evaluating a company's real capabilities in the marketplace. In particular, the resource-based perspective, and particularly relating this to marketing activities (Möller and Anttila, 1987; Day, 1994), provides a basis for defining the key marketing capabilities that can be used to create competitive advantage. These capabilities all stem from the central processes with which marketing is concerned (see chapter 1).

5.6.1 Strategic marketing capabilities

At the strategic level, marketing capabilities can be assessed as:

➤ **Market sensing capability** – the capacity for understanding what is happening in the external environment with respect to demand, customers, competitors and wider macro-environmental change. Specific capabilities include the ability to undertake marketing research and competitor analysis and effectively to disseminate the resulting information throughout the organization as a basis for decision-making.
➤ **Market targeting and positioning capabilities** – the ability to identify alternative opportunities and then select appropriate market targets, where the firm's resources and capabilities are aligned for the best effect. In aligning current resources and capabilities with changing markets, market targeting involves the competencies of top management and several other functions (such as operations, finance and R&D) as well as marketing.

5.6.2 Functional marketing capabilities

At the level of managing the marketing process, capabilities to evaluate include:

➤ **Customer relationship management** – the ability to acquire, retain, expand and (where necessary) to delete customers. Key account management skills are becoming increasingly important, together with the increased focus in many markets on relationship building through customer service. Direct marketing also has a role to play here.
➤ **Customer access capabilities** – the ability to employ existing channels

and/or develop new distribution methods for servicing customer. Customer access includes competence for efficient management of traditional distribution channels, but also developing and managing franchising networks and new electronic channels. This is a broad capability drawing on several organizational and individual competencies.

➤ **Product management capability** – the ability to manage existing products, including the ability to influence others in the organization, where their activities impact on customer satisfaction. This involves the marshalling of all resources (which may cut across traditional organizational boundaries) to deliver customer value.

➤ **New product development capability** – the ability to innovate and develop the next generation of goods and services. Effective new product development requires both an outside-in (customer sensing) capability and typically strong R&D skills. It relies on multidisciplinary inputs from marketing, R&D, finance, operations and other functional disciplines.

5.6.3 Operational or task marketing capabilities

At the level of action in the marketplace, capabilities can be described as:

➤ **Implementation capabilities** – the ability to implement marketing activities, such as promotions, personal selling, public relations, price deals, special offers to customers, packaging redesign, and so on. Increasingly companies are outsourcing many of these activities to enable them to buy in best practice and expertise from outside (see chapter 8). Design consultancies, PR agencies, packaging specialists and the like are emerging as service providers to marketers in these specialist areas of implementation. Within the focal firm, however, the key competencies required are increasingly in the selection, management and co-ordination of these specialist outside suppliers.

5.7 Conclusions

We started this chapter with the debate about the resource-based view of the firm and core competencies. We expressed certain reservations about how competencies and capabilities are understood, but noted that our focus on competition positioning (i.e. the choice of target markets and the competitive advantage exploited) provides a mechanism for reconciling the internal focus on competencies and resources with the *external* focus demanded by market orientation.

The practical reality faced in building robust marketing strategies is that each company has its own unique strengths and weaknesses with respect to the competition and its own distinctive competence. While the overarching imperative is customer focus, a key factor for competing successfully in ever more competitive markets is to recognize these factors and utilize them to the full.

At a fundamental level each organization needs to be understand its core competencies and its resource base. These are the particular skills and processes at which the company excels, and that can produce the next generation of products or services.

At the next level the organization should be aware of its exploitable marketing assets. The asset-based marketing approach encourages organizations to examine systematically their current and potential assets in the marketplace and to select those for emphasis where they have, ideally, a defensible uniqueness. Assets built up in the marketplace with customers are less prone to attack by competitors than low prices or easily imitated technologies.

Combined, these different perspectives come together in the assessment of the critical marketing capabilities of the firm.

CHAPTER 6

Customer analysis

*... when the future becomes less visible, when the fog descends,
the forecasting horizon that you can trust comes closer and
closer to your nose. In those circumstances being receptive to
new directions becomes important. You need to take account of
opportunities and threats and enhance an organisation's
responsiveness.*

Igor Ansoff, quoted by Hill (1979)

Introduction

Information is the raw material of decision-making. Effective marketing decisions
are based on sound information; the decisions themselves can be no better than the
information on which they are based. Marketing research is concerned with the provision of information that can be used to reduce the level of uncertainty in decision-
making. Uncertainty can never be eliminated completely in marketing decisions, but
by the careful application of tried-and-tested research techniques it can be reduced.

The first section of this chapter looks at the information needed about customers
to make effective marketing decisions. This is followed by a brief discussion of the
various research techniques available for collecting data from the marketing environment. The use of these techniques in a typical marketing research study aimed
at creatively segmenting a market and identifying current and potential product/
service positions is then discussed. The chapter concludes with a discussion of
how marketing-related information can be arranged within an organization and the
development of marketing decision support systems (MDSS).

6.1 What we need to know about customers

Information needed about customers can be broadly grouped into current and
future information. The critical issues concerning current customers are who the
prime market targets are; what gives them value; how they can be brought closer;
and how they can be better served.

For the future, however, we also need to know how customers will change; which
new customers to pursue; and how to pursue them.

6.1.1 Information on current customers

The starting point is to define who the current customers are. The answer is not
always obvious as there may be many actors in the purchase and use of a particular

product or service. Customers are not necessarily the same as consumers. A useful way to approach customer definition is to recognize five main roles that exist in many purchasing situations. Often several, or even all, of these roles may be conducted by the same individuals, but recognizing each role separately can be a useful step in more accurately targeting marketing activity.

The roles are:

1. **The initiator:** This is the individual (or individuals) who initiates the search for a solution to the customer's problem. In the case of the purchase of a chocolate bar it could be a hungry child who recognizes her own need for sustenance. In the case of a supermarket the re-ordering of a particular line of produce nearing sellout may be initiated by a stock controller, or even an automatic order processing system.
2. **The influencer:** Influencers are all those individuals who may have some influence on the purchase decision. A child may have initiated the search for a chocolate bar, but the parents may have a strong influence (through holding the purse strings) on which product is actually bought. In the supermarket the ultimate customers will have a strong influence on the brands ordered – the brands they buy or request the store to stock will be most likely to be ordered.
3. **The decider:** Taking into account the views of initiators and influencers some individual will actually make the decision as to which product or service to purchase. This may be back to the initiator or the influencer in the case of the chocolate bar. In the supermarket the decider may be a merchandiser whose task it is to specify which brands to stock, what quantity to order, and so on.
4. **The purchaser:** The purchaser is the individual who actually buys the product or service. He or she is, in effect, the individual that hands over the cash in exchange for the benefits. This may be the child or parent for the chocolate bar. In industrial purchasing it is often a professional buyer who, after taking account of the various influences on the decision, ultimately places the order attempting to get the best value for money possible.
5. **The user:** Finally comes the end-user of the product or service, the individual who consumes the offer. For the chocolate bar it will be the child. For the goods in the supermarket it will be supermarket's customers.

What is important in any buying situation is to have a clear idea of the various actors likely to have an impact on the purchase and consumption decision. Where the various roles are undertaken by different individuals it may be necessary to adopt a different marketing approach to each. Each may be looking for different benefits in the purchase and consumption process. Where different roles are undertaken by the same individuals, different approaches may be suitable depending on what stage of the buy/consume process the individual is in at the time.

A central theme of this book is that most markets are segmented; in other words, different identifiable groups of customers require different benefits when buying or using essentially similar products or services. Identifying who the various customers are and what role they play then leads to the question of what gives them value. For each of the above members of a decision-making unit (DMU) different aspects of the purchase and use may give value.

For the child's purchase of a chocolate bar a number of benefits may emerge. The child/initiator/decider/user gets a pleasant sensory experience and a filled stomach. The parent/influencer gets a feeling of having steered the child in the direction of a product that is nutritious and good value for money. In an industrial purchase such as a tractor the users (drivers) may be looking for comfort and ease of operation, the deciders (top management) may be looking for economical performance, while the purchaser (purchasing officer) may be looking for a bulk purchase deal to demonstrate his/her buying efficiency. Clearly, the importance of each actor in the decision needs to be assessed and the benefits each gets from the process understood.

Having identified the motivators for each actor attention then shifts to how they can be brought closer to the supplier. Ways of offering increased benefits (better sensory experiences, enhanced nutritional value, better value for money) can be examined. This may involve extending the product service offering through the 'augmented' product (see Levitt, 1986; and chapter 13).

For industrial purchases a major route to bringing customers closer is to develop mutually beneficial alliances that enhance value for both customer and supplier. A characteristic of Japanese businesses is the closeness developed with suppliers so as to ensure continuity of appropriate quality supply of semi-finished material 'Just in Time' for production purposes.

Better service is at the heart of improving customer relations and making it difficult for customers to go elsewhere. Surveys in the US have shown that of lost business, less than 20 per cent is down to poor products and only 20 per cent down to high (relative) prices. The major reason for losing business is predominantly poor service – more than 40 per cent of cases.

6.1.2 Information on future customers

The above issues have been concerned with today's customers. Of importance for the future, however, is how those customers will change. There are two main types of change essential to customer analysis.

The first is changes in existing customers: their wants, needs and expectations. As competition intensifies so the range of offerings open to customers increases. In addition, their experiences with various offers can lead to increased expectations and requirements. As pointed out in chapter 1, a major way of dealing with this type of change is continuous improvement (or the *Kaizen* approach of the Japanese).

In the hi-fi market continuous product improvements, coupled with some significant innovations such as the CD player, have served to increase customer expectations of both the quality of sound reproduction and the portability of equipment. A manufacturer still offering the products of the 1970s or even 1980s in the 1990s would soon find its customers deserting in favour of competitors' offerings.

The second type of change comes from new customers emerging as potentially more attractive targets. Segments that may be less attractive at one point in time might become more attractive in the future. As social, cultural and economic change has affected living standards so has it affected the demand for goods and services. There is now increased demand for healthy foods, sports and leisure equipment and services such that markets which might have been less attractive in the 1960s are now booming (*The Economist*, 1997).

The main ways in which organizations go about analyzing their customers is through marketing research (to collect relevant data on them) and market modelling (to make sense of that data). Each is discussed below.

6.2 *Marketing research*

The use of marketing research services by a variety of organizations, from commercial firms to political parties, has increased dramatically in recent years. The sector is now worth more than £400 million. Not only large companies and organizations benefit from marketing research. It is possible, through creative design of research studies, for organizations with smaller budgets to benefit from marketing research studies. Commercial research organizations will conduct studies for clients costing as little as £2,000, depending on the research being undertaken.

Figure 6.1 shows the range of marketing research activities engaged in by research agencies. In the UK there are currently around 200 agencies providing research services. Some companies, such as NOP (part of MAI Research) and AGB (the Taylor Nelson group), offer a wide variety of services. Others specialize in particular types of research (e.g. A.C. Nielsen specialize in retail audits). For a full listing of companies in the UK providing marketing research services, and where appropriate their specializations, see the Market Research Society Yearbook. Each type of research is discussed below.

6.2.1 Company records

An obvious, but often underutilized, starting point for gathering marketing data is through the effective use of the company's own records. Often large amounts of data that can be used to aid marketing decisions (both strategic and tactical) are held in unlikely places within the company (e.g. in the accounts department). Data on factors such as who purchases and how much they purchase may be obtained from invoice records. Similarly purchase records may show customer loyalty patterns, identify gaps in customer purchasing and highlight the most valuable customers.

The value of internally collected data is dependent, however, on how it is collected in the first place. Unfortunately, sales data are often not collected or maintained in a form that facilitates use for marketing decision-making. As a general rule it is desirable to collect routine data on as detailed a basis as possible to allow for unforeseen data analysis requirements. For example, sales records should be kept by customer, customer type, product, product line, sales territory, salesperson and detailed time

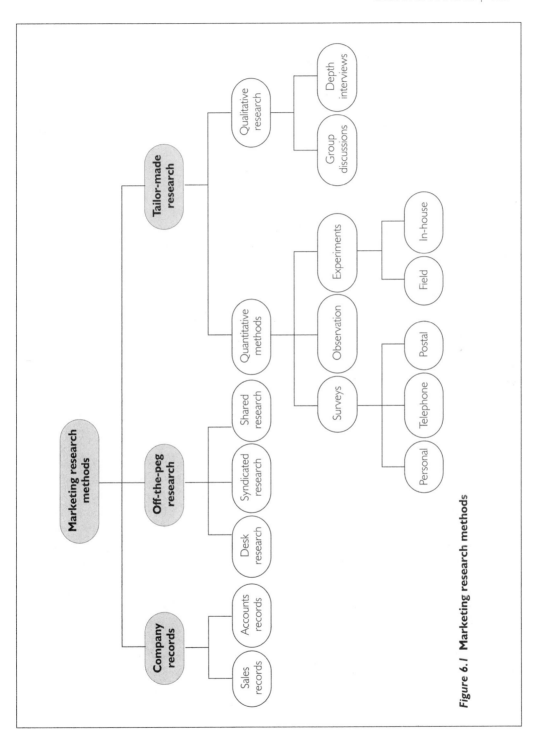

Figure 6.1 **Marketing research methods**

period. Data of this type would allow the isolation of profitable and unprofitable customers, territories and product lines, and identify trends in the marketplace.

In direct marketing it is said that the best customer prospects are often existing customers. Adequate sales records should reveal frequencies of purchase, latent and lapsed customers, and may suggest alternative products that could be of interest. In the mail order business catalogue companies keep records of the types of product customers have bought from them. This enables additional catalogues, more specialist in nature, to be targeted at the most likely prospects.

6.2.2 Off-the-peg research

As the name implies, off-the-peg research consists of tapping into existing research services, often locating and using data that are already in existence but held externally to the company. Much basic information, such as market sizes and growth rates, broad social and economic trends, customer firms and competitor firms, is already available in some form or another. Crouch and Housden (1996) classifies three main types of off-the-peg research:

1. Research using the very large body of already published data, usually termed secondary or desk research.
2. Research using data available from regular market surveys of syndicated research. Both the costs of the research and the data collected are shared by the syndicate of research buyers.
3. Research in which the method of data collection is shared, but the data are not. Off-the-peg research instruments, such as omnibus surveys, are employed to collect client specific data.

Secondary desk research
Secondary desk research uses data that have already been published by someone else. The researcher is a 'secondary' user of the research. Secondary data have the advantages of being relatively cheap and quick to obtain (when you know where to look!), and can also be reliable and accurate. Unfortunately, secondary data are often out of date and not specific enough to answer the majority of marketing questions. Secondary data will, for example, often tell you how many customers buy each competitors' offering but won't tell you why.

In the UK there are very many sources of secondary data; the major problem facing the inexperienced researcher is finding them. The government publishes a great deal of statistical information about industry, trade, commerce and social trends. Most of these data are free, or charged for at the cost of publishing only. The starting point for identifying relevant government statistics is the booklet 'Government Statistics: a brief guide to sources'. Increasingly, it is possible to use on-line information services such as Harvest to search through alternative sources and to scan quickly what data are already available.

Secondary data vary dramatically in quality, both from country to country and from supplier to supplier within a particular country. In assessing the accuracy of secondary data the following questions should be borne in mind:

1. Who collected the data and why?
   (Are they likely to be biased in their reporting?)
2. How did they collect the data?
   (Sample or census? Sampling method? Research instruments?)
3. What level of accuracy do they claim?
   (Does the methodology support the claim?)
4. What use did they put the data to?
   (Is its use limited?)

Primary, or field, research is undertaken where the secondary sources cannot provide the detail of information required to solve a particular problem or to aid sufficiently the decision-making. Primary research involves the collection of new data, often directly from customers, or distribution intermediaries (such as retailers of wholesales).

Syndicated research

Syndicated research occurs where a group of research buyers share the costs and the findings of research amongst themselves. The majority of such syndicated research services are conducted by the larger marketing research agencies and the results are sold to whomever will buy.

In the UK syndicated research is carried out in a wide variety of markets, though primarily consumer markets. The most widely used services are the Retail Audits of A.C. Nielsen, the Television Consumer Audit (TCA) (a consumer panel) of AGB, the Target Group Index of British Market Research Bureau Ltd (BMRB) and the various media research services, including the National Readership Survey currently administered by Research Bureau Ltd (RBL), and the television viewing survey, BARB, researched and administered by AGB.

There are a great many sources of syndicated research covering a wide variety of markets. They have the major advantages that the methodology is usually tried and tested, the samples are often bigger than individual companies could afford to survey on their own and they are considerably cheaper than conducting the research for one company alone.

The disadvantages are that the data are limited in their usefulness to monitoring sales over time, identifying trends in markets and competitors and tracking advertising and other promotional activity. They do not allow further probing of motivations for purchase, nor indeed any additional, company-specific questioning.

Shared research

The final type of research to be classified as off-the-peg is research where some of the costs and fieldwork are shared by a number of companies, but the results are not. Omnibus surveys are regular research surveys which are being undertaken using a predetermined (off-the-peg) sampling frame and methodology. Individual clients then 'buy a seat' on the omnibus by adding their own questions. These are asked, along with the questions of other clients, and the results tabulated against such factors as social class, ACORN category, age, etc.

Typical Omnibus surveys in the UK are the NOP Random Omnibus of 2,000 adults per week, the RSGB Motoring Omnibus of 1,000 motorists monthly and the BMRB National Children's Survey of 1,100 7–17-year-olds monthly. Omnibus research has the major advantages of low cost, as the fieldwork costs are shared by all participating companies, and added flexibility in that each client can ask his or her own questions of a typically large sample of respondents. The number of questions that can be added to an Omnibus is, however, generally limited to between 6 and 10 and, because the respondent will be asked questions about a variety of product fields in the same interview, questions are best kept short and factual to avoid respondent fatigue.

In summary, there is a wide variety of off-the-peg sources from which the company or organization wishing to conduct market or social research can choose. They have the advantages over conducting primary research in that they have established methodologies and are relatively quick and cheap to tap into. The disadvantages lie in the scope and number of the questions that can be asked. Before undertaking costly primary research, however, marketing managers are well advised to examine the possibilities that off-the-peg research offers.

6.2.3 Tailor-made research

Tailor-made research, in contrast to off-the-peg, provides the organization undertaking the research the flexibility to design the research to exactly match the needs of the client company. Depending on those needs there is a variety of techniques available (see Figure 6.1). The techniques are broadly categorized as qualitative and quantitative.

In qualitative research emphasis is placed on gaining understanding and depth in data that often cannot be quantified. It is concerned with meaning rather than numbers, usually involving small samples of respondents but probing them in-depth for their opinions, motivations and attitudes. Quantitative research, on the other hand, involves larger samples, more structured research instruments (questionnaires and the like) and produces quantifiable outputs. In major studies both types of technique may be used hand in hand. Qualitative research is often used in the early, exploratory stages of research, and quantitative research then used to provide quantification of the broad qualitative findings.

Qualitative techniques
Qualitative techniques are essentially unstructured or semi-structured interviewing methods designed to encourage respondents to reply freely and express their real feelings, opinions and motivations. There are two main techniques used in qualitative research: the group discussion (variously termed focus group or group depth interview) and the individual depth interview.

Group discussions usually take the form of a relaxed, informal discussion amongst 6–9 respondents with a group leader or moderator ensuring that the discussion covers areas relevant to the research brief. The discussions are typically held in the moderator's home (in the case of consumer studies) or in a hotel room (for industrial groups). The advantage of the group set-up is that it encourages interaction amongst the participants, which can generate broader discussion than a one-to-one interview-and-answer session. Its value as a research technique rests with the quality of the group moderator (usually a trained psychologist) and his or her ability to encourage wide-ranging but relevant discussion of the topics of interest. Products can be introduced into the group for trial and comment in an informal setting conducive to evaluation.

Group discussions were used effectively in the development of the advertising message 'naughty but nice' for fresh cream cakes (see Bradley, 1987). A series of group discussions discovered feelings of guilt associated with eating fresh cream cakes and that the advertising could capitalize on this by emphasizing the sheer pleasure of cream cakes and the slightly naughty aspects of eating them. Feelings and emotions of this sort could not have been obtained from quantitative research. The relaxed, informal settings of the group discussion were essential to obtaining the clues that led to the advertising copy development.

The depth interview takes place between one interviewer (again often a trained psychologist) and one respondent. It is used extensively for deeper probing of motivations, especially in areas of a confidential nature, or on delicate subjects where it is necessary that rapport and trust is built up between the interviewer and the respondent. Many of the techniques used in depth interviews have been developed from clinical psychology including the use of projective techniques such as word associations and Kelly Repertory Grids.

Qualitative research is often used as preliminary research prior to a more quantitative investigation. In this context it can help in the wording of questions on a further questionnaire, indicate what questions to ask and to elicit important product and brand features and image dimensions. Qualitative research is also used on its own in motivation studies, for the development and pretesting of advertising messages, for package design evaluation, for concept testing and new product testing. The major limitation of qualitative research is that its cost and its nature make it impossible to employ large samples and hence it can be dangerous applying it to large populations on the basis of the small sample involved.

Quantitative techniques
Quantitative research techniques include surveys, observation methods and experimentation of one type or another.

Surveys are a vast subject in themselves. There are three main types of survey depending on how the interviews are conducted: personal interviews are where the interviewer and the respondent come face-to-face for a question-and-answer session; telephone interviews, an increasingly used research techniques, are conducted over the telephone; and postal surveys use the mail services to send self-completion questionnaires to respondents.

Each technique has its advantages and drawbacks. Personal interviews are the most expensive to conduct, but offer the greatest flexibility. They are particularly useful where respondents are asked to react to attitudinal statements and more complex questions that may require some clarification by the interviewer.

Telephone interviews are particularly useful when data are required quickly. They do not entail the costs of physically sending interviewers into the field, can be closely controlled and the data collected entered directly onto computer for analysis. The majority of opinion polls are now conducted in this manner facilitating next day reporting in the sponsoring newspapers. The drawbacks of telephone interviews are that not everybody has a telephone and hence the sample achieved may be biased towards the more affluent in society (this problem is now less acute than a few years ago as more households now have telephones) and that the interview is less personal than a face-to-face encounter requiring it to be kept relatively short. It is not possible to show prompts and other stimuli during a telephone conversation.

Postal surveys are the cheapest method of all. They are useful in locating geographically disperse samples and for situations where the questionnaire is long and detailed. Response rates, however, can be low and there is little control over who responds. The lack of personal contact requires a very clearly laid out questionnaire, well pretested to ensure clarity.

Observation techniques can be particularly useful where respondents are unlikely to be able or willing to give the types of information required. Crouch (1992) cites the example of research into what items a shopper has taken from a supermarket shelf, considered for purchase but not bought. Direct questioning after the shopping trip is unlikely to produce accurate data as the respondent simply will not remember. Observation of shopping behaviour in the store can provide such data.

Observation can be conducted by individuals, as in the case of the supermarket behaviour noted above, or observation of traffic density on particular roads, or by instruments designed to monitor behaviour. The prime example of the latter is the 'PeopleMeter' recording device used in television viewing research. A black box is attached to the television sets of a sample of viewers and records when the set was turned on and what channel was tuned to. Each individual in the household has a code key which is activated when he/she is in the room. Data are transmitted from the home to the research company via the telephone network overnight enabling rapid analysis of viewing data.

In recent years PeopleMeters have been widely adopted throughout the developed and developing world as methods of monitoring TV viewing and audiences. Figure 6.2 shows the use of the technique world-wide.

The final type of quantitative research of interest here is experimentation. Experiments are either carried out in the field or in-house (laboratory). Field experiments take place in the real world and the subjects of the experiments typically do not know that they are part of an experiment. The prime example is test marketing where a new product will be marketed in a limited geographic region prior to a

Country	AGB	Nielsen	Others
Australia	●	●	
Belgium Flemish	●		●
French			●
Brazil			○
Canada		●	
Finland			●
France	●	●	●
Germany			●
Greece	●		
Hong Kong	○		
Ireland	●		
Italy	●		
Japan		○	○
Netherlands	●		
New Zealand	●		
Philippines	●		
Portugal	●		
Spain			●
Switzerland			●
Thailand	●		
Turkey	●		
UK	●		
US National		●	
Local		○	○
Total number of countries where PeopleMeter services operate	13	4	6

● PeopleMeter   ○ Set Meter

Source: SRG News, No. 63 (May 1990).

Figure 6.2 TV meters world-wide

decision on whether to launch the brand nationally or internationally. In-house experiments are conducted in a more controlled but less realistic setting where the respondents knows he or she is taking part.

Broadbent (1983) describes the use of regional experiments in the development and testing of advertising copy for Cadbury Flake. Cadbury Flake competes in the confectionery countline market. The brand sales had grown steadily until the total countline market went into decline. Flake sales, however, declined at twice the market rate. An attitudinal study was undertaken which showed a high proportion of lapsed users found the product too messy/crumbly. As this represented the major reason for purchase by the heavy users of the brand it was not considered desirable to change the product design.

An alternative advertising message was developed emphasizing 'every little piece of flake is sheer enjoyment' and making an art out of eating Flake. There were various techniques shown for getting the last crumbs – tipping back the chair, using a paper plate and sucking the last crumbs through a straw.

The new advertisements were tested in the Lancashire and Yorkshire television regions and sales closely monitored compared to the rest of the country. Using syndicated sources and specially commissioned surveys it was estimated that in the 18 months of the test unit sales had increased by 16 per cent over and above what would have been expected. Both initial purchase and repeat purchase rates were shown to have increased. The campaign was judged to have turned the negative (mess) into a positive (delicious morsels of Flake) through the humour of the ads and was extended on a limited basis to other areas.

There have been several recent innovations in test marketing. Full-scale testing, as described above, suffers from a number of problems. It is costly, time-consuming and alerts the competition to changes in marketing strategy or new products about to be launched. As a result there has been an increase in other smaller-scale testing methods (some of these are described in chapter 11).

Mini-test markets, such as the Taylor Nelson 'Model Test Market' and the RBL 'Minivan', offer the opportunity to introduce products into the real market on a limited and controlled distribution basis. They are good at estimating initial and repeat purchase rates but poor at evaluating the overall impact of the complete marketing mix.

Simulated supermarket tests make grocery products available in a simulated environment. They can be helpful in estimating trial rates, testing purchase intents created by exposure to test advertisements and testing individual elements of the marketing mix such as packaging, pricing and branding. Supermarket panels, recruited within the shoppers of a particular chain, have their purchases recorded through laser scanning and related to purchase card numbers. These panels can be particularly useful in the limited market testing of new brands.

As with off-the-peg research the variety of tailor-made research available is very wide indeed. There are a great many market research agencies available with varying expertise and skills. While it is still true to say that the majority of expenditure on marketing research comes from the larger fast-moving consumer goods companies, it is possible for smaller companies to take advantage of the research services and sources available (especially off-the-peg research).

Market research techniques are also increasingly being used to investigate noncommercial problems. Research was used heavily, for example, to investigate drug abuse by young people prior to an advertising campaign designed to tackle the problem. The OXFAM charity has used survey research to help it understand the motivations behind charity donations and to help identify 'prime donor segments'. During the run-up to the 1997 General Election in the UK both major political parties spent heavily on market and opinion research to gauge the mood of potential voters. Opinion poll results (sponsored by the media and political parties) were published almost daily in the three week run-up to the election.

In the context of competitive positioning marketing research provides the raw data with which it is possible to segment the market creatively and can help to identify current and potential product positionings.

6.3 *The marketing research process*

A typical segmentation and positioning research project might combine the use of several of the techniques described above to investigate a particular market. Figure 6.3 shows the various stages.

Problem definition
The first step is to define clearly the problem to be tackled. Typically, a series of discussions between marketing research personnel (internal or external to the company) and marketing decision-makers are necessary to ensure that the research project is tackling the correct issues.

Exploratory research
As part of problem definition, and a starting point in the research process itself, exploratory research will be used to identify information gaps and specify the need for further research.

Initially, secondary sources can be utilized. Company records can be employed, alongside off-the-peg desk research, to quantify the market and draw its preliminary boundaries.

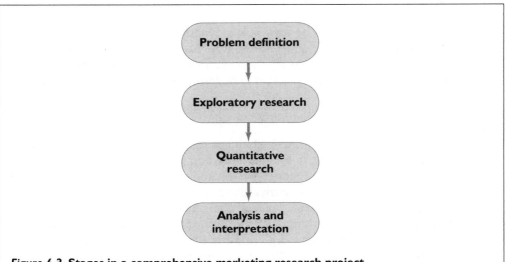

Figure 6.3 **Stages in a comprehensive marketing research project**

Qualitative research might then be used to explore with customers and/or potential customers why and how the particular product was used. At this stage group discussions may be relevant in many consumer markets. In industrial markets, while group discussions are successfully employed, a preferred route is often personal, depth interviews with key customers.

In a segmentation and positioning study the focus of this qualitative research will be to identify the prime motivators to purchase (i.e. the major benefits being sought) and any demotivators. The research should also seek to identify relevant competitors and explore their strengths and weaknesses in serving the market. Finally, hypotheses about how the market could be segmented should be developed which can be further researched during the later stages of the research project.

Quantitative research phase
While qualitative research will help in formulating hypotheses about how the market is segmented and what factors influence purchase, because of the small and normally non-representative samples involved it is unlikely to be adequate in itself for segmentation purposes. Typically it will be followed by a quantitative study (a personal survey most often) utilizing a sufficiently large and random sample to enable market segment sizes to be estimated and strength of opinions to be gauged.

Such a quantitative study might ask respondents to evaluate competing products on a series of attributes that have been identified as important during the qualitative research. Further, respondents could be asked to rate how important to them personally each attribute is and to express what characteristics their 'ideal' product would have. Background customer characteristics could also be collected to enable any market segments uncovered to be described in ways helpful to further marketing activity (see chapter 9).

Experimentation might also be used in the quantitative phase of a segmentation and positioning study. Product samples might be placed with existing and potential customers to gauge reaction to new or improved products. Conjoint analysis experiments might be used to estimate reaction to hypothetical product combinations (see chapter 10).

Analysis and interpretation
Following data collection, statistical techniques and models can be employed to turn the data generated into meaningful information to help with the segmentation. Factor analysis might be used to reduce a large number of attitudinal statements to their underlying dimensions, or underlying factors. Cluster analysis could be used to group respondents on the basis of several characteristics (attitudes, likes, dislikes or background demographics) into meaningful segments. Perceptual mapping techniques could be employed to draw models of customer perceptions on two, three or more relevant dimensions. These techniques are discussed in more detail in chapter 9.

Finally, the results will be presented to and discussed with the senior marketing decision-makers to aid their interpretation of the market in which they are operating.

The essence of a successful research project is to use the data-gathering and analysis techniques that are relevant both to the product type being investigated and the stage in the research project where they are being employed. By utilizing innovative techniques and looking at markets afresh it is often possible to gain new insights into market structure and hence aid the sharpening of target market definition.

The final section in this chapter looks at how information is organized within the organization.

6.4 *Organizing the customer information*

Information is organized within the company through the Marketing Information System (MIS). This system may be formally structured, physically consisting of several personnel and a variety of computer hardware and software, or it may be a very informal collection of reports and statistics piled on an executive's desk or even in his/her head!

Conceptually, however, the system can be represented as in Figure 6.4 (developed from Little, 1979). The information system has five basic components: a market research interface concerned with collecting and gathering raw data from the marketing environment; the raw data collected through the market research interface; statistical techniques that can be used to analyze, synthesize and collate the raw data, to turn it into information; market models that utilize both the raw data and statistical techniques to describe the marketplace, to simulate it or to predict it; and finally a managerial interface that allows the decision-maker access to the information and models to aid his or her decision-making.

Raw data

As discussed above data come into the system from a variety of sources, from internal and external, secondary and primary sources. The data are stored in various forms (e.g. on paper, in people's heads, on computer). Increasingly data are being stored on machine-readable media such as magnetic tape or hard and soft disk. The increased availability of computer hardware and software (especially with the advent of the microcomputer) has made it increasingly possible to store large amounts of data in a form that is readily accessible and easily analyzed.

Statistical techniques

The processes available to synthesize and summarize the raw data are called statistics. A wide variety of statistics is available but often the most important are the simple ones that allow data to be summarized (such as averages, means, standard deviations, ranges, etc.) so that many small, often diverse observations can be condensed into a few important numbers. (For a comprehensive review of statistical techniques available to analyze marketing data, see Green, Tull and Albaum, 1993; and Diamantopoulos and Schlegelmilch, 1997.)

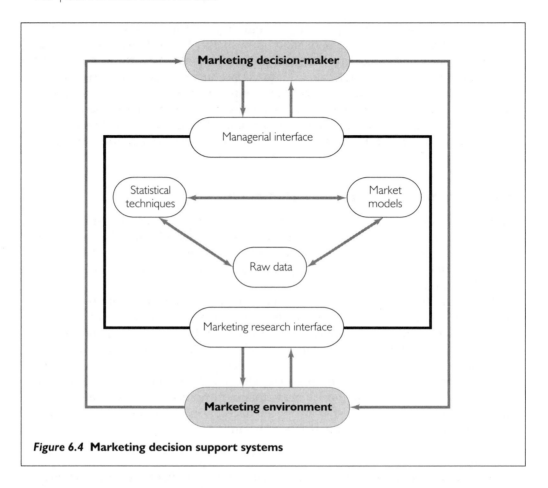

Figure 6.4 **Marketing decision support systems**

Market models

A model is a representation of the real world. Most managers have an implicit model of the markets in which they operate in their own minds. For example, they can give an expectation of the effect of changing price on sales of the product based on their experiences. This is essentially their internal model of the price/sales relationship. In examining data through the use of statistical techniques the analyst may wish to test out the model of the market he or she already has. Alternatively, the objective may be to build a new model of the market to help managerial understanding of the forces that affect demand and overall company performance. There are models covering all parts of marketing activity. Lilien *et al.* (1992) Undertook a comprehensive review of these attempts 'to bring order to the chaos of collected facts' (Little, 1979).

Managerial interface

If the information system is to be of value to the marketing decision-maker, he or she must have access to that system in such a way as to facilitate and encourage easy use. The interface between the manager and the MIS can consist of an individual (a marketing information officer), a report or set of reports produced on a regular or intermittent basis, or, increasingly commonly, a computer terminal or a micro-computer. With the relevant software to facilitate use of the MIS direct, 'hands on', access for the decision-maker can encourage wider use of the system and experimentation with the various models developed.

Marketing decision support systems (MDSS)
In the 1990s there has been a change in emphasis in marketing from information systems (MIS) to marketing decision support systems (MDSS). The distinction may seem merely of semantics but is, in fact, fundamental. While MIS placed emphasis on provision of information, primarily in the form of facts and figures, MDSS changes the emphasis to aiding decision-making through the provision of question and answer facilities. In other words, MDSS allows analysis rather than merely retrieval of information.

Decision support systems can have several types of output. These have been grouped into two types: data-oriented and model-oriented.

1. **Data-oriented decision support systems** focus on data retrieval and simple analysis using statistical techniques. This can include, for example, straightforward data retrieval of such items as stock levels. Systems of this type are effectively information systems rather than decision support systems as defined above.

2. **Model-oriented decision support systems**, on the other hand, focus on simulation and representation of aspects of the real world. Accounting models, for example, calculate the consequences of planned actions on the financial performance of the company. Representational models estimate the consequences of action of one type or another. An advertising model may estimate the effects of running a particular advertising campaign. Optimization models provide guidelines for action by generating the optimal solutions consistent with a series of constraints. For example, given an advertising budget, a target audience and a required average viewing frequency an optimization model could be used to select the most effective combination of media and insertions.

Implementation of MDSS in marketing has, however, been slower than predicted, but with the advent of PCs and user-friendly programs the use of decision support systems in marketing is now developing rapidly. Several characteristics of MDSS that differentiate them from their predecessors (the information systems of the 1970s) deserve emphasis:

1. MDSS support decisions! They are not merely data retrieval systems, but are actively designed to help managers make better decisions. In addition they support, rather than replace, managerial decision-making.

2. MDSS are essentially interactive. They allow the manager to ask questions, receive inputs and experiment with decisions to estimate the likely outcomes. As such they are more effective where a manager has the scope to use the system directly.

3. MDSS should be flexible and easy to use. Ease of use is a major characteristic essential to gaining widespread use of an innovation such as MDSS poses in many organizations. Flexibility is desirable to allow the system to respond to a variety of information and decision support needs.

Expert systems for marketing decision support
More recent developments in computer hardware and software offer exciting opportunities for marketing management. The developments in expert systems and artificial intelligence which enable not only the modelling of marketing phenomena but also the decision-making processes of 'experts' in the field promise to revolutionize the whole field of decision support.

The directions in which these developments will move is difficult to predict at present (Hooley and Hussey, 1994). What is certain, however, is that marketing decisions will become more data-based (there is already a data explosion in marketing) and there will be an increased need to organize those data in meaningful ways to enable them to be used quickly and effectively. In particular increased computing and modelling power will enable decisions to be tested in simulated environments prior to implementation in the real world.

6.5 Conclusions

Understanding customers is central to developing a coherent positioning strategy. This chapter has examined first, the types of information about customers that can be useful in determining competitive position; and second, the marketing research methods available for collecting that information. The process typically undertaken to identify potential market segments and their needs was then discussed. Finally, developments in organizing and presenting data were examined.

CHAPTER 7

Competitor analysis

A horse never runs so fast as when he has other horses to catch up and outpace.
Ovid, The Art of Love, *AD8*

Introduction

Sun Tzu (see Clavell, 1981, for a recent, accessible, translation), the great fourth-century BC Chinese general, encapsulated the importance of competitor analysis:

> If you know your enemy as you know yourself, you need not fear the result of a hundred battles. If you know yourself but not the enemy, for every victory you gain you will suffer a defeat. If you know neither the enemy nor yourself, you will succumb in every battle.

What was true of war in the fourth century BC is equally true of business today. However, as we shall see in chapter 8 the complexity facing the modern business is that its main competitor, customer and collaborator may be the same company! For example, Kodak and Fuji are intense rivals in the photographic film business, yet in 1996 they collaborated to bring the Advanced Photographic System (APS) to market while at the same time fighting in the Japanese courts over market protection issues. Similarly, the Efficient Consumer Response programme involves groups of competing manufacturers working together with retailers to streamline supply-chains – an alliance of competitors, customers and collaborators. The complexity and ambiguity faced by executives in many modern markets underline yet further the imperative of identifying and understanding competitors.

The reason is that without a knowledge of competitors' strengths and their likely actions, it is impossible to formulate the central component of marketing strategy – finding a group of customers for whom one has a competitive advantage over the competition. It must also be true that, since competitive advantage is a relative concept, a company that has poor understanding of its competitors can have no real understanding of itself.

Japan's leading companies retain Sun Tzu's obsession with competitor analysis. Although successful Eastern and Western companies are alike in many ways (Doyle, Saunders and Wong, 1986), the commitment of Japanese companies to gathering information remains a distinguishing feature (Kotler, Fahey and Jatusripitak, 1985). As one example, Lehmann and Winer (1991) report that one Mitsubishi intelligence unit in the US fills two entire floors of an office building in New York. Indeed, as long ago as the early 1980s *Business Week* described how Japanese companies had established surveillance posts throughout the heartland of the US computer industry in California's Silicon Valley, monitoring US technology development by hiring American software experts.

This chapter provides a framework for the essential activities of gathering, disseminating and acting on competitor intelligence. It covers four areas:

1. Benchmarking against rivals.
2. The dimensions of competitor analysis.
3. The choice of 'good' competitors.
4. The origin, sources and dissemination of competitive information.

7.1 *Competitive benchmarking*

Competitive benchmarking is the process of measuring your company's strategies and operations against 'best-in-class' companies, both inside and outside your own industry (Swain, 1993). The purpose is to identify best practices that can be adopted or adapted to improve your own performance. Benchmarking usually involves four main steps.

7.1.1 Identifying who to benchmark against

Industry leaders are obvious firms to compare your own activities against. Central to such an analysis will be identifying the keys to their success in the market. What is it they do differently from others? What makes the difference to their operations? Why are they winners?

Benchmarking may also, however, be undertaken against lesser players in the overall market. New entrants or smaller, more focused firms, may have particular strengths from which the firm can learn. These strengths may be in a particular aspect of their operations, rather than their operations in total. One firm may be an exemplar, for example, in terms of customer service, while another may be the best in the industry at cost control.

Finally, firms may benchmark specific activities (such as procurement and purchasing) against firms outside the immediate industry where lessons can be transferred. When Xerox wanted to improve their order processing and warehousing they benchmarked themselves against L.L. Bean, the mail order company, which were believed to be far more 'cutting edge' than Xerox's main competitors (Swain, 1993).

7.1.2 Identifying what aspects of business to benchmark

All aspects of business across the complete value-chain (see below) are targets for benchmarking. Scarce resources and time constraints generally dictate the selection of a few key central processes for detailed benchmarking. These will initially centre on the key factors for success in the industry. Initial focus will also typically be on processes which account for significant costs, make a significant impact on customer satisfaction and show greatest room for improvement. Subsequently, analyses may be further broadened out in attempts to create fresh competitive advantages in new areas of operation.

7.1.3 Collecting relevant data to enable processes and operations to be compared

Data on own operations may be relatively easily available, but where competitors are benchmarked commercial secrecy may make access to relevant data difficult. Swain (1993) suggests three main sources of competitor information for benchmarking: published sources; data sharing; and interviews.

Published sources include company reports, technical (trade) reports, industry studies and surveys commissioned by governments or industry associations. For consumer goods, for example, *Which?* reports provide useful published data comparing product performance from the consumer perspective.

Data-sharing may take place in industry forums such as conferences, through direct, formal contacts or more informal contacts. In most industries employees and managers of competing firms meet from time to time and swap information with each other, either consciously or subconsciously.

Direct interviews with customers, distributors, industry experts, former employees of competitors, regulators, government officials, etc. may also be useful in collecting data on competitor operations for benchmarking purposes. Often competitors' customers in particular are a rich source of information on competitor processes. Questioning customers on the levels of service they received, for example, or the manner in which complaints were handled, can help to identify the processes used behind the scenes to deliver that service.

7.1.4 Comparison with own processes

The final stage in the benchmarking process is to compare and contrast the processes of the identified 'best-in-class' with the firm's own processes, to identify actions that need to be taken as a consequence, and the setting-up of processes to measure and monitor improvement.

Once the comparisons have been made and the areas for direct attention identified a number of options may be apparent. First, the firm may conclude that its own operations are close to best practice and will continue with them, striving to improve where possible. Second, the firm may conclude that their processes are inadequate or suboptimal and need to be overhauled. This may involve setting up new processes which mirror those of the best practices identified. Alternatively, it may involve adopting best practice processes from other industries which will enable the firm to leapfrog the competition and gain competitive advantage from process innovation.

Where new processes are proposed, or existing processes reinforced, measurable targets should be set that will enable the firm to assess its progress towards achieving better practices. These targets should be specific (e.g. 'answer 95 per cent of telephone calls by the third ring') and achievable within specified timeframes.

Beyond the benchmarking value of competitor analysis, a clearer picture of competitor strategies, strengths and weaknesses also helps firms to develop more effective competitive strategies. We now go on to discuss the main processes involved in competitor analysis for the purposes of strategy formulation.

7.2 The dimensions of competitor analysis

In the medium term the focus of competitor analysis must be firms within the same strategic group as the company concerned. In the longer term, however, there is a danger in the analysis being so constrained. The industry as a whole must be scanned for indirect competitors who may have the resources or the need to overcome the entry barriers to the incumbent's strategic group. Although entry barriers may be high, if the incumbent's strategic group shows high profits or growth potential beyond the rest of the market, it is likely to attract new entrants.

The European luxury car makers showed some myopia with their focus being concentrated upon each other rather than upon the Japanese mass manufacturers. For a long time the Japanese have been building up a reputation in terms of quality and technology which they are now exploiting, together with their huge resources, to compete against the Europeans in the American market.

The UK financial services sector is an example where conventional competitors have lost much business to the entry of new-style competitors with the powerful weapons of both major sources of competitive differentiation and significant cost advantages. These include direct marketing operations such as Direct Line, based on telemarketing, Virgin Direct exploiting brand strength and product simplification in another form of direct marketing, the entry to banking by major supermarkets such as Sainsbury and Tesco, exploiting their customer base and existing retail locations, and the piecemeal entry of diverse firms like British Gas, British Airways and the oil companies who cherry-pick certain financial products. The probability is that turbulence will continue. In 1996 Bill Gates, head of Microsoft, was quoted as saying 'Give me a share of the transactions business and the banks are dead!' The jury is out, but it is possible that the real competitive question for banks and other conventional players is whether there will be a separate and distinguishable financial services sector at all in the future!

It follows, then, that a second source of threat could be potential entrants into an industry, or substitutes. Part of the failing of EMI in the body scanner market was their neglect of the entrants that their hugely profitable success in the new market would be likely to attract. Rather than build defences or coalitions against the almost inevitable onslaught, the company chose to continue to exploit the market as if it was the sole supplier. Perhaps the greatest failing was their falling behind in product quality and their inability to develop a support network for their product (Kay, 1993).

In the longer term, substitutes are the major threat to an industry. These not only bring with them new processes and products with advantages that can totally undermine the incumbents' capabilities (as the scanner did for certain forms of X-ray machine), but they are also likely to bring with them new and hungry competitors who are willing to question conventional industry practices. Once IBM entered the PC market they were quite successful relative to their target competitors (Apple and Hewlett Packard) but had great difficulty in handling the new competition, (Compaq, Toshiba and Dell), which their standardized PC attracted.

Competitor analysis, therefore, involves evaluating a series of concentric circles of adversaries: innermost are the direct competitors within the strategic group, next companies within the industry that are driven to overcome the entry barriers to the strategic group, and outermost potential entrants and substitutes (Figure 7.1).

Lehmann and Winer (1991) suggest four main stages in competitor analysis (Figure 7.2):

1. **Assessing competitors' current and future objectives**. Understanding what the competitor is setting out to achieve can give clues as to the direction it will take and the aggressiveness with which it will pursue that direction.
2. **Assessing the competitors' current strategies**. By understanding the strategies used by competitors in pursuit of their goals and objectives the firm can identify opportunities and threats arising from competitor actions.
3. **Assessing competitors' resources**. The asset and capability profile of competitors show what they are currently able to do. Those resources may not be fully deployed at present but can give further clues into how the competitor will move in the future, or how the competitor will react to threats.

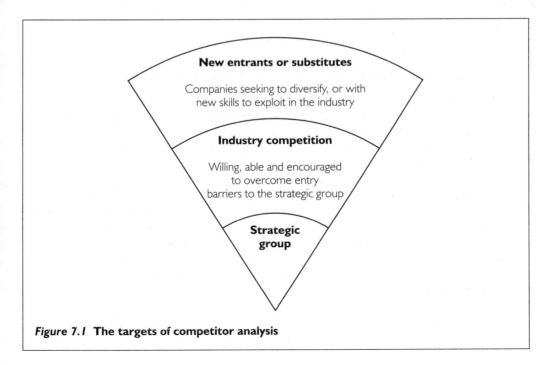

Figure 7.1 The targets of competitor analysis

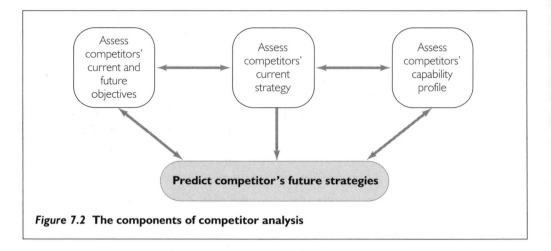

Figure 7.2 **The components of competitor analysis**

4. **Predicting competitors' future strategies**. By combining the above analyses the firm can begin to answer perhaps the most fundamental question in competitor analysis: what is the firm likely to do in the future?

Each of the above is now discussed in detail. In particular, potential sources of information are suggested, together with ways in which the analyses might be conducted. The aim of the analysis is not just to describe the competitor, but to be able to gauge the competitor's future intentions or, more importantly, what the competitor is likely to do in response to the evaluating firm's own actions.

7.2.1 Assessing competitors' current and future objectives

Understanding the goals or objectives of competitors can give guidance to strategy development on three levels. Goals can indicate where the company is intending to develop and in which markets, either by industry or internationally, major initiatives can be expected. The areas of expansion could indicate markets which are to be particularly competitive but may simultaneously signify companies not so committed.

Where the intention is profitable coexistence, it is often better to compete in areas which are deemed of secondary interest to major companies rather than to compete directly. Such was the opportunity created when both General Motors and Ford declared that the small car markets in America and Europe were intrinsically unprofitable and therefore of little interest to them. Interestingly, both are now actively pursuing this market as the full potential is becoming apparent. Pressures on the environment from automobile pollution and road crowding are leading governments to consider measures to encourage smaller cars with more efficient engines. Ford's response in Europe has been the launch of the Ka, a small, fuel-efficient, commuter and family second car. This illustrates that goals change as circumstances change and competitors' need to be constantly monitored for shifts in strategic direction.

Goals may also give a guide to the intensity of competitor activity and rivalry. When the likes of Procter & Gamble or General Electric declare that they are only interested in being the number 1 or the strong number 2 in markets in which they operate, it is to be anticipated that they will compete very hard for every new market they enter.

Finally, a company's goals can indicate the type of trade-off it is likely to make when faced with adversity. The obsession of many American overseas subsidiaries with the need to report back steady and slowly increasing profits has meant that they have often been willing to relinquish market share in order to achieve their short-term profit goals.

The goals can have implications across the broad portfolio of a company's activities. When competing against a diversified company, ambitious goals in one sector may indicate that commitment to another is diminishing. Equally, very large and diversified companies may often not be able to take advantage of their huge financial strengths because of their unwillingness to make strategic shifts in their resources. There is also a chance that financially driven companies may be unwilling to take the risks of new ventures, preferring instead to pick the bones of those who were damaged in taking the risk.

Competitor goals and objectives can best be inferred from observations of the strategies they are pursuing, together with pronouncements they make through company reports, press releases, etc. For example, decisions to build additional production facilities are a clear signal of growth objectives. The recruitment of staff with particular skills (identified through observation of recruitment advertisements) can indicate new directions in which the competitor may go.

Reward structures for staff can also indicate objectives. Where sales staff, for example, are rewarded on a percentage of sales commission that practice suggests that sales volume (rather than profitability) is a key objective (Lehmann and Winer, 1991).

Also indicative of future goals can be the ownership structure of the competitor. Competitors owned by employees and/or managers may set higher priority in providing continuity of employment than those owned by conventional shareholders. Likewise, competitors run through the public sector may set higher priorities on social goals rather than profitability. Competitors owned as part of diversified conglomerates may be managed for short-term cash rather than long-term market position objectives.

Underlying assumptions

Assumptions that a firm has about itself and the market affect the goals and objectives it sets and can be a source of opportunity or threat. Examples of flawed assumptions being made by companies and their dire consequences are many. In the 1960s, Cunard assumed that as the cost of transatlantic travel was so high, people would want a leisurely crossing rather than spending a large amount of money in flying the Atlantic in a few hours. The result of this faulty logic by Cunard and other operators of passenger liners was a massive increase in the tonnage of liners being constructed in their last few years of useful life. Similarly, Dunlop's assumption that they were pre-eminent in rubber technology in tyres meant that they neglected Michelin's development of steel-braced radials. The result was a catastrophic decline in their own market share, accompanied by a decline in the total market size which occurred because of the longer life of Michelin's new development. Having assumed its pre-eminence in an established market, Dunlop's position was made intractable by their inability to develop new products.

Dunlop and Cunard were not atypical in their inability to see changing market conditions. As Foster (1986) says, there is a tendency for incumbent companies to dismiss incipient new technologies as of little significance or maybe catering for some faddish segment of the market. Such was the case of the Swiss watch industry when first faced by the competition from Japanese digital alternatives. Thus, the evaluation of assumptions of competitors and those made by a firm itself, can be of major strategic significance to a company. Having said this, there is a clear gap between the need and the ability of firms to questions their own assumptions.

Analyses of how major firms often react to technological threats shows they are rarely able to change their historic orientation. O'Shaughnessy (1995) explains how incumbents often avoid the problems rather than taking evasive action. He suggests that there is a tendency for firms to force the evidence to fit preconceptions; become deaf to any evidence at odds with their beliefs; predict the most feared competitive action as a defence in case there is any future post-mortem after such action occurs; predict that competitive action will be that to which the manager's favourite strategy is an effective counter-strategy as a way of getting support for that strategy.

7.2.2 Assessing competitors' current strategies and activities

Assessing the current strategy involves asking the basic question: 'What exactly is the competitor doing at the moment?' This requires making as full as possible a statement of what each competitor is trying to do, and how they are trying to achieve it. It is an essentially complex activity where the components of marketing strategy outlined in chapter 2 can give some structure.

Three main sets of issues need to be addressed with regard to understanding current competitor strategies. First, identification of the market or markets they have chosen to operate in: their selection of target markets. Second, identification of the way in which they have chosen to operate in those markets: the strategic focus they are adopting with regard to the type of competitive advantage they are trying to convey. Third, the supporting marketing mix that is being adopted to enable the positioning aimed for to be achieved. Beyond these three core elements of strategy it can also be helpful to assess the organization of the marketing effort – the structures adopted – to facilitate implementation of the strategy.

Competitors' market targets
The broad markets and more specific market segments competitors choose to

compete in can often be inferred from an analysis of the products and services they are offering, together with the ways in which they are pricing, promoting and distributing them. These elements of the marketing mix are generally highly visible aspects of a firm's activities on display in the public domain and available for competitors to analyze.

The features built into products and the type and extent of service offered will be good indicators of the types of customer the competitor is seeking to serve. In the automobile industry, for example, the products made by Jaguar, a subsidiary of Ford, indicate clearly the types of customers being pursued. Skoda, now owned by Volkswagen, on the other hand, offers very different cars to the market, suggesting a completely different target market. Prices charged will also often be an indicator of the target market aimed for. In grocery retailing, for example, Aldi and Netto have consistently pursued a minimum-range, low-price strategy in attempts to attract price-sensitive, bulk grocery purchasers rather than compete directly with industry leaders such as Tesco and Sainsbury on quality and service.

Advertisements and other promotional materials can also give clues as to the target markets aimed for. The wording of advertisements indicates the values the advertiser is attempting to convey and imbue in the product/service offered. Again in automobiles traditional Volvo advertising has clearly focused on safety appealing to safety-conscious, middle-class families. BMW advertising concentrates on technical quality and the pleasures of driving, suggesting a younger market target. The media in which the advertisements appear, or the scheduling adopted, will also give indications of the target market aimed for. Similarly, the distribution channels the competitor chooses to use to link customers physically with offerings may give clues as to the targets aimed for.

Competitors' strategic focus

Most successful companies attempt to build their strategies on a differential advantage they have over others in the market. This is an important consideration in two ways. It is clearly necessary to base the differential advantage on customer targets and it is important to avoid basing one's competitive strategy on trying to build strengths where one is always going to be weak relative to competitors. For instance, in the jewellery trade it is possible to compete through design or distribution, but absolutely impossible to try to compete with the De Beers through securing one's own supply of uncut diamonds.

As discussed in chapter 13, there are two main routes to creating a competitive advantage. The first is through low costs relative to competitors. The second through providing valued uniqueness, differentiated products and services that customers will be willing to pay for.

Signals of competitors adopting a low-cost focus include their attention to overheads in the balance sheet, the vigour with which they pursue low-cost factor inputs and the tight financial controls they exert on all functions and activities. The cost leadership route is a tough one for any firm to follow successfully and requires close, relentless attention to all cost drivers. As noted above, in the UK grocery market

Aldi and Netto have adopted this rigorous approach, restricting product lines and providing 'no frills' service.

Providing something different, but of value to customers, is a route to creating competitive advantage all players in a market can adopt. The creative aspect of this strategy is to identify those differentiating features on which the firm has, or can build, a defensible edge. Signals of differentiation will be as varied as the means of differentiation. Greater emphasis on customer service, added features to the product, special deals for volume or continued custom and loyalty schemes are all means of differentiation. All are highly visible to competitors and show the ground on which a given supplier has chosen to compete.

Competitors' supporting marketing mix

As discussed above, analysis of the marketing mix adopted by competitors can give useful clues as to the target markets at which they are aiming and the competitive advantage they are seeking to build with those targets. Analysis of the mix can also show areas where the competitor is vulnerable to attack.

Detailed analysis of competitors' products and services, particularly through the eyes of customers, can be used to highlight competitor weaknesses. Rowntree, the UK confectionery firm now owned by the Swiss firm Nestlé, noted that chocolate bars offered by its prime competitor Cadbury were getting thinner and thinner as Cadbury attempted to absorb increased raw material costs by reducing the size of chocolate bars. Customer market research showed that many customers wanted 'chunky' bars of chocolate and Rowntree responded by launching its own, highly successful Yorkie brand.

Analysis of competitor pricing strategies may identify gaps in the market. For example, a firm marketing vodka in the US market noted that the leader offered products at a number of relatively high price points but had left others vacant. This enabled the firm to position its own offerings in a different market sector.

Both the message and the media being used by competitors warrant close analysis. Some competitors may be better than others at exploiting new media such as satellite or cable. Others may be adept at their use of public relations. Again, analysis will show where competitors are strong and where they are vulnerable.

Finally, understanding the distribution strengths and weaknesses of competitors can also identify opportunities. Dell, for example, decided to market their PCs direct to businesses rather than distribute through office retail stores where their established competitors were already strong.

Competitors' marketing organization

Consideration of organization is important because of the way that it can dictate strategy. For a long time Procter & Gamble's brand management structure was held up as a marketing ideal. This was probably the case when the American market was dominant and lessons learnt there were relatively easily transferred downstream to less developed parts of the world. However, with America's relative economic decline compared to the rest of the world, Unilever's more flexible structure allowed them to transfer ideas across boundaries more easily and be more flexible to emerging local needs. Indeed, Procter & Gamble themselves have now moved away from their product management structure.

Understanding the competitors' organizational structure can give clues as to how quickly, and in what manner, the competitor is likely to respond to environmental change or competitive actions. Competitors where responsibility for products are clearly identified are often able to respond more quickly than firms where responsibility is vague or confused. Firms organized around markets, rather than products, are most likely to spot market changes early and be in a position to lead change rather than simply react to it.

The position of marketing within the organizational structure can also provide clues to current and future strategy. In many traditional companies marketing is considered merely part of sales, responsible simply for advertising and other promotional activities. In such cases the voice of marketing may not be easily heard at the strategic decision-making level. In still other firms marketing may be seen as a guiding philosophy which will ensure a much more market responsive set of actions. Clues to the position of marketing may lie in the background of the CEO, the visibility within the firm of senior marketing executives, and indeed, their previous career tracks. The appointment of a new marketing director from FMCG at Madam Tussaud's, the waxworks, signalled a far more customer-responsive and aggressive approach to the marketing of the attraction.

A useful tool for analyzing current activities of competitors is the value-chain.

Value-chain analysis
Porter (1985) identifies five primary activities which add value to the final output of a company (Figure 7.3).

1. **Inbound logistics** involves managing the flow of products into the company. Recent attention to just-in-time manufacturing has shown how important this can be to the efficient operation of a company and how by management of its suppliers and their quality, a company can add to the quality of its final products.
2. **Operations** have long been seen as the central activity of businesses. These comprise the processes whereby the inbound items are changed in form, packaged and tested for suitability for sale. Traditionally, this has been seen as the area where value is added to a company's products. At this stage, value can be added beyond the normal capital and manpower inputs by the maintenance of high quality, flexibility and design.
3. **Outbound logistics** carry the product from the point of manufacture to the buyer. They therefore include storage, distribution, etc. At this stage, value can be added through quick and timely delivery, low damage rates and the formulation of delivery mechanisms which fit the operations of the user. Within the fertilizer industry, for instance, ICI have added value to their products by offering blends which fit the specific needs of farmers at certain

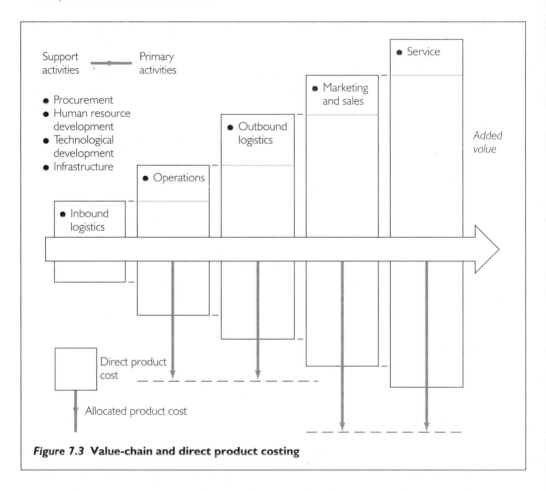

Figure 7.3 Value-chain and direct product costing

times of the year and delivery modularization which fits the farmers' own systems. Taking it a stage further, deliveries can be taken to the field rather than to the farm or even as far as spreading being undertaken by the supplier.

4. **Marketing and sales** activities inform buyers about products and services, and provide buyers with a reason to purchase. This can concern feedback which allows the user company to fit their operation's outbound logistics to user requirements or by helping customers understand the economic value of products that are available. Taking the ICI example again, part of their marketing activity involves showing how some of their products can be used to equalize the workload on a farm throughout the year and therefore use the overall labour force more efficiently.

5. **Service** includes all the activities required to keep the product or service working effectively for the buyer, after it is sold and delivered. This can involve training, return of goods policies, consultation hot-line and other

facilities. Since customer satisfaction is central to achieving repeat sales and word-of-mouth communication from satisfied customers, after-sales service is clearly a major part of added value.

In support of the primary activities of the value-chain, Porter also identified support activities. These are procurement, human resource development, technological development and infrastructure. These, of course, feed into each stage of the primary activities of the value-chain.

There are several ways in which analysis of the value-chain can provide an insight into competitors.

- It can reveal cost advantages that competitors may have because of their efficient manufacture, inbound or outbound logistics. It may also reveal why with better marketing, sales and service a company making intrinsically similar products may be achieving higher added value through their operations.
- Many conventionally oriented companies perceive operations as their primary source of added value and therefore leave opportunities for competitors to gain by taking a more extended view of the value they can add in the customer's eyes.
- Where the value added is costed effectively, it can help locate economical ways of adding value to the customer. There are often numerous ways of achieving this, such as in the efficient management of single sourcing and just-in-time inbound logistics; total quality being incorporated in the operations and so reducing the service requirements and maybe adding to the appeal of the marketing and sales activity by offering extended warranties; well-targeted marketing and sales activities which assure that maximum perceived added value is communicated to the customer while incurring lower marketing and sales activity than if blanket sales activity was attempted.

A company's assumptions about how its costs are allocated across products and elements of the value-chain can provide clear competitive guidelines. For instance, many companies add most of their overheads to manufacturing operations where inputs can usually be measured. This occurs despite products having vastly different inbound logistics, outbound logistics, marketing, sales and service expenditures. The result can be that the final price of the products in the marketplace has little bearing upon the overall inputs and the value-chain.

Similarly, where the overheads are allocated equally across products, direct product pricing can show where some products are being forced to carry an excessive burden of overheads, so allowing a competitor to enter the market and compete effectively on price. When a company is competing in many different markets, it is very likely that their allocated product costs are completely out of line with some of the markets in which they are competing. This can act as an overall constraint upon their intention to support those products or give them little commitment to it. IBM encountered this problem in their PC marketing where the margins are incapable of carrying the allocated overheads which were borrowed from their mainframe and mini business. This became particularly true in their venture into the home computer market with the 'Peanut' which was launched with a totally inappropriate performance:price ratio.

7.2.3 Assessing competitors' capability profiles

The above discussion has highlighted what the competitor is seeking to achieve and what it is doing now. Also critical, of course, are the degrees of freedom open to the competitor. What might it do in future?

The assessment of a competitor's resources involves looking at their strengths and weaknesses. Whereas a competitor's goals, assumptions and current strategy would influence the likelihood, time, nature and intensity of a competitor's reactions, its resources, assets and capabilities, will determine its ability to initiate and sustain moves in response to environmental or competitive changes.

Competitor resource profiles (see section 7.1 above on benchmarking) can be built in much the same way as a firm conducts an analysis of its own assets and capabilities. A useful starting point is to profile competitors against the key factors for success in the particular industry. Among these could be operational areas (such as research and engineering or financial strength) or generic skills (such as the company's ability to grow, quick response capability, ability to adapt to change, staying power, or innovativeness).

Lehmann and Winer (1991) suggest concentrating the analysis under five key competitor abilities:

➤ **Ability to conceive and design.** Assessing the ability of a competitor to innovate will help the firm to predict the likelihood of new products being brought to market, or of new technologies being employed to leapfrog existing products. Indications of this type of ability come from assessing technical resources (such as patents and copyrights held), human resources (the calibre of the creative and technical staff employed) and funding (both the total funds available and the proportion devoted to research and development, relative to industry average).

➤ **Ability to produce.** In manufacturing industries this will include production capacity and utilization, while in service industries capacity to deliver the service will be critical. Firms with slack capacity clearly have more opportunities to respond to increased demand. Similarly service firms that can manage their resources flexibly by, for example, calling on temporary but sufficiently skilled and motivated staff may enjoy more flexibility than those with a fixed staff with rigid skills. Ability to produce is signalled by physical resources (such as plant and equipment) to gather with human resources (including the skills and flexibility of the staff employed).

➤ **Ability to market.** Despite strong innovation and production abilities a competitor may be relatively weak at marketing its products or services to customers. Assessing marketing capability is best accomplished through examining the elements of the marketing mix. Central to this analysis, however, will be the assessment of the skills of the people involved in sales, marketing, advertising, distribution, and so on. Also important will be the funds available and devoted to marketing activities. How well does the competitor understand the market? The answer to this question may lie in the extent and type of marketing research being undertaken.

➤ **Ability to finance.** Financial resources act as a constraint in any organization. In Hungary, for example, a major constraint on marketing activity for indigenous firms during the transition period of the 1990s has been the limited funds available for investment. Many successful Hungarian firms overcame this problem through joint ventures with Western firms seeking entry into the market. The Hungarian firms provided the local market knowledge and contacts while the Western partners provided capital and managerial expertise. Examination of published accounts can reveal liquidity and cash flow characteristics of competitors. Again, however, such hard data should be supplemented with assessments of the qualities and skills of the human resources available within finance.

➤ **Ability to manage.** The characteristics of key managers can send clear messages on strategic intentions. Indicators include the previous career paths and actions of powerful managers, the reward systems in place, the degree of autonomy allowed to individual managers, the recruitment and promotions policies of the firm.

Figure 7.4 shows a summary sheet which a company has used to assess the relative capability of 'self' against three competitors: A, B and C. In this, six dimensions have been determined as critical and a company has rated itself and three competitors on each key factor using a scale ranging from −2 (very poor) to +2 (very good). The result are profiles which suggest the companies are quite similar in their overall capabilities and average scores, which clearly identify the company on a par with competitors A and B overall. However, the total score should not be allowed to cloud the differences of the main protagonists in the market, since their relative strengths clearly show that they may move in different directions given similar opportunities. For instance, Company A could build upon its European strength in marketing applied technology, whereas Company B may be forced to depend upon differentiation achieved through technological breadth and strength in R&D to maintain its market position. However, if the technology or market shift in a direction which required major expenditures, Company B may be weaker compared to A or 'self'. An inspection of the competitive capabilities also suggests that, although Company C looks weak overall, it could be a good acquisition by 'self'. Although weak in the financial and technological areas, it has a strong European marketing presence and therefore may be capable of providing 'self' with rapid access to the European markets.

7.2.4 Predicting competitors' future strategies

The ultimate aim of competitor analysis is to determine competitors' response

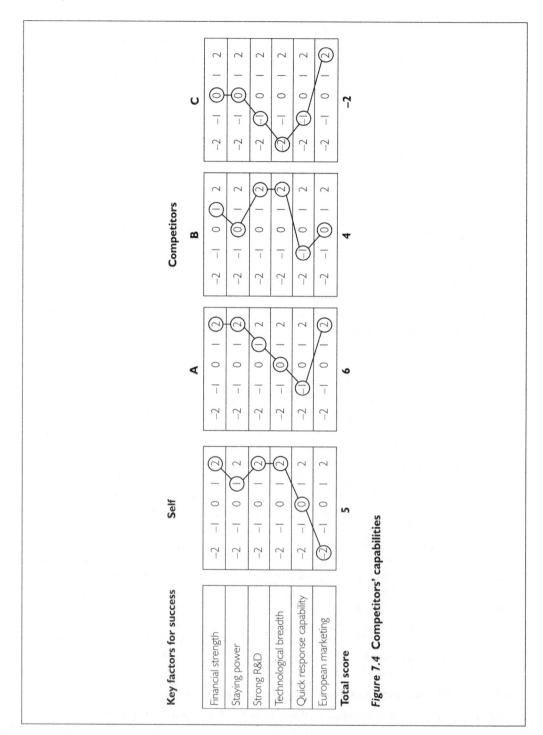

Figure 7.4 Competitors' capabilities

profiles – that is, a guide to how a competitor might behave when faced with various environmental and competitive changes. This covers such questions as:

➤ **Is the competitor satisfied with the current position?** One that is satisfied may allow indirect competitors to exploit new markets without being perturbed. Alternatively, one that is trying to improve its current position may be quick in chasing market changes or be obsessed by improving its own short-term profits performance. A knowledge of a company's future goals will clearly play an important part in answering this question.

➤ **What likely moves or strategy shifts will the competitor make?** History can provide some guide as to the way that companies behave. Goals, assumptions and capabilities will also give some guidance to how the company can effectively respond to market changes. After looking at these a company may be able to judge which of its own alternative strategies is likely to result in the most favourable reaction on the part of the competitors.

➤ **Where is the competitor vulnerable?** In commerce, as in war, success is best achieved by concentrating strength against weakness (Clausewitz, 1908). It takes no great insight to realize that it would be foolish for a company to take on a market leader in the areas where they are strongest, but successions of large companies (including Xerox, GE and ICL) took on IBM at their own game and lost. Much better to compete against IBM in niche markets which their size means they cannot cover effectively, i.e. in rapidly changing markets where their bureaucracy means they cannot move swiftly or in high-volume/low-margin markets where they have no understanding of distribution systems. The complacency of leaders in markets can provide major opportunities. The competitor's own feeling of invulnerability may be their own weakness which could lead them to a downfall. In truth businesses, like armies, cannot defend on all flanks, from all positions, at all times. No company is ever all-powerful at all places. Richard Branson at Virgin has proved particularly skilful at identifying opportunities in markets where existing competitors had key vulnerabilities: attacking financial services suppliers through branding, high value and product simplicity in his direct marketing strategy; attacking the powerful Coca-Cola and Pepsi brands on low price with Virgin Cola, knowing that those firms will never get involved in a price war.

➤ **What will provoke the greatest and most effective retaliation by the competitor?** Whereas market leaders may accept some peripheral activity, because of the low margins they perceive, anti-trust laws or the scale involved, other actions are likely to provoke intense retaliation. This is what Rolls-Royce learnt to expect whenever they approached the American market for aero engines, what Freddie Laker found when he openly challenged the major carriers on the Atlantic route, and what the small Yorkshire-based company Dale-Pack found when their chopped meat burgers starting making inroads into Unilever's market share. There is little sense in even the most powerful company unleashing the wrath of a strong competitor when there are less sensitive routes to success available. Early in 1997, for example, Sainsbury was reported to be considering price-cuts to retrieve some of its lost market share. The next day, Ian MacLaurin, then leading Tesco, said in the financial press that each and every price-cut would be matched. He was believed by Sainsbury, as Tesco has a reputation and track-record of sensitivity on price that underlines their determination on this issue. No price war ensued.

Beside providing a general guideline, a competitor's response profile depends on obtaining a view of how a competitor is likely to respond, given various stimuli. Porter (1980) suggests examining the way a competitor may respond to the feasible strategic moves by a firm and feasible environmental changes. This first involves assessing the vulnerability of a competitor to the event, the degree to which the event will provoke retaliation by the competitor and, finally, the effectiveness of the competitor's retaliation to the event.

The aim is to force a company to look beyond its own moves and towards those of its competitors and, like a great player of chess, think several moves ahead. It involves a firm thinking of its moves in a broad, strategic framework rather than the incremental manner in which strategies often emerge. Or, by following a series of seemingly small incremental shifts in pricing and promotion, a firm may be perceived to be making a major play in the marketplace and incur the wrath of major players. It is clearly better for Black to consider the alternative moves carefully rather than make a series of moves, each one of which makes local sense, without regard to White's counter-moves and the long-term consequences of incremental action.

7.3 Choosing good competitors

When a company chooses to enter a market, it also chooses its competitors. In the selection of new opportunities, therefore, it is important to realize that not all competitors are equally attractive. Just as markets can be attractive and a company's strengths can fit those markets, so competitors can be attractive or unattractive. Porter (1985) lists the characteristics which make a good competitor. In Figure 7.5 these features are organized to show how certain features of competitors can make them attractive.

The competitively mature company understands the market it is operating in and enhances, rather than destabilizes, the environment of the strategic group. The good competitor can help promote the industry's stability by understanding the rules governing the market and by holding realistic assumptions about the industry and its own relative position. In this way, it is unlikely to embark upon strategies which are unprofitable and result in zero-sum competition, such as precipitating price wars or unprofitable practices. Among the British clearing banks in the late 1980s both Midland and Lloyds introduced interest-bearing current accounts. This gave them a short-term competitive edge, but once the market leaders followed, the

	Balance	Strength	Weakness
Competitive maturity	• Understand the rules • Realistic assumptions • Support industry structure	• Credible/ viable • Know the industry costs	• Clear weaknesses • Limited strategic concept
Reconcilable goals	• Moderate strategic stake • Accept current profitability • Desire cash generation	• Comparable ROI targets	• Short time horizons • Risk-averse

Figure 7.5 Good competitors

result was everyone losing money on this major part of their business. Once locked in, it was difficult for any of the banks to extricate themselves from this self-defeating position.

A company making unrealistic assumptions about itself and the market can equally damage industry stability. Within the European and American automobile market it is clear that an excess of capacity is being constructed. In the medium to long term this can be nothing but suicidal for the industry as a whole.

A good competitor can support industry structure if it invests in developing its own product and enhancing quality differentiation and market development, rather than confrontational price-cutting or promotional strategies. In that way, barriers to entering the industry are enhanced because the market becomes relatively fragmented and the impact of one company or new entrant is diminished. The global pharmaceutical industry tends to have this structure where legislation and the differentiation of drugs allows a large number of medium-sized companies to survive in many of the world's leading markets.

A further advantage of a competitively mature company is that it can provide a steady pressure towards the efficient operations of those with whom it is competing. It can provide a respectability and standards in the way that IBM did in the PC market and ensure that the market does not become too comfortable for the incumbents. The danger, then, as many state monopoly industries have shown, is that once the protection is removed, or competition is allowed, they find themselves too weak, fat or rigid to change themselves. Pressure increases when the leading competitor has a thorough understanding of industry costs and therefore sets standards for cost-efficient services.

Finally, the existence of the credible and viable large company within the strategic group can act as a deterrent to other entrants. A good competitor, therefore, can provide both a pressure to keep its competitors lean and an umbrella under which the industry can develop steadily.

A good competitor is a company which has a clear understanding of its own weaknesses and therefore leaves opportunities for others in the market. Within the British banking market after the Big Bang, there was clearly a shortage of good competitors when, once the market was deregulated, many clearing banks acquired diverse activities and offered excessive salaries in areas which they did not understand. The result was over-capacity, collapsing profits and a weakening of the British banking industry generally. A wiser competitor would have been more aware of its strengths and weaknesses and would have avoided ventures which would not only weaken its profitability but also damage the market generally. In that sense, a company with a limited strategic concept or a clear idea of the business it is in, is a better competitor than one with wider or more vague statements about its intent.

A good competitor will have reconcilable goals which makes it comfortable within the market it operates, less likely to make massive strategic shifts and tolerant of moderate intrusion. Where its strategic stake is moderate, a good competitor may not see market dominance or the maintenance of its own market position as a principal objective. If under pressure, it may be willing to retreat from the market or, when faced with greater opportunities, may choose to grow elsewhere.

Moderation in desired profitability is also an advantageous characteristic of a competitor. If driven by the need to increase the returns it is obtaining, the industry's ability is likely to be disturbed by major investments in new products, promotional activity or price cutting. A company that accepts its current profitability will be a seeker of stability rather than new opportunities.

The desire of a competitor to maintain its cash flow can have a further impact on promoting industry's stability. Most ventures which involve destabilizing an industry depend upon investing in research and development, marketing and/or construction of new cost-cutting plant. A company with strict cash requirements is therefore less likely to embark upon such costly ventures.

The reconcilable goals of a good competitor can also provide a beneficial steady pressure upon the other companies within the industry. If a competitor has comparable return on investments targets to its stakeholders' it will face similar competitive pressures to the rest of the industry. In contrast, a state-owned competitor, which does not face the same profitability requirements, or one that is funded from markets with different expectations from one's own, can be unhealthy. Within the EU, the British Steel Corporation for a long time faced a regulated market against European competitors which were heavily subsidized by their respective state governments. Rather than competing with these, however, it chose to concentrate on speciality steels where the competitors were often in the private sector and therefore faced similar expectations. In a global context, many firms have found it very difficult competing with the Japanese who have a lower cost of money from their home stock market, which is also less volatile and responsive to short-term changes than their Western counterparts.

A feature of many Western companies which had made them good competitors for the Japanese has been their short time-horizon. This means that when faced with adversity, the Western companies which the Japanese face have often cut back investment to maintain short-term profitability or have taken a fast route to corporate success rather than investing for internal growth. With the UK market for dried milk products, Cadburys found Carnation a particularly attractive competitor, because its American owners were seeking a quick return on their investment while Cadburys, which had a longer term commitment to the market, was willing to invest to gain market share. Risk-aversion can also lead to a competitor being more attractive. Where there is a fear of making errors, there are likely to be followers within an industry, which gives more agile companies a chance to gain an advantage when the technology or market changes.

Clearly, finding a market in which the competitors are good on all fronts is unlikely, just as it is impossible to find a market which is completely attractive and consistent with a company's own strengths. But by examining competitors and looking for markets where they tend to be good rather than wayward, a company is likely to face a more stable environment and have one in which opportunities are there to be taken.

The diversity of competition makes it difficult to draw generic classes of companies which are likely to be good competitors. Some groups can be identified as likely to be the good or bad competitors but, in all these cases, there are likely to be many exceptions to the rule. Porter identifies smaller divisions of diversified firms as one likely group of good competitors. These may not be viewed as essential to the long-term corporate strategy and often face tough profitability targets. In a global sense, this is particularly true of American multinationals, which have shown a remarkable willingness to retreat home when faced with adversity. They are also often given particularly tough profitability objectives with little support or understanding in the overseas market. Part of this comes from the belief that what is good enough for the home market is good enough for the overseas subsidiaries, and that all the major lessons can be learnt at home (Wright *et al.*, 1990).

Another group of potentially good competitors can be old-established companies with a dynastic interest in the industry. This can be because the companies are strong and set high standards but are careful (as in the case of Sainsbury and Marks & Spencer in the UK) or because they are moderate in their expectations (as many British textile companies have been).

Among groups that are unlikely to be good could be new entrants from other industries who break the mould of established competition in the markets. Within microcomputers these would be Amstrad in the UK and Compaq in the USA. They could also be new entrants into a market who have made major investments and therefore have a large stake in terms of ego and money in making a venture a success. By not understanding the market they may destabilize competition and be willing to forgo profits for a long time. These can be very large companies at times, such as Unilever in the American market which has a number 3 position in terms of household products and a desperation to grow in order to become viable; or Japanese automobile companies in Europe and America which have been building industrial capacity which requires their taking a huge market share in both continents. To the incumbents these are bad competitors. Of course, the issue here is not good or bad from an ethical point of view. They are just bad competitors to compete with, although the new standards they bring to an industry and the services they provide to the consumer can do great good to the consumers and the economies concerned. Moreover they *are* good at competing, just not good to be competing against.

7.4 *Obtaining and disseminating competitive information*

The inability of commanders to obtain and use military intelligence is one of the major reasons for displays of military incompetence (Dixon, 1976). The same is true of competitive intelligence. Also, given the competitive nature of both war and commerce, it is not surprising that the means of gathering information on an enemy or the competition are similar in both method and ethics. And, in both cases, the legality of methods has not been a barrier to their use. The final section of this chapter draws together the alternative means of gathering competitive information. In doing so, it follows a sequence of declining morality, but seeks to make no judgement about the ethics of many approaches mentioned.

At the most basic level a company can collect *published statistical information* on competitors and markets. Many companies will have such information on their records from market studies or from published sources on public companies. A problem with many of these sources is their disaggregation and the frequent inconsistency between various government statistics and those provided by a range of market research companies. Some of this is due to sampling problems, particularly in some government statistics, such as Business Monitors, where the respondents are little controlled. Although factual and quantitative, this sort of information is limited by its historic basis.

A company's own *propaganda* – in other words, its public relations activities – can add texture to background statistical information. The need to communicate to shareholders and intermediaries in markets means that frequent marketing or technological initiatives are broadcast widely. A danger here, clearly, is the source credibility of the public relations involvement of the competitors. Investigative journalism can lead to more open disclosures but here again usually the press is dependent upon the goodwill of a company in providing information. Nevertheless, such sources can give a splendid feel for a company's senior executives. In that light it can be akin to the information that great generals try to gather on each other.

An increasingly frequent source of information on a company is *leakages* from employees which get into the hands of press, either intentionally or unintentionally. Since these often have to be newsworthy items, such information is usually limited in context but, once again, can give texture to background information. Firms that are more aggressive seekers of information may take positive steps in precipitating the giving of information: for instance, grilling competitors' people at trade shows or conferences, or following plant tours and being a particularly inquisitive member of a party. Although leakages may involve one of the competitor's employees being indiscreet they do not involve the researching company in unethical activities. Many of the practices that follow hereon may be deemed as less worthy by some.

A company can gather information from *intermediaries* or by posing as an intermediary. Both customers and buyers can have regular contact with competitive companies and can often be a source of valuable information, particularly with the salespeople or buyers from a researching company with whom they have regular contact. It is also possible to pose as a potential buyer, particularly over the phone, to obtain some factual information, such as price, or to obtain performance literature.

Many industries have policies of not recruiting between major companies or, as in the United States, have regulations regarding the nature of an individual's work after he has moved from company to company. However, a company would be naïve if it did not thoroughly debrief *competitors' former employees* if they did join the company and, where there is a strong market leader, it is very frequent for that company's employees to be regularly recruited by smaller companies. For a long time in the UK Procter & Gamble and Unilever, for instance, have been a training ground for marketing people in many other industries. When they move they also carry with them a great deal of useful information on their previous employers' products, methods and strategies. Many such large employers are very much aware of this and often request people who are leaving to clear their desks and leave within minutes once their intent to move is known. Even if competitors' employees may not be eventually recruited, the interviewing process itself can often provide useful information, particularly since the person being interviewed may be eager to impress the potential employer.

Surveillance is widely used within counter-espionage, but is less common as a means of gathering competitive information. Some of the methods used can be quite innocuous, such as monitoring competitors' employee advertisements or studying aerial photographs. Others are very sensible business practices, such as reverse engineering, i.e. tearing apart the competitors' products for analysis. Less acceptable, and certainly less hygienic, is the possibility of buying a competitor's garbage to sift for useful memoranda or components. Bugging is a controversial means of surveillance which is becoming more common now equipment is inexpensive, reliable and small enough to be concealed. Not only were Richard Nixon's presidential campaign organizers found using this method, but also the retailer Dixons, during their acquisition of Currys.

Dirty tricks have always been a danger of test marketing, but with the current availability of mini-test markets (Saunders *et al.*, 1987), a new dimension has emerged. Their speed means that while a company is test marketing its products over a matter of months, a competitor can buy supplies, put them through a mini-test market, find their market appeal and maybe experiment with alternative defensive strategies, before the test marketed product is launched fully. Unilever's subsidiary Van den Berghs is reputed to have done just this when Kraft launched their Carousel margarine. Using mini-test markets they were able to find that although the Kraft product had a high trial rate, few people adopted it in the long term and therefore it was of no great danger to Unilever's leading products.

A final means of gathering information is the use of *double agents*, either placed in a competitor's company purposely or recruited on to the pay roll while still working for the competitor. One can easily imagine how invaluable such people could be over the long term. We know that such individuals are common within military espionage, although few examples have come to light in business circles. One wonders how many leading companies would be willing to admit that they have been penetrated, even if a double agent was found within them.

Disseminating competitor intelligence
Intelligence itself is an essentially valueless commodity. It becomes valuable only when it researches the right people within the organization and is subsequently acted on. Successful dissemination requires two things. First, the destination must be clearly identified. Basically the question is: who needs to know this? Second, the data must be presented in a manner that the recipient can understand and assimilate. Too many competitive intelligence reports, like market research reports, are far too detailed and cumbersome for busy executives to extract and use the relevant information.

Bernhardt (1993) suggests the use of a hierarchical approach to dissemination. For senior management (including CEOs and strategy formulation groups) intelligence should be limited to that which is of high strategic value. There is little point burdening top managers with the minutiae of everyday operations. Indeed, too much operational detail in their menu of intelligence may mask the really important issues that they need to act on.

Information to senior managers should include special intelligence briefings, typically one- or two-page reports identifying and summarizing specific issues and showing where more detailed information can be obtained. Senior managers may also require regular (monthly or quarterly depending on the rate of change in the industry and market) intelligence briefings, which address regularly occurring issues systematically, so that trends can be identified and priorities made.

Middle and junior managers at a more operational level may require more detailed information to enable them to formulate tactical decisions. Here, more detailed profiles of competitor products and services will be required, together with detailed analysis of competitor marketing mix strategies. Increasingly, middle management (where it has survived the downsizing of the 1990s!) is becoming conversant with database manipulation enabling managers to directly interrogate intelligence data rather than simply relying on information specialists to extract and present relevant information (see Fletcher, 1996).

7.5 Conclusions

Over the last few years competitive strategy has emerged as one of the major foundations of business strategy. Just as understanding markets is fundamental to business success, so is a complete understanding of competitors, their strengths, weaknesses and likely responses. This chapter suggests that the focus of competitor analysis should be on strategic groups, but should not neglect other firms within the industry with the ability to overcome entry barriers or potential entrants to the industry. It provides some frameworks for analyzing competitors and suggests the importance of thinking through their likely responses. It also suggests that when entering markets and instituting strategies firms should be looking for 'good' competitors who can stabilize markets, provide opportunities and a downward pressure upon performance. Finally, means of gathering and disseminating competitive information are presented.

Although as important as market information, these data are rarely gathered systematically or comprehensively. There is also such a multiplicity of sources which have to be assessed that there is little chance of doing so on an *ad hoc* basis. There is therefore good reason for incorporating a competitive information system within any marketing information system that exists, and having people responsible for ensuring its maintenance. In competitive strategy, just as in war, it is impossible to exaggerate the importance of gathering information on the adversaries a company faces. As Sun Tzu says: 'An army without spies is like a man without ears or eyes' and, because of this 'to remain in ignorance of the adversary's condition simply because one grudges the outlay of a few hundred ounces of silver in honours and emoluments, is the height of inhumanity.'

CHAPTER 8

Strategic alliances and networks

The competitive realities of surviving and prospering in the complex and rapidly changing business environment encourage teaming up with other companies. Co-operative strategic relationships among independent companies are escalating in importance.
David W. Cravens (1997)

'There's a new beast in the jungle ...'
An executive describing her competitor's network organization, quoted in Snow (1997)

Introduction

We suggested in chapter 1 that in the late 1990s, executives in many organizations throughout the world have no choice but to become accustomed to the fact that they must go to market in an environment which has changed forever. The fuller implications of this fundamental environmental change are explored in chapter 19, but briefly that new environment is increasingly characterized by:

- **scarce resources** – both literally in the physical environment, but also in terms of the down-sized, leaner, strategically focused corporation;
- **increased competition**, frequently from new sources, new types of competitor, and new technologies, at home and overseas;
- **higher customer expectations** for service and quality requiring specialized expertise at the market level, from more sophisticated and informed customers;
- **pressures from strong distributors** like retailers in consumer goods marketing, to achieve ever-greater economies in supply-chain costs;
- the unavoidable **internationalization of markets and competition**, driven by such technological forces as the Internet and the world wide web;
- **faster rates of change in markets and technologies**; and
- **more turbulent, unpredictable markets**.

Changes of this kind have been associated with the evolution of new organizational forms, which disaggregate and devolve functions:

> Organizations of the future are likely to be vertically disaggregated: functions typically encompassed within a single organization will instead be performed in independent organizations. The functions of product design and development,

manufacturing, and distribution ... will be brought together and held in temporary alignment by a variety of market mechanisms. (Miles and Snow, 1984)

One of the most important responses to these competitive and market conditions has been the emergence of strategies of collaboration and partnership with other organizations as a key element of the process of going to market – these have variously been termed marketing partnerships, strategic alliances and marketing networks (Piercy and Cravens, 1996). In many ways, this is the other face of relationship marketing. There is the priority of managing better the relationship with the customer, but this is accompanied by the need for efforts to be made in managing the relationship with the collaborator as well. These new collaborative organizations are distinctive and different. They are:

characterized by flexibility, specialization, and an emphasis on relationship management instead of market transactions ... to respond quickly and flexibly to accelerating change in technology, competition and customer preferences. (Webster, 1992)

The emergence of networks of collaborating organizations linked by various forms of alliance has become a dominant strategic development in many industries. For example:

➤ at Corning Inc almost 50 per cent of revenue comes through alliances and joint ventures;
➤ at the leading computer company Compaq, the strategy is to pursue the information superhighway through twenty strategic alliances with telecommunications and software companies;
➤ the international airlines business is dominated by a small number of groupings of airlines operating as competing alliances across the world;
➤ outsourcing and networking has become a major strategy at marketing research agencies like A.C. Nielsen (Piercy and Cravens, 1996).

For these reasons, it is important that our thinking about the implementation of our own strategies, and also our understanding of the emerging forms of competition we face in the market, should embrace the strategic alliance and the resulting growth of networks of organizations linked by various forms of collaborative relationship. However, it is also important to emphasize that some of the strategic issues faced in alliances and networks go far beyond simple inter-organizational co-operation, but are leading to new organizational forms and new ways of doing business with the customer.

This chapter examines the following issues as a framework for evaluating the importance of strategic alliances and networks in our markets:

➤ the implications of an era of strategic collaboration for our strategic choices;
➤ the types of partnership, collaboration and strategic alliance which are emerging in the marketplace, as important ways of building networks;

➤ the forms which networks of collaborating organizations are taking, and the development of new organizational forms for marketing based on networks;
➤ the importance of strategic alliances as a competitive force in global markets;
➤ the risks involved in strategies of collaboration and alliance;
➤ a management agenda which details the issues which should be addressed in evaluating alliance-based strategies as a way for us to go to market.

8.1 *The era of strategic collaboration*

Cravens and Piercy (1994) argued that factors like rapidly changing markets, a complex array of technologies, shortages of important skills and resources, and more demanding customers present organizations with an unprecedented set of challenges (e.g. Tapscott and Castor, 1993; Gummesson, 1994). A central feature of responding to these challenges is the recognition by many business executives that building relationships with other companies is essential to compete effectively in the turbulent and rapidly changing post-industrial era confronting the developed world economies. In effect, we are experiencing an important change from an era of competition to an era of strategic collaboration. Figure 8.1 illustrates some of the types of interorganizational relationships which we have increasingly to consider in building effective marketing strategies: vertical channel relationships and supplier/manufacturer collaborations, and horizontal relationships in the form of strategic alliances and joint ventures – all share a growing emphasis on collaboration and partnership rather than simple contractual obligations.

These new collaboration-based relationships with customers, suppliers, distributors and even competitors are resulting in a variety of new organizational forms, which are commonly grouped together and classified as 'networks', where members may constitute 'virtual corporations' (Achrol, 1991; Quinn, 1992; Ring and Van de Ven, 1992; Webster, 1992; *Business Week*, 1993). As we shall see, many of the pioneers have been in the services sector, but networks spanning complexes of supply-chains are becoming more usual. In fact, the network paradigm may become the dominant organization form of the twenty-first century – the revolutionary nature of the changes occurring in the traditional hierarchical forms of organizations and the adjustment of their traditional adversarial relationships with suppliers and competitors is underlined by the comment of John Sculley, then the Chairman of Apple Computer: 'the network is *the* paradigm, not the Catholic Church or the military' (Sculley, 1992).

We shall examine a variety of examples of network organizations below, but the characteristics of network organizations can be discussed in the following terms. A defining characteristic of the network organization is the performance of marketing and other business functions by different independent organizations and individuals – the process of 'vertical disaggregation' (Cravens *et al.*, 1994). The network is a flat organizational form, involving interaction between network partners rather than the multi-layered functions of the traditional hierarchical organization.

In fact, dramatic changes are taking place in the traditional hierarchical forms of

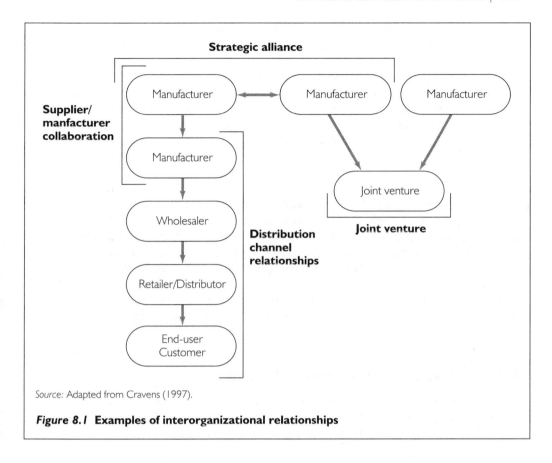

Source: Adapted from Cravens (1997).

Figure 8.1 Examples of interorganizational relationships

organizations as a result of alliance and network strategies. Although in some ways similar to channel of distribution networks (e.g. suppliers/producers, marketing intermediaries and end-users), network organizations may display both horizontal and vertical structures (e.g. collaborations between suppliers as well as supply-chain linkages). Moreover, networks are frequently complex and liable to change more frequently than traditional distribution channels. Interestingly, recently network concepts have fed back into traditional channel structures, in the form of collaborative 'channel partnerships' which go far beyond conventional channel relationships (Buzzell and Ortmeyer, 1994).

Typically, network operations are guided by sophisticated information and decision support systems, often global in their scope, which perform many of the command and control functions of the traditional hierarchical organization (Tapscott and Castor, 1993). The resulting network is flexible and adaptable to change, and the more successful network designs are customer-driven – guided by the needs and preferences of buyers (Powell, 1990).

Quinn (1992) characterizes networks as 'intelligent enterprises', and outlines various structural concepts such as infinitely flat, spider's web, starburst and inverted organizations. As we shall see below, the resulting networks may be complex and unfamiliar.

The interorganizational ties in a network may span organizations from suppliers to end-users, and/or actual or potential competitors. The network may also include service agencies, such as advertising, research, consulting services and distribution specialists. The relationships among the firms in a network may include: simple transactional contracts of the conventional buyer–seller type; supplier–producer collaborative agreements, strategic alliances or partnerships, consortia, franchising and distribution linkages, joint ventures or vertical integration (Doz, 1988; Achrol, 1991; Anderson and Narus, 1993; Bucklin and Sengupta, 1993; Cravens *et al.*, 1993). We shall examine these relationships in more depth below.

Developing from these general points about networks, we shall attempt in this chapter to build a framework for evaluating and designing network organizations as part of the implementation of marketing strategy and as a fundamental change in the competitive scenario. However, it is important to recognize that our under-standing of the network paradigm is limited, although we know that it is different: 'These relationships vary in significant ways from those governed by markets or hierarchies, and pose very different issues for researchers and managers' (Ring and Van de Ven, 1992).

8.2 *The drivers of collaboration strategies*

A starting point is to identify the potential drivers or motivating factors that lead organizations towards collaboration in delivering their strategies to market (Cravens *et al.*, 1994). Such driving forces include factors like the following.

8.2.1 **Market complexity and risk**

Modern markets are frequently characterized by complexity and high degrees of risk. One way of coping with that complexity and reducing (or sharing) risk is through collaboration. For example, Microsoft invested some $150 million in devel-oping Windows NT, but this product was pre-sold to PC manufacturers prior to production, when the PC partners could offer 5 million unit sales, then the product was manufactured. This type of complexity and risk may be exhibited in various situations:

> **Blurring of market boundaries** – conventional market definitions may become outdated and expose a company to new types of customer demand and new types of competition. The information industry is a prime example, where we see the convergence of telecommunications, consumer electronics, entertainment media, publishing and office equipment industries becoming intermingled. A converging industry greatly increases the complexity for a single firm trying to compete in the face of a widening range of customer

requirements and technologies to satisfy customer needs. Many of the products required are likely to be beyond the design, manufacturing and marketing capabilities of a single company, thus driving companies to pool their skills. This pooling of capabilities may be very effective – Hewlett Packard and Matsushita combined their relative capabilities in ink-jet and fax technologies to enter the market for an ink-jet fax machine far more rapidly than either could have done alone.

➤ **Escalating customer diversity** – in many markets buyers are demanding increasing value but also uniqueness in their purchases: one-to-one marketing, or microsegmentation, is becoming a reality. To respond positively to this demand may be beyond the scope of a single company in terms of expertise and economy, and may require new ways of doing business. For example, Calyx & Corolla (C&C) has reinvented the US market for fresh flowers by developing a network organization (see Figure 8.2). Traditionally, fresh flowers are a week old when purchased and displays are expensively made to order at a retail flower shop level, if a standard display is not what the customer wants (and if the shop has a wide enough range in stock). The C&C network markets fresh flowers by catalogue, offering more than 100 flower arrangements and designs. Customer orders are phoned/faxed to C&C, the information is transmitted by computer link to one of the growers in the network and to Federal Express. The growers make up the chosen design, branded by its packaging as a C&C product, which is then collected by

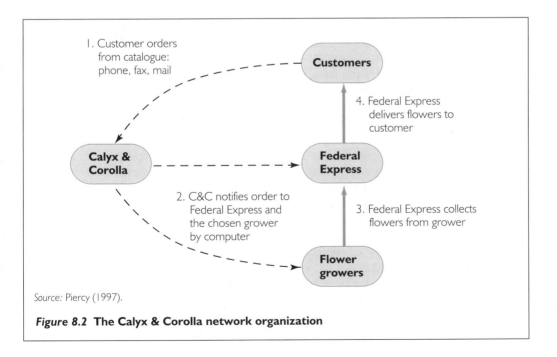

Source: Piercy (1997).

Figure 8.2 **The Calyx & Corolla network organization**

Federal Express and shipped to the customer. The customer has a far greater choice, the flowers received are up to nine days fresher, and three middlemen are avoided. This is a new way of going to market that reflects the need for 'mass customization', but that offers superior value at the same time. It has only been achieved by developing an effective network organization.

➤ **A borderless world** – Ohmae (1990) wrote about the interlinked economy of *The Borderless World*. Companies are increasingly driven to compete globally, and collaboration offers an attractive alternative to competing alone in a new environment. For example, British Airways' globalization strategy is driven by international partnerships with other carriers – a partnership with USAir offered access to the US internal market. (In fact, this partnership collapsed and BA is attempting to replace it with an alliance with the stronger American Airlines to control more than 60 per cent of transatlantic traffic. The competitive importance of this alignment is demonstrated by the outraged opposition provided by the other international airlines, led by Richard Branson of Virgin.)

8.2.2 Skills and resource gaps

It follows that there are growing pressures on firms to collaborate to compete effectively in globalized, technology-driven markets. The costs of developing internally the full range of skills and capabilities needed to compete effectively may be beyond the resources of a single company, or simply more cheaply available through alliances with specialized partners – where each partner can concentrate on applying its own core competencies, i.e. what it does best. For example, Apple Computer, Motorola and Sony collaborated to develop a pocket-sized cellular phone that also functions as an electronic notepad – Apple brought software expertise, Motorola the electronics, and Sony the design and manufacturing skills for a miniaturized product. The result is a better product, developed more quickly than any of the companies could have done alone. General Electric has more than 100 collaborative relationships with other companies throughout the world. The GE strategy is one of partnering to gain the core competencies needed and to gain faster access to both technology and markets. Similarly, NEC is renowned for its strategy through the 1980s of entering into a large number of alliances with other companies, with the goal of learning and absorbing other companies skills to build its core competencies rapidly and at relatively low cost. At a lower scale of operation, Daewoo Cars has taken 1 per cent of the UK car market in the fastest time ever achieved, by a strategy of customer focus and dealing direct with customers rather than through distributors. However, while customers will travel to visit a Daewoo showroom, they will not travel similar distances to have the car serviced and maintained. To overcome this barrier to a small car supplier, Daewoo has entered an alliance with Halfords, the national retail chain, to provide servicing of Daewoo cars at Halfords outlets. Daewoo's strategy underlines the power of focus on core activities and exploiting alliances to fill gaps (Piercy, 1997).

8.2.3 Supply-chain management

A more recent manifestation of the pressure to collaborate has come through the proposal for the 'lean enterprise' (Womack and Jones, 1996), and perhaps most clearly in the related Efficient Consumer Response programme in the grocery business:

➤ **Lean enterprise**: Womack and Jones (1996) describe the lean enterprise as a collaborative form spanning the supply chain. Their model argues that supply chains should be organized around value streams to drive out waste, responding to the pull of the product through the supply chain by customers, to eliminate stocks by organizing value-creating activities around flow. The enemy is waste or *muda*. The advantage is also to reduce markets to stable, predictable demand through collaboration and co-operation, rather than the turbulence created by conventional inter-firm competition and aggressive uncoordinated sales promotions. Their model organizations are companies like Toyota and Pratt and Whitney. This is a powerful and persuasive argument led by operations management, which substitutes collaboration for competition.
➤ **Efficient Consumer Response**: one new manifestation of this type of thinking is ECR, which is advanced in the US and starting to impact in Europe. ECR is based on 'co-operative partnerships' between retailers and manufacturers who commit to collaborate in reducing costs in the supply chain. Three years after launch in the US, 90 per cent of firms in the grocery business were participants in ECR. Launched in 1996 in the UK, participants included the six major retailers and the leading manufacturers of packaged goods. The key elements of ECR are: category management instead of the traditional product and brand approach, and the elimination of weak brands; more efficient promotion by substituting value pricing for special offers; continuous replenishment systems and cross-docking to reduce and possibly eliminate stocks in the channel; electronic data interchange for automated ordering and information flow; and organizational change – Procter & Gamble in the US has replaced its sales organization with its new Customer Business Development organization. ECR is a powerful weapon which demonstrably reduces supply-chain costs, but has been criticized for reducing consumer choice and competition and restricting manufacturer strategic development (Piercy, 1997).

These developments are dangerous to ignore as they provide powerful pressures towards collaboration between companies conventionally viewed as having only a buyer–seller relationship, or who were traditionally competitors.

It is important that in evaluating our markets and our strategies for the future we should carefully and systematically consider the emergence of factors like those listed above, which may drive our competitors' and our own strategies into collaborative network forms.

The next questions to consider are the types of networks which can be identified and the nature of the links which hold them together.

8.3 *Types of network*

There is no broadly accepted typology of network organizational forms. However, two approaches are useful in clarifying our ideas about the types of network which exist and may emerge in our markets.

First, Cravens *et al.* (1996) integrated the perspectives offered by Achrol (1991), Powell (1990), Quinn (1992) and Webster (1992) to propose the model of network organization types shown in Figure 8.3. They argued that networks differed and could be classified in two important respects:

1. **The type of network relationship,** which can vary from the highly collaborative (involving various forms of interorganizational co-operation and partnership), to the mainly transactional (the traditional buyer–seller transaction, for example).
2. **The volatility of environmental change** – the argument that in highly volatile environments, external relationships with other organizations must be flexible enough to allow for alteration – and possibly termination – in a short time period. On the other hand, when the environment is more stable, more enduring forms of collaboration are more attractive.

Using these dimensions to classify networks produces the model in Figure 8.3, suggesting that there are at least four types of network prototype:

1. **The hollow network** – a transaction-based organizational form, associated with highly volatile environments. The term 'hollow' emphasizes that the core organization draws heavily on other organizations to satisfy customer needs. For example, organizations that compete in this way are often specialists that co-ordinate an extensive network of suppliers and buyers. An illustrative case is The Registry Inc in the USA. The Registry's core competence is recruiting software engineers and technical specialists to perform services on corporate customers' computing projects. The Registry's customer account managers

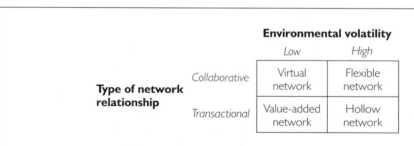

Source: Adapted from Cravens *et al.* (1996).

Figure 8.3 Types of network organization

identify client needs, and then form customized technical teams to service client projects. The Registry has a database of 50,000 technical experts, but fewer than 100 employees. Founded in 1987, by 1995 sales were running at $100 million. The 'marketing exchange company' described by Achrol (1991) is a possible design for a hollow network (see Figure 8.4), with the characteristics of a brokerage or marketing information-based clearing house, and the core organization operates as a hub of a worldwide network of marketing offices and information systems. The hollow organization offers a buffer against the risks in a frequently changing environment (Achrol, 1991).

2. **The flexible network** – associated with conditions of high environmental volatility but characterized by interorganizational links which tend to be collaborative and long-term in duration, where the network co-ordinator manages an internal team that identifies customer needs and establishes sources of supply to satisfy customer requirements. For example, many of the multinational pharmaceutical firms are tied to core competencies in organic and inorganic chemistry and are seeking to establish alliances with entrepreneurial biotechnology firms. The larger firms have too much invested in their current technology to switch completely to biotechnology, but want to exploit partnerships to ensure they have a source of biotechnology-based products. The Calyx and Corolla (C&C) example discussed earlier also provides a model of a flexible network, where C&C acts as a hub performing internally product design, packaging design, promotion and pricing, but using a network of external partners to provide the flowers and deliver them to the customer. It is notable, for example, that ICL, once the 'British' computer company, no longer owns factories to manufacture computers; it focuses on service and design and sources hardware from partner organizations.

3. **The value-added network** – associated with less volatile environments and based mainly on transactional relationships between network members. For example, the network co-ordinator may use a global network of suppliers, but still maintain substantial internal operations – the core organization may contract for many added-value functions such as production, but retain responsibility for innovation and product design. The Bombay Company, a highly successful speciality furniture retailer in the USA is an example of this network form. The Bombay Company has transactional (buyer–seller) links with over 150 speciality producers throughout the world. A particular supplier may produce only a contracted quantity of table tops, which are assembled by another company along with other items produced by other suppliers to produce tables. The transactional relationship is appropriate because the supplier is simply filling a contract for one of their standard products. Members of the network are specialists in performing certain value-adding functions at low cost. The Bombay Company's ability to construct and market a unique product selection through its network has achieved substantial success in the US marketplace. Other industries using this type of network are clothing manufacture, furniture, eye-glasses and some services – the link is that the

value-added network fits situations where complex technologies and customized product offerings are not required.

4. **The virtual network** is associated with situations where environmental volatility is relatively low, and the core organization seeks to establish collaborative relationships with other organizations. This is similar to what has been called the 'virtual corporation' (*Business Week*, 1993), which seeks to achieve adaptability to meet the needs of segmented markets through long-term partnerships rather than internal investment. Examples of companies forming virtual networks include GE, Hewlett Packard and Motorola. In these cases market access and technology access are the key drivers, and as with the flexible network, formal strategic alliances are the most common method for collaborating. The virtual network provides a buffer against market risks and access to new technology.

More recently, a broader and more complex view of network types has been provided by Achrol (1997), who has attempted to reflect three important characteristics that may differentiate different types of network: whether they are single-firm or multi-firm, whether they are single-industry or multi-industry; and, whether they are stable or temporary. Achrol's (1997) view of networks identifies the following types:

➤ **Internal market networks** – this describes the re-formation of major companies to break free of the restrictions of traditional hierarchies and multi-divisional forms, by organizing into internal enterprise units that operate as independent profit centres. For example, General Motors have reorganized their rigid and inefficient component manufacturing units into eight internal market units, each specialized in an automotive system area and able to sell its products on the open market as well as to GM, including GM's competitors in automotive manufacture.

➤ **Vertical market networks**, or **marketing channel networks**, reflect the traditional view of vertical channel relationships, but go further to recognize the focal firm that co-ordinates upstream supplier firms and downstream distributor firms. Often the integrator specializes in marketing functions and uses specialists for manufacture and distribution. Early forms included the 'hollow corporation', for example Casio, Nike, Liz Claiborne. In such networks, the typical pattern is that the integrator is the firm which owns the brand and which specializes in the marketing function, while alliance partners are specialized resource centres providing some aspect of product or production technology. Another example is provided by IKEA, the retailer of Swedish furniture, which successfully operates a global sourcing network of 2,300 suppliers in 67 countries, to get 10,000 products on the shelf at prices up to 30 per cent cheaper than traditional rivals (*Economist*, 1994). On the other hand, in technology-based markets the integrator may well be a technology specialists – Sun Microsystems has subcontracted chip manufacturing, distribution and service functions to specialize in designing advanced computers. Achrol suggests this is not so much a strategic alliance as a functional alliance.

➤ **Intermarket or concentric networks** – this is largely the province of the Japanese and Korean economies – the well-known *keiretsu* and *chaebol* 'enterprise groups' representing alliances among firms operating in a variety of unrelated industries. The intermarket network involves institutionalized affiliations among firms operating in different industries and the firms linked in vertical exchange relationships with them. They are characterized by dense interconnections in resource-sharing, strategic decision-making and culture and identity. The centre may be a trading company – possibly functioning as the marketing arm of the network – associated with manufacturing affiliates, which

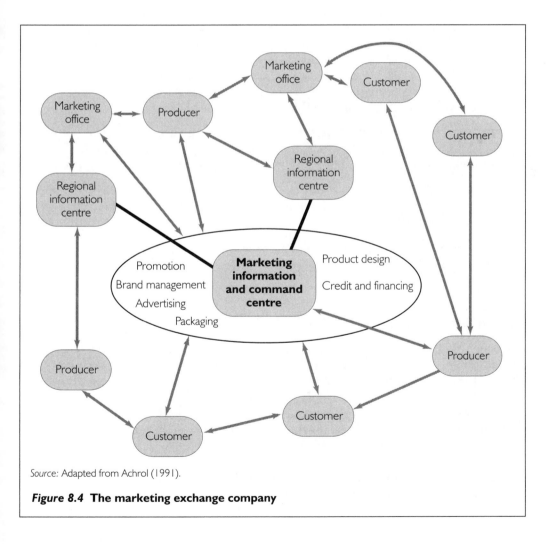

Source: Adapted from Achrol (1991).

***Figure 8.4* The marketing exchange company**

in turn have large vertical clusters of subcontractors, distributors and satellite companies, and are often involved in technology alliances with competitors. For example, Toshiba has around 200 companies in a direct exchange relationship, and another 600 'grandchild companies' below them (Gerlach, 1992). While the Japanese and Korean networks may appear impenetrable, it is interesting to note that recent commentators have attempted to explain the operation of Virgin as a *keiretsu* (Piercy, 1997) to explain the growth of the business through music and entertainment, transportation, financial services and diverse branded goods linked primarily by the Virgin brand and mainly funded by partner organizations.

➤ **Opportunity networks** – this is represented as a set of firms specializing in various products, technologies or services that form temporary alignments around specific projects or problems. Characteristically, the hub of the network is a marketing organization specializing in collecting and disseminating market information, negotiating, co-ordinating projects for customers and suppliers, and regulating the network. Achrol (1991) has described this as the 'marketing exchange company', as we saw earlier (see Figure 8.4). One prototype is the direct marketing company using media like the Internet to market a wide variety of consumer products and novelties.

This review illustrates the diversity and potential complexity of network organizational forms as they are emerging and as we are trying to classify and understand them. In fact, it remains true that our general understanding is not well developed:

> network and virtual organizations have been here for a long time, although our ability to define them and communicate their true content is still limited.
> (Gummesson, 1994)

We may be able to improve that understanding if we turn our attention next to the nature of the links which ties organizations together in these various forms of collaboration.

8.4 *Alliances and partnerships*

Achrol (1997) underlines the importance of thinking of networks in the terms of relationship marketing, where the relationships between network partners go beyond those that would be defined by contract or written agreement or buyer–seller exchanges in the channel of distribution. He argues that 'the mere presence of a network of ties is not the distinguishing feature of the network organization', but that 'the quality of the relationships and the shared values that govern them differentiate and define the boundaries of the network organization' (Achrol, 1997).

This said, a starting point in understanding the dynamics of the network organization, and its attractiveness or otherwise in developing a specific marketing strategy lies in analyzing *partnership*. It is important that we do not see strategic alliances and network formation as ends in their own right, but as a means to an end – the implementation and regeneration of our marketing strategy and the enhancement of our process of going to market – to be used selectively and appropriately based on our objectives and our capabilities for managing collaborations with other organizations.

One way of categorizing collaborative relationships is shown in Figure 8.5. These relationships form a spectrum running from a largely traditional, transactional relationship to full-scale vertical integration. The relationships shown in Figure 8.5 have the following characteristics.

8.4.1 Outsourcing

At one extreme is an 'arm's length' relationship, where we may simply buy in goods and services from outside, as the alternative to producing them internally. This

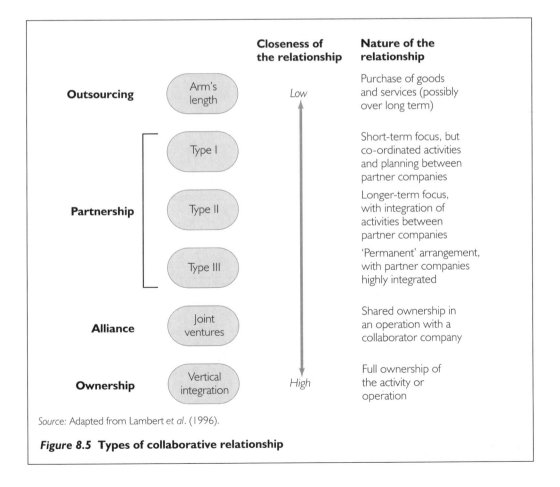

Source: Adapted from Lambert et al. (1996).

Figure 8.5 Types of collaborative relationship

might involve outsourcing for services like advertising, market research and direct marketing expertise. It may also describe how we buy in goods for resale, or handle relationships with our distributors. However, increasingly even at this end of the spectrum people may see suppliers and distributors as partners and use terms like 'strategic alliance' to describe relationships. This may be inaccurate, but underlines Achrol's point above that networks are about more than the nature of the legal ties between partners. Transactional relationships of this kind also characterize what Cravens *et al.* (1996) described as value-added and hollow networks (see above). It is also true that in many situations, arm's length relationships are reshaping into closer collaborative relationships – for example, in the Efficient Consumer Response programme (see above), and in the customer pressure in business-to-business marketing for suppliers to build closer relationships between all their resource departments and the equivalents in customer organizations (see Figure 8.6). In such cases, what starts as outsourcing may acquire many of the collaborative characteristics of a formal strategic alliance.

For example, British Airways is outsourcing significant sections of its business, as part of an array of franchising, alliance and partnership relationships with other companies, in moving towards the concept of a 'virtual airline'.

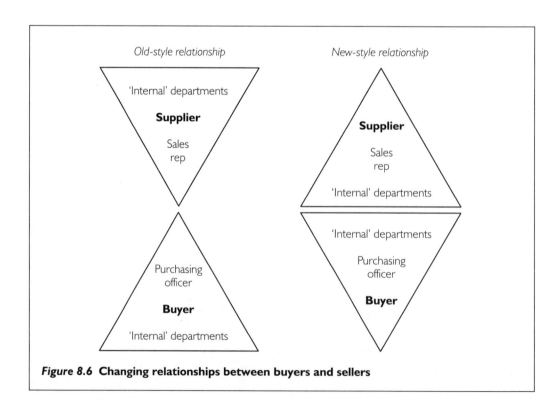

Figure 8.6 Changing relationships between buyers and sellers

8.4.2 Partnerships

These are alliances that involve a closer relationship between organizations, but stopping short of shared ownership in a joint venture or vertical integration. Lambert *et al.* (1996) suggest that partnerships vary in the degree and type of integration. They suggested that: Type I partnerships are short-term in focus and involve limited co-ordination; Type II partnerships have a longer-term focus and move beyond co-ordination to integration of activities; and, Type III partnerships are viewed as 'permanent' and each party views the other as an extension of its own firm.

For example, in 1997 Vickers and British Aerospace (BAe) announced a partnership arrangement under which BAe will market Vickers armoured vehicles in the Middle East. In another novel partnership arrangement Shell has recently established a consortium of retailers to use the Shell 'smart card' to handle 70 per cent of the average consumer's purchases. The card will allow the user to shop, bank, make phone calls and be rewarded with discount points and airmiles, and to claim the discounts in any of the member businesses. Also in 1997, Microsoft and Hewlett Packard announced a 'corporate computing alliance', in which HP will 'aggressively integrate' Microsoft's Windows NT network operating system into its computers.

A different form a marketing alliance is shown by the marketing consortium formed by Cadbury-Schweppes, Unilever, Kimberley-Clark and Bass to attack the consumer market. The goal is to share information about consumer trends and the individual companies' consumer databases. Possible applications are joint marketing programmes, for example, combining into a single programme complementary products like Huggies and Pull-Ups nappies from Kimberley-Clark with toiletries and cleaners from Unilever in the 'mother and baby market' (Becket, 1997).

8.4.3 Joint ventures

These are alliances where the ownership of a project or operation is shared between the parties concerned. For example, in 1997 Dixons, the electrical retailer, sold a 40 per cent stake in its communications offshoot Link (a retailer of mobile phones, pagers and faxes) to Cellnet, one of its major suppliers. The effect is two-fold: Dixons and Cellnet are both committed jointly to the Link retailing project, and they have largely shut Cellnet's competitor Vodafone out of the Link retail outlets.

The computer world was shocked in 1997 by the decision of Microsoft to invest $150 million in Apple computers – the companies have long been deadly rivals, and Microsoft's chief executive, Bill Gates, was loudly booed at the meeting when the new relationship was announced. In fact, if the parties are capable of collaborating after their historical antipathy, the collaboration makes much sense. Microsoft has committed to providing Mackintosh-compatible releases of its Office package and its Internet Explorer Web browser, which will support Apple's growth. In return, Microsoft gains a wider base of users for its software, and another ally against the threat from Sun Microsystems which is attacking the Windows operating system.

Some joint ventures go much further towards what is being called 'constellation marketing' (Mitchell, 1997; see p. 191). Mercedes, the German car company, and Swatch, the Swiss watch company, are in a joint venture to produce the Smart minicar, supported by partnership sourcing by its ten key suppliers, which have relocated their operations to a 'smart ville' in France. This relationship focuses on partners from different industries sharing innovative design abilities, technological expertise and marketing capabilities to innovate. The concept is that the partners see themselves as selling 'mobility' as a total product not just a car – the product may include the ability to borrow larger cars when needed for particular mobility needs.

8.4.4 Vertical integration

An activity is fully owned by the core organization, although the relationship may still be seen as a strategic alliance. For example, HFS Inc in the US has spent seven years acquiring a variety of travel and relocation services to create one-stop shopping for home buyers, holiday travellers, and business travellers. Someone moving to a new job contacts a Century 21 agent to find a new home, rent an Avis car and reserve rooms at Ramada Inns along the route. HFS has purchased Coldwell Banker, the world's largest estate agency, Avis, the world's second largest car rental company, and timeshare rental businesses, as well as relocation specialists and mortgage lending businesses. HFS is also the world's largest franchiser of hotels. Sales had grown to $550 million by 1996. HFS is essentially a marketing hub in a network, in which the ties are ownership and franchising.

It is important that we consider the strengths and weaknesses of these different degrees and types of partnership in developing appropriate alliance strategies, and that we recognize that in reality networks may contain a mix of different partnership styles.

8.5 *Strategic alliances as a competitive force*

It is also important that we recognize in our marketing strategy development that in some markets, competition is increasingly based on the relationship between alliances and the networks they create and no longer between individual companies. This is particularly true in the global airline business. Other cases which underline this reality are:

➤ The new alliance between Microsoft and Hewlett Packard. Described above, this is a direct response to the alliance between IBM, Sun Microsystems and Oracle. Microsoft and HP aim for leadership in network computing by combining Windows NT and the UNIX system, while IBM's alliance focuses on supporting technologies like Sun Microsystem's Java programming language as a lever to weaken Microsoft's control over technology standards in computing.

➤ In the international telecoms business British Telecommunication's (BT) £13 billion bid for MCI, the US's second largest long-distance carrier, was one of the largest financial manoeuvres ever attempted. Although strictly a takeover, the goal was alliance. The strategy was to create a new company, Concert, which would operate the three businesses as BT, MCI and International. The BT strategy failed because WorldCom, a US competitor, outbid BT, leaving BT's international strategy in disarray. Although offering a variety of gains in cross-fertilization and a new style of organization, Concert represented primarily the goal of gaining leadership in the global telecoms business by providing a competitive force large enough to beat the AT&T Unisource consortium, and the Franco-German alliance of Deutsche Telekom and France Telecom. Further inroads were being made by 'poaching' Telefonica of Spain from the AT&T consortium into the Concert alliance. BT had to look elsewhere to build its international strategy. The basis for competition is the alliance not the individual company.

➤ In many markets alliances are also the source of new forms of competition: in 1996 it was rumoured that BT was looking to move into gas and electricity supply through a marketing alliance with a power company; BP is jointly marketing petrol and groceries in partnership with Safeway; IBM may become the core of a new on-line banking consortium.

➤ The term 'constellation marketing' (Mitchell, 1997) has been coined to describe companies collaborating to build unique combinations of products and services that add more value to the customer than purchasing any of the brands or products separately. The sophisticated joint loyalty card scheme, the Smart card, operated by companies like Shell, Menzies, Victoria Wine, Dixons and others, is an example of such collaboration.

At the very least, our analysis of competitive structures would be potentially misleading if we did not account for the potential impact of strategic alliances.

8.6 *The risks in strategic alliances*

We stressed earlier that strategic alliances are no panacea. They may be an important way to achieve the things we need, but there are significant risks also.

To begin with, we should be aware that, for one reason or another, strategic alliances sometimes simply do not work, and they may crash spectacularly:

➤ IBM and Microsoft were partners in the 1980s, and Microsoft provided the DOS operating system that drove IBM's PCs. However, IBM did not have exclusive rights to DOS and it was adopted by their competitors in clones of the IBM PC. IBM lost much market share and profit, while Microsoft benefited from the additional sales of DOS under licence. In 1985 IBM signed a formal Joint Development Agreement with Microsoft to create the next generation operating system – OS/2. The development of OS/2 proceeded slowly. Meanwhile Microsoft developed Windows, which was quickly taken up by the market – the same market IBM wanted for OS/2. The alliance exploded in an acrimonious press conference in Las Vegas in 1989. The partners finally parted company in 1991. As a partnership, the alliance had been a total failure. However, as in many 'divorces' the division of costs and benefits was far from equal: Microsoft got the time and space to develop the worldwide success of Windows, while IBM was left with the unpopular OS/2 system in a market now dominated by Microsoft. Perhaps unsurprisingly, Microsoft and IBM are now deadly rivals (see above) (Sengupta and Bucklin, 1994; Chesbrough and Teece, 1996).

➤ A key component of British Airways' globalization strategy was its partnership with USAir, to gain access to the critical internal US market. By 1996 the two companies were in court because BA had announced a new alliance with American Air. The first that the chairman of USAir knew of this was when he read the news in the *Wall Street Journal*. The USAir/BA alliance crumbled immediately. However, competitors including Virgin and a new alliance of US airlines is doing its utmost to prevent the BA/AA alliance.

➤ Rover and Honda formed an early R&D and marketing partnership in the UK automotive industry. Some fifteen years into that partnership, in secret negotiations, Rover was sold to BMW, the German car company. Rover appeared to believe that the Honda partnership was part of the deal. The acquisition came as a surprise to Honda, who on considering their options, withdrew from the partnership to avoid allowing BMW access to Honda technology.

➤ A study by Cravens *et al.* (1993) found that in 82 large multinational corporations, fewer than half the companies operating strategic alliances were satisfied with the effectiveness of those alliances.

It is perhaps wise not to overestimate the strength and durability of strategic alliances. Quinn noted some time ago:

> Like earlier decentralization and SBU concepts, some of these newer organizational modes have been touted as cures for almost any managerial ill. They are not. Each form is useful is certain situations, and not in others. But more importantly, each requires a carefully developed infrastructure of culture, measurements, style and rewards to support it. When properly installed, these disaggregated organizations can be awesomely effective in harnessing intellectual resources for certain purposes. When improperly supported or adapted, they can be less effective than old-fashioned hierarchies. (Quinn, 1992)

Indeed, as well as the outright failure of an alliance and the crash of the network involved, there are a number of other important issues to bear in mind as potential limitations to the application of strategies of collaboration.

Achrol (1997) argues that we should consider the following factors as key elements of designing and operating network organizations:

➤ **Power**: we need to take a careful look at the relative dependence and power within a network, both in terms of whether the relative position we take is acceptable to us and if we are going to be able to cope with the way power is likely to be exercised in the network, and how vulnerable this may make us.

➤ **Commitment and interdependence**: at its simplest are the people in the partnering companies going to be behind the alliance, and what mechanisms may be needed like interlocking directorships and exchange of personnel or other liaison mechanisms? In the *keiretsu*, the Japanese refer to what is necessary to 'keep each other warm' (Gerlach, 1992); their example suggests we should not underestimate the importance of people's commitment, or lack of it, in an effective network organization.

➤ **Trust**: the network organization requires that each partner gives up some influence or control over important issues and becomes vulnerable to ineffective or hostile actions by other network members. This is a key aspect of relationship management in a network. The cases of network failure cited above illustrate the vulnerability involved. Compare this to the risk of lack of commitment to a collaboration through an unjustified lack of trust in the partner organization, and the significance of the issue becomes clearer. This point is underlined in Morgan and Hunt (1994).

➤ **Social norms**: it is suggested that network organizations should be considered in terms of behavioural issues like (a) solidarity – the unity of action among network members, (b) mutuality – network partners acting in the common good and receiving a payoff in terms of benefits from the collaboration, (c) flexibility – the willingness of partners to change the joint arrangements as conditions change, (d) role integrity – clarity in what each partner organization is to do, (d) conflict handling – agreement on how conflicts will be handled in the network. The important point to bear in mind is that while organizations are familiar with how to handle these questions in conventional, independent, hierarchical structures, we are still learning how best to manage them in the very different setting of the collaborative network of organizations.

We need to consider the attractiveness of a collaborative or alliance-based strategy in terms not simply of the pressures of factors like resource gaps and market access, but also in the light of whether we can design and implement an effective network, and whether we have the skills and capabilities to manage through a network of relationships with other companies.

We shall consider these points in more detail in the managerial agenda in the next section. The practical importance of this point can be underlined, however, by looking at the experiences of alliance partners like KLM and Northwest in the airline business. The logic of an alliance between these two airlines is impeccable: the partnership formed in 1990 helped Northwest to return to profitability, and generated more than $100 million in additional revenue for both airlines. The alliance enables Northwest to market its own flights (via KLM) from Amsterdam to many cities in Europe and the Middle East, while KLM gets access to the internal US market. However, by 1995 a battle for power had emerged in the alliance. KLM threatened to sue Northwest because it planned to change shareholder rights, requiring KLM to reduce its holding of Northwest stock. This was a result of Northwest executives' belief that KLM was trying to gain control of Northwest. KLM's management believes that Northwest's top management is primarily interested only in short-term financial gains. The partnership is plagued by a lack of trust between the two companies and a clash of management cultures. What is more, there have been suggestions that Northwest's flights do not offer service to the level offered by KLM, thus alienating KLM customers who are offered Northwest flights to the US. These hidden frictions may suggest that the partnership was logical but possibly not wise (Cravens *et al.*, 1997). By mid-1997, KLM was reported to have made a secret deal to collaborate with the proposed new BA/American Airlines alliance (Gribben, 1997).

8.7 Strategic alliances: the management agenda

The discussion above and the examples examined in this chapter suggest that the managerial issues that should be addressed carefully and systematically in evaluating the strategy of collaboration and alliance as a route to market are the following.

8.7.1 Core competencies

One of the fundamental attractions of collaboration and partnership with other organizations is that it allows each organization to focus on its own core competencies and to benefit from the specialization of other organizations in their own areas of expertise (Achrol, 1991; Webster, 1992). Quinn (1992) notes:

> If one is not 'best in world' at a critical activity, the company is sacrificing competitive advantage by performing that activity internally or with its existing techniques.

Certainly, research by Buffington and Frabelli (1991) in the telecommunications industry suggests that when partners in a collaboration do not contribute their core competencies, then the probability of success for the alliance is substantially reduced. This suggests that clarity in defining those core competencies may be critical to negotiating and sustaining effective interorganizational relationships of this type.

However, there are two problems. First, it is clear that the identification of core competencies may be far from straightforward within an organization or between partners (e.g. see Piercy and Cravens, 1996). Second, we have to factor in not just existing and recognized core competencies, but issues of complementarity and 'fit' between potential partners, and the potential for synergy through collaboration (Sengupta and Bucklin, 1994).

8.7.2 Strategic priorities

The issue of core competencies also raises important questions about competitive strategy and the choices faced in when, where and how to compete (Prahalad and

Hamel, 1990). While networking offers a company the opportunity to focus on and exploit its core competencies, it will rarely create such capabilities for a company.

This focusing may be highly effective. For example, GE's top management vision for competing in the 1990s illustrates the significance of establishing priorities and making important strategic choices. GE moved away from consumer electronics because of intense competition and the lack of attractiveness of this product market in terms of profitability and growth. GE assigned top priority to a few key businesses, such as jet engines, where the company had a leading market position and a clear competitive advantage. It is in these key areas that GE has used networks of collaborators to reinforce this advantage.

However, this focus and concentration may create vulnerabilities as well. We saw earlier that the British Airways alliance with USAir has collapsed before the new alliance with American Airlines has been approved. This leaves BA potentially with no US-based collaborator and highly exposed to competitive attack by other alliances. While there is much current favour in corporate thinking for strategic focus and concentration, using collaborations as a vehicle, we should be aware of the risks involved in this prioritizing. Reliance on partners to perform critical activities involves risks if the partnership fails or underperforms, and may leave us without the capacity to develop new competencies.

8.7.3 **Managing network organizations**

It is apparent from the case examples we have used that organizations differ markedly in their ability to manage effectively in networks. Forming and managing networks calls for a different set of management skills and issues compared to the conventional organization. *Business Week* (1993) concludes that for managers in the 'Virtual Corporation':

> They'll have to build relationships, negotiate 'win-win' deals, find the right partners with compatible goals and values, and provide the temporary organization with the right balance of freedom and control.

Before making the commitment to enter an alliance, we should consider the following factors:

➤ **Drivers** – which of the drivers of collaboration strategies (see pp. 178–81 above) apply in this case? What does a collaboration strategy offer us in terms of: asset/cost efficiencies; customer service improvements; marketplace advantage over the competition, profit stability/growth (Lambert *et al.*, 1996)?

➤ **Choice of partners** – which potential partners are available, and what basis do we have for believing that we could create an environment of trust, commitment and co-operation between the members of the alliance (Cravens *et al.*, 1997)?

➤ **Facilitators** – are the circumstances and environment favourable for a partnership? Lambert *et al.* (1996) suggest that partnerships are more likely to be successful if the following conditions prevail:

corporate compatibility: the cultures and business objectives of the partners must mesh;

managerial philosophy and techniques: are the partners' organizational structures, attitudes towards employees and method of working compatible?

mutuality: are there equally important benefits for both partners?

symmetry: are the partners similar types of company who understand each other?

exclusivity: are partner organizations willing to shut out others who are not part of the network?

shared competitors: partnerships work best as an alliance against a common foe;

prior history: experience in successful collaboration is a plus;

shared end-user: when partners serve the same customer, collaboration is likely to be more successful.

➤ **Components** – these are the activities and processes that management establishes and controls throughout the life of the partnership, and effective partnerships understand these from the outset (Lambert *et al.*, 1996). This includes arrangements for joint planning, joint operating controls, communications between partners, equitable risk/reward sharing, facilitating trust and commitment between partner organizations, a contract acceptable to both sides, the definition of the scope of the partnership and clarity about the financial investments to be made by partners.

➤ **Network effectiveness** – we saw earlier that Cravens *et al.* (1993) found that many companies pursuing alliance-based strategies were dissatisfied with the results. Defining realistic expectations at the outset and evaluating progress against them is required. We may have to think in terms of somewhat different measures to the conventional evaluation of effectiveness – network stability and sustainability, relationship strength, network synergy, and the like. If we cannot provide convincing evidence that the network provides a superior way of going to market, it is unlikely to endure.

➤ **Organizational change** – it is highly likely that the formation of network organizations will be stimulated by, and in turn lead to further changes in, alliance companies' internal organizational structures and processes. The requirements for effectiveness here may be complex and currently outside the experience of many senior managers in traditional organizations (Cravens *et al.*, 1996). The complexity of this issue is underlined by Gummesson (1994): 'organizing a network business requires continuous creation, transformation and maintenance of amoeba-like, dynamic processes and organizational structures.'

➤ **Market orientation and customer service** – a particular point of concern for the marketing strategist is the impact of networked operations on the market orientation of the new type of organization and its ability to deliver the required levels of customer service and superior customer value. Where the primary motivation for collaboration is technological or supply-chain efficiency, this may be a particularly significant concern. For example, we reported elsewhere that some companies in the airline business are moving towards the concept of the 'virtual airline' which owns no aircraft or facilities and exists primarily as a brand and information system with a small core staff. Some executives suggest that while the core organization is highly market-oriented and committed to high service quality, in a networked organization they lack the means to share these imperatives with their partners. Quite simply, we may believe in service quality at the core airline, but is this shared by the people who run the operation the customer experiences at check-in (Piercy and Cravens, 1996)? This suggests that one of the major questions we need to consider is what mechanisms we may need to create to drive goals like service and quality through a network to the end-user.

➤ **The role of marketing in network organizations** – there is some lack of clarity about how marketing is located and operated in a network organization. In some models, like the 'marketing exchange company', the hub of the network is the marketing facility (Achrol, 1991). Others suggest that the critical role for marketing in the alliance-based network is applying relationship marketing skills to managing the links between partners in the network (Webster, 1992). Certainly, there is a compelling argument that the concepts and processes of relationship marketing are pivotal to the management of networks. Relationship marketing involves the creation and distribution of value through mutual co-operation and interdependence (Sheth, 1994), and we have seen that co-operation and interdependence are central features of network organizations. It is too early to reach conclusions about the role that marketing can and will take generally in these new organizational forms, although it is highly likely that there will be some redefinition of its role which may be radical.

8.8 *Conclusions*

We have argued in this chapter that there are many factors compelling organizations to collaborate and forms alliances with others, rather than to compete independently – we may be entering an era of collaboration rather than competition. The network paradigm is impossible to ignore for two reasons: it may be how we take our strategy to market; and it may be how our competitors build their market power. The factors driving this process include market complexity and risk, skills and resource gaps, supply chain management imperatives, and the strategic priority of focusing on core competencies and outsourcing to partners for other activities and resources.

We attempted to identify the types of networks which are emerging in the modern marketplace. One approach looks at the type of relationship on which alliance is based and market volatility in order to identify the hollow network, the flexible network, the value-added and the virtual network (Cravens *et al.*, 1996). A broader view suggests that there are internal market networks, vertical market networks, intermarket or concentric networks and opportunity networks (Achrol,

1997). Related issues concerned the type of relationship ties between network members, ranging from outsourcing, through partnership, to joint venture and vertical integration.

The conclusion we reached at this point was that strategic alliances are a major competitive force, which in some industries like the airlines, computing and telecommunications is replacing conventional competition between individual companies. However, the cases and studies available to date suggest that while the potential gains may be great, strategic alliances and networks carry major risks.

This led us to an important management agenda to be considered in evaluating the importance of strategic alliances and networks as part of marketing strategy. We suggest that in considering a strategy of alliance, managers should focus on the issue of core competencies brought to the alliance by each partner, and the benefits and vulnerabilities associated with focus and outsourcing, and the capabilities that a company has to manage its strategy through a very different organizational environment. Questions to raise regarding those managerial capabilities include: understanding the underlying drivers favouring collaboration strategies, the choice of partners, the facilitators and components important to effective collaboration, the ability to define and evaluate network effectiveness in achieving marketing goals, and the capacity of a network to deliver the customer value on which our marketing strategy is based. The redefinition of the role of marketing also falls into this area.

Strategic alliances and networks are not a panacea for strategic problems. They are an important development with many potential benefits. They also carry major strategic risks and vulnerabilities, and demand new managerial skills. This is an issue requiring particularly careful and detailed analysis.

PART III

Identifying current and future competitive positions

The third part of the book addresses in more detail the issues and techniques behind segmentation and positioning research.

Chapter 9 discusses the underlying principles of competitive positioning and market segmentation, and their impact on the choice of target markets. The chapter continues by discussing in detail the logic of segmentation as an approach to identifying market targets, and by comparing the alternative bases for segmenting both consumer and industrial markets. The chapter closes by considering the benefits of identifying and targeting market segments, but also the importance of integrating market segment-based strategies with corporate characteristics and competencies, as well as external factors.

Chapter 10 examines the techniques of segmentation and positioning research in detail. Two fundamentally different approaches are discussed. Under the first, termed *a priori*, the bases for segmenting are decided in advance and typically follow product/brand usage patterns or customer demographic characteristics. The second approach, *post-hoc* or cluster-based, searches for segments on the basis of a set of criteria, but without preconceived ideas as to what structure in the market will emerge. The chapter then discusses methods for collecting segmentation data (relating back to the marketing research methods discussed in chapter 6), ways of analyzing those data to identify and describe market segments, and addresses the issue of validating empirically the segmentation structure uncovered. The chapter next discusses both qualitative and quantitative approaches to positioning research. In the former the use of focus groups and depth interviews to identify images and positions is examined. The chapter concludes with a discussion of quantitative approaches to creating perceptual maps.

Chapter 11 looks at forecasting techniques that can be used to predict changes in segments and positions in the future. The chapter examines methods for analyzing and extrapolating past trends, testing current options through concept and market testing, and more qualitative judgements of future outcomes. The chapter concludes by offering a set of recommendations for how to choose the most appropriate forecasting technique in any given situation, and lists a number of pitfalls of which to be beware.

CHAPTER 9

Segmentation and positioning principles

Focussed competitors dominate their target segments – by fending off broad-coverage competitors who have to compromise to serve the segment, and outperforming rivals with the same focus ... Focussed strategies also gain meaning from the differences between the segments covered and the rest of the market.

George S. Day (1994)

Introduction

Our approach to marketing analysis so far has rested largely on the identification and exploitation of key differences – in marketing capabilities and competitive strengths, for example. Our attention now focuses on two particularly important areas of differentiation: the differences between alternative market offerings as far as customers are concerned, i.e. the *competitive positioning* of suppliers, products, services and brands; and the differences between customers – in terms of their characteristics, behaviour and needs – that are important to marketing decisions-makers in developing strong marketing strategies, i.e. *market segmentation.*

The distinction between competitive positioning and market segmentation is illustrated in Figure 9.1, which suggests that the key issues are:

➤ **Competitive positioning** – concerned with how customers perceive the alternative offerings on the market, compared to each other, e.g. how do Audi, BMW and Mercedes medium-price saloon cars compare in value, quality and 'meaning' or image?

➤ **Market segmentation** – described as how we as marketers can divide the market into groups of similar customers, where there are important differences between those groups, e.g. what are the characteristics of medium-price saloon car buyers that relate to their product preferences and buying behaviour?

➤ **Customer needs** – while positioning and segmentation are different concepts, ultimately they are linked by customer needs, in the sense that the most robust form of segmentation focuses on the customer benefits that matter most to different types of customer, while the strongest competitive positions to take are those where customers recognize that a supplier or product is the one they choose because it best meets their needs.

In this sense, positioning and segmentation are distinct parts of the strategy process

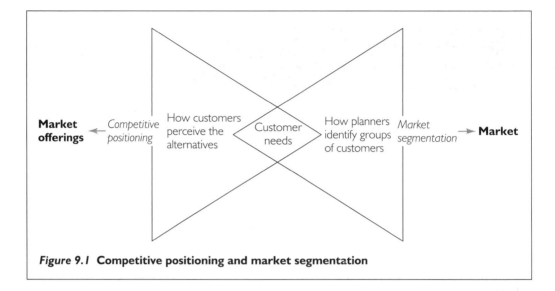

Figure 9.1 **Competitive positioning and market segmentation**

and provide us with some extremely powerful tools; but ultimately they are linked by the central issue of focusing on satisfying the customer's needs in ways that are superior to competitors'.

Operationally, positioning and segmentation may be linked in the way shown in Figure 9.2. This suggests that the sequence in planning can be of the following type:

➤ **Market segmentation** – identifying the most productive bases for dividing a market, identifying the customers in different segments and developing segment descriptions.

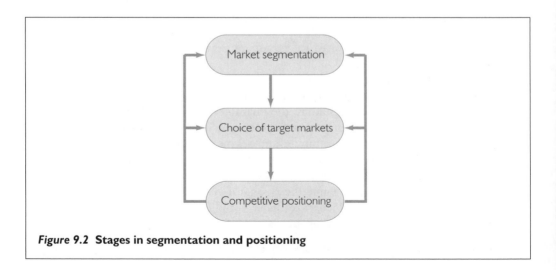

Figure 9.2 **Stages in segmentation and positioning**

➤ **Choice of target markets** – evaluating the attractiveness of different market segments, parts of segments (niches) or groups of segments, and choosing which should be targets for our marketing.

➤ **Competitive positioning** – identifying the positioning of competitors (in the market and in target segments or niches), to develop our own positioning strategy.

➤ **Iteration** – understanding competitors' positioning and the possible positioning strategies open to us should influence our thinking about the attractiveness of different market segments and the choice of market targets, and may change the way we segment our market, leading to revised target choices and positioning approaches.

While they are distinct strategy concepts, there are important similarities between positioning and segmentation: both start as issues of perception – how customers compare and understand alternative market offerings and how marketers understand the customer benefits different buyers seek from products and services. But both are also susceptible to quantitative research-based analysis.

We approach these issues in the following way. The role of this chapter is to distinguish between positioning and segmentation, and to clarify the underlying concepts and principles. From this foundation, we move to an evaluation in chapter 10 of the technical aspects of developing positioning and segmentation models. The implications for developing marketing strategies are found in chapter 13 (on developing defensible positions in target markets) and chapter 18 (on the integration of positioning and segmentation to build robust marketing strategies for the future).

9.1 *Principles of competitive positioning*

Competitive positioning as an issue in developing marketing strategy has been defined in the following terms:

> POSITIONING is the act of designing the company's offering and image so that they occupy a meaningful and district competitive position in the target customers' minds. (Kotler, 1997)

The essential principle of competitive positioning is that it is concerned with how customers in different parts of the market perceive the competing companies, products/services or brands. It is important to bear in mind that positioning may apply to any of these levels:

➤ **Companies** – for example, in grocery retailing in Britain the major competitors include Tesco, Sainsbury and Asda, and positioning is based on these identities.

➤ **Products and services** – positioning also applies at the level of the product, as shown in the example of the Dyson vacuum cleaner compared to similar priced products from Hoover and Electrolux.

➤ **Brands** – competitive positioning is perhaps most frequently discussed in terms of brand identities: Coca-Cola versus Pepsi, and the like.

Indeed, some cases show the importance of these levels as they relate to each other – Virgin, for example, is a company that stands for certain values in customers' minds, which translates to the company's simplified financial services products, and provides the brand identity for diverse products and services.

Competitive positioning may be seen in some ways as the outcome of companies' attempts to create effective competitive differentiation for their products and services (see chapter 4). However, Kotler (1997) suggests that not all competitive differences will create a strong competitive position; attempts to create differentiation should meet the following criteria:

➤ **Importance** – a difference should create a highly valued benefit for significant numbers of customers.
➤ **Distinctive and pre-emptive** – the difference cannot be imitated or performed better by others.
➤ **Superior** – the difference should provide a superior way for customers to obtain the benefit in question.
➤ **Communicable** – the difference should be capable of being communicated to customers and understood by them.
➤ **Affordable** – the target customers can afford to pay for the difference.
➤ **Profitable** – the difference will command a price adequate to make it profitable for the company.

One way of describing the outcome of the search for differences which matter to target customers, and how we perform them in a distinctive way, is the concept of the value proposition – the promise made to customers that encapsulates the position we wish to take compared to competitors.

For example, in the mid-1990s the Korean car company Daewoo gained 1 per cent of the British car market from a standing start in the fastest time ever achieved by any car manufacturer. There was nothing distinctive about the cars they sold – they were old General Motors designs produced under licence. What was distinctive was an explicit and clear value proposition to their target market segment. The four pillars of this company's distinctive value proposition were:

1. **Direct** – treating customers differently by dealing direct instead of through traditional distributors, and staying in touch throughout the purchase and use of the product.
2. **Hassle-free** – clear communications with customers, and no sales pressure or price haggling.
3. **Peace of mind** – all customers pay the same price, and many features traditionally sold as extras are included in the deal.
4. **Courtesy** – demonstrating respect for customer needs and preferences throughout the process.

Daewoo quickly established a strong competitive positioning in a specific segment of the car market on the basis of this proposition.

A competitive position may be built on any dimensions of product or service that produce customer benefits in the market, but an importance emphasis in positioning is that what matters is customer perceptions.

In fact, the term 'positioning' was brought to prominence by Al Ries and Jack Trout (1982) to describe the creative process whereby:

> Positioning starts with a product. A piece of merchandise, a service, a company, or even a person ... But positioning is not what you do to a product. Positioning is what you do to the mind of the prospect. That is, you position the product in the mind of the prospect.

The Ries and Trout approach to the 'battle for your mind' is highly oriented towards marketing communications and brand image, while as we have seen, competitive positioning is somewhat broader in recognizing the impact of every aspect of the market offering that is perceived by customers as important in creating distinctive value. One way of summarizing the underlying thinking is about focus on customer benefits and positioning in the customer's mind:

> You don't buy coal, you buy heat; you don't buy circus tickets, you buy thrills; you don't buy a paper, you buy news; you don't buy spectacles, you buy vision; you don't sell products, you create positions.

The importance of clear and strong competitive positioning is underlined by Kotler's (1997) warning of the major positioning errors which can undermine a company's marketing strategy:

➤ **Under-positioning** – when customers have only vague ideas about a company or its products, and do not perceive anything special about it, the product becomes an 'also-ran'.

➤ **Over-positioning** – when customers have too narrow an understanding of the company, product or brand: Mont Blanc sells pens that cost several thousand pounds, but it is important to that company that the consumer is aware that a Mont Blanc pen can also be purchased for under £100.

➤ **Confused positioning** – frequent changes and contradictory messages may simply confuse customers about a company's positioning: the indecisiveness of the retailer Sainsbury about whether or not to have a loyalty card to rival Tesco's launch of its card, and about its price level compared to others, has contributed to its loss of market leadership in the 1990s.

➤ **Doubtful positioning** – the claims made for the company, product or brand may simply not be accepted, whether or not they are true: the goal at British Home Stores to position that retail business as 'the first choice store for dressing the modern woman and family' failed in a market that remains dominated by Marks & Spencer.

In essence, positioning is concerned with understanding how customers compare alternative offerings on the market and building strategies that describe to the customer how the company's offering differs in important ways from those of existing or potential competitors. Together with market segmentation, competitive positioning is central to the development of effective marketing strategies (see chapter 13).

These characteristics of competitive positioning can be compared to the principles of market segmentation.

9.2 Principles of market segmentation

Two major features of modern markets are the extent to which they are capable of being segmented (because of growing differences between customers and their demands to be treated as individuals) and the existence of the vastly superior technologies of communication, distribution and production, which allow the pursuit of segmentation strategies. In some cases, this leads to 'micro-segmentation' or 'one-to-one marketing', in which each customer is treated as a different segment (see chapter 5).

Where there are differences in customer needs or wants, or in their attitudes and predispositions towards the offerings on the market, between groups or individuals in the market, then there are opportunities to segment the market, i.e. to subdivide the larger market into smaller groups (segments) which provide market targets.

The history of thinking about market segmentation can be traced to Wendell Smith (1956), who distinguished between strategies of product differentiation (applying promotional techniques to influence demand in favour of the product) and market segmentation (adjusting market offerings in various ways to more closely meet the requirements of different customers). Baker (1992) acknowledges this as the first coherent statement of a distinctive marketing view of market structure, representing a compromise between the economist's view of markets as single entities, and the behavioural scientist's focus on individual buyer differences. Seen in this light, segmentation is a logical extension of the marketing concept and market orientation (see chapter 1).

9.3 The underlying premises of market segmentation

Consider the underlying requirements for market segmentation and an overview of segmentation issues.

9.3.1 Underlying requirements for market segmentation

It is possible to describe three basic propositions which underpin market segmentation as a component of marketing strategy:

1. For segmentation to be useful, customers must differ from one another in some important respect, which can be used to divide the total market. If they were not different in some significant way, if they were totally homogeneous, then there would be no need or basis on which to segment the market.

However, in reality all customers differ in some respect. The key to whether a particular difference is useful for segmentation purposes lies in the extent to which the differences are related to different behaviour patterns (e.g. different levels of demand for the product or service, or different use/benefit requirements) or susceptibility to different marketing mix combinations (e.g. different product/service offerings, different media, messages, prices or distribution channels), i.e. whether the differences are important to how we develop a marketing strategy.

2. The operational use of segmentation usually requires that segment targets can be identified by measurable characteristics to enable their potential value as a market target to be estimated and for the segment to be identified. Crucial to utilizing a segmentation scheme to make better marketing decisions is the ability of the marketing strategist to evaluate segment attractiveness and the current or potential strengths the company has in serving a particular segment. Depending on the level of segmentation analysis, this may require internal company analysis or external market appraisal (see pp. 230–2 below). The external market evaluation of segments and selection as market targets is discussed in chapter 10.

3. The effective application of segmentation strategy also requires that selected segments be isolated from the remainder of the market, enabling them to be targeted with a distinct market offering. Where segments are not distinct they do not form a clear target for the company's marketing efforts.

For any segmentation scheme to be useful it must possess the above three characteristics.

9.3.2 Major issues in market segmentation

By way of overview, our general understanding of the issues to be addressed in studying and applying market segmentation falls into the four areas suggested by Piercy and Morgan (1993):

➤ the methodology of market segmentation;
➤ the criteria for testing segments as robust market targets;
➤ the strategic segmentation decision itself;
➤ the implementation of segmentation strategy in the company.

The methodology of market segmentation
The methodological tools available for use in developing segmentation schemes are concerned with two issues. First, there is the question of the choice of the variables or customer characteristics with which to segment the market – the 'bases' of market segmentation. Second, there is the related question of the procedures or techniques to apply to identify and evaluate the segments of the market. The bases for segmentation are considered in the next sections of this chapter, and the techniques for market segmentation analysis are discussed in chapter 10.

Testing the robustness of segments

If segments can be identified using the bases and techniques chosen, then there is the question of how they should be evaluated as prospective targets. In a classic paper, Frank *et al.* (1972) suggested that to provide a reasonable market target, a segment should be: measurable, accessible, substantial and unique in its response to marketing stimuli. These criteria remain the basis for most approaches (e.g. see Kotler, 1997). In fact, evaluating market segments may be more complex than this suggests (see p. 231).

Strategic segmentation decision

If the market is susceptible to segmental analysis and modelling, and attractive segments can be identified, then the decision faced is whether to use this as the basis for developing marketing strategies and programmes, and whether to target the entire market or concentrate on part of it. These issues of strategy are discussed in chapter 13.

Implementation of segmentation strategies

Finally, there is the question of the capabilities of the organization for putting a segmentation approach into effect, and indeed, the extent to which corporate characteristics should guide the segmentation approach in the first place. These questions are considered at the end of this chapter.

9.4 *Bases for segmenting markets*

Some of the major issues in market segmentation centre on the bases on which the segmentation should be conducted and the number of segments identifiable as targets in a particular market. The selection of the base for segmentation is crucial to gaining a clear picture of the nature of the market – the use of different bases can result in very different results. In fact, the process of segmentation and the creative selection of different segmentation bases can often help to gain new insights into old market structures which in turn may offer new opportunities – this is not merely a mechanical piece of statistical analysis.

In addition to choosing the relevant bases for segmentation, to make the segments more accessible to marketing strategy, the segments are typically described further on common characteristics. Segments formed, for example, on the basis of brand preference may be further described in terms of customer demographic and attitudinal characteristics to enable relevant media to be selected for promotional purposes and a fuller picture of the chosen segments to be built.

In the next section we examine the major bases used in consumer markets, and in the following section we turn to industrial and business-to-business markets.

9.5 *Segmenting consumer markets*

The variables used in segmenting consumer markets can be broadly grouped into three main classes:

➤ background customer characteristics,
➤ customer attitudes,
➤ customer behaviour.

The first two sets of characteristics concern the individual's predisposition to action, whereas the final set concerns actual behaviour in the marketplace.

9.5.1 Background customer characteristics for segmenting markets

Often referred to as classificatory information, background characteristics do not change from one purchase situation to another. They are customer-specific but not specifically related to his or her behaviour in the particular market of interest. Background characteristics can be classified along two main dimensions (see Figure 9.3).

The first dimension is the origin of the measures. The measures may have been taken from other disciplines and are hence not marketing-specific but believed to be related to marketing activity. Non-marketing-specific factors include demographic and socio-economic characteristics developed in the fields of sociology and demography. Alternatively they may have been developed specifically by marketing researchers and academics to solve marketing problems. Typically they have been developed out of dissatisfaction with traditional (sociological) classifications. Dissatisfaction with social class, as a predictor of marketing behaviour, for example, has led to the development of lifestyle segmentation and to the ACORN (A Classification of Residential Neighbourhoods) and related classification schemes.

	Objective measures		*Subjective measures*
Non-marketing-specific	**Demographics** Sex, age, geography, subculture **Socioeconomics** Occupation Income Education	P s y c h o g r a p h i c s	**Personality inventories**
Marketing-specific	**Consumer life cycle** **ACORN** **Media usage**		**Lifestyle**

Figure 9.3 **Background customer characteristics**

The second dimension to these characteristics is the way in which they are measured. Factors such as age or sex can be measured objectively, whereas personality and lifestyle (collectively termed 'psychographics') are inferred from often subjective responses to a range of diverse questions.

The commonest variables used are as follows.

Demographic characteristics

Measures such as age and gender of both purchasers and consumers have been one of the most popular methods for segmenting markets:

1. **Gender**: a basic approach to segmentation of the market for household consumables and for food purchases is to identify 'housewives' as a specific market segment. For marketing purposes 'housewives' can include both females and males who have primary responsibility for grocery purchase and household chores. This segmentation of the total potential market of, say, all adults will result in a smaller (around half the size) identified target. Many segmentation schemes use gender as a first step in the segmentation process, but then further refine their targets within the chosen gender category, e.g. by social class. In some markets, the most relevant variable is gender-preference, e.g. the 'gay' market for certain products and services.

2. **Age**: age has been used as a basic segmentation variable in many markets. The market for holidays is a classic example with holiday companies tailoring their products to specific age groups such as 'under 30s' or 'senior citizens'. In these segmentation schemes it is reasoned that there are significant differences in behaviour and product/service requirements between the demographic segments identified.

   The main reasons for the popularity of age and gender as segmentation variables have been the ease of measurement of the these characteristics (they can be objectively measured) and their usefulness for media selection purposes. Widely available syndicated media research studies present data on viewing and reading habits broken down by these characteristics. Matching media selected to segments described in these terms is, therefore, quite straightforward.

   Age may also combine with other characteristics like social class. For example, Taylor Nelson AGB analyzed the alcoholic drinks market into age/social class groups and linked this to drinks consumption (Grant, 1996):

   (a) *Downmarket/young* – favour alcopops and premium canned lagers.
   (b) *Upmarket/young* – preferences were for premium bottle lagers and cider.
   (c) *Downmarket/older* – favouring stout, and spirits like rum, brandy and whisky.
   (d) *Upmarket/older* – characteristic preferences for super premium lager and gin.

3. **Geographic location**: geographic segmentation may be a useful variable, particularly for small or medium-sized marketing operations which cannot hope to attack a widely dispersed market. Many companies, for example,

choose to market their products in their home country only, implicitly excluding world-wide markets from their targets. Within countries it may also be possible to select regional markets where the company's offerings and the market requirements are most closely matched. Haggis, for example, sells best in Scotland, while sales of jellied eels are most successful in the East End of London.

4. **Subculture**: each individual is a member of a variety of subcultures. These subcultures are groups within the overall society which have peculiarities of attitude or behaviour. For a subculture to be of importance for segmentation purposes, it is likely that membership of the subculture has to be relatively enduring and not transient, and that membership of the subculture is of central importance in affecting the individual's attitudes and/or ultimate behaviour.

   The major subcultures used for segmentation purposes are typically based on racial, ethnic, religious or geographic similarities. In addition subcultures existing within specific age groupings may be treated as distinct market segments. For example, targeting 'micro-communities' has become important in relationship marketing – one Canadian bank has focused to great effect on the tightly knit but affluent Filipino community in Canada (Svendsen, 1997).

The major drawback of all demographic characteristics discussed above as bases for segmenting markets is that they cannot be guaranteed to produce segments which are internally homogeneous but externally heterogeneous in ways that are directly relevant to the marketer. Within the same demographic classes there can be individuals who exhibit very different behavioural patterns and are motivated by quite different wants and needs. Similarly there may be significant and exploitable similarities in behaviour and motivations between individuals in different demographic segments. As a consequence a generally low level of correspondence between demographics and behaviour has been found in the academic marketing research literature. Despite these drawbacks, their relative ease of measurement makes them popular amongst marketing practitioners.

Socio-economic characteristics
Factors, such as income, occupation, terminal education age and social class have been popular with researchers for similar reasons to demographics: they are easy to measure and can be directly related back to media research for media selection purposes. More importantly, the underlying belief in segmenting markets by social class is that the different classes are expected to have different levels of affluence and to adopt different lifestyles. These lifestyles are, in turn, relevant to marketing-related activity, such as propensity to buy certain goods and services. Socio-economic measures are best seen in the use of social class groups.

Marketing researchers use several social class stratification schemes. In the UK the Market Research Society uses the standard scheme presented in Table 9.1.

For many marketing purposes the top two and bottom two classes are combined to give a four-group standard classification by social class: AB, C1, C2, DE. In the

Table 9.1 UK socio-economic classification scheme

Class name	Social status	Occupation of head of household
A	Upper-middle	Higher managerial, administrative or professional
B	Middle	Intermediate managerial, administrative or professional
C1	Lower-middle	Supervisors or clerical, junior managerial, administrative or professional
C2	Skilled working	Skilled manual workers
D	Working	Semi-skilled and unskilled manual
E	Those at lowest levels of subsistence	State pensioners or widows, casual or lower-grade workers

US several alternative social class schemes have been used for segmentation purposes (see Frank *et al.*, 1972). The most widely adopted, however, is that proposed by Warner (see Table 9.2).

Social class has been used as a surrogate for identifying the style of life that individuals are likely to lead. The underlying proposition is that consumers higher up

Table 9.2 The Warner index of status characteristics

Class name	Description	Consumption characteristics
Upper-upper	Elite social class with inherited social position	Expensive, irrelevant, put purchase decisions not meant to impress; conservative
Lower-upper	*Nouveau riche*; highly successful business and professional; position acquired through wealth	Conspicuous consumption to demonstrate wealth, luxury cars, large estates, etc.
Upper-middle	Successful business and professional	Purchases directed at projecting successful image
Lower-middle	White-collar workers, small businesspeople	Concerned with social approval; purchase decisions; conservative; home- and family-oriented
Upper-lower	Blue-collar workers, technicians, skilled workers	Satisfaction of family roles
Lower-lower	Unskilled labour, poorly educated, poorly off	Attraction to cheap, 'flashy', low-quality items; heavy exposure to TV

the social scale tend to spend a higher proportion of their disposable income on future satisfactions (such as insurance and investments) while those lower down the scale spend proportionately more on immediate satisfactions. As such, socio-economic class can be particularly useful in identifying segments in markets such as home purchase, investments, beer and newspapers.

The financial services industry makes extensive use of socio-economic groups for marketing, such as developing pensions and life assurance products aimed at particular social groups. One company is launching an occupational annuity to pay a higher pension to those in stressful or unhealthy jobs. Premiums and terms for private health insurance are partly determined by social class groupings (Gardner, 1997).

However, as with the demographic characteristics discussed above, it is quite possible that members of the same social class have quite different purchase patterns and reasons for purchase. Consider, for a moment, your peers – people you work with or know socially. The chances are they will be classified in the same social class as you. The chances are also that they will be attracted to different sorts of products motivated by different factors and make quite different brand choices.

Concern has been expressed amongst both marketing practitioners and academics that social class is becoming increasingly less useful as a segmentation variable. Lack of satisfaction with social class in particular and other non-marketing specific characteristics as segmentation variables has led to the development of marketing specific measures such as stage of customer life cycle, the ACORN classification system and the development of lifestyle research.

Consumer life cycle
Stage of the family life cycle, essentially a composite demographic variable incorporating factors such as age, marital status and family size, has been particularly useful in identifying the types of people most likely to be attracted to a product field (especially consumer durables) and when they will be attracted. The producers of baby products, for example, build mailing lists of households with newborn babies on the basis of free gifts given to mothers in maternity hospitals. These lists are dated and used to direct advertising messages for further baby, toddler and child products to the family at the appropriate time as the child grows.

Stage of family life cycle was first developed as a market segmentation tool by Wells and Gubar (1966) and has since been updated and modified by Murphy and Staples (1979) to take account of changing family patterns. The basic life cycle stages are presented in Table 9.3.

In some instances segmentation by life cycle can help directly with product design, as is the case with package holidays. In addition to using age as a segmentation variable, holiday firms target very specifically on different stages of the life cycle, from the Club Med emphasis on young singles, to Butlins family holidays and coach operators' holidays for senior citizens.

In the UK, the Research Services Ltd marketing research company has developed a segmentation scheme based on a combination of consumer life cycle,

Table 9.3 **Stages of the family life cycle**

Stage	Financial circumstances and purchasing characteristics
Bachelor stage Young, single, not living at parental home	Few financial burdens, recreation-oriented; holidays, entertainments outside home
Newly wed Young couples, no children	Better off financially, two incomes; purchase home, some consumer durables
Full nest I Youngest child under 6	Home purchasing peak; increasing financial pressures, may have only one income earner; purchase of household 'necessities'
Full nest II Youngest child over 6	Financial position improving; some working spouses
Full nest III Older married couples with dependent children	Financial position better still; update household products and furnishings
Empty nest I Older married couples no children at home	Home ownership peak; renewed interest in travel and leisure activities; buy luxuries
Empty nest II Older couples, no children at home, retired	Drastic cut in income; medical services bought
Solitary survivor Still in labour force	Income good, but likely to sell home
Solitary survivor Retired	Special needs for medical care, affection and security

occupation and income. The scheme, termed SAGACITY, defines four main life cycle stages (dependent, pre-family, family and late), two income levels (better off and worse off) and two occupational groupings (white-collar and blue-collar – ABC1 and C2DE). On the basis of these three variables twelve distinct SAGACITY groupings are identified with different aspirations and behaviour patterns (see Crouch and Housden, 1996).

ACORN and related classificatory systems
As a direct challenge to the socio-economic classification system the ACORN (A Classification Of Residential Neighbourhoods) system was developed by the CACI Market Analysis Group. The system is based on population census data and classi-

fies residential neighbourhoods into thirty-six types within twelve main groups (see Table 9.4). The groupings were derived from a clustering of responses to census data required by law on a ten-yearly basis. The groupings reflect neighbourhoods with similar characteristics.

Early uses of ACORN were by local authorities to isolate areas of inner city deprivation (the idea came from a sociologist working for local authorities), but was soon seen to have direct marketing relevance, particularly because the data base enabled post codes to be ascribed to each ACORN type. Hence its use particularly in direct mail marketing.

Other 'geodemographic' data sources are provided by such firms as Marketing Information Consultancy, Equifax Europe and The Data Consultancy (Cramp, 1996).

Personality characteristics
Personality characteristics are more difficult to measure than demographics or socio-economics. They are generally inferred from large sets of questions often involving detailed computational (multivariate) analysis techniques.

Several personality inventories have been used by segmentation researchers. Most notable are the Gordon Personal Profile (see Sparks and Tucker, 1971), the Edwards Personal Preference Schedule (see Alpert, 1972), the Cattell 16-Personality Factor Inventory (see, for example, Oxx, 1972) and the Jackson Personality Inventory (see Kinnear, Taylor and Ahmed, 1974). All were developed by psychologists for reasons far divorced from market segmentation studies and have, understandably, achieved only varied levels of success when applied to segmentation problems.

Perhaps the main value of personality measures lies in creating the background atmosphere for advertisements and, in some instances, package design and

---

Table 9.4 ACORN: a classification of residential neighbourhoods

ACORN group	Description
A	Agricultural areas
B	Modern family housing, higher incomes
C	Older housing of intermediate status
D	Poor quality older terraced housing
E	Better-off council estates
F	Less well-off council estates
G	Poorest council estates
H	Multiracial areas
I	High-status, non-family areas
J	Affluent suburban housing
K	Better-off retirement areas

branding. Research to date, however, primarily conducted in the US, has identified few clear relationships between personality and behaviour. In most instances personality measures are most likely to be of use for describing segments once they have been defined on some other basis. As with the characteristics discussed above, behaviour, and reasons for behaviour, in personality homogeneous segments may be diverse.

Lifestyle characteristics

In an attempt to make personality measures developed in the field of psychology more relevant to marketing decisions, lifestyle research was pioneered by advertising agencies in the US and the UK in the early 1970s. This research attempts to isolate market segments on the basis of the style of life adopted by their members. At one stage these approaches were seen as alternatives to the social class categories discussed above.

Lifestyle segmentation is concerned with three main elements: activities (such as leisure-time activities, sports, hobbies, entertainment, home activities, work activities, professional work, shopping behaviour, house work and repairs, travel and miscellaneous activities, daily travel, holidays, education, charitable work); interaction with others (such as self-perception, personality and self-ideal, role perceptions, as mother, wife, husband, father, son, daughter, etc., and social interaction, communications with others, opinion leadership); and opinions (on topics such as politics, social and moral issues, economic and business–industry issues and technological and environmental issues).

A typical study would develop a series of statements (in some instances over 200 have been used) and respondents asked to agree or disagree with them on a 5- or 7-point agree/disagree scale. Using factor analysis and cluster analysis groups of respondents are identified with similar activities, interests and opinions. Examples include the following:

➤ In classic studies, Segnit and Broadbent (1973) found six male and seven female lifestyle segments on the basis of responses to 230 statements. These have been used to segment markets by publishers of newspapers (such as the *Financial Times* and *Radio Times*) and manufacturers (Beechams used the technique successfully to segment the shampoo market in the mid-1970s).

➤ Martini advertising is directed at individuals on the basis of what lifestyle they would like to have. It appeals to 'aspirational lifestyle' segments.

➤ Ford Motor Company identifies four basic lifestyle segments for their cars: Traditionalists (who go for wood, leather and chrome); Liberals (keen on environmental and safety features); Life Survivors (who seek minimum financial risk by going for the cheapest options); and Adventurers (who actually like cars and want models to suit their own self-images) (*The Economist*, 30 September 1995).

➤ Marketing strategy at the House of Fraser department stores group relies on attracting three types of women clothes shoppers to the stores: the 'Follower of

Fashion', the 'Smart Career Mover' and the 'Quality Classic – The Woman of Elegance'. The company has turned its back on the 'Young Mum' and other buyers. Unfortunately, at present, House of Fraser products and merchandising do not attract the target segments (they tend to shop at House of Fraser only for the concession areas like Oasis, Alexon and Morgan) (Rankine, 1996).

The most significant advantages of lifestyle research are again for guiding the creative content of advertising. Because of the major tasks involved in gathering the data, however, it is unlikely that lifestyle research will supplant demographics as a major segmentation variable.

Summary of background customer characteristics
The background customer characteristics discussed above all examine the individual in isolation from the specific market of interest. While in some markets they may be able to discriminate between probable users and non-users of the product class, they can rarely explain brand choice behaviour. Members of the same segments based on background characteristics may behave differently in the marketplace for a variety of reasons. Similarly, members of different segments may be seeking essentially the same things from competing brands and could be usefully grouped together. While traditionally useful for the purposes of media selection and advertising atmosphere design, these characteristics are often too general in nature to be of specific value to marketers. They are essentially descriptive in nature. They describe who the consumer is, but they do not uncover the basic reasons why the consumer behaves as he or she does.

9.5.2. Customer attitudinal characteristics for segmenting markets

Attitudinal characteristics attempt to draw a causal link between customer characteristics and marketing behaviour. Attitudes to the product class under investigation and attitudes towards brands on the market have both been used as fruitful bases for market segmentation.

Benefit segmentation
Classic approaches (e.g. Haley, 1968, 1984) examine the benefits customers are seeking in consuming the product. Segmenting on the basis of benefits sought has been applied to a wide variety of markets such as banking, fast moving consumer products and consumer durables. The building society investment market, for example, can be initially segmented on the basis of the benefits being sought by the customers. Typical benefits sought include high rates of interest (for the serious investor), convenient access (for the occasional investor) and security (for the 'rainy day' investor).

Benefit segmentation takes the basis of segmentation right back to the underlying reasons why customers are attracted to various product offerings. As such it is perhaps the closest means yet to identifying segments on bases directly relevant to marketing decisions. Developments in techniques such as conjoint analysis make them particularly suitable for identifying benefit segments (Hooley, 1982).

Perceptions and preferences
A second approach to the study of attitudes is through the study of perceptions and preferences. Much of the work in the multidimensional scaling area (Green *et al.*, 1989) is primarily concerned with identifying segments of respondents who view the products on offer in a similar way (perceptual space segmentation) and require from the market similar features or benefits (preference segmentation). This approach to market segmentation is discussed further in chapter 10, where we are concerned with segmentation research.

Summary of attitudinal bases for segmentation
Segmentation on the basis of attitudes, both to the product class and the various brands on offer, can create a more useful basis for marketing strategy development than merely background characteristics. It gets closer to the underlying reasons for behaviour and uses them as the basis for segmenting the market. The major drawback of such techniques is that they require often costly primary research and sophisticated data analysis techniques.

9.5.3 Customer behavioural characteristics for segmenting markets

The most direct method of segmenting markets is on the basis of the behaviour of the consumers in those markets. Behavioural segmentation covers purchases, consumption, communication and response to elements of the marketing mix.

Purchase behaviour
Study of purchasing behaviour has centred on such issues as the time of purchase (early or late in the product's overall life cycle) and patterns of purchase (the identification of brand loyal customers):

➤ **Innovators**: because of their importance when new products are launched, innovators (those who purchase a product when it is still new) have received much attention from marketers. Clearly, during the launch of new products isolation of innovators as the initial target segment could significantly improve the product's or service's chances of acceptance on the market. Innovative behaviour, however, is not necessarily generalizable to many different product fields. Attempts to seek out generalized innovators have been less successful than looking separately for innovators in a specific field. Generalizations seem most relevant when the fields of study are of similar interest.
➤ **Brand loyalty**: variously defined, brand loyalty has also been used as a basis for segmentation. While innovators are concerned with initial purchase, loyalty patterns are concerned with repeat purchase. As such they are more applicable

to repeat purchase goods than to consumer durables, though they have been used in durables markets (see the example below). As with innovative behaviour, research has been unable to identify consumers who exhibit loyal behaviour over a wide variety of products. Loyalty, like innovativeness, is specific to a particular product field.

Volkswagen, the German automobile manufacturer, has used loyalty as a major method for segmenting its customer markets. It divides its customers into the following categories: First Time Buyers; Replacement Buyers – (a) Model-loyal replacers, (b) Company-loyal replacers, and (c) Switch replacers. These segments are used to analyze performance, market trends and for forecasting purposes.

Consumption behaviour

Purchasers of products and services are not necessarily the consumers, or users, of those products or services. Examination of usage patterns and volumes consumed (as in the heavy user approach) can pinpoint where to focus marketing activity. There are dangers, however, in focusing merely on the heavy users. They are, for example, already using the product in quantity and therefore may not offer much scope for market expansion. Similarly they will either be current company customers or customers of competitors.

Cook and Mindak (1984) have shown that the heavy user concept is more useful in some markets than in others. In the soap market they note that heavy users of soap account for 75 per cent of purchases. However, heavy users account for nearly half the population and constitute a very diverse group. By contrast Bourbon whiskey is consumed by around 20 per cent of adults only, and the heavy users account for 95 per cent of consumption, making this a much tighter target market.

In the latter case brand loyalty patterns may be set and competition could be fierce. Companies may be better advised to research further the light or non-users of the product to find out why they do not consume more of the product. In the growth stage of the product life cycle the heavy user segment may well be attractive, but when the market reaches maturity it may make more sense to try to extend the market by mopping up extra potential demand in markets that are not adequately served by existing products.

Product and brand usage has a major advantage over many other situation-specific segmentation variables in that it can be elicited, in the case of many consumer products, from secondary sources. The 'heavy users' of beer, for example, can be identified through the Target Group Index (TGI) (see chapter 6) and their demographic and media habits profiled. For this main reason consumption is one of the most popular bases for segmenting consumer markets in the UK.

Communication behaviour

A further behavioural variable used in consumer segmentation studies has been the degree of communication with others about the product of interest.

Opinion leaders can be particularly influential in the early stages of the product life cycle. Recording companies, for example, recognize the influence that disc jockeys have on the record-buying public and attempt to influence them with free records and other inducements to play their records. In many fields, however, identifying opinion leaders is not so easy. As with innovators, opinion leaders tend to lead opinion only in their own interest areas. A further problem with satisfying opinion leaders is that they tend to have fairly strong opinions themselves and can often be a very heterogeneous group (the 'pop' disc jockeys providing a good example).

In addition to information-giving behaviour (as displayed by opinion leaders) markets could be segmented on the basis of information-seeking behaviour. The information seekers may be a particularly attractive segment for companies basing their strategy on promotional material with a heavy information content.

Response to elements of the marketing mix
The use of elasticities of response to changes in marketing-mix variables as a basis for segmentation is particularly attractive as it can lead to more actionable findings, indicating where marketing funds can best be allocated. Identifying, for example, the deal-prone consumer or the advertising-responsive segment has immediate appeal. There are, however, methodological problems in research to identify factors such as responsiveness to changes in price.

Relationship-seeking characteristics
A related characteristic for segmentation which is attracting some attention in the light of the move towards relationship marketing (see chapter 15) is the relationship requirements of customers (Piercy, 1997). One initial model suggests that the relationship-seeking characteristics of customers differ in the type of relationship customers want with suppliers (for example, long-term versus short-term and transactional) and the intimacy customers want in the relationship (for example, close or distant). This suggests the potential for segmenting markets into such groups as the following, and linking this to other variables:

➤ **Relationship seekers,** who want a close long-term relationship with the supplier or retailer.
➤ **Relationship exploiters,** who want only a short-term relationship with the supplier, but are happy with a close relationship, which they will exploit for any advantages on offer.
➤ **Loyal buyers** – those who want a long-term relationship, but at a distance.
➤ **Arm's-length transaction customers,** who do not want close relationships with suppliers and will shop around for the best deal because they see no value in a long-term relationship.

An example of an integrated study of consumer characteristics on a global scale is work done by the US agency Roper Starch (Shermach, 1995). International business has much interest in whether consumer segments cut across national boundaries and may be more useful than traditional geographical approaches to planning marketing. The study identified the following segments from 40,000 respondents in 40 countries:

➤ **Deal-makers** – well-educated, aged in the early 30s, with average affluence and employment (29 per cent of the sample).
➤ **Price-seekers** – a high proportion of retirees and lowest education level with an average level of affluence and more females than males (23 per cent of the sample).
➤ **Brand loyalists** – mostly male, aged in mid-30s, with average education and employment, and the least affluent group (23 per cent of the sample).
➤ **Luxury innovators** – the most educated and affluent shoppers, mostly male in professional and executive employment, they seek new, prestigious brands (21 per cent of the sample).

The proportions of consumers in these groups varied in interesting ways across the geographic areas: deal-makers predominate in the US, Asia, Latin America and the Middle East; price-seekers exist mainly in the competitive developed markets like Europe and Japan. Although producing only stereotypes, the study suggests that consumer behavioural and purchase characteristics may be stronger predictors of purchase behaviour than the traditional country-market definitions used in export and international marketing.

Summary of behavioural bases for segmentation
Many variables have been tested as bases for consumer segmentation, ranging from behaviour, to attitudes to background characteristics. The most often used characteristics are product and brand usage and demographics/socio-economics, primarily because of the ease of obtaining this sort of data from secondary sources. Ultimately, however, for a segmentation scheme to be useful to marketing management it should seek not only to describe differences in consumers, but also to explain them. In this respect attitudinal segmentation can offer better prospects.

9.6 *Segmenting industrial markets*

As with consumer markets, a wide variety of factors has been suggested for segmenting industrial markets, but in fact, industrial segmentation variables can be considered under the same headings as those for consumer markets:

➤ background company characteristics,
➤ attitudinal characteristics,
➤ behavioural characteristics.

It should be noted, however, that market segmentation is substantially less well-developed in industrial marketing than consumer marketing, which may affect both the acceptability of different approaches to companies (see pp. 230–2 below) and the availability of information and support to use a particular approach. It should also be noted that in business-to-business marketing, it is far more common to find a one-to-one relationship between supplier and customer. In this situation, the segmentation approach may best be applied inside the customer organization. The segmentation structure below follows the model developed in Shapiro and Bonoma (1990).

9.6.1 Background company characteristics

Demographic characteristics of companies can be a useful starting point for industrial segmentation. Indeed, they characterize the approaches most commonly used by industrial marketing companies. Factors that can be considered here include demographics like industry type, customer size and location, but also operating variables like customer technology and capabilities, different purchasing policies and situational factors like product application.

Industry type
Factors such as the Standard Industry Classification (SIC) provide a first stage of analysis, both for identifying target industries and subdividing them into groups of companies with different needs or different approaches to buying. This may be the basis for vertical marketing to industry sectors. Retailers and hospitals, for example, both buy computers, but they have different applications and different buying strategies. ICL as a computer company has always lagged behind IBM and other international competitors. None the less, the ICL strategy of vertical marketing to industry groups was highly effective against international competitors – a decade after the strategy of vertical marketing to the retail industry was introduced, ICL computer equipment can be seen as the point-of-sale in the retail outlets of major chains throughout the world.

Company size
Size may also be highly significant, if, for instance, small companies have needs or buying preferences which are distinctly different from those of larger companies. Typical measures would be variables like number of employees and sales turnover. Size may be very significant because it impacts on issues like volume requirements, average order size, sales and distribution coverage costs and customer bargaining power, which may alter the attractiveness of different segments as targets. Company size may be analyzed alongside other demographics. Companies, for example, selling ingredients for paint manufacture in the UK could initially segment the market by SIC to identify paint manufacturers, then by size of company as indicated by number of employees (there are only seven companies employing more than 750 employees and they together account for over 60 per cent of the paint market).

Customer location
The geographic location of customers may be a powerful way of segmenting the market for an industrial product for several reasons. Domestically location will impact on sales and distribution costs and competitive intensity may vary if there

are strong local competitors in some regions. Product demand may vary also – the demand for chemicals for water softening in operating cooling equipment in factories will vary according to local water hardness conditions. Internationally, product preferences may also be different by location – medical diagnostic products sell to the National Health Service in the UK, but to private testing agencies and medical practices in the US, and to hospital laboratories in the developing world, all of whom display very different product and price requirements.

Company technology
The customer's stage of technology development will impact directly on its manufacturing and product technology, and hence on its demand for different types of product. Traditional factories operating mixed technologies and assembly methods require different product and sub-assembly inputs (e.g. test equipment, tooling, components) compared to the automated production unit. High-technology businesses may require very different distribution methods — Tesco requires suppliers to have the capability to co-operate in electronic stock control and cross-docking to avoid retail stockholding. Increasingly, high-technology firms require that their suppliers are integrated to their computer systems for all stages of the purchase process.

Customer capabilities
Industrial customers may differ significantly in their internal strengths and weaknesses, and hence their demand for different types of product and service. For example, in the chemicals industry customers are likely to differ in their technical competencies – some will depend on their suppliers for formulation assistance and technical support far more than others. For many years, in the computer business Digital Equipment specialized in selling minicomputers to customers who were able to develop their own software and systems, and did not need the full-service offering of IBM and others: they targeted a segment on the basis of the customers' technical strength in computing.

Purchasing organization
How customers organize purchasing may also identify important differences between customers. For example, centralized purchasing may require suppliers to have the capability to operate national or international account management, while decentralized purchasing may require more extensive field sales operations. Depending on a supplier's own strengths and weaknesses, the purchasing organization type may be a significant way of segmenting the market. IBM, for example, has always maintained a strong position in companies with a centralized Information Technology (IT) department, while other suppliers have focused on companies where IT is less centralized.

Power structures
The impact of which organizational units have greatest influence may also be effective in segmenting a market to identify targets matching a supplier's strengths.

Digital (in the computer business) traditionally targeted engineering-led customers, where its strengths in engineering applications gave it a competitive edge.

Purchasing policies
The way different customers approach purchasing may also be a source of targeting information. Customers might divide, for example, into: those who want a lease-based deal versus those who want to purchase; those with affirmative action policies versus those dominated by price issues; those who want single supply sources versus those who want to dual-source important supplies; public sector and similar organizations where bidding is obligatory versus those preferring to negotiate price; those actively pursuing reductions in their supplier base compared to others. Indeed, the model proposed above (see pp. 220–1) of the customer's relationship requirements as a basis for segmenting may be even more useful in the industrial market, where the demand for partnership between suppliers and customers characterizes many large companies' approaches to purchasing.

Product application
The product application can have a major influence on the purchase process and criteria and hence supplier choices. The requirements for a small motor used in intermittent service for a minor application in an oil refinery will differ from the requirements for a small motor in continuous use for a critical process.

9.6.2 Attitudinal characteristics

It is possible also to segment industrial markets on the basis of the benefits being sought by the purchasers. As we saw, benefit segmentation in the consumer market is the process of segmenting the market in terms of the underlying reasons why customers buy, focusing particularly on differences in why customers buy. Its strength is that it is segmentation-based on customer needs. In the industrial market, the same logic applies to the purchasing criteria of different customers and product applications (see above).

This may be reflected, for example, in urgency of order fulfilment – the urgency of a customer's need to keep a plant in operation or to solve a problem for its own customers may change both the purchase process and the criteria used. Urgent replacements may be bought on the basis of availability, not price. A chemical plant needing to replace broken pipe fittings will pay a premium price for a supplier's applications engineering, flexible manufacturing capacity, speed of delivery and installation skills, while a plant buying pipe fittings to be held in reserve would behave quite differently.

One corporate bank struggled to find a way of segmenting the UK market for corporate financial services; they concluded that the most insightful approach was to examine their customers' own strategies as a predictor of financial service product need and purchasing priorities.

An added complication in industrial markets, however, is the decision-making unit (see chapter 6). For many industrial purchases decisions are made or influenced by a group of individuals rather than a single purchaser. Different members of the DMU will often have different perceptions of what the benefits are, both to their organization and to themselves.

In the purchase of hoists, for example, the important benefit to a user may be lightness and ease of use, whereas the purchasing manager may be looking for a cheaper product to make his purchasing budget go further. Architects specifying installations for new plant may perceive greater benefit in aesthetically designed hoists and maintenance personnel may look for easy maintenance as a prime benefit.

Benefit segmentation is at the centre, however, of conventional wisdom on industrial selling which emphasizes selling benefits rather than features in any product or service. In communicating with the different members of the DMU different benefits may be emphasized for each.

9.6.3 Behavioural characteristics

Behavioural issues relevant to segmenting industrial markets may include: buyers' personal characteristics and product/brand status and volume.

Buyers' personal characteristics
Although constrained by company policies and needs, industrial products are bought by people in just the same way that consumer products are. Industrial goods markets can be segmented by issues like:

➤ **Buyer–seller similarity** – compatibility in technology, corporate culture or even company size may be a useful way of distinguishing between customers.
➤ **Buyer motivation** – purchasing officers may differ in the degree to which they shop around and look at numerous alternative suppliers, and dual-source important products and services, as opposed to relying on informal contacts for information and remaining loyal to existing personal contacts.
➤ **Buyer risk perceptions** – the personal style of individual, intolerance for ambiguity, self-confidence and status within the company may also provide significant leverage.

For example, for many years in the computer industry IBM focused on IT buyers in major corporates, providing training information and career development support, to build the 'IBM closed shop' where other suppliers were largely excluded.

Product/brand status and volume
The users of a particular product, brand or supplier may have important things in common that can make them a target. For example, customers may differ in the rate and extent of the adoption of new safety equipment in plants. Companies loyal to a specific competitor may be targeted – for instance, to attack that competitor's

weaknesses in service or product. Current customers may be a different segment from prospective customers or lost customers.

High-volume product users may be different from medium and low users in how they purchase. Even more than in consumer markets the 80/20 rule (80 per cent of sales typically being accounted for by only 20 per cent of customers) can dominate an industrial market. Identifying the major purchasers for products and services through volume purchased can be particularly useful. Also of interest may be the final use to which the product or service is put. Where, for example, the final consumer can be identified, working backwards can suggest a sensible segmentation strategy.

The paint market, for example, can be segmented at various levels. At the first level it can be divided into 'decorative paints', mainly used on buildings, and 'industrial paints', used in manufactured products. In 1982 general industrial paints by volume represented 24 per cent of the market, the automobile industry 14 per cent, professional decorative 42 per cent and DIY decorative 22 per cent. Demand for vehicle paints relates to automobile sales (derived demand) and relates closely to demand in this market. In the general industrial paints sector there are various specialist segments such as marine coatings. Here ultimate product use dictates the type of paint and its properties and is the basic method for segmentation.

9.6.4 Summary of bases for segmenting industrial markets

The segmentation bases available for industrial marketing follow industrial buying behaviour as those in consumer marketing follow consumer behaviour. Because of the presence, however, of particularly large individual customers in many industrial markets usage-based segmentation is often employed. For smaller companies geographic segmentation may be attractive, limiting their markets to those that are more easily served. Ultimately, however, in industrial and consumer markets the basic rational for segmentation is that groups of buyers exist with different needs or wants (benefits sought) and it is segmentation on the basis of needs and wants that offers the closest approach to implementing the marketing concept.

9.7 Identifying and describing market segments

It will be clear from the above that the first task the manager faces is to decide on what bases to segment the market. If product usage or background characteristics are selected in many markets the segmentation can be accomplished from secondary sources (e.g. from TGI or AGB/TCA in consumer markets, or from SIC or Kompass in industrial markets). Where segmentation is based on attitudes, however, there will often be insufficient data available from secondary sources. In these cases primary research will be necessary.

A typical primary research segmentation study could include initial qualitative research to identify major benefits to users and purchasers of the product or service under consideration. This would be followed by quantitative research to estimate the size of the potential segments and to describe them further in terms of other background characteristics. This methodological approach is described in the seminal work by Haley (1968).

9.7.1 First-order and second-order segmentation

There is a frequent misconception amongst marketing managers as to what constitutes a market segment.

In consumer marketing, in particular, many managers will describe the segmentation of their market and their selected market targets in terms of customer background characteristics. Thus, for example, a marketer of quality wines might describe the segmentation of the market in terms of social class, the prime target being the ABC1 social classes. From our discussion above, however, it can be seen that this way of segmenting the market is rigorous only if all members of the ABC1 group purchase quality wine for the same reasons and in the same way. Where use/benefits of wine purchase differ substantially within a given social class, there is the opportunity to segment the market in a more fundamental way.

In reality, the most fundamental way of segmenting markets is the market-oriented approach of grouping together customers who are looking for the same benefits in using the product or service. All other bases for segmenting markets are really an approximation of this. The wine marketer assumes that all ABC1s have similar benefit needs from the wines they purchase. Hence use/benefit segmentation can be referred to as *first-order segmentation*. Any attempt to segment a market should commence by looking for different use/benefit segments.

Within identified use/benefit segments, however, there could be large numbers of customers with very different backgrounds, media habits, levels of consumption, and so on. Particularly where there are many offerings attempting to serve the same use/benefit segment concentration on subsegments within the segment can make sense. Subsegments, for example, who share common media habits, can form more specific targets for the company's offerings. Further segmentation within use/benefit segments can be termed *second-order segmentation*. Second-order segmentation is used to improve the ability of the company to tailor the marketing mix within a first-order segment.

In the wine example the marketing manager may have identified a first-order segmentation in terms of the uses to which the wine was being put (e.g. as a meal accompaniment, as a home drink, as a social drink, as a cooking ingredient). The quality level of the wine might suggest use in the first segment as a meal accompaniment. Further research would then reveal within this segment further benefit requirements (e.g. price bands individual customers are prepared to consider, character of the wine preferred, etc.).

Having further refined the target through matching the company's offerings to specific customer group requirements the marketer may still find a wide variety of potential customers for his wines. Within the identified first order segment subsegments based on demographic characteristics could be identified (e.g. AB social class, aged 35–55, male purchaser) enabling a clearer refinement of the marketing strategy.

9.8 *The benefits of segmenting markets*

There are a number of important benefits that can be derived from segmenting a market, which can be summarized in the following terms:

➤ Segmentation is a particularly useful approach to marketing for the smaller company. It allows target markets to be matched to company competencies (see chapter 5), and makes it more likely that the smaller company can create a defensible niche in the market.

➤ It helps to identify gaps in the market, i.e. unserved or underserved segments. These can serve as targets for new product development or extension of the existing product or service range.

➤ In mature or declining markets it may be possible to identify specific segments that are still in growth. Concentrating on growth segments when the overall market is declining is a major strategy in the later stages of the product life cycle.

➤ Segmentation enables the marketer to match the product or service more closely to the needs of the target market. In this way a stronger competitive position can be built.

➤ The dangers of not segmenting the market when competitors do should also be emphasized. The competitive advantages noted above can be lost to competitors if the company fails to take advantage of them. A company practising a mass marketing strategy in a clearly segmented market against competitors operating a focused strategy can find itself falling between many stools.

9.9 *Implementing market segmentation*

It should also be noted that there is evidence that companies often struggle with the implementation of segmentation-based strategies, and fail to achieve the potential benefits outlined above (see e.g. Piercy and Morgan, 1993; Dibb and Simkin, 1994) – this is the difference between segmentation as a normative model and as a business reality (Danneels, 1996).

9.9.1 **The scope and purpose of market segmentation**

There is growing recognition that conventional approaches may pay insufficient attention to identifying the scope of market segmentation (Plank, 1985). Indeed, a seminal paper by Yoram Wind (1978) proposed that in selecting segmentation approaches it is necessary to distinguish between segmentation that has the goal of gaining a general understanding of the market and for positioning studies, and segmentation concerned with marketing programme decisions in new product launches, pricing, advertising and distribution. These are all valid and useful applications in segmentation analysis, but they are fundamentally different.

9.9.2 Strategic, managerial and operational levels of segmentation

One approach to making the scope of market segmentation clearer is to distinguish between different levels of segmentation, in the way shown in Figure 9.4 (Piercy and Morgan, 1993).

This approach is similar to the first-order and second-order segmentation distinction made above, but goes further in relating the levels of segmentation to organizational issues as well as customer issues. The nature of the different levels of segmentation can be described as follows:

➤ **Strategic segmentation** is related to management concerns for strategic intent and corporate mission, based on product/service uses and customer benefits.
➤ **Managerial segmentation** is concerned primarily with planning and allocating resources like budgets and personnel to market targets.
➤ **Operational segmentation** focuses on the issue of aiming marketing communications and selling efforts into the distribution channels which reach and influence market targets (and their subdivisions).

These differences are important to gaining insight into what segmentation can contribute to building marketing strategy and competitive positioning, but also to understanding the sources of implementation problems with segmentation-based strategies.

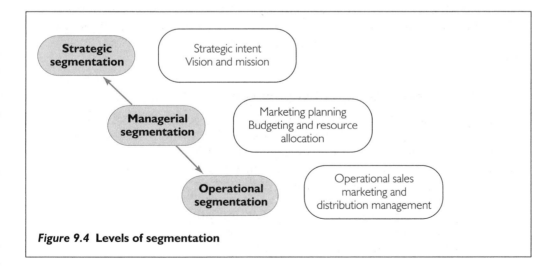

Figure 9.4 **Levels of segmentation**

For example, when the manager responsible for marketing replacement car exhausts to car owners groups his customers in terms of their fears, ignorance and transport dependence, rather than their requirements for different product specifications and engineering, he or she is concerned with creating a new understanding of the market (strategic segmentation), not a model for the detailed application of marketing resources (operational segmentation).

When British Rail identified customer 'types' as the 'realistic', the 'fatalistic' and the 'analytic', it is defining broad targets for different marketing strategies, not measurable customer niches (Elgie, 1990).

When the corporate banker looks at the corporate banking market in terms of the strategic financial services needs of customers, based on their own corporate strategies (Carey, 1989), the goal is to create a framework for strategy, not a mechanism for advertising and salesforce allocation.

On the other hand, when advertisers and sales managers describe buyers in terms of socio-economic groups, geographic location or industrial sector, they are concerned with the effective targeting of advertising, sales promotion, selling and distribution resources, rather than describing customer benefit-based market segments. Market segmentation studies describing consumer groups in terms of their media behaviour – for example, as 'mainstream media rejecters', 'genteel media grazers', 'thirty-somethings', and so on (Laing, 1991) – are concerned with operational effectiveness, not strategic positioning.

Confusing these very different roles for segmentation may be why segmentation is sometimes seen as a failure in organizations:

> Failed segmentation efforts tend to fall into one of two categories: the marketer-dominated kind, with little data to support its recommendations, or the purely statistical type that identifies many consumer differences that aren't germane to the company's objectives. (Young, 1996)

The implication is that clarifying the role and purpose of an approach to segmentation may be important to avoid unrealistic expectations. However, it is clear that segmentation-based strategies do sometimes fail at the implementation stage.

9.9.3 Sources of implementation problems

The recognition of implementation problems with segmentation-based strategies may be traced back over the years: Wind (1978) noted that little was known about translating segment research into marketing strategies; Young et al. (1978) accused marketers of being preoccupied with segmentation technique rather than actionability; Hooley (1980) blamed segmentation failures on the use of analytical techniques for their own sake and poor communication between managers and marketing researchers. Shapiro and Bonoma (1990) wrote: 'Much has been written about the strategy of segmentation, little about its implementation, management and control', and this would still seem a valid conclusion.

Piercy and Morgan (1993) attempted to catalogue the sources of implementation failure with segmentation-based strategies, and these issues provide a further screening device for evaluating the suitability of a segmentation model generated through market research. Issues to assess include the following:

➤ **Organization structure**: companies tend to organize into functional departments and sub-units of one kind or another, depending on their task allocation and how they deal with the outside world. A customer benefits approach to establishing market targets may cut across these internal divisions – they may not 'fit' with the jurisdiction of departments or regional organizations for sales and marketing. Segment targets which fall between departments and regions may be neglected and lack 'ownership', and the strategies built around them will fail. We need to map carefully how segment targets will match the internal organization structure.

➤ **Internal politics**: Young (1996) argues that strategic segmentation is essentially a cross-functional activity, requiring expertise and involvement by many functional specialists. If functions cannot collaborate or work together because people are vying for power and withholding their knowledge and expertise, the segmentation strategy is likely to fail. If our segmentation-based strategy relies on internal collaboration and co-operation, we need to be sure this can be achieved or the strategy will fail.

➤ **Corporate culture**: in some circumstances customer benefit segmentation is unacceptable to people inside an organization, because it is not how they understand the world. Organizations dominated by strong professional groups frequently have struggles with customer benefit segments – examples are traditional financial service companies and professional service firms like lawyers and accountants. The problem may be overcoming bankers' preferences for 'prudent banking' to develop customer focus.

➤ **Information and reporting**: novel segmentation schemes may not fit with existing information systems and reporting systems. This may mean it is difficult to evaluate the worth of segment targets, or to allocate responsibilities and monitor performance in doing business with them.

➤ **Decision-making processes**: if segmentation schemes identify new market targets which are not recognized in plans (they are not currently part of the served market, they are spread across existing segment targets for which responsibility has been allocated, or they are subsumed within an existing segment), then they may be ignored in the planning process and when plans are implemented. Similarly, segment targets which are not recognized by existing resource allocation processes may face difficulty in getting a marketing budget. We should examine carefully how a new segmentation approach can be integrated with planning and budgeting and in evaluation systems.

➤ **Corporate capabilities**: it is easy for marketing researchers and analysts to develop attractive market targets, where a company has little basis for

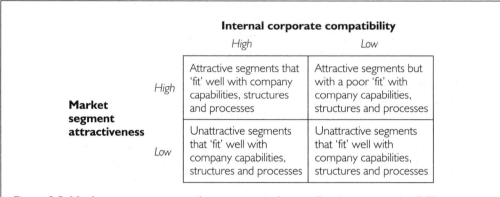

Figure 9.5 **Market segment attractiveness versus internal company compatibility**

achieving a competitive advantage simply because it lacks the capabilities for dealing with this type of customer (see chapter 5).

➤ **Operational systems**: segmentation strategy may fail because it underestimates the problems faced at the operational level in translating segmentation strategy into effective reality – Can salespeople deal with this target customer? Do we have access to the distribution channels we need? Do we have the expertise to develop and operate segment-based advertising and promotion? Do we have market research organized around the segment targets so we can identify them, measure opportunities and evaluate progress? Do we have the technical facilities to price differently to different customer types if this is required? We should look very carefully at the operational capabilities we have in sales, advertising, promotion and distribution and question their ability to adapt to a new segmentation-based strategy.

Many of these issues are covert and hidden inside the organization, yet to ignore them is to place the strategy at risk. One proposal is that in addition to the conventional evaluation of market targets, each potential target should be tested for internal compatibility, as suggested in Figure 9.5.

This analysis may suggest that some market targets are unattractive because the have a poor 'fit' with the company's structures and processes, or even that the company is not capable of implementing a segmentation-based strategy at the present time, or it may identify the areas that need to be changed if the segment target is to be reached effectively.

9.10 *Conclusions*

In increasingly fragmented markets, marketers in both consumer and industrial markets are turning more and more to segmentation methods to identify prime market targets. In approaching market segmentation, companies must confront the sometimes quite sophisticated methodology of segmentation, test the market targets identified and make the strategic segmentation decision of how to use a segmentation model in developing its market strategy.

This suggests that one of the major decisions faced is: 'What bases to segment on?' We have seen that there are a great many potential bases for segmentation in consumer and industrial markets, and for product and service (and non-profit) marketing.

Arguably, the segmentation approach closest to extending the marketing concept is use/benefit segmentation suggested originally some thirty years ago by Haley (1968). While it does require considerable primary investigation, understanding the benefits customers derive in buying and/or consuming products and services is central to designing an integrated marketing strategy.

There are substantial potential benefits from basing marketing strategy on rigorous market segmentation. However, the organizational issues impacting on the implementation of segmentation-based strategies should also be evaluated to test for the internal compatibility of segment targets and the costs of organizational change which may be involved in segmentation-based marketing strategies.

The next chapter, on segmentation research, concentrates on the methodology for developing bases for segmentation.

CHAPTER 10

Segmentation and positioning research

... researchers are anxious to find a magic formula that will profitably segment the market in all cases and under all circumstances. As with the medieval alchemist looking for the philosopher's stone, this search is bound to end in vain.
Joel P. Baumwoll (1974)

Introduction

While the last chapter was concerned with the underlying concepts and principles for the key strategic issues of competitive positioning and market segmentation, the subject of this chapter is the research and modelling techniques which can be applied to evaluate these issues operationally.

The first section of the chapter focuses on segmentation research, and in particular the critical questions of whether or not to pursue a segment-based approach, and if so whether these are based *a priori* on some predefined segmentation scheme or developed *post-hoc* on the basis of creative, empirical research. The second part of the chapter turns to positioning research, which may often be carried out in parallel to segmentation research, applying both qualitative techniques such as focus groups and depth interviews, together with quantitative modelling methods such as perceptual mapping through multidimensional scaling.

The process of identifying potential market targets can be one of the most creative aspects of marketing. There is no single 'right way' to segment any market. Different competitors may adopt different approaches in the same market. All may be intrinsically valid, but each may lead to a different conceptualization of the market, and subsequently a different marketing approach and a different strategy. The creative aspect of segmentation research lies in finding a new way to conceptualize your market, a way that will offer some competitive advantage over the ways competitors choose.

Two broad approaches to segmentation research are typically pursued. First, the *a priori* approach. This entails using an 'off-the-peg' segmentation scheme, such as socio-economic or geodemographic classifications. Central to this approach is that the segmentation scheme is known in advance and the number of segments predetermined by the scheme chosen. By its very nature *a priori* segmentation uses schemes that are in the public domain and hence also available to competitors.

The second approach is a *post-hoc* or *cluster-based* approach to segmentation. In this approach the final segmentation scheme is not known in advance, nor is the

234

appropriate number of segments. The criteria on which to segment are defined in advance, but may typically be multidimensional (e.g. usage and attitude data). Data are then collected on these criteria (through the use of qualitative and/or quantitative marketing research) and analyzed to identify underlying patterns or structure. The segmentation scheme emerges from the data analysis reflecting patterns identified in response. The data analysis itself is part-science (using statistical techniques) and part-art (employing judgement in which criteria to include and how to interpret the output). In this way the segmentation scheme emerging is likely to be unique to the specific analysis. This offers potential for looking at the market afresh and identifying new opportunities not necessarily seen by competitors. It also, of course, requires that any segmentation scheme created be rigorously tested to ensure that it is not merely an artefact of the specific data-set or the analytical technique employed.

Following the discussion of segmentation approaches, the chapter goes on to discuss alternative methods for researching and presenting positions in the marketplace. Two broad approaches are discussed. First, the use of *qualitative* research methods to uncover brand, product and company images. These approaches are particularly popular in the development of advertising programmes. Second, *quantitative* approaches to modelling positions are explored, from simple profiling on semantic or similar scales, through the more complex modelling available through multidimensional scaling and correspondence analysis techniques.

To segment or not to segment? That is the question

Although a central part of most marketing programmes, there are circumstances in which segmentation may be inappropriate. It could be, for example, that customer needs and wants in a particular market are essentially homogeneous, and hence similar offerings can be made to appeal across the whole market, or that the costs associated with pursuing individual market segments with tailored marketing programmes outweigh their longer-term economic value.

A company following a segmented approach has either to choose a single market segment at which to aim, and therefore have a marketing mix which is inappropriate for other customers, or develop a series of marketing mixes appropriate for customer segments with different needs. Within British retailing the two approaches have clearly been used by Next, which expanded its retailing chains to cater for more and more needs of young professionals, and the Burton Group, which has used the differently positioned Top Shops, Evans, Harvey Nichols stores, etc. to appeal to a variety of segments.

Both these approaches have limitations depending on the company's longer-term objectives. A single-focus company has limitations to its potential because the market segment itself is limited. If the company has expansion and growth objectives, these may be constrained by the size of its target market. This, of course, would be less of a problem to a small- or medium-sized company following the dictum *think small – stay small*. A company taking the multiple segment approach may face diseconomies in managing, supplying and promoting in a different way to each of the segments it has chosen. In some cases an economic alternative is to use an undifferentiated mix designed to appeal to as many segments as possible. The company does not fine-tune its offering to any one segment but hopes to attract a sufficient number of customers from all segments with one mix. The company can, therefore, benefit from economies of scale in a simple operation but may be damaged by the 'sameness of the mix' not appealing to the customers in each segment completely, or by better targeted competitors.

The appropriateness of segmenting or not segmenting depends on economies of scale, the cost of developing separate marketing mixes and the homogeneity of needs of different markets – issues that are pursued further in chapter 12. Such are the similarities in demand for petroleum, for example, that the products being supplied by competitors converge as they all seek to develop a mix with broad market appeal. Certainly segments do exist, but not of significant magnitude or difference to justify separate appeals. The aerospace industry and automobile industry have markets which are diverse but in which development and manufacturing costs are such that it is not feasible to develop products to fit all market needs exactly. The successful companies, therefore, focus on a relatively small product range with variations which appeal to individual customer preferences.

Even in markets whose main body does not demand segmentation, however, there are often small-scale opportunities where companies can thrive by pursuing a focus strategy. Examples include Marks & Spencer in food retailing and Rolls-Royce in the luxury car market. Therefore, even in markets where the major players may be using a mass strategy, segmentation offers an opportunity for some smaller participants. For small market share companies in particular, the advice is: segment, segment, segment!

Whereas the previous chapter concentrated on the concept of segmentation and possible bases for segmentation, this chapter follows the process of identifying usable market segments. First we discuss *a priori* approaches to segmentation. The chapter then goes on to discuss *post-hoc, cluster-based* approaches. For the latter we follow a model developed by Maier and Saunders (1990), which takes segmentation research from initiation through to eventual tracking. Within this framework the wide range of approaches and techniques for segmentation are discussed.

10.1 A priori *segmentation approaches*

10.1.1 Single variable segmentation

A priori, or off-the-peg, methods are the easiest way of segmenting markets. In their original form this involved searching amongst demographic or socio-economic characteristics and identifying which of these form significant and useful splits within the marketplace. Usually the search for appropriate criteria would be guided by some expectation of how the market could be divided.

The major advantage of this approach is that it can be undertaken from secondary sources and can be related directly to advertising media and messages. In consumer markets, studies such as the Target Group Index (TGI) enable managers to identify heavy users of a product group and relate this directly to their media usage. Crimp (1990) cites an example from TGI which shows that the proportion of wine users is higher among *Daily Express* readers and lower among *News of the World* readers than the national average. Wine users are also shown to be light viewers of television. A marketing manager responsible for wine sales may have segmented the market on wine use and can then use the TGI data to help select appropriate media.

There are some clear cases where *a priori* segmentation has proved a powerful tool. The successful toy company Lego, for example, has carefully developed assembly toys to fit the development of children from birth to mid-teens, segmenting the market on the basis of age. Duplo, their pre-school product, starts with rattles and manipulative toys, which are not immediately intended for assembly but do have fixture mechanisms which allow the child to progress into Duplo proper (chunky and brightly coloured bricks and shapes which can be assembled into all manner of toys). Duplo overlaps with Lego, a system of building bricks upon which the Lego empire was formed. Almost identical to Duplo parts in every other way, the Lego units are half the size and therefore suitable for a child's enhanced manipulative ability and allow more detail in construction. They are also cleverly designed to link with the Duplo units and therefore allow relatively easy progression from one to the other. As the children get older so they can progress to Technical Lego, and other specialist variants, which again build on the manipulative, assembly and design skills inculcated with earlier sets.

Age is also used as a powerful segmentation variable in the package tour market. ClubMed and Club 18–30 are aimed at the single or young couples market while Saga holidays are aimed at the over-fifties.

Despite their ease of use and intuitive appeal, attempts to validate demographic and socio-economic bases in terms of product preferences have met with little success. One of the earliest reported attempts to validate this approach was by Evans (1959), who sought to use demographic variables to distinguish between Ford and Chevrolet owners in the US. He concluded that 'demographic variables are not a sufficiently powerful predictor to be of much practical use … [they] point more to the similarity of Ford and Chevrolet owners than to any means of discriminating between them. Analysis of several other objective factors also leads to the same conclusion.'

In other markets the conclusions have been similar. Some relationships were found, but no more than could have been expected to occur by chance if the data were random. Unfortunately, study after study throws doubt upon the direct usefulness of demographic characteristics as a predictor for product purchase.

These findings do not dispute the certainty that some products with clearly defined target consumers depend heavily on demographic characteristics. For instance, nappies are purchased by families with babies, incontinence pads by older people and sanitary towels by women. However, evidence does seem to show that demographic characteristics alone are incapable of distinguishing between the subtle differences in markets which are not explained by the physiological differences between human beings. Perhaps most limiting, they have been found to be poor differentiators of individual products within the broad categories identified (i.e. brand of nappy or sanitary towel).

In business markets perhaps the most often used segmentation variable is Standard Industrial Classification (SIC) code. The industry classification can be very specific. Hindle and Thomas (1994) cite the SIC in the US for manufacturers of a pair of pliers. The full code is '342311' made up as follows:

> '34' indicates a classification for fabricated metal products.
> '2' shows the industry group as cutlery, handtools and hardware.
> '3' indicates the specific industry of hand and edge tools.
> '1' shows the product class of mechanics hand service tools.
> '1' shows the product – pliers.

By selecting appropriate SICs a business marketer can identify the other businesses that may be most receptive to its offerings. Again, however, for businesses selling products and services that can be used across industry classifications (such as stationery, machine tools or consultancy services) SIC may be of little practical value as a segmentation base. While giving the impression of detail (six-figure classifications), the codes do not offer many clues as to why specific products are purchased or what is likely to appeal to individual customers.

10.1.2 Multiple variable *a priori* methods

Recently the traditional demographic and socio-economic means of off-the-peg segmentation have been supplemented by more sophisticated methods being promoted, in consumer marketing at least, by advertising and market research agencies. These encompass the subjective methods and the marketing-specific objective measures in discussed in chapter 9. The distinction between these and the approaches discussed above is that multiple criteria are considered simultaneously and segments created on the basis of these multiple measures. A number of different consumer classification schemes have been suggested such as ACORN, MOSAIC, VALS. These schemes have been created through analysis of large data-sets (in the case of the former two official census data) using cluster analytical techniques. They are still considered *a priori* because once formed they are then available for any users off-the-peg from the agencies concerned.

Earliest of the multiple variable *a priori* techniques was the extensive use of personality inventories in the 1960s and 1970s. At that time researchers were seeking to identify personality typologies that could be related, in much the same way as socio-economic factors were, to purchase decisions and consumption patterns. Techniques of personality measurement were borrowed by marketing from psychologists. Set psychological tests such as the Edwards Personality Preference

Schedule (EPPS) and the Catell 16 PF Inventory were tested in a marketing context. Unfortunately, these tests showed them to be of little more discriminating power than the less sophisticated demographic and socio-economic methods.

Compared with demographic and socio-economic off-the-peg methods, personality inventories have a slight but insubstantial advantage. They do appear to be able to discriminate to a small extent between some high involvement products, but even in these cases they leave the majority of variance unexplained. Like demographic and socio-economic methods, they seem to have most power to discriminate in markets where their measurement has a clear role, such as smoking which reflects a drug dependency, and deodorants which suggest anxiety. However, the subtlety of personality measurement renders it less useful as an off-the-peg measure in most cases because the personality differences are less strong and obvious than the physiological differences which demographics can measure: introversion and dependency are well-defined personality traits, but they are nowhere near as easily measured or as linked to behaviour as gender or age.

At the same time as personality traits were being explored as potential bases for segmentation, marketers were also experimenting with combining demographics characteristics to create the idea of the consumer life cycle. Under this model, age, marital status and family size were combined to identify a life cycle stage. This approach has been used for the marketing of holidays, insurance, housing, baby products and consumer durables. A recent development is the SAGACITY classification scheme, developed by the Research Services Ltd marketing research agency. This scheme combines life cycle (dependent, pre-family, family, late) with income (better off, worse off) and occupation (blue-collar, white-collar). Crouch and Housden (1996) list twelve resulting SAGACITY segments and show the types of products the different segments are considered likely to purchase.

The introduction of CACI's ACORN geodemographic database represented one of the biggest steps forward in segmentation and targeting techniques. Its basis was segments derived from published census information which provides a classification of neighbourhoods based on housing types. Although the measure is crude, the great strength of the service depends on CACI's own research linking the neighbourhood groups to demographics and buyer behaviour, together with the ability to target households. The system, therefore, provides a direct link between off-the-peg segmenting and individuals, unlike earlier methods which provided indirect means only of contacting the demographic or personality segments identified.

Like the other *a priori* techniques, the limitations of CACI's approach is the variability within neighbourhoods and the similarity between their buying behaviour for many product classes. English (1989) provides an example of this where five enumeration districts (individual neighbourhood groups of 150 households) are ranked according to geodemographic techniques. Of the five, two were identified as being prime mailing prospects. However, when individual characteristics were investigated, the five groups were found to contain 31, 14, 10, 10 and 7 prospects respectively: the enumeration districts had been ranked according to the correct number of prospects, but neighbourhood classifications alone appeared to be a poor method of targeting. With only 31 prime target customers being in the most favoured enumeration district, 119 out of 150 households would have been mistargeted. To be fair, like other means of off-the-peg segmentation discussed, geodemographics are powerful when related to products linked directly to characteristics of the neighbourhood districts; for instance, the demand for double glazing, gardening equipment, etc. Even in the case provided, targeting upon the best enumeration districts increases the probability of hitting a target customer from less than 10 per cent to over 20 per cent, but misses are still more common than hits. More recent developments have included CCN's MOSAIC, Pinpoint's PIN and SuperProfiles, all based on census data but using different items and different clustering techniques (Crimp and Wright, 1995).

Lifestyle segmentation provides an opportunity to overlay geodemographic data with lifestyle characteristics. In this descriptive form they have existed for some time and have been associated with the original success of Storehouse's Habitat chain or the success of the Conservative Party in the 1986 British General Election. These have sometimes been used in conjunction with demographics and form the second part of two stage segmentation. Third Age Research have done this after first identifying the over-65s as a target market and then breaking them up into lifestyle segments of apathetic, comfortable, explorer, fearful, organizer, poor me, social lion and status quo. To anyone who has contact with more than one older person, it is clear that these labels provide a much more powerful way of putting a face on the over-65 customer than does their age alone.

Stanford Research Institute in the US developed a lifestyle segmentation scheme called Values and Lifestyles (VALS) which has seven categories: *belongers* (patriotic, stable traditionalists content with their lives); *achievers* (prosperous, self-assured, middle-aged materialists); *emulators* (ambitious young adults trying to break into the system); *I-am-me group* (impulsive, experimental and a bit narcissistic); *societally conscious* (mature, successful, mission-oriented people who like causes); *survivors* (the old and poor with little optimism for the future); *sustainers* (resentful of their condition and trying to make ends meet). A similar scheme has been developed for use in pan-European marketing including: *successful idealists*; *affluent materialists*; *comfortable belongers*; *disaffected survivors*; and *optimistic strivers* (Hindle and Thomas, 1994).

Recent developments have linked lifestyle segments to customer databases. In the UK there are several of these (Coad, 1989);

➤ **The Lifestyle Selector**. A UK database started in 1985 by the American National Demographics and Lifestyle Company. The Lifestyle Selector collects data from questionnaires packed with consumer durables or by retailers and holds over 4.5 million returned, self-completed questionnaires.

➤ **Behaviour Bank**. The UK service provided by the American Computerized Marketing Technologies company. This collects data from syndicated questionnaires distributed directly to consumers via magazines and newspapers, and holds over 3.5 million returned questionnaires.

➤ **Omnidata**. This is a result of a joint venture between the Dutch Post Office and the Dutch *Reader's Digest*. The company mails its questionnaires to all Dutch telephone subscribers and tries to induce them to respond by arguing that by doing so they would receive less junk mail. Twenty-three per cent of consumers responded, and Omnidata has 730,000 households on file from a total of 5 million in Holland.

➤ **Postaid**. This is a Swedish organization by PAR, a subsidiary of the Swedish Post Office. It was started in the early 1980s and similar to the Dutch system was based on the thesis that people should be given the chance to determine the kind of mail they want to receive. The result is a database containing one million of Sweden's 3.7 million households.

Most research carried out so far has been on generalized lifestyle typologies and their comparative use in discriminating consumer attitudes and behaviour (Wilmott, 1989). The results are mixed, but a recent study (O'Brien and Ford, 1988) suggests that such generalized typologies are less efficient than traditional variables like social class or age as discriminators. While the relative merit of demographic variables and lifestyle tends to vary from situation to situation overall, in the comparisons that have been conducted, lifestyle comes out worst. It must therefore be concluded that, like their less sophisticated demographic brethren, lifestyle segments are no panacea for marketing. Although, when added to databases, they provide a powerful means of shifting from target markets to individual customers, their low coverage renders them of limited value. On the other hand, lifestyle segments, where valid, do provide a more graphic portrayal of customers than do demographics, and hence can give suggestions for advertising copy platforms. As with single demographic variables, it is too much to hope that a single classification will work beyond markets for which they are particularly well suited.

To return to Lego, which has been so successful in using age as a way of discriminating between sectors in the market for construction toys, once the individuality of children starts to develop they have found it necessary to develop a wide range of products covering the different needs of children: Lego Basic for the 3–12-year-olds, which specializes in using the original Lego components as they were initially contrived; Fabuland aimed at the 4–8-year-old girls and which revolves around a fantasy theme based on animal characters; Legoland for the 5–12-year-olds, which are sub-themes of space, medieval life, pirates and modern suburbia; and Legotechnic for the 7–16-year-old which has a focus on engineering mechanisms. Although the company found demographics as the first basis of segmentation, to go further depended upon identifying customer characteristics specific to the product in question.

All the above approaches are in the public domain and hence, even where they do offer reliable segmentation schemes of a market, they will rarely offer the marketer any originality in viewing it. The essence of a competitively useful segmentation scheme is that it is fresh, new, original and provides insights into the market that competitors do not have. To achieve this originality requires primary research where preconceptions about the market structure are put on one side and patterns sought from the original data.

10.2 Post-hoc *cluster-based segmentation approaches*

Unlike the methods discussed above for segmenting markets, the *post-hoc* approach does not commence with a preconception of market structure. The analysis is undertaken with a view to uncovering naturally existing segments rather than shoe-horning customers into predefined categories.

The remainder of this chapter discusses how firms can go about this more creative approach to segmentation. In doing so it follows a model developed by Maier and Saunders (1990) (see Figure 10.1). The process flows from initiation of the desire to segment the market creatively through to tracking of continuing segment usefulness.

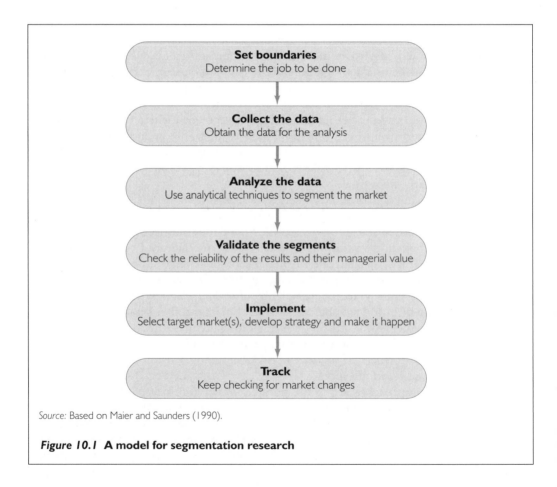

Source: Based on Maier and Saunders (1990).

Figure 10.1 **A model for segmentation research**

10.2.1 Setting the boundaries

Original and creative segmentation research needs both market and technical expertise. This often necessitates a dialogue between a manager commissioning a segmentation study and an agency or individual conducting the necessary research. The value of the final segmentation results will depend on the effort the individuals concerned have taken in bridging the gap between the technical requirements of segmentation methods and the practical knowledge of marketing and sales management. It is customary to see this bridge-building role as a responsibility of the researcher (who will typically be a modeller or marketing scientist) but, since the marketing manager is going to depend on the results and is going to be responsible for implementing them, he or she has a clear vested interest in ensuring a mutual understanding is achieved. Whereas the expert or modeller faces rejection if the technical gap is not bridged, the marketing manager may face failure in the marketplace if the relationship fails. When employing an agency, the marketing manager will certainly need to know how to cross-examine the agency to ensure their methods are appropriate and assumptions valid.

The entry of the marketing researcher or marketing modeller into the segmentation process is similar to opening a sale. If good initial relationships are not formed, the chance of further progress is slight. The researcher has to establish credibility by showing relevant expertise while fitting into the client's culture. As in selling, the prior gathering of information about the industry, the company and the personnel is beneficial. A grasp of terminology popular in the company is particularly useful. This preparation accelerates the formation of the mutual understanding necessary for successful model implementation.

The role of the saleswoman or man and the marketing researcher should be different because, although a salesperson usually has a limited set of products to sell, the marketing researcher should theoretically be able to choose without bias from a wide portfolio of appropriate techniques. Unfortunately this perspective is an ideal, for many marketing research agencies have a predisposition towards techniques with which they are familiar, or may even have developed in-house. So, in commissioning segmentation research, the marketing manager has to have sufficient knowledge to resist being supplied from a limited portfolio of solutions. Beware the researcher adopting the *'have technique – will travel'* approach!

The major lessons for starting a segmentation project are that the first contact is critical and that successful segmentation depends upon the marketing manager and the marketing researcher being sympathetic to each others' needs – not necessarily knowing each others' business perfectly, but certainly having the ability to ask the right questions.

At this initial stage it is essential to agree the focus of the project, the product market to be investigated and the way in which the results are intended to be used. Multi-product companies may choose to start with one application and proceed to others if the trial is successful. There may also be market structures – such as the division between industrial and consumer markets – which suggest a two-stage approach: the first stage breaking the market down into easily definable groups, and the second being involved with the segmentation analysis proper. In their segmentation analysis of the general practitioner (GP) market Maier and Saunders (1990) used such a process by first dividing doctors into general practitioners and hospital doctors, this distinction being necessary because of the different jobs of the two groups. The second stage then focused upon determining the product usage segments within the GP markets.

Agreeing on a focus reduces the chance of initial misunderstandings leading to dissatisfaction with the final results and maximizes the chances of the results being actionable.

10.2.2 Collect the data

The data required for segmentation studies can be broken down into two parts: that which is used in conjunction with cluster analysis to form the segments, and that which is used to help describe the segments once they are formed. Cluster analysis will allow any basis to be used, but experience has shown that the most powerful criteria are those that relate to attitudes and behaviour regarding the product class concerned. These could include usage rate, benefits sought, shopping behaviour, media usage, etc.

Before such data can be collected, however, it is necessary to be more specific about the questions to be asked. Typically qualitative techniques, such as group discussions, are used to identify the relevant attitudes, or benefits sought, prior to their incorporation in representative surveys.

For effective benefit segmentation, in particular, it is vital that exhaustive prior qualitative research is undertaken to ensure that all possible benefits of the product or service are explored in depth. The benefits that the firm believes the product offers may not be the same as the ones the customers believe they get. For the subsequent analysis to be valid the customers' perspective is essential, as is the use of the customers' own language in subsequent surveys.

Following qualitative research a segmentation study will usually involve a quantitative survey to provide data representative of the population, or market, under study. The method of data collection depends on the usage situation. Where the aim is to define target markets based on attitudes or opinions, the data collection is usually by personal interviews using semantic scales which gauge strength of agreement with a number of attitude statements. The results then provide a proxy to the interval-scaled data which is the usual basis for cluster analysis.

By contrast where the segmentation in a study is to be used in conjunction with a database which can rely on direct mailing, the data sources are much more limited. For example, the lifestyle classifications mentioned earlier use simple checklists so that consumers can be classified according to their interests. In the database segmentation study conducted by Maier and Saunders (1990), the basis was product usage reports by general practitioners. It is clearly a limitation of database methods that their data collection is constrained by the quality of data that can be obtained from a guarantee card or self-administered questionnaire. There inevitably tends to be an inverse correlation between the coverage in segmentation databases and the quality of the data upon which they are formed.

Where surveys are conducted to collect data for segmentation purposes these data are usually of two main types. The primary focus is on the data that will be used to segment the market: the benefits sought, usage patterns, attitudes, and so on. In addition, however, the survey will also collect information on traditional demographic and socio-economic factors. These can then be related back to the segments once formed (they are not used to form the segments) to enable a fuller picture of the segments to be painted. For example, a benefit segmentation study may find that a significant segment of car purchasers are looking for economical and environmentally friendly cars. To enable a marketing programme to be directed to them, however, requires a fuller picture of their purchasing power, media habits and other factors. Often age and social class are used as intermediary variables; where these factors discriminate between segments they can be used to select media.

10.2.3 Analyze the data

Once the data on which the segments are to be based have been collected they need to be analyzed to identify any naturally occurring groups or clusters. Generically, the techniques used to identify these groups are called *cluster analysis* (see Saunders, 1994).

It should be realized that cluster analysis is not a single analytical technique but a whole class of techniques which, while sharing the same objective of identifying classifications with homogeneity internally but heterogeneity between them, use different methods to achieve this. This diversity of approach is both an opportunity and a problem from the practitioner's point of view. It means that the approach can be tailored to the specific needs of the analysis, but requires a degree of technical expertise to select and implement the most appropriate technique. Not surprisingly, it has been found that cluster analysis is relatively little used and understood amongst marketing practitioners, but is much more widely used by marketing research companies. In a recent set of surveys Hussey and Hooley (1995) found that across the top European companies only 1 in 7 (15 per cent) reported regular use of cluster analysis in their marketing analysis, whereas the usage figures rose to 3 out of 5 (60 per cent) among specialist marketing research companies. The techniques are particularly widely used among researchers in the Netherlands (73 per cent), France (68 per cent) and Germany (67 per cent), but less so in Spain (47 per cent) and the UK (52 per cent).

The most common approach to clustering is called hierarchical clustering. Under this approach all the respondents are initially treated separately. They are then each joined with other respondents who have given identical or very similar answers to the questions on which the clustering is being performed. At the next stage the groups of respondents are further amalgamated where differences are small. The analysis progresses in an interactive fashion until all respondents are grouped as one large cluster. The analyst then works backwards, using judgement as well as the available statistics, to determine at what point in the analysis groups that were unacceptably different were combined.

Even within hierarchical clustering, however, there is a multiplicity of ways in which respondents can be measured for similarity and in which groups of respondents can be treated. Grouping can be made, for example, on the basis of comparing group averages, the nearest neighbours in two groups or the furthest neighbours in each group. Table 10.2 summarizes the main alternatives.

Comparative studies consistently show two methods to be particularly suitable for marketing applications: Ward's (1963) method, which is one of the minimum variance approaches listed in Table 10.2; and the K-means approach of interactive partitioning. In fact, an analyst does not have to choose between these two, because they can be used in combination, where Ward's method is used to form the initial number of clusters, say seven, and the K-mean approach used to refine that seven-cluster solution by moving observations around. If desired, after finding the best seven-cluster solution, Ward's method can then be re-engaged to find a six-cluster solution which is again optimized using K-mean, etc. This may seem a computationally cumbersome approach, but fortunately packages are available to allow this process to be used. The leading package is now the PC version of the popular SPSS (Norusis, 1992) package. So, at a stroke, by realizing Ward's method in conjunction with K-means is the best approach for forming cluster-based segments, the analyst has removed the necessity to sort among numerous cluster alternatives and is able to choose between the clustering programs which are available.

While there is plenty of advice available on which techniques to use, the determination of the most appropriate number of segments to select following the analysis is very much more judgemental. The statistics produced will offer a guide as to where amalgamation of groups results in two quite dissimilar groups being joined. The internal homogeneity of the group will suffer. This is a starting point and in some circumstances, where segmentation is very clear-cut, will be the best choice.

Figure 10.2 shows an example where there are three fairly clearly defined segments on the basis of the two dimensions studied. In this case 'eyeballing' a plot of the positions of each object (in segmentation studies the objects are usually individual respondents) shows three clusterings of objects scoring similarly, but not identically, on each of the two dimensions.

In most situations, however, there will be several dimensions on which the clustering is being conducted, and several candidate solutions, possibly ranging from a three-group to a ten-group solution. After narrowing down through examination of the statistics, the analyst will then need to examine the marketing implications of each solution, basically addressing the question: if I treat these two groups separately rather than together, what differences will it make to my marketing to them? If the answer is 'little difference', the groups should usually be amalgamated. This is the creative element of segmentation where judgement is crucial!

Finally, it should also be noted that lifestyle and geodemographic databases depend upon some form of cluster analysis to group customers who are alike. The results obtained for ACORN and MOSAIC, for example, are based on judgement as to how many clusters are needed to represent the population adequately just as tailor-made approaches are.

Table 10.1 Clustering methods

Favoured name	Method	Aliases
Hierarchical methods		
Single linkage	An observation is joined to another if it has the lowest level of similarity with at least one member of that cluster	Minimum method, linkage analysis, nearest neighbour cluster analysis, connectiveness method
Complete linkage	An observation is joined to a cluster if it has a certain level of similarity with all current members of that cluster	Maximum method, rank order typal analysis, furthest neighbour cluster analysis, diameter method
Average linkage	Four similar measures which differ in the way they measure the location of the centre of cluster from which its cluster membership is measured	Simple average linkage analysis, weighted average, centroid method, median method
Minimum variance	Methods which seek to form clusters which have minimum within-cluster variance once a new observation has joined it	Minimum variance method, Ward's method, error sum of squares method, H GROUP
Interactive partitioning		
K-means	Starts with observation partitioned into a pre-determined number of groups and then reassigns observation to cluster whose centroid is nearest	Non-hierarchical methods
Hill-climbing methods	Cases are not reassigned to a cluster with the nearest centroid but moved between clusters dependent upon the basis of a statistical criterion	

Source: Based on G. Punj and D.W. Stewart (1983), 'Cluster analysis in marketing research: review and suggestions for applications', *Journal of Marketing Research*, Vol. 20, No. 2, Table 2, published by the American Marketing Association.

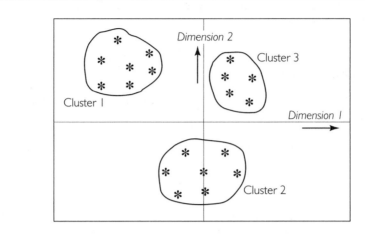

Figure 10.2 Clustering of objects in two-dimensional space

Once the segments have been identified, and described across other criteria, there is a need to validate the segments found.

10.2.4 Validate the segments

One of the beauties and problems of cluster analysis is its ability to generate seemingly meaningful groups out of meaningless data. This, and the confusion of algorithms, has frequently led to the approach being treated with scepticism. These uncertainties make validation an important part of segmentation research.

One favoured method of validation was mentioned above. Where product class behaviour or attitude was used to form the clusters, the extent to which those clusters also vary on demographic or psychographic variables is a measure of the cluster's validity. If the cluster is found to describe people with different beliefs and attitudes and behaviour, it would be expected that they could also have different demographic or psychographic profiles. Equally, from an operational point of view, if the market segments are demographically and psychographically identical, it is going to be very difficult to implement any plan based upon them.

Where sample data have been used to suggest segments and there is a hope to extrapolate those results to the fuller population, there is a need to test the reliability of the solution, to ask the question: do the results hold for the population as a whole? The most common way to test for this is cross-validation. This involves randomly splitting the data that have been collected into two, using one set to form the set of clusters and the second set to validate the results. A simple approach is to conduct the same cluster analysis on both samples and to compare them to see the similarity of the clusters in terms of their size and characteristics.

Since comparing two cluster analysis solutions tends to be rather subjective, several authors have recommended using discriminate analysis for cross-validation. This approach once again involves taking two samples and performing a separate cluster analysis on each. One sample is then used to build a discriminate model, into which cases from the other samples are substituted. The reliability is then measured by comparing the allocation using discriminate analysis with the allocation by cluster analysis. Integrated data analysis packages, such as SPSS PC, enable such linked analyses to be conducted quickly and efficiently.

It is necessary to supplement this statistical validation mentioned above with operational validation, which checks if the segments have managerial value. At a first level, this means the segments having face validity and appearing to provide marketing opportunities. If further endorsement is needed, an experiment can be run to test if the segments respond differently or not. For example, Maier and Saunders (1990) used a direct mailing campaign to a sample of GPs to show their segments captured major differences in the doctors' responses to certain self-reported activity.

10.2.5 Implement the segmentation

Implementation is best not viewed as a stage in segmentation research, but should be seen as the aim of the whole research process. Implementation has become one of the central issues in market modelling. A successful (validated) model adequately represents the modelled phenomena, and implementation changes decision-making, but a successful implementation improves decision-making. In many cases it is worth going beyond the concept of implementation to implantation. By this we mean the results of the exercise, not just being used once, but adopted and used repeatedly once the marketing scientist has withdrawn from the initial exercise. This again suggests that implementation not only begins at the start of the segmentation research process, but continues long after the results have been first used by the marketing manager.

Successful implementation, therefore, depends on more than the correct transfer of a model into action. The whole model-building process needs to be executed with implementation in mind. In particular, the segmentation researcher must be involved with the potential user in order to gain their commitment and ensure the results fit their needs and expectations. An unimplemented segmentation exercise is truly academic in its more cynical sense.

Segment selection and strategy development are two critical stages which follow the technical activity of segmentation research. These are managerial tasks which are central to marketing strategy and upon which successful implementation depends. Chapter 12 focuses upon these and links them to the broader issues of strategic positioning.

10.2.6 Tracking

A segmentation exercise provides a snapshot of a market as it was some months before the results were implemented. Inevitable time delays mean that, from the start, the results are out of date and, as time goes on and consumers change, it will inevitably become an increasingly poor fit to reality. Modelling myopia (Lilien and Kotler, 1983) occurs when successful implementation leads to the conviction that market-specific 'laws' have been found that make further analysis unnecessary. The converse is true: success means modelling should continue. Customers and competition change. Successful implementation itself may also change the market and competitors' behaviour.

Tracking of segmentation schemes for stability or change over time is essential in rapidly changing markets. As segmentation and positioning strategies are implemented they inevitably change the pattern of the market and customer perceptions, wants and needs. Through tracking the impact of various campaigns on segmentation, it may be possible to refine and detail the sort of promotional activity which is appropriate for them. If the segments do not prove to be stable, either showing gradual changes or a radical shift, that itself can create a major opportunity. It may indicate a new segment is emerging or that segment needs are adjusting and so enable an active company to gain a competitive edge by being the first to respond.

Positioning research is often carried out in parallel with segmentation research. Indeed, the quantitative approaches discussed below typically have as their aim the development of a multidimensional model representing both the positioning of objects (typically brands or companies) and customer segments.

10.3 *Qualitative approaches to positioning research*

The images of brands, products, companies and even countries have long been of interest to marketing researchers. Qualitative research approaches to this are semi-structured techniques aimed at gaining a more in-depth understanding of how respondents view aspects of the world (or more specifically markets) around them. They include focus groups and depth interviews (see chapter 6).

Calder (1994) relates a qualitative research study into the image of a for-profit hospital in the US. The hospital chain was opening a new 100-bed facility in a town with two existing and much larger hospitals. The problem was how to position the new hospital given its relatively small size and lack of established reputation. A number of focus group sessions were held which showed that the relative size was known by respondents, but not seen as necessarily negative. Indeed, the smaller size led to expectations of a friendlier, personalized service. Comments during the discussions included:

> Very friendly and you get a lot of good care there. The others are a little big for that kind of care.

> From what I hear it has a more personalized service. Mealwise and otherwise. You even get wine [with meals]. It's more of a personalized hospital.

> I understand it has quite an excellent menu to choose from. Wine. They have the time to take care of you.

The researchers concluded that the new hospital could be positioned very differently from the existing ones and built on the friendly, caring image in subsequent marketing.

Through the use of projective techniques during qualitative research, images can be uncovered that serve to show how the brand product of the company is positioned in the mind of the respondent. Some of the most popular techniques include:

➤ **The brand or company as animal or person**. Under this approach respondents are asked to name a person or an animal that embodies their view of the product or company under study. Calder (1994) cites the use of the technique to uncover the image of the US army among potential recruits. Respondents were asked '*If you were to think of the army as an animal, which would it most be like?*' The answers were, in order: tiger, lion, bull, wolf, bear. The army was not seen as: mule, horse, dog, squirrel, elephant, or cow! The researchers concluded that the army was symbolized (positioned) as strong, tough, aggressive, powerful and dominating. This positioning had some negative effects on potential recruits who feared failure in the training/induction period. It is interesting to note that more recent recruitment advertising in the UK has served to stress the 'family' and 'team' nature of military service – an attempt at some repositioning.

➤ **Role-play**. In role-playing the respondent is asked to assume the role or behaviour of another person, or of an object under research. Tull and Hawkins (1993) give an example of research for a premium brand of Canadian whisky marketed by Schenley, called O.F.C. During a group discussion a member of the group was asked to role-play a bottle of O.F.C. and explain his feelings. The player explained that he didn't think anyone could like him as he didn't have a real name and hence no real identity. Further probing and discussion resulted in the name 'Old French Canadian' being suggested (using the letters of the original name, building on the origin of the liquor in the French Canadian area of Quebec, and on the favourable image of 'Canadian Club'). The brand was relaunched with the new name, a stronger personality and a clearer positioning in the market.

➤ **The friendly Martian**. In this approach the interviewer or group moderator assumes the role of an alien recently landed from space and asks members of the group to explain a particular product and how it is used. By acting the alien the moderator can ask basic questions which the respondents would normally assume the moderator knew the answers to. In a group discussion for the British Home Sewing and Needlecrafts Association the researcher (a male in a female-dominated market) was able, through use of this technique, to discover that knitting was 'positioned' as a craft hobby that could be undertaken as a background activity while doing other sedentary activities such as watching television. Sewing, on the other hand, was 'positioned' as a thrift activity, undertaken primarily to save money, especially with children's garments, and required full attention to the exclusion of other activities.

A number of stimuli can be used to prompt respondents and aid them in articulating the images they hold of objects. These include:

➤ **Association techniques**. Here respondents are asked for associations with a particular stimulus. They may, for example, be asked what words, or values, or lifestyles, they associate with a BMW car. The words elicited can then be further explored through discussions and other techniques.

➤ **Concept boards**. Boards with pictures of the brand or the brand logo on them. These are shown to respondents and their reactions sought through probing.

➤ **Animatics**. Drawings of key frames from a commercial with 'bubble' speech. Respondents are then asked for their reactions and helped to describe the feelings they have towards the items being advertised.

➤ **Cartoon and story completion**. Cartoons of situations, such as the purchase of a specific brand, where the speech 'bubbles' are left blank for the respondent to fill in. Tull and Hawkins (1993) relate the use of story completion in researching changing drinking habits for Seagram. The unfinished scenario used was:

> Sarah hadn't seen Jane for a long time. She seemed very sophisticated and self-assured these days. At the bar she ordered ...

Completion of the scenario by female drinkers most often had Jane ordering a glass of wine reflecting, as the researchers interpreted it, her higher level of knowledge of drinks and general sophistication. Based on this and further qualitative research, the company developed a wine-based drink with a twist of citrus to liven it up – 'Taylor California Cellar's Chablis with a Twist'.

➤ **Visual product mapping**. This is a qualitative form of the perceptual mapping approaches discussed below under quantitative techniques. Here respondents are given a large piece of paper – the size of a flip-chart – with two dimensions drawn at right-angles to each other. Respondents are then given a number of objects (such as brands or companies) on small cards, or in the case of small pack products such as shampoos they may even be given a number of real packages. They are then asked to position the cards or packs on the chart with similar brands close to each other but far apart from dissimilar brands. The dimensions which can be used to explain these differences are then discussed and written onto the maps. Alternatively, the identity of the dimensions may have been elicited from earlier parts of the interview (such as 'price', 'quality', etc.) and respondents are asked to 'position' the objects on the dimensions directly.

Qualitative approaches to uncovering the images and positions of objects in the minds of respondents have been particularly popular among advertising agencies who value the in-depth, rich data that can be derived. The images and positions articulated are in the respondents' own language and hence offer insights for direct communication with them as customers.

The classic concern of qualitative research, however, remains. That is, how representative of the population in their normal everyday shopping and consumption experiences are the responses of a relatively small number of respondents in often very artificial settings completing strange and unfamiliar tasks? In most instances positioning research needs to go beyond the qualitative to develop models of images and positions based on more representative samples in a quantitative study.

10.4 *Quantitative approaches to positioning research*

While qualitative approaches to image research often focus on the core object (brand, product, company, etc.) in isolation, the more quantitative approaches typically consider positioning relative to the positioning of major competitors and relative to the desires, wants and needs of target customer segments.

As a starting point, therefore, it is necessary to define the competitive set that will be analyzed along with the focal brand, product or company. While positioning studies can focus at the level of the company or the product, most typically focus at the brand level.

For example, a company analyzing the market for hover-mowers might be interested in how customers perceive competitors' brands (i.e. Flymo, Qualcast, and Black and Decker) and the products they sell. When buying such a product a customer is likely to have a reasonable idea about the likely size and cost of the item they wish to buy and, therefore, give most attention to products within that price performance envelope. Among the competitors the customer is likely to see various dimensions of importance, such as value for money, reliability, safety, convenience, etc. and it is the relationships between the direct competitors with which positioning is particularly involved. If the direct competitors have not been correctly identified, the researcher may include within the survey manufacturers of sit-upon mowers, i.e. Lawnflight, Laser or Toro. This would not only add to the burden of respondents whose perceptions are being sought, but could also change the perceptions since, when compared with sit-upon mowers, conventional handmowers may all look similarly inexpensive, time-consuming and compact.

The mower market is relatively simple compared with some others. Consider the problem faced by a company wishing to launch a low alcohol lager. Should the competitors be other low alcohol lagers or should it include low alcohol beers as well? Or maybe the study should be extended to include other low alcohol drinks such as shandy, cider or wine. In Britain, the rapid increase in the consumption of soft drinks which has been associated with the concern for the health and safety of alcohol consumption may suggest that they also should be considered as an alternative to low alcohol lagers, but should diet and caffeine-free versions also be considered? Maybe it is a matter of just taste, and it is more appropriate to low alcohol drinks with variants with normal alcohol content. Production orientation is a danger when trying to reduce the number of product alternatives. A brewer may well consider low alcohol lagers or other lagers as the direct competitors, but certain customer groups may easily associate low alcohol drinks with cokes or other beverages. It is clearly necessary to take a customer-oriented view of the direct competitors.

One way of defining direct competitors is to look at panel data to see what customers have done in the past. By tracking the past purchases of customers, it may be possible to identify product alternatives when switching takes place. The danger in this approach is the dissociation of the purchasers with the usage situation and the user. For instance, a buying pattern which shows the purchase of low alcohol lagers, lemonade, beer and coke could represent products to be consumed by different people at different times, rather than switching between alternatives. Another approach is to determine which brands buyers consider. For consumer durables, customers might be asked what other brands they considered in their buying process. For low involvement products it may be inappropriate to ask a buyer about a particular purchase decision, so instead they could be asked what brands they would consider if their favourite one was not available.

Day *et al.* (1979) proposed a more exhaustive process (introduced in chapter 2) as a cost-effective way of mapping product markets. Start by asking twenty or so respondents the use context of a product, say a low alcohol lager. For each use context so identified, such as the lunchtime snack, with an evening meal, or at a country pub, respondents are then asked to identify all appropriate beverages. For each beverage so identified, the respondent has to identify appropriate use context. Once again the process is continued until an exhaustive list of contexts and beverages is produced. A second group of respondents would then be asked to make a judgement as to how appropriate each beverage would be for each usage situation, the beverages then being clustered on the basis of their similarity of their usage situation. For instance, if both low alcohol lager and coke were regarded as appropriate for a company lunchtime snack but inappropriate for an evening meal, they would be considered as direct competitors.

Rather than using consumers, it can be tempting to use a panel of experts or retailers to guide the selection of direct competitors. This could be quicker than using customers, but is likely to lead to a technological definition of preference. There can be a vast difference between what is perceived by experts and what is perceived by customers. Since the focus of positioning is to gauge customers' images of offerings and their preferences for them it is difficult to justify using any other than customers to define competitors.

10.4.1 Attribute profiling methods

One of the simplest ways of collecting quantitative position data is through the use of attitude or attribute scaling. Under this approach the dimensions that respondents use to differentiate and choose between alternative offerings are included in a survey (usually personally administered, though it is also possible to collect these data by mailed or telephone surveys) and presented as semantic scales for respondents to give their views on.

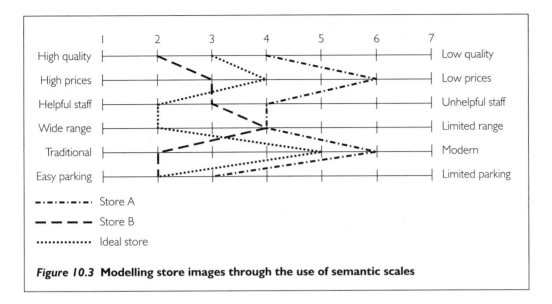

Figure 10.3 **Modelling store images through the use of semantic scales**

An example from a survey of store images and positioning is given in Figure 10.3. Here respondents were asked to rate two competing stores on six attributes identified as important in prior qualitative research: quality, price, staff attitudes, range of goods, modernity and ease of parking. Results are shown from one respondent only. Also shown is that respondent's ideal store profile – what s/he would ideally like in terms of the features listed. For most purposes the responses from the sample would be averaged* and those averages used to show the differences in positioning and requirements. Where ideal requirements differ across the sample they could be first grouped together (using cluster analysis – see above) to identify alternative segment requirements.

This approach examines each dimension separately, bringing them together in the diagram to enable a more complete image to be drawn. Some dimensions may, however, be more important to particular market segments than others. For instance, in the store positioning example above it might well be that for one segment price considerations outweigh convenience, range and other factors. It is therefore essential to examine the relative importance of the dimensions, either through weighting them differently to reflect importance, or through assessing the dimensions simultaneously such that more important dimensions come to the fore.

10.4.2 Multidimensional positioning analysis

Increasingly, researchers and managers are seeking to create multidimensional models

* Note that where there is wide variation in the evaluations from individual respondents it may be necessary first to group respondents by perceptual segments, i.e. those sharing a common view of the market, prior to analyzing alternative segment requirements.

of the markets in which they are operating. The essence of these models is that they seek to look at a number of dimensions simultaneously, rather than separately, in an attempt to reflect more closely the way in which customers view the market.

To explain this approach we shall follow a case involving the positioning of leisure facilities accessible from the East Midlands. For the sake of simplicity only the major attractions and segments are considered in this case. Interviews with respondents revealed six leisure centres which, although very different in their provision, were all seen as major attractions. These were:

➤ **The American Adventure theme park**: a completely modern facility, with a Wild West emphasis but also includes other American themes such as GI and Space exploration.

➤ **Alton Towers**: acquired by Madame Tussaud's, this is a large leisure facility based around a derelict country house. It has inherited several natural features, such as the house itself, the gardens and lakes, but particularly focuses upon dramatic, white-knuckle rides.

➤ **Belton House**: one of many country houses owned by the National Trust and, like most of these, has splendid gardens and furnished accommodation, which visitors may see. Atypical of National Trust properties, the house also has a large adventure playground in a wood beside the house, this being a venture started by the family who owned the house prior to its passing on to the National Trust.

➤ **Chatsworth House**: one of the largest stately homes in Britain and is still the residence of the owning family. Its extensive grounds and the house itself make it a popular place for families to visit.

➤ **Warwick Castle**: one of the best kept and most visited medieval castles in Britain. Like many estates, it has been lived in from medieval times and in this case the owners have built a country house into the fabric of the building. Now owned by Madame Tussaud's, the castle's attractions have been extended beyond the building and its gardens, to include contemporary waxworks within the furnished accommodation, medieval knights cavorting, torture chambers, etc.

➤ **Woburn Abbey and Safari Park**: like Chatsworth, still the residence of the family owning the estate. However, the family in this case have developed two distinct attractions, the house and the safari park, the latter also having a fairground, etc.

Although widely different in their appeals, ownership and background, the respondents' interviews clearly indicated that these were direct competitors and were alternatives they would choose between when deciding on an outing.

The positioning research process (Figure 10.4) shows the determination of competitive dimensions, competitors' positions and the customers' positions as parallel phases. This is because there are certain techniques which can be used to extract all these simultaneously. In this case the phases are taken in sequence. Details of other approaches that are available are given later.

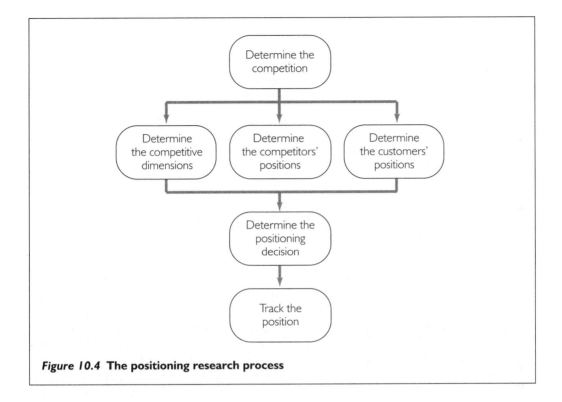

***Figure 10.4* The positioning research process**

Identifying product positions

It is an odd feature of many of the techniques used in positioning research that the competitors' positions can be determined before it is understood how the customer is differentiating between them. Such an approach was used to represent the leisure park market in the East Midlands. The approach is called similarities-based multi-dimensional scaling. In this, respondents were given a shuffled stack of cards which contained all possible combinations of the six leisure parks. There were fifteen pairs in all, ranging from American Adventure linked to Alton Towers, to Warwick Castle linked with Woburn Safari Park. The respondents were then asked to rank the pairs in accordance with their similarity, the pair most alike being on the top and the pair least alike being on the bottom. Since this can be a rather cumbersome process, it is sometimes advisable first to ask respondents to stack the cards into three piles representing those pairs that are very similar, those pairs that are very unalike and a middling group. The respondent then has to rank the pairs within each group.

Figure 10.5 presents the ranking from one such process. It shows that this particular respondent (one of many) thought Belton House and Woburn Safari Park were the most similar. As the next most similar, the pair of Belton House and Chatsworth House were chosen, and so on, until the least similar pair of the American Adventure and Chatsworth House. An indication that the respondent is

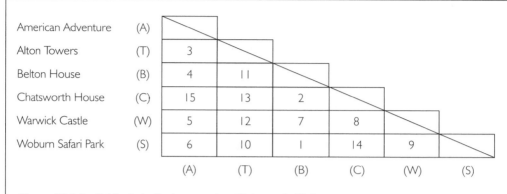

Figure 10.5 Individual similarity matrix of leisure facilities

using different criteria to judge each pair is shown by the judgement that Belton is similar to Woburn and Chatsworth, but Woburn and Chatsworth are not alike. Such are the permutations and combinations of pairs each respondent can choose that it is almost inevitable that each individual's similarity matrix is different.

The objective from this point is to develop a plot of the stimuli (leisure parks) which shows those that respondents said were similar close together, and those that respondents said were dissimilar far apart. Although this is a difficult task to conduct manually, computers are particularly adept at finding such solutions and researchers in the field of multidimensional scaling have produced many computer packages which can be used (for a recent summary, see Green *et al.*, 1989). A multidimensional scaling package called KYST can be used to produce perceptual maps from the similarities matrix provided and many other data formats (Kruskal *et al.*, 1973). The map produced (Figure 10.6) shows some of the detail from a similarity matrix (Figure 10.5). Chatsworth House, Alton Towers and Woburn Safari Park are some distance apart, while American Adventure, Alton Towers and Belton House are somewhat closer together.

There are two reasons why the fit is not perfect:

➤ The perceptual map presented in Figure 10.6 is in two dimensions, whereas the customers' perception of the market is rather more complex than that; and
➤ The perceptual map is an aggregate of a number of customers' views whereas the similarity matrix in Figure 10.5 represents the views of one customer.

KYST can produce a perceptual map for a single customer, but it is more common to produce a map which aggregates either all customers or a segment's view.

Uncovering the dimensions of perception
While the map shows a representation of the similarities between objects (leisure attractions) in itself it tells us little of why they are seen as similar or dissimilar. We

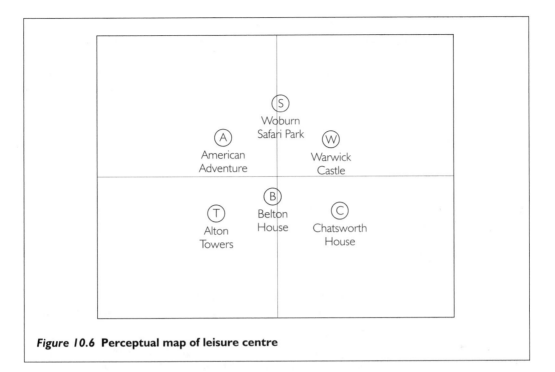

Figure 10.6 **Perceptual map of leisure centre**

need to go further to identify and understand the dimensions, or criteria, that were being used by respondents in giving their similarity judgements.

Two methods of determining the dimensions or criteria are not recommended. The first is using experts' judgements which, like their judgements of competitors, is likely to be different from that of customers. And second, trying to eyeball the perceptual map to try to work out what the dimensions represent. Such maps are often ambiguous and there is a particular danger of researchers superimposing their own views of what is going on. A better, but still imperfect, technique is to ask customers directly how they differentiate the market. The problem here is that customers may give a relatively simplistic answer, which may not represent all the dimensions they may, sometimes subconsciously, use to differentiate product offerings.

More useful is a research-based approach where respondents are asked first to choose two or more similar products and asked to say why they consider them to be alike, then to choose some products they consider to be quite dissimilar and ask them why they see them as unalike. An approach like this was used to determine the dimensions of the perceptual space for the leisure facilities. The respondents were first asked why they chose the first pair (Woburn Safari Park and Belton House) as most alike. They were then asked what made Belton House and Chatsworth House alike, and so on, until the respondents had difficulty saying that pairs were alike at all. The opposite tack was then taken, where the respondents were asked to explain why they considered pairs to be unalike; first of all, the most dissimilar pair of Chatsworth House and American Adventure, then Chatsworth House and Woburn Safari Park, etc. The result was a long list of attributes, which was reduced to ten after some similar ones were combined and less frequently used ones were deleted. The ones remaining were:

➤ Big rides
➤ Educational
➤ Fun and games
➤ Sophisticated
➤ Noisy
➤ For teenagers
➤ Strong theme
➤ For all the family
➤ Synthetic/artificial
➤ Good food.

Kelly Grids are a popular marketing research technique which could also have been used to identify the dimensions underlying the perceptual map. A four-step approach is typically taken:

1. Respondents are presented with three stimuli (in our case, leisure attractions) and asked to state one way in which two of them are alike and yet different from the third.
2. The criteria upon which the two were said to be alike (say 'noisy') is labelled 'the emergent pole' and associated dissimilarity (say 'quiet') is labelled 'the implicit pole'.
3. The remaining stimuli (leisure attractions) are then sorted equally between the two poles.
4. Another three stimuli are selected and the process repeated until the respondent can think of no new reasons why the triad are alike or dissimilar.

To find how the dimensions fit the perceptual map in Figure 10.6, respondents were asked to rank each of the leisure facilities on the basis of the attributes identified. Once again, the result is a series of matrices which are difficult to analyze manually and, once again, computers come to our aid. In this case, a package called PREFMAP (Chang and Carroll, 1972) which takes the perceptual map of product positions in Figure 10.6, and fits the dimensions as they best describe the respondents' perceptions was used. To identify the meaning of these vectors, each one can be traced back through the centre of the perceptual map (see Figure 10.7).

The score of each of the leisure centres (stimuli) on the dimension (vector) is measured by their relative position as the vector is traced back through the centre. For instance, the respondents see Chatsworth House as being the most 'sophisticated' (on the east–west dimension), followed by Warwick Castle, Woburn Safari Park, Belton House, American Adventure and Alton Towers. In almost complete

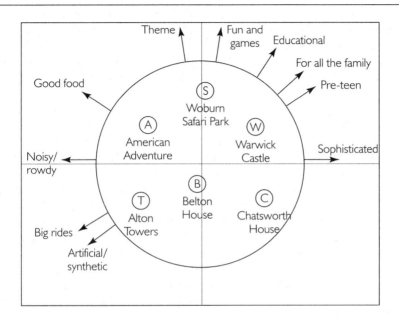

Figure 10.7 **Perceptual map of leisure centres with dimensions identified**

opposition to sophistication is the vector representing noisy and rowdy, on which Alton Towers and American Adventure scored the highest. Projecting back the vector which represents a strong theme shows the highest scoring leisure centre to be Woburn Safari Park, followed by the American Adventure and Warwick Castle with an almost equal rating, and finally, Belton House, Alton Towers and Chatsworth House. Once again, it is likely that the respondents' individual or aggregated scores are not perfectly represented by the map that has been generated. This is inevitable, considering that the picture is now trying to represent even more information in the same two dimensions. The magnitude of this problem can be reduced by resorting to portraying the picture using three or more dimensions, but usually the situations becomes less understandable rather than more understandable as the map goes beyond our normal experience. It may also be that segments of the market have distinctly different views and therefore it is more appropriate to produce maps which represent their different perceptions rather than aggregating the market as has been done so far.

Identifying market segment locations
A two-stage process was used to add customer positions to the perceptual map of leisure centres. First, respondents were asked to rate the leisure centres in terms of their preference. Cluster analysis was then used to form segments with similar

preferences (see above). This indicated the presence of three main clusters. Analysis of their demographic characteristics revealed these to be mature couples or young sophisticates who found Chatsworth House and Belton House most attractive; young families who preferred American Adventure and Woburn Safari Park, and 'wild young things' who were most attracted by Alton Towers and American Adventure.

Once again, PREFMAP was used to locate these segments in relation to product position. However, in this case the segments were to be expressed as ideal points within the body of the map rather than as vectors in the way that the dimensions were examined. Figure 10.8 gives the final map. This shows clearly the strategy of American Adventure, the latest of the leisure centres to enter the market. Aimed at the family market, it has big rides, good food and plenty of opportunity for fun and games, particularly for the very young children. Although lacking sophistication and being perceived as artificial, it is well positioned for young families and for wild young things. Less successful appears to be Belton House, where the National Trust have found themselves running a country estate, with which they are very familiar, and an adventure playground, with which they are unfamiliar. Although the house and gardens may provide the sophistication and tranquillity desired by the mature couples, the existence of the adventure playground would make it too rowdy for

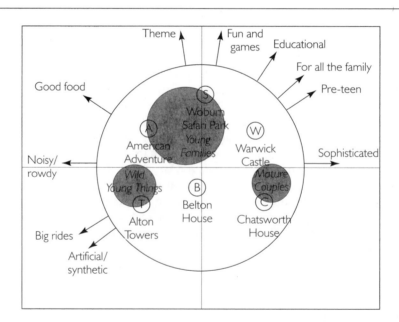

Figure 10.8 **Perceptual map of leisure centres with dimensions identified and segment ideal locations**

them. Equally, the direction of so many resources into maintaining the house and gardens to National Trust standards provides facilities which are unlikely to be attractive to the wild young things (which the National Trust probably thinks is good) or young families.

The map also shows the dangers of product positioning without consideration of market segments. The positions of the leisure centres suggest there may be an opportunity to develop one which excels in the provision of an educational experience for the pre-teens, or for all the family. Vacant that position may be, but it is dangerously away from the needs of the three major segments which have been identified in this case. Maybe the mums and dads would have liked such a leisure centre, but the kids would be happier with a less pretentious, synthetic attraction providing fun and games.

10.4.3 Alternative algorithms

In developing positioning maps, researchers are spoilt by the number of alternative approaches that can be used (see Green *et al.*, 1989). For instance, PREFMAP allows the stage where segments were formed from individuals to be missed out and so produces a map representing the ideal point of each individual. Rather than the picture seen in Figure 10.8, which presents the ideal points of each segment, the map would then show the product positions, the market dimensions and the position of each individual relative to the product. From there it may be possible to eyeball the positions of individual respondents to identify a group which are worthy of being targeted. Another package, MDPREF (Chang and Carroll, 1969) can be used to combine the identification of the perceptual map of product positions and underlying dimensions. This would have required respondents to have rated leisure parks along each of the dimensions, such as 'for all the family' or 'sophisticated', and then aggregating the results to arrive directly at a map similar to Figure 10.7.

A further approach is offered through correspondence analysis. Correspondence analysis (see Carroll, Green and Schaffer, 1986, 1987) is a multivariate method for analyzing tables of categorical data in order simultaneously to identify relationships between the variables (both rows and columns). It can therefore operate with commonly collected data, such as usage and attitude data, to produce perceptual maps that simultaneously show the positions of objects (brands or segment ideals) and attributes (dimensions). Originally developed in France as an alternative approach to multidimensional scaling, correspondence analysis is now available in leading MDS packages such as that provided by Smith (1990).

Anyone who starts to use this diversity of approaches will find that the map produced depends upon the approach used. This is because of the differences in the data-gathering techniques and the assumptions and methods used to optimize the results. In that way, the use of multidimensional scaling to produce perceptual maps is similar to cluster analysis where the results depend on the clustering algorithm used. But just as in cluster analysis, this should not be seen as a defect but the realization that there are numerous ways of looking at a market. Life would be more convenient if there were just one map which represented a market, but any attempt to compress the richness of a market into so simple a perspective is likely to result in opportunities being lost, or never seen.

Only a few years ago, the access to the packages was difficult, and the programmes themselves were poorly documented and hard to use. Now the situation has changed completely. They, along with other reasonably user-friendly data analysis packages, are available in PC form (Smith, 1990) and are routinely used by leading market research companies.

10.5 *Conclusions*

Considerable research has shown that the naive practitioner of segmentation and positioning research can be easily confused and disappointed. The traditional *a priori*, off-the-peg methods of segmentation have proved to be a poor guide to segmenting markets other than those which have a direct and immediate link to the markets concerned, e.g. gender-, age- or race-based products. Although more expensive, and providing a much more graphic view of the marketplace, the more modern off-the-peg psychographic methods appear to provide little advantage. Like demographic bases for segmentation, they do work in certain circumstances, but only when the product class or form and the segmentation criteria are very closely related. Within a product class or a product form, however, they rarely differentiate between brands.

The need to find segmentation bases which are closely associated with the product market in question means that successful implementation often involves a company developing product-specific bases. Here there is a potential barrier because of the perceived complexity of the approach and the confusion that researchers have created by their own misunderstandings. Although once a major block to implementation, sufficient case law on using cluster analysis in marketing has been accumulated to allow some of the confusion to be removed. Comparative studies come down firmly in favour of Ward's method in conjunction with iterative partitioning. Few of the computer packages available can do this, so a selection of clustering algorithms and the computer package used to run it becomes routine.

There is rightly much scepticism about the results from cluster analysis. This is justifiable, given the confusion of the algorithms used, the tendency of cluster analysis to produce results even if the data are meaningless, and the lack of validation of those results. Being aware of these dangers, it is vital that validation – both statistical and operational – has a central role within segmentation research. In particular tests should be done to see if the segments formed can be replicated using other data, that the segments are managerially meaningful and respond differently to elements of the marketing mix.

As with segmentation research there is a wide variety of positioning research approaches and techniques available. Typically they require the collection of primary data relating to brand images and customer requirements. Multidimensional scaling techniques can be used to summarize the mass of data collected in visually appealing and easily communicable ways. They are perhaps best seen as visual models of the customer's mind. As such they should be treated with caution, as any model is a simplification of reality, and used with care. They can never replace the individual manager's insights, which are central to creative marketing decision-making. At best they are an aid to that process.

Segmentation and positioning researchers have indeed failed to find a single criterion which will fit all markets, despite the claims of those selling lifestyle segmentation. However, rather than finding a single criterion, researchers have found consistently reliable methods of using product market data to segment customers into groups which are of managerial significance and to represent their views and opinions in visually communicable ways. While Baumwoll (1974) was right in predicting that no philosopher's stone would be found, researchers have perhaps discovered how to make philosopher's stones!

CHAPTER 11

Forecasting

What's small, dark and knocking at the door? The future.
Greek proverb

Introduction

The economist Ralph Harris defined a forecast as 'a pretence of knowing what would have happened if what does happen hadn't'. People are rightly cynical about forecasting, but forecasting is at the heart of marketing strategy and competitive positioning. As part of the marketing information system in chapter 6, forecasting feeds into many of the stages of marketing strategy formulation. There is little point in developing strategies to fit the past, so forecasting needs to extend the environment and industry analyses of chapters 1 and 2 into the future. Portfolio analysis (chapter 3) starts with historic information, but ends by projecting the portfolio forward to help decide what to do. From that stage onwards plans depend upon forecasts. Target markets are chosen because of what markets are forecast to be (chapter 12) and new product development programmes (chapter 16) build upon market and technology forecasts.

Companies that have not mastered forecasting are likely to build positions that defend against yesterday's competitors or appeal to yesterday's customers. Yet forecasting is often neglected or done naively. Why? The perceived complexity and sheer variety of forecasting methods are two reasons. These barriers have risen as people try to develop evermore sophisticated ways of doing the impossible: looking into the future.

Fortunately forecasts do not have to complicated to be good, although the methods do have to be understood if they are to be useful. This chapter introduces the forecasting alternatives for sales, markets, technology and society. It gives examples of their use and suggests what to use and when.

11.1 Forecasting what?

Market demand measurement calls for a clear understanding of the market involved. A *market* is the set of all actual and potential buyers of a product or service. A market is the set of buyers, and an *industry* is the set of sellers. The size of a market hinges on the number of buyers who might exist for a particular market offer. Potential buyers for something have three characteristics: interest, income and access.

Companies commonly use a three-stage procedure to arrive at a sales forecast. First, they make an *environmental forecast*, followed by an industry *demand forecast*, followed by a company *sales forecast*. The environmental forecast calls for project-ing inflation, unemployment, interest rates, consumer spending and saving, business investment, government expenditures, net exports and other environmental events important to the company. The result is a forecast of gross national product used, along with other indicators, to forecast industry sales. Then the company prepares its sales forecast assuming a certain share of industry sales.

Companies use many techniques to forecast their sales. All are built on one of four information bases: what there is, what has happened, what happens when, or what people think will happen. There are numerous forecasting methods for each use with each information base (Saunders, Sharp and Witt, 1987). Figure 11.1 relates the important ones.

11.2 *What there is*

Companies have developed various practical methods for estimating total market demand (Barnett, 1988). We illustrate three.

11.2.1 Market build-up method

The *market build-up* method identifies all the potential buyers in each market and estimates their potential purchases.

Suppose Polygram wants to estimate the total annual sales of recorded compact discs. A common way to estimate total market demand is as follows:

$$Q = n \times q \times p$$

where:

    Q = total market demand;
    n = number of buyers in the market;
    q = quantity purchased by an average buyer per year; and
    p = price of an average unit.

If there are 10 million buyers of CDs each year and the average buyer buys six CDs a year and the average price is £15, then the total market demand for CDs is $10,000,000 \times 6 \times £15.00 = £900$ million.

The market build-up method faces the problem of all demand measurement methods: it is about the present, not the future. To find out what the market will be, forecasters have to estimate the future number of buyers, quantity purchased and prices. This disaggregation has its advantages. The three components are easier to forecast than sales alone. For example, existing population distributions make it easy to forecast an increased demand for medical support as the population ages.

11.2.2 Chain ratios

The *chain ratio* method multiplies a base number by a chain of adjusting percentages.

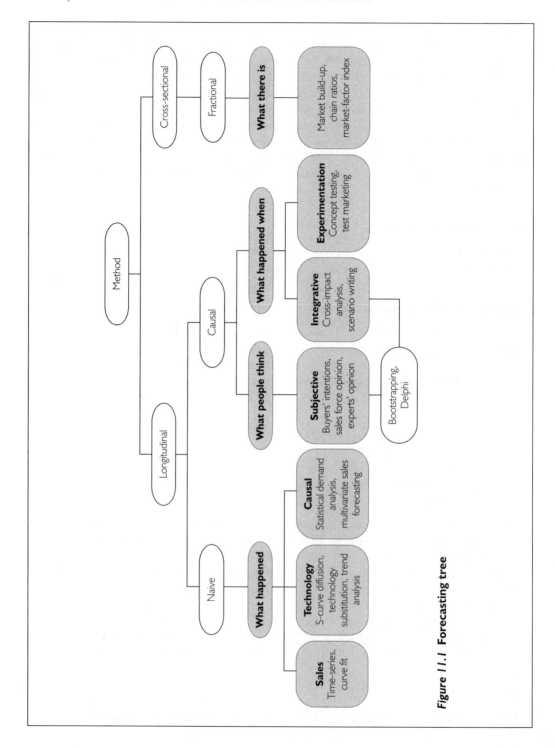

Figure 11.1 **Forecasting tree**

For example, Britain has no national service, so the British Army needs to attract 20,000 recruits each year. There is a problem here, since the Army is already under-strength and the population of 16–19 year olds is declining. The marketing question is whether this is a reasonable target in relation to the market potential. The Army estimates market potential using the following method:

Total number of males in age group:	1,200,000
Percentage who are militarily qualified (no physical, emotional or mental handicaps):	50%
Percentage of those qualified who are potentially interested in military service:	5%
Percentage of those qualified and interested in military service who consider the Army the preferred service:	60%

This chain of numbers shows a market potential of $1,200,000 \times 0.5 \times 0.05 \times 0.6 = 18,000$ recruits, fewer than needed. Since this is less than the target number of recruits sought, the Army needs to do a better job of marketing itself. They responded by doing motivational research which showed existing advertising did not attract the target age group, although a military career did give them what they wanted. A new campaign therefore aimed to increase the attractiveness of a military career.

11.2.3 Market-factor index method

The *market-factor index* method estimates the market potential for consumer goods. A manufacturer of shirts wishes to evaluate its sales performance with market potential in Scotland. It estimates total national potential for dress shirts at £400 million per year. The company's current nationwide sales are £4,800,000 – about a 1.2 per cent share of the total potential market. Its sales in Scotland are £1,200,000. It wants to know whether its share of the Scottish market is higher or lower than its national market share. To find this out, the company first needs to calculate market potential in Scotland.

One way of calculating this is to multiply together population and the area's income per capita by the average share of income spent on shirts. The product then compares with that for the whole country. Using this calculation, the shirt manufacturer finds that Scotland has 8 per cent of the UK's total potential demand for dress shirts. Since the total national potential is £400 million each year, total potential in Scotland is $0.08 \times £400m = £32$ million. Thus the company's sales in Scotland of £1,200,000 is $£1,200,000/£32$ million $= 3.75$ per cent share of area market potential. Comparing this with the 1.2 per cent national share, the company appears to be doing much better in Scotland than in other parts of the UK.

11.3 *What happened*

Time-series analyses use the pattern of past sales, or other items, to estimate the future. Although it is basically naive, it often outperforms more complicated methods. Its objectivity is one reason for its success. Time-series analyses are so mechanistic that there is little room for managerial intervention to bias results.

11.3.1 Time-series analysis

Many firms base their forecasts on past sales. A method our cynical Ralph Harris 'vividly compared to steering a ship by its wake'. They assume that statistical analysis can uncover the causes of past sales. Then analysts can use the causal relations to predict future sales.

Time-series analysis consists of breaking down sales into four components – trend, cycle, season and erratic components (see Figure 11.2) – then recombining these components to produce the sales forecast.

1. **Trend** is the long-term, underlying pattern of growth/decline in sales resulting from basic changes in population, capital formation and technology. It is found by fitting a straight or curved line through past sales.
2. **Cycle** captures the medium-term, wavelike movement of sales resulting from changes in general economic and competitive activity. The cyclical component can be useful for medium-range forecasting. Cyclical swings, however, are difficult to predict because they do not occur on a regular basis.
3. **Seasonality** refers to a consistent pattern of sales movements within the year. The term *season* describes any recurrent hourly, weekly, monthly or quarterly

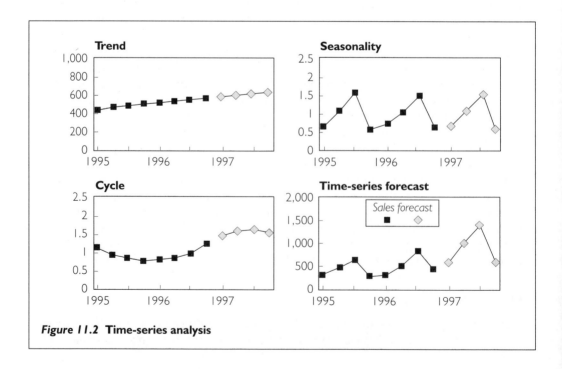

***Figure 11.2* Time-series analysis**

sales pattern. The seasonal component may relate to weather factors, holidays and trade customs. The seasonal pattern provides a norm for forecasting short-range sales.

4. **Erratic events** include fads, strikes, earthquakes, riots, fires and other disturbances. These components, by definition, are unpredictable and should be removed from past data to see the more normal behaviour of sales. One British retailer found that the best predictor of daily sales was the depth of snow falling. A true, but not useful result!

In this method sales volume, V_t, in period t is calculated from the product past sales, V_{t-1}, trend, T_t, cyclical, C_t, and seasonal, S_t, components.

$$V_i = V_{t-1} \times T_t \times C_t \times S_t$$

Having sold 12,000 life insurance policies this year $(V_{t-1} = 12,000)$, a life insurance company wants to predict next year's December sales. The long-term trend shows a 5 per cent sales growth rate per year $(T_t = 1.05)$. This suggests sales next year of £12,000 × 1.05 = £12,600. However, a business recession is expected next year, which will probably result in total sales achieving only 90 per cent of the expected trend-adjusted sales $(C_t = 0.90)$. Sales next year are therefore more likely to be £12,000 × 1.05 × 0.90 = £11,340. If sales were the same each month, monthly sales would be £11,340/12 = £945. However, December is an above-average month for insurance policy sales, with a seasonal index, S_{12}, standing at 1.30. Therefore December sales may be as high as £945 × 1.30 = £1,228.

The central issue in time-series analysis is estimating the seasonal, cyclical and trend components. A simple approach is to average these over several years, although this does not give any extra weighting to recent events and there is always a problem about how many periods to average. Exponentially weighted moving averages overcomes this problem by including all past statistics but weighting recent ones more highly. This avoids the truncation problem, but the exponential decay rates that weight the past figures then become an issue. Many methods have been developed to adjust weights automatically but all have the same limitation of all time-series analysis: they assume past patterns will continue.

11.3.2 Trend analysis

Curve fitting
Trend analysis is the most widely used and abused method of strategic forecasting. It is popular because it is quick and easy to use. It is abused when it is used thoughtlessly to give naive but statistically reliable results. The approach fits an equation to historical time-series data then projects that curve into the future to produce a forecast. Figure 11.3 is a typical case where the objective is to use the sales history from 1990 to 1994, S_Y, to produce a forecast for 1995 and 1996.

The basic form of trend analysis fits a straight line to the time-series and then uses the result to extrapolate to future sales levels. This assumes that VCR sales will

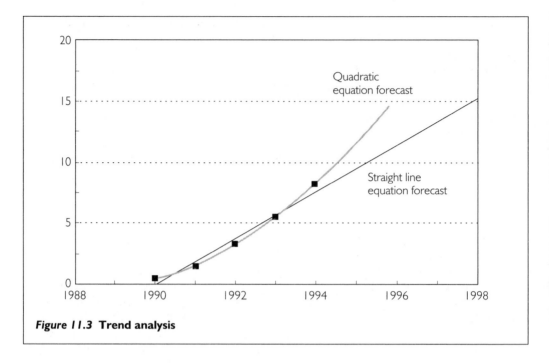

Figure 11.3 Trend analysis

increase by the same amount each year, a trend explained by the linear equation:

$$F_Y = a + b \times T$$

where:

F_Y is the forecast video tape recorder sales in year Y, where $T = Y - 1980$, a and b are unknown coefficients to be estimated.

The basic question of trend analysis, and many other statistical forecasting tools, is the estimation of the unknown coefficients. Regression analysis is the most common way of doing this. It calculates the values of the coefficient that minimize the sum of the squares of the differences between actual and forecast sales, minimizing

$$\sum_{Y=1980}^{1984} u_Y^2,$$

where u_Y is the error term, $F_Y - S_Y$.

The approach gives the equation:

$$F_Y = 0.14 + 1.65 \times T + u_Y$$

$$R^2 = 0.987$$

The R^2 value indicates a reasonably good fit since its value can range between 1, meaning a perfect fit to the data, and 0, meaning no fit at all.

This statistically excellent result reveals the dangers of trend analysis. The result is naive; only a fool would expect VCR sales to increase linearly with time for ever! Visual inspection also shows that the sales trend is not a straight line but one that curves upwards. Trend analysis can overcome this problem by fitting a more complex equation. A quadratic equation allows regression analysis to produce an equation with a better fit and shape:

$$F_Y = 0.44 + 1.05 \times T + 0.15 \times T^2 + u_Y$$

$$R^2 = 0.999$$

substituting $T = 5$, for 1985 and $T = 6$, for 1986. The results also give upper and lower limits (95 per cent) of the estimate – figures that are a useful by-product of regression analysis.

The linear and quadratic forms are two of many equations that can be used to fit trends. Other forecast could be:

Log quadratic $RF_Y = EXP(-0.67249 + 1.1727 \times T + 0.13112 \times T^2)$, $R^2 = 0.999$

Exponential $F_Y = 0.66348 \times EXP(0.64821 \times T)$, $R^2 = 0.945$

Modified
hyperbola $F_Y = 1/(1.5006 - 0.4181 \times T)$, $R^2 = 0.730$

The fits are good but what do they forecast? The quadratic and exponential forms both forecast sales growing increasingly rapidly, but the exponential form at such a rapid rate that it produces a forecast of over 30,000,000 units in 1996 – more than one per household in the UK. Unfortunately, the two curves with the best fit give the most contrasting forecasts. While quadratic suggests a reasonable exponential increase, the log quadratic forecasts declining sales after 1984.

The results show the danger of collapsing the shape and curve fitting parts of trend analysis. Curve fitting using regression analysis should only be attempted after the desired shape and expression have been chosen. If in doubt, use a straight line to fit the series. It may be obviously wrong, but at least its limitations are known. Alternatively, the careful choice of series to be analyzed and the use of constrained trend analysis can overcome some of the problems with wayward curves.

Despite its limitation, there are several useful applications of trend analysis. Sales are the most common but the adoption rate of new products, the substitution of one technology for another and technology forecasting are other areas where trend analysis is effective. Trend analysis also inherits several advantages from regression analysis. It is relatively quick and easy to use and, because it is based on a well-understood technique, it provides statistical measures of the reliability and validity of the results.

The S-curve
S-shaped time-series, or curves that saturate to an upper limit, are particularly suited to time-series analysis. In technology and sales forecasting there is often an upper limit beyond which performance or sales can never go. Take, for example,

the motor car engine. There is a theoretical limit to the thermal efficiency that the internal combustion engine can ever achieve, so it is expected that gains from spending on R&D would decline as the theoretical limit is approached. Similarly, for VCR sales, there is obviously some upper limit to the sales that can be made. By taking into account these rational or practical constraints the quality and reliability of trend analysis can be significantly increased.

When forecasting the potential of a new product group, like a VCR, it is easier and more reliable to forecast penetration rather than sales. This is because penetration always follows a particular type of curve that has an upper limit. For domestic appliances the absolute upper limit must be 100 per cent of households although there are some goods, such as dishwashers, that appear to have saturated at a much lower level.

Figure 11.4 contains penetration figures and a forecast for VCRs. The forecast is produced using a Gompertz curve which is S-shaped and saturates. The expression has the form

$$F_T = a_0 \times a_1^{a_2^T}$$

where a_0, a_1 and a_2 are parameters to be estimated and T is time. After solution a_0 is the saturation level, the level beyond which sales will never go, and $a_0 \times a_1$ is the forecast when $T = 0$. Unfortunately, the Gompertz equation has to be solved using

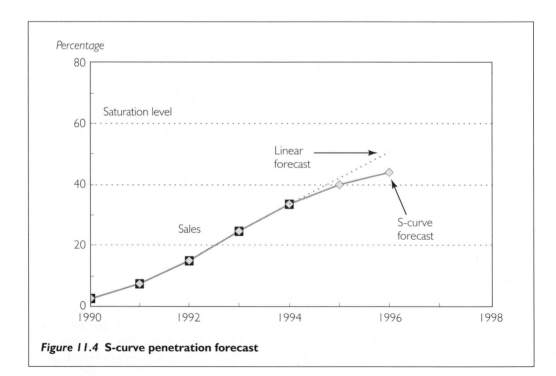

Figure 11.4 S-curve penetration forecast

non-linear estimation techniques rather than regression. These are iterative procedures that use rules to guide the search for the coefficients that would otherwise be
estimated using regression analysis. There is a wide range of procedures, but they
are not all robust.

The Gompertz equation for the VCR penetration series is:

$$VCRF_Y = 59.2 \times 0.0420^{0.647^T}$$

where T = the year 1980.

This suggests a saturation level of penetration to be 59.2 per cent of households,
with sales declining after 1994. As an alternative to using non-linear estimation to
estimate an S-curve, the Gompertz equation, or a similar *logistic model*, can be
solved using regression analysis if saturation level (a_0) is assumed.

These transformations allow reliable S-shaped expressions to be estimated, but
if an inappropriate saturation level is chosen, the results will provide a poor fit to the
data. When this occurs alternative saturation levels should be tried until a more sat-
isfactory result is obtained. If the search procedure is conducted systematically, the
process would become one of non-linear estimation. The following specialized cases
of the diffusion of innovations and technology substitution provide other examples
of where constrained trend analysis can be profitably used.

The similarity between the S-shaped curve explaining the adoption of a product
and a plot of the early stages of the product life cycle is misleading. The S-curve
tracks first uses of a product and leads to a saturation level when all users have
adopted the product. In contrast, the product life cycle tracks sales that include
repeat purchases as well as first-time uses. These curves are often out of phase. For
example, in Europe almost everyone has travelled by bus so the S-curve of the
adoption has levelled off and will not go up and cannot go down. Conversely the
product life cycle for buses is declining as more people take to their cars. An opposite case occurs for UK wine consumption. Again the S-curve for adoption has levelled out as most people who are willing and able to try wine have done so. However
the product life cycle curve for wine in the UK continues to increase as people
consume more table wine.

The 'market build-up' model discussed above (section 11.2.1) links the adoption
and product life cycle curves. In this the S-curve plots closely follows 'the number
of buyers in the market' while the product life cycle represents 'total market
demand'.

Diffusion of innovations
Some insights into the mechanism of the diffusion of innovations have led to trend
analysis models with some behavioural detail. Bass (1969) has produced a new
product growth model for consumer durables which is based on the innovative and
imitative behaviour of consumers. For VCRs this suggests that I_T, the increase in
penetration in time T will be

$$I_T = r(M - P_T) + p(M - P_T)P_T/M$$

where:

$r(M - P_T)$ is the *innovation effect*, proportional to the untapped potential;
$p(M - P_T)P_T/M$ is the *imitation effect*, proportional to the potential already tapped;
M is the final potential achieved as a fraction of the maximum potential;
P_T is the penetration achieved at time T.

This makes the realistic assumption that some individuals make their adoption decision independently (innovators), while others (imitators) are influenced by the number of people who have already adopted. The shape of the cumulative penetration curve depends upon the relative magnitudes of the *innovation rate* (r) and the *imitation rate* (p). If the *innovation rate* is larger than the *imitation rate* sales will start quickly then slowly approach saturation. However, if *imitation rate* dominates, an S-shaped curve will occur. Once sufficient data have been collected r and p can be using regression analysis.

The diffusion equations are a useful variation on conventional trend analysis. Unlike other time-series methods, they are based on ideas about consumer behaviour. Actual diffusion processes are obviously far more complex than the simple dichotomy into innovators and imitators suggests, but the resulting equations are robust and can produce reliable forecasts.

There have been attempts to produce more sophisticated diffusion models by adding extra dimensions. These have had limited success. Most add the effect of one or two marketing variables (usually advertising and promotion), but there is no unified theory of how to incorporate marketing or exogenous variables. The few comparisons that have been made tend to show that the extra sophistication offers little improvement over the simple models. A major limitation of the more sophisticated models is their need to be estimated early in a product's life when little data are available.

Technology substitution
Technology substitution is a special case of the diffusion of innovation that occurs when a new technology replaces an old one; for example, the substitution of air for sea/rail travel, or the replacement of vinyl albums by pre-recorded tapes or compact discs. Substitution can be forecast in the same way as conventional diffusion processes by the very neat method devised by Fisher and Pry (1978).

The Fisher–Pry method represents a series showing a new idea replacing an older one, in this case, the per capita consumption of margarine and butter where:

$$f_T/(f_T - 1) = e^{d + bT}$$

where:

f_T is the fraction of people having adopted the new technology (margarine) at time T,
d and b need estimating.

Regression analysis gives the result:

$$f_T/f_T - 1) = e^{-0.261 + 0.284T}, \qquad R^2 = 0.928$$

Although an equation can be solved using regression, the beauty of the substitution process is its regularity which allows a clever transformation to show the process as a straight line that can be projected without resorting to statistics. This result shows the proportion of margarine consumed continuing to increase from 81 per cent in 1995 to 91 per cent by 2005.

The Fisher–Pry method is a simple way of looking at a very complex process. Over the decades covered by the substitution the economic, trade and health reasons for the change must have undergone many changes. An attempt to model the change causally would have to find some way of representing all the mechanisms involved. Like the other trend analysis methods, the Fisher–Pry approach observes the aggregate effect of all the influences and assumes that together they will produce the same pattern of substitution in the future as they did in the past. However, sometimes one of the major influences does undergo a major change and affect the rate of substitution.

Technology trend analysis
Technology trend analysis seeks to forecast changes in technological performance rather than sales. It has grown out of the realization that, for most of the time, technological progress proceeds at a steady pace. Figure 11.5 is a case that shows how

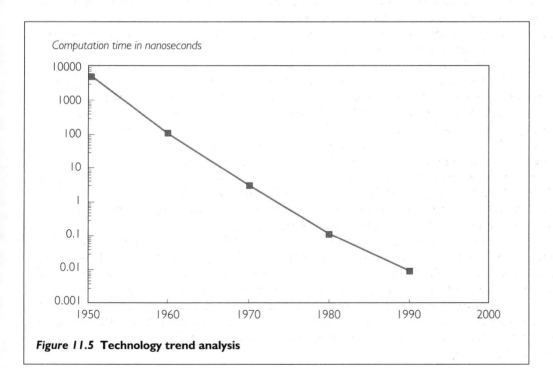

Figure 11.5 **Technology trend analysis**

this is true for computational speeds that have changed dramatically over the last 40 years.

The trend analysis of technological progress appears to be at odds with the popular view of unexpected scientific progress, but unexpected breakthroughs are much rarer than commonly supposed. The much quoted example of penicillin is the exception rather than the rule. Most of the innovation in the early decades of the new millennium will be based upon scientific and technological knowledge existing now. The pattern of technological progress tends to be uniform because it is usually achieved as the result of designers selecting and integrating a large number of innovations from diverse technological areas to produce the higher performance achieved.

Often the impact of a radically new innovation is swamped by the steady progress of evolutionary developments in related areas. This is shown by the change of computational speeds. The period covers major discontinuous innovations (from vacuum tubes in 1950 to transistors in 1960, silicon chips in 1970 and gallium arsenide in 1980), but the progress is regular. The transistor itself provides a good example of the relative impact of breakthroughs. It is often credited with being responsible for the size reduction in electronic equipment, yet without the parallel development of ancillary technologies, it is estimated that transistor-based electronic equipment would be only marginally smaller (about 10 per cent) than a vacuum tube version.

So technological trend analysis is based on the same assumption as the Fisher–Pry approach to technological substitution. Both are the result of very complex processes, but their cumulative effect tends to be regular, and the past trends can be a good indication of the immediate future.

The recognition of the S-shaped path of technological progress is a major feature of technology trend analysis. Initially technological progress is slow, maybe because few people are involved, basic scientific knowledge must be gained, and engineering obstacles cleared. Conventional wisdom and the establishment can hold back development for a long time. Combat aircraft technology progressed rapidly in the First World War, but then became almost frozen for 20 years as military budgets were cut and the senior services resisted flying machines. Advances start to accelerate exponentially once the importance of a technology is realized and technological effort and funds are expanded. The threat of the Second World War stimulated the rapid increase in combat aircraft performance and this continued after the war and the introduction of radically new jet engine technology.

Finally, technological advances cease to accelerate and may stop growing altogether. There are two reasons why rapid technological progress ends. First, there may be an absolute limit to the technology. For example, the maximum speed of operational helicopters has saturated at just above 350 kph. Above that speed either the forward moving rotor becomes supersonic (so loses lift), or the rearward moving rotor stalls (also losing lift). By using radically new technology the barrier can be overcome, but not satisfactorily or economically for most helicopter roles, even with military R&D budgets.

Sometimes the barrier is purely economic. For example, the 'sound barrier' did not slow combat aircraft development, so why should civil aircraft not be supersonic? Concorde and the Tu-144 (maybe) have shown there is no technological barrier, but all economically successful aircraft are subsonic. Practical technologies stop advancing when rapidly diminishing returns set in. At the moment, the limited economic value to the customer of supersonic air travel, in conjunction with its high economic and social costs, make the speed of sound an economic barrier. Even combat aircraft appear to have reached a non-technological barrier to their development. Faster combat aircraft could be built but at too great a cost to other performance criteria, and speed, just like size, isn't everything! These days it is much better to be invisible than fast, like the B-2 and F-117 stealth aircraft.

The S-shaped curve of technological trends is more prone to uncertainty than that of sales trends. The initial slow growth may not exist if the potential of a new idea is grasped quickly. Both helicopter and laser technology developed rapidly from the start because their significance was obvious and they were no challenges to established power-bases. Levelling of development is usually due to a combination of technological and economic factors. Often the trend line continues across several major technological innovations but new technologies can sometimes cause rapid changes as is now occurring in telecommunications where satellites and deregulation have destroyed the relationship between the distance of phone calls and cost, if not price.

The normally regular pace of technological development makes technology trend analysis a useful planning tool. It can help set realistic performance targets for new developments and prevent heavy expenditure on technologies when the likely returns are diminishing. However, it is a tool that can be dangerous if used thoughtlessly.

Often it is not obvious which performance trends are central. US aero engine manufacturers, and the British government, initially rejected jet engines for transport aircraft because some experts were preoccupied with specific fuel consumption as the criterion for comparing aero engines. Relative to piston engines, jet engines still have poor specific fuel consumption, but they are supreme in terms of passenger miles per unit cost. To overcome this myopia, identifying at least half a dozen attributes or, more likely, twice that is necessary. The criteria should then be used, compared and reviewed periodically.

Technology trend lines are often fitted manually rather than using regression analysis. Regression analysis is limited because transformations are often unable to follow the rapid saturation that sometimes occur. It provides a good statistical fit to the data but produces a shape which overshoots natural or economic barriers. A second disadvantage of regression is the need to envelop data points rather than fit a line of best fit through them. It is usually the extremes of performance, rather than the average, that are tracked. However, developments in envelope methods are overcoming this problem (Bultez and Parsons, 1998).

The direction and limits of trends should be explored carefully. It is easy to neglect the limits to performance improvement when competition has focused attention on a particular criterion for a long time. Potential technical, economic, social, political and ecological reasons for barriers should be considered. Often, as was the case with Concorde, the actual limit is not due to one factor, but a combination of factors.

11.3.3 Leading indicators

Many companies try to forecast their sales by finding one or more *leading indicators*: that is, other time-series that change in the same direction but ahead of company sales. For example, a plumbing supply company might find that its sales lag behind the housing starts index by about four months. An index of housing starts would then be a useful leading indicator. Other leading indicators, such as birth rates and life expectancy, show huge shifts in markets in the next millennium. Many developed countries, including France, Germany and Japan, will have huge problems funding the greying population's pensions. Other countries with funded pension schemes, including the Netherlands, the US and the UK, will have an increasingly wealthy ageing population. Despite the wide difference in country's preparedness for this easy to forecast demographic shift, all will enjoy one rapidly growing market over the next few decades: the funeral market.

It can be dangerous to assume that the indicators that served in the past will continue to do so in the future, or will transfer from one market to another. For example, Disney places great stress on a model of concentric circles around its theme park sites, in which travel time and population numbers indicate demand. Part of the initial failure of EuroDisney was because the company clung to this model, ignoring the fact that Europeans have different vacation spending and travel behaviour from Americans.

11.3.4 Multivariate statistical analysis

Time-series analysis treats past and future sales as a function of time, rather than as a function of any real demand factors. But many real factors affect the sales of any product.

Statistical demand analysis
Statistical demand analysis uses statistical procedures to discover the most important real factors affecting sales and their relative influence. The factors most commonly analyzed are prices, income, population and promotion. It consists of expressing sales (Q_T) as a dependent variable and trying to explain sales as a function of a number of independent demand variables $X_1, X_2, ..., X_n$. That is:

$$Q_T = f(X_1, X_2, ..., X_n)$$

Using multiple-regression analysis, various equations can be fitted to the data to find the best predicting factors and equation.

For example, the South of Scotland Electricity Board developed an equation that predicted the annual sales of washing machines (Q_T) to be (Moutinho, 1991):

$$Q_T = 210{,}739 - 703P_T + 69H_T + 20Y_T;$$

where:

P_T is average installed price;
H_T is new single-family homes connected to utilities;
Y_T and per capita income.

Thus in a year when an average installed price is £387, there are 5,000 new connected homes, and the average per capita income is £4,800, from the equation we would predict the actual sales of washing machines to be 379,678 units:

$$Q = 210{,}739 - 703(387) + 69(5{,}000) + 20(4{,}800)$$

The equation was found to be 95 per cent accurate. If the equation predicted as well as this for other regions, it would serve as a useful forecasting tool. Marketing management would predict next year's per capita income, new homes and prices and use them to make forecasts. Statistical demand analysis can be very complex and the marketer must take care in designing, conducting and interpreting such analysis. Yet constantly improving computer technology has made statistical demand analysis an increasingly popular approach to forecasting.

Multivariate sales forecasting
Information gathered by the company's marketing information systems often requires more analysis, and sometimes managers may need more help in applying it to marketing problems and decisions. This help may include advanced statistical analysis to learn more about both the relationships within a set of data and their statistical reliability. Such analysis allows managers to go beyond means and standard deviations in the data. In an examination of consumer non-durable goods in the Netherlands, regression analysis gave a model that forecast a brand's market share (B_t) based upon predicted marketing activity (Alsem, Leeflang and Reuyl, 1989):

$$B_t = -7.86 - 1.45P_T + 0.084_{T-1} + 1.23D_T$$

where:

P_T is relative price of brand;
A_{T-1} is advertising share in the previous period;
D_T is effective store distribution.

This, and models like it, can help answer marketing questions such as:

➤ What are the chief variables affecting my sales and how important is each one?
➤ If I raised my price 10 per cent and increased my advertising expenditures 20 per cent, what would happen to sales?
➤ How much should I spend on advertising?

➤ What are the best predictors of which consumers are likely to buy my brand versus my competitor's brand?

➤ What are the best variables for segmenting my market and how many segments exist?

Information analysis might also involve a collection of mathematical models that will help marketers make better decisions. Each model represents some real system, process or outcome. These models can help answer the questions of *what if?* and *which is best?* During the past twenty years, marketing scientists have developed numerous models to help marketing managers make better marketing-mix decisions, design sales territories and sales-call plans, select sites for retail outlets, develop optimal advertising mixes and forecast new-product sales.

11.4 *What happens when*

Where buyers do not plan their purchases carefully or where experts are not available or reliable, the company may want to conduct a direct test market. This is especially useful in forecasting new-product sales or established-product sales in a new distribution channel or territory. New-product forecasting methods range from quick and inexpensive concept testing that tests products before they even exist, to highly expensive test markets that test the whole marketing mix in a geographical region.

11.4.1 Concept testing

Concept testing calls for testing new-product concepts with a group of target consumers. The concepts may be presented to consumers symbolically or physically. Here, in words, is *Concept 1*:

> An efficient, fun-to-drive, electric-powered subcompact car that seats four. Great for shopping trips and visits to friends. Costs half as much to operate as similar petrol-driven cars. Goes up to 90 km per hour and does not need to be recharged for 170 km. Priced at £6,000.

In this case, a word or picture description might be sufficient. However, a more concrete and physical presentation of the concept will increase the reliability of the concept test. Today, marketers are finding innovative ways to make product concepts more real to concept-test subjects.

After being exposed to the concept, consumers may be asked their likelihood of buying the product. The answers will help the company decide which concept has the strongest appeal. For example, the last question asks about the consumer's intention to buy. Suppose 10 per cent of the consumers said they 'definitely' would buy and another 5 per cent said 'probably'. The company could project these figures to the population size of this target group to estimate sales volume. Concept testing offers a rough estimate of potential sales, but managers must view this with caution. They must recognize that the estimate is only a broad pointer and is uncertain largely because consumers do not always carry out stated intentions. Drivers, for example, might like the idea of the electric car that is kind to the environment, but might not want to pay for one! It is, none the less, important to carry out such tests with product concepts so as to gauge customers' response as well as identify aspects of the concept that are particularly liked or disliked by potential buyers. Feedback might suggest ways to refine the concept, thereby increasing its appeal to customers.

11.4.2 Pre-test markets

Companies can also test new products in a simulated shopping environment. The company or research firm shows, to a sample of consumers, ads and promotions for a variety of products, including the new product being tested. It gives consumers a small amount of money and invites times to a real or laboratory store where they may keep the money or use it to buy items. The researchers note how many consumers buy the new product and competing brands. This simulation provides a measure of trial of the commercial's effectiveness against competing commercials. The researchers then ask consumers the reasons for their purchase or non-purchase. Some weeks later, they interview the consumer by phone to determine product attitudes, usage, satisfaction, and repurchase intentions. Using sophisticated computer models, the researchers then project national sales from results of the simulated test market.

Simulated test markets overcome some of the disadvantages of standard and controlled test markets. They usually cost much less (£25,000–£50,000), can be run in eight weeks, and keep the new product out of competitors' view. Yet, because of their small samples and simulated shopping environments, many marketers do not think that simulated test markets are as accurate or reliable as larger, real-world tests. Still, simulated test markets are used widely, often as 'pretest' markets. Because they are fast and inexpensive, one or more simulated tests can be run to assess a new product or its marketing programme quickly. If the pretest results are strongly positive, the product might be introduced without further testing. If the results are very poor, the product might be dropped or substantially redesigned and retested. If the results are promising but indefinite, the product and marketing programme can be tested further in controlled or standard test markets.

11.4.3 Mini-test markets

Several research firms keep controlled panels of stores which have agreed to carry new products for a fee. The company with the new product specifies the number of stores and geographical locations it wants. The research firm delivers the product to the participating stores and controls shelf location, amount of shelf space, displays and point-of-purchase promotions, and pricing according to specified plans. Sales results are tracked to determine the impact of these factors on demand.

Controlled test-marketing systems are particularly well developed in the US. Systems like Nielsen's Scantrack and Information Resources Inc.'s (IRI) BehaviorScan track individual behaviour from the television set to the checkout counter. IRI, for example, keeps panels of shoppers in carefully selected cities. It uses microcomputers to measure TV viewing in each panel household and can send special commercials to panel member television sets. Panel consumers buy from co-operating stores and show identification cards when making purchases. Detailed, electronic-scanner information on each consumer's purchases is fed into a central computer, where it is combined with the consumer's demographic and TV viewing information and reported daily. Thus BehaviorScan can provide store-by-store, week-by-week reports on the sales of new products being tested. And because the scanners record the specific purchases of individual consumers, the system also can provide information on repeat purchases and the ways that different types of consumers are reacting to the new product, its advertising and various other elements of the marketing programme.

Controlled test markets take less time than standard test markets (six months to a year) and usually cost less. However, some companies are concerned that the limited number of small cities and panel consumers used by the research services may not be representative of their products' markets or target consumers. And, as in standard test markets, controlled test markets allow competitors to get a look at the company's new product.

11.4.4 Full test market

Full test markets test the new consumer product in situations similar to those it would face in a full-scale launch. The company finds a small number of representative test cities where the company's salesforce tries to persuade resellers to carry the product and give it good shelf space and promotion support. The company puts on a full advertising and promotion campaign in these markets and uses store audits, consumer and distributor surveys, and other measures to gauge product performance. It then uses the results to forecast national sales and profits, to discover potential product problems and to fine-tune the marketing programme.

Standard market tests have some drawbacks. First, they take a long time to complete – sometimes 1–3 years. If the testing proves to be unnecessary, the company will have lost many months of sales and profits. Second, extensive standard test markets may be very costly. Finally, full test markets give competitors a look at the company's new product well before it is introduced nationally. Many competitors will analyze the product and monitor the company's test market results. If the testing goes on too long, competitors will have time to develop defensive strategies and may even beat the company's product to the market. For example, prior to its launch in the UK, Carnation's Coffee-Mate, a coffee-whitener, was test marketed over a period of six years. This gave rival firm Cadbury ample warning and the opportunity to develop and introduce its own product – Cadbury's Coffee Compliment – to compete head on with Coffee-Mate.

There are other dangers. In 1997, Sainsbury was conducting price tests by charging different prices at different stores to gauge customer response. When discovered, this made headline news, with the company criticized for the unfairness of differential pricing even in market test. Market testing which endangers brand equity is unlikely to be pursued by many companies.

Furthermore competitors often try to distort test market results by cutting their prices in test cities, increasing their promotion or even buying up the product being tested. Despite these disadvantages, standard test markets are still the most widely used approach for significant market testing. But many companies today are shifting towards quicker and cheaper controlled and simulated test-marketing methods.

Full test marketing tests its entire marketing programme for the product – its positioning strategy, advertising distribution, pricing, branding and packaging, and budget levels. The company uses it to learn how consumers and dealers will react to handling, using and repurchasing the product. The results can be used to make better sales and profit forecasts. Thus a good test market can provide a wealth of information about the potential success of the product and marketing programme.

The cost of a full test market can be enormous and test marketing takes time that may allow competitors to gain advantages. When the costs of developing and introducing the product are low or when management is already confident that the new product will succeed, the company may do little or no test marketing. Minor modifications of current products or copies of successful competitors' products might not need standard testing. But when the new-product introduction requires a large investment, or when management is not sure of the product or marketing programme, the company should do a lot of test marketing. In fact, some products and marketing programmes are tested, withdrawn, changed and retested many times during a period of several years before they are finally introduced. The costs of such test markets are high, but they are often small compared with the costs of making a serious mistake.

Whether or not a company test markets, and the amount of testing it does, depends on the cost and risk of introducing the product on the one hand, and on the testing costs and time pressures on the other. Test marketing methods vary with the type of product and market situation, and each method has advantages and disadvantages.

11.4.5 Test marketing industrial goods

Business marketers use different methods for test marketing their new products, such as: product-use tests; trade shows; distributor/dealer display rooms; and standard or controlled test markets.

➤ **Product-use tests**: Here the business marketer selects a small group of potential customers who agree to use the new product for a limited time. The manufacturer's technical people watch how these customers use the product. From this test the manufacturer learns about customer training and servicing requirements. After the test, the marketer asks the customer about purchase intent and other reactions.

➤ **Trade shows**: These shows draw a large number of buyers who view new products in a few concentrated days. The manufacturer sees how buyers react to various product features and terms, and can assess buyer interest and purchase intentions.

➤ **Distributor and dealer display rooms**: Here the new industrial product may stand next to other company products and possibly competitors' products. This method yields preference and pricing information in the normal selling atmosphere of the product.

➤ **Standard or controlled test markets**: These are used to measure the potential of new industrial products. The business marketer produces a limited supply of the product and gives it to the salesforce to sell in a limited number of geographical areas. The company gives the product full advertising, sales promotion, and other marketing support. Such test markets let the company test the product and its marketing programme in real market situations.

11.5 *What people think will happen*

11.5.1 **Buyers' intentions**

One way to forecast what buyers will do is to ask them directly. This suggests that the forecaster should survey buyers. Surveys are especially valuable if the buyers have clearly formed intentions, will carry them out and can describe them to interviewers.

Several research organizations conduct periodic surveys of consumer buying intentions. These also ask about consumers' present and future personal finances and their expectations about the economy. Consumer-durable goods companies subscribe to these indexes to help them anticipate significant shifts in consumer buying intentions, so that they can adjust their production and marketing plans accordingly. For *business buying*, various agencies carry out intention surveys about plant, equipment and materials purchases. These measures need adjusting when conducted across nations and cultures. Overestimation of intention to buy is higher in southern Europe than it is in northern Europe and the United States. In Asia, the Japanese tend to make fewer overstatements than the Chinese (Lin, 1990).

11.5.2 **Salesforce opinions**

When buyer interviewing is impractical, the company may base its sales forecasts on information provided by the salesforce. The company typically asks its salespeople to estimate sales by product for their individual territories. It then adds up the individual estimates to arrive at an overall sales forecast.

Few companies use their salesforce's estimates without some adjustments. Salespeople are based observers. They may be naturally pessimistic or optimistic, or they may go to one extreme or another because of recent sales setbacks or successes. Furthermore they are often unaware of larger economic developments and do not always know how their company's marketing plans will affect future sales in their territories. They may understate demand so that the company will set a low sales quota. They may not have the time to prepare careful estimates or may not consider it worthwhile.

Accepting these biases, a number of benefits can be gained by involving the salesforce in forecasting. Salespeople may have better insights into developing trends than any other group. After participating in the forecasting process, the sales-people may have greater confidence in their quotas and more incentive to achieve them. Also, such 'grassroots' forecasting provides estimates broken down by product, territory, customer and salesperson.

11.5.3 Dealer opinions

Motor vehicle companies survey their dealers periodically for their forecasts of short-term demand. Although dealer estimates have the same strengths and weak-nesses as salesforce estimates, forecasting accuracy can be improved by using role playing exercises, involving both sales people and dealers (Armstrong and Hutcherson, 1989).

11.5.4 Expert opinion

Companies can also obtain forecasts by turning to experts: distributors, suppliers, marketing consultants and trade associations. Experts can provide good insights, but they can be wildly wrong. In 1943 IBM's Chairman, Thomas J. Watson, pre-dicted 'a world market for five computers'. Soon after that another expert, Twentieth Century Fox's head Darryl F. Zanuck, predicted that 'TV won't be able to hold on to any market it captures after the first six months. People will soon get tired of staring at a plywood box every night.' Where possible, the company should verify experts' opinions with other estimates.

11.5.5 Delphi method

Occasionally companies will invite a special group of experts to prepare a forecast. They exchange views and come up with a group estimate (group discussion method). Or they may supply their estimates individually, with the company analyst combining them into a single estimate (pooling, of individual estimates). Or they may supply individual estimates and assumptions reviewed by a company analyst, revised and followed by further rounds of estimation using the Delphi method (Cassino, 1984).

This systematic gathering of subjective opinions considerably increases the reli-ability of subjective forecasting (Armstrong, 1985). This process is not as expen-sive, in terms of the cost of experts, as it at first seems. Delphi is designed to gather estimates from people who are geographically dispersed so the experts do not need to be called to even one meeting. In addition, few experts are needed, typically 5–20, and people with modest expertise work as well as true experts (Hogarth, 1978). Ironically, true expertise appears to be a real problem with Delphi since it is generally wise to involve some people who are not involved with the products being forecast in order to avoid bias (Tyebjee, 1987).

11.5.6 Bootstrapping

Bootstrapping strives to convert judgements into objective measures. A way to do this is to obtain protocols of experts: descriptions of the process the expert uses in making forecasts. This process is then converted to a set of rules which is used to make forecasts. Another approach is to create a series of situations and to ask an expert to make forecasts for each. These judgemental forecasts are then regressed against data that the experts used to make their forecasts. This method provides estimates of how the experts relate each variable to sales volume. Bootstrapping models offer a low-cost procedure for making additional forecasts. They usually provide a small but useful improvement in accuracy over judgemental forecasts.

11.5.7 Scenario writing

According to Cornelius Kuikon, the head of strategic analysis and planning at Shell, the reason why many firms are disenchanted with planning is that they committed themselves too much to specific future predictions. To overcome the problem Shell, and many other companies including GE, now use scenario planning to generate a series of possible futures against which strategic plans can be tested.

The subset of individual forecasts to be combined into a scenario can be chosen in many ways. Cross-impact analysis can be used to generate a single 'most probable' scenario, although this approach is limited by its dependence on the forecasts making up the matrix. Once a most probable scenario has been chosen other boundary scenarios can be generated by examining deviations from the core. Alternatively, several 'individual theme scenarios' can be chosen automatically or by groups. The military were one of the earliest users of scenario planning and they have used a process where events and trends are combined randomly to produce alternative views. A more popular managerial approach brings a group of imaginative experts together to discuss a pre-prepared series of trends, topics and hypotheses. Each scenario is then developed around a theme and given a title that focuses attention on their major features. For example, 'the violent society' where crime and civil disobedience grow exponentially, or 'the limits to growth' where the world economy and population collapse when material limits are reached.

How many scenarios should be produced? The answer is: a few. A single most probable scenario is likely to retain too many of the problems of myopic planning. It is also obvious that the strategic planning process would be ridiculous if there were dozens of scenarios against which each strategy had to be tested. So, the number chosen must be a compromise between a desire for safety and a need for simplicity.

11.5.8 Cross-impact analysis

Cross-impact analysis is used to examine the potential interaction between forecasts. Some events may interact to reduce the impact of either, while others may interact to facilitate accelerated development or a disaster. For example, Malthus's (1777–1834) prediction that the world would starve because of exponential population growth with fixed land resources was wrong because population growth has been more than balanced by agricultural productivity. Two developments that have had a mutually amplifying effect were liquid crystal and silicon chip technology. Without the other, neither would have revolutionized the watch or computer in the way they did.

In its simple form cross-impact analysis involves cross tabulating possible events on a matrix which allows the interaction between every pair of events to be reviewed (Figure 11.6). The matrix is then examined asking, if event 1 is true, what would be the impact on events 2, 3, 4, etc.? Typically, three forms of impact are considered:

1. **Impact**: will event 1 amplify or diminish the impact of events 2, 3 …?
2. **Timing**: will it accelerate or retard the occurrence of the other events?
3. **Probability**: will it ensure, require or prevent the other events occurring?

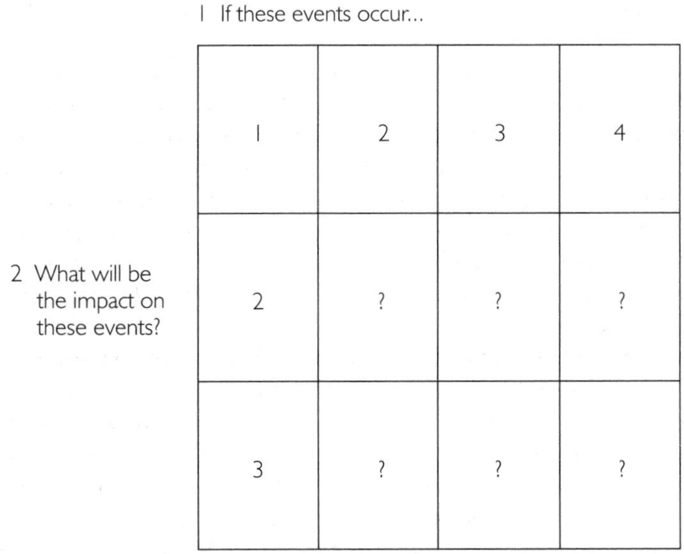

Figure 11.6 **Cross-impact analysis**

It is sometimes imputed that the evaluation should be conducted by an analyst, but the process is one that is likely to be enhanced by team work. In a first passthrough experts may be asked the likely level of cross-impact for each cell, and then required to give more information where interactions are high. Cross-impact analysis could stop at this stage having forced participants to consider the complex dynamics of events. Even at this level the technique has a potential for improving the internal consistency of forecasts and clarifying assumptions.

Cross-impact lends itself to the development of more sophisticated analyses. Interactions are likely to be more than one to one making the whole matrix interactive with, for example, event 1 affecting events 2, 5 and 6; event 2 affecting 5, 7 and 9; and event 5 affecting 1, 2, etc. To evaluate such patterns iterative computer simulations have been used to produce likely probability distributions of the times of events.

11.6 Conclusions

Although our review of forecasting methods is no way near comprehensive, there is clearly no shortage of forecasting methods. The managerial questions are, which ones work? which ones to use? and when? One important principle is to understand the limitations of the methods used and only to use them in the way they are intended. Table 11.1 suggests what to use and when. In this the categories are not rigid and it is likely that any method could fit in one of its adjacent boxes. For example, expert opinion could be used of *medium-term demand* forecasting as well as for *technology forecasting*. Moving beyond adjacent boxes is dangerous. Time-series analysis could sometimes accurately forecast sales three years ahead but it wrongly assumes the past will be repeated forever.

Studies comparing the accuracy of methods help in two ways: they show which methods work best and that complicated mathematical methods do not always outperform simple ones. For short-term forecasting. the *time-series analysis* has been made technically more sophisticated by statisticians. Fortunately for managers, but not for statisticians, comparative studies show that *simple exponential smoothing* usually outperforms other methods (Gardner, 1985). In addition, that hugely complex methods, such as the *Box-Jenkins* method, offers no improvement in forecasting accuracy (Makridakis *et al.*, 1993). For obvious reasons, these exquisitely complicated alternatives were not discussed here.

For medium-term forecasting *subjective methods*, which depend solely people's judgement, and simple extrapolations, such as *curve fitting*, do equally well (Lawrence *et al.*, 1985). However, this result is contingent on circumstances. Subjective methods can be improved by using the *Delphi method* with *bootstrapping* (Armstrong and Hutcheson, 1989). *Judgemental methods* also outperform *trend analysis* when there are large recent changes in sales levels and there is some knowledge about what influences the sales to be forecast. This weakness of trend analysis occurs because of its naiveté – *trend analyses* have no way of absorbing external information or quickly responding to step changes. In contrast, *trend analyses*

Table 11.1 Forecasting methods, roles and ranges

Forecasting	Time period		
	Short up to 1 year	Medium 1 to 3 years	Long beyond 3 years
Company sales	Salesforce opinion Time-series analysis	Buyers' intentions Chain ratios Concept testing Market factor Multivariate sales forecasting Test marketing	
Demand	Time-series analysis	Curve fitting Expert opinion Market build-up Statistical demand analysis	Diffusion Leading indicators
Technology		Diffusion Expert opinion S-curve	Bootstrapping Delphi Substitution Trend analysis
Futures			Cross-impact analysis Scenario writing

outperform *judgemental methods* when there is plenty of historic sales data or when regular increases in sales are large (Sanders and Ritzman, 1992).

Econometric methods, including *multivariate demand analysis* and *multivariate sales forecasting*, are useful in exploring the impact of influences that are known and modelled. In these cases the influences have to be large and direct otherwise the margins of error swamp variations. *Econometric methods* do outperform *trend analyses* and *expert judgement* when changes are large. Once again, trend analyses suffer from their inability to learn quickly and 'experts' find it hard to imagine dramatic changes.

Comparative results for *new product forecasting* are particularly convenient. Forecasting new product sales is hard – an early estimate suggesting the average error is 65 per cent (Tull, 1967). Luckily, the error does not increase with the earliness of forecasts. Relatively unrealistic but inexpensive *pre-test marketing* forecast as well as full *test markets*. *Concept testing* also gives results as good as test marketing if the product being tested is an incremental change. This changes the role of new product forecasting. Rather than checking what sales will be with the product in hand, managers can test what sales would be if it existed! If a concept does not work, it is easy and quick to try an alternative. Developments in *conjoint analysis* have made it relatively easily to test and refine several product concepts simultaneously. From these conjoint experiments it is even possible to forecast the likely sales of some concepts not even tested (Cattin and Wittink, 1992).

Part of the answer to the difficult question of which forecasting method to use, is not to choose just one. Combining forecasts irons out some of the problems with individual methods. In particular, combine forecasts derived using different approaches, such as econometric and subjective methods (Blattberg and Hoch, 1992). Do not worry about the weighting used in combining them, equal weighting is as accurate as any other schemes (Clemen, 1989).

Follow a few simple guidelines in choosing forecasting methods:

1. Use the simple methods you understand rather than complex methods that few people do.
2. Simple methods are often as good as complicated ones.
3. Do not choose a forecasting method based on its past forecasting accuracy but on its fitness for the job in hand.
4. Use different methods and combine them.
5. Expensive does not necessarily mean good.
6. Before making decisions based on forecasts, be aware of the way they were produced, and the limitations and risks involved.

Remember:

1. For existing markets, where there is not major change, it is hard to beat a naive model that assumes that tomorrow will be like today (Brodie and de Kluyver, 1987).
2. The past is unlikely to contain the information that forecasts major changes, so scan the environment for these.

If the environment is uncertain, flexibility not forecasting is the key!

Competitive positioning strategies

Part IV looks at implementation of competitive positioning strategies.

Chapter 12 discusses ways of selecting market targets from those uncovered through segmentation and positioning research. Two key dimensions are suggested for making the selection of target markets. First, the relative attractiveness of each potential segment. This will be dependent on many factors, including size, growth prospects, margins attainable, competitive intensity, and so on. The second key dimension is the strength of the organization in serving that potential target market. This is determined by the core competencies of the organization, its current and potential marketing assets and the resources it is prepared to put into the market all relative to competitors.

Chapter 13 focuses on methods for building defensible market positions once the target market has been decided. Routes to achieving cost leadership and differentiation are examined and the critical factors for maintaining position addressed.

Chapter 14 examines strategies for building position, holding position, harvesting, niching and divesting. Finally, the issues of the managerial skills and competencies necessary for each strategy are discussed.

Chapter 15 looks at the role of service and relationship marketing in building stronger competitive positions. The goods and services spectrum is introduced to show the increasing importance of the service element in the marketing implementation mix, even for goods marketers. Relationship marketing is discussed in the context of building and maintaining long-term relationships with key customers and customer groups. Techniques for monitoring and measuring customer satisfaction are presented with particular emphasis on the use of Gap Analysis to track problems in customer satisfaction back to their root causes.

Chapter 16 assesses the role of innovation and new product/service development in creating competitive positions. The new critical factors for success in new product development are identified, together with common reasons for failure. The processes of new product development are discussed along with suggestions for speeding up and enhancing the likelihood of success. The chapter concludes by considering organizational issues in new product development and innovation.

Chapter 17 is concerned with the use of internal marketing to build effective implementation approaches for marketing strategy. The internal market of employees, managers and processes is seen as a parallel target to the external market, and one which will determine the effectiveness of external marketing strategy. The chapter provides a framework for planning internal marketing, and examines the potential for partnership with human resource management in marketing strategy implementation, and the growing emphasis of behaviour-based approaches to management to link marketing strategy to sales and distribution operations.

CHAPTER 12

Selecting market targets

Attacking a fortified area is an art of last resort.

Sun Tzu (c. 500 BC)

Introduction

One of the most fundamental decisions a company faces is its choice of market or markets to serve. Unfortunately, many firms enter markets with little thought to their suitability for the firm. They are entered simply because they may appear superficially to be an attractive market for the firm's products or services. As we shall see in this chapter, Porter (1980) makes a strong case for choosing markets and industries where the prospects are attractive, and also where we can take a strong position. Figure 12.1 suggests that if we compare, in general terms, the attractiveness of markets and the strength of the competitive position we can take, then there are several traps to be avoided:

➤ **Peripheral business** – areas where we can take a strong and secure competitive position, but where the market simply does not deliver the benefits that the company needs. It is easy for those with great enthusiasm for a product or service in which they specialize to drive us into these areas, but they will never deliver the margin and growth that we need and will absorb resources and management time.

➤ **Illusion business** – areas where the market appears very attractive to us, because it is large, dynamic, expanding, and so on. However, these are areas where we can only ever hold a weak position – perhaps because these are typically the markets defended most fiercely by entrenched competitors. It is easy for managers to be seduced into entering these markets because of the potential they offer, without acknowledging that we can never reach that potential.

➤ **Dead-end business** – markets which are not attractive and where we can only take an 'also-ran' position. Few managers will deliberately take us into these markets, but this may describe markets from which we should exit – they may have been attractive in the past, but have declined, or our competitive position may have been undermined by new competitors and technologies.

➤ **Core business** – markets offering the benefits we want, where we should take a strong position. Clearly, these are the highest priority for investment of time and resources. The major issue here is how well we understand what makes a market attractive for a particular company, and what makes a competitive market strong (Piercy, 1997).

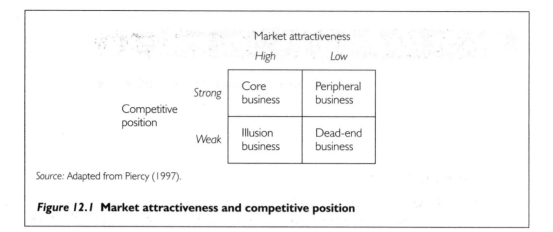

Source: Adapted from Piercy (1997).

Figure 12.1 **Market attractiveness and competitive position**

While these strategic traps are easily described, the importance of the issue is underlined by the fact that market choices are just that – choice may mean that we turn our back on some markets and some customers and some ways of business, to focus on the areas where we can achieve superior performance and results. Making such choices may be difficult. Michael Porter has suggested the heart of the problem:

> To put it simply, managers don't like to choose. There are tremendous organisational pressures toward imitation and matching what the competitor does. Over time this slowly but surely undermines the uniqueness of the competitive position. (Porter, quoted in Jackson, 1997)

Porter's argument is that a key challenge is to make clear trade-offs and strategic choices. The alternative is that a company risks destroying its own strategy:

> They start off with a clear position, and over time they're drawn into a competitive convergence where they and their rivals are all basically doing the same thing. Those kinds of competitions become stalemates. (Porter, quoted in Jackson, 1997)

However, the importance of market and segment choices must be put in the context of the potential complexity of markets and the consequent uncertainty surrounding the ideal choices to make. Indeed, as we shall see, defining markets and segments is not simply an exercise in statistical analysis, it is also a subjective and highly creative process (e.g. see Aaker, 1995). Considering alternative perspectives on market and segments is a way to enrich our understanding of the customer, and to establish competitive differentiation in the way we go to market.

The role of this chapter can be described as follows. Chapter 9 was concerned with the different ways in which markets could be segmented. Alternative bases for segmentation were examined and the benefits of adopting a segmentation approach discussed. Chapter 10 then looked at the research techniques available to help segment markets. In this chapter market definition and market targeting is discussed in more detail. In particular, the process of identifying the market segments where the company's capabilities can be used to the best advantage is considered, together with the selection of the appropriate marketing strategy.

In deciding on the markets and segment(s) to target four basic questions need to be asked:

1. How do we define the market – what is its scope and constitution?
2. How is the market segmented into different customer groups?
3. How attractive are the alternative market segments?
4. How strong a competitive position could we take – where do our current or potential strengths lie?

12.1 *The process of market definition*

The definition of the markets a company serves, or those which it is evaluating as possible targets, is partly a question of measurement and conventional competitive comparisons. It is also in part a creative process concerned with customer needs. Stanley Marcus of Neimann Marcus is frequently cited on this point: 'Consumers are statistics. Customers are people.'

A number of points are worth bearing in mind in approaching market definition:

➤ **Markets change** – the development of marketing strategy takes place in the context of a constant process of change. From this perspective it is unreasonable to assume that a company's definition of markets should remain static.

➤ **Markets and industries** – we have made before the point that markets are not the same as industries or products. Industries are groups of companies that share technologies and produce similar products. Markets are groups of customers with similar needs and problems to solve. Defining markets around industries and products exposes a company to its competitive position being overturned by competition from outside the conventional industry. Developing robust marketing strategies and strong competitive positions requires both understanding the existing industry (see chapters 4 and 7) but also the market from the customer's perspective (see chapter 6).

➤ **Different definitions for different purposes** – Day (1990) makes the point that we may need different market definitions for different types of marketing decision: tactical decisions like budgeting and salesforce allocation are likely to require narrow and easily understood market definitions (existing customers, similar products, existing channels), while strategic decisions require broader market definitions (including new market opportunities, changes in technology and substitute products, and potential new types of competitive entrant).

12.1.1 Different ways of defining markets

Day (1990) suggests that markets can be defined in two ways: on the basis of customers, or on the basis of competitors:

➤ **Customer-defined markets:** This approach takes us beyond products which are 'substitutes in kind', i.e. the same technology as our own, to 'substitutes in use', i.e. all the products and services which may meet the same customer needs and problems.

➤ **Competitor-defined markets:** This approach focuses on all the competitors who could possibly serve the needs of a group of customers, and reflects technological similarity, relative production costs and distribution methods.

In general, competitor-based definition will be important for allocating marketing resources and managing the marketing programme – responding to price-cuts, salesforce coverage, and so on. On the other hand, customer-defined approaches are likely to be more insightful in understanding the dynamics of the market, the attractiveness of alternative markets, and in developing strong competitive position.

One practical approach to evaluating the characteristics of markets is the product-customer matrix.

12.1.2 Product–customer matrix

Figure 12.2 suggests that the underlying structure of a market can be understood as a simple grouping of customers and products/services. The challenge is to examine a market using this matrix to identify no more than five or six groups of products and services and five or six groups of customers, who constitute the market. If this is impossible, then this is probably not a single market, but several, and the exercise should be subdivided.

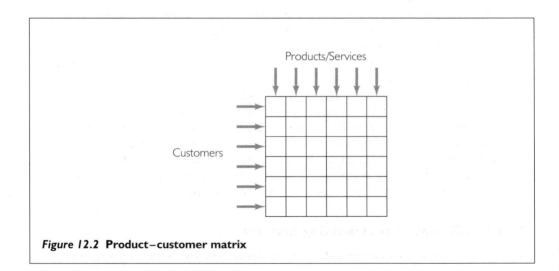

Figure 12.2 **Product–customer matrix**

The important perspective that can be built using this approach is one which recognizes:

➤ **Products/services** – in terms of what they do for customers, not in terms of how they are produced or by whom.
➤ **Customers** – in terms of important differences between groups in needs, preferences, priorities or ways of buying.

For example, vast arrays of retail financial services products provided by banks and their competitors can be reduced to six categories of products by considering what customer benefits they provide. Rather than hundreds of products, the market consists of only six groups of products and services to: provide access to cash; provide security of savings; buy-now pay-later; make cashless payments; to get a return on assets like savings; and acquire a range of specialist services. The same process of reduction can be applied to products/services. For example, do not describe the market as 'computers', but as what different mixes of computer hardware, software and services actually deliver to customers in a particular market, such as accounting systems, internal communications, management information, and so on.

This approach provides a start in defining markets in such a way that we move past the core market of similar products, to find the extended market:

> to encompass all competitive possibilities for satisfying customer needs, including substitutes and potential entrants. [because] this latter perspective is especially needed to help understand why some markets are attractive and others are not. (Day, 1990)

This analysis can be used for a variety of purposes, but one advantage of this type of initial approach is that it starts to identify the way a market divides into distinctly different segments.

12.2 *Defining how the market is segmented*

As discussed in chapter 9, there are many ways in which markets can be segmented. Often a useful starting point is to ask how management views the market, on the basis of their experience in the marketplace. Management definition of market segments may typically be on the basis of products/services offered or markets served.

12.2.1 Products or services offered

Describing segments on the basis of products or services offered can lead to broad based segmentation of the market. John Deere, for example, competing against the much larger Caterpillar company in the US crawler tractor (bulldozer) market initially segmented the market into 'large' and 'small' bulldozers. On the basis of their marketing assets (defined in terms of better service support through local dealer networks and lower system price) Deere decided to concentrate their efforts in the small bulldozer market thus avoiding head-on competition with Caterpillar who were stronger in the large bulldozer market.

Many market research companies, operating in the service sector, define their market segments in terms of the services they offer, e.g. the market for retail audits, the market for telephone surveys, the market for qualitative group discussions, the market for professional (industrial) interviewing.

Underlying this product- or service-based approach to identifying markets is a belief that segments defined in this way will exhibit the differences in behaviour essential to an effective segmentation scheme. The strategy adopted by Deere made sense, for example, only because the requirements of purchasers and users from large and small bulldozers were different. Where the requirements of customers are essentially the same, but satisfied by different products or services, this segmentation approach can lead to a myopic view of the market.

12.2.2 Market or markets served

Many companies now adopt a customer-based or markets-served approach to segmenting their markets. Segments are defined in terms of the customers themselves rather than the particular products they buy. In consumer markets, management may talk in terms of demographic and socio-economic segments while in industrial markets definitions may be based on SIC or order quantity. A particularly useful approach in many markets is to segment on the basis of the benefits the customer is seeking in consuming the product or service and/or the uses to which the product or service is put.

Van den Berghs (a subsidiary of Unilever) have been particularly successful in segmenting the market for 'yellow fats' on the basis of the benefits sought by consumers (see Broadbent, 1983). The market, which comprises butter, margarine and low fat spreads stood at £600 million at retail selling price (RSP) in 1979. It was a static market with no overall growth. Within the market, however, there were some important changes taking place. There had been a marked trend away from butter to margarine, primarily because of the increasing price differential (butter and margarine were roughly equivalent prices in the mid-1970s but since then butter prices had increased more rapidly widening the gap). Coupled with this came increased price sensitivity as the UK economy entered the recession of the late 1970s/early 1980s. Van den Berghs were quick to spot a market opportunity as they segmented the market. There were at least five benefit segments identified:

➤ **Segment 1** consisted of customers who wanted a 'real butter taste' and were not prepared to forego that taste at almost any price. This segment chose butter, the top-selling brands being Anchor, Lurpak and Country Life.
➤ **Segment 2** were customers who wanted the taste, feel and texture of butter but were concerned about the price of butter. They were typically not prepared to sacrifice on taste etc. and not convinced that existing margarines

could satisfy them. These customers would typically choose the cheapest butter available, such as supermarket own label.

➤ **Segment 3** were ex-butter users who were prepared to accept existing margarines as a substitute and even found they offered additional benefits over butter, such as softness and ease of spreading. Also attractive to this segment was tub packaging and larger packs. They were more price sensitive than Segment 2. The leading brand in this segment was Stork margarine.

➤ **Segment 4** were a growing minority segment concerned with diet and weight control. In particular they were concerned with calories and with fat content. Outline was a leading brand. More recently St Ivel Gold has been particularly successful in appealing to this segment.

➤ **Segment 5** were concerned with health in general and particularly the effects of cholesterol. Of special appeal to this segment were spreads low in cholesterol and high in polyunsaturated fats. The market leader in this segment was Flora.

Van den Berghs had achieved around 60 per cent of the total market in 1980 through recognizing the segmentation described above and positioning their brands such that they attracted specific individual segments. Segment 1 was deliberately not targeted specifically. Krona, a block margarine with (in blind tests) a very similar taste to butter, was launched at a premium price and high margins to attract Segment 2 customers as they traded down from butter. Segment 3 was secured by Van den Berghs' leading brand Stork, while Segments 4 and 5 were served by Outline and Flora respectively. During the 1980s and 1990s, competition to serve Segment 2 intensified. Following the initial success of Krona, Dairy Crest launched Clover in 1983 as a dairy spread. In 1991, Van den Berghs launched the amazingly named 'I Can't Believe It's Not Butter', as a brand that gave a butter taste but with much lower fat intake levels. Within just nine months of its launch, ICBINB (as it became to be known in the trade), took 2.3 per cent of the margarine low fat spreads market. In 1995, it was followed by St Ivel's new brand, positioned directly in opposition, 'Utterly Butterly'.

Central to the success of Van den Berghs and other creative marketers has been an unwillingness merely to accept the segmentation of the market adopted by others. In many fast-moving consumer products markets, and in grocery marketing in particular, there has been a tendency to over-segment on the basis of background customer characteristics or volume usage. By looking beyond these factors to the underlying motivations and reasons to buy companies can often create an edge over their competitors.

Once the segments have been identified, the alternatives need to be evaluated on the basis of market attractiveness and company strength, or potential strength, in that particular market segment. This evaluation is carried out across a number of factors.

12.3 *Determining alternative market or segment attractiveness*

It is clear that many factors may be considered in evaluating market, or specific segment, attractiveness. In chapter 3, we discussed multi-factor approaches to evaluation in the context of assessing the portfolio of product offerings, while here they are discussed as strategic tools for deciding which markets to enter in the first place. There have been many checklists of such factors, but one way of grouping the issues is as follows:

➤ Market factors;
➤ Economic and technological factors;
➤ Competitive factors;
➤ Environmental factors.

However, it should be noted at the outset that a general checklist of this kind is only a starting point – the factors important to making a market attractive or unattractive to a specific company are likely to reflect the specific characteristics of that company and the priorities of its management. For example, one company may see a market segment which is growing as highly attractive, while in the same industry another company may look for slower rates of growth to avoid stretching its financial and other capacities. Similarly, a company which has cost advantages over its rivals may see a price-sensitive segment as highly attractive, while its competitors do not. In fact, there is a group of factors which impact on judgements of market attractiveness which are wholly subjective (see pp. 308–9).

12.3.1 Market factors

Among the market characteristics which influence the assessment of market attractiveness are the following.

Size of the segment
Clearly, one of the factors that makes a potential target attractive is its size. High-volume markets offer greater potential for sales expansion (a major strategic goal of many companies). They also offer potential for achieving economies of scale in production and marketing and hence a route to more efficient operations.

Segment growth rate
In addition to seeking scale of operation, many companies are actively pursuing growth objectives. Often it is believed that company growth is more easily achieved in growing markets.

Stage of industry evolution
We looked earlier (see chapter 4) at the characteristics of markets at different stages of evolution. Depending on the company's objectives (cash-generation or growth) different stages may be more attractive. For initial targeting markets in the early stages of evolution are generally more attractive as they offer more future potential and are less likely to be crowded by current competitors (see competitive intensity below). Typically, however, growth requires marketing investment (promotion, distribution, etc.) to fuel it so that the short-term returns may be modest. Where more immediate cash and profit contribution is sought, a mature market may be a more attractive proposition requiring a lower level of investment.

Predictability

Earlier we stressed the predictability of markets as a factor influencing their attractiveness to marketers (see chapter 4). Clearly the more predictable the market, the less prone it is to discontinuity and turbulence, the easier it is to predict accurately the potential value of the segment. The more certain, too, is the longer-term viability of the target.

Price elasticity and sensitivity

Unless the company has a major cost advantage over its main rivals markets which are less price-sensitive, where the price elasticity of demand is low, are more attractive than those that are more sensitive. In the more price-sensitive markets there are greater chances of price wars (especially in the mature stage of industry evolution) and the shake-out of the less efficient suppliers.

Bargaining power of customers

Those markets where buyers (ultimate customers or distribution chain intermediaries) have the strongest negotiating hand are often less attractive than those where the supplier can dominate and dictate to the market.

In the UK grocery market the buying power of the major supermarket chains is considerable. Together the top ten chains supply around 80 per cent of the nation's food shopping needs. Food manufacturers and processors compete vigorously for shelf space to make their products available to their ultimate consumers. Indeed some supermarket chains are now moving towards charging food manufacturers for the shelf space they occupy.

Similarly, in the market for military apparel a concentration of buying power (by the government) dictates to potential entrants on what basis they will compete.

Seasonality and cyclicality of demand

The extent to which demand fluctuates by season or cycle also affects the attractiveness of a potential segment. For a company already serving a highly seasonal market a new opportunity in a counter-seasonal market might be particularly attractive, enabling the company to utilize capacity all year round.

The Thompson publishing group found the package tour market highly attractive primarily for cash flow reasons. The company needed to bulk purchase paper for printing during the winter months and found this a severe drain on cash resources. Package holidays, typically booked and paid for during the winter months, provided a good opportunity to raise much needed cash at the crucial time. Thompson Holidays, founded originally as a cash flow generator, has gone on to become a highly successful package tour operator.

12.3.2 Economic and technological factors

Issues reflecting the broader economic characteristics of the market and the technology used include the following:

Barriers to entry
Markets where there are substantial barriers to entry (e.g. protected technology or high switching costs for customers) are attractive markets for incumbents but unattractive markets for aspirants. While few markets have absolute barriers to entry in the long term, for many companies the costs of overcoming those barriers may make the venture prohibitively expensive and uneconomic.

Barriers to exit
Conversely, markets with high exit barriers, where companies can become locked in to untenable or uneconomic positions are intrinsically unattractive. Some new target opportunities, for example, may have substantial investment hurdles (barriers to entry) that, once undertaken, lock the company in to continuing to use the facilities created. In other markets powerful customers may demand a full range of products/services as the cost of maintaining their business in more lucrative sectors. When moving into high-risk new target markets a major consideration should be exit strategy in the event that the position becomes untenable.

Bargaining power of suppliers
The supply of raw materials and other factor inputs to enable the creation of suitable products and services must also be considered. Markets where the suppliers have monopoly, or near-monopoly power, are less attractive than those served by many competing suppliers (see Porter, 1980).

Level of technology utilization
Use and level of technology affects attractiveness of targets differently for different competitors. The more technologically advanced will be attracted to markets which utilize their expertise more fully and where that can be used as a barrier to other company entry. For the less technologically advanced, with skills and strengths in other areas such as people, markets with a lower use of technology may be more appropriate.

Investment required
Size of investment required, financial and other commitment, will also affect attractiveness of market and could dictate that many market targets are practically unattainable for some companies. Investment requirements can form a barrier to entry that protects incumbents while deterring entrants.

Margins available
Finally, margins will vary from market to market, partly as a result of price sensitivity and partly as a result of competitive rivalry. In grocery retailing margins are notoriously low (around 2 – 4 per cent) whereas in other markets they can be nearer 50 per cent or even higher.

12.3.3 Competitive factors

The third set of factors in assessing the attractiveness of potential market targets relate to the competition to be faced in those markets.

Competitive intensity
The number of serious competitors in the market is important. Markets may be dominated by one (monopoly), two (duopoly), a few (oligopoly) or none ('perfect competition') of the players in that market. Entry into markets dominated by one or a few key players requires some form of competitive edge over them that can be used to secure a beachhead. In some circumstances it may be that the existing players in the market have failed to move with changes in their markets and hence create opportunities for more innovative rivals.

Under conditions of perfect, or near-perfect, competition price competitiveness is particularly rife. The many small players in the market offer competitively similar products so that differentiation is rarely achieved (the stalemate environment – see chapter 4), and it is usually on the basis of price rather than performance or quality. To compete here requires either a cost advantage (created through superior technology, sourcing or scale of operations) or the ability to create a valued uniqueness in the market. In segments where there are few, or weak, competitors there may again be better opportunities to exploit.

In the early 1980s Barratt Developments made a major impact on the house building market. Their segmentation of the market identified the need for specialist housing at various consumer life cycle phases. The first venture was Studio Solos, designed for young single people. In the first year of sales Barratt sold over 2,000 (2 per cent of total new home sales). In the US the same strategy was adopted to spearhead the company's international expansion (70 per cent of Barratt's US sales coming from solos). At the same time in the UK the company successfully developed retirement housing for pensioners, one- and two-bedroom apartments in blocks featuring communal facilities and wardens. In both retirement homes and solos housing Barratt were amongst the first aggressively to pursue the markets they had identified. Indeed they would argue they were amongst the first to recognize that the housing market was segmented beyond the traditional product-based segmentation of terraces, semis and detached.

Quality of competition
Chapter 7 discussed what constitutes 'good' competitors – those that can stabilize their markets, do not have over-ambitious goals and who are committed to the market. Good competitors are also characterized by their desire to serve the market better and hence will keep the company on its toes competitively rather than allow it to lag behind changes in the environment. Markets that are dominated by less predictable, volatile competitors are intrinsically more difficult to operate in and control and hence less attractive as potential targets.

Threat of substitution
In all markets there is a threat that new solutions to the customers' original problems

will be found that will make the company's offerings obsolete. The often quoted example is substitution of the pocket calculator for the slide rule, though other less dramatic examples abound. With the increasing rate of technological change experienced in the 1980s and 1990s it is probable that more products will become substituted at an accelerating rate.

In such situations, two strategies make sense. First, for the less technologically innovative, seek market targets where substitution is less likely (but beware being lulled into believing substitution will never occur!). Second, identify those targets where your own company can achieve the next level of substitution. Under this strategy companies actively seek market targets which are using an inferior level of technology and are hence vulnerable to attack by a substitute product. Hewlett Packard's success with laser printers followed by ink jet printers in the PC peripherals market (attacking dot matrix printers) is a classic example. The importance of changing the competitive rules by collaboration is important (see pp. 178–81).

Degree of differentiation
Markets where there is little differentiation between product offerings offer significant opportunities to companies that can achieve differentiation. Where differentiation is not possible often a stalemate will exist and competition will degenerate into price conflicts, which are generally to be avoided.

12.3.4 Environmental factors

Lastly, there is the issue of more general factors surrounding the market or segment in question.

Exposure to economic fluctuations
Some markets are more vulnerable to economic fluctuations than others. Commodity markets in particular are often subject to wider economic change hence meaning less direct control of the market by the players in it. For example, the New Zealand wool export industry was badly affected in mid-1990 by an Australian decision, in the face of declining world demand and increasing domestic stockpiles, to lower the floor price on wool by 20 per cent. Australia is such a dominant player in the essentially commodity world market that New Zealand exporters were forced to follow suit.

Exposure to political and legal factors
As with exposure to economic uncertainty markets which are vulnerable to political or legal factors are generally less attractive than those which are not. The exception, of course, is where these factors can be used positively as a means of entering the markets against entrenched but less aware competitors (e.g. when protection is removed from once government-owned monopolies).

Degree of regulation
The extent of regulation of the markets under consideration will affect the degrees

of freedom of action the company has in its operations. Typically, a less regulated market offers more opportunities for the innovative operator than one which is closely controlled.

Again there is an exception, however. Regulated markets might afford more protection once the company has entered. This might be protection from international competition (e.g. protection of European car manufacturers from Japanese car imports by quotas) which effectively creates a barrier to (or a ceiling on) entry. The warning should be sounded, however, that experience around the world has generally shown that protection breeds inefficiencies and when that protection is removed, as is the current trend in world trade, the industries thrown into the cold realities of international competition face major difficulties in adjusting.

Social acceptability and physical environment impact
Increasingly, with concern for the environment and the advent of green politics, companies are looking at the broader social implications of the market targets they chose to go after. Especially when the company is widely diversified the impact of entering one market on the other activities of the company must be considered.

With increasing concern for the natural world, its fauna and flora, some cosmetics companies are now looking to non-animal ingredients as bases for their products and manufacturers of aerosols are increasingly using non-ozone depleting propellants in place of CFCs. The Body Shop, a cosmetics and toiletries manufacturer and retailer, has built its highly successful position in the market through a clear commitment to the use of non-animal ingredients.

Summary
The quality of a market is dependent on a number of factors. Other factors being equal segments which are big and growing offer the best prospects for the future. Other factors rarely are equal, however, and size and growth are not the only criteria that should be taken into consideration. Of prime importance is the scope for building a valuable and defensible position for the company in that segment. This will also require a clear identification of the company's strengths with regard to the proposed segment.

12.3.5 Making the criteria clear and explicit

We made the point earlier that the factors making a market or segment attractive to a particular company are likely to be unique to that company, rather than simply reflecting a general checklist of the type discussed above. We also made the point that it is likely that the direction of a decision criterion will also vary – high growth markets are attractive to some companies and unattractive to others in the same industry.

It is also the case that some of the real criteria for evaluating market/segment attractiveness may be highly subjective and qualitative. For example, a brewery evaluating alternative markets for its by-products identified the criteria of market attractiveness as:

➤ **Market size** – they defined a minimum market value to be of interest.
➤ **Market growth rate** – moderate growth was preferred (they did not want to invest large amounts in keeping up with a by-products market).
➤ **Low competitive intensity** – they wanted to avoid head-on competition with others.
➤ **Stability** – they wanted a stable income flow.
➤ **Low profile** – they did not want to invest in any area which would attract media criticism, or regulatory activity by the government.

What we see is a mix of the qualititative and the quantitative, and the objective and subjective. None the less, these are the issues that matter to that management group. There is much advantage in making the real criteria as explicit as possible, notwithstanding that some reflect corporate culture and management preferences, rather than economic market analysis.

Indeed, a recent development at the Virgin group has been making explicit the criteria that make further markets attractive to Virgin. The head of corporate development, Brad Rosser, states that Virgin will invest in a market only if it meets at least four out of the following criteria (Piercy, 1997):

➤ the products must be innovative;
➤ they must challenge established authority;
➤ they must offer customers good value for money;
➤ the products must be high quality;
➤ the market must be growing.

This describes Virgin's mission of offering 'first-class at business-class prices' and applying the brand to new market opportunities.

12.3.6 The impact of change

It should also be remembered that nothing is static – things change, and sometimes they change rapidly in a number of ways:

➤ **Company change**: As companies evolve, their views about market attractiveness may develop. In the Virgin example given above, these criteria may describe the company's view of how it is developing, they do not describe how it has invested in markets in the past.
➤ **Markets change**: The attractiveness of a market can alter dramatically. Matthew Clark, the UK drinks group, reported at the end of 1996 that sales of Diamond White and K Ciders had dropped 40 per cent with declining profits following. The reason was a switch by young drinkers to alcopops like Bass's 'Hooch' brand of alcoholic lemonade. Disparaged by the industry experts, a year after launch alcopops were selling 100 million litres a year.
➤ **Competitors change**: The UK market for household vacuum cleaners had

been dominated by Hoover and Electrolux since the 1950s, with very conventional technology. James Dyson offered his new product, 'the world's first bagless vacuum cleaner', to the existing players and was laughed at. After many difficulties he launched his own product – with unknown technology and a high price. He sold £3 million of vacuum cleaners in the first year and has tripled sales every 12 months. Hoover's share of the upright vacuum cleaner market has halved, and in the high-margin market for cleaners priced over £180, Dyson in 1995 took 58 per cent of the market compared to Hoover's 14 per cent. The attractiveness of market and segments within them can change dramatically.

➤ **Reinventing the market**: Market attractiveness can change dramatically also as a result of those who 'reinvent the business', by establishing new ways of doing business. At the time of writing, Eagle Star has attacked the car insurance market by offering the cheapest products in Britain from its Internet site. Daewoo took 1 per cent of the British car market (and a much higher share of its segment) in the fastest time ever, by establishing a new direct distribution channel and a brand proposition of high value and 'hassle-free' car buying.

➤ **Market boundaries change**: The issue of market definition we considered earlier cannot be separated from the question of market attractiveness – attractiveness always means in a specific market. As we saw earlier (pp. 297–9), a characteristic of many markets is that traditional boundaries and definitions are in flux. Avoiding the investment traps we described at the outset may involve constant awareness of how boundaries are changing as a result of new technologies and new types of customer demand.

12.4 *Determining current and potential strengths*

The importance of the resource-based theory of the firm, and the practicalities of assessing a company's strengths (and weaknesses) was considered in chapter 5. The issue to consider now is how those resources, capabilities and competencies can be deployed in a specific market or segment. One approach to this evaluation divides the issue into:

➤ the firm's current market position;
➤ the firm's economic and technological position;
➤ the firm's capability profile.

12.4.1 Current market position

A start in evaluating strengths in a particular market or segment can be made with consideration of the following issues.

Relative market share
In markets which the company already targets, market share serves two main

functions. First, it acts as a barometer of how well the company is currently serving the target: a higher share will indicate better performance in serving the needs of the customers. Second, market share can, of itself, confer an advantage in further penetrating the market: high share brands, for example, typically have high levels of customer awareness and wide distribution. Share of market is a prime marketing asset that can be used to further develop the company's position (see chapter 5).

Rate of change of market share

Absolute market share in itself can confer a strength to the company; so too can rapidly increasing share. Growing share demonstrates an ability to serve the market better than those competitors currently losing share. A company with a low but increasing share of market can demonstrate to distributors the need for increased shelf-space and availability.

Exploitable marketing assets

Central to this book has been the identification and exploitation of the company's marketing assets (see pp. 115–29). In target markets where marketing assets have potential for further exploitation (e.g. a favourable image, brand name, distribution network, etc.) the company has potential strength from which to build. Identifying marketing assets was discussed at length in chapter 5. Of interest here is how those marketing assets affect the strength of the company in serving particular market segments. What may, for example, be a strength with one target segment may be a weakness with another.

The image of John Player No. 6 as an ordinary, everyday cigarette was seen to be an advantage in the mass, filter-tipped cigarette market. When used in the king-size sector of the market, however, where prestige and sophistication are more important, that image was a clear disadvantage. The company, therefore, developed other brands to cater to that market (such as the Lambert and Butler brand).

Unique and valued products and services

In potential markets where the company has superior products and services, which are different in a way valued by the customers, there is potential for creating a stronger competitive position. Similarly, a competitive advantage based on low price relative to the competition is likely to be attractive to price-sensitive segments, but may actually deter segments more motivated by quality.

12.4.2 Economic and technological position

The evaluation should also address the company's relative economic and technological characteristics and resources.

Relative cost position

The company's cost structure relative to competitors was listed as a potential marketing asset in chapter 5. Low relative production and marketing costs – through technological leadership, exploitation of linkages or experience and scale effects – give a financial edge to the company in the particular market.

Capacity utilization
For most companies the level of capacity utilization is a critical factor in its cost structure. Indeed the PIMS study has shown that capacity utilization is most crucial to small and medium-sized companies (see Buzzell and Gale, 1987). Few companies can hope to achieve 100 per cent utilization (there will inevitably be downtime in manufacturing and slack periods for service companies), and indeed running at 'full' capacity may produce strains on both systems and structures. What is clearly important in any operation is to identify the optimum level of utilization and seek to achieve that.

Technological position
Having an exploitable edge in technology again creates a greater strength for the company in serving a market. That may or may not be leading-edge technology. In some markets a lower technology solution to customer requirements may be more suitable than state of the art applications. Again, the key is matching the technology to the customers' problems or requirements.

12.4.3 Capability profile

The third set of factors affecting competitive strength centres on the resources that can be brought to bear in the market.

Management strength and depth
A major asset, and hence potential strength, of any company is its human resources and particularly its management strength and depth. The skills and competencies of the staff working in an organization are the strengths on which it can exploit opportunities in the marketplace. In service organizations (such as consultancy companies, health services, etc.) in particular the strength of the supplier often comes down to the individual skills of the managers who deal directly with the customers.

Marketing strength
Marketing strength stems from experience and synergy with other product areas. Companies operating primarily in consumer markets often believe they have superior marketing skills to those operating in slower moving industrial markets. They then see these markets as areas where they can use the FMCG skills they have learned elsewhere to good effect. Experience of transferring skills from one business sector to another, however, has not been universally successful.

Forward and backward integration
The extent of control of the supply of raw materials backward integration) and

distribution channels (forward integration) can also affect the strength or potential strength of a company in serving a specific target. Where integration is high, especially in markets where supplier and buyer power is high (see above) the firm could be in a much stronger position than its rivals.

Summary
The important points to consider when assessing company or business strength is that strength is relative to competitors also serving the segment and to the requirements of customers in the segment.

12.5 *Making market and segment choices*

Conventional approaches suggest the use of portfolio matrices as a useful way of summarizing the alternative business investment opportunities open to a multi-product company, and for making explicit choices between markets and segments. While such matrices have been used to assess the balance of the portfolio of businesses the company operates (see chapter 3). The same techniques can be usefully adapted to help with the selection of market targets.

Classic portfolio techniques include the Directional Policy Matrix developed by the UK Chemical Division of Royal Dutch Shell (Robinson *et al.*, 1978) or the McKinsey/GE Business Screen (Wind and Mahajan, 1981). These are generally considered as methods for modelling existing portfolios; they are actually, in many instances, better suited to deciding which markets to target in the first place. An adapted model is presented in Figure 12.3; this is the operational version of the conceptual model we saw in Figure 12.1 at the start of our evaluation of market targets.

Using this approach the factors deemed relevant in a particular market are

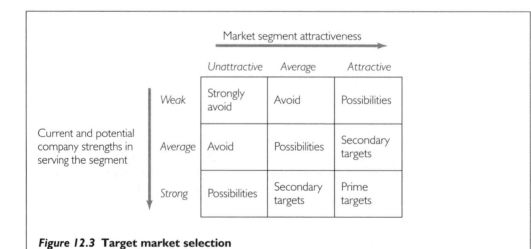

Figure 12.3 Target market selection

identified (typically from the factors listed above) and are each assigned weights depending on their perceived importance. The subjective choice and weighting of the factors to be used in the analysis ensure that the model is customized to the needs of the specific company. The process of selecting and weighting the factors can, in itself, prove a valuable experience in familiarizing managers with the realities of the company's markets. Where appropriate factors can be more objectively assessed through the use of marketing research or economic analysis.

Once the factors have been determined and weighted, each potential market segment is evaluated on a scale from 'excellent = 5' to 'poor = 1' and a summary score on the two main dimensions of 'market segment attractiveness' and 'company business strength in serving that segment' computed using the weightings. Sensitivity analyses can then be conducted to gauge the impact of different assumptions on the weight to attach to individual factors and the assessments of targets on each scale.

The resulting model, such as that shown in Figure 12.4 for a hypothetical company, enables the alternatives to be assessed and discussed objectively.

Ideally, companies are looking for market targets in the bottom right hand corner of Figure 12.4. These opportunities rarely exist and the trade-off then becomes between going into segments where the company is, or can become strong, but that are less attractive (e.g. target opportunity 1), or alternatively tackling more attractive markets but where the company is only average in strength (target 2).

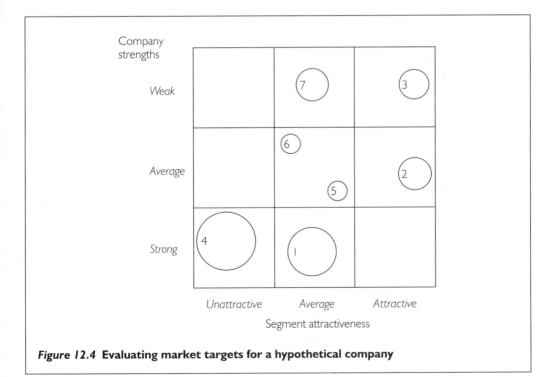

Figure 12.4 **Evaluating market targets for a hypothetical company**

To develop defensible positions in the marketplace the former (sticking to areas of current or potential strength) often makes the most sense. Indeed, many would argue (see Ohmae, 1982) that most companies are better advised to consolidate in apparently less attractive markets where they have considerable exploitable strengths than to 'chase the rainbows' of seemingly attractive markets where they are only average or weak players.

Where business strength is weak, investment should be avoided in average or unattractive markets (target 7) unless in very attractive market segments where some strengths could be built or bought in through merger/acquisition (e.g. target 3). Similarly investment in unattractive segments should be avoided unless particular company strengths can lead to a profitable exploitation of the market (target 4). Market segments of medium attractiveness where the company has medium strength should be invested in selectively (targets 5 and 6).

A further factor in selecting target markets for the overall business is how those individual targets add up – i.e. the overall portfolio of businesses or markets the company is operating in (see chapter 3). Companies are typically seeking to build a balanced portfolio of activities. Balanced in terms of cash use and generation, risk and return, and focus on the future as well as on the present.

A prime example of a company using the above approach to selecting new market targets on a world scale is Fletcher Challenge Ltd. With assets in 1990 valued at over £6 billion, turnover of £4.11 billion and pre-tax profit of £345 million, it is New Zealand's largest and most successful company. Fletcher Challenge examines opportunities for acquisition or further investment on the basis of two sets of factors – industry attractiveness and potential business strength in serving that market. Industry, or target *market attractiveness*, is determined by the following key factors: Fletcher Challenge looks for markets with a steady demand growth (growing markets are easier to exit if difficulties arise); which are low in customer concentration (are not dominated by a handful of large customers); where there are substantial barriers to entry (in scale of operations, level of technology employed and control of the inputs and supporting industries); where participants are few and competitors are 'good' (up to two or three major players, in the market for the long haul); where prices are stable (absence of price wars or wild fluctuations); and where there is a steep cost (experience) curve where Fletcher Challenge's scale of operations will yield lower costs. *Company strength* in serving the targets are examined in the following main areas: Fletcher Challenge looks for markets where it is, or believes it can become, the market leader; it seeks to utilize its technological expertise to the full; looks for markets where it can achieve a cost leadership position; seeks markets where it can manage intergroup (competitor) understandings; and markets where it can keep control of the market (especially in pricing). The acquisitions and expansion strategies of Fletcher Challenge from the mid-1980s have consistently met the above criteria.

12.6 *Alternative targeting strategies*

The classic approach to segmentation or targeting strategies is provided by Kotler, most recently in Kotler (1997). Kotler's model suggests that there are three broad approaches a company can take to a market, having identified and evaluated the various segments that make up the total. The company can pursue:

➤ **Undifferentiated marketing**, essentially producing a single product designed to appeal across the board to all segments;
➤ **Differentiated marketing**, offering a different product to each of the different segments; or
➤ **Concentrated marketing**, focusing attention on one, or a few, segments.

12.6.1 Undifferentiated marketing

An undifferentiated marketing approach entails treating the market as one whole, rather than as segmented, and supplying one standard product or service to satisfy all customers. It is the approach carried out in Porter's (1980) cost leadership strategy. This approach was particularly prevalent in the mass marketing era in the days before the emergence (or recognition!) of strongly identified market segments. More recently, however, as the existence of market segments has become more widely accepted the wisdom of such an approach in all but markets where preferences are strongly concentrated, has been called into doubt.

12.6.2 Differentiated marketing

Differentiated marketing is adopted by companies seeking to offer a distinct product or service to each chosen segment of the market. Thus a shampoo manufacturer will offer different types of shampoo depending on the condition of the hair of the customer. The major danger of differentiated marketing is that it can lead to high costs, both of manufacturing and marketing a wide product line.

Depending on the company's resources, however, differentiated marketing can help in achieving overall market domination (this is the strategy pursued in the yellow fats market by Van den Berghs, see pp. 300–1 above).

12.6.3 Focused marketing

For the organization with limited resources, however, attacking all or even most of the potential segments in a market may not be a viable proposition. In this instance concentrated or focused marketing may make more sense. Under this strategy the organization focuses attention on one, or a few, market segments and leaves the wider market to its competitors. In this way it builds a strong position in a few selected markets, rather than attempting to compete across the board (either with undifferentiated or differentiated products).

The success of this approach depends on clear, in-depth knowledge of the customers served. The major danger of this strategy, however, is that over time the segment focused on may become less attractive and limiting on the organization.

The Lucozade brand of soft drink was first marketed in the 1920s. It was originally developed by a Newcastle chemist as an energy drink for his son, who was recovering from jaundice. The brand was bought by Beechams in 1938 and marketed in a distinctive yellow cellophane wrapper, with the slogan 'Lucozade Aids Recovery'. During the 1950s and 1960s it was Beechams' biggest selling brand. By the 1970s, however, lower levels of sickness, less frequent 'flu epidemics and price increases had contributed to a decline in sales. From 1974 to 1978, sales fell by 30 per cent. The company decided that the brand needed to be repositioned.

The first repositioning was as an in-house 'pick-me-up' for housewives in the late 1970s. Sales initially increased by 11 per cent, but growth was not maintained, and by the end of 1979, sales has levelled out. In 1980, a new 250 ml bottle was launched and the new slogan 'Lucozade Replaces Lost Energy' was developed. But by 1982, a usage and attitude survey showed that the brand character had not changed significantly – it was still used primarily for illness recovery.

More radical repositioning was considered. In the carbonated soft drinks (CSD) market, Lucozade was competing head-on with well-established brands like Coca-Cola and Pepsi. Lucozade also suffered from a poor image at the younger end of the market – it had been given to them by their mums when they were ill! A new positioning was developed around the theme: 'Lucozade is not only delicious and refreshing but can quickly replace lost energy'. The potential of the sports market became apparent and in July 1982 the advertising started to use Daley Thompson, an Olympic decathlete. Initially, however, the target customers liked Daley, but did not connect him with the brand.

The next phase of repositioning was the 'traffic lights' TV commercial, using Daley and the heavy metal music of Iron Maiden to 'portray' rather than 'explain' the message. The advertisements graphically conveyed the energy replacement message in a way younger users immediately identified with. In the first year of the new campaign, sales volume increased by 40 per cent. Qualitative research showed the message getting across to existing users and, crucially, to the younger target market.

Since then, Lucozade has enjoyed continued success, and new flavour variants have been launched. 1988 saw the launch of the Lucozade Sport isotonic drink and 1995 the launch of the NRG teen drink. The same positioning strategy has been pursued successfully in Ireland, Asia and Australasia. From 1985 to 1995, worldwide sales had grown from £12 million to £125 million (Salmon, 1997).

The most effective strategy to adopt with regard to target market selection will vary from market to market. Certain characteristics of both the market and the company, however, will serve to suggest the type of strategy that makes most sense in a given situation.

The classic statement on how to approach the segmentation strategy choice comes from Frank et al. (1972). They propose that the choice of strategy should be based on:

➤ segment size – to determine its value and prospects;
➤ the incremental costs faced in differentiating between segments – which may be small, or may be high enough to undermine a full segmentation strategy;

➤ the extent and durability of segment differences – if segments are only marginally differentiated, they may not be worth taking as separate targets, and if the differences are transitory, then the viability of a segmentation strategy may be questionable;

➤ the stability and mutual compatibility of segment targets;

➤ the 'fit' between segments characteristics and company strengths (see chapter 9); and

➤ the level and type of competition in the prospective segment targets.

12.7 *Conclusions*

The selection of which potential market segment or segments to serve is the crucial step in developing a robust and comprehensive marketing strategy. Until the targets have been clearly identified, their requirements and motivations fully explored, it is not possible to develop a robust competitive positioning.

CHAPTER 13

Building and maintaining defensible positions

Competitive Strategy is the search for a favourable competitive position in an industry. Competitive Strategy aims to establish a profitable and sustainable position against the forces that determine industry competition

Michael E. Porter (1985)

Introduction

Chapter 11 discussed the choice of target market suited to the strengths and capabilities of the firm. This chapter focuses on methods for creating a competitive advantage in that chosen target market. While few advantages are likely to last forever, some bases of advantage are more readily protected than others. A key task for the strategist is to identify those bases which offer the most potential for defensible positioning.

As noted in chapter 3, Porter (1980) has identified two main routes to creating a competitive advantage. These he termed cost leadership and differentiation. In examining how each can be achieved Porter (1985) takes a systems approach likening the operations of a company to a 'value-chain' from the input of raw materials and other resources through to the final delivery to, and after sales servicing of, the customer. The value-chain was discussed in the context of competitor analysis in chapter 7 and was presented in Figure 7.3.

Each of the activities within the value-chain, the primary activities and the support functions, can be used to add value to the ultimate product or service. That added value, however, is typically in the form of lower cost or valued uniqueness.

The main factors affecting each route are discussed below.

13.1 Creating cost leadership

Porter (1985) has identified several major factors that affect costs. These he terms 'cost drivers', they are shown in Figure 13.1 and each is reviewed briefly below.

Economies of scale
Economies of scale are perhaps the single most effective cost driver in many industries. Scale economies stem from doing things more efficiently or differently in

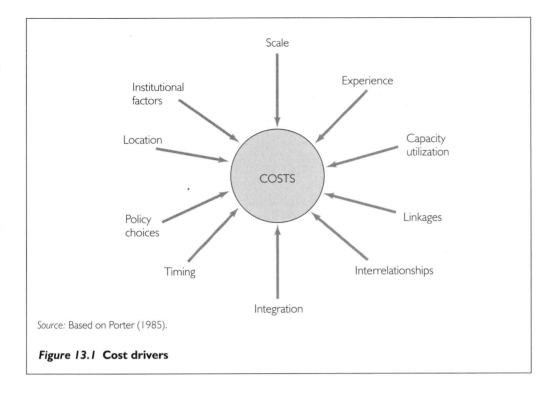

Source: Based on Porter (1985).

Figure 13.1 Cost drivers

volume. In addition, sheer size can help in creating purchasing leverage to secure cheaper and/or better quality (less waste) raw materials and securing them in times of limited availability.

There are, however, limits to scale economies. Size can bring with it added complexity which itself can lead to diseconomies. For most operations there is an optimum size above or below which inefficiencies occur.

Experience and learning effects
Further cost reductions may be achieved through learning and experience effects. Learning refers to increases in efficiency that are possible at a given level of scale through having performed the necessary tasks many times before.

In the 1960s the Boston Consulting Group extended the recognized production learning curve beyond manufacturing and looked at the increased efficiency that was possible in all aspects of the business (e.g. in marketing, advertising and selling) through experience. BCG estimated empirically that, in many industries, costs reduced by approximately 15–20 per cent each time cumulative production (a measure of experience) doubled. This finding suggests that companies with larger market share will, by definition, have a cost advantage through experience, assuming all companies are operating on the same experience curve.

Experience can be brought into the company by hiring experienced staff, and be enhanced through training. Conversely competitors may poach experience by attracting away skilled staff.

The experience curve as an explanation of costs has come under increasing scrutiny recently. Gluck (1986) argues that when the world changed from a high growth, 'big is beautiful', mentality to low growth, 'big is bust', realization the experience curve fell into disfavour. He concludes that in today's business environments competitive advantages that rely too heavily on economies of scale in manufacturing or distribution are often no longer sustainable. In addition, a shift in the level or type of technology employed may result in an inexperienced newcomer reducing costs below those of a more experienced incumbent, essentially moving onto a lower experience curve. Finally, the concept was derived in manufacturing industries and it is not at all clear how applicable it is to the service sector.

13.1.1 Capacity utilization

Capacity utilization has been shown to have a major impact on unit costs. The PIMS study (see Buzzell and Gale, 1987) has demonstrated a clear positive association between utilization and Return on Investment (ROI). Significantly, the relationship is stronger for smaller companies than for larger ones. Major discontinuities or changes in utilization can add significantly to costs, hence the need to plan production and inventory to minimize seasonal fluctuations. Many companies also avoid segments of the market where demand fluctuates wildly for this very reason (see chapter 11 on factors influencing market attractiveness).

13.1.2 Linkages

A further set of cost drivers are linkages. These concern the other activities of the firm in producing and marketing the product that have an effect on the costs. Quality control and inspection procedures, for example, can have a significant impact on servicing costs and costs attributable to faulty product returns. Indeed, in many markets it has been demonstrated that superior quality, rather than leading to higher costs of production, can actually reduce costs (Peters, 1987).

External linkages with suppliers of factor inputs or distributors of the firm's final products can also result in lower costs. Recent developments in just in time (JIT) manufacturing and delivery can have a significant impact on stockholding costs and work in progress. Beyond the cost equation, however, the establishment of closer working links have far wider marketing implications. For JIT to work effectively requires a very close working relationship between buyer and supplier. This often means an interchange of information, a meshing of forecasting and scheduling and the building of a long-term relationship. This in turn helps to create high switching costs (the costs of seeking supply elsewhere) and hence barriers to competitive entry.

13.1.3 Interrelationships

Interrelationships with other SBUs in the overall corporate portfolio can help to share experience and gain economies of scale in functional activities (such as marketing research, research and development, quality control, ordering and purchasing).

13.1.4 Degree of integration

Decisions on integration, e.g. contracting out delivery and/or service, also affect costs. Similarly the decision to make or buy components can have major cost implications. The extent of forward or backward integration extant or possible in a particular market was discussed in chapter 11 as one of the factors considered in assessing target market attractiveness to the company.

13.1.5 Timing

Timing, though not always controllable, can lead to cost advantages. Often the first mover in an industry can gain cost advantages by securing prime locations, cheap or good quality raw materials, and/or technological leadership. Second movers can often benefit from exploiting newer technology to leap-frog first mover positions.

As with other factors discussed above, however, the value of timing goes far beyond its impact on costs. Abell (1978) has argued that a crucial element of any marketing strategy is timing, that at certain times 'strategic windows' are open (i.e. there are opportunities in the market that can be exploited) while at other times they are shut. Successful strategies are timely strategies. An example was the impact of the more economical and 'honest' German and Japanese cars in the US market after the oil crisis and subsequent price rise, while Detroit kept 'gas guzzling jukeboxes on wheels' (Mingo, 1994).

13.1.6 Policy choices

Policy choices, the prime areas for differentiating discussed below, have implications for costs. Decisions on the product line, the product itself, quality levels, service, features, credit facilities, etc. all affect costs. They also affect the actual and perceived uniqueness of the product to the consumer and hence a genuine dilemma can arise if the thrust of the generic strategy is not clear. The general rules are to reduce costs on factors which will not significantly affect valued uniqueness, avoid frills if they do not serve to differentiate significantly and invest in technology to achieve low-cost process automation and low-cost product design (fewer parts can make for easier and cheaper assembly).

13.1.7 Location and institutional factors

The final cost drivers identified by Porter (1985) are location (geographic location to take advantage of lower distribution, assembly, raw materials or energy costs), and institutional factors such as government regulations (e.g. larger lorries on the roads can reduce distribution costs but at other environmental and social costs). The sensitivity of governments to lobbyists and pressure groups will dictate the ability of the company to exercise institutional cost drivers.

13.1.8 Summary of cost drivers

There are many ways in which a company can seek to reduce costs. In attempting to become a cost leader in an industry a firm should be aware first, that there can only be one cost leader, and second, that there are potentially many ways in which this position can be attacked (i.e. through using other cost drivers). Cost advantages can be amongst the most difficult to sustain and defend in the face of heavy and determined competition.

That said, however, it should be a constant objective of management to reduce costs that do not significantly add to ultimate customer satisfaction.

13.2 *Achieving differentiation*

Most of the factors listed above as cost drivers could also be used as 'uniqueness drivers' if the firm is seeking to differentiate itself from its competitors. Of most immediate concern here, however, are the policy choices open to the company. These are summarized in Figure 13.2.

13.2.1 Product differentiation

Product differentiation seeks to increase the value of the product or service on offer to the customer. Levitt (1986) has suggested that products and services can be seen on at least four main levels. These are the core product, the expected product, the augmented product and the potential product. Figure 13.3 shows these levels diagrammatically. Differentiation is possible in all these respects.

At the centre of Levitt's model is the core, or generic, product. This is the central product or service offered. It is the petrol, steel, banking facility, mortgage, information, etc. Beyond the generic product, however, is what customers expect in addition, the expected product. When buying petrol, for example, customers expect easy access to the forecourt, the possibility of paying by credit card, the availability of screen wash facilities, air for tyres, radiator top-up and so on. Since most petrol forecourts meet these expectations, they do not serve to differentiate one supplier from another.

At the next level Levitt identifies the augmented product. This constitutes all the extra features and services that go above and beyond what the customer expects to convey added value and hence serve to differentiate the offer from that of competitors. The petrol station where, in the self-serve 1990s, one attendant fills the car with petrol while another cleans the windscreen, headlamps and mirrors, is going beyond what is expected. Over time, however, these means of

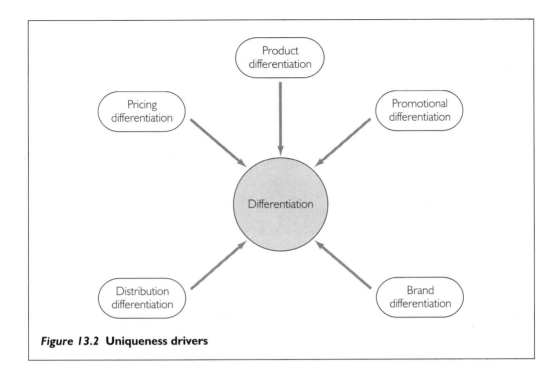

Figure 13.2 **Uniqueness drivers**

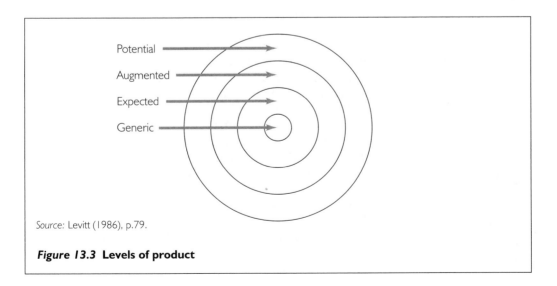

Source: Levitt (1986), p.79.

Figure 13.3 **Levels of product**

distinguishing can become copied, routine and ultimately merely part of what is expected.

Finally, Levitt describes the potential product as all those further additional features and benefits that could be offered. At the petrol station these may include a free car wash with every fill-up, gifts unrelated to petrol and a car valeting service. While the model shows the potential product bounded, in reality it is only bounded by the imagination and ingenuity of the supplier.

Peters (1987) believes that, while in the past suppliers have concentrated on attempts to differentiate their offerings on the basis of the generic and expected product that convergence is occurring at this level in many markets. As quality control, assurance and management methods become more widely understood and practised, delivering a performing, reliable, durable, conforming offer (a 'quality' product in the classic sense of the word) will no longer be adequate. In the future he predicts greater emphasis on the augmented and potential product as ways of adding value, creating customer delight and hence creating competitive advantage.

Differentiating the core and expected product
Differentiation of the core product or benefit offers a different way of satisfying the same basic want or need. It is typically created by a step change in technology, the application of innovation. Calculators, for example, offered a different method of solving the basic 'calculating' need from the slide rules that they replaced. Similarly the deep freeze offers a different way of storing food from the earlier coldstores, pantries and cellars.

Augmenting the product
Differentiation of the augmented product can be achieved by offering more to customers on existing features (e.g. offering a life-time guarantee on audio tape as Scotch provide, rather than a one- or two-year guarantee) or by offering new features of value to customers. There are two main types of product features that can create customer benefit. These are performance features and appearance features.

Analysis of product features must relate those features to the benefits they offer to customers. For example, the introduction of the golf ball typewriter did not change the core benefit (the ability to create a typewritten page of text or numbers). It did, however, allow different typefaces and different spacings to be used, thus extending the value to the customer who wanted these extra benefits. In estimating the value to the consumers of additional product features and their resulting benefits conjoint measurement (see Green and Wind, 1975) can be particularly useful. This technique has been successfully applied, for example, to deciding on product features by companies operating in the audio market and to service features offered by building societies in high interest accounts.

In the lawnmower market Flymo introduced the rotary blade hover mower as a means of differentiating from the traditional rotating cylinder blade. In some markets, especially where lawns were awkwardly shaped or steeply sloping, the ease of use of the hover mower made it a very attractive, differentiated product. In other markets, however, the market leader, Qualcast, was able to retaliate by showing the advantage of the conventional mower in having a hopper in which to catch the grass cuttings. Under the Flymo system the cuttings were left on the lawn. More recent developments have seen the introduction of rotary, hover mowers with hoppers.

A prime factor in differentiating the product or service from that of competitors is quality. Quality concerns the fitness for purpose of a product or service. For manufactured products that can include the durability, appearance or grade of the product while in services it often comes down to the tangible elements of the service, the reliability and responsiveness of the service provider, the assurance provided of the value of the service and the empathy, or caring attention, received (see Parasuraman *et al.*, 1988). Quality can reflect heavily both on raw materials used and the degree of quality control exercised during manufacture and delivery.

Of central importance is consumer perception of quality which may not be the same as the manufacturers perception. Cardozo (1979) gives an example of where the two do not coincide:

> The marketing research department of a manufacturer of household paper goods asked for consumer evaluation of a new paper tissue. The reaction was favourable but the product was not thought to be soft enough. The R&D department then set about softening the tissue by weakening the fibres and reducing their density. In subsequent usage tests the product fell apart and was useless for its designed purpose. Further tests showed that to make the product 'feel' softer required an actual increase in the strength and density of the fibres.

Quality has been demonstrated by the PIMS project to be a major determinant of commercial success. Indeed, Buzzell and Gale (1987) concluded that relative perceived quality (customers' judgements of the quality of the supplier's offer relative to its competitors) was the single most important factor in affecting the long-run performance of a business. Quality was shown to have a greater impact on ROI level and be more effective at gaining market share than lower pricing.

Closely related to perceptions of quality are perceptions of style, particularly for products with a high emotional appeal (such as cosmetics). In fashion-conscious markets such as clothes, design can be a very powerful way of differentiating. Jain (1990) notes that Du Pont successfully rejuvenated their market for ladies' stockings by offering different coloured tints and hence repositioned the stockings as fashion accessories – a different tint for each different outfit.

Packaging too can be used to differentiate the product. Packaging has five main functions, each of which can be used as a basis for differentiation:

1. Packaging stores the product, and hence can be used to extend shelf-life, or facilitate physical storage (e.g. tetra-packs for fruit juice and other beverages).
2. Packaging protects the product during transit and prior to consumption to ensure consistent quality (e.g. the use of film packs for potato crisps to ensure freshness).

3. Packaging facilitates use of the product (e.g. applicator packs for floor cleaners, wine boxes, domestic liquid soap dispensers).
4. Packaging helps create an image for the product through its visual impact, quality of design, illustration of uses, etc.
5. Packaging helps promote the product through eye-catching, unusual colours and shapes, etc. Examples of the latter are the sales of wine in carafes rather than bottles (Paul Masson California Wines) and the sale of ladies' tights in egg-shaped packages (L'eggs).

A particularly effective way of differentiating at the tangible product level is to create a unique brand with a favourable image and reputation. As discussed in chapter 5, brand and company reputation can be powerful marketing assets for a company.

Brand name or symbol is an indication of pedigree and a guarantee of what to expect from the product – a quality statement of a value-for-money signal. Heinz baked beans, for example, can command a premium price because of the assurance of quality the consumer gets in choosing the brand. Similarly, retailers such as Sainsbury and Marks & Spencer are able to differentiate their own branded products from other brands because of their reputation for quality that extends across their product ranges. Branding is also a highly defensible competitive advantage. Once registered, competitors cannot use the same branding (name or symbol).

Service can be a major differentiating factor in the purchase of many products, especially durables (both consumer and industrial). Certainly, enhanced service was a major factor in the success of Wilhelm Becker, a Swedish industrial paints company. Becker developed 'Colour Studios' as a service to its customers and potential customers to enable them to experiment with different colours and combinations. Volvo, the Swedish auto manufacturer, used the service in researching alternative colours to use on farm tractors and found that red (the colour used to date) was a poor colour choice as it jarred, for many farmers, with the colours of the landscape. Changing the colour scheme resulted in increased sales.

In domestic paints, too, there has been an attempt to add service, this time provided by the customer him or herself. Matchpots were introduced by a leading domestic paint supplier to allow, for a small outlay, customers to try different colours at home before selecting the final colour to use. In this case, however, unlike Becker's Colour Studios, copy by competitors was relatively easy and the advantage quickly disappeared.

Service need not be an addition to the product. In some circumstances a reduction can add value. The recent growth in home brewing of beers and wines is a case where a less complete product (the malt extract, hops, grape juice, yeast, etc.) is put to market but the customer is able to gain satisfaction through self completion of the production process. Thus the customer provides the service and becomes part of the production process.

Providing superior service as a way of creating a stronger link between supplier and customer can have wide-reaching consequences. In particular, it makes it less likely that the customer will look for alternative supply sources and hence acts as a barrier to competitor entry.

To ensure and enhance customer service Peters (1987) recommends that each company regularly conduct customer satisfaction studies to gauge how well it is meeting customers' expectations and to seek ways in which it can improve on customer service.

Further elements of the augmented product that can be used to differentiate the product include installation, credit availability, delivery (speedy and on time, when promised) and warranty. All can add to the differentiation of the product from that of competitors.

Deciding on the bases for product differentiation

Each of the elements of the product can be used as a way of differentiating the product from competitive offerings. In deciding which of the possible elements to use in differentiating the product three considerations are paramount.

First, what do the customers expect in addition to the core, generic product? In the automobile market, for example, customers in all market segments expect a minimum level of reliability in the cars they buy. In the purchase of consumer white goods (fridges, freezers, washing machines, etc.) minimum periods of warranty are expected. In the choice of toothpaste, minimum levels of protection from tooth decay and gum disease are required. These expectations, over and above the core product offering, are akin to 'hygiene factors' in Hertzberg's Theory of Motivation. They must be offered for the product or service to be considered by potential purchasers. Their presence does not enhance the probability of consumers choosing products with them, but their absence will certainly deter purchase.

The second consideration is what the customers would value over and above what is expected. In identifying potential 'motivators' the marketer seeks to offer more than the competition to attract purchasers. These additions to the product beyond what is normally expected by the customers often form the most effective way of differentiating the company's offerings. Crucial, however, is the cost of offering these additions. The cost of the additions should be less than the extra benefit (value) to the customers and hence be reflected in a willingness to pay a premium price. Where possible an economic value should be placed on the differentiation to allow pricing to take full account of value to the customer (see Forbis and Mehta, 1981).

The third consideration in choosing a way of differentiating the product from the competition is the ease with which that differentiation can be copied. Changes in the interest rates charged by one building society, for example, can easily be copied in a matter of days or even hours. An advantage based, however, on the location of the Society's outlets in the major city high streets takes longer and is more costly to copy.

Ideally, differentiation is sought where there is some (at least temporary) barrier precluding competitors following. The most successful differentiations are those that use a core skill, competence or marketing asset of the company that competitors do not possess and will find it hard to develop. In the car hire business, for example, the extensive network of pick-up and drop-off points offered by Hertz, the market leader, enables them to offer a more convenient service to the one-way customer than the competition. Emulating that network is costly, if not impossible, for smaller followers in the market.

Peters (1987) has argued that many companies over-emphasize the core product in their overall marketing thinking and strategy. He suggests that as it becomes increasingly difficult to differentiate on the basis of core product, greater emphasis will need to be put on how to 'add service' through the augmented (and potential) product. This change in emphasis is shown in Figure 13.4, which contrasts a product focus (core product emphasis) with a service added focus (extending the augmented and potential products in ways of value and interest to the customer).

A focus away from the core product towards the 'outer rings' is particularly useful in 'commodity' markets where competitive strategy has traditionally been based on price. Differentiation through added service offers an opportunity for breaking out of an over-reliance on price in securing business.

In summary, there are a great many ways in which products and services can be differentiated from their competitors. In deciding on the type of differentiation to adopt, several factors should be borne in mind: the added value to the customer of the differentiation; the cost of differentiation in relation to the added value; the probability and speed of competitor copy; and the extent to which the differentiation exploits the marketing assets of the company.

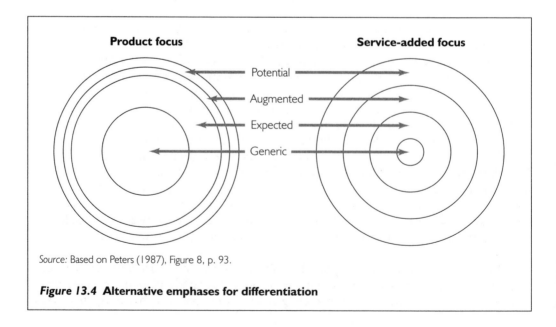

Source: Based on Peters (1987), Figure 8, p. 93.

Figure 13.4 **Alternative emphases for differentiation**

13.2.2 Distribution differentiation

Distribution differentiation comes from using different outlets, having a different network or a different coverage of the market.

Recent developments in direct marketing are not only related to creating different ways of promoting products. They also offer new outlets for many goods. Shopping by phone through TV-based catalogues has yet to take off in any big way, but there are certainly opportunities for innovative marketers.

13.2.3 Price differentiation

Lower price as a means of differentiation can be a successful basis for strategy only where the company enjoys a cost advantage, or where there are barriers to competing firms with a lower cost structure competing at a lower price. Without a cost advantage starting a price war can be a disastrous course to follow, as Laker Airways found to their cost.

Premium pricing is generally only possible where the product or service has actual or perceived advantages to the customer and therefore is often used in conjunction with and to reinforce a differentiated product.

In general, the greater the degree of product or services differentiation the more scope there is for premium pricing. Where there is little other ground for differentiation, price competition becomes stronger and cost advantages assume greater importance.

Promotional differentiation

Promotional differentiation involves using different types of promotions (e.g. a wider communications mix employing advertising, public relations, direct mail, personal selling, etc.), promotions of a different intensity (i.e. particularly heavy promotions during launch and relaunch of products) or different content (i.e. with a clearly different advertising message).

Many companies today make poor use of the potential of public relations. Public relations essentially consists of creating relationships with the media and using those relationships to gain positive exposure. Press releases and interviews with key executives on important topical issues can both help to promote the company in a more credible way than media advertising.

A small, UK-based electronics company brilliantly exploited a visit by Japanese scientists to its plant. The company gained wide coverage of the event, presenting it as an attempt by the Japanese to learn from this small but innovative company. The coverage was in relevant trade journals and even the national media. The result was a major increase in enquiries to the company and increasing domestic sales of its products.

The PR had two major advantages over media advertising. First, it was very cheap in relation to the exposure it achieved (the company could never have afforded to buy the exposure at normal media rates). Second, the reports appearing in the press called more credibility because they had been written by independent journalists and were seen as 'news' rather than advertising. (*Source*: 'The Marketing Mix', television series by Yorkshire TV.)

Using a different message within normal media advertising can also have a differentiating effect. When most advertisers are pursuing essentially the same market with the same message an innovative twist is called for.

Most beers were promoted in the 1970s by showing gregarious groups of males in public houses having an enjoyable night out. Heineken managed to differentiate their beer by using a series of advertisements employing humour and the caption 'Heineken refreshes the parts other beers cannot reach'.

When Krona was launched by Van den Berghs into the margarine market (see chapter 11) aimed at consumers who were increasingly sensitive to the price of butter but who still required the taste of butter the company had a major communications problem. Legislation precluded stating that the product tasted like butter (Clark, 1986) and the slogan 'four out of five people can't tell the difference between Stork and butter' had already been used (with mixed success) by one of the other company brands.

The solution was to use a semi-documentary advertisement featuring a respected reporter (René Cutforth) which majored on a rumour that had circulated around a product of identical formulation in Australia (Fairy). The rumours had been that the product was actually New Zealand butter being dumped on the Australian market disguised as margarine to overcome trade quotas. The slogan selected was 'the margarine that raised questions in an Australian parliament' and the style of the advertisement, while never actually claiming taste parity with butter, cleverly conveyed the impression that people really couldn't tell the difference.

More recently Van den Berghs have promoted the low-fat margarine Flora as the spread bought by women who care about the health of their men while their originally branded I Can't Believe It's Not Butter returns to Stork's old taste appeal.

Brand differentiation

Brand positioning places the customer at the centre of building a maintainable hold on the marketplace. It shifts from the classic idea of companies developing a 'Unique Selling Proposition' (USP) to establishing a 'Unique Emotional Proposition' (ESP).

Competing products may look similar to the hapless parent buying a pair of Nike trainers, but not to their children. They want Nike trainers, and the parent is pressured to pay the extra to get them. Nike's success at brand differentiation flowed from their Air Jordan range which built upon the USP of air cells in the heels and their ESP of being associated with top athletes. So powerful did this combination become that even in crime-free Japan people paid huge price premiums for their Air Jordans but would not jog in them for fear of being mugged (called jugging) for their Nikes. Adidas and Reebok promote their products using athletes and air in their heels, but Nike have won the battle for the minds of teenagers and their parents' pockets.

Nike is an exemplary case of gaining market strength by using Ries and Trout's (1986) ladder of awareness. Even though there may be numerous products on the market, consumers are rarely able to name more than a few. This was the problem faced by Audi, when they realized that people mentioned Mercedes, BMW and Volkswagen as German cars, with all the connotations of quality and reliability that entails, but often omitted Audi. The result was the Vorsprung Durch Technik campaign which concentrated upon the Germanness of the product and, through rallying and the Quatro, upon their technical excellence. Ever the number 4, in 1990 Audi had to change tack once again to maintain a foothold on the product ladder by successfully associating themselves with green issues.

Trout and Ries noted that the second firm in markets usually enjoys half the business of the first firm, and the third firm enjoys half the business of the second, etc. This flows through into profitability and return investments where, in the long term, profitability follows the market share ranking of the companies. Leading companies can also achieve major economies in advertising and promotion (Saunders, 1990). Part of the reason for this is the tendency for people to remember the number 1. When asked who was the first person to successfully fly alone across the Atlantic, most people would correctly answer Charles Lindberg, but how many people can name the second person? Similarly with the first and second people to set foot on the moon, or climb Mount Everest.

The importance of being number 1 is fine for market leaders such as Nike in sports shoes, Mercedes in luxury cars, Coca-Cola in soft drinks and Nescafé in coffee, but it leaves lesser brands with an unresolved problem. Positioning points to a way of these brands establishing a strong place in the minds of the consumer despite the incessant call for attention from competing products. This involves consistency of message and the association of a brand with ideas that are already held strongly within the consumer's mind.

A matrix of alternative generic positions and positioning strategies is available (Figure 13.5). Generic positions provide the broad alternatives: consolidation, latent position, deposition and membership position. The consolidation position might be used by market leaders, such as Boeing in civil aircraft. The consolidation position can work for non-leaders with a strong reputation. Throughout the world Land Rover has a reputation for ruggedness, tradition and real cross-country capability. With its reputation, the BMW subsidiary could launch less expensive and stylish models, such as the Discovery, which now outsell the original Land Rover military and agricultural vehicles.

While making headway against established competition can be difficult, where there is an unfulfilled need or want, a company can use latent positioning to establish a reputation. Such was the appeal of Sensodyne toothpaste, the first product to focus on the comfort of people with sensitive teeth, or Lever's highly successful Radion automatic soap powder, which focused upon removing 'dirt and odours'. The Radion campaign took unsubtlety to the extreme. A brutal name with possible association with strength and radioactivity, a brash, day-glo orange, green, yellow and blue pack, and the parody on an advert which displays the wife's distaste at the smell of her husband's armpit. Although Lever Brothers received no advertising awards, they did achieve 9 per cent market share in the UK market in

	Generic position			
	Consolidation	**Latent position**	**Deposition**	**Membership**
Attributes	Land Rover	Radion		Lloyds Bank
Price/quality	Sainsbury		MBNA Gold Advantage	
Competition			MBNA Gold Advantage	Swiftair Express
Application		Polaroid		
User	Swissair			
Product class				Toyota

Figure 13.5 **Positioning alternatives**

the first year. Helped by their radical positioning, this massive gain within an established market was achieved without particularly cannibalizing any of Unilever's other brands.

Depositioning is directly competitive, although the competitors may not always be mentioned – for instance, the Barclaycard campaign where Alan Whicker comments on the universal usability of Visa which is 'More than can be said for certain other charge cards I could mention'. Although American Express is not mentioned, it is certainly imputed by referring to charge cards and the exotic locations involved in the ads. Beside promoting the advantage of Barclaycard, it also tends to undermine the prestige position occupied by American Express. Within the Visa market itself MBNA's Gold advantage depositions other Visa suppliers by promoting its low interest rate and no fees that it charges its well-shod customers.

Membership positioning is attractive for lower-order companies within a product market. This Lloyds Bank does by identifying itself as one of the Big Four and projecting the range of facilities and services it provides for the consumer and the business user.

Within each of the generic positions, the positioning strategy determines the means by which each of the product's positions are communicated. Aaker (1982) identified six of these:

➤ **Positioning by attribute** as used by Land Rover, Radion and MBNA Gold Advantage, where their distinctiveness or similarity to other products are stated. Sainsbury's use price/quality as a basis for their dominant position in the marketplace: 'Good food costs less at Sainsbury's'.

➤ **Competition** is the main emphasis of British Rail's Intercity campaign, although the generic strategy is to deposition the competitor. An alternative competitor-based position is used by the Royal Mail's Swiftair service which, although less expensive, seeks to be seen as a courier service: 'By air, by land, by Swiftair, by hand'.

➤ **Application/application-based positioning** is used by Polaroid to position their EMI System range as a piece of communication equipment rather than a fun camera: 'Now when you describe it, everyone will get the picture What will Polaroid do for you today?'

➤ **User portraits** are used to position Swissair within the overcrowded and protected European airline industry. For instance, 'Swissair customer portrait 69, photographed by Nikolaus Schmid-Burgk, Elizabeth Princess of Shchsen-Weimar and Eisenach, managing directrice of an eminent jewellery company, Munich ... She chooses Swissair because it's a gem of an airline.' In contrast, Lufthansa, who have a similar profile in the marketplace, focus upon their attributes of safety and reliability: 'We have people who check the people who check the people who check the aircraft.'

➤ **Product class association** is now being used strongly by the Japanese motor manufacturers, as they move up-market. The advertising of Toyota and Nissan particularly associates them with Porsche and, more creatively, Mazda associates their sports cars with the golden age of MG, Austin Healey and Triumph.

A feature of many successful products is their ability to hold their position over many years and so give themselves a strong identity. Even though the product may have many different attributes, as does Coffeemate, the emphasis has remained upon it making 'good coffee taste great'. This is despite the alternative claim that it contains fewer calories and is more economical to use than ordinary milk. To help them retain this consistency throughout generations of competitors, common brand managers and advertising campaigns, Unilever developed the concept of the positioning bridge which provides a clear focus and eases internal communications about the brand's identity. This is a deceptively simple tool, which seeks to anchor the product to its core identity. It involves using two words – one functional, one emotional or psychological – that give the essence of a brand's position in the marketplace; for instance, for the fabric conditioner Comfort, loving softness; for the washing powder Persil, caring whiteness; and for the washing up liquid Fairy, gentle relationships.

Like marketing in general, the essence of positioning is simplicity and tenacity: the distillation of the miscellaneous features of a product, its competitors and the marketplace into a simple message that is easy to understand and then focusing the promotional effort of a company on to retaining that idea. Simple to say; hard to do; easy to forget.

Summary
Where the route to competitive advantage selected is differentiation the key

differentiating variables, those that offer the most leverage for differentiation using the company's skills to the full, should be identified. Where possible differentiation should be pursued on multiple fronts to enhance differentiation. In addition, value signals should be employed to enhance perceived differentiation (e.g. building on reputation, image, presence, appearance and pricing of the product). Barriers to copy should be erected, through patenting, holding key executives and creating switching costs to retain customers.

13.3 *Maintaining a defensible position*

It will be clear from the above that there is a variety of ways in which companies can attempt to create for themselves a competitive advantage. Some of these ways will be easier for competitors to copy than others. The most useful ways of creating defensible positions lie in exploiting the following.

13.3.1 Unique and valued products

Fundamental to creating a superior and defensible position in the marketplace is to have unique and valued products and services to offer to customers.

Dow Jones maintains high margins from unique products. *The Wall Street Journal* is a product that customers want and are willing to pay for. Central to offering unique and valued products and services is the identification of the key differentiating variables – those with the greatest potential leverage.

Uniqueness may stem from employing superior, proprietary technology, utilizing superior raw materials, or from differentiating the tangible and augmented elements of product.

Unique products do not, however, stay unique forever. Successful products will be imitated sooner or later so that the company that wishes to retain its unique position must be willing, and indeed even eager, to innovate continually and look for new ways of differentiating. This may mean a willingness to cannibalize its own existing products, before the competition attacks them.

13.3.2 Clear, tight definition of market targets

To enable a company to keep its products and services both unique and valued by the customers requires constant monitoring of, and dialogue with, those customers. This in turn requires a clear understanding of who they are and how to access them. The clearer the focus of the firm's activities on one or a few market targets the more likely is it successfully to serve those targets. In the increasingly segmented markets of the 1990s the companies that fail to focus their activities are less likely to respond to changing opportunities and threats.

13.3.3 Enhanced customer linkages

Creating closer bonds with customers through enhanced service can help establish a more defensible position in the market. As suggested above, a major advantage of JIT manufacturing systems is that they require closer links between supplier and buyer. As buyers and suppliers become more enmeshed so it becomes more difficult for newcomers to enter.

Creating switching costs, the costs associated with moving from one supplier to another, is a further way in which customer linkages can be enhanced. Loomis writing in *Fortune* (30 April 1984) pointed to the success of Nalco in using its specialist expertise in the chemicals it markets to counsel and problem solve for its customers. This enhancement of the linkages with its customers makes it less likely they will shop around for other sources of supply.

13.3.4 **Established brand and company credibility**

Brand and company reputation are amongst the most defensible assets the company has, provided they are managed well and protected. Brands can take many years to build, but can be destroyed overnight by a lack of attention to issues such as quality control or safety.

> Worthington Steel in the US have an enviable reputation for superior quality workmanship. The company also has a high reputation for customer service. Combined they make it hard for customers to go elsewhere. (Peters, 1987)

The rate of technological and market change is now so fast, and products so transient, that customers find security and continuity in the least tangible of a company's assets: the reputation of its brands and company name. Brand, styles and products change year on year, but people the world over desire Nike, Sony, Mercedes, Levi and Rolex. They 'buy the maker', not the product (Sorrell, 1989).

13.4 *Conclusions*

While two basic approaches to creating a competitive position have been discussed it should be clear that the first priority in marketing will be to decide on the focus of operations: industry-wide or specific target market segments. Creating a competitive advantage in the selected area of focus can be achieved either through cost leadership or differentiation. To build a strong, defensible position in the market the initial concern should be to differentiate the company's offerings from those of its competitors on some basis of value to the customer. The second concern should then be to achieve this at the lowest possible delivered cost.

CHAPTER 14

Offensive and defensive competitive strategies

Companies fail in the market-place because their strategies are ill-conceived, poorly prepared and badly executed in relation to those of their competitors.
Barrie James (1984)

Introduction

Successful strategy amounts to combining attacking and defensive moves to build a stronger position in the chosen marketplace. In recent years several writers, most notably Kotler and Singh (1981), James (1984) and Ries and Trout (1986), have drawn an analogy between military warfare and competitive battles in the market-place. Their basic contention is that lessons for the conduct of business strategy can be learned by a study of warfare and the principles developed by military strategists. Indeed, the bookshelves of corporate strategists around the world now often contain the works of Sun Tzu (Khoo, 1992; Trai, 1991) and von Clausewitz (1908).

There are five basic strategies that an organization can pursue to reach its overall objectives. It may pursue a build (or growth) strategy, a holding (or maintenance) strategy, a niching strategy, a harvesting strategy, or a deletion (divestment) strat-egy. Each type of strategy is discussed below. The structure of the discussion draws from both Kotler (1997) and James (1984).

14.1 Build strategies

Build strategies are most suited to growth markets. In such markets it is generally considered easier to expand, as this need not be at the expense of the competition and does not necessarily provoke strong competitive retaliation. During the growth phase of markets companies should aim to grow at least as fast as the market itself.

Build strategies can also make sense in non-growth markets where there are exploitable competitor weaknesses. In the UK chocolate bar market Rowntree iden-tified an exploitable competitor weakness. Cadbury Dairy Milk, the market leader, had responded to escalating costs of raw materials by making the product progres-sively smaller. One manifestation was that the product was made thinner.

Customer research carried out by Rowntree showed that a significant proportion of customers were dissatisfied with the 'thinner' bars and were prepared to pay

336

higher prices for a chocolate that was thicker, or more 'chunky'. The Rowntree product 'Yorkie' to emerge was a major marketing success, capturing a large slice of the mature chocolate bar market.

Similarly where there are marketing assets that can be usefully deployed a build strategy may make sense. Rank Hovis MacDougall successfully exploited the granule technology developed for their Bisto gravy product in the market for instant packet soups with the launch of the 'Welcome' range of granular soups.

Build strategies are often costly, particularly where they involve a direct confrontation with a major competitor. Before embarking on such strategies the potential costs must be weighed against the expected gains.

14.1.1 Market expansion

Build strategies are achieved through market expansion or taking customers from competitors (confrontation). Market expansion, in turn, comes through three main routes: new users; new uses; and/or increased frequency of purchase.

New users
As products and services progress through their life cycles different purchasers will emerge at different times. During the introductory phase innovators may be attracted to the offering. Once the market amongst innovators has been exhausted new customers must be sought. For many expensive consumer-durable products, such as compact disc players or home computers, a trickle-down effect has been observed, with the products selling first to wealthy consumers at the top end of the social scale. As the product moves more into growth, competition intensifies and prices typically begin to fall so newer customers are attracted to purchase the product. These are less wealthy and lower down the social scale.

For products which have reached the mature phase of the life cycle a major task is to find new markets for the product. This could involve geographic expansion of the companies' activities domestically and/or internationally. Companies seeking growth but believing their established market to be incapable of providing it roll out into new markets.

New uses
For some products the market may be expanded through introducing existing (or new) users to different uses. The recent campaign for Hellman has stressed the versatility of their mayonnaise product and the fact that it can be used as an accompaniment to a variety of dishes, not just the traditional salad usage.

Increased frequency of use
The third route to market expansion is through encouraging existing users to use more of the product. Clearly this route is most applicable to repeat purchase (both consumer and industrial) products. Segmentation by volume of consumption can

help to identify medium or light users who can be targeted in an attempt to increase their frequency.

When segmenting by volume purchased or consumed the typical approach is to focus activity on the heavy users. In mature markets, however, it is probable that the heavy users are already consuming near to maximum amounts of the products or services offered and that growth for one competitor in that segment will be only at the expense of another, initiating a confrontation strategy. Depending on their reasons for using the product or service less medium or light users may prove an easier target.

14.1.2 Market share gain through competitor confrontation

When a build objective is pursued in a market that cannot, for one reason or another, be expanded, success must, by definition, be at the expense of competitors. This will inevitably lead to some degree of confrontation between the protagonists for customers. Kotler and Singh (1981) have identified five main confrontation strategies (see Figure 14.1).

Frontal attack
The frontal attack is characterized by an all-out attack on the opponent's territory. It is often countered by a fortification, or position, defence (see below). The outcome of the confrontation will depend on strength and endurance.

James (1984) points to the successful use of the frontal attack by Montgomery at El Alamein in 1942 when the attackers had a superiority of forces (men, guns, tanks and air support) of between 2 and 3 to 1. The attackers also had the reserves to sustain the heavy casualties normally associated with a frontal attack.

The requirement of a similar 3 to 1 advantage to ensure success in a commercial frontal attack has been suggested (Kotler and Singh, 1981), further calibrated (Cook, 1983) and questioned (Chattopadhyay, Nedungadi and Chakravarti, 1985). All agree, however, that to defeat a well-entrenched competitor, who has built a solid market position, requires substantial superiority in at least one key area of the marketing programme.

IBM's attack on the PC market in the early 1980s is a classic example of the frontal attack. The market pioneer (Apple) was attacked partly as a defensive move by IBM as the company saw the likelihood that PCs would become executive workstations and hence threaten IBMs traditional dominance of the mainframe business market. There were several aspects to IBM's attack on the market. It was spearheaded by a technological improvement (16-bit processors gave increased power and speed over the competitive 8-bit machines).

At the same time IBM made the technical specification of their machines widely available to software houses and other peripheral equipment manufacturers so that software became readily available and soon established an industry standard ('IBM-compatible'). The creation of the industry standard was made possible by the use of that prime marketing asset – the IBM name and reputation. Finally, a massive

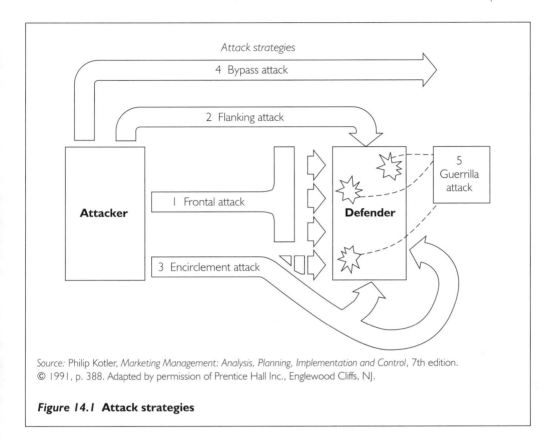

Source: Philip Kotler, *Marketing Management: Analysis, Planning, Implementation and Control*, 7th edition.
© 1991, p. 388. Adapted by permission of Prentice Hall Inc., Englewood Cliffs, NJ.

***Figure 14.1* Attack strategies**

promotional campaign was launched in the small business market. The results were not only a dominant share of the market for IBM, but they also managed to encourage the further growth of the market as a whole.

Frontal attacks, however, can be costly failures. The Charge of the Light Brigade at Balaclava in the Crimean War of 1854 resulted in the death of 500 officers and men in the space of 30 minutes (Regan, 1992). Trench warfare in France during the First World War saw millions of casualties. In one 5-month period during 1916 over 1,250,000 men died in attempts to break through enemy lines. In April 1915 thousands of Australian and New Zealand (ANZAC) troops lost their lives in frontal attacks on Turkish-held positions on the Galipoli Peninsula. Their beachhead was abandoned a few weeks later when it became clear that the Turkish positions were unassailable (Liddel Hart, 1972; Regan 1992).

In business, too, the frontal attack can prove suicidal. Laker Airways attacked the major airlines in the late 1970s on a low-price platform but with a matched product and service offering. When the other airlines reacted by cutting their prices Laker was eventually forced out of business as the company's cost structure was no lower than the competitors and the reserves, badly affected by currency fluctuations in the early 1980s, were inadequate to sustain the losses.

For a frontal attack to succeed requires sufficient resources, a strength advantage over the competitors being attacked, and that losses can be both predicted and sustained.

Flanking attack

In contrast to the frontal attack the flanking attack seeks to concentrate the aggressor's strengths against the competitor's weaknesses. In warfare a flanking attack would seek to shift the battleground away from the enemy's strength to the unguarded or less well-defended flanks. As Sun Tzu (Khoo, 1992) says:

> In battle, use direct methods to engage the enemy's forces [but] indirect methods [flanking] to secure victory.

History has proved him right. Almost all the major battles in history have been won by a successful flanking manoeuvre (Keegan, 1993).

In business a flanking attack is achieved either through attacking geographic regions where the defender is under-represented or through attacking underserved competitor segments.

In many markets Japanese industries first attacked established Western companies in their weak Southeast Asian flank. Only after building up their strengths in those markets did they attack the Western firms in their home markets. We have already seen the impact of this in the car, motor-cycle and consumer electronics industry but Japanese cosmetics, homecare and retailers are now building attacking the Southeast Asian flank.

World-wide Coca-Cola dominates the soft drinks market but in some specific locations Pepsi Cola has exploited Coca-Cola's weaknesses and dominates.

Segmental flanking involves serving distinct segments that have not been adequately served by existing companies. James (1984) gives as an example the development of grocery retailing in the USA. During the 1980s US supermarkets were getting bigger, emphasizing one-stop-shopping and (because of their sheer size) locating out of town. The problems for the smaller grocery stores were acute. There was, however, a limited market for convenience stores, those with a limited product range but local availability and long opening hours. Importantly customers were prepared to pay more for convenience, and smaller chains such as 7–11 emerged.

The entry of Japan into the UK motor-cycle market and subsequently the automobile market is a classic example of a flanking strategy. In autos especially the Japanese took advantage of the OPEC-induced oil crisis of the early 1970s to cater to customer needs in the sub-compact car segment. The Japanese cars were cheap, reliable and offered good fuel consumption to the hard-hit motorist. Having established a toehold in the market, the Japanese car manufacturers have subsequently moved into other segments.

Crucial to a successful flanking strategy can be timing. The Japanese entry into the US sub-compact car market was timed to take advantage of the recession and power. The strategy requires the identification of competitor weaknesses, inability or unwillingness to serve particular sectors of the market. In turn identification of market gaps often requires a fresh look at the market and a more creative approach to segmenting it.

Encirclement

The encirclement attack, or siege, consists of enveloping the enemy, cutting him off from routes of supply to force capitulation. In warfare the analogy would be with castle sieges of the Middle Ages where attackers would force defenders into their castles and cut the supply lines to starve the defenders into submission.

In business there are two approaches to the encirclement attack. The first is to attempt to isolate the competitor from the supply of raw materials on which he depends and/or the customers he seeks to sell to. The second approach is to seek to offer an all-round better product or service than the competitor. After their original flanking attack on the small car market, the Japanese employing an encirclement attack aimed at many segments simultaneously: Toyota pickups and Land Cruisers, luxury cars such as the Lexus, the Lexus 4×4 in the US, the MX-5 sports car, Honda's Ferrari bashers, etc.

Bypass strategy

The bypass strategy is characterized by changing the battleground to avoid competitor strongholds. The Maginot Line, built by France to protect itself from invasion, was simply bypassed and ignored by the invading German Army in the Second World War. Bypass in business is often achieved through technological leap-frogging. Casio bypassed the strength of the Swiss watch industry through the development and marketing of digital watches. They similarly bypassed slide rule manufacturers with pocket calculators. After decimating the traditional watch industry Swatch bypassed Casio's dull digital with their fashionable and inexpensive Swatch.

Guerrilla tactics

Where conventional warfare fails guerrilla tactics often take over. During the Second World War the French Resistance harassed the occupying German forces. Terrorist activities in Northern Ireland, the Basque Country, Nicaragua and Sri Lanka are all designed to weaken the morale and determination of their enemies.

In business guerrilla, or unconventional, tactics can be employed primarily as 'spoiling' activities to weaken the competition. Selective price-cuts, especially during a competitor's new product testing or launch, depositioning advertising (as attempted by the Butter Information Council Ltd in its campaign against Krona margarine), alliances (as used against Laker Airways), executive raids and legal manoeuvres can all be used in this regard. Guerrilla tactics are used by companies of all sizes in attempts to soften up their competitors, often before moving in for the kill. Their effectiveness lies in the difficulty the attacked has in adequately defending against them due to their unpredictability.

One of the most long lasting guerrilla actions is Virgin Atlantic's campaign against British Airways (BA). Despite being in an alliance that carries more people across the Atlantic than BA, Virgin Atlantic still successfully positions itself as the little victim of BA's proposed alliance with American Airlines. Virgin's approach contrasts with that of Freddie Laker in the 1970s who failed in a price-based frontal attack on British Airways.

14.2 *Hold strategies*

For market leaders, especially in mature or declining markets, the major objective may not be to build but to maintain the current position against potential attackers. It could also be that, even in growing markets, the potential rewards judged to be possible from a build strategy are outweighed by the expected costs due, for example, to the strength and nature of competition (Treacy and Wiersema, 1995).

A hold strategy may be particularly suitable for a business or product group designated as a cash generator for the company, where that cash is needed for investment elsewhere.

14.2.1 Market maintenance

The amount and type of effort required to hold position will vary depending on the degree and nature of competition encountered. When the business dominates its market it may have cost advantages through economies of scale or experience effects which can be used as a basis for defending through selective price-cutting. Alternatively, barriers to entry can be erected by the guarding of technological expertise where possible and the retention of key executive skills.

14.2.2 Defensive strategies

While in some markets competitor aggression may be low, making a holding strategy relatively easy to execute in most, especially where the potential gains for an aggressor are high, more constructive defensive strategies must be explicitly pursued. Kotler and Singh (1981) suggest six basic holding strategies (see Figure 14.2).

Fortification
Market fortification involves erecting barriers around the company and its market offerings to shut out competition. The military analogy is the opposite side of the wall from the siege. The defender creates the largest walls and moats possible and sits tight until the aggressor gets weary, or finds other more pressing priorities, and withdraws. During the Second World War Leningrad was besieged by the German Army for 900 days but never taken. Eventually, in 1944, Hitler had other preoccupations and called off the siege (Liddel Hart, 1973).

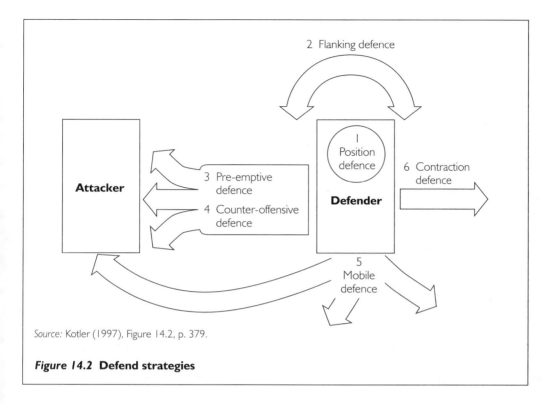

Source: Kotler (1997), Figure 14.2, p. 379.

Figure 14.2 **Defend strategies**

In business a position defence is created through erecting barriers to copy and/or entry. This is most effectively achieved through differentiating the company's offerings from those of competitors and potential competitors. Where differentiation can be created on non-copyable grounds (e.g. by using the company's distinctive skills, competences and marketing assets) that are of value to the customers, aggressors will find it more difficult to overrun the position defended.

For established market leaders, brand name and reputation are often used as the principal way of holding position. In addition, maintaining higher quality, better delivery and service, better (more appealing or heavier) promotions or lower prices based on a cost advantage, can all be used to fortify the position held against a frontal attack.

Flanking defence
The flanking defence is a suitable rejoinder to a flanking attack. Under the attack strategy (see above), the aggressor seeks to concentrate his strength against the weaknesses of the defender, often (especially in military warfare) using the element of surprise to gain the upper hand.

A flanking defence requires the company to strengthen the flanks, without providing a weaker and more vulnerable target elsewhere. It requires the prediction of competitor strategy and likely strike positions. In food marketing, for example, several leading manufacturers of branded goods, seeing the increasing threat posed by retailer own-label and generic brands. have entered into contracts to provide own-label products themselves rather than let their competitors get into their markets.

The major concerns in adopting a flanking strategy are, first, whether the new positionings adopted for defensive reasons significantly weaken the main, core positions. In the case of retailer own-labels, for example, actively co-operating could increase the trend towards own-label and lead to the eventual death of the brand. As a consequence, many leading brand manufacturers will not supply own-label and rely on the strength of their brands to see off competition (effectively a position, or fortification, defence). Kellogg's are a prime example in the breakfast cereal market where they have adopted the slogan 'If it doesn't say Kellogg's on the label it isn't Kellogg's in the box'.

After creating the luxury off-the-road vehicle market with the Range Rover, sometimes referred to as the Hollywood Jeep, Land Rover came under attack from many American and Japanese car manufacturers selling lower priced products. They responded by defending the Range Rover by moving it upmarket with a 4.6 litre BMW engined version while defending its flank with the Land Rover Discovery. The design and the off-the-road credibility of the Land Rover brand gave the Discovery a huge advantage in the market which successfully pushed back the sales of the attackers.

The second concern is that the new position is actually tenable. Where it is not based on corporate strengths or marketing assets it may be less defensible than the previously held positions.

Pre-emptive defence
A pre-emptive defence involves striking at the potential aggressor before he/she can mount their attack. The objective is to strike a physical or demoralizing blow which will prevent the aggressor from attacking in the first place.

In military conflict the classic attempt at a pre-emptive strike was the attack by the Japanese on the American Fleet in Pearl Harbor in 1941. In that conflict the pre-emptive strike did not deter the Americans from entering the Second World War; indeed, it may have hastened their entry (James, 1984). More successful was the Israeli strike on Lebanon in 1982 to prevent a major offensive on Israel's home ground. The NATO strategy of threatening first use of nuclear weapons in the event of a Warsaw Pact aggression in Northern Europe during the Cold War was also a pre-emptive defence strategy signalling the threat of retaliation.

In business the pre-emptive defensive can involve an actual attack on the competition (as occurs in disruption of competitor test marketing activity) or merely signalling an intention to fight on a particular front and a willingness to commit the necessary resources to defend against aggression.

When Goldenfry gravies were about to launch a major offensive on the gravy granule market the defender, Bisto, launched a major pre-emptive strike with heavy account calling and detailed marketing research demonstrating Bisto product superiority.

Sun Tzu (Khoo, 1992) summed up the philosophy behind the pre-emptive defence:

The supreme art of war is to subdue the enemy without fighting.

Unfortunately it is not always possible to deter aggression. The second-best option is to strike back quickly before the attack gains momentum, through a counter-offensive.

Counter-offensive

Where deterrence of a potential attack before it occurs may be the ideal defence, a rapid counter-attack to 'stifle at birth' the aggression can be equally effective. The essence of a counter-offensive is to identify the aggressor's vulnerable spots and to strike hard.

When Xerox attempted to break into the mainframe computer market head on against the established market leader, IBM launched a classic counter-offensive in Xerox's bread and butter business (copiers). The middle-range copiers were the major cash-generators of Xerox operations and were, indeed, creating the funds to allow Xerox to attack in the mainframe computer market. The IBM counter was a limited range of low-priced copiers directly competing with Xerox's middle-range products with leasing options that were particularly attractive to smaller customers. The counter-offensive had the effect of causing Xerox to abandon the attack on the computer market (they sold their interests to Honeywell) to concentrate on defending in copiers (James, 1984).

The counter-offensive defence is most effective where the aggressor has made him/herself vulnerable through overstretching resources. The result is a weak underbelly which can be exploited for defensive purposes.

Mobile defence

The mobile defence was much in vogue as a military strategy in the 1980s. It involves creating a 'flexible response capability' to enable the defender to shift the ground which is being defended in response to environmental or competitive threats and opportunities. The US Rapid Deployment Force is one example of flexible response.

In business a mobile defence is achieved through a willingness continuously to update and improve the company's offerings to the marketplace. Much of the success of Persil in the UK soap powder market has been due to the constant attempts to keep the product in line with changing customer requirements. The brand, a market leader for nearly half a century, has gone through many reformulations as washing habits have changed and evolved. Reformulations for top-loading washing machines, front loaders, automatics, and more recently colder washes, have ensured that the brand has stayed well placed compared to its rivals.

Interestingly, however, Persil went too far twice in recent years: first, when it was modified to a 'biological' formula. Most other washing powders had taken this route to improve the washing ability of the powder. For a substantial segment of the population, however, a biological product was a disadvantage (these powders can cause skin irritation to some sensitive skins). The customer outcry resulted in an 'Original Persil' being reintroduced. A few years later Persil came back again with even more disastrous Persil Power with its magnesium accelerator. Initially, Unilever denied P&G's claim that Persil Power damaged cloths in many washing conditions. However, within months 'Original Persil' was back again.

The mobile defence is an essential strategic weapon in markets where technology and/or customer wants and needs are changing rapidly. Failure to move with these changes can result in opening the company to a flanking or bypass attack.

Contraction defence

A contraction defence, or strategic withdrawal, requires giving up untenable ground to reduce overstretching and allow concentration on the core business which can be defended against attack.

In 1980/1, in response to both competitive pressures and an adverse economic environment, Tunnel Cement rationalized its operations. Capacity was halved and the workforce substantially reduced. Operations were then concentrated in two core activities where the company had specialized and defensible capabilities: chemicals and waste disposal.

In UK retailing Woolworth rationalized their operations to six key areas in 'Operation Focus' in 1987 where the company believed it had a defensible position. BHS have recently withdrawn from food retailing, and Boots from electrical goods to concentrate on their core retail areas.

Strategic withdrawal is usually necessary where the company has diversified too far away from the core skills and distinctive competences that gave it a competitive edge. Many of the tobacco companies diversified into totally unrelated fields in the 1990s only to find themselves in untenable positions and having to divest in the next millenium.

14.3 *Market nicher strategies*

Market nicher strategies, focusing on a limited sector of the total market, make particular sense for small and medium-sized companies operating in markets which are dominated by the larger operators. The strategies are especially suitable where there are distinct, profitable, but underserved pockets within the total market, and where the company has an existing, or can create, a differential advantage in serving that pocket.

The two main aspects to the nicher strategy are first, choosing the pockets, segments or markets on which to concentrate; and second, focusing effort exclusively on serving those targets.

14.3.1 Choosing the battleground

An important characteristic of the successful nicher is an ability to segment the market creatively to identify new and potential niches not yet exploited by major competitors.

The battleground, or niches on which to concentrate, should be chosen by consideration of both market (or niche) attractiveness and current or potential strength of the company in serving that market.

For the nicher the second of these two considerations is often more important than the first. The major automobile manufacturers, for example, have concentrated their attentions on the large-scale segments of the car market in attempts to keep costs down, through volume production of standardized parts and components and assembly-line economies of scale.

This has left many smaller, customized, segments of the market open to nichers where the major manufacturers are not prepared to compete. In terms of the overall car market, these segments (such as for small sports cars) would be rated as relatively unattractive, but to a small operator such as Morgan Cars, with modest growth and return objectives, they offer an ideal niche where their skills can be exploited to the full. The Morgan order book is full, there is a high level of job security and a high degree of job satisfaction in manufacturing a high quality, hand-crafted car.

14.3.2 Focusing effort

The essence of the nicher strategy is to focus activity on the selected targets and not to allow the company blindly to pursue any potential customer. Pursuing a niching strategy requires discipline to concentrate effort on the selected targets.

Hammermesh, Anderson and Harris (1978) examined a number of companies that had successfully adopted a niching strategy and concluded that they showed three main characteristics:

1. An ability to segment the market creatively, focusing their activities only in areas where they had particular strengths that were especially valued. In the metal container industry (which faces competition from glass, aluminium, fibrefoil and plastic containers) Crown Cork and Seal has focused on two segments: metal cans for hard-to-hold products such as beer and soft drinks, and aerosol cans. In both these segments the company has built considerable marketing assets through its specialized use of technology and its superior customer service.
2. Efficient use of R&D resources. Where R&D resources are necessarily more limited than amongst major competitors they should be used where they can be most effective. This often means concentrating not on pioneering work, but on improvements to existing technologies that are seen to provide more immediate customer benefits.
3. Think small. Adopting a 'small is beautiful' approach to business increases the emphasis on operating more efficiently rather than chasing growth at all costs. Concentration of effort on the markets the company has chosen to compete in leads to specialization and a stronger, more defensible position.

14.4 *Harvesting strategies*

Building, holding and niching strategies are all applicable to the products and services of the company that offers some future potential either for growth or revenue-generation.

At some stage in the life of most products and services it can become clear that there is no long-term future for them. This may be because of major changes in customer requirements that the product as currently designed cannot keep pace with, or it may be due to technological changes that are making the product obsolete. In these circumstances a harvesting (or 'milking') strategy may be pursued to obtain maximum returns from the product before its eventual death or withdrawal from the market.

Kotler (1997) defines harvesting as:

> a strategic management decision to reduce the investment in a business entity in the hope of cutting costs and/or improving cash flow. The company anticipates sales volume and/or market share declines but hopes that the lost revenue will be more than offset by lowered costs. Management sees sales falling eventually to a core level of demand. The business will be divested if money cannot be made at this core level of demand or if the company's resources can produce a higher yield by being shifted elsewhere.

Candidate businesses or individual products for harvesting may be those that are losing money despite managerial and financial resources being invested in them, or they may be those that are about to be made obsolete due to company or competitor innovation.

Implementing a harvesting strategy calls for a reduction in marketing support to a minimum, to cut expenditure on advertising, sales support and further R&D. There will typically be a rationalization of the product line to reduce production and other direct costs. In addition, prices may be increased somewhat to improve margins while anticipating a reduction in volume.

Occasionally a harvested product can continue to produce healthy revenues for some time into the future. The John Player Special (Blacks) brand of cigarettes was effectively harvested when marketing support was reduced to a minimum and returns from the brand were used to support new ventures such as the relaunch of the Lambert and Butler range. The brand declined to a steady state of core, loyal customers who continued to buy the brand. More recently, with changing customer tastes and requirements from a cigarette, the brand has been revived and enjoyed increased marketing support to rebuild its market position.

14.5 *Divestment/deletion*

Where the company decides that a policy of harvesting is not possible, for example when, despite every effort, the business or product continues to lose money, attention may turn to divestment, or deletion from the corporate portfolio.

Divestment – the decision to get out of a particular market or business – is never taken lightly by a company. It is crucial when considering a particular business or product for deletion to question the role of the business in the company's overall portfolio.

One company, operating both in consumer and industrial markets, examined its business portfolio and found that its industrial operations were at best breaking even, depending on how costs were allocated. Further analysis, however, showed that the industrial operation was a crucial spur to technological developments within the company which were exploited in the consumer markets in which it operated. The greater immediate technical demands of the company's industrial customers acted as the impetus for the R&D department to improve on the basic technologies used by the company. These had fed through to the consumer side of the business and resulted in the current strength in those markets. Without the industrial operations it is doubtful whether the company would have been so successful in its consumer markets. Clearly, in this case, the industrial operations had a non-economic role to play and divestment on economic grounds could have been disastrous.

Once a divestment decision has been taken, and all the ramifications on the company's other businesses carefully assessed, implementation involves getting out as quickly and cheaply as possible.

14.6 *Matching managerial skills to strategic tasks*

The above alternative strategies require quite different managerial skills to bring them to fruition. It should be apparent that a manager well suited to building a stronger position for a new product is likely to have different strengths to those of a manager suited to harvesting an ageing product. Wissema, Van der Pol and Messer (1980) have suggested the following types of manager for each of the jobs outlined above.

Pioneers and conquerors for build strategies
The pioneer is particularly suited to the truly innovative new product that is attempting to revolutionize the markets in which it operates. A pioneer is a divergent thinker who is flexible, creative and probably hyperactive. Many entrepreneurs would fall into this category.

A conqueror, on the other hand, would be most suited to building in an established market. The conqueror's main characteristics are a creative but structured approach, a systematic team builder who can develop a coherent and rational strategy in the face of potentially stiff competition.

Administrators to hold position
The administrator is stable, good at routine work, probably an introverted conformist. These traits are particularly suited to holding/maintaining position. The administrator keeps a steady hand on the helm.

Focused creators to niche

In many ways similar to the conqueror but in need, especially initially, of more creative flair in identifying the area for focus. Once that area has been defined, however, a highly focused approach is necessary at the expense of all other distractions.

Economizers for divestment

The diplomatic negotiator (receiver, or hatchet man!) is required to divest the company of unprofitable businesses, often in the face of internal opposition.

14.7 Conclusions

A variety of strategies might be pursued once the overall objectives have been set. The strategies can be summarized under five main types: build; hold; harvest; niche; divest. To implement each type of strategy different managerial skills are required. An important task of senior management is to ensure that the managers assigned to each task have the necessary skills and characteristics.

CHAPTER 15

Competing through superior service and customer relationships

Why is it that Land's End remembers your last order and your family members' sizes, but after 10 years of membership with American Express you are still being solicited to join? Don't the people at AmEx know that you're a customer?
Treacy and Wiersema (1995)

Introduction

One of the most significant trends in marketing thinking and practice during the 1990s has been the shift in focus from achieving single transactions to establishing longer-term relationships with customers (see, for example, Gummesson, 1987; Webster, 1992; Grönroos, 1994; Morgan and Hunt, 1994; Payne, 1995; Zielke and Pohl, 1996). While transactional marketing is concerned with making a single sale, relationship marketing is more concerned with establishing a rapport with the customer that will result in repeat business and opportunities for further business development.

Many markets in developed countries are now mature, or at best growing only slowly, and there are fewer new customers to compete for. Competition is intense, and the costs of attracting new customers high. It has been estimated that the costs of attracting new customers can be up to five times as much as the costs of adequately serving existing ones to ensure that they stay with you. As the RSA (1994) put it:

> The fundamental strategic battle is for the customer: only those companies which have as their goal the winning and retention of customers will succeed.

Customer retention is becoming a key predictor of profitability. Reichheld and Sasser (1990) showed the value to companies operating in a variety of markets of cutting customer defections (lost customers) by as little as 5 per cent. For an automobile service chain a 5 per cent cut in customer defections resulted in a 30 per cent increase in profits, for an industrial laundry 47 per cent increase in profits, for an insurance brokerage 51 per cent increase and for a bank branch a staggering 84 per cent increase. Customers that have been with a company longer tend, on average, to spend more on each transaction, offer more opportunities for cross-selling (selling them other products and services), and give better recommendations to their friends and colleagues. In the bank, customer relationships of ten years or more accounted for 29 per cent of the account base but 71 per cent of the profits.

A recent survey of 500 marketing practitioners for *Marketing Business* (Wells, 1994/5) showed the most important driver of success to be customer loyalty. Forty-nine per cent of respondents placed this as the single most important success driver in their business, compared with only 13 per cent for second-placed new product development.

However, in all this it is important that we distinguish between customer retention and customer loyalty, together with the relationship each of these has with customer satisfaction. There is a danger, in practice, that these concepts become confused. Customer retention is essentially a measure of repeat purchase behaviour and there are many reasons why customers may come back even if we have failed to provide them with a high level of satisfaction – they may have no choice or they may not know any better. Customer loyalty, however, is more to do with how customers feel about us: Do they trust us? Do they actively want to do business with us? Will they recommend us to others? Customer loyalty in this sense is more closely related to customer satisfaction.

To confuse retention and loyalty can be dangerous. Retention may be achieved through a 'bribe' – discounts for repeat purchase, and so on. Achieving high customer loyalty is likely to be far more difficult and requires greater long-term investment. The practical difference is great. The 'customer loyalty' card schemes at Tesco and Sainsbury are more about customer retention than loyalty and satisfaction, and it is likely that their effects will last only until there is a better offer available. On the other hand, Marks & Spencer and John Lewis achieve high customer loyalty through satisfaction building and see no need for such 'loyalty cards'. As airlines have discovered, for example, if all competitors offer the same thing, then customer 'loyalty' programmes such as frequent flyer awards become a cost of being in business rather than a differentiator.

To build customer retention for the major financial benefits it brings, let alone longer-term customer loyalty, requires companies to invest in strategies focused on these goals, not just on sales volume. This may involve brand-building (of the type practised at Virgin) or specific programmes (like the retailer 'loyalty' card schemes or product innovation), but increasingly it involves emphasis on achieving excellence in the service activities that augment the basic product offering.

This chapter explores the concept of 'service' and examines methods for competing through providing superior service.

15.1 *The goods and services spectrum*

Most offerings in the marketplace are some combination of tangible and intangible elements. This is shown diagrammatically in Figure 15.1.

Tangible elements can be seen, touched, smelled, heard or tasted. They constitute the physical aspects of the offer, such as the product itself and the surroundings

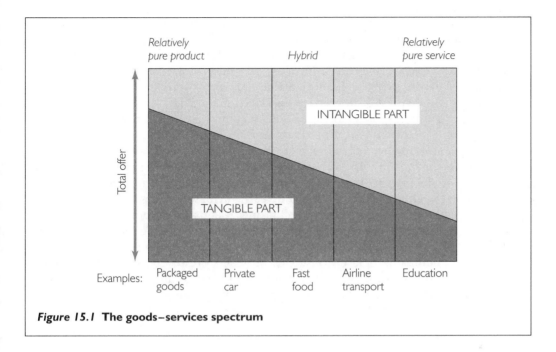

Figure 15.1 **The goods–services spectrum**

in which it is bought or consumed. The intangible elements are often more elusive. They comprise the level of service offered in support of the tangible and the image or beliefs that surround the product.

At the left-hand end of the spectrum the offer to customers is primarily physical and hence tangible. Examples include packaged goods such as baked beans and batteries, and consumer durables such as stereos and televisions. From the customers' perspective, however, the benefits derived from purchase and consumption may well be less tangible – baked beans defeat hunger, batteries provide portable light, stereos provide entertainment and televisions are the 'opiate of the people'! The distinguishing factor is that these benefits are primarily delivered by the physical features and characteristics of the product. There are also, of course, even less tangible elements to these purchases. Physical products are sold through retail outlets where sales staff may provide advice and demonstrations. Individual brands, through their media advertising and other promotional activities, will have established images and reputations in the minds of customers that may enhance value to them.

At the right-hand end of the spectrum the relative importance of intangibles and tangibles is reversed. In education, for example, the essence of the 'offer' is intangible. It is concerned with the service provided to the student/customer and the way in which the student interacts with teacher, colleagues and course materials. There are some tangible, physical elements involved, such as textbooks, audio-visual aids and the physical surroundings. The essence of education, however, is the intangible process that takes place in the development of skills, knowledge or understanding of the student. Ultimately, the success of the educational process is determined by the way the student responds to and interacts with the educational service provided.

Between these two extremes lie offers which combine tangible and intangible elements in more equal proportions. In fast-food outlets, for example, the offer is a combination of the physical food (tangible) together with the ambience of the restaurant and the speed of the service provided (intangible).

As more companies have embraced quality control and assurance techniques in the production of their physical products so the scope for differentiation between one supplier and another on the tangible elements of offer has diminished. Total quality management (TQM) has been increasingly applied to the physical element of products, reducing variability, tightening tolerances and ensuring fewer (or even approaching the cherished goal of zero) defects. Increasingly, companies operating at the left-hand end of the spectrum are looking to enhance differentiation through focus on the intangible elements of offer. These include branding the offer and the delivery of service to augment the physical product offer. At the right-hand end of the spectrum companies and other service providers are recognizing that the type and quality of the service they offer is their major means of differentiation. The line between tangible and intangible elements is becoming blurred and moving downwards, so that the intangible elements are becoming increasingly important across the whole spectrum.

15.2 *Relationship marketing*

To improve the probability of retaining customers organizations are increasingly turning to the techniques of relationship marketing. The focus of relationship marketing is on building bonds and ties between the organization and its customers to improve feedback and ultimately enhance the prospects of customer loyalty.

Figure 15.2 shows the 'relationship marketing ladder' developed by Payne *et al.* (1995). The ladder shows graphically a number of identifiable stages in relationship-building. At the bottom of the ladder is the prospect, or the target customer. The initial emphasis will be to secure the prospect as a customer. To achieve this, marketing effort is concentrated on customer-catching. Once the customer has been caught, however, the emphasis shifts to securing a longer-term, ongoing relationship. While a customer may be essentially nameless and have done business with the company once or only occasionally, a client is more individual and does business on a repeat basis. Clients may, however, be ambivalent or neutral towards the supplier company. Relationship marketing seeks to convert clients to supporters, those who have positive feelings towards the supplier, and even advocates, those who may actively recommend the supplier to others. The top rung of the ladder is partner. At this level the supplier and the customer are working together for mutual benefit. The focus of relationship marketing is moving customers up the ladder, finding ways of enhancing the value both parties get from the relationship.

Not all customers will be equally worth the effort needed to move them up the ladder, however. Critical to a successful relationship marketing strategy is the

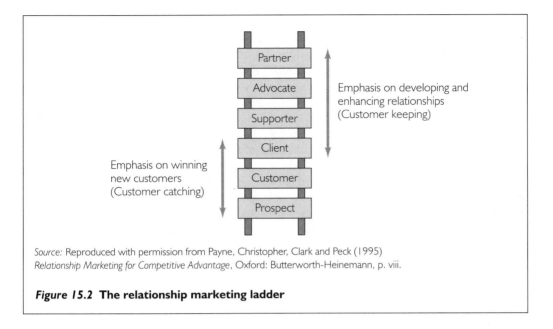

Emphasis on developing and enhancing relationships (Customer keeping)

Emphasis on winning new customers (Customer catching)

Partner

Advocate

Supporter

Client

Customer

Prospect

Source: Reproduced with permission from Payne, Christopher, Clark and Peck (1995) *Relationship Marketing for Competitive Advantage*, Oxford: Butterworth-Heinemann, p. viii.

Figure 15.2 **The relationship marketing ladder**

targeting of customers of sufficient value (current or potential) to warrant the investment in creating a relationship with them.

For relationship marketing to be effective requires sound reasons on both sides for the relationship (Figure 15.3). In some markets, such as rail travel, customers may not see advantages in becoming 'partners' and may prefer to stay at arm's length from the supplier. One respondent filling in a customer satisfaction questionnaire on a train was overheard to say: 'I wish I could go back to being just a passenger rather than a customer!'

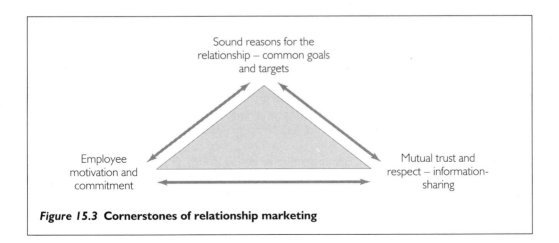

Sound reasons for the relationship – common goals and targets

Employee motivation and commitment

Mutual trust and respect – information-sharing

Figure 15.3 **Cornerstones of relationship marketing**

One recent commentary suggests that there is an element of spuriousness about the relationship offering made by some companies. From the customers' perspective, the British Airways relationship does not offer more seat-room, and the Tesco and Sainsbury relationship does not offer much more than a bribe to come back next time. The only tangible aspects of the customers' relationship with these companies seems to be becoming the target of large quantities of junk mail, selling financial services (Piercy, 1997).

In other markets firms may misjudge the value customers would put on a relationship. In financial services, for example, attempts to create closer relationships with individual clients may have been naive in assuming the client will automatically see a value in having a 'personal banking manager'. Fundamental to establishing a relationship is to determine what each party gets, or could get, from that relationship. Too many organizations still look primarily from their own perspective, recognizing the value to them of customer retention or loyalty, but not thinking through clearly what the customer will get from the deal.

In contrast, other firms are now coming to realize that the type of relationship customers want with a supplier can in itself be an effective way of segmenting markets around fundamental customer needs. This can lead to focusing relationship-building resources on those customer groups where this is mutually advantageous, and significantly cut the cost and the ill-will created through more scatter-gun approaches.

Also essential for more advanced relationships such as partnering, especially in business markets, is the establishment of mutual trust and respect between the parties (Crosby, Evans and Cowles, 1990). This involves being prepared to share sometimes commercially sensitive information. Marks & Spencer is a prime example of an organization in close partnership with its suppliers, sharing information about customer wants and needs to facilitate joint development of well-targeted product offerings over an extended period.

Recent research in the US suggests that the challenge to companies in business-to-business markets is no longer simply to sell, but to become the 'outsource of preference' through a collaborative relationship between vendor and customer, where the customer expects the vendor to know the customer's business well enough to create products and services that the customer could not have designed and created, and to give proof in hard evidence that the supplier has added value in excess of price. The excellent suppliers are those that add value to the customer's business by being close enough to measure the customer's needs, develop added services to improve the customer's business performance, and prove to the customer this has been done. This is a long way removed from simple, transaction-based business (H.R. Chally Group, 1996).

The third cornerstone of relationship marketing stems from employee involvement and commitment to the relationship-building and maintaining process. While companies may set strategies in the boardroom for relationship marketing, the success of those strategies ultimately rests with the employees who are charged with putting them into practice. Employees, from front-line sales staff through accounts personnel to car park attendants, need to understand their role in relationship-building, be committed to it and be motivated to achieve it. In many situations, as far as the customer is concerned, the employee they meet at the point of sales or service delivery *is* the company and its brand. We shall consider the importance of this relationship in examining the growing importance of internal marketing in Chapter 17.

15.2.1 Building relationships with customers

A number of methods have been suggested for building closer links with customers, and hence moving them higher up the relationship marketing ladder. These can be grouped into three main categories: building enhanced benefits of loyalty; creating structural ties; and creating delighted customers.

Building enhanced benefits of loyalty
A basic approach to building relationships is through the development of enhanced benefits of loyalty for customers. These might be financial benefits or social benefits.

Financial benefits give the customer a financial reason to enter into a longer-term relationship and remain loyal to the supplier. These might include discounts for bulk or repeat purchase or other rewards for loyalty. Typical examples include store loyalty cards where shoppers build credits towards free purchases (e.g. the ABC Card offered by the grocery supermarket Safeway), or the collection of Airmiles through the use of National Westminster Bank credit cards.

Social benefits might include the establishment of regular social groupings such as the Weight Watchers Clubs sponsored by Heinz and used to promote its own brand of low-calorie foods. Other social benefits might include corporate hospitality or social events sponsored by a firm where its clients can meet other clients with a view to developing their mutual business interests. British Airways operates a 'Premier Club' for senior executives and other influential decision-makers. The club is limited to 1,000 members, by invitation only, and offers exclusive VIP treatment in airports and in the air. Members also receive preferential treatment in seat bookings and a service whereby their favourite wine can be provided while in flight.

Creating structural ties and bonds
Through offering enhanced benefits companies may create structural ties with their clients, which then make it difficult, or costly, for their clients to defect (Storbacka, Strandvik and Grönroos, 1994). Professional medical equipment supply companies, for example, provide hospital surgeons with the equipment needed to help perform knee and hip implants with their own make of implant. The equipment works poorly with competitors' implants and is hence a major incentive for the surgeons to remain loyal. Sponsorship of the surgeons at symposia and conferences to enable them to stay up-to-date with medical advances also helps to strengthen their relationship with the supplier and build corporate goodwill.

In some industries the structural ties might be based on legal agreements and commitments, particularly where the use of protected patents is concerned. Ties are also created through the sharing of knowledge and expertise that the client otherwise would not have access to.

When structural ties are strong even dissatisfied clients may stay loyal due to the high switching costs involved (Gronhaug and Gilly, 1991). Clark and Payne (1995) discuss 'strategic bundling' whereby companies build barriers to customer defections through offering groups of interrelated products. Banks, for example, may offer several different types of accounts, together with mortgage and loan facilities. Despite dissatisfaction with one or more of these services the costs to the customer of switching to a competitor may be substantial when all the services are taken into account. The growing significance of collaborative relationships with customers and the formation of networks of collaborative organizations is discussed in more detail in chapter 8 on strategic alliances and networks.

Creating delighted customers

Perhaps most fundamental as a basis for establishing a lasting relationship with clients, and moving them up the ladder to become supporters, advocates or even partners is to ensure that customers get more from the relationship than they were originally looking for.

Research has shown that merely satisfying customers is rarely enough to give them a reason for staying loyal and becoming advocates rather than merely clients (Jones and Sasser, 1995; Reichheld, 1995). Depending on the level of competition in the market which can directly impact the level of choice available to the customer, and the degree of involvement the customer feels with the product or service, customer retention rates amongst 'satisfied' customers may vary dramatically. British Airways has found, for example, that its retention rate is exactly the same among satisfied and dissatisfied customers. As noted earlier, customer retention is not the same thing as customer satisfaction and loyalty. Reichheld (1993) reports that 65–85 per cent of customers who defect say they were satisfied with their former supplier. Amongst dissatisfied customers (with freedom of choice) retention rates rarely exceed 20 per cent, and amongst the seriously dissatisfied 'terrorists' or 'well poisoners' can pose a significant threat to the business as they tell others about their poor experiences.

To improve the probability of customer retention it is now necessary to go beyond what is expected and deliver even greater value to customers. Among very satisfied or delighted customers retention rates are significantly higher and they are more likely to become 'apostles', or advocates, telling others of their good experiences.

Creating delighted customers demands a high priority be given to customer service both in the strategies the organization designs and the actions it takes in the marketplace.

15.3 *The three 'S's of customer service*

There are three critical ingredients to successful service provision. These have been called the 'three 'S's of service': strategy, systems and staff.

First, there is a need to have a clear service strategy which is communicated throughout the organization so that everyone knows their role in providing service to customers and clients. The strategy needs to demonstrate the company's commitment to service and its role in overall corporate strategy. Increasingly companies are using customer satisfaction measures alongside financial and other criteria for measuring overall performance, signalling the higher priority they now give to creating customer satisfaction. Indeed, some of these companies now promote and reward staff on the basis of customer satisfaction ratings achieved.

Not only do firms need to be committed to superior service in their strategies, but they need to put in place the systems to enable their staff to deliver service to their clients (Payne, 1993). This may entail computer systems to share information rapidly and easily throughout the firm, or more mundane but no less critical queuing practices. A hallmark of good service providers in the 1990s has been their ability to embrace and use (rather than be swamped by) new technologies to improve service to customers.

Third, and perhaps most important of all, the staff must recognize the importance of customer service and be committed to providing it. That means recruiting, training and empowering employees to provide the levels of service that will create customer delight and then rewarding them appropriately. Bowen and Lawler (1992) suggest a number of factors in empowering employees to deliver excellent service. Central is the provision of information, both on what customers require and how well the organization is doing in providing that level of service. Also important is the power to make decisions that will affect the level of service provided.

15.4 *Providing superior service*

There has now been a great deal of research published in the US (e.g. Berry and Parasuraman, 1991) and in Europe (e.g. Gummesson, 1987; Grönroos, 1994; Payne *et al.*, 1995) looking at the nature of 'service' and what constitutes excellent or superior service in the eyes of customers.

Much of the literature on customer satisfaction measurement (e.g. Berry and Parasuraman, 1991) concludes that customers measure their experiences against a benchmark of the service they expect to receive. The quality of a service provision, and subsequently the level of satisfaction of the customer, is directly related to the difference (or 'gap') between expectations and experiences (see Figure 15.4).

15.4.1 Expectations

Berry and Parasuraman (1991) discuss two different ways in which expectations may be used as comparison standards. First are expectations of what customers believe will occur in a service encounter. These they call predictive expectations. Second are what customers want from the service encounter, their desires. These two levels constitute adequate and desired levels of service. Between these two levels

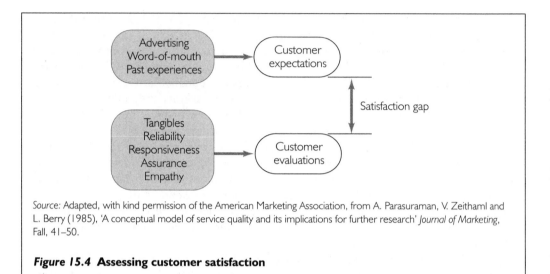

Source: Adapted, with kind permission of the American Marketing Association, from A. Parasuraman, V. Zeithaml and L. Berry (1985), 'A conceptual model of service quality and its implications for further research' *Journal of Marketing*, Fall, 41–50.

Figure 15.4 Assessing customer satisfaction

Berry and Parasuraman (1991) suggest lies a 'zone of tolerance'. A performance level above the zone of tolerance will pleasantly surprise the customer and strengthen loyalty, while performance below the zone of tolerance will create customer dissatisfaction, frustration and ultimately may lead to decreased customer loyalty (see Figure 15.5). Their research showed that both types of expectations are

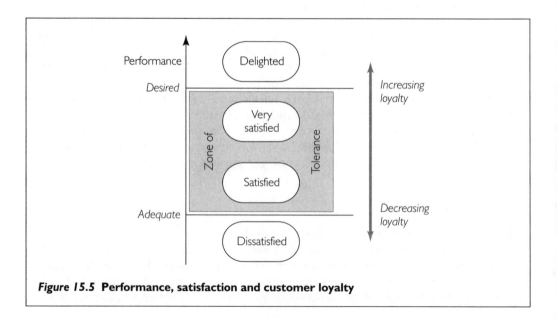

Figure 15.5 Performance, satisfaction and customer loyalty

dynamic – over time expectations generally increase. There was some suggestion, however, that desired levels change more slowly than adequate levels.

A number of factors have been found to influence expectations, ranging from the personal needs of the customer, through the alternative services considered, to the specific promises made by service providers in their bid to win business in the first place. Word-of-mouth communications with influencers and the customers' past experiences also affect the service level expectations.

Prior experiences of the service provider, or of similar providers, are often the starting point in creating expectations. When customers step into a restaurant they are often judging the experience based on other restaurants they have visited. They typically make verbal comparisons : 'It was more relaxed than ...'; 'The food was better than at ...' In addition to their own prior experiences expectations are also often affected by the opinions of friends, relatives or colleagues, who have related their own experiences. Depending on the standing of these opinion-makers in the customer's esteem they can have a significant influence on what is expected, and even deter trial of a particular service.

A third major determinant of expectations are the promises the company itself makes prior to customers using it. These promises, by way of advertising messages, sales pitches and general image created through pricing strategies and the like, set standards that the company is expected to live up to. Pitching them can be difficult. Promising too little may result in failing to attract the customers in the first place (they may be seduced by more attractive competitor promises), promising more than can be delivered may result in dissatisfied customers.

Managing and exceeding customer expectations

From Figure 15.5 it can be seen that in order to create delighted customers organizations need to exceed customer expectations. There are two main ways to achieve this: provide an excellent service; or manage customer expectations downwards so that they *can* be exceeded. They are not, of course, mutually exclusive but should be used together. Berry and Parasuraman (1991) offer a number of suggestions for managing customer expectations:

➤ **Ensure promises reflect reality**. Explicit and implicit promises are directly within the control of the organization yet many promise what they can never deliver in the desire to win business. Promises should be checked beforehand with the personnel responsible for delivering them to ensure they are achievable and attention paid to methods that might be employed to demonstrate to customers that promises have been kept (or exceeded).

➤ **Place a premium on reliability**. Below we discuss the main elements of service evaluation. A key aspect of most services is reliability: doing what you say you will do when you say you will do it. Where services are reliably performed they may fall down on other criteria (e.g. the manner of their performance), but overall evaluation is likely to be acceptable. Where services are reliably performed they also reduce the need for rework, or redoing the service, a highly visible indicator of poorly performed service. During rework customer expectations are likely to be raised and the chances of successful completion diminished.

➤ **Communicate with customers.** Keeping in touch with customers to understand their expectations and explain the limits of service possibilities can be a powerful way of managing their expectations. Communication can encourage tolerance, demonstrate concern for the customer and may serve to widen the tolerance zone. Phoning ahead to warn a customer of being late for an appointment is a simple example of communication being used to reduce the probability of customer frustration (though not a guarantee it will be eliminated altogether!).

15.4.2 Evaluations

Against expectations customers evaluate the performance of a service provider. Again, there are a number of factors that customers typically take into account when evaluating the service they have received. The most enduring classification is the five-dimensional model proposed by Parasuraman, Zeithaml and Berry (1988) and easily remembered by the acronym **RATER**: **R**eliability, **A**ssurance, **T**angibles, **E**mpathy and **R**esponsiveness.

➤ **Reliability** is the ability of the provider to perform the promised service dependably and accurately. In other words, it is conformance to specification – doing what you said you would do when you said you would do it. In many service situations reliability has been shown to be the single most important aspect to many customers. Besides contributing to customer satisfaction or delight, reliable service reduces the costs of redoing the service and can contribute to employee moral and enthusiasm (Berry and Parasuraman, 1991).

➤ **Assurance** stems from the knowledge and courtesy of employees and their facility to convey trust and confidence in their technical abilities. Customers want to be assured that the chef in the restaurant can cook without endangering their life, that the garage mechanic can fix the car, and that their accountant will not have them convicted for tax evasion. Assurance stems from professional competence. It is not enough, however, merely to have a high level of competence. It must also be demonstrated to the customers, often through the use of tangible cues.

➤ **Tangibles** are the appearance of physical features: equipment, personnel, reports, communications materials, and so on. Chartered accountants, for example, are critically aware of the impression their physical appearance creates with their clients. Care and attention is exercised when choosing company cars for partners and managers. Too expensive or luxurious a car might signal to clients that they are paying too high a fee for the services they are getting, while too cheap a car might signal that the firm is not particularly successful. Tangibles can be used in this way as indicators of professional competence.

➤ **Empathy** is the provision of caring, individualized attention to customers. It is the quality good doctors have of being able to convince patients that they really care about their welfare beyond addressing the current ailment. Empathy implies treating customers as individual clients and being concerned with their longer-term interests.

➤ **Responsiveness** is the ability of the organization to react positively and in time to customer requests and requirements. Some businesses, such as Richardson Sheffield Ltd who make kitchen knives under the Laser brand, have built their positions on being more responsive to the customer than their competitors. The company claims to respond to written enquiries within the day, faxed enquiries within minutes, and telephone enquiries instantly. They can also provide samples of products the next working day, even to new specifications. In some markets instantaneous, or near-instantaneous, responsiveness is critical. In Japan, for example, a key factor for success in the elevator business is the speed with which faults are fixed as the Japanese hate to get stuck in a faulty lift! Responsiveness typically requires flexibility. Customer requests can often be off-beat, unexpected. The highly responsive organization will need to predict where possible, but build into its systems and operations capacity to respond to the unpredictable.

These five main dimensions of service quality have been found in many different service situations, from banking to restaurants, construction to professional services (Parasuraman *et al.*, 1988). The relative importance of each might vary, and the way in which each is manifest in any situation will be different, but time and again these factors have been shown to be relevant to customers in their evaluation of the services they receive.

15.5 *Measuring and monitoring customer satisfaction*

A start to measuring customer satisfaction can be made through complaint and suggestion systems. These catch those highly dissatisfied customers who bother to complain. The problem, of course, is that it may be too late to retrieve the situation, though swift attention to customer problems has actually been shown to help bond closer relationships – what Berry and Parasuraman (1991) refer to as 'doing the service *very* right the second time' (see also Hart, Heskett and Sasser, 1990).

For every dissatisfied customer who complains, however, it is estimated that around twelve others will be equally dissatisfied but not bother to complain. They will simply take their business elsewhere and may even tell others about their bad experiences (the 'well poisoners'). There is, therefore, a need for a more systematic assessment of customer satisfaction rather than sitting back and waiting for problems to emerge.

A more systematic approach is the use of regular customer satisfaction surveys, as now used by many service providers from railway companies to the leading international accounting firms. A four-step approach is typically adopted (Figure 15.6).

1. Identify the factors that are important to customers. These are not necessarily the same as the factors that managers think are important. Qualitative research techniques such as group discussions and depth interviews can be useful here. Depth interviews with the clients of a large accountancy firm showed that partners demonstrating that they really cared about the development of the client's business (showing empathy) was critical to building a long-term relationship.

2. Assess the relative importance of the factors identified and measure customer expectations on those factors. While some clients may expect their problems to be dealt with immediately, others may have more relaxed expectations. While for some reliability may be paramount, for others cost could be more critical.

3. Assess performance of the service provider on the factors important to the clients. Here it can be useful to assess performance relative to expectations directly (Parasuraman, Zeithaml and Berry, 1994). Did performance live up to, fall short of, or exceed expectations? At this stage a useful summary can be made of the factors under consideration in a performance-importance matrix (Figure 15.7). Here the factors are plotted in terms of their importance to customers and the performance of the firm on them.

A typical example is shown in Figure 15.8 for a firm of chartered accountants (disguised data). The evaluations were made by a client, a finance

Figure 15.6 **Monitoring customer satisfaction levels**

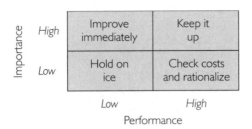

Figure 15.7 Performance–importance matrix

director of a large national company. The factors were identified through depth interviews and the evaluations of performance made against 'what would be expected of a leading firm of accountants'. The matrix can be used to focus attention on those aspects of the service of particular importance ('essential') to the client but where performance is judged to be below par.

In the example five elements of service were identified as being 'essential' to this client. On three of the factors performance exceeded expectations, while on two it fell below. Technical competence ('assurance' of technical ability to perform the audits), efficient use of the client's time ('reliability' in taking the time originally specified) and discussing charges in advance (and 'reliably' keeping to them) all constitute differentiators for this firm with their client. Where they fall down, however, are in showing an interest in the client's business (a lack of 'empathy') and some problems in the punctuality of staff or reports ('unreliable' delivery). Clearly these factors need to be addressed as a priority.

At the next level of importance the firm is poor at demonstrating flexibility ('responsiveness' to client requirements, especially when they change) and in being readily available to help when needed (again, a lack of 'responsiveness' to the client). On the other hand, they are well organized and have a good standard of written documents ('tangibles'). Again, areas for action are suggested.

Finally, the chart also shows that the firm excels in areas less important to the client. They rate highly on showing creative thinking and in providing detailed invoices. It may be that providing these less important aspects of service is distracting attention from getting the basics right on the more important factors, and hence might be candidates for rationalization. As a warning, however, we should note that sometimes factors are not important to customers until they start to go wrong! If the detailed invoices were not provided, for example, it could be that they start to become 'essential'!

4. Analyze the differences between expectations and performance through gap analysis. For important factors, where there is a significant gap, there is a need to identify the reasons behind it and identify suitable remedial action.

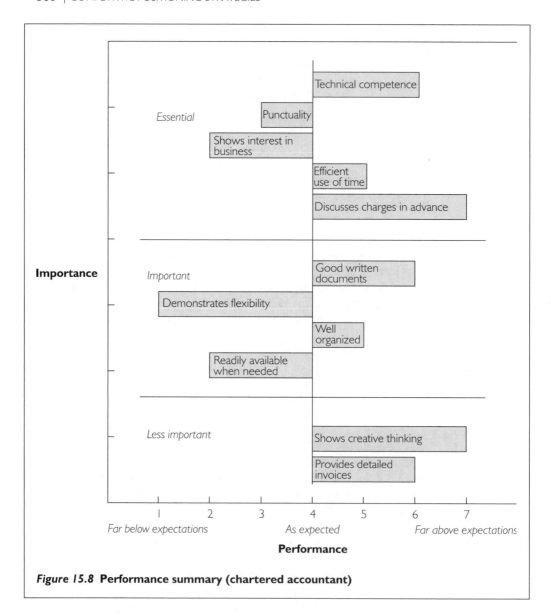

Figure 15.8 **Performance summary (chartered accountant)**

15.5.1 Gap analysis

Figure 15.9 shows the ways in which a satisfaction gap could have arisen. By working systematically through the framework, the root causes of dissatisfaction can be identified and dealt with.

A starting point is to determine whether the provider really understood the expectations and needs of the client in the first place. The market intelligence gap

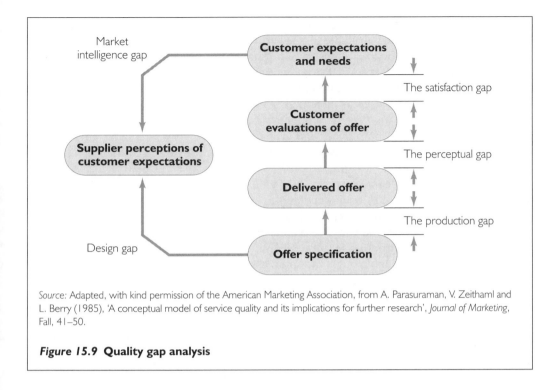

Source: Adapted, with kind permission of the American Marketing Association, from A. Parasuraman, V. Zeithaml and L. Berry (1985), 'A conceptual model of service quality and its implications for further research', *Journal of Marketing*, Fall, 41–50.

Figure 15.9 **Quality gap analysis**

is the difference between customer expectations and supplier understanding, or perception, of those expectations. This could be brought about through inadequate research of customer wants and needs, or through arrogance on the part of the supplier in assuming knowledge of the customer. It could also be brought about through poor internal communications such that customer requirements are not passed on from the marketing researchers through to those responsible for designing the service that will be provided.

Where customer expectations are understood, they may still not be adequately catered to in the service specification. The design gap is the difference between what the supplier believes the customers expect and the service specification. This could typically be caused by resource constraints where a service provider is too stretched to provide the service he/she knows the customer expects. Rather than increase the resource, or admit that the expected service cannot be provided, the service provider attempts to get as close as possible to customer expectations.

Even where the service specification is closely aligned to customer expectations there is a possibility that the actual service delivered falls short. The production gap is the difference between the service specification and the service that is actually delivered to the customer. There are a number of reasons why there may be a gap here. First, the service design might be so complex as to make accurate delivery unlikely. Service promises may be unrealistic given the resources put into them.

Response times planned for telephone enquiries, for example, may be unrealistic given the number of staff available to answer the phone or the number of lines available to take the calls. Second, staff may not have the skills or the systems back-up to deliver the service as specified. Poor employee training, poor technology provision or even inadequate internal communications can result in frustrated employees unable to deliver the service as specified to the customer. Third, a major problem in service provision is the very heterogeneity of services. The quality of service can vary from employee to employee, and from time to time for the same employee. Quality control systems are more difficult to implement in services than in manufacturing; they can be no less important however.

The final gap that can lead to a satisfaction gap is the perceptual gap. Here it may be that the service has been delivered to specification and that the specification was in tune with customer expectations, but that the client, for one reason or another, does not believe the service has been delivered as expected. This could be brought about through poor use of tangible cues, lack of reinforcement of delivery, poor delivery manner or through the intercession of external influencers. In many ways a perceptual gap is the easiest to rectify. It requires the service provider to demonstrate to the client that the service really has been delivered to original expectations.

15.6 *Conclusions*

This chapter has examined the recent recognition by many companies that successful positioning is increasingly about creating ongoing relationships with selected target customers rather than relying on more sporadic transactions. Relationship marketing seeks to build longer-term relationships with selected customers, moving them up the relationship marketing ladder from customers to clients to supporters to advocates and ultimately, where applicable, to partners. A major factor in creating longer-term relationships is the provision of superior service, beyond original customer expectations.

Customer satisfaction monitoring is suggested as a means of assessing the quality of the service offered. Where there is a gap between expectations and customer evaluations of the service provided a systematic gap analysis can be used to identify and eliminate the causes.

CHAPTER 16

Competing through innovation and new product development

The key to long-term success in business is what it always has been: to invest, to lead, to created value where none existed before.

Robert Hayes and William Abernathy

Introduction

Innovation may emerge on many fronts: an innovation in customer service to reinvent a business by a firm like Daewoo in car retailing, a brand extension strategy by Virgin, or a new access method for conventional products by First Direct in financial services. However, the nature of innovation in marketing strategy is best understood by examining the new product development process. The lessons here may be applied more generally to understanding innovation in the services and brand elements of marketing strategy.

It is imperative for new product managers to appreciate the reasons for new product failure, and to avoid these pitfalls. By understanding the drivers of new product success, managers can check if their firm has the requirements for effective product innovation. It not, they should develop means by which the requisites of successful innovation are acquired to minimize the likelihood of market failure.

This chapter starts by examining new product success and failure then uses that knowledge to help understand the new product development process and how to organize for innovation.

16.1 New product success and failure

Studies that compare new product successes with failures are consistent in their observations of the key factors that govern a new product's success in the marketplace. Getting to grips with these helps us understand successful product innovation.

16.1.1 Successful new brands

Successful new brands provide better performance than existing brands; they succeed often, despite being offered at higher prices than competing offerings. Most failures offer price parity or inferior value. Successful brands offer advantages that matter to customers. Failures too have performance advantages, but in fringe areas where customers see little benefit (Davidson, 1987).

Besides the price-and-performance advantage, successful new brands often provide benefits that are dramatically different from current offerings. New products need to have a significant advantage over existing brands; 'me-toos' are basically a waste of time. Even though companies such as Spring Ram Corporation in kitchen and bathroom products, Honda in motor-cycles and Amstrad in PCs have succeeded despite their late market entry, it is almost always better to be first.

Despite the inevitable risk of being a pioneer, first is often best for several reasons. The news value of an innovation peaks in the early stages, and this offers maximum communication impact and a chance for widespread consumer trial. The innovator catches consumers first; this means that competitors who follow must improve their market positioning and produce better and cheaper products to make consumers switch. This is not so easy to achieve once the pioneer has secured strong consumer loyalty and a reputation for innovation in the marketplace.

16.1.2 Industrial product success

Studies of new industrial product successes and failures make the following distinctions between successes and failures (Cooper and Kleinschmidt, 1993):

➤ product uniqueness (innovativeness) or superiority;
➤ management's possession of market knowledge and marketing proficiency;
➤ presence of technical and production synergies and proficiency.

The first dimension – industrial product uniqueness/superiority – is very close to that for consumer brands. In this respect industrial and consumer products are similar. It is likely that industrial and consumer products are similar in other ways too. Successful industrial innovators study their customers and market well. They carry out market research to gain knowledge of customer's requirements/needs; they are sensitive to price as well as to the intricacies of buyer behaviour.

Successful innovators acquire as much of the required information as possible to enable them to forecast market size and determine potential demand for their new product. They test market prior to product launch. There is strong and often well-targeted sales support, which recognizes the need for forceful communications to stimulate primary demand and to prise open new markets. Glaxo's forceful and focused marketing efforts were significant factors contributing to the astounding market success of their anti-ulcer drug, Zantac, while Wellcome's failure to maximize new drugs sales has been attributed to the company's poor marketing skills.

Successful industrial innovations are clearly not the result of sophisticated technology alone. Mismanagement of technical and technological resources can have a detrimental effect on new product performance. Successful industrial innovators ensure there is synergy between the firm's engineering and production capabilities and the new product project. They also undertake a range of technical activities and do these proficiently – preliminary technical assessment, product development, prototype testing with customers, production start-up, with facilities well geared for launch. Their technical staff know the product technology well. They are familiar with the product design.

16.1.3 Types of new product failure

In what way do new products fail? Answering this question helps us appreciate what actions the firm should take to avoid different types of product failure. There are six classes of product failures (Cooper and Kleinschmidt, 1990): the better mousetrap no one wanted, the me-too meeting a competitive brick wall, competitive one-upmanship, environmental ignorance, the technical dog product and the price crunch.

1. **The better mousetrap no one wanted** is the classic 'technology-push' type innovation for which little or insufficient market demand exists. Customers do not perceive they have a real need for the technology and, consequently, are not prepared to buy the innovation. Video telephones, and possibly the Channel tunnel, fall into this category.
2. **The me-too meeting a competitive brick wall** is the result of followers failing to reconcile with the market leader's or established competitors' strengths (e.g. Lidl's and Aldi's attack on the UK grocery market against Asda, Sainsbury and Tesco).
3. **Competitors** can spring surprises and come up with a better product that is preferred by customers. 'Competitive one-upmanship' is not easy to predict but can be seen in the case of decaffeinated Nescafé Gold Blend upstaging innovative Café Haag in the coffee market. Innovations may achieve great short-term advantage, but if competitors can easily and simply imitate the innovation (and have other advantages as well), then the innovator is likely to achieve little long-term value. For example, Direct Line had a major impact on the financial services market by offering simple products and fast telephone access for customers. This was a major success story in the early 1990s. By 1997 Direct Line was close to a loss-making position. Direct telephone marketing is easily copied by established firms and this is exactly what they have done.
4. **Environmental ignorance** occurs when the innovating firm fails to study market or customer requirements or to monitor and scan its external environment for signals of change. Socio-economic, technological, political and/or legislative conditions and/or changes are ignored, overlooked or misunderstood, resulting in poor sales after launch. In the case of Concorde, society's resistance to the noise it makes was grossly underestimated – this resistance was a major barrier to rapid adoption of supersonic aircraft by other airlines.
5. **The technical dog** product does not work or users of the product are dogged by technical problems when using the product (e.g. Amstrad's PC2000 business computer, or first the Rover SD1 and then the Rover Stirling in the US market).

6. **The price crunch** comes when the innovating firm sets too high a price for a new product whose value is not perceived by target customers to be better or greater than existing products. Often if competition offers a lower-cost product, the innovating firm has to cut price so fails to obtain the required return on investment from the innovation. Despite repeated relaunches, Sony's mini-disc seems to be falling into this category, as did video discs.

16.2 *Planned innovation*

Since innovation is so uncertain, can innovation be managed? By using formalized new product development processes achieve greater new product success than businesses that use an *ad hoc* approach to product innovation. There is, however, a distinction between invention and innovation. The former is the discovery of a new device or a new process. It is fair to say that managers cannot specify deadlines for the discovery of new ideas or predict when a particular invention will occur or, indeed, when exactly a scientific discovery will be made. Invention cannot be planned for. Often, the latter is left to chance, or the perseverance and ingenuity of the scientist/inventor. Innovation is different. Once the new scientific or technical discovery is being made or a novel product idea has been conceived, its chances of being successfully commercialized rest predominantly upon the astuteness of the firm's management in new product planning and strategy determination as well as the proficiency with which certain new product developments and launch activities are undertaken. From discovery/conception of the idea to marketplace, management and employees of the firm have direct control and influence over the fate of the discovery/idea.

Businesses can reduce the risk of product innovation whilst improving the likelihood of success by adopting a planning orientation and sophisticated new product development process (Wong, Saunders and Doyle, 1992). There was nothing accidental or *ad hoc* about the results achieved by Glaxo for Zantac in the anti-ulcer drugs market, or McDonald's in fast foods – they succeeded through careful preparation of the strategies for product development and market entry.

16.2.1 The new product planning

Most successful innovating companies develop a new product process, like that in Figure 16.1, which is linked to their company's overall longer term planning process.

First, companies should define their business mission by asking: What business are we in? And what business do we want to be in? By considering the growth potential of the sales and market share and profitability of the company's current range of products, and the extent to which growth objectives will be fulfilled, management can begin to identify gaps in achievable and desired growth. The role of new products and how the firm's portfolio of businesses might be changed to achieve planned growth can be determined.

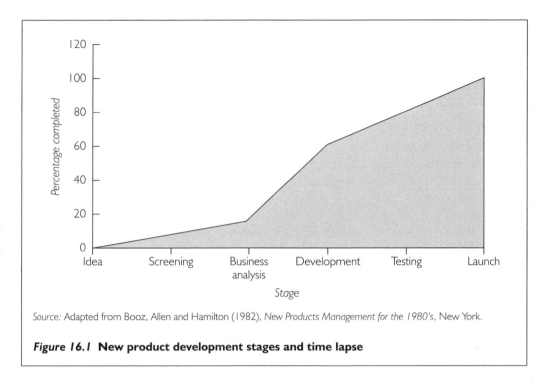

Source: Adapted from Booz, Allen and Hamilton (1982), *New Products Management for the 1980's*, New York.

Figure 16.1 New product development stages and time lapse

Firms also have to decide on the types of new product that are to be developed. It is usual to classify new products according to the degree of newness to the company and to the customers (Figure 16.2).

Six categories of new products emerge, each one taking the company further and

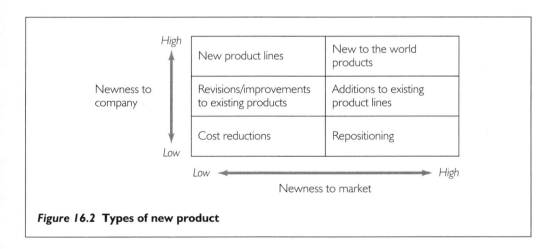

Figure 16.2 Types of new product

Table 16.1 **The strategic role of new product types**

Strategic role	New product type
Maintain technological leadership	New to the world
	New product line
Enter future/new markets	New to the world
Pre-empt competition or segment of the market	New to the world
	New product line
	Repositioning
Maintain market share	New product line
	Repositioning
	Additions to existing product line
Defend market share position/prevent decline	Repositioning
	Cost reduction
	Revisions/improvements to existing product lines
Exploit technology in a new/novel way	New to the world
	New product line
Capitalize on distribution strengths	Additions to existing product line

Source: Based on Veronica Wong (1993), 'Ideas generation', section II of *Identifying and Exploiting New Market Opportunities*, London: Department of Trade and Industry.

---

further away from its current activities and, therefore, being more risky:

1. **Cost reductions,** which provide similar performance at lower cost, as Mercedes achieved with their new C series saloon.
2. **Repositionings,** which are current products targeted at new customer segments or new markets. For example, Lucozade, a soft drink, traditionally aimed at the 'convalescent', is now targeting the youth and sporty user segment.
3. **Improvements** or revisions to existing products, which enhance performance or perceived value and replace existing products. Japanese car manufacturers tend to upgrade existing models giving 'new products' with improved performance and/or more features, as opposed to developing radically new models from scratch.
4. **Additions** to existing product lines which supplement a firm's established product lines. Mr Brain's Faggots in sweet and sour sauce was an addition to the company's 'traditional' line.
5. **New product lines,** which enable a company to enter an established market for the first time, such as Virgin's entry into Personal Equity Plans.

6. **New to the world products**, which create an entirely new market, for example Sony's personal hi-fi, the 'Walkman', Psion's palm top computers and JCB's original digger.

Depending on the sales, market share and financial objectives set by the firm, and the overall strength of its current range of products, management has to select the appropriate type, or combination of types, of new product to develop. Usually, a firm would have to invest in various types of new product development to maintain a healthy and balanced portfolio of products. The firm's functional capabilities and available resources have to be taken on board when deciding the strategic direction to be taken. Table 16.1 shows the various strategic roles for new products and the types of new product that are likely to fulfil each of these roles.

The magnitude of the risk attached to innovation alters with the type of new product being developed. Planning can help, failure to do so increases the risks, whilst decreasing the chances of new product success.

16.3 *The new product development process*

Figure 16.3 presents the key stages in the new product development process that show the mortality rate on new product ideas. It shows two rates of decay: the first

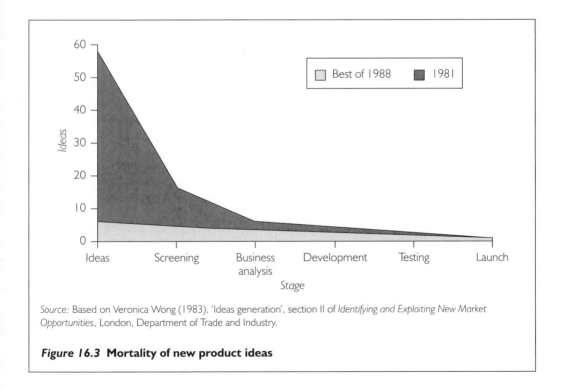

Source: Based on Veronica Wong (1983), 'Ideas generation', section II of *Identifying and Exploiting New Market Opportunities*, London, Department of Trade and Industry.

Figure 16.3 Mortality of new product ideas

shows average performance; the second contrasts the achievements of best performing companies.

16.3.1 Idea generation

For new products, a firm has to find novel ideas, do new things and do things differently. This is the essence of product innovation. New ideas trigger the innovation process and the development of new products. Ideas are where all new products start. Both the creativity of individuals and the methods of idea generation can be employed to obtain novel ideas.

Creativity and productive ideation
Really innovative ideas come out of inspiration and use appropriate techniques. Because of the high mortality rate of new ideas it is desirable to generate and consider a large number of ideas. The use of appropriate methods to generate new product ideas can improve the productivity of in-house ideas generation. A company can also facilitate the generation of innovative new product ideas by creating an environment which will induce and facilitate creativity. How can the creative potential of individuals be harnessed, and what techniques aid the creative ideas generation process?

Defining creativity
Creativity is the combining of previously unrelated parts into a useful whole so that one can get more out of the emergent whole than one has put in (Miller, 1996). This explanation of creativity suggests that one condition has to be satisfied for really novel ideas to emerge, that is, that many widely disparate ideas must coexist long enough in the individual's mind to combine, to yield a 'useful whole'.

The creative process is not easily achieved and many managers would assert that creativity cannot be supervised like the pursuit of quality or other functional operations. It is not possible to predict when a creative person will generate a novel idea. It is almost as if management should leave outbursts of creative thinking to nature and chance. However, contrary to conventional wisdom, creativity can be managed. Apart from spotting creative individuals within the firm and encouraging them to tap their creative potential, the manager would do better by asking if barriers to creative thinking exist and, if so, how these barriers might be overcome.

Aids to ideas generation
Some of the many techniques that can help creative thinking are shown in Table 16.2. Avoid using one of these methods all the time. It is best to use a variety of approaches, where possible; leeway is a must; try out, adapt and fit approaches to the problem at hand. There are many other approaches: suggestion box, competitive products analysis or negative engineering, patents search, customer need assessment and problem-detection studies; there are almost as many techniques as there are creative people (Townsend and Favier, 1991).

16.3.2 Screening

Take ten new product ideas. The chances are, two will pay, seven will fail, and only one will be a big winner. New product idea screening and selection is not about dropping bad ideas but catching the winner. Picking a potential 'winner' is not an easy task. What should managers take into account when evaluating new product ideas? What are the critical screening criteria? How do managers choose the best from among a pool of apparently viable ideas?

Systematic screening

If resources are committed to the development of a new product idea, management should assess the commercial potential and technical (including production) feasibility of the idea. If there are alternative ideas or projects competing for development funds and management time, these have to be screened and the more viable and attractive ideas selected.

Ideas screening is, therefore, an important component of the product innovation process. Screening can take up management's time. It is often tempting for the management team to devote a minimum amount of time and effort to it, and even to skip the exercise, in the rush to get idea development started and new products out to market quickly. An idea coming from a senior manager in the firm may sometimes also escape thorough screening and evaluation because of the assumed credibility of the source – which could turn out to be a costly error of misplaced confidence! Or ideas may not be systematically evaluated because management regards screening as a superfluous exercise given the lack of concrete data, in the early stages, on what is still apparently vague and ill-formed ideas.

Whatever the barriers, it pays to give serious attention to screening. There are good reasons for doing this. Screening helps avoids potentially heavy losses by reducing the possibility of bad ideas being accepted, and raises the chances of good ideas being developed. It encourages more efficient resource allocation by directing the firm's attention to the 'best' ideas and encourages firms to pursue those ideas which build on its core strengths. Also, as screening experience accumulates, it improves the managers' precision in ideas selection, so increasing the chances of success.

Initial screen

Screening can be conducted at different levels of detail. The preliminary screening may be treated as a course filter enabling managers quickly to separate out useful ideas for further investigation. Figure 16.4 shows the key screening questions. Remember that the initial screen is only a crude filtering device. Sometimes a new product idea might fit a legal, technical or marketing barrier which might not be all that insurmountable. It is therefore important for the management team to use the tool cautiously, taking on board internal company, as well as market and technological, developments which could be exploited to avoid premature closure of new product opportunities.

Table 16.2 Aids to thinking

Thinking aid	Process	Blocks confronted
Question the problem (ask, ask, ask a lot of questions about the problem at hand)	Inculcate a questioning attitude; ask questions about the problem to gain familiarity with it rather than hiding ignorance	● Perceptual (overcomes problem of having narrow viewpoints, clarifies problem) ● Emotional (addresses fear of looking like a fool, betraying ignorance – individual is forced to ask questions instead of hiding ignorance by not questioning) ● Intellectual (questions about the problem stimulate generation of information/ideas which later help conception of solution to problem)
Listing (force individual to make a list of ideas to facilitate generation of many ideas)	Encourage problem-solvers/ideas-generators to make a list of the ideas, whatever comes to mind. Once the individual's thoughts are flowing, this simple but disciplined ideas-listing exercise can facilitate 'fluency' of thought (i.e. aid individual to generate many ideas)	● Emotional (attacks inflexibility of thinking and triggers creation of a large volume of ideas)
Attribute listing	Break a product into its main components. For each component, list all the physical attributes or functions and then examine possible alternatives for fulfilling each of these in isolation	● Perceptual (helps individual examine the problem from a variety of angles/see it more clearly)

Applied imagination checklist

Use an explicit checklist to identify new product opportunities. Questions act as triggers:

- Can the product be used in any new way?
- What else is like it and what/whom could we copy?
- Can the product be changed in meaning, function, form, usage pattern?
- What can be added to the product? To make it bigger; stronger; longer; thicker; etc.?
- What can be deleted from it? How to make it smaller? lighter, etc.?
- What can be substituted? Other material, process, ingredient, etc.?
- Can we rearrange its components?
- Can it be combined with other things?

- Perceptual (by encouraging problem-solver to extend thinking/look at problem from a variety of perspectives)
- Emotional (pushes the imagination)

1. Is idea compatible with company objectives?	Yes – (go to 2) No – (terminate)
2. Is idea legally accepted?	Yes – (go to 3) No – (terminate)
3. Can idea be technically developed within desired time and budget constraints?	Yes – (go to 4) No – (terminate)
4. Is there a demand for proposed product? (i.e. What market/market segment is it likely to appeal to? Why? Is it large enough to be profitable? What product is the new product likely to compete with? Under the most optimistic conditions, what share of the market/market segment can it expect to achieve?)	Yes – (go to 5) No – (terminate)
5. Does the idea fit the firm's current and desired marketing objectives and strengths?	Yes – (go to 6) No – (terminate)
6. Are the commitments and risks involved acceptable?	Yes – (proceed further: investigation and development) No – (terminate)

Figure 16.4 **Initial screening of new product ideas**

Formalized screening system

Potentially viable ideas should be evaluated more thoroughly for selection purposes. It is important for management to appreciate that full screening requires identification of specific information and the investment of resources to obtain these data. Formalized screening means that new product ideas are evaluated logically and within a systematic structure. It is less impressionistic than initial screening and attempts to increase the objectivity of idea selection.

When actual data are unobtainable, the management team doing the screening must exercise subjective qualitative judgements. It is important to record all major assumptions and quantitative estimates made so that they can be used as control standards for future reference.

The screening devices are not a panacea for poor innovation record. The analyses rely on the ability of the firm's management team to combine high quality subjective judgements with good objective data. The tools do not absolve management using them from exercising creativity. These techniques are not a substitute for management vision either.

The analyses are time- and resource-consuming. The many uncertainties at the early stage of ideas selection make detailed and sophisticated evaluation somewhat meaningless. This encourages rejection of screening. But it is certainly misguided to make no attempt to consider the determinants of project success and failure, or the attendant risk and uncertainty when committing resources to major product innovation programmes.

The output of screening and evaluation is only as good as the input data. This means that, to benefit from utilizing screening systems, management must commit time and resources to building an information system geared to supporting ideas screening, evaluation and selection decisions. Like building any management information system, this takes time, but if implemented properly, yields a lasting and positive effect.

Screening based upon the opinions and judgements of staff within the firm can be highly biased. Judgements can be distorted because of undue pressure applied on individuals, information sparseness/inaccuracy, psychological pressures, personal influences, etc. The market viability of an idea should always be tested against criteria judged important by the customer/potential customer.

16.3.3 Business analysis

Business analysis considers the attractiveness of the market for the proposed new product idea and the company's capabilities and whether it has the business skills required to cater to the needs of the market in a way that gives it a distinct edge over competition.

Sales, costs and profit projections for a new product show whether they satisfy the company's objectives. To estimate sales, the company looks at the sales history of similar products and survey market opinion. Estimates of minimum and maximum sales give the range of risk. Starting with sales forecast (see chapter 12) the expected costs and profits for the product, including marketing, R&D, manufacturing, accounting and finance costs are calculated.

Management have to decide which criteria are the most critical and which level of accuracy in the data are needed for decision-making. This is to avoid wasting resources on refining information pertaining to factors to which the project's viability is relatively insensitive. Whilst the desired criteria may vary according to the nature of the industry and the circumstances of the individual firm, some criteria are likely to be relevant to most companies. With measures of market attractiveness and business position decided, the process becomes similar to segment selection described in chapter 13. If the market is attractive and the company has a sufficiently strong position relative to the competition, the product can move to the product development stage.

16.3.4 Product development

At this stage R&D or engineering convert the concept into a physical product. So far the new product development process has been relatively inexpensive, the product has existed only as a word description, a drawing or perhaps a crude mock-up. In contrast product development calls for a large jump in investment. It will show whether the product idea can he turned into a working product.

The R&D department will develop physical versions of the product concept: a prototype that will satisfy and excite consumers and that can be produced quickly and at budgeted costs. Depending on the product class, developing a successful prototype can take days, weeks, months or even years. It will be over a decade before the prototype of Airbus's proposed 550-seater A3XX, superjumbo airline flies, while Schweppes developed a prototype of their Oasis soft drink within a week.

Prototypes must have the required functional features and convey the intended psychological characteristics. Mercedes' new 'Swatchmobile' small city car, for example, should strike consumers as being well built and safe. Management must learn what makes consumers decide that a car is well built. Some consumers slam the door to hear its 'sound'. If the car does not sound like other Mercedes doors, consumers may think it is poorly built.

When the prototypes are ready, they must be tested. Functional tests are then conducted under laboratory and field conditions to make sure that the product performs safely and effectively. The new car must start easily; it must be comfortable; it must be able to corner without overturning. Consumer tests are conducted, in which consumers test-drive the car and rate its attributes.

When designing products, the company needs to look beyond simply creating products that satisfy consumer needs and wants. Too often, companies design their new products without enough concern for how the designs will be produced – their main goal is to create customer-satisfying products. The designs are then passed along to manufacturing, where engineers must try to find the best ways to produce the product.

Increasingly, businesses use Design For Manufacturing and Assembly (DFMA) to fashion products that are *both* satisfying *and* easy to manufacture. This often results in lower costs while achieving higher quality and more reliable products at the same time. For example, using DFMA analysis, Texas Instruments redesigned an infra-red gun-sighting mechanism which it supplies to the Pentagon. The redesigned product required 75 fewer parts, 78 per cent fewer assembly steps and 85 per cent less assembly time. The new design did more than reduce production time and costs; it also worked better than the previous, more complex version. Thus DFMA can be a potent weapon in helping companies to get products to market sooner, while offering higher quality at lower prices.

16.3.5 **Market testing**

By this point in the product innovation process, you have a physical product or complete specifications for a new service. The product has passed a use test and the use test has suggested that the product works and fulfils the need as originally embraced by the concept. The next phase is market testing or trial sell. Test marketing is not one, but a range of techniques, ranging from a simulated sale using a carefully selected customers to a full test market in one or more regions of a country (for more details of the alternatives, see chapter 11).

Up to this stage in the overall new product development process, testing has not been conducted under realistic market conditions. It is dangerous to trust any customer judgement wholeheartedly until made under typical market conditions. This is where market testing plays a role in helping the firm to gauge whether its marketing plan for the new product will work and to confirm that the product, with its attendant claims, do, in fact, motivate customers to buy it and that they keep on doing so, if repeat purchase is an important factor. Market testing could be regarded as a form of 'dress rehearsal' which enables management to gather information to forecast new product sale and test effectiveness of the marketing plan (i.e. pricing, advertising and promotion, distribution). It checks that all key operations fit with each other and are adequately geared up for launch, and provides diagnostic information to help managers revise/refine the marketing plan. Full test markets can test competitive response and gauge if their efforts affect the judgements of customers. This is a mixed blessing since full test markets can be deliberately spoilt by competitors and give competitors an early warning of intended activities.

16.3.6 Commercialization

Commercialization is often the 'graveyard' of product innovation, not because new products die here but because real innovation often stumbles at this point of the process of innovation. By this we mean that things are going wrong and the product concept that seemed so feasible in the beginning now is tarnished and facing considerable pressure to compromise because of time, cost and other resource. Managers who are impatient to get the product to market fail to allocate sufficient time and resources to developing an effective launch campaign. Surprisingly, after all that has gone into development, products often fail because they are launched with insufficient marketing support behind them. Most new product fails, not because of any inherent deficiency, but because the market launch strategy and tasks were poorly conceived and executed.

The launch managers should work closely with sales and other operating staff to achieve good co-ordination of the timing and scheduling of all these activities. Every effort must be made to ensure that critical activities (e.g. salesforce training, sales materials, promotions materials) are completed proficiently to secure launch success. In conjunction with key operating personnel, the launch manager has also to put together a launch plan which consists of a programme outlining the sequence of tasks to be performed, a schedule that relates the programme to a time sequence, and budgets for the programme and schedule.

Launch programmes easily turn into a complicated and unwieldy task. There is little point in turning out project control or milestone events charts hundreds of pages long because this is bound to break down, providing hardly any basis for effective project control. Except for the most complex technological developments, as found in car, aerospace and defence projects, complex, computer-based systems for project control are usually not necessary. For the small to medium-sized company simple 'checklists' may suffice. Remember, there is also 'eyeball control', which relies upon managers being constantly on the go, visiting every area of the firm (daily, if possible), gathering their own information, and becoming 'expert' enough to exercise sound judgement and keeping launch tasks under control.

16.4 *Speeding new product development*

Managers must appreciate the value of being fast at innovation. A company that takes less time to develop and commercialize a new product can be expected to be more competitive than a slower competitor. The firm would be able to launch more new products in a given period of time, therefore building a strong innovation leadership image. Speedy companies are also able to respond faster to changing customer requirements, thereby securing sales and building customer loyalty. Also, by increasing the frequency with which it introduces new products into the market, the firm could pre-empt competition, thereby creating and maintaining a market leadership position.

The cost of new product development could be reduced by undertaking innovation of an incremental, as opposed to radical, nature, with substantial reduction in the risks of innovation. Companies should, however, ascertain if they have the capabilities for accelerating new product development. Also, management should ensure that the film supports a balanced innovation programme such that opportunities are not forgone because of failure to fund more radical (and longer term) product innovation programmes in view of the obsession with speed.

Speeding the new product development process needs action at all stages of the process. At the start avoid delays in approving budget for developing product idea and pay early attention to 'snagging' at the end of the process. Overlap product and process design and development phases have two benefits. It means that process take place in parallel and forces the formation of multi-functional project teams (design, engineering, production, sales, marketing, etc.). Big technological breakthroughs are not necessary to make big commercial gains so take an incremental approach to product improvement and development, making many small steps rather than attempting giant leap forward. New product innovation often clashes with the systems and controls designed to make firms 'well managed'. To overcome this, successful businesses adapt operational and organizational procedures to give the flexibility and freedom that new product innovation needs.

16.5 *Organization for innovation*

'Mental walls ... block the problem solver from correctly perceiving a problem or conceiving its solution' (Adams, 1987) The nature and intensity of these blocks vary from individual to individual, but organizations that innovate recognize and avoid them.

16.5.1 Blocks and bugs

➤ **Perceptual blocks** prevent the person from perceiving clearly either the problem itself or the information needed to solve the problem (e.g. problem isolation difficulty; narrow definition of problem; limited viewpoints examined).

➤ **Cultural blocks** are acquired as a result of exposure to a given set of cultural values or patterns (e.g. tradition is preferable to change; intolerance of subjectivity; fantasy/reflection/playfulness is a waste of time; humour is out of place where problem-solving is concerned).

➤ **Environmental blocks** are imposed by our immediate social and physical environment and are, therefore, closely linked to cultural barriers (e.g. autocratic boss; lack of trust/co-operation among colleagues; distractions, unsupportive organization; lack of financial support to implement ideas).

➤ **Emotional blocks** interfere with the freedom with which we explore and play with ideas, and prevent us from communicating them effectively to others (e.g. fear of failing or looking like a fool; intolerance of ambiguity; preference for judging ideas, rather than generating them; inability to incubate and 'sleep on it').

➤ **Intellectual and expressive blocks** arise because intellectual capabilities are limited and verbal/writing skills needed to communicate ideas not only to others, but to yourself, are deficient (e.g. lack of information; incorrect information; poor language skill; failure to apply appropriate mental problem-solving tactics).

16.5.2 Organizational needs for innovation

It is people, not plans or committees, that create ideas and achieve innovation. It is their efforts that truly determine whether businesses succeed or fail. If managers have grand visions for their business, the surest way to bringing these to fruition is to have their staff on their side, to encourage, enthuse and motivate them and, above all, to reward them for their achievements.

Three conditions are required for a firm to innovate successfully:

1. **Closeness to customers** – managers must know their customers and understand their needs and requirements well.
2. **Cross-functional communications** - innovation in most companies (except the 'one-man-band' which is not stereotypical of the average established small/medium-sized firm anyway) is about the flow of information between key functions.
3. **Multi-functional teamwork** – successful product innovations are almost invariably the result of people in the firm working together in teams rather than independently.

These are three deceptively simple criteria for innovation success. In practice, they are difficult for the firm to achieve. Large, bureaucratic firms face this problem most of all. Small-sized companies which can still maintain a cohesive unit may find criteria 2 and 3 easy to achieve, but, if led by excessively product-oriented tech-nocrats, frequently drift away from 1. The manager of a small company must, however, take note of the 'fast-forgetting' syndrome: as the business grows and the organization expands the three principal requirements for innovation – closeness to the market, good interfunctional communications and team work – become increasingly more difficult to preserve, frequently resulting in management losing sight of the very factors that brought success to the business in the first place. Entrepreneurship, although highly desirable, is, on its own, insufficient for successful innovation, especially continual innovation. To remain successful innovators, business managers must continually review their firm's ability to meet the above three conditions for effective innovation.

16.5.3 Organizational alternatives

Although marginal product changes can be managed within conventional organizations, radical innovations need suitably radical organizations. Six broad approaches are suggested that differ in their isolation from day-to-day business activities. All help small groups escape from entrenched departments and attitudes.

1. **The functional approach** has people from different business areas (such as finance or marketing). Tasks are done by the various departments. Individuals meet to make the necessary decisions. Usually a new products or product planning committee reviews project progress. Members do not commit all their time to the project, which must mesh with their normal duties.
2. **A taskforce** consists of several individuals who either are hand-picked by the boss or have volunteered to join the team. Taskforce members come together more regularly to work on the project which they pursue with slightly greater urgency than in the previous approach. The taskforce should have a balance of engineering, production and marketing talents. Members' primary commitment is still very much to their function rather than the project.
3. **A project team–functional matrix** is appropriate when project demands are high. Team members commit themselves to the project as much as their normal functional responsibilities. However, this type of 50/50 thinking often results in indecision and delay because members involved are still needed to see to their regular job while project needs require greater push. There may also be a conflict between what the project team needs to achieve and their parent function's main interests.
4. **Venture teams** are mostly associated with very small firms which have few people and no entrenched departments. The venture group should contain a mix of people with different functional skills, not just specialists. For bigger companies the venture option is used to free people from current functional pressures so that they can focus their entire effort on the project. The group is given complete autonomy and power to forge ahead, and incentive compensation for taking the risks.
5. **Spin-outs** are completely detached from the parent company. Big companies use this option to support very risky product innovation projects which do not

currently fit the corporation's core business. Outside capital could be sought. The venture is sold off for an equity stake in the new start-up firm. For small firms, spin-offs are not a logical route for nurturing innovation but they could consider another type of venture approach – the joint venture.

6. **Inside–outside venture** approaches fit both big and small/medium-sized firms. Smaller firms with the advantages of advanced technology, flexibility, vigour and/or entrepreneurial flair could team up with larger firms with the capital, distribution network and marketing muscle to gain market entry. The big firm gains through achieving entry into promising technologies which were too risky and ill-fitted to their mainstream business (the alliances between pharmaceuticals and biotechnology firms are a case).

The more radical the new product project (which means higher risk), the greater the need for project focus and its protection from current departmental and operational influences and constraints. The **functional** and **taskforce** options are therefore appropriate for low risk, incremental product innovations (e.g. improvements, repositionings, new sizes, etc. involving present product lines).

A **project team–functional matrix** is most suitable for marginally riskier projects, involving expansion in the number of product lines. **Venture teams**, **spin-outs** and **inside–outside venture** options are for radical, high-risk projects where internal constraints and opposition are expected to be very high (e.g. the IBM PC project and GM's Saturn car).

The proposed radical structures help large firms capture the benefits of a small firm. Ironically, the idea that 'small is good' stems from the observations that large innovative firms work in non-bureaucratic, smaller settings. They try to gain the advantages of being small (Quinn, 1985). But, of course, size is not a determinant of innovation success. Many new products introduced by small firms fail because a lot of them should never have come about – it may be that they were badly conceived, they failed to meet market needs, or the company lacked marketing skills required to prise open new markets.

16.6 Conclusions

Product innovation is not a one-off activity. A successful, profitable innovation can see a firm through for a while, but long-run survival depends on new products to balance its future portfolio (chapter 3), replace declining products and to cater for new customer needs. Glaxo cannot thrive on the back of its blockbuster drug Zantac alone.

Many businesses are caught out because management has failed to use the profits from current innovations to develop more innovations for future markets. Today's breadwinners will eventually dry up as competitive forces intensify over the product's life cycle. New products – tomorrow's breadwinners – are necessary to maintain the firm's position in the market place. One win is insufficient; multiple wins are necessary for corporate longevity!

The more the firm innovates, the greater the experience accumulated; the greater the experience gained, the better it gets at innovation; the better the firm becomes at this daunting activity, the greater its chances of competitive survival. A virtuous cycle of innovation is established.

Increasingly, a multidisciplinary, team-based approach to product innovation is required. Team work is important and has been one of the most significant organizational factors behind Japanese companies' ability to accelerate new product development in the drive to achieve lasting competitive advantage as observed, for example, in the consumer electronics, computer and motor vehicle markets.

There are many factors that affect new product performance. Neglect of one factor alone can bring about failure. Management should check that their firm is pursuing a balanced and realistic, new product development strategy, that customer/market needs are clearly identified and well understood, and that requisite technical and technological skills are married with a market orientation to ensure success.

CHAPTER 17

Implementation through internal marketing

A company is either customer-focused from top to bottom, or it simply is not customer-focused ... To become genuinely customer-focused you have to be prepared to change your culture, processes, systems and organization.

George Cox, Chief Executive, Unisys Ltd, June 1995

Introduction

Part IV of the book concludes our consideration of competitive positioning strategies, by considering the role of internal marketing in enhancing and sustaining a company's ability to compete. We will see that there are, in fact, several different notions of internal marketing which overlap to a degree and require some clarification (since as a consequence there are a number of different roles that internal marketing can play in a company's strategic development in different situations). For example, linkages between internal marketing and certain of the issues we have examined earlier include the following:

➤ Much new thinking and practice in strategic marketing is concerned with *managing relationships*: with the customer (see chapter 15), and with partners in strategic alliances (see chapter 8). However, a further aspect of relationship management and relationship marketing is the relationship with the employees and managers, upon whose skills, commitment and performance the success of a marketing strategy unavoidably relies. This is the internal market inside the company. The logic being followed by an increasing number of companies is that building effective relationships with customers and alliance partners will depend in part (and possibly in large part), on the strengths and types of relationships built with employees and managers inside the organization.

➤ We have emphasized the centrality of *competitive differentiation* to build market position. Yet truly exploiting a company's potential competitiveness and its capabilities in reality is often in the hands of what Evert Gummesson (1990) has called the 'part-time marketers', i.e. the people who run the business and provide the real scope for competitive differentiation. Indeed, in some situations, the employees of a company may be the most important resource that provides differentiation – Avis achieves high customer satisfaction and customer retention through its superior employee skills and attitudes, not because the cars it rents out are any different from those of its competitors (Piercy, 1997) (see p. 395 below).

➤ In a similar way, the growing emphasis on competing through superior *service quality* relies ultimately on the behaviour and effectiveness of the people who deliver the service, rather than the people who design the strategy.

➤ Indeed, increasingly it is recognized that one of the greatest barriers to effectiveness in strategic marketing lies not in a company's ability to conceive and design innovative marketing strategies or to produce sophisticated marketing plans, but in its ability to gain the effective and enduring *implementation* of those strategies. A route to planning and operationalizing implementation in strategic marketing is 'strategic internal marketing' (Cespedes and Piercy, 1996). For example, in the strategic turnaround at British Airways, branding has been a critical element in competitive positioning, and because customers gain their understanding of the brand not just from advertising and the product itself, but from every contact with the company, the company's marketing director describes how it was 'important to bring a unified brand message to consumers and employees' in implementing British Airways' (BA) successful repositioning in the market (Brierley, 1996). The breaking down of relationships with employees in 1997 is more than an industrial relations problem for Robert Ayling (disruptive though industrial actions has been for the company and its customers); it is a threat to the company's brand. Indeed, the BA example is particularly apposite. The strategic turnaround led by John King and Colin Marshall at BA was characterized by dramatic improvements in customer service and satisfaction, in parallel with high staff morale, evidenced by published surveys. In 1994, for the first time, those internal climate surveys showed downturns. The City took this evidence extremely seriously and, by 1997, BA was experiencing strike action by its staff. There is some sign that the company's strategies are not supported by the staff and this is the major implementation barrier faced, at a critical moment in the company's development.

These applications suggest that, depending on the particular circumstances, the internal marketing process might include the following types of activity and programme:

➤ Gaining the *support* of key decision-makers for our plans – but also all that those plans imply in terms of the need to acquire personnel and financial resources, possibly in conflict with established company 'policies', and to get what is needed from other functions like operations and finance departments to implement a marketing strategy effectively;

➤ Changing some of the *attitudes and behaviour* of employees and managers, who are working at the key interfaces with customers and distributors, to those required to make plans work effectively (but also reinforcing effective attitudes and behaviour as well);

➤ Winning *commitment* to making the plan work and 'ownership' of the key problem-solving tasks from those units and individuals in the firm whose working support is needed; and

➤ Ultimately, managing incremental *changes in the culture* from 'the way we always do things' to 'the way we *need* to do things to be successful' and to make the marketing strategy work.

The potential importance of internal marketing to relationship marketing strategies, to strategic alliances, to competitive differentiation, to delivering superior service quality and to effective marketing implementation is underlined by the growing emphasis placed by companies in this issue. For example, research conducted at the Marketing Forum suggests that internal marketing is claiming an increasing share of total marketing budgets – of the major companies participating in the Forum in 1997, 78 per cent claimed to have a formal commitment to internal communications programmes for employees, and for companies with a total marketing budget of more than £20 million, 70 per cent had a dedicated internal marketing budget (*Marketing Business*, 1997a).

However, it remains true that internal marketing means very different things in different companies and different situations. If we are to evaluate the potential contribution of internal marketing to building and implementing our competitive strategy and achieving our chosen positioning in the market, then we need to consider such issues as the following:

➤ the sources of internal marketing theory;
➤ the types of internal marketing practice in companies;
➤ how internal marketing can be planned as part of our competitive strategy; and
➤ the implication for other significant relationships such as the potential partnership between marketing and human resource management within organizations to achieve the effective implementation of marketing strategies.

17.1 *The development of internal marketing**

The conventional training and development of marketing executives, quite reasonably, has focused primarily on the *external* environment of customers, competitors and markets, and the matching of corporate resources to marketplace targets. The argument we now present is that, while analyzing markets and developing strategies to exploit the external marketplace remains quite appropriately a central focus, it is frequently not enough on its own to achieve the effective implementation of marketing strategies. In addition to developing marketing programmes and strategies aimed at the external marketplace, in order to achieve the organizational change that is needed to make those strategies work, there is a need to carry out essentially the same process for the *internal marketplace* within companies.

*This section draws heavily on Nigel F. Piercy and Neil A. Morgan (1990), 'Internal marketing strategy: leverage for managing marketing-led strategic change', *Irish Marketing Review*, Vol. 4, No. 3, 11–28.

That marketplace is made up of the people, the culture, the systems, the procedures, the structures and developments inside the company, whose skills, resources, participation, support and commitment are needed to implement marketing strategies. Indeed, the internal marketplace may increasingly extend to include our partners in alliances and network organizations (see pp. 195–7).

It seems that the reality in many organizations is that often an implicit assumption is made by executives that marketing plans and strategies will 'sell' themselves to those in the company whose support and commitment are needed. When made explicit in this way, it is apparent that this is just as naive as making similar assumptions that, if they are good enough, products will 'sell themselves' to external customers. It is often surprising that those same executives who have been trained and developed to cope with behavioural problems – like 'irrational' behaviour by consumers and buyers, or the problems of managing power and conflict in the distribution channel, or the need to communicate to buyers through a mix of communications vehicles and media, or the problems of trying to outguess competitors – have taken so long to arrive at the conclusion that these same issues have to be coped with *inside* the company. The paradox is that we discuss the 'better mousetrap' syndrome for our external markets, but adopt exactly this approach in expecting managers and operatives, whose support we need, to make a 'beaten path' to the marketing planner's office. In particular, we suggest that it is not acceptable to adopt a 'don't blame me' attitude as a response to organizational barriers to strategic change and to the 'unreasonable' behaviour of those who hold different views about the desirability of that market-led change. Real commitment to strategic marketing must involve a managerial role of creating the conditions necessary to permit strategic change to happen.

What we are calling strategic internal marketing here has the goal of developing a marketing programme aimed at the internal marketplace in the company that *parallels* and *matches* the marketing programme aimed at the external marketplace of customers and competitors. This model comes from the simple observation that the implementation of external marketing strategies implies changes of various kinds within organizations – in the allocation of resources, in the culture of 'how we do things here', and even in the organizational structure needed to deliver marketing strategies to customer segments. In practical terms, those same techniques of analysis and communication, which are used for the external marketplace, can be adapted and used to market our plans and strategies to important targets within the company. The goals of the internal marketing plan are taken directly from the implementation requirements for the external marketing plan, and the objectives to be pursued.

This is not as radical as it may at first seem. The marketing literature has traditionally displayed some attempts to link the marketing concept to the 'human resource concept' (e.g. Cascino, 1969; Dawson, 1969) and more recent attention has been given specifically to the interaction between the human and organizational context and the effectiveness of marketing (Arndt, 1983). Other evidence relating to the impact of the internal market on marketing effectiveness has focused on various aspects of the intervention of organizational issues as a determinant of marketing strategies rather than a result of them: Leppard and MacDonald (1987) attempted to relate the effectiveness and appropriateness of marketing planning to the different stages of organizational evolution; John and Martin (1984) have analyzed the credibility and use of marketing plans in terms of characteristics of the surrounding organizational structure; Cunningham and Clarke (1976) studied product managers as self-serving manipulators of targets and marketing information; Deshpandé (1982) and Deshpandé and Zaltman (1984) have attempted an analysis of the cultural context of marketing management and commented on the lack of a marketing theory of culture; while Bonoma (1985) has commented on the problems of a lack of 'marketing culture' in the specific context of implementation obstacles. More recently, in a similar way, Ruekert and Walker (1987) have studied the interaction between marketing and other functional units and the role of marketing in implementing business strategies.

While this focus on the significance of various dimensions of organizational context provides a foundation, the most specific attention given to acting on the organizational environment through internal marketing, to achieve marketing goals, is found in the services literature. One of the earlier conceptualizations of the employee as 'internal customer' was provided by Berry (1981) in the context of bank marketing, and this theme has been pursued by others, and it is heavily oriented towards the identification of employee training and development needs to improve quality in the delivery of services. Similarly, the interdependence of internal and external markets has been stressed by Flipo (1986), who emphasized the need to overcome conflict and challenges to marketing strategies from the internal market, implicitly following Arndt's (1983) conceptualization of internal markets in a political economy model of marketing.

Perhaps the best-known conceptualizations of internal marketing come from the 'Nordic School of Services', where amongst other contributions Grönroos (1984, 1985) has written of the need for strategic and tactical internal marketing, and Gummesson (1987) has studied the use of internal marketing to achieve culture change in organizations. The practical application of these concepts is reflected in the literature of 'customer care' (e.g. Moores, 1986; Thomas, 1987; Lewis, 1989), which emphasizes customer perceptions of quality, and the importance of fostering this perception through the training and development of personnel at the point-of-sale. (An interesting aside on the customer care issue from one organization was that, when presented with top management's new customer care strategy, employees reacted with some hostility and the message 'If you care about customers why don't you care about us?' (Piercy, 1997).)

None the less, there is some established precedent for use of the terms 'internal marketing' and the 'internal customer'. We see these developments as important for two main reasons. First, the internal marketing paradigm provides an easily accessible mechanism for executives to analyze the organizational issues which may need to be addressed in implementing marketing strategies. Quite simply, concepts of marketing programmes and targets are familiar to marketing executives and they are 'comfortable' with them. The second point is that the internal marketing model provides a language which actually legitimizes focusing attention on issues like power, culture and political behaviour which appear quite often to be avoided by executives as somehow 'improper'.

17.2 *The scope of internal marketing*

It follows from the emergence of the internal marketing paradigm from diverse conceptual sources that the practice of internal marketing and its potential contribution to marketing strategy are similarly varied. It is possible to consider the following 'types' of internal marketing, although they are probably not equal in importance:

> internal marketing that focuses on the development and delivery of high standards of *service quality* and customer satisfaction;
> internal marketing that is concerned primarily with development *internal communications programmes* to provide employees with information and to win their support;
> internal marketing which is used as a systematic approach to managing the *adoption of innovations* within an organization;
> internal marketing concerned with providing products and services to users *inside the organization*; and
> internal marketing as the *implementation strategy* for our marketing plans.

17.2.1 Internal marketing and service quality

The original and most extensive use of internal marketing has been in efforts to improve the quality of service at the point-of-scale in services business like banking, leisure, retailing, and so on – the so-called 'moment of truth' for the services marketer. Some call this 'selling the staff', because the 'product' promoted is the person's job as a creator of customer service and value. This tends to be seen in customer care training programmes and similar initiatives. These types of internal marketing programme are, in practice, essentially tactical and often restricted to the operational level of the organization.

The logic is that it is apparent and obvious that marketplace success is frequently largely dependent on employees who are far removed from the excitement of creating marketing strategies – service engineers, customer services departments, production and finance personnel dealing with customers, field sales personnel, and so on. As we noted earlier, these are all people Evert Gummesson (1990) called 'part-time marketers' – they impact directly and significantly on customer relationships, but are normally not part of any formal marketing organization, nor are they typically within the marketing department's direct control.

Indeed, recent US research suggests we should think more carefully about the impact of the organization's external communications on employees – as 'advertising's second audience' (Gilly and Wolfinbarger, 1996). The chances are that employees are more aware and more influenced by our advertising than are our customers, so the suggestion is that we should use that awareness productively to deliver messages to employees. Some companies take this very seriously to good effect. In the US, Day's Inn TV advertising says 'Thank you for staying with us' – to the *staff* not just the guests.

Indeed, completing the communications circle may result in employees actually becoming the focus of the advertising. McDonald's is fighting to regain lost market position in the fiercely competed US fast-food market with TV advertising starring employees and outlet operatives linked by the key message 'My McDonald's'. Tracking studies suggest these advertisements to be highly effective. In the same industry, Pizza Hut has built the opportunity to appear in the company's advertising into its employee rewards programme. Similarly, in the UK, B&Q hardware stores currently use employees in television advertising as spokespersons promising personal service and value to external customers.

An illustrative case of the importance of managing the synergy between external and internal communications is Kinko's Copiers. Kinko's is a US company which positions itself as 'the world's branch office' – it offers 24-hour facilities for photocopying, computer services, audio-visual production, video-conferencing and Internet access, and post office services. In fact, the company started as a single rented Xerox machine in an old hamburger stand in California and has expanded to locations throughout the US, and is growing in Europe and the Far East. The founder, Paul Orfalea, is adamant that 'If you never take care of your co-workers, you won't be able to take care of your customers.... The attitude of our workers is our *biggest* competitive advantage' (Rubel, 1996). This belief is central to how he has successfully differentiated and grown this simple service business. His view is that anyone can open a copy shop – but it won't be a Kinko's.

More supporting evidence comes from the highly successful and long-lasting 'We Try Harder' strategy at Avis, the car rental business. Underpinning Avis's successful differentiation of its 'commodity' business is the close measurement and careful balancing of both employee and customer satisfaction at all their retail locations. For example, from the earliest days of the 'We Try Harder' advertising campaign, copies of advertisements have been inserted in employee pay packets as well as in conventional external advertising media, and all employees in all functions and jobs have regular opportunities to 'hear the tills ringing' by working in a retail outlet. Management policies in areas like recruitment and promotion are carefully geared to maintaining standards in employee *and* customer satisfaction (Piercy, 1997).

It can be argued that there is no one 'right' strategy in any given product market situation, but there are good and bad ways of *delivering* market strategies, which determine if they succeed or fail. The critical issue is becoming the consistency between strategies, tactics and implementation actions. This suggests that real culture change is a central part of the process of going to market effectively. At its simplest, the disgruntled employee produces the disgruntled customer. Tom Bonoma (1990) summarizes this point succinctly: 'treat your employees like customers, for your customers will get treated like employees'.

However, it is apparent that successfully exploiting the linkage between employee and customer satisfaction may not always be straightforward. Research into the way in which customer satisfaction is measured and managed in British companies is revealing (Piercy, 1995). Studies suggest that:

1. There is a need to create clarity for all employees regarding customer service quality policies and customer satisfaction targets. It is not enough to pay lip-service to these ideals and to expect success in attaining them. The starting point must be to identify what has to be achieved in customer satisfaction to implement specific market strategies, and to position the company against the competition in a specific market. It is unlikely that achieving what is needed will be free from cost. We need to take a realistic view of the time needed and the real costs of implementation in aligning the internal market with the external market.

2. Internal processes and barriers suggest the need to consider both the internal and external markets faced in implementing customer satisfaction measurement and management systems. To ignore the internal market is to risk actually damaging the company's capacity to achieve and improve customer satisfaction in the external market. If, for example, management uses customer feedback in a negative and coercive way, then it may reduce employee enthusiasm for customer service, or create 'game-playing' behaviour where people compete for 'Brownie points' in the system at the expense of both the company and the customer. This said, we have also to recognize not just the complementarity between internal and external markets, but the potential for conflict of interest. Achieving target levels of customer service and satisfaction may require managers and employees to change the way they do things and to make sacrifices they do not want to make. This may take more than simple advocacy or management threat.

3. Related to the above argument, recognizing the internal market suggests that there may be a need for a structured and planned internal marketing programme to achieve the effective implementation of customer satisfaction measurement and management. This has been described elsewhere as 'marketing our customers to our employees' (Piercy, 1995), and can be built into the implementation process to address the needs of the internal customer and to confront the types of internal processual barrier we have encountered.

4. Also related to the recognition of the internal market, is the need to question the relationship between internal and external customer satisfaction. This can be discussed with executives using the structure shown in Figure 17.1. This suggest four possible scenarios that result when internal and external customer satisfaction are compared:

    (a) **Synergy**, which is what we hope for, when internal and external customer satisfaction are high, and we see them as sustainable and self-regenerating. As one hotel manager explained it: 'I know that we are winning on customer service when my operational staff come to me and complain about how I am

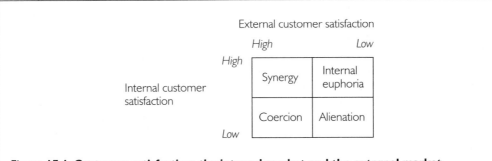

Figure 17.1 Customer satisfaction: the internal market and the external market

getting in their way in providing customer service, and tell me to get my act together!' This is the 'happy customers and happy employees' situation, assumed by many to be obvious and easily achieved.

(b) **Coercion** is where we achieve high levels of external customer satisfaction by changing the behaviour of employees through management direction and control systems. In the short term this may be the only option, but it may be very difficult and expensive to sustain this position in the longer term, and we give up flexibility for control.

(c) **Alienation** is where we have low levels of satisfaction internally and externally, and we are likely to be highly vulnerable to competitive attack on service quality, and to the instability in our competitive capabilities produced by low staff morale and high staff turnover.

(d) **Internal euphoria** is where we have high levels of satisfaction in the internal market, but this does not translate into external customer satisfaction – for example, if internal socialization and group cohesiveness actually shut out the paying customer in the external market. These scenarios are exaggerated, but have provided a useful way of confronting these issues with executives.

5. A critical mistake is to ignore the real costs and challenges in sustaining high service quality levels and the limitation which may exist in a company's capabilities for improving customer satisfaction levels. While advocacy is widespread and the appeal is obvious, achieving the potential benefits requires more planning and attention to implementation realities than is suggested by the existing conventional literature.

17.2.2 Internal marketing as internal communications

As well as customer care training and a focus on service quality, internal marketing may also be seen as internal communications. In fact, the largest growth in this area has been investment by companies in broader internal communications pro- grammes of various kinds – where 'communications' is understood as providing our employees with information and delivering messages which support the business strategy. The goal is to build both understanding and commitment. Conventionally, these activities tend to be a responsibility of the Human Resource Department (Mitchell, 1994a).

A 1994 study of British companies by the Industrial Society suggested that some 60 per cent saw internal communications as an HRM responsibility, compared to 2 per cent who said the marketing department took responsibility. It is perhaps worth noting that in the same study only one in three of the responding companies linked employee communications policy to a strategic business plan (*Marketing Business*, 1997b).

Indeed, Mitchell (1994b) suggests that internal communications is becoming one of the most important tools available to companies to hone competitive edge:

➤ for the delivery of brand promises;
➤ for improving levels of customer service;
➤ for faster and better innovation; and
➤ for smooth yet rapid organizational, technological and cultural change.

One industry study (Pounsford, 1994) suggested that managers saw the role of internal communications in the following terms and with the following advantages:

Perceived role	Illustrative comments
Team building	Educate employees about breadth and diversity of the organization.
	Assist co-operation between divisions.
Damage control	Prevent managers getting communications wrong.
	Suppress bad news.
	Counter pessimism.
Morale builders	Build confidence.
	Increase motivation.
Involvement	Represent employee opinions upwards.
	Create channel to share problems/values.
	Increase people recognition.
Change management	Increase understanding of the need for change.
	Test new ideas.
	Help people relate to rapidly changing environment.
Goal-setting	Help organization steer in a co-ordinated direction.
	Provide focus on corporate goals.
	Generate support for policies.

In fact, the most visible sign of investment in internal communications programmes to build employee commitment to strategies of customer service is the huge expenditures made by companies like British Telecommunications, and retailers like Sainsbury and Safeway. These companies have built programmes of communications that justify management changes to employees and explain the background to things like media stories about the company (Brierley, 1996). Indeed, British Telecommunications has actually formally merged internal communications with public relations. Employees on such companies are increasingly treated as 'trusted insiders'.

The manifestations of this form of internal marketing include: company newsletters, employee conferences and training, video-conferencing, satellite TV transmissions, interactive video, e-mail, and so on. These delivery mechanisms are important, but are in danger of obscuring an important point. Instructing and informing people about strategic developments is not the same as winning their real involvement and participation. Communication is a two-way process – listening as well as informing.

This may be why internal communications appear ineffective in some companies. For example, an industry expert, Peter Bell of the Added Value Internal Communications Consultancy, discusses the emergence of in-company barriers to internal communications 'that halt or distort the flow of information, whether they take the form of misunderstandings and misconceptions, hidden agenda and internal politicking, or even myths' (Mitchell, 1994a).

Even more revealing about how companies may use internal communications programmes badly is the view of Chris Argyris of Harvard Business School (Mitchell, 1994b). Argyris argues that many internal communications strategies are misconceived to the point of being counter-productive. He cites the case of one chief executive who was determined to improve his company's performance in innovation and time to market, and formed special taskforces to work on this issue. The taskforces found that every new idea in the company was subjected to 275 separate checks. By redesigning channels of internal communication, 200 of these checks were eliminated which dramatically reduced the time to get a new idea to market. Argyris suggests the chief executive *failed*, because at no stage did he ask the really unsettling questions like 'how long have you known that we have had an excessive number of barriers to innovation?' or 'what is it that prevented you from questioning these practices?'

This highlights a fundamental problem in some internal communications programmes – they become about telling and persuading, not listening. This may be said to be internal *selling* not internal *marketing*.

In fact, the businesses using internal communications effectively are companies like Avis, CIGNA and British Telecommunications, which are actually going to enormous efforts to *listen* to their employees' feedback, and to react positively to it, to improve the value they deliver to their external customers. Examples include Asda's 'Tell Archie Campaign' to encourage staff to make comments and suggestions direct to their senior managers, and in-store terminals at Safeways to collect staff suggestions.

An interesting illustration of the gains from two-way communications comes from Dana Corp, the US car parts manufacturer. At that company, the 'suggestions box' is described by the CEO as 'a core part of our value system'. Employees contribute ideas to improve operations and service, and 70 per cent are actually used. Dana is an example of an organization where employees have taken a share of the responsibility for keeping the company competitive. This underlines the important practical difference between producing company newsletters and taking internal communications seriously.

17.2.3 **Internal marketing and innovation management**

Somewhat different is the use of the internal marketing framework to place, and gain use of, innovations like computers and electronic communications in the IT field. These applications use tools of market analysis and planning to cope with and avoid resistance and to manage the process of change. This may be particularly important where the effectiveness of a marketing strategy relies on the adoption of new technologies and ways of working. The argument here is that people in an organization are 'customers' for our ideas and innovations. This view encourages us to consider:

➤ **looking at customer needs** – even in hierarchical companies people are not robots waiting to be told what to do, so making the effort to understand their needs increases the likely effectiveness of innovation;
➤ **delivering the goods** – the needs of customers tell us what matters most to them;
➤ **raising unrealistic expectations** – is as dangerous with internal customers as it is with external customers (Divita, 1996).

An example of a company using this approach is OASIS, the IT consultancy firm, which has a well-developed systems for the internal marketing of IT applications. The use of laptop computers by a geographically dispersed salesforce in one company was guided by the analysis of the 'internal market' using the classic diffusion of innovation model to identify opinion leaders as key influencers in the adoption process.

17.2.4 **Internal markets instead of external markets for products and services**

The terms 'internal market' and 'internal marketing' have been applied to internal relationships between different parts of the same organization – making them suppliers and customers as a way of improving the focus on efficiency and value. This is common in total quality management programmes, and in wider applications like the reform of the UK National Health Service.

This can lead to some interesting issues. For example, work with the R&D division of a major brewery suggested that the internal customer issues were really about the type and degree of dependence between the internal supplier (in this case the provider of R&D solutions to process problems in the brewery) and the internal customer (here the production and sales units of the brewery), which in turn reflects the freedom of either internal supplier or customer to deal with third parties outside the company.

17.2.5 **Strategic internal marketing and implementation**

Lastly, we should note the use of strategic internal marketing (SIM) as an approach to the structured planning of marketing implementation and analysis of underlying implementation problems in an organization. This form of internal marketing is a direct parallel to our conventional external marketing strategy and marketing programme, which aims at winning the support, co-operation and commitment we need inside the company, if our external market strategies are to work. This is a somewhat different view of internal marketing compared to those discussed above, although it is informed by the other types of internal marketing which have a longer history. The key underlying issue here is the organizational and cultural change needed to make marketing strategies happen.

A structure for an internal marketing programme is shown in Figure 17.2. The underlying proposal is that the easiest way to make practical progress with this type of internal marketing, and to establish what it may achieve, is to use exactly the same structures that we use for planning *external* marketing. This suggests that we should think in terms of integrating the elements needed for an internal marketing mix or programme, based on our analysis of the opportunities and threats in the internal marketplace represented by the company with which we are working. This is shown in Figure 17.2 as a formal and legitimate part of the planning process.

In fact, in this model, we take the internal marketing programme not only as an *output* of the planning process and the external marketing programme, but also as

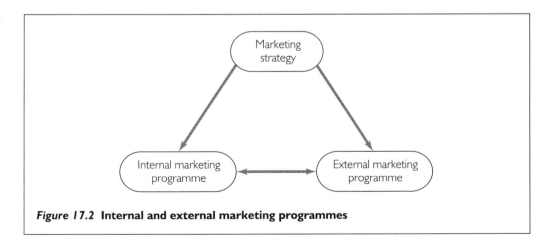

Figure 17.2 **Internal and external marketing programmes**

an *input*, i.e. constraints and barriers in the internal marketplace should be considered and analyzed as a part of the planning at both strategic and tactical levels. For the proposals to make sense in practice, we rely on this iterative relationship.

The starting point for this approach is that the marketing strategy and the planning process may define an external marketing programme in the conventional way, and less conventionally the internal barriers suggest that some external strategies are not capable of being implemented in the time-scale concerned, and we have to feed back into the planning process the message that some adjustments are needed while there is still time to make those adjustments to plans.

More positively, however, it is equally true that our analysis of the internal market may suggest new opportunities and neglected company resources which should be exploited, which in turn impact on our external marketing plan and thus on the planning process. What we are trying to make explicit for executives is the need to balance the impact of both internal and external market attributes on the strategic assumptions that they make in planning.

The structure of such an internal marketing programme can be presented in the following terms:

➤ **The product**: At the simplest level the 'product' consists of the marketing strategies and the marketing plan. Implied, however, is that the product to be 'sold' is those values, attitudes and behaviours which are needed to make the marketing plan work effectively. These hidden dimensions of the product may range from increased budgets and different resource allocations, to changed control systems and criteria used to evaluate performance, to changed ways of handling customers at the point of sale. At the extreme the product is the person's job – as it is redefined and reshaped by the market strategy so it will make people's working lives more enjoyable. There may also be negatives – changes people will not like, which brings us to price.

➤ **The price**: The price element of the internal marketing mix is not *our* costs, it is concerned with what we are asking our internal customers to 'pay', when they buy in to the product and the marketing plan. This may include the sacrifice of other projects which compete for resources with our plan, but more fundamentally the personal psychological cost of adopting different key values, and changing the way jobs are done, and asking managers to step outside their 'comfort zones' with new methods of operation. The price to be paid by different parts of the internal marketplace, if the marketing plan is to be implemented successfully, should not be ignored as a major source of barriers and obstacles of varying degrees of difficulty.

➤ **Communications**: The most tangible aspect of the internal marketing programme is the communications media and the messages used to inform and to persuade, and to work on the attitudes of the key personnel in the internal marketplace. This includes not only written communications, such as plan summaries and reports, but also face-to-face presentations to individuals and groups who are important to the success of the plan. Broadly, we should remember that to assume that simply 'telling' people will get them on our side is likely to be as naive inside the company as it is outside. We suggest it is important to consider the full range of communications possibilities and associated goals, as we would with external customers, and we should not forget to budget the time and financial costs which may be associated with these activities. At the simplest level, the purpose of our internal marketing communication may be served by a video presentation explaining things, or a roadshow taking the message out to the regions and the distributors. But real communication is two-way – we listen, we adapt, we focus on our audience's problems and needs (see pp. 397–400 above).

➤ **Distribution**: The distribution channels element of the mix is concerned with the physical and socio-technical venues at which we have to deliver our product and its communications: meetings, committees, training sessions for managers and staff, seminars, workshops, written reports, informal communications, social occasions, and so on. Ultimately, however, the real distribution channel is human resource management, and in the lining up of recruitment training, evaluation and reward systems behind marketing strategies, so that the culture of the company becomes the real distribution channel for internal marketing strategies. In fact, Ulrich (1992) makes some radical points about this, which are worth confronting. He says that if we really want complete customer commitment from our external customers, through independent, shared values and shared strategies, then we should give our customers a major role in our:

➤ staff recruitment and selection decisions;
➤ staff promotion and development decisions;
➤ staff appraisal, from setting the standards to measuring the performance;
➤ staff reward systems, both financial and non-financial;
➤ organizational design strategies; and
➤ internal communications programmes.

In effect this means using our human resource management systems as the internal marketing channel, thus taking the internal and external customer issue to its logical conclusion (see section 17.5 below). Companies developing such approaches in the US include General Electric, Marriott, Borg-Warner, DEC, Ford Motor Company, Hewlett Packard and Honeywell.

For example, a simple internal marketing analysis for two companies is illustrated in Tables 17.1 and 17.2. These examples concern a key customer account strategy in a financial services organization and a vertical marketing strategy in a computer company. In both cases we can see a 'formal' level of internal marketing which concerns the marketing plan or strategy, but also levels of internal marketing concerned with the informal organization and the processes of decision-making and change inside the company. In the computer company, vertical marketing is not a simple strategy because it is linked to changing resource allocation and departmental

Table 17.1 Internal marketing in a computer company

Internal market targets
(1) Business unit management
(2) Product group management
(3) Salesforce

Internal marketing	Internal marketing levels		
	Formal	Informal	Processual
Product	Marketing plan to attack a small industry as a special vertical market, rather than grouping it with many other industries as at present, with specialized products and advertising	Separation of resources and control of this market from the existing business unit	Change from technology-oriented management to recognition of differences in buyer needs in different industries – the clash between technology and customer orientation
Price	Costs of developing specialized 'badged' or branded products for this industry	Loss of control for existing business units	Fear of 'fragmentation' of markets leading to internal structural and status changes
Communications	Written plan Presentations to key groups	Support for plan by key board members gained by pre-presentation 'softening up' by planners	Action planning team formed, including original planners, but also key players from business unit and product group – rediscovering the wheel to gain 'ownership' Advertising the new strategy in trade press read by company technologists and managers
Distribution	Business unit board meeting Product group board meeting Main board meeting Salesforce conference	Informal meetings	Joint seminars in applying IT to this industry, involving business unit managers and key customers Joint charity events for the industry's benevolent fund

Source: Adapted from Piercy (1997).

Table 17.2 Internal marketing in a financial services organization

Internal market targets (1) Branch managers of retail banks and finance company offices
(2) Divisional chief executives for the banks and the finance company

Internal marketing	Internal marketing levels		
	Formal	Informal	Processual
Product	Integration of selling efforts around key customers, as a key marketing strategy	Head office group-based planning and resource allocation with greater central control	Change in the individual managers' role from independent branch entrepreneur to group-based collaborator
Price	Branch profit/commission from independent selling to smaller customers, to be sacrificed to build long-term relationships with key accounts	Loss of freedom/independence of action in the marketplace Potential loss of commission-earning power	Time, effort and psychological 'pain' of collaborating with former 'competitors' with different ethnic/educational/professional backgrounds – the 'banker versus the hire purchase salesman' Fear that the other side would damage existing customer relationships
Distribution	Written strategic marketing plans Sales conferences	Written communications Informal discussion of chief executive's 'attitude' Redesign of commission and incentives systems in both companies	Joint planning/problem-solving teams for each region – built around central definition of target market segments Combining/integrating management information systems, and changing its structure to reflect new segments
Communications	Formal presentation by chief executive at conferences Written support from chief executive Redesign market information systems to be more up-to-date	Sponsorship by chief executive – 'the train is now leaving the station, you are either on it or …' (written memo sent to all branches)	Social events Joint training course Redefinition of markets and target segments

Source: Adapted from Piercy and Morgan (1991).

responsibilities, and also to a change of management culture. In the financial services company, a key account strategy involves not simply a new marketing direction, but a change in line management freedom and ways of doing business. These
cases are indicative of the types of implementation and change problem which can
be addressed by internal marketing.

It also follows that we can use conventional market research techniques inside
the company to get to grips with who has to change, in what way, how much and
what the patterns are in our internal marketplace.

Finally, as with the external marketing programme, we should not neglect the
importance of measuring results wherever possible. This may be in terms of such
criteria as people's attitudes towards the market strategy and their commitment to
putting it into practice, or customer perceptions of our success in delivering our
promises to them – or, perhaps more appositely, our lack of success as presented
by complaints, and so on.

Again, in exact parallel with the conventional external marketing plan, our internal marketing programmes should be directed at chosen targets or segments within
the market. The choice of key targets for the internal marketing programme should
be derived directly from the goals of the external marketing programme, and the
types of organizational and human changes needed to implement marketing strategies. The internal marketplace may be segmented at the simplest level by the job
roles and functions played by groups of people, e.g. top management, other departments and marketing and sales staff.

Alternatively, we might look beyond job characteristics to the key sources of
support and resistance to the external marketing plan which are anticipated, to identify targets for reinforcement, or for persuasion and negotiation. Perhaps at the
deepest level we might choose our targets on the basis of the individual's attitudes
towards the external market and customers, and the key values that we need communicated to external customers, together with people's career goals.

It can be seen, therefore, that internal marketing can be used in different ways,
and that the role may vary from developing customer care and service quality programmes to improve and maintain service standards and customer satisfaction at
the point-of-scale, through to internal communication programmes, to providing a
structured approach to planning the full implementation of marketing strategy. We
noted also that internal marketing may be of particular importance in the alliance-
based network organization.

17.3 Planning for internal marketing

There is a variety of situations when strategic thinking about competitive strategy
should address the possible role of internal marketing:

➤ where performance in critical areas of customer service are unsatisfactory and
not sufficient to establish a strong competitive position;

➤ where customer satisfaction is consistently low and complaints suggest that the underlying causes are employee attitudes and behaviour, rather than poor product standards or inadequate support systems;
➤ when market conditions and customer requirements have shifted, so that continuing the standards and practices of the past will no longer bring success;
➤ when new marketing strategies require new skills and ways of behaving – a 'stretch' strategy,
➤ when bridging the gap between planning and implementation has proved problematic in the past.

In such situations, we may wish to consider an internal marketing strategy with the following components:

➤ **Internal market strategy**: In broad terms what is needed to gain the successful implementation of an external market strategy. It is here that we need to confront the real implications of our external market strategy for the internal customer – the decision-makers, managers, operatives and others without whose support, co-operation and commitment, the external strategy will fail. This is the most critical question in the whole internal marketing exercise. It may be worth consulting the people directly concerned – doing internal market research. It is certainly worth incorporating some diversity of opinion. As we learn more, we can come back and redraft and rethink our conclusions here. It is here that we should take a view of what it is likely to cost us to achieve these things and the deadline for achieving them to implement the external marketing strategy on time.
➤ **Internal market segmentation** is about identifying the targets in the internal marketplace around which we can build internal marketing programmes, which are different in what we have to achieve and how we are going to do it. This may not be straightforward, but is the route to real insights into the internal market problem and effectiveness in how we cope with that problem. The most obvious way of identifying internal segments may be by role or function, or location, and this may be sufficient. It might be more productive to think of who are the innovators and opinion leaders who will influence others. We might approach this more directly in terms of the role that different people will play in implementing the external strategy and the problems they may face in this, or simply how much different people will have to change to get the external strategy to work.
➤ **Internal marketing programmes** specify which internal marketing programmes will be needed in each internal market segment to achieve the objectives we have set. In each area we need to collect our thoughts about the rational issues but also the human and cultural issues. To us the product may be a new marketing plan that we need to inform people about (internal marketing communications), through formal presentations (internal marketing distribution), adjusting commission and evaluation systems as need be (internal marketing price). To the internal customer, the same plan may be about

disruption and threat (product), loss of initiative and status (price), imposed without consultation by management (communication) and rigorously 'policed' through coercion (distribution). If internal marketing is about anything, it is about confronting and coping with this conflict. It is this confrontation which will drive us away from thinking about internal marketing as simply writing customer care brochures and doing great plan presentations, towards coping with the human and organizational realities of what strategic change involves and costs. This is also the stage to take a look at the cost implications of what we now see to be necessary in our internal marketing: does the internal marketing cost mean that the external market strategy is no longer attractive? Do we have to account for internal marketing cost which is more than we expected, but bearable? Do we have to change the external strategy to reduce the internal marketing cost? Are there cheaper ways of achieving the critical internal marketing goals?

➤ **Internal marketing evaluation** – what we can measure to see if we are getting there, ideally quantified and objective: reduced customer complaint rates or higher customer satisfaction scores. This may be ambitious and we should not abandon important objectives because they are difficult to evaluate – we may have to settle for a subjective or qualitative evaluation, which is better than nothing.

17.4 *Partnership with human resource management*

As we have seen, increasingly major companies are recognizing that they compete through the people they employ: the managers and operational staff who create the service and quality in the customer's terms, upon which so much of modern thinking about marketing strategy relies.

One way in which this can be achieved is through the cross-functional partnership between marketing and human resource management. We discussed earlier the growing importance of the links between the marketing concept and the 'human relations concept', which lies at the heart of human resource management, and the manifestation of such links when some companies actively involve their customers in staff recruitment, selection reward and development programmes.

The main argument advanced is that radical change in the market environments faced by companies, accompanied by equally radical change in the role of marketing in the organization, is placing increasing emphasis on successfully managing interfunctional relationships to implement effectively marketing strategies of service and quality. While there has been some analysis of the relationships between marketing and technical functions in the product marketing field (e.g. see Gupta *et al.*, 1986; Ruekert and Walker, 1987; Olson, 1993), there has not been a similar rigorous analysis of relationships between marketing and human resource management (HRM). In fact, the evidence that suggests that the effective management of this interface is relatively rare in practice, although there are important exceptions.

17.4.1 Rationale for a partnership between marketing and human resource management

We have seen that the organizational role of marketing has been subject to substantial challenge in recent years. For example, Achrol (1991) has examined the emergence of new organizational forms, and Webster (1992) analyzes the role of marketing in organizations developing through networks and alliances. Such internal organizational changes can be seen as responses to increasingly turbulent and complex market strategies (Piercy and Cravens, 1995).

Generally commentators suggest that there is a considerable potential enhancement in marketing effectiveness available through more productive interfunctional relationships, but also that the area is frequently characterized by tensions and the potential for conflicts of interest, jurisdiction and ownership disputes, and political struggles (e.g. Ruekert and Walker, 1987).

In particular, there have been several compelling arguments that the human element is perhaps the single most important factor in implementing service quality and competitive advantage. Pfeffer (1994) argues many companies are failing to recognize the evidence that the single most important factor in achieving and maintaining competitive strength is employees, while Walker (1994) claims in a similar way that competitive advantage is achieved by managing people more effectively than do competitors. The underlying case is that distinctive human resources provide the real core competencies of the business as the source of competitive advantage (Cappelli and Crocker-Hefter, 1996), underlining the importance of aligning workforce capabilities with market strategies (McDowell, 1996). As a result, others suggest that a critical challenge is to recognize that external strategies require direct counterparts in human resource management, focusing on learning and adaptation, strategic culture management and developing new communications patterns (Burack *et al.*, 1994). Similarly, Gratton (1994) explains the challenge as aligning strategic intent with human resources.

General conclusions of this type regarding the importance of better linking human resource polices with market strategies have led to a small number of more specific proposals for redesigning the HRM/marketing interface.

It has been suggested, for example, that marketing and human resource management have developed along parallel paths which are now converging to provide a shared view of customer and employee needs (Pollock, 1995). The strongest case has been made by Glassman and McAfee (1992), who argue that the major issue facing modern business is how to integrate marketing with human resource management, since these can no longer be effective as separate functions. The integration mechanisms they prescribe range from interdepartmental committees to full merger of the traditional functions. Indeed, Hulbert and Pitt (1996) have a similar view of convergence of functions in the era of 'post-functional marketing', which is similar to suggestions of the need to consider the marketing/human resource management relationship as a 'strategic partnership' (Micolo, 1993), a 'partnership for change' (Eisenstat, 1993), or a 'business partnership' (Ulrich, 1992).

More operational views of the interface between marketing and HRM issues come from the link between HRM and relationship marketing strategies (Perrien *et al.*, 1993; Perrien and Ricard, 1995), and the need to direct HRM policies to focus on customer service and customer value (Cripe, 1994; Gubman, 1995). Conversely, Sheth and Mittal (1996) have recently examined the use of HRM skills in the management of customer expectations.

17.4.2 Evidence of current practice

Notwithstanding these arguments and prescriptions, evidence from practice suggests that the marketing/HRM interface is generally not closely or well managed.

There is some general evidence that human resource management is not closely integrated with business and market strategies in British or European companies (Story, 1992; *IRS Employment Review*, 1996). Where there is evidence of closer and more effective integration between HRM and the implementation of customer-focused market strategies, it is associated with the benchmarks provided by major global companies, such as: Rank Xerox (Anon., 1993); Hewlett Packard (Laabs, 1993); Pepsi Cola (McNerney, 1994); Coca Cola (Anfuso, 1994), AT&T (Plevel *et al.*, 1994); and Colgate-Palmolive (Anfuso, 1995). These companies provide us with important benchmarks in this area.

For example, Avis provides an illustrative example of partnership between HRM and marketing. The company has achieved sustained market leadership, a profit record superior to competitors and consistent growth in shareholder value. There is widespread external recognition that Avis approaches are effective shown in: a higher level of product innovation in product development than any competitor; more service awards than any other car rental company; and regular success in major quality award programmes spanning three continents. It is telling, however, that even with these achievements, managers in both HRM and marketing at the company describe their success far more in terms of what their customers think of Avis, than in the usual figures. The Avis culture drives customer satisfaction through employee satisfaction as the route to the financial results.

There is a compelling case that one of the keys to effective implementation of marketing strategies of service and quality, and to the competitive advantage to be gained, lies in exploiting the potential synergy between marketing and human resource management. However, the evidence is that this interfunctional partnership is relatively unusual in practice.

In lead company examples like Avis, it is striking that there is truly a partnership between human resource management and marketing, which transcends traditional functional boundaries and is genuinely collaborative rather than competitive or political. The sharing and ownership of customer issues outside marketing and sales has dramatic effects. This is achieved through a variety of mechanisms: cross-functional teams focusing on customer issues; the rotation of personnel across traditional functional boundaries; 'hands-on' involvement of managers at the retail business level – 'hearing the tills ringing' as company executives describe it;

widespread promotion of executives from within the business. Notwithstanding the specific mechanisms used, the effect is that executives in all functions are focused on the customer above all else. If partnering human resource management and marketing is effective, the intangible of customer obsession is probably the sign of success, more than the specific organizational mechanisms used.

Part of the effect of this cross-functional collaboration and shared focus on market strategy is reflected in the internal processes of the company. In particular, two process exchanges are most significant. First, human resource processes are directly linked to market strategy – in recruitment and selection, training and development, reward systems, the real empowerment and involvement of people at the operating level of the business, and internal communications programmes. Second, marketing processes and the visible components of marketing strategy – primarily advertising and customer satisfaction measurement – are directly linked to human resource management. Indeed, it is possible that the outcome of HRM/marketing collaboration will lead to the disappearance of both functions as traditional departments in such organizations, to be replaced by customer functions managing employees and buyers as joint customers for the business.

Less speculatively, it is clear that much of the effective implementation of marketing strategies relies on the realignment of organizational processes and structures with customer issues. While interfunctional relationships with technical functions has often been stressed, the link to HRM has been given relatively little attention. Given the association of many marketing implementation failures with lack of employee commitment and inappropriate skill bases, the potential from this collaboration appears substantial.

It may be that these interfunctional mechanisms are what effective internal marketing requires. It is also evident that successful marketing implementation may rely heavily on a company's ability to manage critical aspects of the behaviour of employees, rather than just evaluating outcome results like sales and accounts visited. This may be considered further as the move to behaviour-based management rather than outcome-based management, in the particular context of linking marketing strategy to salesforce management.

17.4.3 Behaviour-based management: linking marketing strategy to sales operations

One area that illustrates particularly well the growing importance of people management skills in achieving marketing strategy implementation, and correspondingly an area frequently ripe for joint action by marketing and HRM, is linking marketing strategy to the management of salespeople in the field.

Traditionally, salesforce management has mainly involved the evaluation of the salesperson's outcome performance (sales results, market share, profitability of a salesperson's accounts, and so on). Correspondingly, the motivation of salespeople has conventionally been seen as a matter of designing appropriate commission and financial incentive schemes. However, in an era when marketing strategy emphasizes relationship-building, customer partnership, service quality and customer satisfaction, many companies have questioned the appropriateness of these traditional management approaches in linking marketing strategy to sales operations. At its simplest, salespeople who are primarily evaluated and rewarded on the basis of sales volume may have little incentive to build enduring customer relationships or undertake activities which support those relationships but which do not directly generate short-term sales revenue.

A research model which has been evaluated in recent studies of sales management in different countries including the US, Australia and the UK is shown in Figure 17.3. For the purposes of evaluating this model, the effective sales organization was taken as the one which is meeting and beating the objectives set for it by management, and which is meeting and beating the competition in sales, profitability, market share and customer satisfaction (Piercy *et al.*, 1997).

This model suggests that while salesforce effectiveness is linked to outcome performance, the important influence on salesforce outcome performance is behavioural performance by salespeople, which is in turn driven by sales management control activities, organization design and salesperson characteristics. We can expand briefly on this model below.

The conclusions reached in the study of effective sales organizations in the UK can be summarized as follows. The more effective sales organizations have a number of things in common:

➤ Their salespeople share several similar success characteristics.
➤ Their salespeople perform exceptionally well on a number of critical
dimensions of behaviour – these are the drivers of salesforce performance.

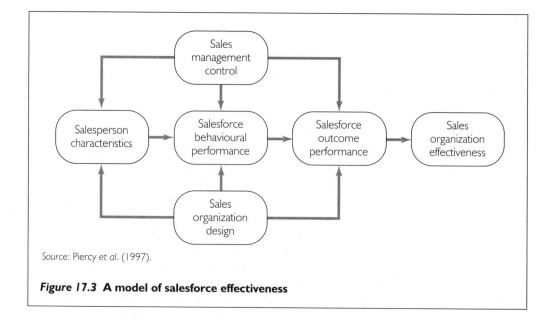

Source: Piercy et al. (1997).

Figure 17.3 A model of salesforce effectiveness

➤ Their field sales managers play a critical role as coaches rather than as commanders – sales management control is more about managing behaviour than simply outcomes.
➤ They are 'right-sized' and soundly organized at the sales unit level.
➤ They focus throughout on building long-term customer relationships.

What we have found is that looking across many different selling situations and market conditions, superiority in sales organization effectiveness is strongly associated with: the characteristics of salespeople, the behavioural drivers of salesforce performance, the critical sales manager role in managing salesperson behaviour, the soundness of sales organization design to allow salespeople to perform well, and cutting across all these other factors the supreme importance of customer relationships.

We can summarize the conclusions of this research in the following terms:

➤ **The characteristics of successful salespeople**: The more effective sales organizations have salespeople who are rated higher in their *motivation*, particularly relating to the sense of personal achievement they get from their work and the enthusiasm they display, but they are also outstanding in their *customer orientation*, their *team orientation*, and their *sales support* orientation. Sales people in effective sales organizations are highly motivated, are driven by customer issues, are team players and are prepared to invest in support activities, even where these are not directly producing sales results in the short term. These findings have a number of important implications for how we recruit, train and develop effective salespeople, which may cause us to question some of the traditional views about the competencies and capabilities we need in salespeople. The view sales managers take is that in the more effective sales organizations salespeople are committed team players and are willing to co-operate in implementing company selling strategies rather than operating on an independent basis. Selling skills are important, but being a sales-oriented superstar is not the key to sales effectiveness.
➤ **The behavioural drivers of salesforce performance**: We have also found that one source of sales organization effectiveness certainly lies in superior outcome performance in the salesforce. This means that the salesforce can be seen to perform at high levels in gaining market share, focusing on selling high margin products and on major accounts for long-term business, and exceeding sales targets and objectives. Outcome performance is important and should form part of our evaluation, but we have also seen that it is partly driven by superior behavioural performance in the salesforce. Traditionally, sales management has focused on developing selling skills. We found that effective sales organizations did, indeed, outperform the rest in selling capabilities reflected in sales presentations and technical knowledge. However, we found these capabilities to be necessary but not sufficient to generate superior results. The major drivers of salesforce performance that characterize the most effective sales organizations come from *adaptiveness* in selling, *teamwork*, *sales planning* and *sales support* activities.

➤ **The critical sales manager role**: We have observed that in the more effective sales organization the sales manager is more a coach and communicator than a commander and scorekeeper. In the effective sales organization: sales manager *monitoring* is really about observing sales performance, reviewing call reports and watching salesperson day-to-day activities; *directing* activities are mainly concerned with helping salespeople to develop their potential, coaching and participating in training; the *evaluating* role of the sales manager focuses on appraising salesperson professional development and the quality of selling, as well as judging sales results; and *rewarding* is associated with providing regular feedback and rewards (often non-financial) linked to results (frequently the quality of work not just the quantity). These findings suggest that the more effective sales organizations and their increased emphasis on behaviour-based management control, have defined a very different role for the sales manager. This critical position combines the role of coach, communicator and facilitator with the more traditional functions of keeping score and allocating financial rewards. In effective sales organizations the sales manager participates in field sales activities and provides a role model, going far beyond the traditional command and control model of sales management.

➤ **'Right-sizing' and organizational design**: It is also apparent that sales organization effectiveness is strongly associated with management confidence that effectiveness cannot be increased by adding or subtracting people at the sales unit level, i.e. 'right-sizing', and a high level of management satisfaction with the design of sales territories and units, and the allocation of resources and market potential. Success here impacts on performance and effectiveness, not least because of its implications for retaining salespeople. This area is problematic. At a time of widespread corporate downsizing and restructuring, staffing levels and allocations may suffer. We suggest that this area should be a high priority in recovering sales effectiveness after large-scale organizational changes.

➤ **Customer relationships**: Cutting across our conclusions in each of these hallmarks of sales organization effectiveness, is our most fundamental finding. The more effective sales organizations are those which build and sustain long-term customer relationships. Effective sales organizations outperform the rest in achieving customer satisfaction. Effective sales organizations do not allow salespeople to neglect customer interests by paying wholly or largely by commission and bonus. Effective salespeople are highly customer-oriented. Effective salesforces adapt their selling to customer characteristics, work in teams to handle customer problems and provide customer service, plan sales strategy around customers and provide support to customers in checking on performance and responding to complaints. The pervasive focusing on activities that develop and maintain productive, long-term customer relationships characterizes the most effective sales organizations and underpins their dramatically superior results. Indeed, many sales executives who have contributed to our studies throughout the world have made precisely this point:

customer relationship building is the most important area in which to focus efforts for improvements in sales organization effectiveness in the future.

The insights from this research may challenge many company beliefs about how best to recruit, train and develop salespeople and sales managers, and how best to manage the sales operation. However, realistically, acting on these insights mean facing new problems. For example, we have found that the more effective sales organizations focus on developing and maintaining long-term customer relationships through teamwork, adaptiveness and customer support in the sales organization. This is highly consistent with the current emphasis on relationship marketing strategy. However, achieving that focus and implementing the relationship marketing strategy may require substantial adjustment to both structural and 'people' issues by sales management.

The goal of those structural decisions is to provide salespeople with high performance situations to exploit – by having a 'right-sized' salesforce, effective territory design, focused sales teams and appropriate spans of control for sales managers. Poor sales management decisions in these areas can establish unnecessary and avoidable performance hurdles. These issues must be addressed alongside the 'people' decisions that aim to develop successful salespeople, capable of winning in the marketplace. These 'people' decisions are critically concerned with having salespeople with the desired success characteristics, and focusing appropriate types of management attention on the underlying drivers of salesforce performance. This is the route to high sales organization effectiveness, based on long-term customer relationships.

However, relationship-oriented selling and team-based sales require very different skills and capabilities to those of the stereotypical 'lone-wolf road warrior' salesperson of the past. In the same way, behaviour-based control by sales managers requires a very different set of skills to the 'command and control' model of sales management.

Sales training will have to emphasize team building, conflict resolution, interpersonal skills and other capabilities relevant to the needed success characteristics and management activities. This will require time and money. It may not always succeed – the truly individualistic 'one-wolf' salesperson may not be easily converted into an effective team player; the 'sales commander and senior salesperson' manager may not take well to coaching and communicating as a management style. None the less, our observations suggest that this is the direction in which many companies will have to move in the future to build the truly effective sales organization.

If we accept the principle that effectiveness in linking marketing strategy to the sales operation is driven by behavioural and managerial factors of the type described above, then the case for a partnership between marketing and HRM becomes far stronger. The foundation for this relationship becomes applying HRM tools and skills to manage the development of supervisory line management and the focus of management on the behavioural performance by people in the organization to support marketing strategies. The most obvious linkages are in recruitment, selection and training, but company experience suggests this will lead to developing different approaches to appraisal and reward systems and organizational design.

It is becoming clear that the marketing/HRM partnership is potentially a powerful mechanism for enhancing the effectiveness of marketing strategy implementation, by facilitating the move towards behaviour-based management approaches.

17.4.4 Alliances and partnerships

Lastly, it should be noted that the importance of internal marketing, the alliance between marketing and HRM, and behaviour-based management, may be even greater in the functionally disaggregated network organization. We have considered earlier (pp. 174–81) the importance of strategic alliances and network organizations in developing and implementing marketing strategies in turbulent and complex modern markets and industries. The underlying logic is one of partnership and collaboration to gain economies and allow the concentration of each company on its core competencies, instead of competition between suppliers at different stages of the supply chain. It may be argued that a parallel to such inter-organizational collaborations is the potential for *intra*-organizational collaborations that will gain access to the capabilities and skills to develop and shape the internal market to enhance an organization's ability to deliver sustained customer value and to innovate in the marketplace. Indeed, such an argument fits well with the view that organizations are moving increasingly away from structures based on functional specializations to new organizational forms built around key value-creating processes (Piercy, 1997).

17.5 Conclusions

This chapter has taken the relatively unusual view that part of thinking about competitive strategy should be concerned with managing the internal market (of employees, functional specialists, managers, and so on) so as to enhance a company's ability to deliver its strategies to customers in the external market. This view is based on the recognition of the importance of relationship management with partners, achieving competition differentiation through the skills of the 'part-time marketers' in the organization, and the problems of marketing implementation.

It was shown that internal marketing may be traced back to early views about the synergy between the marketing concept and the 'human relations' concept, and to have developed operationally in a variety of ways. The scope of internal marketing was seen to encompass: service quality enhancement, internal communications programmes, managing the adoption of innovations inside an organization, cross-functional and cross-divisional supply of products and services, and a framework for marketing implementation. Our interest here is primarily, though not exclusively, in strategic internal marketing as a framework for managing implementation.

In this area we saw that internal marketing offers a framework for evaluating the costs of change and for managing change that utilizes the same concepts, terminology and techniques as planning external marketing.

Lastly, it was argued that one route to consider in managing internal marketing is through internal alliance inside the organization between marketing and human resource management. This alliance has been relatively rarely developed in organizations, but promises great leverage in managing the effective implementation of marketing strategies. The importance is underlined by the example of the significance of behaviour-based management approaches in linking marketing strategy effectively to line management areas like sales operations. One particularly important area where the application of internal marketing tools may be vital is in the management of alliances and networked organizations.

PART V

Conclusions

Chapter 18 concludes the book by looking ahead to marketing strategies for the twenty-first century. Significant environmental changes are highlighted and a number of building blocks are suggested for developing adaptive strategies for a changing world. These include the need to become learning organizations, capturing, internalizing and utilizing knowledge; the need for a clear market orientation and focus on creating superior value and greater levels of satisfaction for customers; the need to base positioning strategies firmly on marketing assets and competencies; the need to establish closer relationships with key customers; and, finally, the need to rethink the role of marketing within the organization. A number of positioning dimensions are discussed that can provide keys to positioning in the future. Price, quality, innovation, service, differentiation and tailoring are compared as fundamental positioning dimensions and strategies, and the competencies and assets required for each explored.

The chapter, and indeed the book, concludes by predicting that marketing in the future will be seen more as a process for achieving a close fit between market requirements on the one hand, and company competencies and assets on the other, than as a functional department within the firm. It is how this strategic, rather than operational, role for marketing is fulfilled in the future that holds much excitement for the discipline of marketing.

CHAPTER 18

Marketing strategies for the twenty-first century*

If it is to achieve sustainable success in the demanding world marketplace, tomorrow's company must be able to learn fast and change fast. To do this a winning company must inspire its people to new levels of skill, efficiency and creativity, supported by a sense of shared destiny with customers, suppliers and investors.
RSA (1994)

Introduction

The emphasis throughout this book has been on developing robust marketing strategies to enable organizations to survive and prosper in the turbulent, competitive and frequently hostile markets they face. From the outset we have stressed the critical need to develop effective ways in which to cope with the change in both customer markets and the ways in which companies go to market. However, we can go further – what of the new century we are entering? As markets and marketing continue to change, what strategies will make most sense in the third millennium AD? This chapter attempts to review some of the major trends which are already apparent, and to propose ways in which new competitive strategies can be fashioned to exploit the opportunities to emerge. As Drucker (1997) has said:

> In human affairs – political, social, economic, or business – it is pointless to try and predict the future ... But it is possible – and fruitful – to identify major events that have already happened, irrevocably, and that will have predictable effects in the next decade or two. It is possible, in other words, to identify and prepare for the future that has already happened.

18.1 The changing competitive arena

Chapter 1 reviewed some of the significant changes taking place in today's markets. Those that are likely to have the most impact on business in the twenty-first century are briefly discussed below.

---

* Some of the ideas presented in this chapter have been explored by one of the authors in a contribution to M. Thomas and C. Egan (eds) (1998), *Handbook of Strategic Marketing*, London: Chartered Institute of Marketing/Butterworth-Heinemann, and in a series of papers appearing in the *Journal of Strategic Marketing* (Hooley and Beracs, 1997; Hooley, Möller and Broderick, 1998).

18.1.1 Changes in the business environment

To claim that 'the only constant is change' is trite but true in today's business environment. The recent Royal Society for the Encouragement of Arts, Manufactures & Commerce (RSA) Inquiry into Tomorrow's Company identified a number of major changes taking place in business markets:

- The pace of economic change is accelerating. During the Industrial Revolution it took 60 years for productivity per person to double. China and South Korea have done the same in 10 years.
- There is an explosion in innovation and new knowledge generation that is also accelerating. Every year as much new knowledge is generated through research and development as the total sum of all human knowledge up to the 1960s.
- Competitive pressures are intensifying. Computer manufacturers, for example, need to reduce costs and improve product performance by around 30 per cent per annum to remain competitive.
- Manufacturing can now take place almost anywhere. Companies are constantly seeking more efficient manufacturing options, and that typically means sourcing from wherever makes economic sense. 1993 figures show UK manufacturing labour costs at half those of Germany but twice those of Korea and Taiwan. Labour costs in Poland, Thailand, China and Indonesia are significantly lower still.
- New organizational structures are emerging as firms seek to make themselves more competitive. Firms have reorganized, reduced overheads, delayered, merged, created alliances and partnerships in attempts to create advantage in the marketplace.
- International trade is being liberalized through the GATT and World Trade Organization, but there are still massive regional trading blocs within which regional, nationalistic, ethnic and religious groupings seek to retain individual identity.
- Company actions are becoming increasingly visible, especially their effects on the environment. Customers are demanding more both economically and environmentally.

At the macro-level these changes can be grouped into economic, technological, social, legal and political issues. Just as water supply companies cannot change weather patterns, most macroenvironmental factors are outside the control of individual firms. Few companies have the ability significantly to influence political, economic, social and technological processes. Most need to ensure they understand and predict the changes going on. Water companies need to predict both weather patterns (supply of water) and demand (water usage) so that they can then put strategies in place to ensure demand is met.

In a recent keynote address to the British Academy of Management (annual conference, Aston University 1996), Professor David Cravens cited an example of a well-known firm that had failed to grasp the significance of technological change on its market (see Sammuels, 1994; Evans and Wurster, 1997). Encyclopaedia Britannica (EB) went from peak US profits in 1990 to severe difficulties in 1996 as it failed fully to appreciate the impact of computer technology, particularly the CD-ROM, on its business. In that period sales plummeted by more than 50 per cent. The business had been built through a highly motivated and successful salesforce selling encyclopaedias to middle-class families (often bought by parents for their children's education) at around $1,500 each.

Then along came home computers, with CD-ROM players and encyclopaedias such as Encarta at around $50. The new entrants may not have had the depth of coverage of EB but they were in a format the children enjoyed using, offered the opportunities for multi-media display (video and audio clips, animations), could be more easily updated, and, perhaps most crucially, offered middle-class parents a justification for the purchase of often expensive home computer systems which in many cases were used primarily for games purposes!

With the advent of the 'information superhighway', the world wide web and Internet the holding of large amounts of data on individual PCs may become a thing of the past, posing potential problems (and, of course, opportunities) for the marketers of CD-ROM-based encyclopaedias.

The experiences of EB are a prime example of the critical importance of market sensing, continuous listening and learning rather than being surprised and wrong-footed when a competitor 'reinvents' the business. By 1997, EB was marketing a CD-ROM version of its encyclopaedia, but by then in a crowded market dominated by Microsoft's Encarta.

Similarly, Hoover and Electrolux were surprised strategically by the success of the Dyson vacuum cleaner and have lost share to the innovation (see below). And yet Dyson offered both the rights to the product before launching it himself. The problem was not that Hoover and Electrolux did not know about the new Dyson technology, rather they were not prepared to listen and learn.

While companies need to operate within the bounds and conditions of the macroenvironment they may have some (limited) ability to influence it. The UK government's Private Finance Initiative (PFI), for example, which is designed to introduce private sector financing into public investment and infrastructure projects, is administered by a steering board including representatives of the construction and other industries. Similarly, most expenditure on scientific research is applied in nature and conducted in commercial companies such that their efforts will directly affect the technological environment in which they, and other firms, operate in the future.

No company can ever hope to understand every aspect of the macroenvironment in which it operates. There will always be surprises and shocks as new technological breakthroughs emerge or political discontinuities occur. What is important, however, is to spot and act on more of the trends and changes than competitors. Shocks are less for companies prepared to think the 'unthinkable' and to challenge the status quo in their strategizing. It may seem outlandish, for example, but the UK brewers and cigarette companies are quite open in admitting that they have contingency plans should cannabis be legalized.

18.1.2 Changes in markets

A number of trends can be seen in modern markets that are likely to continue into the future.

First, customers are becoming increasingly demanding of the products and services they buy. Customers demand, and expect, reliable and durable products with quick efficient service at reasonable prices. They also expect the products and services they buy to meet their needs. Different customers have different wants and needs, and hence companies have an opportunity to select segments where their offerings most closely align with those needs and where they can focus their activities to create a competitive advantage. What is more, there is little long-term stability in customer demands. Positions may be achieved through offering superior customer value, and yet the evidence is that without constant improvement 'value migration' will occur – buyers will migrate to an alternative value offering (Slywotzky, 1996).

For example, an executive in a computer company producing laptop computers complained in 1997: 'First they wanted the notebook with a colour screen – we gave it to them. Then, last year, it had to have a Pentium chip, so we gave them that. Now they tell us they still want all that, but the thing that really matters is that the computer has to have the weight of a feather ...'

A second major trend, one that particularly differentiates the 1990s from the 1980s, is that customers are less prepared to pay a substantial premium for products or services that do not offer demonstrably greater value. While it is undeniable that well-developed and managed brands can command higher prices than unbranded products in many markets, the differentials commanded are now much less than they were and customers are increasingly questioning the extra value they get for the extra expense. Marlboro cigarettes are a case in point. On 2 April 1993 ('Marlboro Friday') Philip Morris announced a 20 per cent reduction in price of its market leading brand of cigarettes to defend market share against aggressive US rivals. The brand had lost substantial market share to lower-priced competitors. Customers were simply not convinced that Marlboro was worth the premium price it had been charging. New strategic thinking has to accommodate the fact that customers are becoming more sophisticated and more marketing literate. The sophisticated customer is less likely to be attracted to cheap products with low quality, and yet neither be won by image-based advertising. The implications are clear. Differentiation needs to be based on providing demonstrably superior value to customers.

A third major trend is in both the level and nature of competition. Competition is becoming more intense and more global in nature. As international trade becomes more liberalized under the aegis of the World Trade Organization (WTO), the successor to the General Agreement on Tariffs and Trade (GATT), so firms face tougher international competition at home and increased opportunities abroad. Time and distance are shrinking rapidly as communications become near instantaneous. When Deng Xiaoping, the Chinese Paramount Leader, died on 18 February

1997 news of his death reached London, Washington and Bonn before many in Beijing knew about it. Firms are increasingly thinking global in their strategies, especially as cross-national segments are beginning to emerge for products and services from fast foods through toys to computers and automobiles. The increasingly widespread use of the Internet for promoting and marketing both products and services now means that communications know no national borders. Ohmae's 'borderless world' (Ohmae, 1990) exists in cyberspace at least!

Not only are markets becoming more competitive through more players emerging in them. Those firms that survive and thrive in these more competitive conditions are, by their very nature, tougher competitors. Weak firms are being shaken out of markets where they do not have clear positionings and attendant capabilities. The implications of heightened, more aggressive competition, both domestic and international, are that firms will need to look even more closely at their scope of operations and targeting in the future.

And yet the executive must confront the central paradox in all this. As markets become harsher in their judgements and in the level of competitiveness faced, companies are under growing pressure to collaborate with and partner others. Increasingly, collaboration is taking place with suppliers, customers and even competitors. The clarity of the past has gone and executives are having to deal with highly ambiguous new roles.

18.1.3 Organizational change

The 1990s saw a major emphasis in many organizations on corporate 'downsizing' or 'restructuring'. In attempts to deal with the difficult economic conditions of the early 1990s in Western, developed markets costs came under increasing pressure and layers of both workers and managers were removed.

While 'downsizing' is now less fashionable, as firms have realized that there is only so much fat that can be cut before you damage the muscle and too aggressive slimming can lead to *anorexia industrialis* (the excessive desire to be leaner and fitter leading to total emaciation and eventual death) its impact on organizational structures for the new millennium has been far broader. These are manifest in two main directions. First the impact within the firm, second the impact on inter-firm relations.

Within firms the boundaries between functional areas are becoming more blurred. Where firms were once organized with clear-cut divisions between marketing, finance and operations it is now recognized that 'functional silos' can result in myopic operations and suboptimal strategies. In leading firms the functional boundaries have long since been replaced by process teams that can view the operations of the organization in holistic terms and will not be hampered by petty rivalries between functions.

At the same time the role of marketing *per se* in the organization has been challenged (Brady and Davis, 1993; Doyle, 1995). In 1994 Lever Brothers abolished the job of marketing director, merged sales and marketing departments into business groups focusing on consumer research and product development. They also created 'customer development teams' responsible for relationship building with key retail customers (*The Economist*, 9 April 1994). Similarly, in 1997 IBM announced a new approach to its global marketing activities. This took the form of the Customer Relationship Management (CRM) initiative, working through core processes such as market management, relationship management, opportunity management, information management and skills management. This is very different from conventional views of how marketing operates (Mitchell, 1997).

Marketing departments can get in the way of serving customers for two main reasons. The first is territorial. They may see dealing with customers as their preserve and wish to retain the power and influence that goes with that. Second, however, they may encourage others in the organization to off-load responsibility for customer building to the marketing department. This creates the dangerous view that others do not need to concern themselves with customers, someone else will take care of it. Indeed, one view is that the days of conventional marketing have long since finished, and the challenge now is to design and implement better ways of managing the process of going to market. That process cuts across traditional functional boundaries as well as external boundaries with partners.

Some writers go further in criticizing the performance of marketing in organizations. Webster (1997) concludes that marketing has been effective in tactics (selling and promotional programmes), somewhat effective in advocating a customer viewpoint, but ineffective in developing robust value propositions and competitive positioning. Doyle (1997) sees marketing departments as the source of radical expansion strategies which can achieve spectacular growth is sales and profit, but which ultimately fail because they do not create customer value. In Doyle's view robust growth strategies come from providing superior customer value and from continuous learning and innovation, based on long-term investments in relationships. A compelling case begins to emerge for radically rethinking the role of marketing as a strategic force in companies.

Between firms the boundaries of where one finishes and the next starts are also increasingly blurred. Boundaries with suppliers, distributors and customers are changing as more businesses understand the need to manage the entire value chain from raw materials through to customers, and work more closely with partner firms to achieve added value through the chain. A number of authors now refer to the 'virtual organization' (Piercy and Cravens, 1995) as networks and alliances create supra-organizational entities.

The above major trends and changes taking place both in markets and organizations lead to a need to reassess business strategy in general and marketing strategy in particular. The strategies that will be successful in the future will need to be responsive and adaptive rather than rigid and fixed. Key will be creating an organizational context in which learning can take place, market changes can be identified and capabilities can be fashioned to ensure a strategic fit between market and firm.

18.2 *Fundamentals of strategy in a changing world*

Figure 18.1 shows a number of factors that are increasingly essential in dealing with complex and changing circumstances.

18.2.1 The learning organization

Central to developing a sustainable competitive advantage in rapidly, and often unpredictably, changing circumstances, is the ability to learn and adapt (see Evans and Wurster, 1997; Prokesch, 1997). The competitive dynamics of markets with new entrants, substitute technologies and shifts in customer preferences can swiftly erode static advantages built on the 'generic' strategies of cost leadership or product differentiation (McKee and Varadarajan, 1995). Organizational learning, however, offers the potential both to respond to, and act on, opportunities in the markets of the firm. Indeed, Dickson (1992) suggests that the ability to learn faster than competitors may be the only real source of sustainable competitive advantage.

Learning is manifest in the knowledge, experience and information held in an organization (Mahoney, 1995). It resides in both people and technical systems. Learning involves the acquisition, processing, storing and retrieval (dissemination)

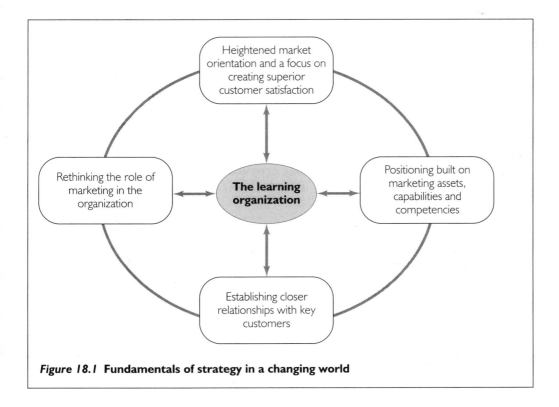

Figure 18.1 **Fundamentals of strategy in a changing world**

of knowledge. A major challenge for many organizations is to create the combination of culture and climate to maximize learning (Slater and Narver, 1995). At the human level managerial systems need to be established to create and control knowledge. At the technical level systems need to be established to facilitate the accumulation and storage of relevant information in a manner that makes it readily accessible to those who need to access it.

Much of an organization's knowledge base typically resides in the heads of managers and workers. When personnel leave through 'downsizing' or recruitment by competitors, that knowledge may be lost or, more damagingly, gained by a competitor. Employment contracts of key personnel are increasingly including 'golden handcuffs' which prohibit critical managers from taking their knowledge to competitors. Organizations are also increasingly looking for ways of extracting the knowledge of their key people and transmitting it to others in the organization, through expert systems and training processes, so that the knowledge is more secure and embedded in the fabric of the organization.

Of particular importance in the context of marketing strategy is the development of knowledge and skills in how to create superior customer value. Slater and Narver (1995) show that a primary focus of market orientation is to create superior customer value, and that in turn needs to be based on knowledge derived from customer and competitor analysis, together with knowledge gleaned from suppliers, businesses in different industries, government sources, universities, consultants and other potential sources. They conclude that learning organizations continually acquire, process and disseminate knowledge about markets, products, technologies and business processes based on experience, experimentation, information from customers, suppliers, competitors and other sources. This learning enables them to anticipate and act on opportunities in turbulent and fragmented markets.

And yet developing learning capabilities need not be complex and sophisticated. Inuit's improvements to Quicken software come from a form of organized 'customer stalking' where employees follow customers home and watch their every move and reaction to the product. The development by Kimberly-Clark of Huggies (training pants for children coming out of nappies) came from sending employees to the homes of customers with small children and listening. They learned essentially that the market is driven by parental guilt about how long a child stays in nappies, not the child's waste disposal problems! Superior learning capabilities may be as much about market sensing and understanding as it is about utilizing technology.

While the central requirement for competing in the future is learning, a number of other more specific building blocks can be suggested as important ingredients in fashioning competitive strategy.

18.2.2 Heightened market orientation and focus on creating superior customer value

In increasingly crowded and competitive markets there is no substitute for being market-oriented. Put simply, a market orientation focuses the firm's activities on meeting the needs and requirements of customers better than competitors. This in turn requires finding out what will give customers value and ensuring that the firm's energies are directed towards providing that. Identifying ways of providing superior customer value is one of the central challenges of management for the new millennium.

A market orientation does not imply over-sophisticated marketing operation. Indeed it has been argued by some that marketing departments can themselves get in the way of providing superior customer value.

As Simon (1996) shows, successful medium-sized German firms (he calls these 'hidden champions') demonstrate a clear focus on providing solutions for their customers. These companies go deep rather than broad (they specialize in narrow niches of the market), but operate across global markets. Their success is based on understanding their customers' needs and being highly responsive to delivering solutions to customers' problems. They typically have dominant market shares of their chosen niches world-wide. For example, Krones has 80 per cent world-wide market share in bottle labelling machines, Hauni is world market leader in cigarette machines with 90 per cent share of high-speed machines, Brita has 85 per cent of the world market for point-of-use water filters, and Baader's share of the world market for fish processing equipment is 90 per cent. All have a narrow focus, but operate across global markets.

Winterhalter Gastronom make dishwashers for commercial use. There are many markets for these products, including hospitals, schools, companies, hotels, military institutions, etc., each with different product requirements. Many products are on the market and Winterhalter found that, globally, they commanded only 2 per cent of the market. This led to a refocusing of the firm's strategy. First, they decided to focus solely on hotels and restaurants (the second part of the company name was added after this decision was made). The business was redefined as the supplier of clean glasses and dishes for hotels and restaurants. In addition to designing the dishwashers to meet the specific requirements of the hotel and restaurant market the company extended its product line to include water-conditioning devices, an own-brand of detergent and round-the-clock service. Thus they were taking full responsibility for the provision of the clean glasses and dishes, going into depth with the chosen segment, rather than simply offering dishwashers across the market and leaving the provision of services and detergent to others. The company now has a 20 per cent world market share of its chosen segment and climbing (Simon, 1996).

In the quest to provide superior customer value no firm can stand still. What offers better value than competitors today will be standard tomorrow. Innovation, the constant improving of the offering to customers, is essential for sustained competitive advantage. Again, Simon's hidden champions demonstrate this clearly. Many of these firms created their own markets through technological breakthroughs but then continued to innovate to stay ahead of further industry entrants. They typically hold relatively large numbers of patents and derive disproportionate amounts of profits from new products. Critically, however, they achieve a balance between being technology-driven and market-led. While they are determined to exploit their technological advantages they also ensure that these are aligned with changing market requirements. W.L. Gore Inc, for example, an American 'hidden champion', maker of semi-permeable Gore-Tex fabrics, has exploited its technological lead in fabric manufacture to develop products suitable for its customers in the garment and shoe industries (Simon, 1996).

The focus of activities in firms that are truly market-oriented and intent on creating superior value for their customers is on finding solutions to those customers' problems. Rather than a focus on selling the firm's own existing products it sets out first to identify current and future customer problems and then to find solutions to them. Solutions may involve creating new products and services, integrating the offerings of other providers (through alliances), and even in some instances accepting that customers cannot be well served and recommending alternative suppliers. After exhausting all other options a truly market-oriented firm can gain more customer goodwill (and ultimately more long-term business) by admitting that it cannot provide exactly what the customer wants rather than trying to persuade the customer to accept second best, or even pretending that the solution offered is appropriate.

18.2.3 Positioning built on marketing assets, capabilities and competencies

Much of the emphasis in the strategy literature in the early 1990s has focused on the 'resource-based theory' of the firm (see Grant, 1995 for a summary). This theory emphasizes the need for strategies to be based on the resources and capabilities of the firm, rather than merely chasing customers irrespective of the ability of the firm to serve them. Resource-based theorists, however, are in danger of losing sight of the fact that resources are valuable only when they are translated into providing something that customers want. This is the essence of the 'asset-based marketing' approach espoused in this book.

Markets change, and so too must assets and competencies. They need to be constantly improved and developed if the firm is to thrive. An essential task for marketing management is to identify the competencies and assets that will be needed in the future, as well as those that are needed today, so that they can be built or acquired in advance.

This may be far from easy, and freedom of manoeuvre may be limited. For example, IBM's core capability in mainframe computers became irrelevant to the PC-dominated market of the 1980s, and the company's performance across the world suffered dramatically. In the 1990s, however, the new head of IBM, Lou Gerstner's strategic goal has been to dominate the global network marketplace, where those mainframe capabilities are critical.

As discussed in chapter 5, marketing assets are any properties that can be exploited in the marketplace to create or sustain a competitive advantage. They range from recognized brand names, through unique use of distribution channels, to information and quality control systems. These assets are the resource endowments the business has created or acquired over time and now has available to deploy in the market. Competencies are the skills that are used to deploy the assets to best effect in the market.

These definitions are in line with resource-based theorists such as Barney (1991), who suggest that it is management that is the most important resource because they make use of the assets and other resources available to them based on their knowledge of the market acquired through their previous learning.

As we saw in chapter 5, Day (1994) goes on to identify three main types of competencies: outside-in; inside-out; and spanning and integrating competencies. Outside-in competencies are those skills and abilities that enable a business to understand its customers and create closer linkages with them. Inside-out competencies are the internal capabilities of the firm and its employees that can be deployed in the marketplace to provide better products and services to customers. Spanning and integrating competencies bring together the inside-out and the outside-in to ensure delivery of appropriate products and services to customers.

Not all assets and capabilities may be vested in the focal firm. Increasingly, companies are creating alliances and networks with others that enable them to leverage further assets and competencies of partner firms (see chapter 8). Alliances can offer four main sets of assets and competencies: access to new markets; access to managerial competence; access to technological competence; and economic benefits.

There are, however, problems in realizing the advantages offered by alliances and networks of collaborating firms. Many of the alliances established in the early 1990s have failed. Understanding of the dynamics of alliances and the critical executive skills required by these new organizations are sadly limited (see chapter 8).

Taken together marketing assets and competencies/capabilities are the basis on which any competitive positioning is built. Ideally firms should seek to build their positions on the basis of assets and competencies which are superior to those of their competitors and difficult to duplicate. They should also seek to create or acquire assets and competencies that can be exploited in many other situations (e.g. extend their brand name into new markets, exploit their technology in new industries, use their networks in different ways). A critical issue for the future is how different assets and competencies can be combined to create new products and services (Hamel and Prahalad, 1994).

18.2.4 Establishing closer relationships with key customers

In chapter 15 we discussed the ways in which firms can build closer relationships with their customers. Fundamental issues include which customers to build those relationships with and how to build them.

Relationship marketing (Payne, 1995) has been one of the most significant developments in marketing thought of recent years. While it has been recognized as important in some markets for some time and under different labels (e.g. the personal account managers in financial services), it is now generally agreed that customer retention, through superior service and relationship-building, is applicable in far wider markets.

In consumer markets relationships can be built initially through branding and reputation creation. In the past relationships in business markets have been stereotyped as between individuals – salesperson and purchasing officer. However, in modern business-to-business markets the pressure is for team-based selling and relationship-building across the whole spectrum of internal departments. The challenge is to become the 'outsource of preference' by understanding the customer's business and adding value in excess of cost. Similarly, Simon (1996) stresses that the relationships which endure in business markets are those based on sound economic and business grounds rather than, perhaps ephemeral, personal/social bases. Relationships and reputations can be far harder for competitors to copy than possibly transitory product features, special offers or deals.

Zielke and Pohl (1996) show that key factors for success in the machine tool industry have changed since the early 1990s. In 1990 the keys to success were cross-functional teams, single sourcing and group working. These factors were seen to differentiate the better performing firms from the weaker ones. By 1996, however, these operational characteristics had become standard in the industry and no longer differentiated winners from losers. What now differentiates the more successful companies is their relationships with customers and suppliers. The market leaders are now managing the complete value chain, with suppliers becoming increasingly concerned with new product development and quality improvement. They are also linking pay and other rewards with customer-related performance targets. While efficiency has been the focus at the start of the decade, the emphasis has now shifted to customer and supplier relationship management.

Not all customers, however, place great value on ever closer relationships with their suppliers. Similarly the costs of creating closer relationships with some customers (in terms of time, effort and financial resource) may well outweigh the long-term commercial benefits. What will become increasingly important will be for firms to decide the optimum intensity of relationship with each customer or customer group and then find effective and efficient means of establishing that level. It is likely that any firm will be operating in a number of different marketing modes depending on the customers served. For some key accounts a heavy emphasis on one-to-one close relationship building to create 'partners' might be applicable, while at the same time other groups are marketed less intensively so as to create 'advocates' rather than partners. For yet other customers of the same firm a mass marketing approach might be applicable to secure their business in the first place. *Multi-mode marketing*, the adoption of different marketing approaches for different customers or customer groups, is likely to take the place of more uniform marketing to all customers.

18.2.5 Rethinking the role of marketing in the organization

The above lead to the inevitable conclusion that the role and function of marketing within the organization (or within the 'virtual network') needs to be redefined and reasserted.

Basic to that rethinking is to escape from the notion that marketing is essentially a business function, a department on the organization chart. Increasingly, marketing is being seen as a process within the value chain, a process responsible for ensuring the creation of value for customers in both the short and long term. This requires a focus on marketing skills rather than on marketing titles (Brown, 1995). Structures need to be created that facilitate rapid response and flexibility rather than hinder it. Indeed, it interesting to note that some of the successful companies, such as Virgin, Marks & Spencer and The Body Shop do not even have marketing departments, yet few would dispute that they are close to their customers and responsive to their needs (Doyle, 1995).

As Brown (1995) notes:

> There are now two types of corporation: those with a marketing department and those with a marketing soul. Even a cursory glance at the latest Fortune 500 shows that the latter are the top performing companies, while the former, steeped in the business traditions of the past, are fast disappearing.

Simon (1996) also notes that many of the firms in his sample of 'hidden champions' do not have marketing departments. They share, however, two main traits. First they are extremely close to their customers and ensure that all employees recognize their role in serving them. Second, they focus on solving customers' problems through innovation to improve on their offerings to customers, continuously providing additional customer value. These two traits are the essence of a market orientation, but are achieved without the trappings of a marketing department.

It is important in defining the role of marketing for the future to recognize that marketing operates at two main levels: strategic and operational. At the operational level brand managers and marketing managers deal with day-to-day marketing tasks such as liaison with market research companies, advertising and public relations agencies and so on. In FMCG companies they also spend much of their time organizing trade and consumer promotions, special deals, competitions, etc.

At the strategic level, however, marketing is more concerned with decisions as to which markets to operate in and how to compete successfully in them. At this level marketing is not a functional activity, but requires input from across the organization of alternative perspectives and skills. As noted earlier, the challenge is then to manage the process of going to market to build superior customer value, through a complex of resources, capabilities and relationships that make up the offering.

Marketing needs to become and remain flexible and responsive to change. That entails distinguishing the philosophy from the trappings. At a strategic level everyone in the organization should place customers at the forefront of their minds because, as the CEO of Xerox says in the firm's mission statement, ultimately, it is customers who will decide whether the firm survives and whether employees and managers have a job or not in the future.

Handy (see Abrahams, 1996) talks of 'shamrock organizations' emerging for the future. These will consist of three leaves. The first will be a small core of professional senior managers on fixed contracts who will run the business and make the strategic decisions such as the markets in which the firm will operate and the ways in which it will create competitive advantage (the positioning decisions discussed in this book). The second leaf will be those on fixed-term contracts providing services such as public relations, database management and advertising. These managers will be specialists in operational and implementation aspects of marketing, but will be closely directed as to where their efforts should go. The third leaf will be *ad hoc* contractors who will supply specialist expertise, such as advertising agencies, marketing research agencies, design consultancies, etc.

In the highly competitive markets envisaged for the foreseeable future ability to assimilate and act on knowledge, to create strategies based on assets and competencies, to establish close, deep relationships with chosen market segments, and finally the ability to redefine the scope and role of marketing within the organization will be the bases for creating competitive advantage.

18.3 *Competitive positioning strategies*

As has been argued above, competitive positioning is about making choices that ensure a fit between chosen market targets and the competencies and assets the firm

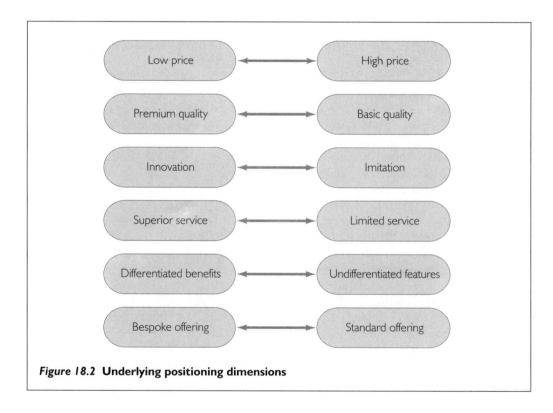

Figure 18.2 **Underlying positioning dimensions**

can deploy to serve those chosen targets more effectively than competitors. While there are, in reality, an infinite number of different ways in which firms might position themselves in their markets, these can be summarized on the basis of the emphasis they give to six main dimensions of differentiation.

Figure 18.2 shows these six dimensions. Positioning could be based on: price; quality (or more correctly, grade); service; tailoring; benefit differentiation; or innovation. While individual firms may choose to position on more than one dimension simultaneously they often find that they are contradictory. For example, offering a higher grade of product is generally incongruent with keeping costs, and hence prices, as low as possible. Indeed, charging low prices for a high-grade product may create confusion in the minds of customers. The key to creating sustainable positions is to ensure that they are built on the marketing assets and competencies of the firm. Figure 18.3 shows the assets and competencies necessary for each positioning strategy.

Position	Customer groups	Strategic focus	Assets & Competencies
Low price	Price-sensitive customers	Internal efficiency	Cost control systems, TQM processes, procurement, information systems
Superior quality	Premium demanding customers	Superior quality, image management	Market sensing, quality control and assurance, brand and reputation, supply chain management
Rapid innovation	Innovators and early adopters	First to market	New Product/Service Development, R&D technical skills, creative skills
Superior service	Service-sensitive customers	Relationship-building	Market sensing, customer linking, service systems, skilled staff, feedback systems, continuous monitoring
Differentiated benefits	Benefit segments	Focused targeting	Market sensing, NP/SD, creativity in segmentation
Bespoke offering	Individual customers	Tailoring to individual customer wants and needs	Market sensing, customer bonding, operations flexibility

Figure 18.3 Basic positioning strategies

18.3.1 Price positioning

Costs must be kept in check – at least as low or lower than competitors – for a low price position to be sustainable. If there is no cost advantage, price wars may put the instigator at a financial disadvantage and the whole positioning strategy may not be sustainable. Positioning as the low-price supplier requires strong inside-out and spanning capabilities. Effective cost-control systems (through activity-based costing) are needed not only within the firm's own operations but also within suppliers' operations. Procurement of raw materials and other factor inputs is organized around keeping costs to a minimum. Distribution logistics are similarly managed for minimum cost.

While the low price position is a viable option for some firms there is a constant need to work at keeping costs down, especially when new competitors enter the market with new operating methods or unique assets that can be used to undercut the costs of incumbents.

For a price positioning strategy to be successful in the marketplace the existence of a viable, price-sensitive customer segment is also required. In most markets there are customers who will buy primarily on price. In the 1990s, however, it became clear that such customers also expect a base level of service and product quality such that rock bottom prices alone are unlikely to be good enough reasons to buy.

In November 1996, for example, the discount grocery retailer KwikSave announced the closure of 107 of its UK stores. KwikSave offered a no-frills, low-price, 'pile it high/sell it cheap' option to its customers. By the mid-1990s, however, this positioning had been eroded. KwikSave was caught between the leading multiples such as Tesco, Sainsbury and Safeway who were offering low prices coupled with superior service and more attractive shopping experiences, and newly entered discounters such as Aldi and Netto offering lower prices than KwikSave could achieve through their high-volume, very minimal service operations. KwikSave admitted that it had not been sufficiently customer-oriented, had gone too much for the deal, tried to expand too rapidly, had not offered 'modern' goods such as fresh produce, health and beauty items, and items for babies. More than 40 per cent of in-store staff were on temporary or part-time contracts, and there were few incentives to provide a high level of customer service. It was also believed that KwikSave was around 3–4 years behind its rivals in its use of technology. It accepted Switch, for example, as a way of directly debiting customer accounts, but failed to capture and analyze the data afforded to allow more detailed understanding of customers and their purchasing patterns. Sales per square foot of space at KwikSave were estimated to be around half those of Sainsbury (*Guardian*, 8 November 1996).

Price positioning can be successful where there is a clearly defined, price-sensitive sector of the market and the firm has a cost advantage in serving that market.

At £5,999 the Skoda Felicia automobile is positioned at the low-price end of the spectrum to attract highly price-sensitive, private car buyers. Indeed, the company describes its target customers as OPTIEs (Over-mortgaged, Post-Thatcherite Individuals) who are carrying negative equity and have concern over their financial futures. These consumers see property, money and job as far less important than family, health and personal relationships. Impressing others with their cars is a low priority to them, 92 per cent of them believing that cars are over-hyped and over-priced, and 66 per cent believing that if you take the badge (brand name) off a car its hard to tell one make from another. The Felicia is marketed as 'sensibly stylish with honest intentions' and the advertisements show the Volkswagen (VW) logo behind the car, building on the solid, quality associations of the parent company. It also takes full advantage of low-cost production in Central Europe (*Marketing Business*, July/August 1995).

Some firms position at the other end of the price spectrum. They deliberately price their products and services more highly than competitors to create an exclusivity for their offerings. High-price positionings are usually accompanied by higher quality, branded offerings requiring strong reputations and clearly superior images (e.g. Harrods department store in Knightsbridge, cosmetics and designer label fashion wear). The competencies required for high-price (premium) positionings to be effective are centred on the ability to create a superior, or exclusive, image, that customers are willing to pay a premium to be associated with. Brand assets in particular need to be built through the use of creative promotional campaigns.

18.3.2 Quality positioning

Positioning as a high quality (grade) supplier also requires effective internal control systems, especially quality assessment and assurance. Beyond control, however, it also requires technical competence, particularly in engineering and manufacturing where physical products are produced. Most significantly, however, it requires a clear view of what constitutes 'quality' in the eyes of the customer. That entails the outside-in capabilities of market sensing and customer bonding. Also important in delivering high quality products and services is supply-chain management, ensuring that the inputs are of the required quality, not simply the cheapest available. Marks & Spencer have a reputation for building long-term, demanding relationships with their suppliers to ensure that the products they put their labels on are of the required quality. To provide high technical quality requires specific expertise.

There are four Betty's Tea Rooms in Yorkshire and one Taylor's. Together they sell 2 million cups of tea each year. They don't advertise, but people flock in their thousands and are prepared to queue for seats. The atmosphere is elegant, sophisticated. Waiters and waitresses are formally dressed in the style of Victorian servants. The tea is perfect and the cakes are delicious. The pastries range from exotic Amadeus Torte to local Yorkshire curd tarts. The company was started in Harrogate by a Swiss confectioner, Frederick Belmont, in 1919. The company's bakers and confectioners still train in Lucerne. The company has built on its brand asset by opening related gift shops on the premises, selling confectionery suited to the tourists who visit. They also sell their products by mail order. More recently they have marketed Yorkshire Tea which has become a major brand in the beverages market (Kotler *et al.*, 1996).

Often critical to a quality positioning are the marketing assets of brand image and reputation (see above). Image and reputation can take years to create and, once established, need to be nurtured and, when necessary, defended vigorously.

To customers quality is manifest through better reliability, durability and aesthetic appearance. For quality positionings to be viable customers must be prepared to pay for superior quality as there are usually, though not always, higher costs associated with offering a higher quality product. In the automotive industry German manufacturers such as Mercedes, BMW and Audi have successfully positioned their offerings at the high quality end of the spectrum through superior design, technical engineering skills ('Vorsprung durch Technik' – leading through technology) and attention to quality control through the manufacturing process.

We should bear in mind in all this, however, that quality and value are decided by customers in the marketplace, not by engineers in the factory, or marketing executives in the marketing department. In what may be a blueprint for other organizations, executives at Royal Mail (RM) are appraised in part by customer-perceived service levels, not actual service levels. RM received many complaints about queuing times in post offices. They reduced queuing times, but customers still complained. They redecorated some post offices and found that in these locations customers ceased complaining about queuing times although the times were the same as elsewhere. RM had learned that quality and value are only what customers perceive them to be.

18.3.3 Innovation positioning

Where markets are changing rapidly, especially as a result of technological developments, there may be opportunities to position on the basis of innovativeness, or speed-to-market. In the PC market, for example, leading firms such as Toshiba are constantly improving on their products and building in technological advances to keep their products ahead of their competitors. Hamel and Prahalad (1991) suggest that firms should encourage 'fast failure', that is, encourage the test launch of new products, in the recognition that many may fail but that some will succeed. Fast failure, they argue, is preferable to smothering new ideas at birth or delaying their launch through over-elaborate screening systems.

In his study of German 'hidden champions', Simon (1996) emphasizes their continuous processes of product and service improvement (*Kaizen*). Constant innovation is shown to be one of the significant characteristics of these world market leaders. By the mid-1990s, however, thinking in Japan, the home of *Kaizen*, had moved on. The challenge for many Japanese firms is now believed to be radical and major change, rather than incremental improvement, to enable them to compete in the future.

The key competencies required include excellent new product development skills together with technical and creative abilities. These are combinations of inside-out and spanning competencies. Once new product ideas have been crystallized, however, it is important to test them out on customers (through fast failure or more conventional means) to avoid the launch of highly innovative, but essentially unwanted, products, such as the Sinclair C5 electric car.

Tellis and Golder (1996), in a study of first-to-market firms, concluded that for many firms a more successful strategy is to be a fast follower. Under this approach firms learn from the mistakes of the pioneers and capitalize on the growth phase of the market without incurring the costs of establishing the market in the first place. Moore (1991), in his study of innovation in high technology markets, concludes that the critical aspect of new product success is bridging the 'chasm' between innovators (those who will be attracted to an innovation because of its innovative nature) and the early majority who represent the beginnings of the mass market. It is this chasm that, in Moore's opinion, accounts for the failure of many new products.

James Dyson is an inventor who has successfully positioned his firm as the provider of innovative solutions to everyday problems. In January 1997 he won the European Design Award for his innovative vacuum cleaner (see below). Dyson started inventing at the age of 28 when he recognized a design fault in conventional wheelbarrows. When full, the barrow, with a single, thin wheel at the front, was prone to tipping over. He replaced the wheel with a large red ball which solved the problem. When he set up in business the 'ball barrow' was an immediate success selling over 60,000 per year. Following that success he designed a new garden roller which was light and manoeuvrable when not in use but heavy enough to roll gardens flat. His innovation was to use a hollow plastic roller that could be filled with water when in use but drained when not in use. The bagless vacuum cleaners followed and he is now considering modernizing other household items such as dishwashers, washing machines and fridges as well as marketing a diesel exhaust cleaner that reduces toxic emissions. The success of the £100 million turnover company has been based on innovation, first to market with revolutionary designs of everyday products, offering superior value to customers.

In the early 1990s Dyson's new vacuum cleaner was launched onto the UK market. The Dyson Dual Cyclone operates in a different way from conventional cleaners in that it creates a cyclone of air (faster than the speed of sound) and does away with the conventional bags to collect the dust. On conventional cleaners the pores of the bags gradually fill so that the cleaner works less well when half full. The Dyson cleaner claims three times the performance of conventional vacuum cleaners but, at around £200, costs up to double the price. Manufacturers of conventional vacuum cleaners were unimpressed by the new product as they derive good on-going profits from the sale of the disposable dust bags (that market alone being worth around £100 million per annum). They fought to keep the Dyson from conventional outlets and Dyson eventually hit on the idea of selling through mail order catalogues (a further innovation in the vacuum cleaner business). Despite the price disadvantage the Dyson had achieved 25 per cent UK market share within three years of its launch. Not content with the UK market, Dyson has also achieved the almost unique success of a British appliance manufacturer with a substantial market share in Japan, rather than vice versa.

Innovation may also come in the form of new processes or approaches to market. Dell, for example, sell PCs direct to businesses (and to a lesser extent household consumers) rather than through retail shops and resellers. Direct marketing eliminates the intermediaries and also speeds up the time to market of the computers. About 80 per cent of the cost of a PC is made up of components (such as micro-processor chips) the price of which is falling at around 30 per cent per annum. Too much inventory, therefore, means high-cost products waiting to be sold at high prices. Similarly, when technology changes (e.g. from 486 to Pentium-based processors) a company can be left with large stocks of out-of-date computers. By selling direct Dell turns over its inventory every 14 days, compared to 50 days for Compaq, its rival. That has been estimated to give Dell a 3 per cent cost advantage. As important, however, has been the market advantage that has been conveyed through the switch from reseller to direct marketing. Dell has been growing at 50 per cent per annum in a market growing at 20 per cent: it is now the fifth largest manufacturer of computers (*The Economist*, 5 October 1996).

18.3.4 Service positioning

Positioning on the basis of offering superior service, or rather service clearly tailored to the needs of the target market, is increasingly being used. Variations in the nature and level of service offered, coupled with differences in requirements across customer groups, mean that service positioning can be viable and attractive for more than one company in a market. Critical to providing superior service are market sensing skills which can identify what level/type of service is required, customer bonding skills that build closer relationships with key customers, service systems that assist the service providers in delivering service to customers and monitoring skills that can regularly assess the customer satisfaction with the level and type of service provided. Most critical of all to providing superior service are the people, or staff, that actually provide the service. Selection, training, motivation and reward of service staff are areas that need high priority in firms seeking to establish a competitive edge through service provision.

Firms seeking to create a service edge to position themselves as offering superior service to that of competitors need first to understand how their customers judge service, what dimensions are important to them and how they are manifest. They then need to put in place strategies and systems to ensure their staff can deliver superior service (see chapter 15).

Otis Elevator recognized the importance of providing excellent service in the elevator business. Customers preferred to deal directly with Otis rather than go through an intermediary, and hence the company set up the OTISLINE through which customers can contact the firm's service centre 24 hours a day. The service has been used to market the firm's offerings and to give customers confidence in them. It also formed the basis for the company making further improvements in information systems, including REM (remote elevator monitoring) identifying problems before lifts break down. The system improved response times through better call management, improved diagnostic capabilities and strengthened the service team by providing them with better communications. The result has been significant increases in customer satisfaction levels (Armistead and Clark, 1992).

18.3.5 Benefit positioning

Benefit positioning rests on clearly identifying alternative benefit segments within markets and then focusing on providing what they want. As discussed in chapter 9, segmenting markets on the basis of the benefits customers are seeking can often help identify new market opportunities and suggest ways in which marketing effort can be more effectively targeted.

Positioning on this basis is dependent on having well-developed outside-in competencies to identify the benefits customers are seeking in the first place and creatively to segment the market into meaningful but commercially viable sectors. It can also require effective new product/service development skills to ensure that the benefits sought are actually delivered to customers through building in the relevant features.

Fairy Liquid is a washing up liquid that has been consistently positioned on the basis of the twin benefits it provides to users: clean dishes but smooth hands for the washer-up. The product was test launched in Birmingham in 1959 when the market was in its infancy, with only 17 per cent of consumers using washing up liquid, the remainder relying on soap powders or household soap to wash their dishes. The national launch in 1960 involved a massive door-to-door programme, which delivered 15 million sample bottles to 85 per cent of houses in the UK. The launch platform stressed that the product was strong enough to remove dirt and grease from plates and dishes but was mild on hands.

By 1980 one billion bottles of Fairy Liquid had been sold. Product improvements in 1982 enabled the advertisements to demonstrate a 20 per cent improvement in the volume of dishes that could be washed with one bottle (a 20 per cent 'mileage' improvement) and the brand had reached 27 per cent market share. Further continuous product improvement followed with the launch of a lemon-scented variant in 1984/5 (share climbed to 32 per cent) and further increased mileage in 1988 (by 15 per cent) and 1992 (by a further 50 per cent and signalled by a change of name to Fairy Excel) taking market share above 50 per cent for the first time. In 1993 Fairy Excel Plus replaced Fairy Excel offering yet a further 50 per cent mileage improvement but still retaining the mildness to hands. One manager was quoted as saying 'the heritage of the brand is so linked with mildness it [putting anything less mild on the market] would be regarded as treachery by the consumer.'

In the over-crowded beer market Boddingtons Draught Bitter has been successfully positioned on the basis of the benefit of 'smoothness'. In a market where most beers have emphasized the sociability of beer drinking, or the personal (generally macho) characteristics of beer drinkers, Boddington advertising has focused on conveying the 'cream of Manchester' attribute through poster and press advertising. Indeed, the advertising campaign won the 1994 IPA Advertising Awards Gold Medal.

Automobile manufacturers have been particularly effective at positioning their offerings to convey particular benefits. Estate cars offer additional carrying capacity, sports cars offer performance benefits, and four-wheel drive cars offer off-road capabilities (though many purchasers never test this out in reality!). Most recently, manufacturers have been developing small cars for city use in anticipation of legislation concerning pollution levels. The Ford Ka, the Renault Twingo and the Mercedes Smart car are early examples. Volkswagen, General Motors and Rover also have similar cars in the pipeline. These cars are typically compact and fuel economical to reduce noxious emissions in city centres.

Yamaha were world market leaders in fine upright and grand pianos. Globally they held 40 per cent of the market, but the market was in decline at around 10 per cent per annum. Market research showed that many pianos were seldom played, gathered dust and were out of tune. Using its competencies in digital music technology (the firm had pioneered electronic keyboards) the firm set about offering additional benefits in the pianos it sold. They developed the 'disklavier' which was a traditional piano (upright and grand) which could be played normally but also had an additional feature. Attached to the piano was an electronic device that enabled the owner to play pre-recorded music on their own piano. The device accepted a 3.5 in disk, similar to a computer floppy disk, which contained the recorded music and played it on the piano. On its launch in Japan the product was an immediate success, rising to 20 per cent market share within three years. The firm also worked on the possibilities retrofitting existing pianos with the device to expand the market potential even further.

The 1996 Harrods catalogue carried an advertisement for a digital grand piano:

> Yamaha DC11 Digital Piano – the perfect choice for real music lovers, the DC11 disklavier is a high quality acoustic piano with an added disc drive. Play as a normal instrument or use the computer facility to play back the disc of your choice. In addition record your own music directly onto disc while you play. Usual price £18,099, SALE PRICE £15,299.

Interestingly the concept was not completely new. In 1930s America pianolas (pianos that could play rolls of punched paper when peddled) were very popular!

The yellow fats market has also been extensively segmented on the basis of benefits sought and individual products positioned to appeal to specific benefit segments (see chapter 12). In the 1960s butter dominated the market, with margarine seen as a cheap, down-market substitute. In the 1970s, however, concerns over healthy eating led to the launch of Flora by Van den Bergh and Vitalite by Kraft, both positioned as more healthy alternatives to butter. The features included polyunsaturated fat rather than the saturated fat of butter (which had been linked with cholesterol and heart disease). Van den Bergh also launched Outline, aimed at the weight-conscious sector conveying low calories as its prime benefit. The competition to offer yet more healthy spreads led to lower fat levels in 'extra light' and 'reduced salt' versions. During the 1980s, however, some consumers began to crave the benefit of a 'real butter taste' once again, but without the health concerns of full fat butter. In the early 1980s Van den Bergh launched Krona, and in 1983 Dairy Crest launched Clover. In 1991 Van den Bergh launched its new butter substitute 'I Can't Believe It's Not Butter' with one of the most innovative brand names to date. The name, though clumsy, was certainly memorable and clearly conveyed the benefit it was designed to offer – butter taste at lower fat levels. St Ivel followed the same positioning in 1995 with 'Utterly Butterly'.

Positioning based on benefits sought by customers is conventionally associated with consumer markets. In fact, the same is true of the strategies of successful firms in business-to-business markets. In both cases, benefit segments provide a powerful basis on which to build positioning directly related to the requirements of customers.

18.3.6 Bespoke positioning (one-to-one marketing)

Perhaps the ultimate in targeting and positioning is the attempt to offer products tailored to the requirements of individual customers. While this has been practised in many business-to-business markets for some time, it is now coming to others and consumer markets too.

The 1996 Paris motor show saw the launch by Mercedes-Benz of its 'Smart Car', a two-seater bubble car jointly developed with MCC (Micro Compact cars), a joint venture with SMH, the Swiss makers of the Swatch. The Smart Car has a small petrol engine (future versions are intended to be battery-driven), seats only two and is aimed at couples living in cities who want a second car. To create the car innovative production methods were used. It is produced in France, where clusters of suppliers around the main factory each produce sub-assemblies, which are then 'snapped' together giving major savings in production time and costs, but also making it possible to tailor the fittings to individual customer requirements even after delivery. The customer can simply return the car and have additional components added (such as air conditioning), current options changed, or even change colours by swapping individual panels. In addition MCC will offer customers a leasing package by which they can rent a larger car for a couple of weeks for annual vacations, etc. (*The Economist* 9 November 1996).

The important skills for bespoke positioning are a combination of outside-in competencies to enable the firm to identify what the customer wants, and to establish relationships with customers, with inside-out competencies of flexible production capability. Recent advances in 'mass customization' (Pine, 1993) make it increasingly possible for firms to enjoy the cost and efficiency advantages of mass production while at the same time tailoring their offerings to individual customer requirements.

In some markets mass customization, by another name, has been around for many years. Supermarkets, for example, provide such a wide range of goods on display and 'employ' customers to do their own selection such that each customer leaving the store has a unique collection of groceries tailored to their individual needs.

The clearest examples of bespoke positioning, however, are generally found in services, both consumer and business, where a bespoke service can be tailored to the requirements of individual customers. Financial consultants offer tailored analysis of investment needs, accountants offer tailored accounts, hairdressers offer tailored haircuts, and architects can offer (if the customer can pay) individual house designs.

Bespoke positioning rests on understanding individual, rather than market segment, needs and having the flexibility to provide for them at a price the customer is willing to pay. While technology can play an important role in enabling economically viable customization, the process needs to be market-led rather than technology-driven. Increasingly, companies are looking to create synergies through the use of new technology to respond to customer demands.

Levi Strauss now offer customized blue jeans – tailored to the tight fit required by customers – by taking measurements in the shop which are sent electronically to the factory to produce a unique garment (and store the data for repeat purchases). The same type of customer offer is made by some shoe suppliers in the US, who respond to customer preferences for unique products by using technology to achieve this at a reasonable cost.

The above alternative approaches to positioning are not necessarily exclusive of each other. They do constitute, however, the main basic alternatives open to firms. The creative application of those alternatives offers an almost infinite variety of ways that firms might build competitive advantage for the new millennium. The task of marketing is to select among the alternatives, basing the choice firmly on the competencies and capabilities of the firm.

18.4 *Conclusions*

Business is changing and so must marketing. Successful strategies for the future will be based on creating a fit between the requirements of the chosen market and the resources of the firm, its ability to meet those requirements.

Marketing will be seen more as a process for achieving this type of matching, rather than a functional specialization or department. To focus on the process of going to market, rather than conventional marketing structures, offers the chance to enhance the role of the customer as a driving force for the company and to finally achieve operationally the goal that 'marketing's future is not as *a* function of business but as *the* function of business' (Haeckel, 1997). The new processes of marketing will require us to learn new ways of doing business in unfamiliar organizations.

Neither resources nor markets are fixed. We may by now be well used to the notion of market requirements changing over time and the need to monitor those changes. We are perhaps less aware of the need explicitly and constantly to examine and develop our resources and capabilities over time. New capabilities must be built or otherwise acquired (e.g. through alliances, mergers or acquisitions) to enable the company to compete in the future. At the same time the firm should examine how it can use its current set of capabilities and assets in different markets or combine its existing capabilities in innovative ways to create new opportunities (as Yamaha did with their digital pianos).

Fundamentally we can expect firms to be more selective and narrower in their choice of markets and customers to serve, but to concentrate their efforts on creating deeper relationships with those chosen to ensure long-term value creation through long-term relationships. There are, of course, an infinite number of ways in which firms can create relationships with their customers. The new millennium will be an exciting period for competitive marketing!

References and further reading

Aaker, D.A. (1982), 'Positioning your product', *Business Horizons*, 25 (3), 56–62.

Aaker, D.A. (1991), *Managing Brand Equity*, New York: The Free Press.

Aaker, D.A. (1995), *Strategic Market Management*, 4th edition, New York: Wiley.

Abell, D.F. (1978), 'Strategic windows', *Journal of Marketing*, 42 (3), 21–6.

Abell, D.F. and Hammond, J.S. (1979), *Strategic Market Planning: Problems and analytical approaches*, Hemel Hempstead: Prentice Hall International.

Abrahams, B. (1996), 'Life after downsizing' *Marketing*, 30 May, 26–7.

Achrol, R. (1991), 'Evolution of the marketing organization: New forms for turbulent environments', *Journal of Marketing*, 55 (October), 77–93.

Achrol, R. (1997), 'Changes in the theory of interorganizational relations in marketing: Toward a network paradigm', *Journal of the Academy of Marketing Science*, 25 (1), 56–71.

Adams, J.L. (1987), *Conceptual Blockbusting: A guide to better ideas*, Harmondsworth, Middlesex: Penguin Books.

Alpert, M.I. (1972), 'Personality and the determinants of product choice', *Journal of Marketing Research*, 9 (1), 179–83.

Alsem, K.J., Leeflang, P.S.H. and Reuyl, J.C. (1989), 'The forecasting accuracy of market share models using predicted values of competitive marketing behavior', *International Journal of Research in Marketing*, 6 (3), 183–98.

Amit, R. and Shoemaker, P.J.H. (1993), 'Strategic assets and organizational rent', *Strategic Management Journal*, 14, 33–46.

Anderson, J.C., Håkansson, H. and Johanson, J. (1994), 'Dyadic business relationships within a business network context', *Journal of Marketing*, 58 (October), 1–15.

Anderson, J.C. and Narus, J.A. (1993), 'A model of distributor firm and manufacturer firm working partnerships', *Journal of Marketing*, 57 (January), 42–58.

Anfuso, D. (1994), 'Coca-Cola's staffing philosophy supports its global strategy', *Personnel Journal*, 73 (11), 116.

Anfuso, D. (1995), 'Colgate's global HR unites under one strategy', *Personnel Journal*, 74 (10), 44–8.

Anon. (1993), 'Quality through customer care', *Industrial Relations Review and Report*, September, 2–5.

Ansoff, H.I. (1984), *Implanting Strategic Management*, London: Prentice Hall.

Armistead, C.G. and Clark, G. (1992), *Customer Service and Support*, London: Pitman Publishing.

Armstrong, J.S. (1985), *Long-range Forecasting: From crystal ball to computer*, New York: Wiley.

Armstrong, J.S. and Collopy, F. (1996), 'Competitor orientation: effects of objectives and information on managerial decisions and profitability', *Journal of Marketing Research*, 33 (May), 188–99.

Armstrong, J.S. and Hutcherson, P. (1989), 'Predicting the outcome of marketing negotiations: role playing versus unaided opinions', *International Journal of Research in Marketing*, 6 (3), 227–39.

Arndt, J. (1983), 'The political economy paradigm: Foundation for theory-building in marketing', *Journal of Marketing*, 47, 44–54.

Baker, M.J. (1992), *Marketing Strategy and Management*, 2nd edition, London: Macmillan.

Barnett, F.W. (1988), 'Four steps to forecast total market demand', *Harvard Business Review*, 66 (4), 28–34.

Barney, J.B. (1991), 'Firm resources and sustained competitive advantage', *Journal of Management*, 17 (1), 99–120.

Barney, J.B. (1997), 'Looking inside for competitive advantage', in A. Campbell and K.S. Luchs (eds.), *Core Competency-Based Strategy*, London: International Thomson Business Press.

Bartlett, C.A. and Ghoshal, S. (1994), 'Changing the role of top management: Beyond strategy to purpose', *Harvard Business Review*, 72 (6), 79–88.

Bass, F.M. (1969), 'A new product forecasting model for consumer durables', *Marketing Science*, 15 (2), 2115–227.

Baumwoll, J.P. (1974), 'Segmentation research: the Baker vs the Cookie Monster', in *Proceedings, American Marketing Association Conference*, 3–20.

Beamish, P.W. and Killing, J.P. (eds.) (1997), *Co-operative Strategies: European Perspectives*, San Francisco: The New Lexington Press.

Becket, M. (1997), 'Top brands to share research on consumers', *The Daily Telegraph*, 21 July, 23.

Bell, E. (1996), ' "Bastards" are losing out to Mr. Clean', *Observer*, 30 June.

Bernhardt, D. (ed.) (1993), *Perfectly Legal Competitor Intelligence*, London: Pitman Publishing.

Bernoth, A. (1996), 'Companies show they care', *Sunday Times*, 8 December.

Berry, L.L. (1981), 'The employee as customer', *Journal of Retail Banking*, 3 (1), 271–8.

Berry, L.L., Conant, J.S. and Parasuraman, A. (1991), 'A framework for conducting a services marketing audit', *Journal of the Academy of Marketing Science*, 19 (3), 255–68.

Berry, L.L. and Parasuraman, A. (1991), *Marketing Services: Competing through quality*, New York: The Free Press.

Blackwell, D. (1997), 'ICI set for bulk chemicals deal', *Financial Times*, 14 July, 19.

Blattberg, R.C. and Hoch, S.J. (1992), 'Database models and managerial intuition: 50% model + 50% manager', *Management Science*, 36 (6), 887–99.

Bonoma, T.V. (1985), *The Marketing Edge: Making strategies work*, New York: Free Press.

Bonoma, T.V. (1990), 'Employees can free the hostages', *Marketing News*, 19 March.

Booz, Allen and Hamilton (1982), *New Products Management for the 1980s*, New York: Booz, Allen and Hamilton Inc.

Boston Consulting Group (1979), *Specialization*, Boston: BCG.

Bowen, D.E. and Lawler, E.E. (1992), 'The empowerment of service workers: what, why, how and when', *Sloan Management Review*, Spring, 31–9.

Bradley, U. (1987), *Applied Marketing and Social Research*, 2nd edition, Chichester: John Wiley & Sons.

Brady, J. and Davis, I. (1993), 'Marketing's mid-life crisis', *The McKinsey Quarterly*, 2 (2), 17–28.

Brierley, S. (1996), 'Shell pours oil on employee relations', *Marketing Week*, 29 November.

Brittan, Sir Leon (1990), 'A compelling reality', *Speaking of Japan*, February, 10 (110), 18–24.

Broadbent, S. (ed.) (1983), *Advertising Works 2*, London: Holt, Reinhart and Winston.

Brodie, R.J. and de Kluyver, C.A. (1987), 'A comparison of the short-term accuracy of econometric and naive extrapolation models of market share', *International Journal of Forecasting*, 3 (3), 423–37.

Brown, A. (1995), 'The fall and rise of marketing', *Marketing Business*, February, 25–8.

Brown, S. (1995), *Postmodern Marketing*, London: Routledge.

Brownlie, D. (1996), 'Marketing audits and auditing: diagnosis through intervention', *Journal of Marketing Management*, 12 (1–3), 99–112.

Bucklin, L.P. and Sengupta, S. (1993), 'Organizing successful co-marketing alliances', *Journal of Marketing*, April, 32–46.

Buffington, B.I. and Frabelli, K.F. (1991), 'Acquisitions and alliances in the communications industry', in H.E. Glass, (ed.), *Handbook of Business Strategy*, 3rd edition, New York: Warren Gorman and Lamont.

Bultez, A. and Parsons, L. (eds) (1998), *Retail Efficiency*, special issue of *International Journal of Research in Marketing*, 15 (5).

Burack, E.H., Burack, M.D., Miller, D.M. and Morgan, K. (1994), 'New paradigm approaches in strategic human resource management', *Group and Organizational Management*, 19 (2), 141–59.

Business Week (1993), 'The virtual corporation', 8 February, 98–102.

Buzzell, R.D. and Gale, B.T. (1987), *The PIMS Principles*, New York: The Free Press.

Buzzell, R.D. and Ortmeyer, G. (1994), *Channel Partnerships: A new approach to streamlining distribution*, Cambridge, Mass.: Marketing Science Institute.

Buzzell, R.D. and Wiersema, F.D. (1981), 'Successful share building strategies', *Harvard Business Review*, 59 (1), 135–44.

Calder, B.J. (1994), 'Qualitative marketing research' in Richard P. Bagozzi (ed.), *Principles of Marketing Research*, Boston, Mass., Blackwell.

Calfee, D.I. (1993), 'Get your mission statement working', *Management Review* January, 54–7.

Cappelli, P. and Crocker-Hefter, A. (1996), 'Distinctive human resources are firms' core competencies', *Organizational Dynamics*, 24 (3), 7–22.

Cardozo, R.N. (1979), *Product Policy*, Reading, Mass.: Addison-Wesley.

Carey, T. (1989), 'Strategy formulation in banks', *International Journal of Bank Marketing*, 7 (3), 4–44.

Carroll, D.J., Green, P.E. and Schaffer, C.M. (1986), 'Interpoint distance comparisons in correspondence analysis', *Journal of Marketing Research*, 23, 271–80.

Carroll, D.J., Green, P.E. and Schaffer, C.M. (1987), 'Comparing interpoint distances in correspondence analysis: a clarification', *Journal of Marketing Research*, 24, 445–50.

Cascino, A.E. (1969), 'Organizational implications of the marketing concept', in E.J. Kelley and W. Lazar. (eds), *Managerial marketing: Perspectives and viewpoints*, Homewood, IL: Irwin.

Cassino, K.D. (1984), 'Delphi method: a practical "crystal ball" for researchers', *Marketing News*, 16 January, 705–6.

Cattin, P. and Wittink, D.R. (1992), 'Commercial use of conjoint analysis: a survey', *Journal of Marketing*, 46 (1), 44–53.

Central Statistical Office (1995), *Annual Abstract of Statistics*, London: HMSO.

Cespedes, F.V. and Piercy, N.F. (1996), 'Implementing marketing strategy', *Journal of Marketing Management*, 12, 135–60.

Chang, J.J. and Carroll, J.D. (1969), 'How to use MDPREF: a computer program for multidimensional analysis of preference data', unpublished paper, *Bell Laboratories*, Murray Hill, N.J.

Chang, J.J. and Carroll, J.D. (1972), 'How to use PREFMAP and PREFMAP 2 – Programs which relate preference data to multidimensional scaling solutions', unpublished paper, *Bell Laboratories*, Murray Hill, N.J.

Chattopadhyay, A., Nedungadi, P. and Chakravarti, D. (1985), 'Marketing strategy and differential advantage – a comment', *Journal of Marketing*, 49 (2), 129–36.

Chesbrough, H.W. and Teece, D.J. (1996), 'When virtual is virtuous', *Harvard Business Review*, 74 (1), 65–73.

Chisnall, P.M. (1985), *Strategic Industrial Marketing*, Hemel Hempstead: Prentice Hall International.

Christopher, M., Payne, A. and Ballantyne, D. (1991), *Relationship Marketing*, Oxford: Butterworth-Heinemann.

Clark, M. and Payne, A. (1995), 'Customer retention: does employee retention hold a key to success?', in A. Payne (ed.), *Advances in Relationship Marketing*, London: Kogan Page.

Clark, P. (1986), 'The marketing of margarine', *European Journal of Marketing*, 20 (5), 52–65.

Clausewitz, C. von (1908), *On War*, London: Routledge & Kegan Paul.

Clavell, J. (ed.) (1981), *The Art of War by Sun Tzu*, London: Hodder and Stoughton.

Clemen, R.T. (1989), 'Combining forecasts: a review and annotated bibliography', *International Journal of Forecasting*, 5 (4), 559–83.

Clover, C. (1996), 'The green shopper is alive and well', *Daily Telegraph*, 11 December.

Coad, T. (1989), 'Lifestyle analysis – opportunities for early entry into Europe with effective customer targeting', Institute of International Research Conference on *Customer Segmentation and Lifestyle Marketing*, London, 11–12 December.

Cook, V.J. (1983), 'Marketing strategy and differential advantage', *Journal of Marketing*, 47 (2), 68–75.

Cook, V.J. and Mindak, W.A. (1984), 'A search for constants: the heavy user revisited', *Journal of Consumer Research*, 1 (4), 80.

Cooper, R. and Kleinschmidt, E. (1990), 'New product success factors: A comparison of kills versus successes and failures', *R&D Management*, 17 (3), 47–63.

Cooper, R. and Kleinschmidt, E. (1993), 'New product success in the chemical industry', *Industrial Marketing Management*, 22 (1), 85–99.

Cooper, R. and Kleinschmidt, E. (1995), 'New product performance: Keys to success, profitability and cycle time reduction', *Journal of Marketing Management*, 11, 315–37.

Cramp, B. (1996), 'Neighbourhood watch', *Marketing Business*, May, 44–7.

Cravens, D.W. (1991), *Strategic Marketing*, 3rd edition, Chicago: Irwin.

Cravens, D.W. (1997), *Strategic Marketing*, 5th edition, Chicago: Irwin.

Cravens, D.W. and Piercy, N.F. (1994), 'Relationship marketing and collaborative networks in service organizations', *International Journal of Service Industry Management*, 5 (5), 39–53.

Cravens, D.W., Greenley, G., Piercy, N.F. and Slater, S. (1997), 'Integrating contemporary strategic management philosophy', *Long Range Planning*, 30 (4), 493–506.

Cravens, D.W., Piercy, N.F. and Shipp, S.H. (1996), 'New organizational forms for competing in highly dynamic environments: The network paradigm', *British Journal of Management*, 7, 203–18.

Cravens, D.W., Shipp, S.H. and Cravens, K.S. (1993), 'Analysis of co-operative interorganizational relationships, strategic alliance formation, and strategic alliance effectiveness', *Journal of Strategic Marketing*, March, 55–70.

Cravens, D.W., Shipp, S.H. and Cravens, K.S. (1994), 'Reforming the traditional organization: The mandate for developing networks', *Business Horizons*, July–August, 19–28.

Crimp, M. (1990), *The Marketing Research Process*, 3rd edition, Hemel Hempstead: Prentice Hall.

Crimp, M. and Wright, L.T. (1995), *The Marketing Research Process*, 4th edition, Hemel Hempstead: Prentice Hall.

Cripe, E.J. (1994), 'Upgrading the service level of HR', *Human Resources Professional*, 7 (3), 7–11.

Crosby, L.A., Evans, K.R. and Cowles, S. (1990), 'Relationship quality in services selling: an interpersonal influence perspective', *Journal of Marketing*, 54, 68–81.

Crouch, S. and Housden, M. (1996), *Marketing Research for Managers*, 2nd edition, Oxford: Butterworth-Heinemann.

Cunningham, M.T. and Clarke, D.C.J. (1976), 'The product management function in marketing', *European Journal of Marketing*, 9 (2), 129–49.

Daily Telegraph (1997), 'Laura Ashley may defeat superman', 27 August.

Danneels, E. (1996), 'Market segmentation: Normative model versus business reality', *European Journal of Marketing*, 30 (6), 36–51.

Davidson, H. (1983), 'Putting assets first', *Marketing*, 17 November.

Davidson, H. (1987), *Offensive Marketing*, London: Penguin Books.

Dawson, L.M. (1969), 'The human concept: New philosophy for business', *Business Horizons*, December, 29–38.

Day, G.S. (1977), 'Diagnosing the product portfolio', *Journal of Marketing*, 41 (2), 29–38.

Day, G.S. (1992), 'Marketing's contribution to the strategy dialogue', *Journal of the Academy of Marketing Science*, 20 (4), 37–52.

Day, G.S. (1994), *Market Driven Strategy: Processes for creating value*, New York: Free Press.

Day, G.S. (1994), 'The capabilities of market-driven organizations', *Journal of Marketing*, 58 (3), 37–52.

Day, G.S. (1997), 'Aligning the organization to the market', in D.R. Lehmann, and K.E. Jocz, (eds.), *Reflections on the Futures of Marketing*, Cambridge, Mass.: Marketing Science Institute.

Day, G.S., Shocker, A.D. and Srivastava, R.K. (1979), 'Customer-oriented approach to identifying product markets', *Journal of Marketing*, 43 (4), 8–19.

de Chernatony, L. and MacDonald, M.H.B. (1992), *Creating Brands*, Oxford: Butterworth-Heinemann.

Deshpande, R. (1982), 'The organizational context of marketing research use', *Journal of Marketing*, 46 (3), 91–101.

Deshpande, R. and Zaltman, G. (1984), 'A comparison of factors affecting researcher and manager perceptions of market research use', *Journal of Marketing Research*, 21 February, 32–8.

Dewar, R. and Schultz, D. (1989), 'The product manager: An idea whose time has gone', *Marketing Communications*, May, 28–35.

Diamantopoulos, A. and Schlegelmilch, B.B. (1997), *Taking the Fear out of Data Analysis*, London: The Dryden Press.

Dibb, S. and Simkin, L. (1994), 'Implementation problems in industrial market segmentation', *Industrial Marketing Management*, 23, February, 55–63.

Dickson, P.R. (1992), 'Towards a general theory of competitive rationality' *Journal of Marketing*, 56, January, 69–83.

Divita, S. (1996), 'Colleagues are customers, market to them', *Marketing News*, 21 October.

Dixon, N.F. (1976), *On the Psychology of Military Incompetence*, London: Futura.

Doyle, P. (1994), *Marketing Management and Strategy*, Hemel Hempstead: Prentice Hall International.

Doyle, P. (1995), 'Marketing in the new millennium', *European Journal of Marketing*, 29 (13), 23–41.

Doyle, P. (1997), 'Go for robust growth', *Marketing Business*, April, 53.

Doyle, P., Saunders, J.A. and Wong, V. (1986), 'A comparative study of Japanese and British marketing strategies in the UK market', *Journal of International Business Studies*, 17 (1), 27–46.

Doyle, P. and Wong, V. (1996), 'Marketing and international competitiveness: An empirical study', Proceedings of the 25th annual conference of the *European Marketing Academy*, May, Budapest, Hungary, 351–70.

Doz, Y.L. (1988), 'Technology partnerships between larger and smaller firms: Some critical issues', *International Studies of Management and Organization*, 17 (4), 31–57.

Drucker, P. (1954), *The Practice of Management*, New York: Harper and Row.

Drucker, P. (1973), *Management: Tasks, responsibilities and practices*, New York: Harper and Row.

Drucker, P. (1997), 'The future that has already happened', *Harvard Business Review*, 75 (5), 20–4.

Dwek, R. (1997), 'Losing the race', *Marketing Business*, March.

Economist (1994), 'Death of the brand manager', 9 April, 79–80.

Economist (1994), 'Furnishing the world', 19 November, 101.

Economist (1997), 'Dr Gallup's finger on America's pulse', 17 September, 133–4.

Egan, C. (1995), *Creating Organizational Advantage*, Oxford: Butterworth-Heinemann.

Eisenstat, R.A. (1993), 'Implementing strategy: Developing a partnership for change', *Planning Review*, 21 (5), 33–6.

Elgie, S.S. (1990), *Travel Problems and Opportunities – Turning adversity to advantage in the 1990s*, London: Elgie Stewart Smith.

English, J. (1989), 'Selecting and analyzing your customer/market through efficient profile modeling and prospecting', *Institute of International Research Conference on Customer Segmentation and Lifestyle Marketing*, London, 11–12 December.

Evans, F.B. (1959), 'Psychological and objective factors in the prediction of brand choice', *Journal of Business*, 32, October, 340–69.

Evans, P.B. and Wurster, T.S. (1997), 'Strategy and the new economics of information', *Harvard Business Review*, 75 (5), 71–82.

Farley, J.U. (1997), 'Looking ahead at the marketplace: It's global and it's changing', in D.R. Lehmann and K.R. Jocz (eds.), *Reflections on the Futures of Marketing*, Cambridge, Mass.: Marketing Science Institute.

Felton, A.P. (1959), 'Making the marketing concept work', *Harvard Business Review*, 37 (4), 55–65.

Ferrell, O.C. and Lucas, G.H. (1987), 'An evaluation of progress in the development of a definition of marketing', *Journal of the Academy of Marketing Science*, 15 (3), 12–23.

Fisher, J.C. and Pry, R.M. (1978), 'A simple substitution model of technological change', *Technological Forecasting and Social Change*, 3 (1), 75–88.

Fitzgerald, L., Johnston, R., Brignall, S., Silvestro, R. and Voss, C. (1991), *Performance Measurement in Service Businesses*, London: Chartered Institute of Management Accountants.

Fletcher, K. (1996), *Marketing Management and Information Technology*, 2nd edition, London: Prentice-Hall International.

Flipo, J.-P. (1986), 'Service firms: Interdependence of external and internal marketing strategies', *European Journal of Marketing*, 20 (8), 5–14.

Forbis, J.L. and Mehta, N.T. (1981), 'Value-based strategies for industrial products', *Business Horizons*, 24 (3), 32–42.

Foster, R.N. (1986), 'Attacking through innovation', *The McKinsey Quarterly*, Summer, 2–12.

Foster, R.N. (1986), *Innovation: The attacker's advantage*, London: Macmillan.

Frank, R.E. , Massey, W.F. and Wind, Y. (1972), *Market Segmentation*, Englewood Cliffs, NJ: Prentice-Hall.

Franks, J.R. and Broyles, J. (1979), *Modern Managerial Finance*, Chichester: Wiley.

Fulmer, W.E. and Goodwin, J. (1988), 'Differentiation: Begin with the customer', *Business Horizons*, 31 (5), 55–63.

Gardner, E.S. (1985), 'Exponential smoothing: The state of the art', *Journal of Forecasting*, 4 (1), 1–28.

Gardner, N. (1997), 'Defining your class is as easy as ABC', *The Sunday Times*, 9 February, 7.

Gerlach, M.L. (1992), *Alliance Capitalism*, Berkeley: University of California Press.

Gershman, M. (1991), *Getting it Right the Second Time*, London: Mercury Books.

Gilly, M.C. and Wolfinbarger, M. (1996), *Advertising's Second Audience: Employee reactions to organizational communications*, Cambridge, Mass.: Marketing Science Institute.

Glassman, M. and McAfee, B. (1992), 'Integrating the personnel and marketing functions: The challenge of the 1990s', *Business Horizons*, 35 (3), 52–9.

Gluck, F. (1986), 'Strategic planning in a new key', *McKinsey Quarterly*, Winter, 173–83.

Gordon, W. and Langmaid, R. (1988), *Qualitative Research: A practitioners' and buyers' guide*, Gower: London.

Grant, R. (1996), 'Message from a bottle', *Financial Mail on Sunday*, 15 December 12.

Grant, R.M. (1995), *Contemporary Strategy Analysis*, 2nd edition, Cambridge, Mass.: Basil Blackwell.

Gratton, L. (1994), 'Implementing strategic intent: Human resource processes as a force for change', *Business Strategy Review*, 5 (1), 47–66.

Green, P.E., Carmone, F.J. and Smith, S.M. (1989), *Multidimensional Scaling: Concepts and applications*, Boston, Mass.: Allyn and Bacon.

Green, P.E., Tull, D.S. and Albaum, G. (1993), *Research for Marketing Decisions*, 6th edition, Englewood Cliffs, NJ: Prentice Hall International.

Green, P.E. and Wind, Y. (1975), 'New way to measure consumers' judgements', *Harvard Business Review*, 53 (4), 107–17.

Greyser, S.A. (1997), 'Janus and marketing: The past, present and prospective future of marketing', in D.R. Lehmann and K.R. Jocz (eds.), *Reflections on the Futures of Marketing*, Cambridge, Mass.: Marketing Science Institute.

Gribben, R. (1997), 'BA has secret global deal, claims Branson', *The Daily Telegraph*, 20 August, 6.

Gronhaug, K. and Gilly, M.C. (1991), 'A transaction cost approach to consumer dissatisfaction and complaint actions', *Journal of Economic Psychology*, 12, 165–83.

Grönroos, C. (1984), *Strategic Management and Marketing in the Service Sector*, London: Chartwell-Bratt.

Grönroos, C. (1985), 'Internal marketing – theory and practice', in T.M. Bloch, G.D. Upah and V.A. Zeithaml (eds.), *Services Marketing in a Changing Environment*, Chicago: American Marketing Association.

Grönroos, C. (1994), 'From marketing mix to relationship marketing: Towards a paradigm shift in marketing', *Management Decision*, 32 (2), 4–32.

Gubman, E.L. (1995), 'Aligning people strategies with customer value', *Compensation and Benefits Review*, 27 (1), 15–22.

Gummesson, E. (1987), 'Using internal marketing to develop a new culture – the case of Ericsson quality', *Journal of Business and Industrial Marketing*, 2 (3), 23–8.

Gummesson, E. (1987), 'The new marketing – developing long-term interactive relationships', *Long Range Planning*, 20 (4), 10–20.

Gummesson, E. (1990), *The Part-Time Marketer*, University of Karlstad, Research Report. 90:3.

Gummesson, E. (1994), 'Service management: An evaluation and the future', *International Journal of Service Industry Management*, 5 (1), 77–96.

Gupta, A.K., Raj, S.P. and Wilemon, D. (1986), 'A model for studying R&D/Marketing interface in the product innovation process', *Journal of Marketing*, 50, 7–17.

H.R. Challey Group (1996), *The Customer Selected World Class Sales Excellence Report*, Ohio: H.R. Challey Group.

Haeckel, S. (1997), 'Preface', in D.R. Lehmann and K.R. Jocz (eds.), *Reflections on the Futures of Marketing*, Cambridge, Mass.: Marketing Science Institute.

Haley, R.I. (1968), 'Benefit segmentation: A decision-oriented tool', *Journal of Marketing*, July, 30–5.

Haley, R.I. (1984), 'Benefit segmentation – 20 years on', *Journal of Consumer Marketing*, 5–13.

Hall, W.A.K. (1980), 'Survival strategies in a hostile environment', *Harvard Business Review*, 58 (5), 75–85.

Hall, W. (1995), *Managing Cultures: Making strategic relationships work*, Chichester: John Wiley.

Hamel, G. (1996), 'Strategy as revolution', *Harvard Business Review*, 74 (4), 9–82.

Hamel, G. and Prahalad, C.K. (1989), 'Strategic intent', *Harvard Business Review*, 67 (3), 63–76.

Hamel, G. and Prahalad, C.K. (1991), 'Corporate imagination and expeditionary marketing', *Harvard Business Review*, 69 (4), 81–92.

Hamel, G. and Prahalad, C.K. (1994), *Competing for the Future*, Boston, Mass.: Harvard Business School Press.

Hammermesh, R.G., Anderson, M.J. and Harris, J.E. (1978), 'Strategies for low market share businesses', *Harvard Business Review*, 50 (3), 95–102.

Harris, L.C. (1996), 'Cultural obstacles to market orientation', *Journal of Marketing Practice: Applied Marketing Science*, 4 (2), 36–52.

Harris, L.C. (1998), 'Cultural domination: The key to a market oriented culture', *European Journal of Marketing*, forthcoming.

Hart, C.W.L., Heskett, J.L. and Sasser, W.E. (1990), 'The profitable art of service recovery' *Harvard Business Review*, 68 (2), 148–156.

Haspeslagh, P. (1982), 'Portfolio planning: Uses and limits', *Harvard Business Review*, 60 (1), 58–73.

Hedley, B. (1979), 'Strategy and the business portfolio', *Long Range Planning*, 10 (1), 9–15.

Henderson, B. (1970), *The Product Portfolio*, Boston, Mass.: The Boston Consulting Group.

Hill, R. (1979), 'Weak signals from the unknown', *International Management*, 34 (10), 55–60.

Hindle, T. and Thomas, M. (1994), *Pocket Marketing*, 2nd edition, Harmondsworth: The Economist Books.

Hogarth, R.M. (1978), 'A note on aggregating opinions', *Organizational Behavior and Human Performance*, 21 (1), 40–6.

Hooley, G.J. (1980), 'Multidimensional scaling of consumer perceptions and preferences', *European Journal of Marketing*, 14 (7), 436–80.

Hooley, G.J. (1982), 'Directing advertising creativity through benefit segmentation', *Journal of Advertising*, 1, 375–85.

Hooley, G.J. (1994), 'The life cycle revisited – aid or albatross?', *Journal of Strategic Marketing*, 3 (1), 23–40.

Hooley, G.J. and Beracs, J. (1997), 'Marketing strategies for the 21st century: Lessons from the top Hungarian companies', *Journal of Strategic Marketing*, 5 (3), 143–65.

Hooley, G.J., Cox, A.J. and Adams, A. (1992), 'Our five year mission – to boldly go where no man has gone before', *Journal of Marketing Management*, 8 (1), 35–48.

Hooley, G.J., Cox, A.J., Shipley, D., Fahy, J., Beracs, J. and Kolos, K. (1996), 'Foreign direct investment in Hungary: Resource acquisition and domestic competitive advantage', *Journal of International Business Studies*, 27 (4), 683–709.

Hooley, G.J. and Hussey, M.K. (eds.) (1994), *Quantitative Methods in Marketing*, London: Dryden Press.

Hooley, G.J., Lynch, J.L. and Shepard, J. (1990), 'The marketing concept: Putting the theory into practice', *European Journal of Marketing*, 7–23.

Hooley, G.J., Möller, K. and Broderick, A.J. (1997), *Competitive Positioning and the Resource-Based View of the Firm*, Aston Business School Research Paper RP9726.

Hooley, G.J., Möller, K. and Broderick, A.J. (1998), 'Competitive Positioning and the resource based view of the firm', *Journal of Strategic Marketing*, forthcoming.

Horovitz, J. and Panak, M.J. (1992), *Total Customer Satisfaction*, London: Pitman Publishing.

Huber, G.P. (1984), 'The nature and design of post-industrial organizations', *Administrative Science Quarterly*, August, 928–51.

Hulbert, J.M. and Pitt, L. (1996), 'Exit left centre stage', *European Management Journal*, 14 (1), 47–60.

Hussey, M.K. and Hooley, G.J. (1995), 'The diffusion of quantitative methods into marketing management', *Journal of Marketing Practice: Applied Marketing Science*, 1 (4), 13–31.

IRS Employment Review (1996), 'HRM is not part of strategic decision making', September, 4.

Imai, M. (1986), *KAIZEN: The key to Japan's competitive success*, Maidenhead: McGraw-Hill.

Imparato, N. and Harari, O. (1994), *Jumping the Curve: Innovation and strategic choice in an age of transition*, San Francisco: Jossey-Bass.

Jackson, T. (1997), 'Dare to be different', *Financial Times*, 19 June.

Jain, S.C. (1985), *Marketing Planning and Strategy*, 2nd edition, Cincinatti, Oh: South Western.

Jain, S.C. (1990), *Marketing Planning and Strategy*, 3rd edition, Cincinatti, Oh: South Western.

James, B.J. (1984), *Business Wargames*, London: Abacus.

Jaworski, B.J. and Kohli, A.K. (1993), 'Market orientation: Antecedents and consequences', *Journal of Marketing*, 57, July, 53–70.

Jobber, D., Saunders, J.A., Hooley, G.J., Guilding, B. and Hatton-Smooker, J. (1989), 'Assessing the value of a quality assurance certificate for software: An exploratory investigation', *MIS Quarterly*, March, 18–31.

John, G. and Martin, J. (1984), 'Effects of organizational structure of marketing planning on credibility and utilization of plan output', *Journal of Marketing Research*, 21 May, 170–83.

Johnson, G. and Scholes, K. (1988), *Exploring Corporate Strategy*, 2nd edition, Hemel Hempstead: Prentice Hall International.

Johnson, G. and Scholes, K. (1993), *Exploring Corporate Strategy*, 3rd edition, Hemel Hempstead: Prentice Hall International.

Jones, T.O. and Sasser, W.E. (1995), 'Why satisfied customers defect', *Harvard Business Review*, 73 (6), 88–99.

Kanner, B. (1996), 'In search of brand loyalty', *Sunday Business*, 30 June, 11.

Kay, J. (1993), *Foundations of Corporate Success*, Oxford: Oxford University Press.

Keegan, J. (1993), *A History of Warfare*, London: Hutchinson.

Keith, R.J. (1960), 'The marketing revolution', *Journal of Marketing*, 24 (1), 35–8.

Khoo, P.C. (1992), *Sun Tzu and Management*, Petaling Jaya, Malaysia: Pelanduk.

King, S. (1985), 'Has marketing failed or was it never really tried?', *Journal of Marketing Management*, 1 (1), 1–19.

Kinnear, T.C., Taylor, J.R. and Ahmed, S.A. (1974), 'Ecologically concerned consumers : Who are they?', *Journal of Marketing*, 38 (2), 20–4.

Kohli, A.K. and Jaworski, B.J. (1990), 'Market orientation: The construct, research propositions and managerial implications', *Journal of Marketing*, 54 (2), 1–18.

Kotler, P.C. (1978), 'Harvesting strategies for weak products', *Business Horizons*, 21 (4), 15–22.

Kotler, P.C. (1997), *Marketing Management: Analysis, planning, implementation and control*, 9th edition, Hemel Hempstead: Prentice Hall International.

Kotler, P.C., Armstrong, G., Saunders, J.A. and Wong, V. (1996), *Principles of Marketing: the European Edition*, Hemel Hempstead: Prentice Hall.

Kotler, P.C., Fahey, L. and Jatusritpitak, S. (1985), *The New Competition*, Hemel Hempstead: Prentice Hall.

Kotler, P.C., Gregor, W. and Rogers, W. (1989), 'The marketing audit comes of age', *Sloan Management Review*, 18 (2), 49–62.

Kotler, P.C. and Singh, R. (1981), 'Marketing warfare in the 1980s', *Journal of Business Strategy*, 1 (3), 30–41.

Kruskal, J.B., Young, F.W. and Seery, J.B. (1973), 'How to use KYST: A very flexible program to do multidimensional scaling', Multidimensional Scaling Program Package of Bell Laboratories, Bell Laboratories, Murray Hill, NJ.

Laabs, J.J.(1993), 'Hewlett Packard's core values drive HR strategy', *Personnel Journal*, 72 (12), 38–48.

Laing, H. (1991), *Brand Advertising Targeting System*, London: Laing Henry.

Lambert, D.M., Emmelhainz, M.A. and Gardner, J.T. (1996), 'So you think you want to be a partner?', *Marketing Management*, Summer, 25–41.

Lattice, J. (1996), 'Blue's legend', *Sunday Business*, 21 April.

Lawrence, M.J., Edmundson, R.H. and O'Connor, M.J. (1985), 'An examination of the accuracy of judgmental extrapolation of time series', *International Journal of Forecasting*, 1 (1), 23–35.

Lehmann, D.R. and Jocz, K.E. (eds.) (1997), *Reflections on the Futures of Marketing*, Cambridge, Mass: Marketing Science Institute.

Lehmann, D.R. and Winer, R.S. (1991), *Analysis for Marketing Planning*, 2nd edition, Homewood IL: Irwin.

Leppard, J. and McDonald, M.H.B. (1987), 'A reappraisal of the role of marketing planning', Proceedings: *Marketing Education Group Conference*, Warwick, July.

Levitt, T. (1960), 'Marketing myopia', *Harvard Business Review*, 38 (4), 45–56.

Levitt, T. (1975), 'Marketing myopia – Retrospective commentary', *Harvard Business Review*, 53 (5), 177–81.

Levitt, T. (1986), *The Marketing Imagination*, New York: The Free Press.

Lewis, B. (1989), 'Customer care in service organizations', *Marketing Intelligence and Planning*, 7 (5/6), 18–22.

Liddel Hart, B.H. (1972), *History of the First World War*, London: Pan.

Liddel Hart, B.H. (1973), *History of the Second World War*, London: Pan.

Lilien, G.L. and Kotler, P.C. (1983), *Marketing Decision Making: A model-building approach*, London: Harper and Row.

Lilien, G.L., Kotler, P. and Moorthy, K.S. (1992), *Marketing Models*, Hemel Hempstead: Prentice Hall International.

Lin, Y.S.L. (1990), 'Comparison of survey response among Asian, European and American consumers and their interpretations' *ESOMAR Conference Proceedings*, Venice, June, 120–32.

Little, J.D.C. (1979), 'Decision support systems for marketing management', *Journal of Marketing*, 43 (3), 9–26.

MacDonald, M. (1984), *Marketing Plans*, London: Heinemann.

McDowell, C. (1996), 'Aligning work force capabilities with business strategies', *Human Resource Professional*, 9 (5), 3–5.

McKee, D. and Varadarajan, P.R. (1995), 'Introduction: Special issue on sustainable competitive advantage', *Journal of Business Research*, 33 (2), 77–9.

McKitterick, J.B. (1957), 'What is the marketing management concept?', Proceedings: AMA Teachers' Conference, Philadelphia.

McLeod, J. (1985), 'Marketing information systems: A review paper', *Quarterly Review of Marketing*, 10 (3).

McNerney, D. (1994), 'Competitive advantage: Diverse customers and stakeholders', *HR Focus*, 71 (6), 9–10.

Mahoney, J.T. (1995), 'The management of resources and the resource of management', *Journal of Business Research*, 33 (2), 91–101.

Maier, J. and Saunders, J.A. (1990), 'The implementation of segmentation in sales management', *The Journal of Personal Selling and Sales Management*, 10 (1), 39–48.

Makridakis, S., Chatfield, C., Hibon, M., Lawrence, M., Mills, T., Ord, K. and Simmons, L. (1993), 'The M2 competition: A real-time judgmentally based forecasting study', *International Journal of Forecasting*, 9 (1), 5–22.

Market Research Society (annual), *Organisations Providing Marketing Research Services in the UK*, MRS.

Marketing Business (1997a), 'Marketing prefers navel gazing to NPD', March, 6.

Marketing Business (1997b), 'Marketplace', March.

Markowitz, H. (1952), 'Portfolio selection', *Journal of Finance*, 7 (2), 77–91.

Mazur, L. (1996), 'Brands', *Marketing Business*, November, 16.

Micolo, A.M. (1993), 'Suggestions for achieving a strategic partnership', *HR Focus*, 70 (9), 22.

Miles, R.E. and Snow, C.C. (1984), 'Fit, failure, and the Hall of Fame', *California Management Review*, Spring, 10–28.

Miller, A.I. (1996), *Insight of Genius*, New York: Springer-Verlag.

Mingo, J. (1994), *How the Cadillac Got its Fins*, New York: HarperCollins.

Mintzberg, H. (1994), 'The fall and rise of strategic planning', *Harvard Business Review*, 72 (1), 107–14.

Mitchell, A. (1994a), 'The people factor', *Marketing Business*, October, 24–7.

Mitchell, A. (1994b), 'The revolution within', *Marketing Business*, December, 22–5.

Mitchell, A. (1995), 'Changing channels', *Marketing Business*, February, 10–13.

Mitchell, A. (1997), 'Speeding up the process' *Marketing Business*, March.

Mitchell, A. (1997), 'Stargazing', *Marketing Business*, June, 32–5.

Möller, K. and Anttila, M. (1987), 'Marketing capability: A key success factor in small business?', *Journal of Marketing Management*, 3 (2), 185–203.

Moore, G.A. (1991), *Crossing the Chasm*, New York: HarperCollins.

Moores, B. (1986), *Are They Being Served?*, Oxford: Philip Alan.

Morgan, R.M. and Hunt, S.D. (1994), 'The commitment–trust theory of relationship marketing', *Journal of Marketing*, 58 (3), 20–38.

Morrison, A. and Wensley, R. (1991), 'Boxing up or boxed in?: A short history of the Boston Consulting Group Share-Growth Matrix', *Journal of Marketing Management*, 7(2), 105–30.

Moutinho, L. (1991), *Problems in Marketing*, London: Paul Chapman Publishing.

Murphy, J. (1991), *Brand Valuation*, 2nd edition, London: Business Books Ltd.

Murphy, P.E. and Staples, W.A. (1979), 'A modernized family life cycle', *Journal of Consumer Research*, June, 12–22.

Narver, J.C. and Slater, S.F. (1990), 'The effect of a market orientation on business profitability', *Journal of Marketing*, 54 (4), 20–35.

Norusis, M.J. (1992), *SPSS for Windows*, Release 5.0, Chicago: SPSS Inc.

O'Brien, N. and Ford, J. (1988), 'Can we at last say goodbye to social class?', *Journal of Market Research Society*, 16(2), 43–51.

Ohmae, K. (1982), *The Mind of the Strategist*, Harmondsworth: Penguin Books.

Ohmae, K. (1990), *The Borderless World*, New York: Harper Business.

Olins, R. (1997a), 'Wilting', *The Sunday Times*, 24 August, 3.

Olins, R. (1997b), 'W.H. Smith stalls on the road to nowhere', *The Sunday Times*, 31 August, 5.

Olson, E.M. (1993), 'The marketing/manufacturing relationship within the new product development process', Proceedings, American Marketing Association Educators' Conference, Chicago, 4, 280–6.

O'Shaughnessy, J. (1992), *Explaining Buyer Behavior*, Oxford: Oxford University Press.

O'Shaughnessy, J. (1995), *Competitive Marketing*, 3rd edition, London and New York: Routledge.

Oxx, C. (1972), 'Psychographics and life style', *Admap*, October, 303–5.

Parasuraman, A., Zeithaml, V.A. and Berry, L.L. (1985), 'A conceptual model of service quality and the implications for further research' *Journal of Marketing*, Fall, 41–50.

Parasuraman, A., Zeithaml, V.A. and Berry, L.L. (1988), 'SERVQUAL: A multiple-item scale for measuring customer perceptic s of service quality', *Journal of Retailing*, 64 (1), 12–40.

Parasuraman, A., Zeithaml, V.A. and Berry, L.L. (1994), 'Reassessment of expectations as a comparison standard in measuring service quality: implications for further research' *Journal of Marketing*, 58 (1), 111–24.

Payne, A. (1993), *The Essence of Services Marketing*, London: Prentice Hall.

Payne, A. (ed.) (1995), *Advances in Relationship Marketing*, London: Kogan Page.

Payne, A., Christopher, M., Clark, M. and Peck, H. (1995), *Relationship Marketing for Competitive Advantage*, Oxford: Butterworth-Heinemann.

Peppers, D. and Rogers, M. (1993), *The One-to-One Future*, London: Piatkus.

Perrien, J. and Ricard, L. (1995), 'The meaning of a marketing relationship', *Industrial Marketing Management*, 24 (1), 37–43.

Perrien, J., Filiatraut, P. and Line, R. (1993), 'The implementation of relationship marketing in commercial banking', *Industrial Marketing Management*, 22 (2), 141–48.

Peters, T. (1987), *Thriving on Chaos*, London: Macmillan.

Pfeffer, J. (1994), 'Competitive advantage through people', *California Management Review*, 36 (2), 9–28.

Piercy, N.F. (1995), 'Customer satisfaction and the internal market: Marketing our customers to our employees', *Journal of Marketing Practice: Applied Marketing Science*, 1 (1), 22–44.

Piercy, N.F. (1997), *Market-Led Strategic Change: Transforming the process of going to market*, 2nd edition, Oxford: Butterworth-Heinemann.

Piercy, N.F. and Cravens, D.W. (1995), 'The network paradigm and the marketing organization', *European Journal of Marketing*, 29 (3), 7–34.

Piercy, N.F., Cravens, D.W. and Morgan, N.A. (1997), 'Sources of effectiveness in the business-to-business sales organization', *Journal of Marketing Practice: Applied marketing science*, 3 (1), 43–69.

Piercy, N.F. and Lane, N. (1996), 'Marketing Implementation: Building and sustaining a real market understanding', *Journal of Marketing Practice: Applied Marketing Science*, 2 (3), 15–8.

Piercy, N.F. and Morgan, N.A. (1991), 'Internal marketing strategy: Leverage for managing market-led strategic change', *Irish Marketing Review*, 4 (3), 11–28.

Piercy, N.F. and Morgan, N.A. (1993), 'Strategic and operational market segmentation: A managerial analysis', *Journal of Strategic Marketing*, 1, 123–40.

Pine, B.J. (1993), *Mass Customization: The new frontier in business competition*, Boston, Mass.: Harvard Business School Press.

Plank, R.E. (1985), 'A critical review of industrial market segmentation', *Industrial Marketing Management*, 14, 79–91.

Plevel, M.J., Martin, J., Lane, F., Nellis, S. and Schuler, R.S. (1994), 'AT&T global business communications systems: Linking HR with business strategy', *Organizational Dynamics*, 22 (3), 59–72.

Pollock, R.B. (1995), 'Linking marketing and human resources in the new employment contract', *Employment Relations Today*, 22 (1), 7–15.

Porter M.E. (1980), *Competitive Strategy*, New York: The Free Press.

Porter M.E. (1985), *Competitive Advantage*, New York: The Free Press.

Porter M.E. (1987), 'From competitive advantage to corporate strategy', *Harvard Business Review*, 65 (3), 43–59.

Porter, M.E. (1996), 'What is strategy?', *Harvard Business Review*, 74 (6), 61–78.

Pounsford, M. (1994), 'Nothing to lose: Is internal communications adding value in today's organizations?', *Internal Communication Focus*, September, 6–8.

Powell, W.W. (1990), 'Neither market nor hierarchy: Network forms of organization', *Research in Organizational Behavior*, 12, 295–336.

Prahalad, C.K. and Hamel, G. (1990), 'The core competence of the corporation', *Harvard Business Review*, 68 (3), 79–91.

Prokesch, S.E. (1995), 'Competing on customer service', *Harvard Business Review*, 73 (6), 101–12.

Prokesch, S.E. (1997), 'Unleashing the power of learning: An interview with British Petroleum's John Browne', *Harvard Business Review*, 75 (5), 146–68.

Punj, G. and Stewart, D.W. (1983), 'Cluster analysis in marketing research: Review and suggestions for applications', *Journal of Marketing Research*, 20, May, 135–48.

Quinn, J.B. (1985), 'Managing innovation: Controlled chaos', *Harvard Business Review*, 63 (3), 73–84.

Quinn, J.B. (1992), *Intelligent Enterprise*, New York: Free Press.

RSA (1994), *Tomorrow's Company: The role of business in a changing world*, London: RSA (Royal Society for the Encouragement of Arts, Manufactures and Commerce).

Rankine, K. (1996), 'Not a happy house', *The Daily Telegraph*, 5 October, B2.

Regan, G. (1992), *Military Blunders* London: Guinness.

Reichheld, F. (1993), 'Loyalty-based management' *Harvard Business Review*, 71 (2), 64–73.

Reichheld, F. and Sasser, W.E. (1990), 'Zero defections: Perfecting customer retention and recovery', *Harvard Business Review*, 68 (5), 105–11.

Ries, A. and Trout, J. (1982), *Positioning: The battle for your mind*, New York: McGraw-Hill.

Ries, A. and Trout, J. (1986), *Marketing Warfare*, New York: McGraw-Hill.

Ring P.S. and Van de Ven, A.H. (1992), 'Structuring co-operative relationships between organizations', *Strategic Management Journal*, 13 (7), 483–98.

Robinson, S.J.Q., Hichens, R.E. and Wade, D.P. (1978), 'The directional policy matrix – tool for strategic planning', *Long Range Planning*, 11 (3), 8–15.

Rowe, A.J., Mason, R.D., Dickel, K.E. and Synder, N.H. (1989), *Strategic Management : A methodological approach*, 3rd edition, Wokingham: Prentice Hall.

Rubel, C. (1996), 'Treating co-workers right is the key to Kinko's success', *Marketing News*, 29 January.

Ruekert, R. and Walker, O. (1987), 'Marketing's interaction with other functional units: A conceptual framework and empirical evidence', *Journal of Marketing*, 51, 1–19.

Salmon, A.-M. (1997), 'Transforming a brand with energy: Lucozade in sickness and in health', *British Brands*, 4, Summer, 3.

Sammuels, G. (1994), 'CD Rom's first big victim', *Forbes*, 28 February, 42–4.

Sanders, N.R. and Ritzman, L.P. (1992), 'The need for contextual and technical knowledge in judgmental forecasting', *Journal of Behavioral Decision Making*, 39–52.

Saunders, J.A. (1990), 'Brands and valuations', *International Journal of Forecasting*, 8 (2), 95–110.

Saunders, J.A. (1994), 'Cluster analysis' in G.J. Hooley and M.K. Hussey (eds.), *Quantitative Methods in Marketing*, London: Academic Press.

Saunders, J.A. and Saker, J. (1994), 'The changing consumer in the UK', *International Journal of Research in Marketing*, 11, 477–89.

Saunders, J.A., Sharp, J. and Witt, S. (1987), *Practical Business Forecasting*, Aldershot: Gower.

Sculley, J. (1992), Chairman of Apple Computer, quoted in *Forbes ASAP*, Technical Supplement, 7 December.

Segnit, S. and Broadbent, S. (1973), 'Life-style research: A case history in two parts', *European Research*, January, 6–13, March, 62–8.

Self, A. (1997), 'Hello Johann, got a new motor?', *The Mail on Sunday*, 12 April, 26.

Sengupta, S. and Bucklin, L.P. (1994), *To Ally or Not to Ally*, Cambridge, Mass.: Marketing Science Institute.

Shapiro, B.P. and Bonoma, T.V. (1990), 'How to segment industrial markets', in R.J. Dolan (ed.), *Strategic Marketing Management, Cambridge*, Mass.: Harvard Business School Press.

Shermach, K. (1995), 'Portrait of the world', *Marketing News*, 28 August, 20.

Sheth, J.N. (1994), 'Relationship marketing: A customer perspective', Keynote address, Relationship Marketing Conference, Emory University.

Sheth, J.N. and Mittal, B. (1996), 'A framework for managing customer expectations', *Journal of Market-Focused Management*, 1, 137–58.

Simms, J. (1996), 'Mission control', *Marketing Business*, July/August, 18–21.

Simon, H. (1992), 'Lessons from Germany's midsize giants', *Harvard Business Review*, 70 (2), 115–23.

Simon, H. (1996), *Hidden Champions*, Boston, Mass.: Harvard Business School Press.

Sinkula, J.M. (1994), 'Market information processing and organizational learning', *Journal of Marketing*, 58 (1), 35–45.

Slater, S.F. and Narver, J.C. (1994), 'Does competitive environment moderate the market orientation-performance relationship?', *Journal of Marketing*, 58 (1), 46–55.

Slater, S.F. and Narver, J.C. (1995), 'Market orientation and the learning organisation', *Journal of Marketing*, 59, July, 63–74.

Slywotzky, A. (1996), *Value Migration*, Boston, Mass.: Harvard Business School Press.

Smith, A. (1997), 'Brand-builders perceive pattern', *Financial Times*, 23 June, 14.

Smith, S.M. (1990), *PC MDS Version 5.1: Multidimensional scaling package*, Prova, Ut: Brigham Young University.

Smith, W.R. (1956), 'Product differentiation and market segmentation as alternative marketing strategies', *Journal of Marketing*, July, 3–8.

Snow, C.C. (1997), 'Twenty-first century organizations: Implications for a new marketing paradigm', *Journal of the Academy of Marketing Science*, 25 (1), 72–4.

Snyder, A.V. and Ebeling, W.H. (1997), 'Targeting a company's real core competencies', in A. Campbell and K.S. Luchs (eds.), *Core Competency-Based Strategy*, London: International Thomson Business Press.

Sorrell, J. (1989), 'Power tools', *Marketing*, 16 November, 45.

Sparks, D.L. and Tucker, W.T. (1971), 'Multivariate analysis of personality and product use', *Journal of Marketing Research*, 8 (1), 67–70.

Spethman, B. (1992), 'Category management multiples', *Advertising Age*, 11 May, 42.

Stalk, G. (1988), 'Time – the next source of competitive advantage', *Harvard Business Review*, 66 (4), 41–51.

Steffens, J. (1994), *Newgames: Strategic competition in the PC revolution*, Oxford and New York: Pergamon Press.

Stonich, P.J. (1982), *Implementing Strategy*, Cambridge, Mass: Ballinger.

Storbacka, K., Strandvik, T. and Grönroos, C. (1994), 'Managing customer relationships for profit', *International Journal of Service Industry Management*, 5 (5), 21–8.

Story, J. (1992), 'HRM in action: The truth is out at last', *Personnel Management*, 24 (4), 28–31.

Svendsen, A. (1997), 'Building relationships with microcommunities', *Marketing News*, 9 June, 13.

Swain, C.D. (1993), 'Competitive benchmarking', in D. Bernhardt (ed.), *Perfectly Legal Competitor Intelligence*, London: Pitman Publishing.

Szulanski, G. (1997), 'Intra-firm transfer of best practices', in A. Campbell and K.S. Luchs (eds.), *Core Competency-Based Strategy*, London: International Thomson Business Press.

Tapscott, D. and Castor, A. (1993), *Paradigm Shift: The new promise of information technology*, New York: McGraw-Hill.

Teece, D.J., Pisano, G. and Shuen, A. (1992), *Dynamic Capabilities and Strategic Management*, Working Paper, University of California, Berkeley.

Teinowitz, I. (1988), 'Brand managers: 90s dinosaurs?' *Advertising Age*, 19 December, 19.

Tellis, G. and Golder, P. (1996), 'First to market, first to fail: Real causes of enduring market leadership', *Sloan Management Review*, 37 (2).

Thomas, M.J. (1987), 'Customer care: The ultimate marketing tool', *Proceedings*: Marketing Education Group Conference, Warwick.

Tighe, C. (1997), 'Lean sales machine', *Financial Times*, 25 June, 26.

Toffler, A. (1981), *The Third Wave*, William Collins/Pan Books.

Townsend, J. and Favier, J. (1991), *The Creative Manager's Pocketbook*, Alresford, Hants: Management Pocketbooks.

Trai, C.C. (1991), *Chinese Military Classic: The art of war*, Singapore: Asiapac Books.

Treacy, M. and Wiersema, F. (1995), *The Discipline of Market Leaders*, London: HarperCollins.

Treacy, M. and Wiersema, F. (1995), 'How market leaders keep their edge', *Fortune*, February, 88–89.

Tull, D.S. (1967), 'The relationship of actual and predicted sales and profit in new product introductions', *Journal of Business*, 40 (3), 233–50.

Tull, D.S. and Hawkins, D.I. (1993), *Marketing Research: Measurement and method*, 6th edition, Englewood Cliffs, NJ: Prentice Hall Inc.

Tyebjee, T.T. (1987), 'Behavioral biases in new product forecasting', *International Journal of Forecasting*, 3 (4), 393–404.

Ulrich, D. (1989), 'Tie the corporate knot: Gaining complete customer commitment', *Sloan Management Review*, Summer, 19–27.

Ulrich, D. (1992), 'Strategic and human resource planning: Linking customers and employees', *Human Resource Planning*, 15 (2), 47–62.

Varadarajan, P.R. (1992), 'Marketing's contribution to the strategy dialogue: The view from a different looking glass', *Journal of the Academy of Marketing Science*, 20 (4), 335–44.

Walker, J.W. (1994), 'Integrating the human resource function within the business', *Human Resource Planning*, 17 (2), 59–77.

Wall, M. (1997), 'Boots to offer health cover', *The Sunday Times*, 1 June, Section 4, 1.

Ward, J. (1963), 'Hierarchical grouping to optimize an objective function', *Journal of the American Statistical Association*, 58, 236–44.

Webster, F.E. (1992), 'The changing role of marketing in the corporation', *Journal of Marketing*, 56 (4), 1–17.

Webster, F.E. (1994), *Market Driven Management*, London: Wiley.

Webster, F.E. (1997), 'The future role of marketing in the organization', in D.R. Lehmann and K.E. Jocz (eds.), *Reflections on the Futures of Marketing*, Cambridge, Mass.: Marketing Science Institute.

Wells, K. (1994/5) 'The road ahead', *Marketing Business*, Dec.-Jan., 18–20.

Wells, W.D. and Gubar, G. (1966), 'Life cycle concepts in marketing research', *Journal of Marketing Research*, 3 (4), 355–63.

Wensley, R. (1981), 'Strategic marketing: Boxes, betas or basics', *Journal of Marketing*, 45 (3), 173–82.

Wernerfelt, B. (1995), 'The resource-based view of the firm: Ten years after', *Strategic Management Journal*, 16, 171–80.

Weyer, M.V. (1997), 'The shop that time forgot', *The Daily Telegraph*, 30 August, 16.

Wheatcroft, P. (1997), 'Bright new look from Persil man', *Financial Mail on Sunday*, 9 February, 9.

Wilmott, M. (1989), 'Whose lifestyle is it anyway?', Institute of International Research Conference on *Customer Segmentation and Lifestyle Marketing*, London, 11–12 December.

Wind, Y. (1978), 'Issues and advances in segmentation research', *Journal of Marketing Research*, 15 (3), 317–37.

Wind, Y. and Mahajan, V. (1981), 'Designing product and business portfolios', *Harvard Business Review*, 59 (1), 155–65.

Wissema, J.G., Van der Pol, H.W. and Messer, H.M. (1980), 'Strategic management archetypes' *Strategic Management Journal*, 1 (1), 37–47.

Womack, J.P. and Jones, D.T. (1996), *Lean Thinking: Banish waste and create wealth in your corporation*, London: Simon and Schuster.

Wong, V. (1993), 'Ideas generation' in *Identifying and Exploiting New Market Opportunities*, London: Department of Trade and Industry.

Wong, V., Saunders, J.A. and Doyle, P. (1992), 'Business orientations and corporate success', *Warwick Business School Research Papers*, No. 52, 41pp.

Wright, P., Kroll, M., Pray, B. and Lado, A. (1990), 'Strategic orientations, competitive advantage and business performance', *Journal of Business Research*, 33, 143–51.

Yoshino, M.Y. and Rangan, U.S. (1995), *Strategic Alliances: An entrepreneurial approach to globalization*, Boston, Mass.: Harvard Business School Press.

Young, D. (1996), 'The politics behind market segmentation', *Marketing News*, 21 October, 17.

Young, S., Off, F. and Fegin, B. (1978), 'Some practical considerations in market segmentation', *Journal of Marketing Research*, 15, August, 405–12.

Zeithaml, V.A., Parasuraman, A. and Berry, L.L. (1990), *Delivering Service Quality*, New York: The Free Press.

Zielke, A. and Pohl, M. (1996), 'Virtual vertical integration: The key to success', *McKinsey Quarterly*, (3), 160–63.

Name index

Company/brand index

Subject index